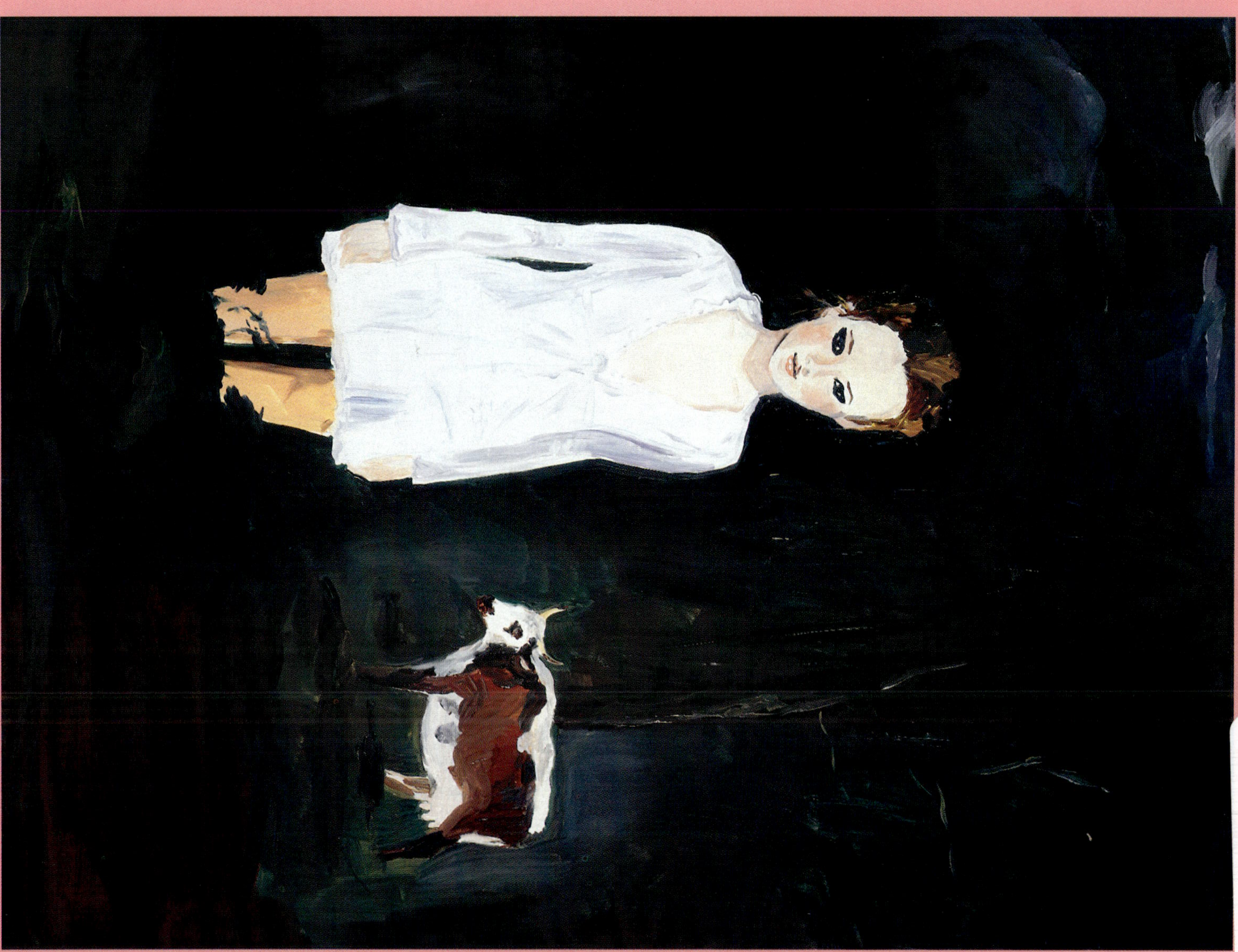

MALCOLM MORLEY, SPRINGBOK, 1997, oil on linen, 44½ x 66" / SPRINGBOCK, Öl auf Leinen, 113 x 168 cm.

UGO RONDINONE, SO MUCH WATER SO CLOSE TO HOME, 1998, wood, loudspeakers, sound, Plexiglas / SOVIEL WASSER SO NAH VON ZUHAUSE, Holz, Lautsprecher, Sound, Plexiglas.

KAREN KILIMNIK, BELGRAVE HALL, 1997, water-based oil on canvas, 18 x14" / Emulsion auf Leinwand, 45,7 x 35,6 cm.

DIE PARKETT-REIHE MIT GEGENWARTSKÜNSTLERN / THE PARKETT SERIES WITH CONTEMPORARY ARTISTS

Book Series with contemporary artists in English and German, published three times a year. Parkett chooses to retain its authors' stylistic variations. Each volume is created in collaboration with artists, who contribute an original work specially made for the readers of Parkett. The works are reproduced in the regular edition and available in a limited and signed Special Edition.

Buchreihe mit Gegenwartskünstlern in deutscher und englischer Sprache, erscheint dreimal im Jahr. Jeder Band entsteht mit Künstlern oder Künstlerinnen, die eigens für die Leser von Parkett einen Originalbeitrag gestalten. Diese Werke sind in der gesamten Auflage abgebildet und zusätzlich in einer limitierten und signierten Vorzugsausgabe erhältlich.

PARKETT NR. 53 ENTSTEHT IN COLLABORATION MIT • ELIZABETH PEYTON, TRACEY MOFFATT, WOLFGANG TILLMANS • WILL BE COLLABORATING ON PARKETT NO. 53

JAHRESABONNEMENT (DREI NUMMERN) / ANNUAL SUBSCRIPTION (THREE ISSUES) SFR. 108.– (SCHWEIZ), DM 130,– (BRD), SFR. 118.– (ÜBRIGES EUROPA), US$ 80 (USA AND CANADA ONLY)

Zürichsee Druckereien AG (Stäfa) Satz, Litho, Druck/Copy, Printing, Color Separations

PARKETT-VERLAG AG, ZÜRICH, MAI 1998 PRINTED IN SWITZERLAND ISBN 3-907582-02-0 ISSN 0256-0917

Special thanks to Lida Morley, Emily Tsingou and Nora Tobbe.

HEFTRÜCKEN / SPINE NO. 52-54: SYLVIE FLEURY
(photograph from *Hot Rod Magazine* 2/98 by Terry Pellegrin & Jeff Koch)

Umschlag unter Verwendung von / Cover with details from:
UGO RONDINONE, NO. 90, ZEHNTERAPRILNEUNZEHNHUNDERTSIEBENUNDNEUNZIG, 1997;
MALCOLM MORLEY, APPROACHING VALHALLA, 1997; KAREN KILIMNIK, THE BLACK PLAGUE, 1995.

PARKETT Zürich New York Frankfurt

Bice Curiger Chefredaktorin/Editor-in-Chief; **Jacqueline Burckhardt** Redaktorin/Senior Editor; **Louise Neri** Redaktorin USA/
Senior Editor US; **Susanne Schmidt** Textredaktion und Produktion/Editing and Production; **Trix Wetter · Hanna Koller**
Graphik/Design; **Catherine Schelbert** Englisches Lektorat/Editorial Assistant for English; **Claudia Meneghini-Nevzadi**
Korrektur/Proof Reading **Karin Klussmann** Volontariat/Traineeship

Beatrice Fässler Vorzugsausgaben/Special Editions; **Beatrice Aschmann** Buchvertrieb, Inserate/Distribution, Advertising;
Sibylle Schellenbauer Abonnemente/Subscriptions; **Linda Pilgrim** Redaktionsassistenz, Vorzugsausgaben und Marketing
USA/Assistant Editor, Editions and Marketing US; **Monika Condrea** Abonnemente USA/Subscriptions US; **Adrian Koerfer**
Deutsche Verlagsvertretung/German Representative

Jacqueline Burckhardt – Bice Curiger – Dieter von Graffenried Herausgeber/Parkett Board; **Jacqueline Burckhardt – Bice Curiger – Dieter
von Graffenried – Walter Keller – Peter Blum** Gründer/Founders

Dieter von Graffenried Verleger/Publisher

PARKETT-VERLAG AG, QUELLENSTRASSE 27, CH-8005 ZURICH, TEL. 41-1-271 81 40, FAX 41-1-272 43 01
PARKETT, NEW YORK, 155 AV. OF THE AMERICAS, N.Y. 10013, PHONE (212) 673-2660, FAX (212) 271-0704
PARKETT-VERLAG AG, TANNENWALDALLEE 17, D-61348 BAD HOMBURG, FAX 06172-937 444

NETZE UND SPRINGFLUT   Das Netz, «the grid», jenes Rastersystem, dessen sich Dürer schon bediente, spielt in Malcolm Morleys Malerei erklärtermassen eine wichtige Rolle. Wie wenig er darauf verzichten mag, erfährt man aus seinen durchaus selbstironischen Äusserungen. Doch das Netz wird im Bild nicht nur unsichtbar, es ist, als ob der Malprozess, einer Springflut gleich, es von innen her attackiert und aufgelöst hätte. Malcolm Morleys Malerei des vergangenen Jahrzehnts thematisiert diesen Fluss, das Hereinbrechenlassen der Farben, der Erinnerung, der psychischen Realität, das Anknüpfen an die selige Abenteuerlust der Kindheit. Die Zellen, Atome des Bildaufbaus, «gems», Juwelen, wie Morley sie nennt, hat er in seiner photorealistischen Phase, beim devoten Abmalen einer Vorlage entdeckt. Innerhalb dieser Partikel fing er an «verbotenen» Malfreuden nachzuleben, sie mit Farben, Spritzern, mit Dynamik zu versehen, um in der Folge dem Ausufern selbst Bedeutung zuzumessen.

In dem von Thomas Bayrle gestalteten INSERT hingegen ist das Netz selber in Schwingung geraten, so dass das Zell-Leben einer verborgenen Ordnung sich zu erkennen gibt.

Auch bei Ugo Rondinone denkt man an Zellen. Es ist eine Art Kokon, in den er sich einspinnt, ein Ort des scheinbaren Stillstands, der Trance, während draussen der Sturm tost. In seiner Edition für Parkett, ALLE AUGENBLICKE HÖREN HIER AUF UND GEMEINSAM WERDEN WIR ZU JEDER ERINNERUNG, DIE ES JEMALS GEGEBEN HAT, hat er sich in das innerste Wesen der perfekt geformten Flusssteine eingefühlt, sozusagen im Namen der Menschheit. Das Polaroidphoto, das er zum Stein mitliefert (jeder einzelne wurde in Rondinones häuslicher Umgebung aufgenommen), enthebt diesen wieder von seinem abstrakten reinen Anspruch, denn es ummantelt ihn mit der persönlich gelebten Aura des Banalen heutiger Alltäglichkeit. Und alle Photos zusammen fügen sich wieder zu einem «grid», einem ordnenden System, herausgewachsen aus dem Jetzt einer unreinen Welt.

Wenn Karen Kilimnik zeichnet, malt, an Objekten bastelt, widmet sie sich mit Hingabe der Gefühlswelt, die aus der Gelben Presse tagtäglich auf uns alle losgelassen wird. Es ist als möchte sie den Wahrheitsgehalt dieses weltumspannenden Fluidums testen, befreit von all dem störend Scheinrationalen, von dem dieser Fluss sonst immer zugedeckt erscheint.

GRIDS AND SPRING TIDES   The network or the grid, which already served Albrecht Dürer, plays a declared role in Malcolm Morley's paintings. Morley's remarks tell us, not without self-irony, how indispensable they are to his work. In his finished pictures, however, the grid is not merely invisible; it seems as if the painting process had attacked and dissolved it from within—like a spring tide. For the past decade, Malcolm Morley has been driven by the idea of flow, of colors crashing in on us, of remembrance, psychic realities and the adventurous excitement of blissful childhood. Morley first discovered the cells and atoms of his constructions, or "gems" as he calls them, in the dedicated act of painting from a source during his photorealist phase. He began to take "forbidden" painterly delight in these particles, lending spatters of paint a startling dynamics, and subsequently endowing the excesses themselves with meaning.

In Thomas Bayrle's INSERT, the network itself begins to vibrate, giving rise to a cellular life of an entirely different order.

Ugo Rondinone also makes us think in terms of cells: the cell as a cocoon in which the artist has encapsulated himself in suspended animation as if in a trance, while the storm rages all around him. In his Edition for Parkett, ALL MOMENTS STOP HERE AND TOGETHER WE BECOME EVERY MEMORY THAT HAS EVER BEEN, he has felt his way into the innermost being of perfectly formed river-bed stones, as if in the name of all humankind. The Polaroid photographs which accompany the stones (shots taken in personal context) relieve them of the onus of abstract purity, for they are thus immersed in the personally experienced aura of banality that envelops everyday life. As a whole the photographs form a grid, an ordered system, that has risen out of today's impure world.

When Karen Kilimnik draws, paints, or assembles her objects, she devotes herself to the emotional world that floods out of the sluices opened daily by the tabloid press. It is as if she were trying to test the veracity of this global spring tide by liberating it from the interference of the fake rationale that ordinarily keeps it in check.

Bice Curiger

JEAN-MICHEL OTHONIEL

EDMUND WHITE

THE INTERPRETATION OF DESIRES

During the last three months of 1997 Jean-Michel Othoniel exhibited crystal works at the Musée des arts décoratifs in Paris. In a raw space, in the process of being converted into a new gallery, these luxurious necklaces and harnesses shimmered in the changing light against a background of concrete walls scrawled with instructions to the builders, exposed electric wires and torn-up parquet floors. On one side the fourth-storey windows give on to the rooftops of the rue de Rivoli and, on the other, they look down on the inner courtyard of the Louvre. In a perfect crystal ball the Louvre was suspended upside down, resembling those spheres in a Matsys painting that refer the viewer to an "offstage" object not otherwise within the range of vision.

As Othoniel explained to me, that one perfect globe is an anomaly. Most of his crystal objects are imperfect, which is a quality hard to achieve. "Crystal is like water—it forms in symmetrical drops. What I wanted were irregular or damaged elements. I'd make them in terra cotta first, then hand them over to a master glass blower, Oscar Zanetti, in Murano. For him it was a real challenge to reproduce these imperfect forms, and he was forced to invent new techniques. For instance, glass has a memory. If you 'wound' a molten ball of glass by cutting into it or by otherwise making an indentation, it heals but later, when the glass cools, the wound will reappear. Zanetti used these wounds to realize some of the forms I was after."

Othoniel strung his giant beads with their baroque irregularities not on thread but wire, interwoven with the sort of strip lights that indicate the exits along the aisles of an airplane. These necklaces hang from an industrial hook touching or, in the case of one extra-long necklace, even pooling on the floor. As the natural light dies in the evening or fades behind a cloud, the inner lights of the crystals glow more strongly. One of the pieces is a harness made out of open circles of clear crystal. Sadomasochists wear such harnesses fashioned out of warm, flexible leather and cold, rigid metal rings, both materials sturdy and functional. Here the material, crystal, is fragile, unyielding—more an idea or a model of a harness than a practical piece of apparel. Another piece is a red and amber pendant that droops in a way suggestive of a full condom, or of the penis itself. A red bead is a rough parody of the traditional Valentine's Day symbol; aubergine-colored crystal takes the form of three small eggplants. The red is derived from gold leaf, the clear crystal from silica; and all the other colors are drawn from earth pigments, a transformation of the humble soil into airy transparency that must appeal to Othoniel's alchemical side.

EDMUND WHITE lives in Paris. His most recent novel is *The Farewell Symphony* published in 1997 by Alfred A. Knopf, New York.

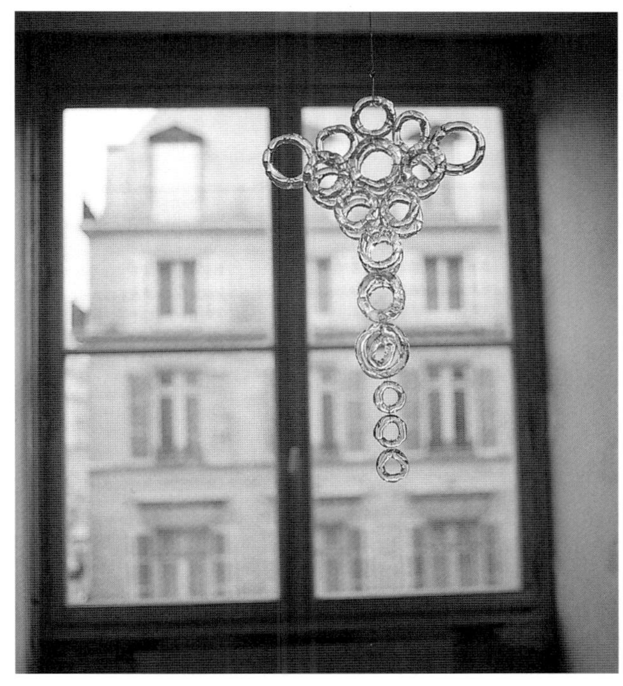

The imagination is forced to play with these objects. Are they religious or erotic or royal finery? A warrior's breastplate? Congealed honey? Are they a primitive form of currency? Are they magical objects in a fairy tale? When they were first exhibited at the Peggy Guggenheim Museum in Venice (June 11–November 9, 1997), they were strung in the trees over the garden. There they had a softer, more bucolic appearance than in Paris. Othoniel refers to the garden as a "closed seraglio." One of the necklaces dangled directly above Peggy's stone throne with its Byzantine motifs. In any event, they represented a rare incursion of the contemporary into a permanent collection devoted to abstraction and surrealism.

The first conversation I ever had with Othoniel was about the turn-of-the-century proto-surrealist writer Raymond Roussel, the author of *Impressions d'Afrique* and *Locus Solus;* Othoniel and I met at a dinner soon after the rediscovery of a trunk that Roussel had put into storage seventy years earlier and that contained many unpublished manuscripts. Othoniel, who is currently working on a fantastic Rousselian CD-ROM machine for the Bibliothèque Nationale which will produce unique books programmed by the visitors to the library, is a fanatical admirer of the eccentric writer, and some of the objects in his new show made me think of Roussel's bizarre contraptions.

When I mentioned that the necklaces reminded me of African cowrie shell necklaces or Indian *wampum*, he said that curiously enough the only authentic eighteenth century Venetian glass beads that still exist appear in African necklaces, since at that time European merchants were trading trinkets in Africa. Othoniel told me that in the early years of this century a European merchant had offered a motorcycle to a tribal ruler in Africa. The king didn't have the petrol to fuel the motorcycle but once a year he'd order his men to push it by hand through the sand. When he noticed the handsome chevron pattern left behind by the tires in the sand, he had it copied in fabric; the chevrons became the royal motif. A literal example of *Impressions d'Afrique,* we agreed, laughing, and of how the quotidian can become regal.

Jean-Michel Othoniel was born in 1964 in Saint-Etienne, a dreary industrial town not far from Lyon, famous for its illustrated catalogues in the eighteenth and nineteenth centuries and for its mines. His father is an engineer for Schlumberger, his mother a teacher; neither are interested in the visual arts, though both are concerned with civic values and virtues. As luck would have it, Saint-Etienne, a progressive communist-run town, had at that time the second most important collection of contemporary

JEAN-MICHEL OTHONIEL, LE COLLIER OUVERT,
November–December 1997, Musée des arts décoratifs, Paris.
(PHOTO: Franck Guignochau)

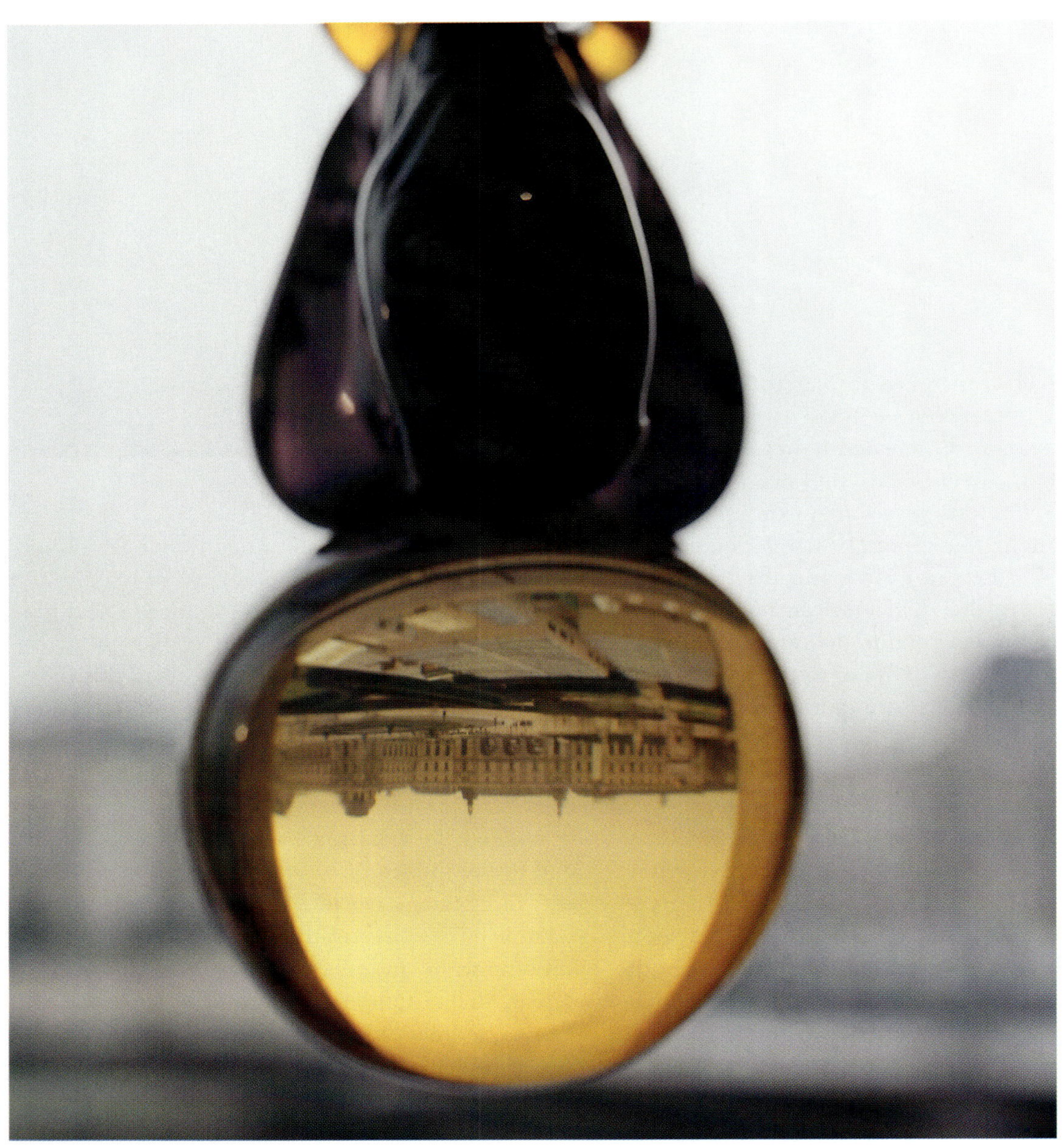

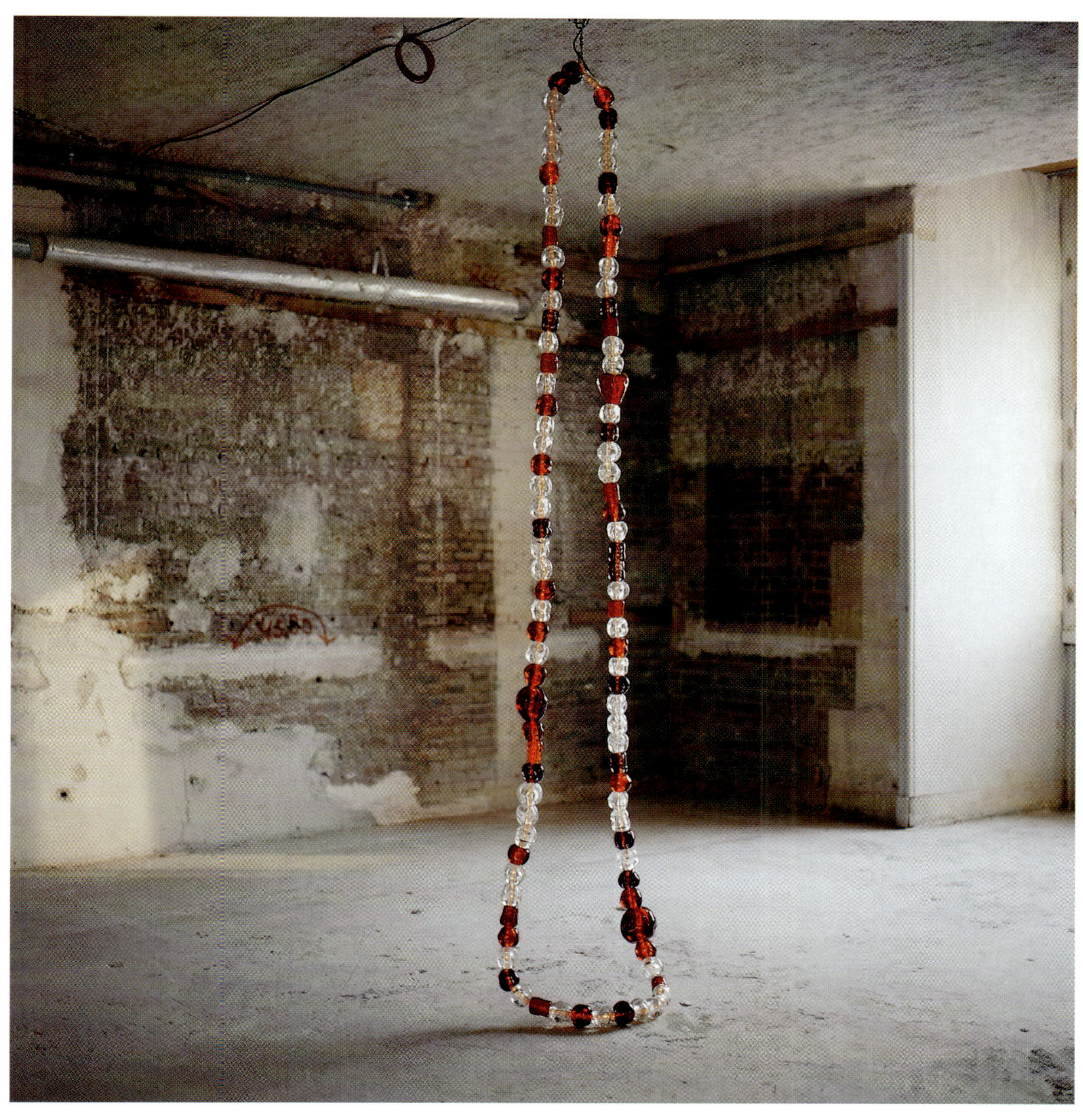

JEAN-MICHEL OTHONIEL, LE GRAND COLLIER,
November–December 1997, Musée des arts décoratifs, Paris.
(PHOTO: Franck Guignochau)

art in France (after the Centre Georges Pompidou), directed by Bernard Ceysson, who is still the chief curator. When Othoniel was just seven years old he saw his first art exhibition there; it was a Robert Morris show. Since Saint-Etienne was an industrial center his friends were the children of Italian, Polish and Arab immigrant workers, which perhaps allowed Othoniel to escape the influence of *le bon goût français,* as much an enemy to serious art as deflating English humor and the English fear of pretentiousness.

When he was eighteen he left Saint-Etienne for one of the new universities created by Jack Lang, the Ecole des Beaux-Arts at Cergy-Pontoise, an experimental school where students were encouraged to work in many different media, including video, poetry, sculpture, painting, ceramics and performance art, and where they chose the professors they wanted to work with and determined what the work should consist of. Othoniel studied primarily with Jean-Claude Silbermann, one of André Breton's last protégés who in 1965, at the last surrealist exhibition during Breton's lifetime, showed THE CONSUMER, a twelve-foot-high sculpture that had a siren for a head, a cab-radio for a voice and a washing machine endlessly churning paper for a stomach. "I enjoyed working with Silbermann," Othoniel confides, "though I rejected surrealism with its dated imagery, misogyny and homophobia. What I did learn at Cergy-Pontoise was to work in many different media—in fact, not to pay too much attention to the medium itself but to the idea behind it, which links my work to conceptual art and minimalism. My generation, the generation of the eighties, was very dogmatic (now things are much more open, of course); I always rejected this closed-mindedness."

One aspect of Othoniel's openness is his love of collaboration and his desire to reach new audiences. In the summer of 1997, when Paris played host to the Pride parade for all Europe, Othoniel took 750 photographic portraits of random parade participants during an eight-hour period. He had hundreds of red glass bead necklaces from Murano around his neck at the beginning. Like one of those traders in Africa, he gave a necklace to each person he photographed (in the pictures they're all wearing their necklaces). The sheer physical labor of taking so many pictures during such a short period of time was a bit of a marathon for him—a performance piece, if you will. He enjoyed the parade immensely with its mixture of gays, lesbians, drags, straight people, including parents with their children—"a real carnival." He has published twenty of the photos but would like to find a way of presenting all 750. The pictures represent the same spirit of tolerance embodied in Othoniel's new children's book, *Tu peux aimer comme tu veux* (You can love any way you like).

Othoniel has been working with sulfur since 1992, when he presented four versions of an anus at documenta IX, each displayed in a glass case with a mirrored base that allowed the viewer a reflection of the bottom of the object—fingers in an anus or a jade amulet, for instance, or a peacock's feather. All of the objects bore names that are dirty French slang for the anus. One sulfur mound was pierced with darts made out of cut-up playing cards—a reference to Saint Sebastian, a "deviationist saint," by which Othoniel understands a saint invoked to ward off evil, as Sebastian survived the arrows that pierced him.

Sulfur led to one of his most remarkable collaborations in 1993. For some time Othoniel had been digging a hole in the earth and then hollowing out a shape with his hand—a shape he had clearly in mind, though he couldn't see how the piece was coming along. He would then fill the earthen mold with liquid sulfur. When the sulfur was cool and dry he would brush away the earth and reveal the "blind sculpture" he had created—a surprising and novel combination of purpose and accident. Then he decided he wanted to use his whole body to make the mold. He went to the sulfur mines in the Pyrenees, at Lacq, and cooperated with a team of workmen. He stripped naked, burrowed into the earth ("like a worm," as he puts it), holding his breath all the while as he hollowed out the shape of his body. When it was cast in sulfur it resembled the ancient statue of the hermaphrodite in the Louvre, the recumbent form that looks like a girl from behind and a boy from the front. "The workers despise the sulfur with which they work," Othoniel told me. "The mine at Lacq was only discovered in the sixties, it's destroying the natural beauty of the landscape—and it smells like rotten eggs.

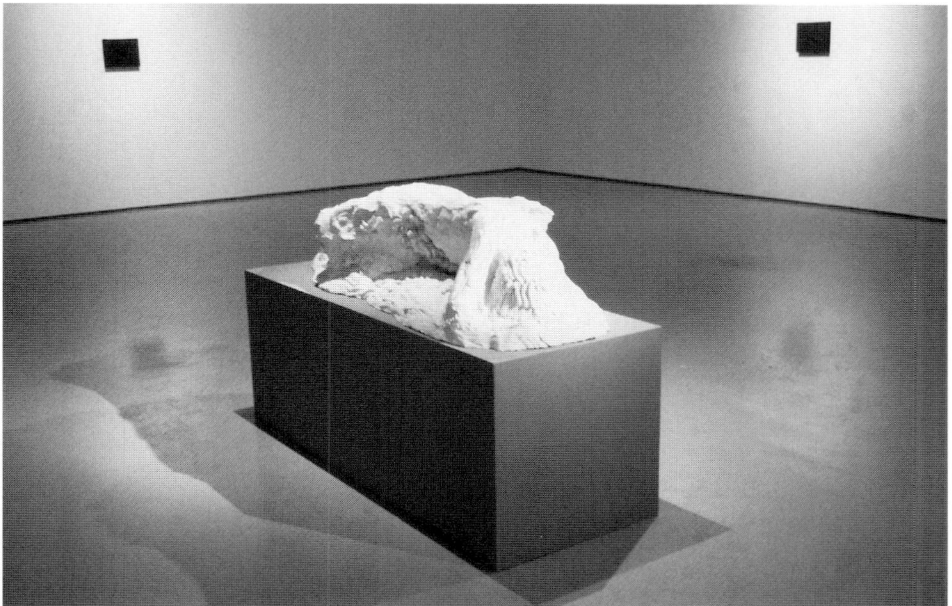

I think it fascinated them that I prized this hated material for its color and light and consistency."

Othoniel enjoyed being naked in front of the laborers, just as at Murano he likes collaborating at the glassworks with men stripped to the waist who must "interpret my desires." No wonder he so admired the "Chambres d'amis" show organized a decade ago by Jan Hoet in Ghent, during which artists were invited to install works in people's houses. Othoniel still recalls Joseph Kosuth's brilliant installation of words and definitions on the walls of a psychiatrist's house.

He is an artist who likes breaking down the barriers between genres, but also between genders. When the Centre Georges Pompidou had its big show, "Féminin-Masculin: Le sexe de l'art" in 1995, Othoniel was discouraged by the rigid separation of art by or about men and art by or about women. He also felt uncomfortable with the unsexy distance between the visitors and the works of art. His piece dissolved these categories. It was MY BEAUTIFUL CLOSET, a narrow chamber entered from one room and exiting into another. The door was opened by pushing a button shaped like a male nipple (molds of these have been used elsewhere to stipple canvases with wax dots). The door would then shudder open. Once the visitor entered the corridor the original door would shut and he or she would be brushed against by dancers, male and female, in the dark. "Gay men are used to dark backrooms," Othoniel told me, "so they didn't react. But the female dancers told me they were quickly exhausted by being felt up by straight men." When the far door would open the visitor would see a spotlit pair of trousers and shoes dipped in sulfur and hanging from the roof by a rope.

In yet another piece Othoniel presented a high school class studying classical Greek with a story in French he'd invented about a misogynist pagan priest in ancient times who receives a single spoken sentence in Greek from the oracle. Othoniel asked the students to translate the sentence and told them that all translations, as far as he was concerned, would be equally "accurate." True to his word, he printed each of the widely diverging translations on a

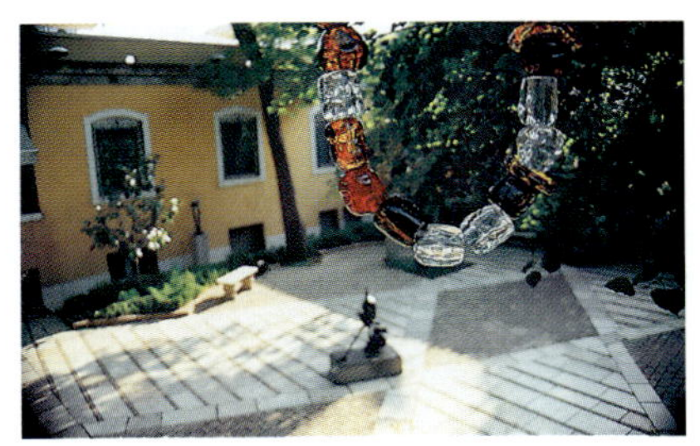

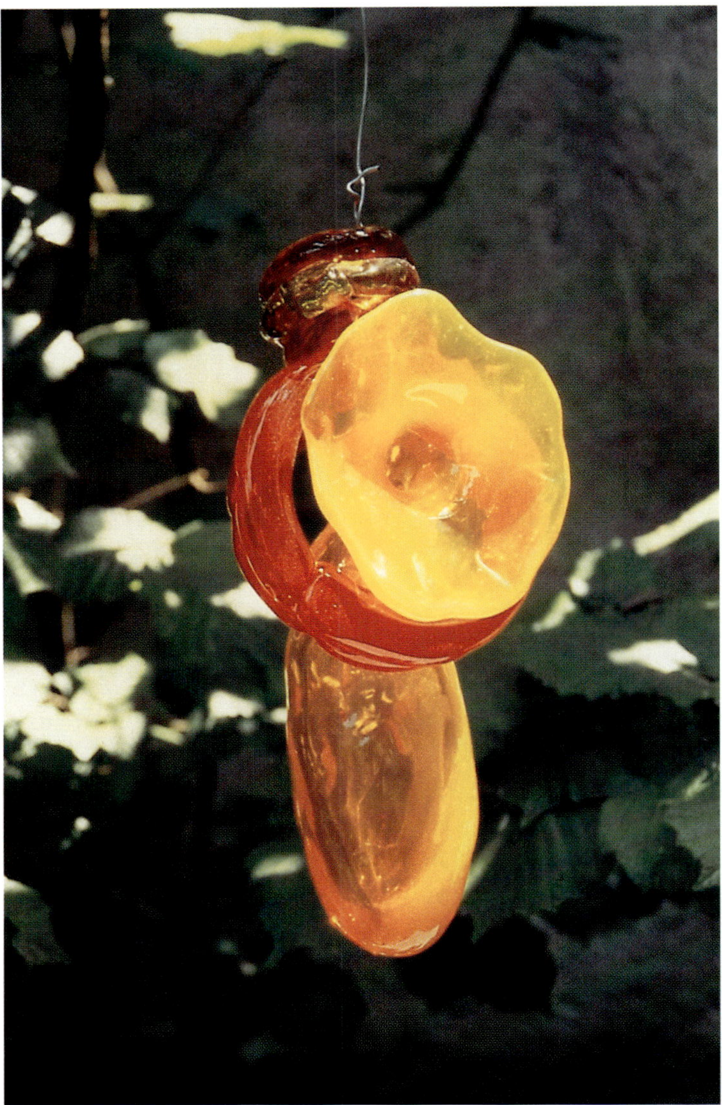

LE COLLIER CICATRICE, 1997,
Murano glass and crystal (4 pictures,
above, below, and on right-hand page) /
Muranoglas und -kristall
(4 Abb., oben, unten und rechte Seite).

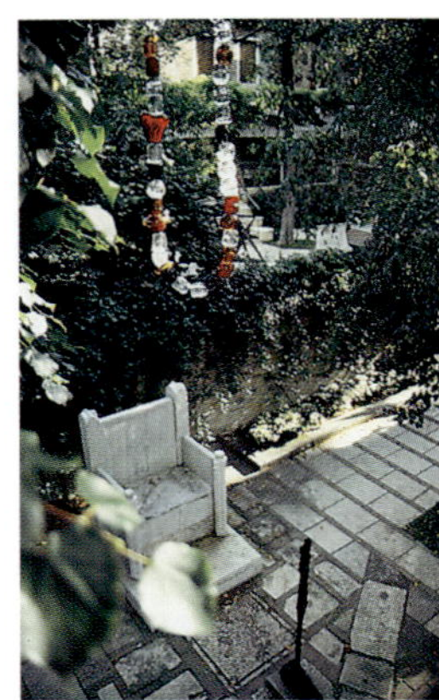

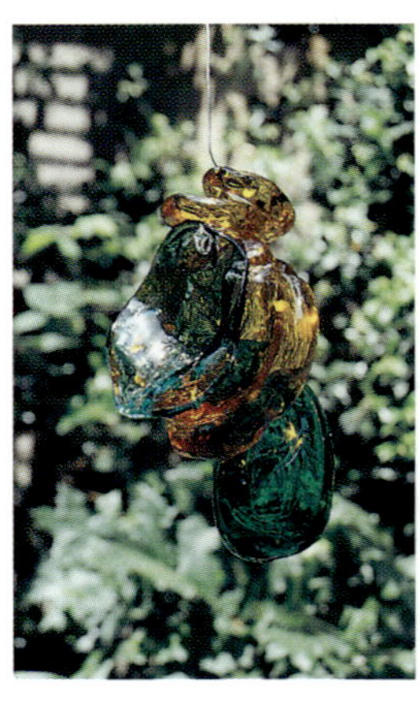

SANS TITRE, 1996,
Murano blown glass /
geblasenes Muranoglas.

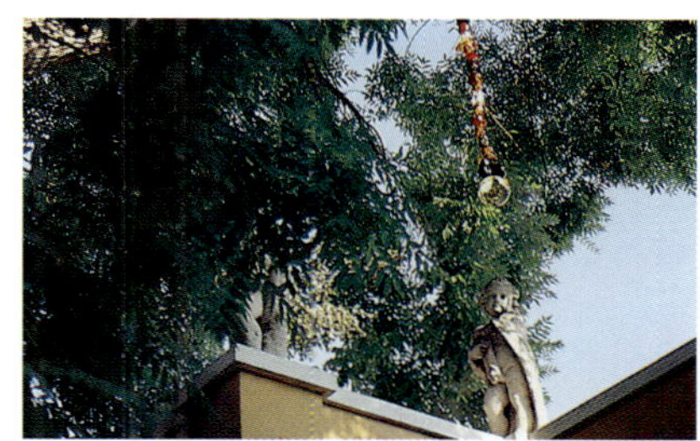

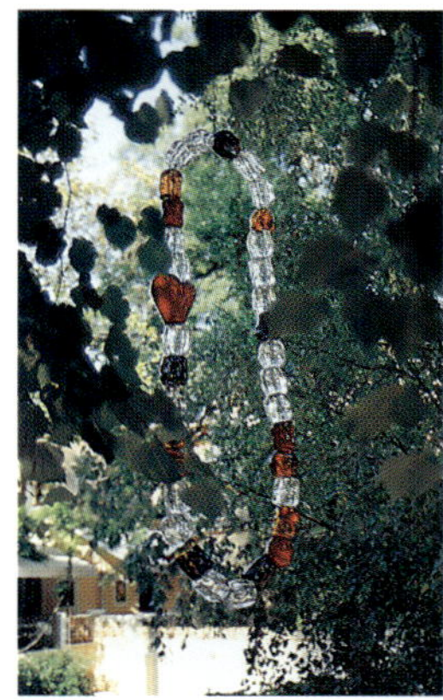

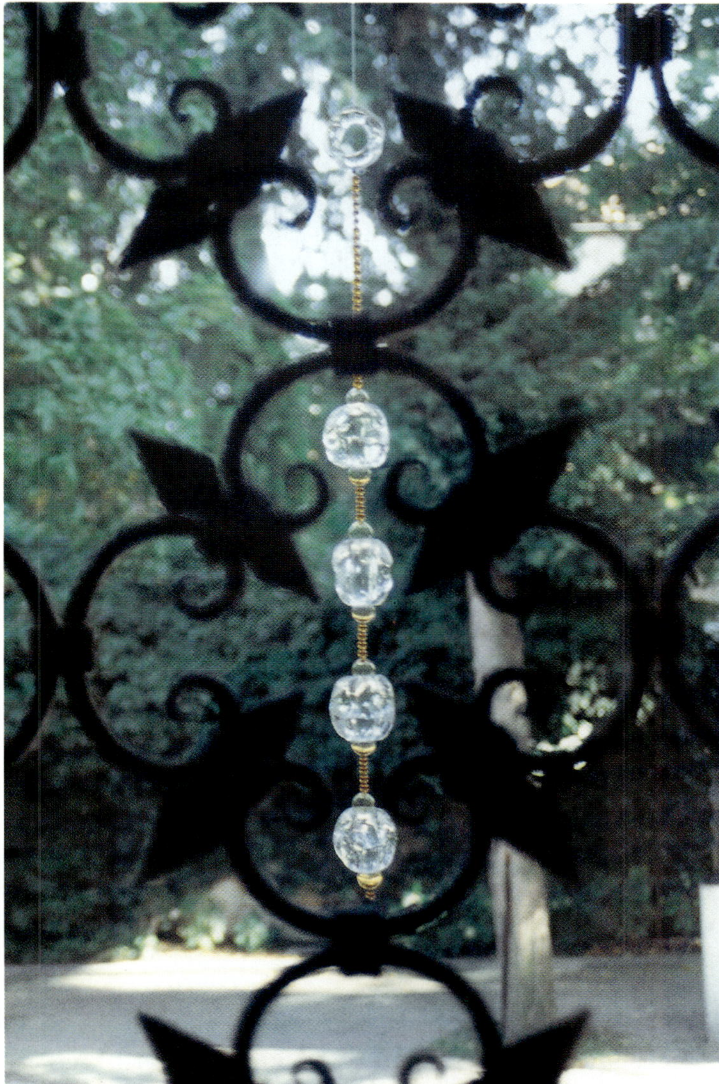

SANS TITRE, 1996,
Murano blown glass /
geblasenes Muranoglas.

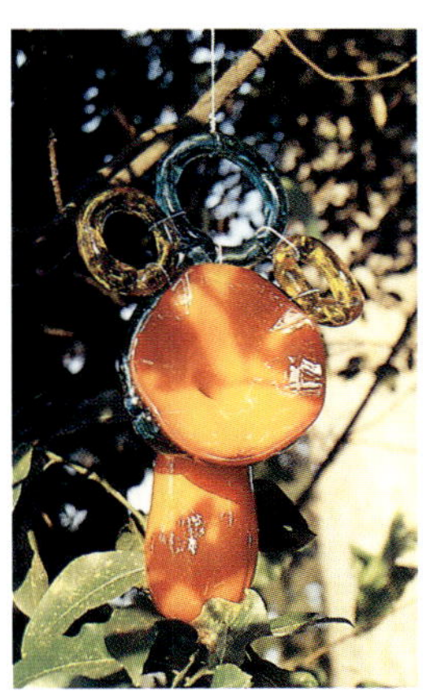

JEAN-MICHEL OTHONIEL, ROSARY, 1997,
Murano glass and crystal, installation at the Peggy Guggenheim Museum, Venice /
ROSENKRANZ, *Muranoglas und Kristall.*

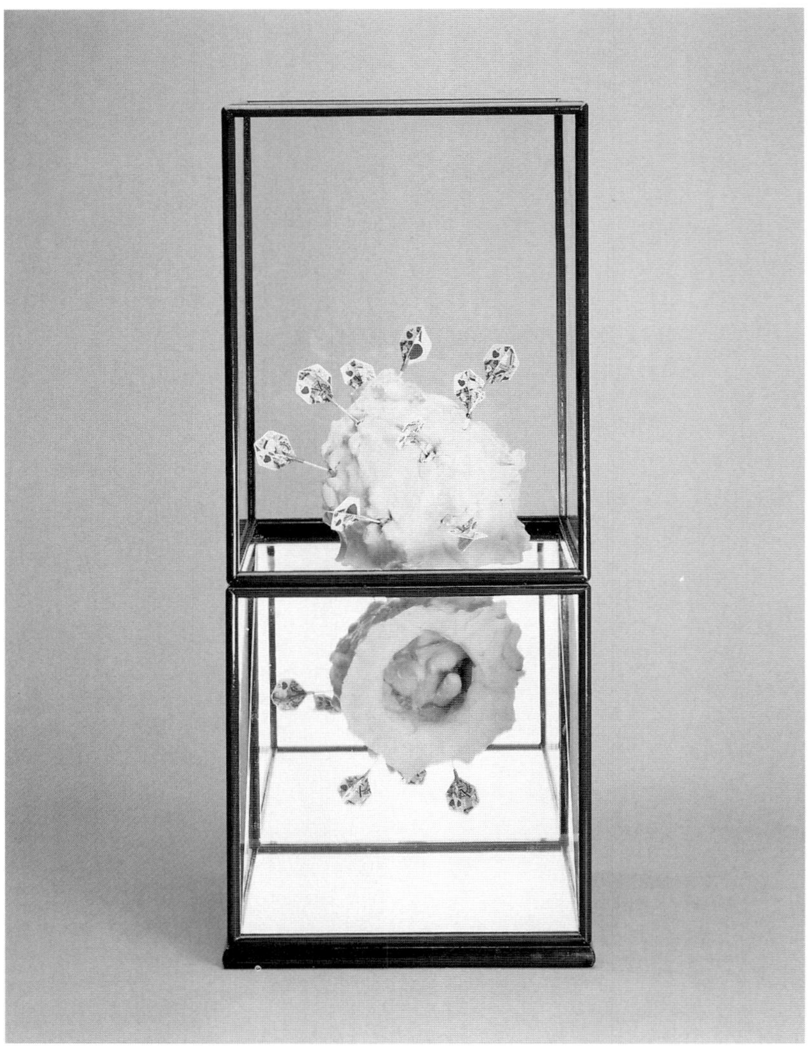

separate page in a little book he made. "I think it puzzled them that I did away with the idea of accuracy in such a highly structured academic subject," Othoniel told me.

Perhaps one of his most interesting collaborations involved dipping dresses in wax and hanging them from a stage ceiling like giant bellpulls of every color. In one five-minute scene, choreographed by Othoniel himself, the dancers were dressed in the flint paper used on the side of match boxes. There was no light on stage except that provided by the matches the dancers struck on each other's costumes. "I loved working with the living bodies of the dancers," Othoniel told me. "The odor of sulfur was

JEAN-MICHEL OTHONIEL, LA MALA DUERTE, 1992,
ground sulfur, small darts, mirror, documenta IX, Kassel,
9⅞ x 9⅞ x 9⅞" /
gemahlener Schwefel, kleine Pfeile, Spiegel, 25 x 25 x 25 cm.

of course an invocation of my sulfur sculptures. But more importantly the dancers brought me out of my solitude as an artist and were able to give a true interpretation of my desires."

Othoniel may believe in collaborations, they may involve people from every walk of life, but every work is generated out of his own powerful desires—as good a place to start as any.

JEAN-MICHEL OTHONIEL DIE INTERPRETATION VON WÜNSCHEN

EDMUND WHITE

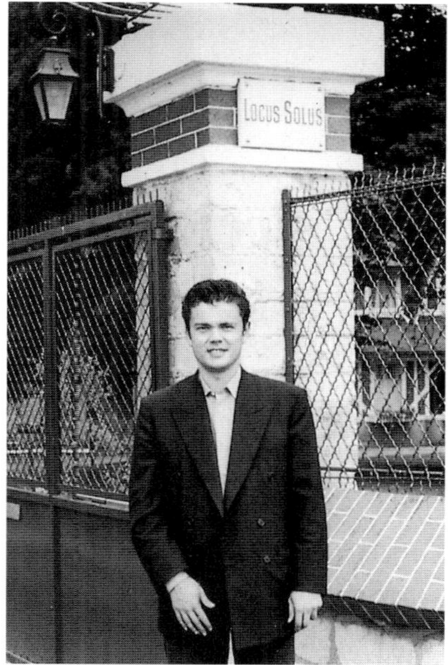

JEAN-MICHEL OTHONIEL, SELF-PORTRAIT AT THE MOMENT
OF DISCOVERING "LOCUS SOLUS," 1992 /
SELBSTPORTRÄT IM MOMENT DER ENTDECKUNG VON «LOCUS SOLUS».

In den letzten drei Monaten von 1997 zeigte das Pariser Kunstgewerbemuseum – heute unter der innovativen Leitung von Marie-Claude Béaud (der ehemaligen Direktorin der Fondation Cartier und danach des amerikanischen Kulturzentrums) – Jean-Michel Othoniels Glasarbeiten. In einem noch unfertigen Raum, der in eine neue Galerie umgewandelt werden sollte, schimmerten diese prachtvollen Ketten und Monturen in wechselndem Licht vor einem Hintergrund aus nackten Betonwänden, die mit Anweisungen für die Arbeiter vollgekritzelt waren, Kabel lagen herum, und die Parkettböden waren aufgerissen. Die Fenster der vierten Etage gingen auf der einen Seite nach den Dächern der rue de Rivoli, auf der anderen nach dem Innenhof des Louvre. Dieser hing mit dem Kopf nach unten in einer vollkommenen Kristallkugel, vergleichbar mit den Kugeln in den Gemälden von Matsys, die den Betrachter auf einen Gegenstand «hinter der Bühne» aufmerksam machen, einen Gegenstand, der ausserhalb seines Blickfelds liegt.

Othoniel erklärte mir, dass eine vollkommene Kristallkugel ungewöhnlich sei. Die meisten dieser Glasobjekte seien unvollkommen, was aber gar nicht so einfach zu bewerkstelligen sei. «Glas ist wie Wasser – es bildet symmetrische Tropfen. Doch ich wollte unregelmässige oder beschädigte Elemente. Gewöhnlich formte ich die Modelle in Terrakotta vor und gab sie dann dem erfahrenen Glasbläser Oscar Zanetti in Murano. Für ihn war es eine echte Herausforderung, diese unvollkommenen Formen hinzukriegen, und er sah sich gezwungen, neue Techniken zu erfinden. Glas besitzt zum Beispiel ein Erinnerungsvermögen. Verletzt man einen geschmolzenen Glasklumpen, indem man ihn anritzt oder anschneidet, so heilt das zwar schnell, aber später, wenn das Glas erkaltet, erscheint die Wunde wieder. Zanetti benutzte diese Wunden, um die Formen zu erreichen, die ich haben wollte.»

Othoniel hat seine riesigen Perlen mit ihren barocken Unregelmässigkeiten nicht auf einem Strang, sondern auf einem Draht aufgereiht, der mit diesen Neonschlangen verwoben ist, die gewöhnlich auf dem Fussboden eines Flugzeugs den Ausgang markieren. Sie hängen an einem Industriehaken und berühren den Boden oder bilden im Fall einer über-

---

EDMUND WHITE lebt in Paris. Sein neuster Roman *The Farewell Symphony* erschien 1997 bei Alfred A. Knopf, New York.

langen Kette ein kleines Häufchen auf ihm. Wenn das Licht gegen Abend abnimmt oder eine Wolke die Sonne verdunkelt, glühen die inneren Lichter des Kristallglases um so intensiver. Eine der Arbeiten ist eine Montur aus offenen Ringen, die aus durchsichtigem Glas bestehen. Sadomasochisten tragen solche Monturen, doch sind sie gewöhnlich aus warmem, weichem Leder und kalten, starren Metallringen, beides robuste, funktionelle Materialien. Das hier verwandte Material, das Glas, ist jedoch zerbrechlich und unbiegsam – eher ein Konzept oder ein Prototyp als ein Kleidungsstück. Eine andere Arbeit, ein roter und bernsteinfarbener Anhänger, suggeriert ein volles Kondom – oder den Penis selbst. Eine rote Perle erscheint wie eine krude Parodie des traditionellen Valentinstag-Symbols, des Herzens; auberginefarbenes Glas nimmt die Form von drei kleinen Auberginen an. Das Rot wird aus Blattgold gewonnen, das durchsichtige Glas aus Kieselerde, zu allen andern Farben werden Erdpigmente verwandt – eine Verwandlung gewöhnlicher Erde in luftige Transparenz, die Othoniels alchimistische Seite ansprechen muss.

An solchen Gegenständen entzündet sich die Phantasie. Sind sie religiöser, erotischer oder königlicher Putz? Die Brustplatte eines Kriegers? Kristallisierter Honig? Eine primitive Form von Geld? Magische Gegenstände in einem Märchen? Als sie vom 11. Juni bis zum 9. November 1997 zum ersten Mal im Peggy Guggenheim Museum in Venedig gezeigt wurden, hingen sie in den Bäumen über dem Garten, wo sie weicher, bukolischer als in Paris wirkten. Othoniel sprach von dem Garten als einem «geschlossenen Serail». Eine der Ketten baumelte direkt über Peggys steinernem Thron mit den byzantinischen Motiven. Jedenfalls waren sie ein seltener Einbruch des Zeitgenössischen in eine ständige Sammlung abstrakter und surrealistischer Kunst.

Mein erstes Gespräch mit Othoniel drehte sich um den Schriftsteller Raymond Roussel, den Verfasser von *Impressions d'Afrique* und *Locus Solus,* der um die Jahrhundertwende gelebt und die surrealistische Ästhetik bereits vorweggenommen hatte. Othoniel und ich trafen uns bei einem Essen kurz nach der Entdeckung eines Schrankkoffers, den Roussel siebzig Jahre zuvor zur Aufbewahrung abgegeben hatte und der viele unveröffentlichte Manuskripte enthielt.

Othoniel, der zur Zeit an einer phantastischen, für die Nationalbibliothek bestimmten rousselianischen CD-ROM-Maschine arbeitet, die einzigartige, von den Besuchern der Bibliothek selbst programmierte Bücher produzieren soll, ist ein fanatischer Bewunderer dieses exzentrischen Schriftstellers, und manche Objekte seiner neuen Ausstellung erinnerten mich an Roussels bizarre Vorrichtungen.

Als ich erwähnte, dass ich afrikanische Ketten aus Kaurimuscheln oder indianische *Wampums* mit ihnen assoziiere, meinte er, die einzigen, aus dem achtzehnten Jahrhundert übriggebliebenen venezianischen Glasperlen würden merkwürdigerweise noch in afrikanischen Halsketten auftauchen, da die europäischen Händler damals Schmuck gegen Waren eingetauscht hätten. Othoniel erzählte mir, ein europäischer Händler habe zu Beginn des Jahrhunderts einem afrikanischen Stammeshäuptling ein Motorrad geschenkt. Dieser verfügte aber nicht über den nötigen Brennstoff, um die Maschine zu starten, doch liess er sie einmal im Jahr von seinen Männern über den Sand schieben. Als er das hübsche Fischgrätmuster entdeckte, das die Reifen im Sand hinterlassen hatten, liess er es auf Stoff nachdrucken, und die Sparren sind seitdem ein Abzeichen königlicher Würde. Afrikanische Eindrücke im wörtlichen Sinn, stellten wir lachend fest, ein Beispiel dafür, wie das Alltägliche höhere Weihen bekommen kann.

Jean-Michel Othoniel wurde 1964 in Saint-Etienne geboren, einer trostlosen Industriestadt in der Nähe von Lyon. Das Schicksal will es, dass Saint-Etienne, eine fortschrittliche, von den Kommunisten regierte Stadt, einst, nach dem Centre Pompidou, die bedeutendste Sammlung moderner Kunst in Frankreich besass, betreut von Bernard Ceysson, der immer noch Chefkurator ist. Als Othoniel gerade sieben Jahre alt war, sah er dort seine erste Kunstausstellung, Werke von Robert Morris. In dem Industriezentrum Saint-Etienne hatte er sich mit den Kindern italienischer, polnischer und arabischer Gastarbeiter angefreundet, ein Umstand, dem es vielleicht zu verdanken ist, dass Othoniel sich dem Einfluss des guten französischen Geschmacks entziehen konnte, der, ähnlich wie der trockene englische Humor und die Angst der Engländer, prätentiös zu wirken, ein Feind jeder ernsthaften Kunst ist.

Mit achtzehn verliess Othoniel Saint-Etienne, um sich an einer der neuen, von Jack Lang eingerichteten Universitäten, der Kunsthochschule von Cergy-Pontoise, einzuschreiben, einer sehr experimentierfreudigen Schule, die ihre Studenten ermutigte, sich mit den unterschiedlichsten Medien wie Video, Lyrik, Skulptur, Malerei, Keramik und Performance auseinanderzusetzen und wo sich die Studenten die Professoren, mit denen sie zusammenarbeiten wollten, aussuchten und auch selbst bestimmen konnten, was sie machen wollten.

Othoniel studierte in erster Linie bei Jean-Claude Silbermann, einem von André Bretons letzten Schützlingen, der 1965, auf der letzten noch zu Bretons Lebzeiten stattfindenden surrealistischen Ausstellung eine dreieinhalb Meter grosse Skulptur, DER KONSUMENT, aufgestellt hatte. Statt eines Kopfes besass sie eine Sirene, statt der Stimme ein Taxiradio und statt des Magens eine endlos Papierfetzen herumwirbelnde Waschmaschine. «Ich hab gern mit Silbermann zusammengearbeitet», gesteht Othoniel, «obwohl ich den Surrealismus mit seiner altmodischen Bilderwelt und seiner Frauen- und Schwulenfeindlichkeit ablehnte. Was ich jedoch in Cergy-Pontoise lernte, war, mit unterschiedlichen Medien umzugehen – ja, dem Medium selbst nicht so grossen Wert beizumessen, sondern mich auf die Idee dahinter zu konzentrieren, was mich in die Nähe der Konzeptkunst und des Minimalismus rückt. Meine Generation, die Generation der 80er Jahre, war sehr dogmatisch (inzwischen ist natürlich alles sehr viel offener). Engstirnigkeit war mir schon immer ein Greuel.»

Von Othoniels Offenheit zeugen auch seine Vorliebe für Teamarbeit und sein Wunsch, ein neues Publikum zu erreichen – selbst Leute, die sich noch nie in eine Galerie oder ein Museum verirrt haben. Im Sommer 1997, als Paris die Pride-Parade für ganz Europa willkommen hiess, lichtete Othoniel innerhalb von acht Stunden 750 willkürlich ausgewählte Teilnehmer ab. Anfangs trug er noch Hunderte von Perlenketten aus rotem Muranoglas um den Hals. Wie einer jener Afrika-Händler gab er jedem Abgelichteten eine Kette (auf den Photos tragen auch alle ihre Ketten). Allein die körperliche Anstrengung, in so kurzer Zeit so viele Photos zu machen, war für ihn eine Art Marathon oder eine Performance, wenn man

will. Er genoss die Parade mit ihrer bunten Mischung aus Schwulen, Lesben, Transvestiten, Heteros und Eltern mit Kindern – «ein echter Karneval». Zwanzig der Photos hat er veröffentlicht, doch sucht er nach einer Möglichkeit, alle 750 zu zeigen. In den Bildern drückt sich dieselbe Toleranz aus wie in Othoniels neuem Kinderbuch *Tu peux aimer comme tu veux* (Du kannst lieben, wie du willst).

Mit Schwefel arbeitet Othoniel seit 1992, als er vier Versionen eines Anus auf der documenta IX in Kassel ausstellte, jede in einem Glaskasten mit einem Spiegel darunter, so dass der Betrachter die Unterseite des Objekts sehen konnte, etwa einen Finger in einem Anus oder ein Jadeamulett oder eine Pfauenfeder. All diese Gegenstände trugen eine Bezeichnung aus der französischen Fäkalsprache. Ein Schwefelhäufchen war von Pfeilen durchbohrt, die aus Spielkarten ausgeschnitten waren – eine Anspielung auf den heiligen Sebastian, einen «Blitzableiter-Heiligen», wie Othoniel Heilige nennt, die angerufen werden, wenn man ein Unheil von sich abwenden will, vergleichbar mit dem heiligen Sebastian, dem es gelungen war, die Pfeile zu überleben, die sich in sein Fleisch bohrten.

Schwefel führte 1993 zu einer äusserst bemerkenswerten Teamarbeit. Othoniel hatte schon seit längerem damit begonnen, ein Loch in die Erde zu graben, um mit der Hand eine Form auszuhöhlen – eine Form, die er sich genau vorstellte, obwohl er nicht sehen konnte, wie die Arbeit sich entwickelte. Anschliessend goss er dann flüssigen Schwefel in die Erdform. Als sich der Schwefel abgekühlt hatte und trocken war, bürstete er die Erde weg und enthüllte die «blinde Skulptur», die er geschaffen hatte – eine neuartige, überraschende Kombination aus Absicht und Zufall. Später beschloss er, seinen ganzen Körper zu benutzen, um eine Form auszuhöhlen. Er

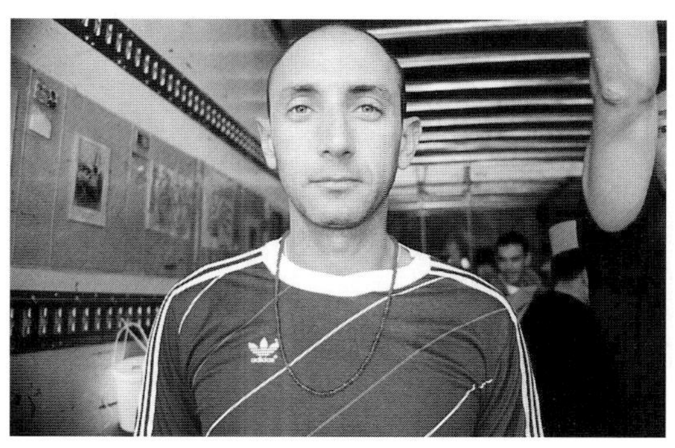

JEAN-MICHEL OTHONIEL, HANGING SCULPTURE, 1994,
trousers and shoes soaked in sulfur, wax hand /
HÄNGENDE SKULPTUR, schwefelgetränkte Hose und Schuhe, Wachshand.

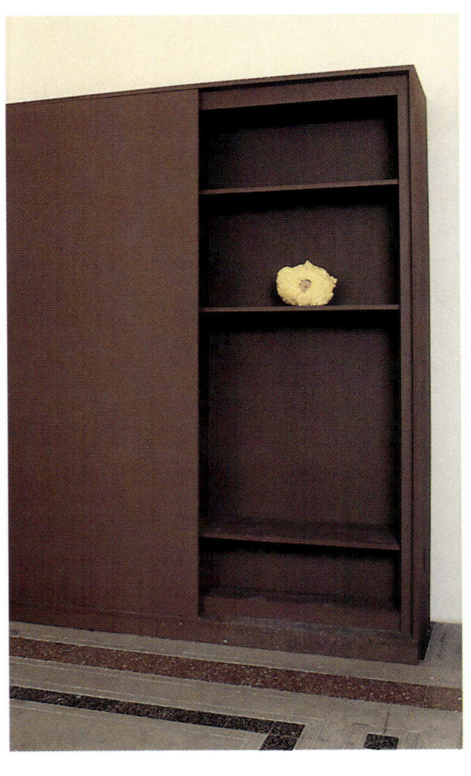

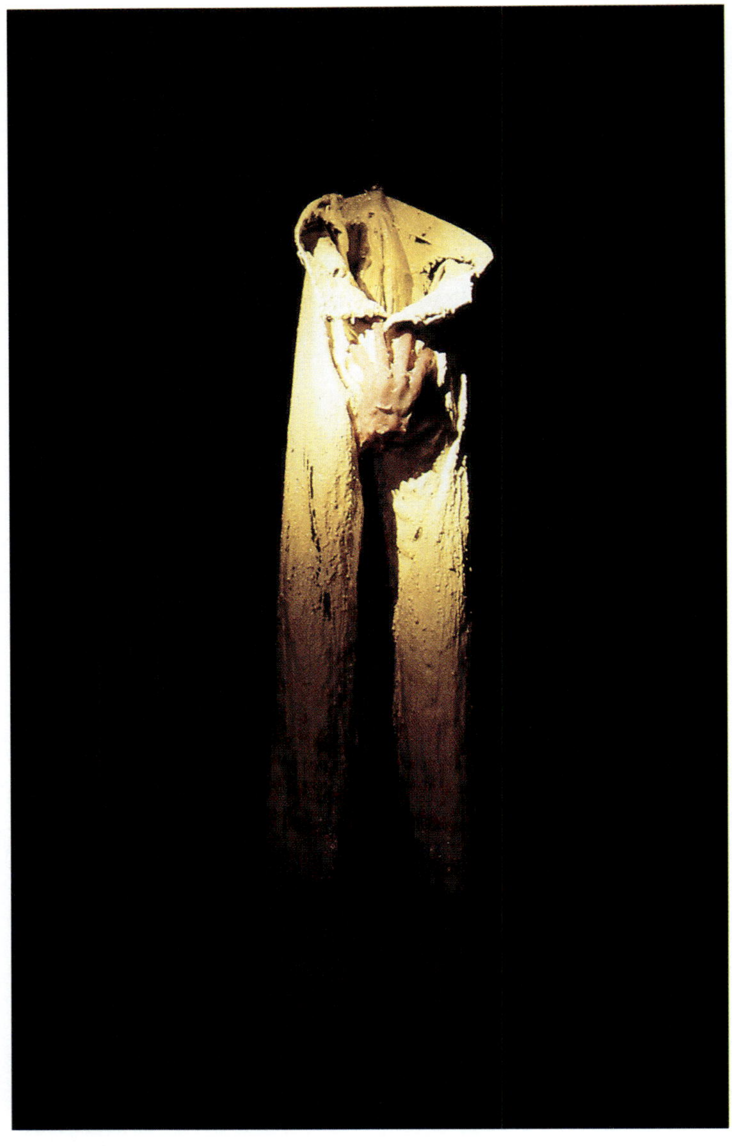

JEAN-MICHEL OTHONIEL,
MY BEAUTIFUL CLOSET, 1994, false closet,
90½ x 63 x 31½ cm /
MEIN SCHÖNES KABINETT, falscher Schrank,
230 x 160 x 80 cm.
(PHOTO: THIERRY BLANDINO)

fuhr in die pyrenäischen Schwefelminen bei Lacq, wo er mit einem Team von Arbeitern zusammenarbeitete; er zog sich nackt aus und kroch in die Erde («wie ein Wurm», so seine Beschreibung), während er mit angehaltenem Atem die Form seines Körpers ausbuddelte. Mit Schwefel ausgegossen, ähnelte diese liegende Figur, die von hinten wie ein Mädchen und von vorne wie ein Knabe aussieht, den antiken Hermaphroditen-Statuen im Louvre. «Die Arbeiter verabscheuen den Schwefel, mit dem sie arbeiten», erklärte mir Othoniel. «Die Mine bei Lacq wurde erst in den 60er Jahren entdeckt; sie zerstört die natürliche Schönheit der Landschaft – ausserdem stinkt es nach fauligen Eiern. Ich glaube, sie waren völlig von den Socken, dass ich mich für dieses von ihnen verachtete Material interessierte, für seine Farbe, seine Helligkeit und Beschaffenheit.»

Othoniel genoss es, nackt vor den Arbeitern zu stehen, so, wie er es auch in Murano genossen hatte, mit den bis zur Taille entblössten Männern in den Glashütten zusammenzuarbeiten, Männern, «die meine Wünsche interpretieren mussten». Kein Wunder, wenn er sich für die *Chambres d'Amis* begeisterte, eine von Jan Hoet ein Jahrzehnt zuvor in Gent organisierte Ausstellung, bei der die Künstler eingeladen waren, ihre Arbeiten in den Häusern von Freunden und Bekannten zu installieren. Othoniel erinnert sich noch an Joseph Kosuths geniale Installation, die Worte und Definitionen auf den Wänden eines von einem Psychiater bewohnten Hauses.

Othoniel ist ein Künstler, der die Schranken zwischen den Gattungen wie auch zwischen den Geschlechtern gerne niederreisst. Als 1995 im Centre Georges Pompidou die grosse Ausstellung «Féminin/ Masculin» über Sex in der Kunst gezeigt wurde, fand Othoniel die starre Trennung zwischen Kunst von Männern oder über Männer und Kunst von oder über Frauen enttäuschend. Auch die unsinnliche Distanz zwischen Besuchern und Kunstwerken behagte ihm nicht. In seiner Arbeit lösten sich diese Kategorien auf. Sie hiess MY BEAUTIFUL CLOSET (Mein schönes Kabinett) und bestand aus einem schmalen Zimmer, das man von einem Raum aus betrat und durch einen andern Raum wieder verliess. Die Tür öffnete sich, wenn man einen Knopf in Form einer männlichen Brustwarze drückte (die gegossenen Brustwarzen dienten bei einer anderen Gelegenheit dazu, Leinwände mit Wachs zu betupfen). Ein kurzer Ruck, und die Tür war auf. Wenn der Besucher in dem Durchgangszimmer stand, schloss sich die erste Tür hinter ihm, und er oder sie wurde im Dunkeln von männlichen und weiblichen Tänzern gestreift. «Schwule sind an dunkle Hinterzimmer gewöhnt», meinte Othoniel, daher liessen sie es geschehen. Doch die weiblichen Tänzerinnen erzählten mir, dass sie es schnell satt hatten, von heterosexuellen Männern begrapscht zu werden. «Wenn sich die andere Tür öffnete, sah der Besucher ein mit Spots beleuchtetes Paar Hosen und Schuhe, die in Schwefel getaucht worden waren und an einem Seil von der Decke baumelten.»

In einer weiteren Arbeit stellte Othoniel einer Klasse, die Altgriechisch lernte, auf französisch eine selbsterdachte Geschichte von einem misogynen Priester im Altertum vor, der von einem Orakel einen einzigen griechischen Satz empfing. Othoniel forderte die Schüler auf, diesen Satz zu übersetzen, und sagte ihnen, alle Versionen seien «richtig», was ihn beträfe. Er hielt sein Wort und druckte jede der ganz unterschiedlichen Übersetzungen auf jeweils einer Seite eines kleinen Buches ab, das er zu diesem Zweck angefertigt hatte. «Ich glaube, sie waren ziemlich fassungslos, dass ich bei einer so akademischen Sache das Konzept der Richtigkeit einfach unter den Tisch fallen liess», meinte Othoniel zu mir.

Eine seiner vielleicht interessantesten Teamarbeiten bestand darin, Kleidungsstücke in Wachs zu tauchen, um sie wie riesige, bunte Klingelzüge von der Bühnendecke baumeln zu lassen. In einem fünfminütigen, von Othoniel selbst choreographierten Sketch steckten die Tänzer in jenem rauhen, auf den Seiten von Streichholzschachteln benutzten Papier. Auf der Bühne war kein Licht, ausser dem der Streichhölzer, die die Tänzer an den Kostümen ihrer Nachbarn entzündeten. «Es machte mir Spass, mit den lebenden Körpern der Tänzer zu arbeiten», sagte Othoniel. «Der Geruch nach Schwefel war natürlich eine Reminiszenz an meine Schwefelskulpturen. Wichtiger war jedoch, dass die Tänzer mich aus der Einsamkeit des Künstlers herausholten und eine echte Interpretation meiner Wünsche lieferten.»

(Übersetzung: Uta Goridis)

RICHARD SERRA'S

NEVILLE WAKEFIELD

There is a well-known photograph of 1857 taken at the Millwall shipyards during the preparations for the launch of the Great Eastern—a leviathan steamship floated on the promise of steam-powered, plate-bending technology and the limitlessness of colonial expansion. The photograph is a portrait of the vessel's architect, the British engineer Isambard Kingdom Brunel standing alone against a wall of chain. Everything about the photograph—from the hands-in-pocket dreamer's contraposto to the sartorial signifiers of aristocrat and navvy—speaks to a golden age of engineering and configurations of progress democratized through industry. Steel, the medium of this revolution, appears in the photograph as both backbone and backdrop, a giant spool of linkage and connection suggestive not just of the launch of the world's largest steel hull but of the extension of the same technology throughout the civic sphere. Monuments to Brunel's vision of an empire engineered out of vastness and plasticity still mark the existing infrastructure of Great Britain. But of the Great Eastern, his culminating achievement, nothing survives bar historical memory—sepia diagrams chaining the launch of curvature to a vision of progress unfulfilled.

In 1943, nearly a century after Brunel eased his behemoth sideways into the river Thames, Richard Serra recalls attending a launch at the marine shipyard in the Bay Area of San Francisco, where his father worked as a pipe fitter. "When we arrived, the black, blue and orange steel-plated tanker was in way, balanced up on a perch. It was disproportionately horizontal and to a four year-old was as large as a skyscraper on its side. I remember walking the arc of the hull with my father, looking at the huge brass propeller, peering through the stays."[1] Like Brunel, Serra would go on to recall the strange epiphany that accompanied the transformation of obdurate mass into buoyant structure. Within the physics of displacement and the bulky maneuverings by which calculation becomes possibility there seemed to be a program of aesthetic possibility. "All the raw material that I needed is contained in the reserve of this memory which has become a recurring dream."[2]

Serra's TORQUED ELLIPSES carry with them the same oneiric sense of vastness set adrift. The products of ship-building technology—the rolled steel plates were produced at the Beth Ship in Maryland using Hugh Smith machines made in Scotland during World War II for the bending of battleship steel—their design follows the same principles by which linear pressure is translated into the compound curvature of maritime architecture. The ellipses themselves take the form of three enclosures, each encircled by slabs of two-inch thick Cor-Ten steel. They are entered via two-foot-wide diagonal slits which repeat the tolerances of the joined slabs in open form. A rotational variance between the ellipse of the footprint and that of the crown sets space in motion, whipping the exterior along a vortex of spatial indeterminacy while transforming the interior into a kind of delirious void. A double ellipse sets one within the other to create between the diametrically opposed entrances a curvilinear corridor

NEVILLE WAKEFIELD is a writer who lives in New York.

TORQUED ELLIPSES

which becomes an elaborately torqued system of compression and decompression. Like the maintenance cavity of a double-hulled vessel, a spatial quarantine is created which is neither the displacement form nor the interior volume. Abstracted from both, a boundary layer is set up where experience, detached from steadfast geometry, undulates along the lines of the steel, transforming its gravity and mass into palpable lightness.

Serra's remarkable use of steel in terms of mass, weight, counterbalance, loadbearing capacity, and so on, traces an evolution of technologies from the earliest days of maritime and industrial engineering through to the phenomenological aesthetics of architects such as Gehry, Himmelblau, and Koolhaas. (Significantly, it was Rick Smith, Gehry's engineer, to whom Serra turned to do the computer math.) For these architects, engineering permits sheer size to instigate a reign of complexity, an aesthetic challenge to the authority of experience. In Koolhaas's words: "A paradox of bigness is that in spite of the calculation that goes into its planning—in fact through its very rigidities—it is the one architecture that engineers the unpredictable."[3] What you see here is no longer quite what you get. Like the unlaunched vessel, the building as perceptual form traces pictorial concerns only to see them cast adrift, displaced from the grounding of phenomenology to the more buoyant realm of mnemonics. "The containers of bigness will be landmarks in the postindustrial landscape—a world scraped of architecture in the way that Richter's paintings are scraped of paint: inflexible, immutable, definitive, forever there, generated through superhuman effort."[4] And as with the Victorian structures envisioned by engineers such as Brunel, the dream of progress is rendered ponderous to the point of extinction. Consumed by scale, the bridges, tunnels, and ships of this era become a form of after-architecture—neither engineering as it was nor sculpture as it might be.

Looking at the photograph of Brunel, it is easy to read into his wry countenance and mixed-message attire the permissions held in the new landscape of architectural and maritime form. Serra, of course, stands at the other end of this tradition. In a portrait of the artist taken by Nancy Lee Katz in 1987, his gaze directly meets ours as he stares out of the picture with the fixed concentration of a prison-yard challenge. Partially obscured by a massive, slanting bulwark of steel, he is pictured literally standing behind his work. It is as if the chains that in earlier times launched the object from the shore of perception to the sea of experience have been severed by the prohibitive diagonal, and what we are left with is an aesthetic which, like the ellipses, has come nearly full circle—to a point where sheer size and mass no longer exhaust the compulsion to decide and determine. With the TORQUED ELLIPSES, this reserve of memory of structures, whose entirety was once animated by intention, becomes a dream of enclosure, drifting and freed from the dunnage of its creation.

1) Richard Serra in *Richard Serra: Writings, Interviews* (Chicago: The University of Chicago Press, 1994), p. 183.
2) ibid., p. 184.
3) Rem Koolhaas, *S, M, L, XL* (New York: Monacelli Press, 1996), p. 511.
4) ibid., p. 514.

RICHARD SERRA, TORQUED ELLIPSES, 1996/97,
Cor-Ten Steel, installation at Dia Center for the Arts, New York (25.09.97–14.06.98).
(PHOTO: ALLEN GLATTER, DIA CENTER FOR THE ARTS)

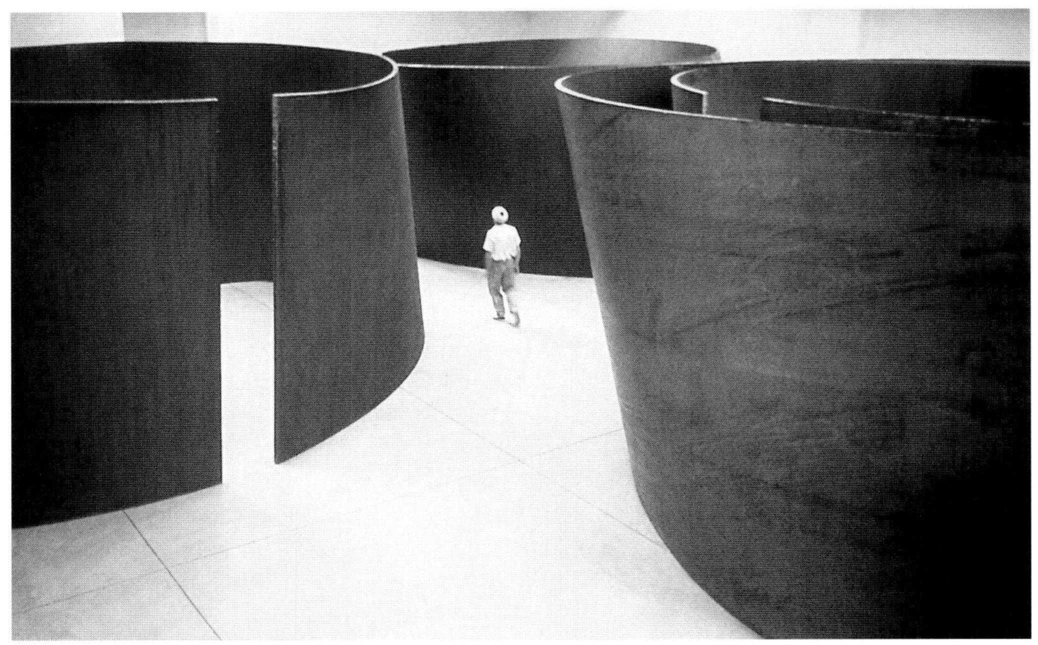

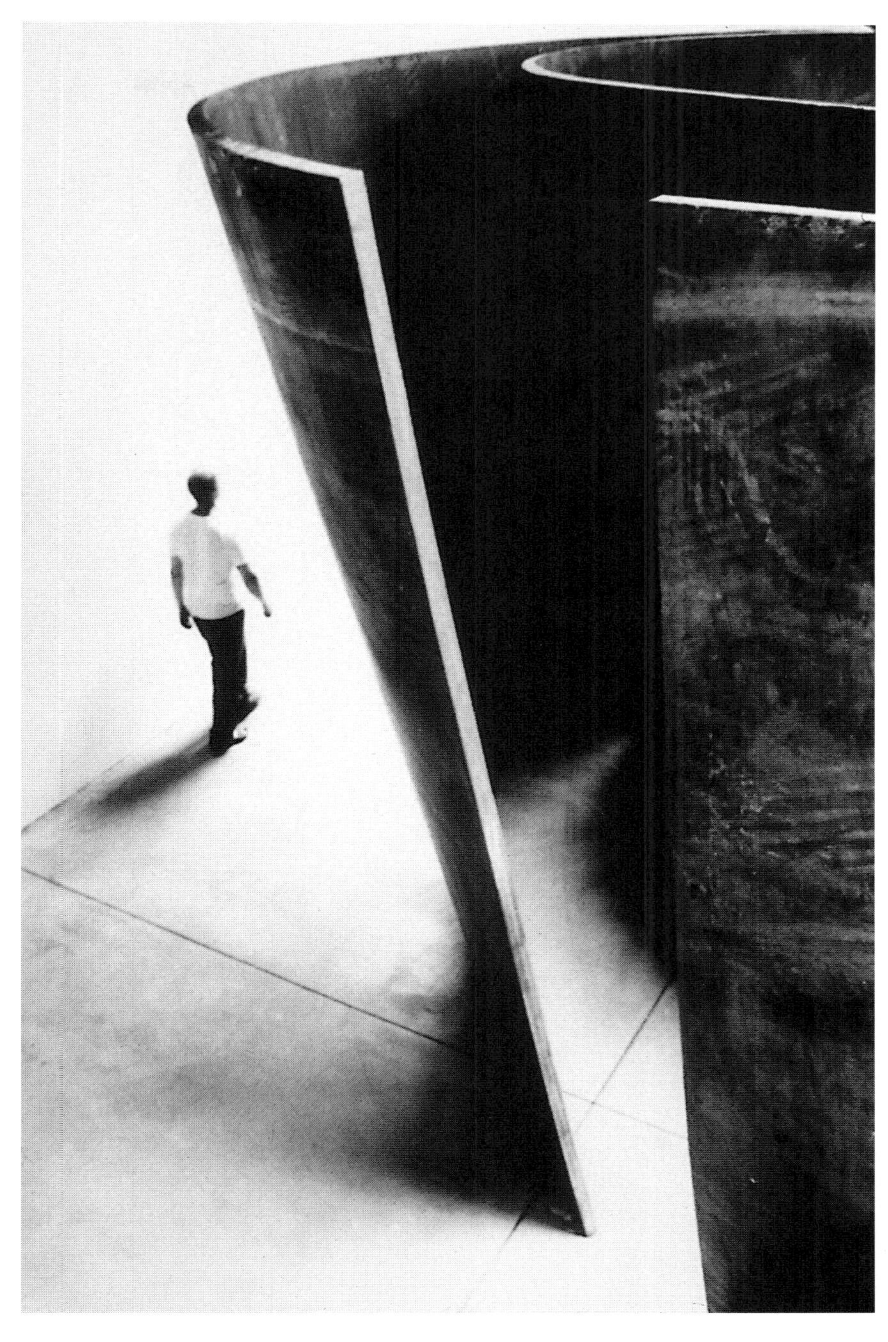

RICHARD SERRA, TORQUED ELLIPSES, 1996/97, Cor-Ten Steel,
installation at Dia Center for the Arts, New York (25.09.97–14.06.98). (PHOTO: IVORY SERRA)

NEVILLE WAKEFIELD

ÜBER SERRAS

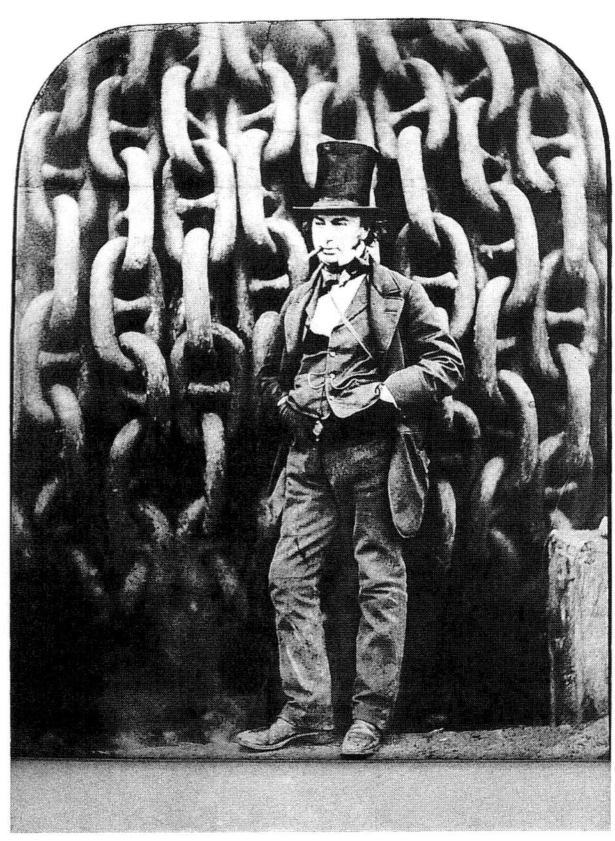

Isambard Kingdom Brunel at the Millwall shipyards /
in der Millwall-Werft, 1837.
(PHOTO: BROWN LENOX & CO. LTD.)

Es gibt ein berühmtes Photo, das im Jahr 1857 während der Vorbereitungen für den Stapellauf des Dampfers *Great Eastern* auf der Schiffswerft von Millwall in England aufgenommen wurde. Die *Great Eastern* war ein Ozeanriese, der seine Entstehung der Verheissung der dampfgetriebenen Walzstahltechnik und der Grenzenlosigkeit kolonialer Expansion verdankte. Das Photo zeigt den Erbauer des Schiffs, den britischen Ingenieur Isambard Kingdom Brunel, der alleine vor einer Mauer aus Ketten steht. Alles an diesem Photo – von dem Kontrapost des mit den Händen in den Hosentaschen dastehenden Träumers bis hin zu den Spuren aristokratischer Schneiderkunst und Schwerarbeit – zeugt von einem Goldenen Zeitalter der Technik und den Grundkoordinaten eines durch Industrie demokratisierten Fortschritts. Stahl, der Träger dieser Revolution, erscheint auf dem Photo zugleich als Rückgrat und als Folie – eine überdimensionale Spule der Verkettung und Verbindung, die nicht nur den Gedanken an den Stapellauf des weltweit grössten Stahlrumpfes aufkommen lässt, sondern die Ausdehnung ebenjener Technologie auf den gesamten zivilen Bereich beschwört. Zeugnisse der Brunelschen Vision von einem auf den Prinzipien Weite und Formbarkeit errichteten Weltreich prägen noch heute die Infrastruktur Grossbritanniens. Von der *Great Eastern*, seiner grössten Leistung, ist jedoch nichts geblieben ausser der geschichtlichen Erinnerung – sepiabraun verfärbte Pläne, in denen sich der Aufbruch der gebogenen Form mit einer Vision unerfüllten Fortschritts verschränkt.

Im Jahr 1943, nahezu ein Jahrhundert nachdem Brunel seinen Koloss seitlings in die Themse manövrierte, war Richard Serra nach eigener Erinnerung zugegen bei einem Stapellauf auf der Marine Shipyard in der Bay Area von San Francisco, wo sein Vater als Rohrleger arbeitete. «Als wir ankamen, balancierte der Tanker mit seinem Rumpf aus schwarzen, blauen und orangefarbenen Stahlplatten wie auf einem Sockel. Er dehnte sich in der Breite unverhältnismässig weit aus und wirkte auf einen Vierjährigen so gross wie ein quer gelegter Wolkenkratzer. Ich entsinne mich, wie ich mit meinem Vater durch den Bogen des Rumpfes ging,

NEVILLE WAKEFIELD ist Schriftsteller und lebt in New York.

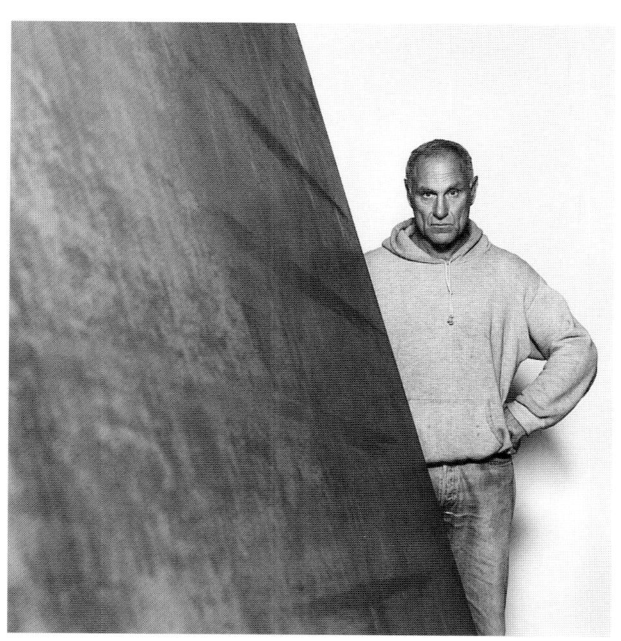

« TORQUED ELLIPSES »

mir die riesige Messingschraube ansah und zwischen den Spanten hindurch spähte.»[1] Ähnlich wie Brunel erinnerte sich Serra dann an die seltsame Epiphanie, die sich mit der Verwandlung von schwerfällig-sperriger Masse in ein schwimmendes Gebilde verband. Innerhalb der Physik der Verdrängung und der massiven Manipulationen, die aus Berechnungen reale Perspektiven werden lassen, schien es ein Programm ästhetischer Perpektiven zu geben. «Das gesamte Rohmaterial, das ich benötigte, war enthalten in dem Fundus dieser Erinnerung, die zu einem regelmässig wiederkehrenden Traum wurde.»[2]

Mit Serras TORQUED ELLIPSES (Gewundene Ellipsen) verbindet sich das gleiche traumhafte Gefühl von etwas Riesenhaftem, das Wind und Wellen preisgegeben wurde. Sie sind eine Frucht der Schiffsbautechnik – die gewalzten Stahlplatten wurden bei der Werft Beth Ship im US-Bundesstaat Maryland mit Hilfe von «Hugh Smith» genannten Maschinen hergestellt, die während des Zweiten Weltkrieges in Schottland zur Fertigung von Walzstahl für Schlachtschiffe gebaut worden waren –, und ihre Form folgt den gleichen Gesetzen, nach denen im Schiffsbau linearer Druck in eine gestaffelte Krümmung umgesetzt wird. Die Ellipsen selbst bilden drei «Einfassungen», die ihrerseits jeweils von fünf Zentimeter starken Corten-Stahlplatten eingefasst werden. Zu betreten sind sie durch ca. 60 Zentimeter breite diagonale Spalten, in denen die Toleranz der aneinandergefügten Platten als Öffnung aufgegriffen wird. Eine durch Drehung bewirkte Abweichung zwischen der Ellipse des Bodenabdrucks und der des oberen Randes setzt den Raum in Bewegung, zieht ihn aussen in einen Strudel räumlicher Unbestimmtheit hinein und verwandelt ihn innen in eine Art deliriöse Leere. Bei einer doppelten Ellipse ist die eine innerhalb der anderen angesiedelt, so dass sich zwischen den einander diametral gegenüberliegenden Eingängen ein krummliniger Korridor mit einem raffiniert gedrehten System der Kompression und Dekompression ergibt. Wie bei dem für Wartungszwecke genutzten Hohlraum eines Schiffes mit doppelter Rumpfwand entsteht eine Art räumliche Quarantäne, die weder Teil des Verdrängungsvolumens ist noch zum Innenraum gehört. Von beiden abgesondert, bildet sich eine Grenzzone, in der sich die Erfahrung, losgelöst von der standhaften Geometrie, an den ondulierenden Linien des Stahls entlangbewegt und dessen Schwere und Masse in tastbare Leichtigkeit verwandelt.

Serras verblüffende Verwendung von Stahl unter dem Gesichtspunkt von Masse, Gewicht, Gegengewicht, Tragfähigkeit usw. folgt einer Geschichte technischer Entwicklungen, die von den Anfängen der modernen Schiffsbau- und Industrietechnik bis hin zu der phänomenologischen Ästhetik von Architekten wie Frank Gehry, Coop Himmelblau und Rem Koolhaas reicht. (Bezeichnenderweise wandte sich Serra für die Computerberechnungen an Gehrys Ingenieur Rick Smith.) Technik ist für diese Architekten etwas, durch das schiere Grösse zum Anstoss für eine Herrschaft des Komplexen werden kann – eine ästhetische Herausforderung der Normativität der Erfahrung. «Es ist ein Paradoxon des Grossen», so Koolhaas, «dass es ungeachtet der Berechnungen, die – eben seiner Sperrigkeit wegen – in seine Planung einfliessen, die einzige Architektur ist, die dem Unberechenbaren Gestalt verleiht.»[3] Was man hier sieht, ist nicht mehr ganz das, was man bekommt. Ebenso wie in dem Schiff auf der Helling finden sich im Bauwerk als Gegenstand der Wahrnehmung bestimmte ikonographische Anliegen ausgeprägt, die sich jedoch verselbständigen und aus der festen Verankerung der Phänomenologie in den eher fliessenden Bereich der Mnemotechnik verlagern. «Die Vehikel der Grösse werden am Ende zu Wahrzeichen in der postindustriellen Landschaft, einer Welt, die in ähnlicher Art und Weise mit Architektur überkrustet ist, wie über Gerhard Richters Gemälde die Farbe geschabt ist: unerbittlich, unwandelbar, endgültig, für immer da, das Werk übermenschlicher Anstrengung.»[4] Und ebenso wie bei den Produkten viktorianischer Baukunst, entworfen von Ingenieuren wie Brunel, findet der Traum vom Fortschritt seinen Ausdruck in einer Schwere und Sperrigkeit, die ebendiesen Traum nachgerade zerstört. Ganz dem Massstab hörig, werden die Brücken, die Tunnel und die Schiffe dieser Epoche zu einer Art Nacharchitektur – weder die Technik, die sie einmal war, noch die Plastik, die sie sein könnte.

Wenn man sich das Photo von Brunel ansieht, kann man aus seinem sarkastischen Gesichtsausdruck und der in ihrer Botschaft mehrdeutigen Kleidung leicht die Freiheiten herauslesen, welche die neue Landschaft architektonischer und schiffsbaulicher Formen bereithielt. Serra, das spricht für sich, steht am anderen Ende dieser Tradition. Auf einem 1987 von Nancy Lee Katz aufgenommenen Photoporträt des Künstlers erwidert er den Blick des Betrachters und stiert mit einer unverwandten Konzentration aus dem Bild heraus, als gelte es, einen Gegner mit blossem Auge niederzuzwingen. Teilweise verdeckt durch eine massive schräge Stahlwand, steht er auf diesem Bild buchstäblich hinter seiner Arbeit. Es ist, als wären die Ketten, an denen einst das Objekt vom Ufer der Wahrnehmung ins Meer der Erfahrung ausgesetzt worden war, nunmehr durch die dazwischentretende Diagonale durchtrennt worden; was uns bleibt, ist eine Ästhetik, die, ähnlich wie die Ellipsen, praktisch einen Kreis schliesst – bis zu dem Punkt, da schiere Grösse und Masse den Zwang, zu entscheiden und zu bestimmen, nicht länger überstrapazieren. Mit den TORQUED ELLIPSES wird dieser Bezirk der Erinnerung an Bauten, die einst zur Gänze von Intention durchwaltet waren, zu einem Traum von etwas in sich Geschlossenem, Planlosem und aus seiner ursprünglichen Verschalung Befreitem.   *(Übersetzung: Bram Opstelten)*

1) Richard Serra: *Writings, Interviews*, The University of Chicago Press, Chicago 1994, S. 183.
2) Ebenda, S. 184.
3) Reem Koolhaas, *S, M, L, XL*, Monacelli Press, New York, 1996, S. 511.
4) Ebenda, S. 514.

Collaborations

Karen Kilimnik,
born 1955 in Philadelphia, PA,
lives and works in Philadelphia /
geboren 1955 in Philadelphia, Pennsylvania,
lebt und arbeitet in Philadelphia.

Malcolm Morley,
born 1931 in London,
lives and works in Brooheaven, NY /
geboren 1931 in London,
lebt und arbeitet in Brooheaven, New York

Ugo Rondinone,
geboren 1963 in Brunnen
(Kanton Schwyz), Schweiz,
lebt und arbeitet in Zürich /
born 1963 in Brunnen, Switzerland,
lives and works in Zurich.

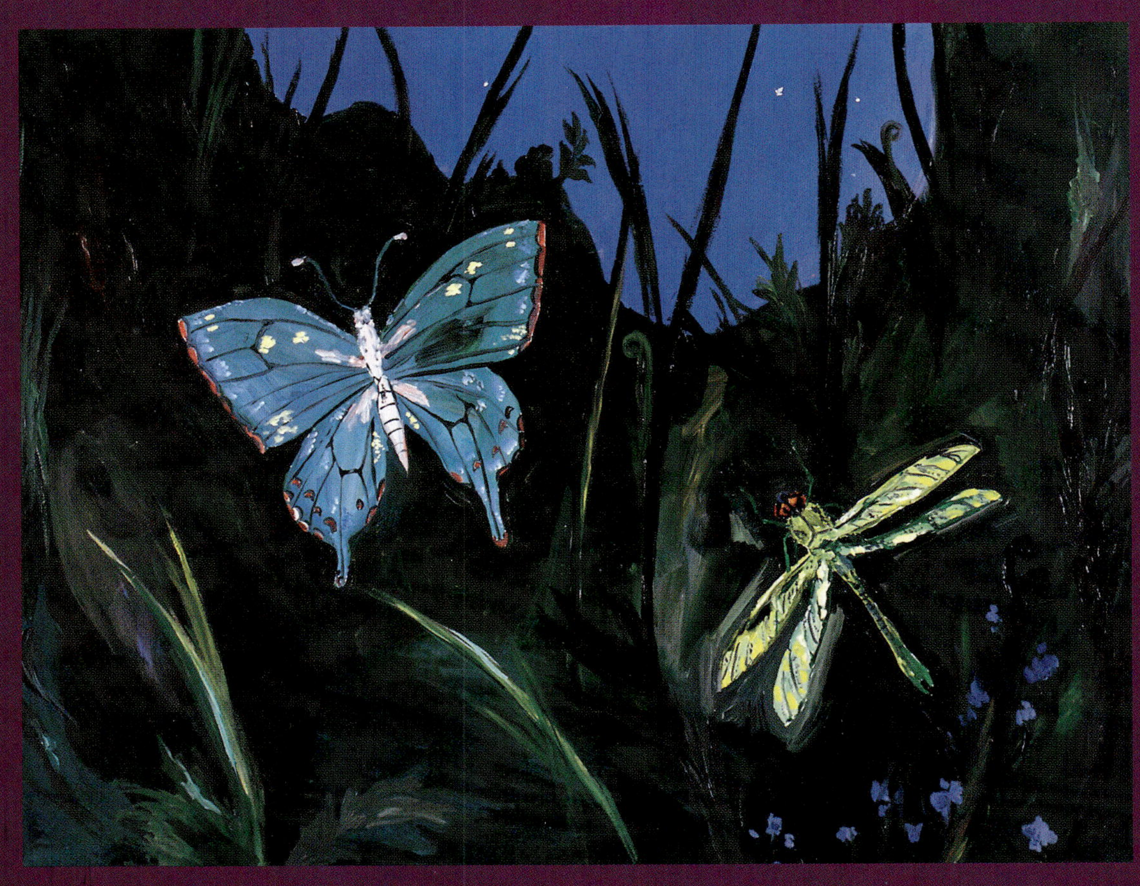

Karen Kilimnik

I can change any perception all the time.   Karen Kilimnik

COLLIER SCHORR

The Good, the Bad, and the Awfully Beautiful

Weather is a significant force in the work of Karen Kilimnik. Storms and brushfires. The aftereffects of a good-sized hurricane or maybe a tornado. There is darkness and then there is the sinister afterdark, when the moon makes mist into a textural flashlight. There is fog in the form of dry ice and a blower. A campfire sputters as do lit candles when drops of rain start to fall. All this is mood music. Organs fingered by Vincent Price or Lonely Widows. Led Zeppelin played backwards in a basement rec room. A light burns in the window on the top floor of an otherwise darkened house. But instead of one of the Brontë sisters, it's the younger sister, Princess Stephanie. Sometimes she is out, living it up at a Parisian hot spot, a disco with a strobe light show and plenty of racing-car drivers and bodyguards. Sometimes she is coursing the narrow winding roads of Monaco, looking for her mother's Ghost. And sometimes she just stays home, roaming the endless corridors of her father's palace. She is a sad Princess, like most, but she also knows how to have a good time. She's the youngest and the black sheep. She's not bad, but she'll never be the good sister.

COLLIER SCHORR is an artist and the U.S. editor of *Frieze Magazine.* She shows in the same gallery as Karen Kilimnik.

At times Kilimnik's work seems overwhelmingly dramatic and nostalgic; candles and candelabras float like apparitions, heavy pastels accentuate rays of light and flushed cheeks. At others, it is so modern, so completely contemporary and sarcastic; the details of a model's outfit are meticulously recorded, as is Cindy Crawford's confession to being marketed on the look of the now dead model-star Gia. From books with characters named Melmoth or Udolpho or Ambrosio to the canonical *Wuthering Heights*, to Deborah Turbeville's photos of nightgowned tribes of women, to Andy Warhol's *Frankenstein* and *Dracula*, to Truman Capote's *Other Voices, Other Rooms*, to Robert Smith's *The Cure*, to models with makeup circles under their eyes, rolling around in the shadows of a Gucci advertisement. This is not stuff for the faint at heart; rather it is material for those who understand that shame, evil, and guilt can be endlessly elaborated, that accusations are a place in which weakened egos breed.

In WITCHCRAFT/THE CRAFT (1995) another dark sky opens above a cluster of candles mimicking a campfire. The wind shifts as a torrential storm approaches. Why else would the campers have fled? Fear at summoning a dead spirit? Sex? Perhaps. The rain, and with it the suggestion of gloom, thunder, and cover of darkness, enable Kilimnik's cross-associations. As she pushes around black paint in a grave-yard or behind a portrait of the late Princess Diana, she shrouds the bright glare of modernity, providing a landscape where romanticism can flourish. What is particularly remarkable is that she is able to endow her work with a timeless quality, all the while insert-ing pop-cultural images. But as much as Kilimnik uti-lizes current iconography—Kate Moss, Calvin Klein, and Amber Valetta, Bulgari, Alicia Silverstone, and Hugh Grant—it is the tenets of Gothic literature that lend her work its pervasive flux. "In the novel, it was the function of Gothic to open horizons beyond social patterns, rational decisions and institutionally approved emotions; in a word to enlarge the sense of reality and its impact on the human being."[1] Homes are consumed by fires or, more oddly, furniture burns like a lovely fireplace awkwardly placed in the center of a room. Windows are used to create bound-aries between nature and home life, to rearrange the dimension of spaces, and to cast doubt upon their very existence. Women are often thin; melancholia abounds. In I'M NOT WHO YOU THINK I AM, AND I HATE YOU TOO (1994), a mask slips down the bridge of a nose, silencing a mysterious masquerader. Most of her characters appear cut out and collaged, travel-ing between languages—Italian and French, always open to mistranslation—and contexts.[2]

There is an odd transparency or hollowness to Kilimnik's sketches; although drawn from photo-graphs her subjects seem to be drifting through, the star in one, an afterthought in another. This is not to say that they ring false, but rather that they express the fast pace of fame and notoriety. Individually, they evoke the feeling of being able to poke your finger through something; together, like anatomical over-lays in medical textbooks, they build a composite site. Drawn with a heavy hand in pastel and a less intense one in choppy crayon, the drawings vacillate, at once seemingly maladroit in gesture and wickedly concrete in notation. Unlike the hobby-sized viscous paintings which generally adhere to one stream of thought and a single backdrop, Kilimnik's drawings play with an assortment of recurring and intermin-gled themes: fallen idols, social strata, career women, public failure. Sibling rivalry, particularly that of sis-ters, is an oft-mentioned construct: Whether it be Cindy Crawford and her look-alike ghost Gia, or the Grimaldi's, or Serena and Samantha Boardman, dis-tinctions are always made: "Stephanie is blond, short-er... Lisa is a professional model."

With a touch of Maxim's longing for his Rebecca, Kilimnik sets up the perfect Gothic plot which runs through her recent book of drawings: the specter of the dead beauty, Gia Carangi, and the appearance of the pretender, Cindy Crawford, to her throne. While her deadpan humor is evident in texts such as "...Death on Thursdays...death on Thursdays, the same club that's hot on a Monday night is death on Thurs-day..." Kilimnik interrupts the organ-playing, cuts the strain of violins which symbolize yearning and unrequited love, inevitably returning to the dichoto-my between internal drama and outside action. A woman named Harriet Neston peers off into space while a window that may or may not represent a premonition frames an embracing couple. Accord-ing to Kilimnik, Neston is engaged to a childhood friend (see Heathcliff and Cathy), and "She had to know what was in his mind, but once again Harriet felt herself to be on the outside, looking in..." This notion was further expanded in Kilimnik's last exhi-bition at 303 Gallery in New York where twice a week, on Wednesdays and Saturdays, velvet curtains drew automatically across the front window of the gallery, enveloping the viewers in darkness in preparation for a SLEEPING BEAUTY sound-and-light show.

Kilimnik forms a bridge between nineteenth- and twentieth-century Gothic literature and neo-Gothic subcultures, using the temperament and accoutre-ments of the former and the gossip and chattiness of the latter. Like James Purdy, the master of the mod-ern southern Gothic novel, she mainstreams histori-cal mannerisms and phraseology with modern benchmarks. In Purdy's *In a Shallow Grave* (itself a play on Gothic grave-speak), a soldier, ravaged beyond recognition, lives from day to day on the caresses of a young boy while writing epistles to a long-lost fiancée. The language shifts back and forth as do the conventions of the time. Kilimnik herself uses stilted dialogue: "...The heart of the house beats warmer" or "Harriet Neston's engagement to her childhood companion...had seemed a natural, happy outcome of their close friendship" or "When I tried

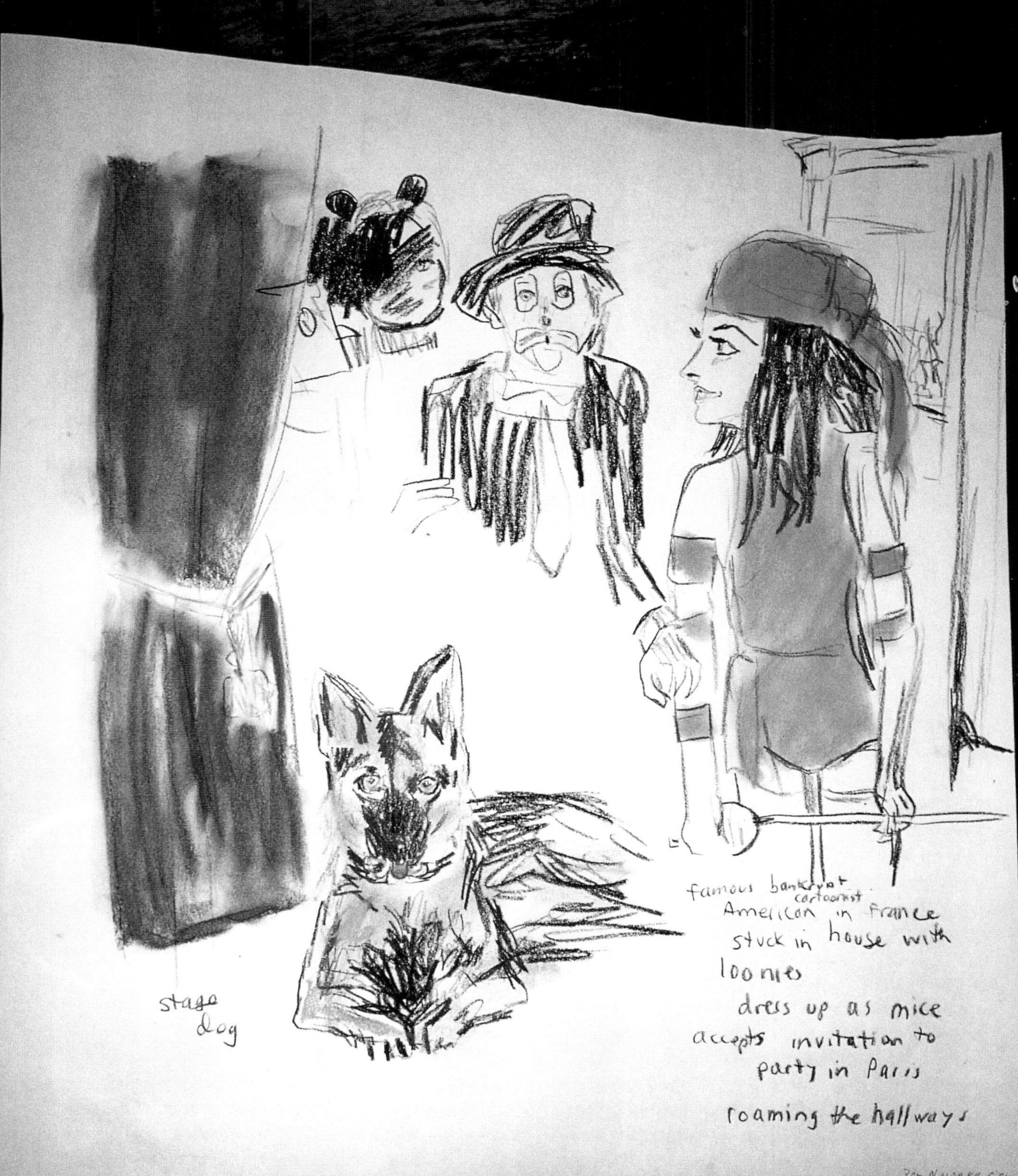

stage
dog
famous bankrupt
cartoonist
American in France
stuck in house with
loonies
dress up as mice
accepts invitation to
party in Paris
roaming the hallways

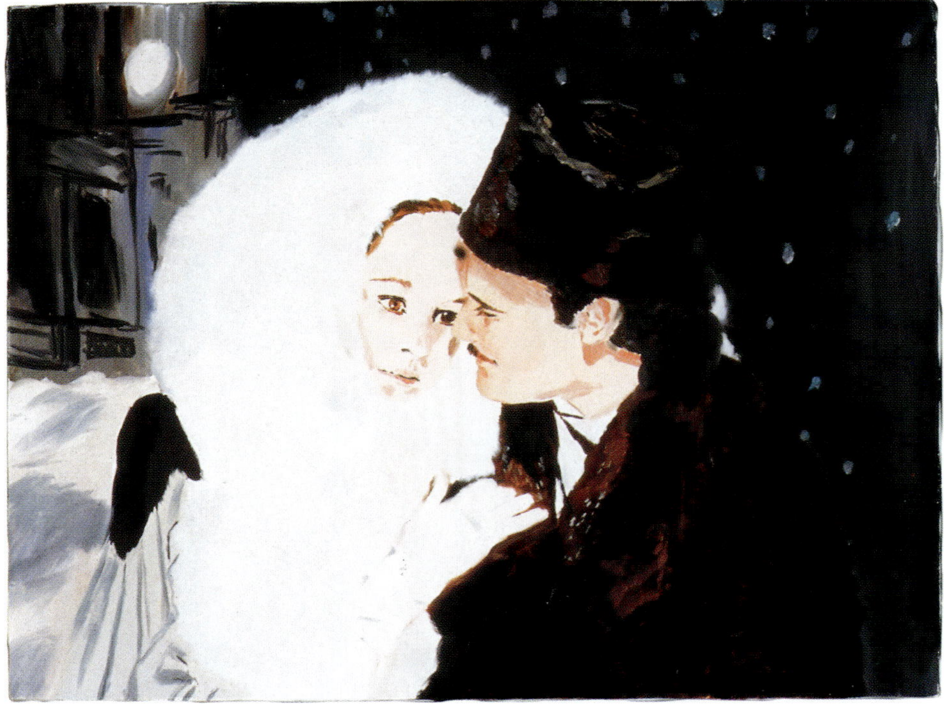

KAREN KILIMNIK, THE SLEIGH RIDE, 1996, oil on canvas, 18 x 24" / DIE SCHLITTENFAHRT, Öl auf Leinwand, 46 x 61 cm.

to understand these things, it was too hard for me; until I entered the sanctuary of god and discerned the end of the wicked"—mixed with quotidian speech—"If it were true he [the priest] were interested in male hustlers I'd have found one or two that would have told me" or "I've never had problems with drugs only policemen and if you close every disco don't think it won't show on your face."

Like institutions, a home in Kilimnik's work is something either to escape from or to intrude on. It is rarely the site of familial harmony. Nowhere is the drama more high-pitched than in the drawing HE ATTEMPTED TO FREE HER FROM THE COFFIN (THE [POUND] 50,000 BREAKFAST) (1984), where an androgynous girl appears poised to paint her toenails. Surrounded by icons such as a calendar page Thursday the 12th, burning candles, and a horseshoe funeral wreath, Kilimnik's entry contains the drama: "His closest sibling, a sister, died when he was five + so close was he to her, that he attempted to free her from the coffin at her funeral." Dressed in a Union Jack suit, her lineage harking back to an eighteenth-century colonel, the girl represents a useful dyad:

Euro-American; old money versus new. Modeling and royalty; celebrity and wealth. Royalty always has an impenetrable fortress, an illegitimate child, a locked-away wife, a bad seed or an idiot. In Princesses Stephanie and Caroline of Monaco, Kilimnik has the ideal double to play with. One is good, one made a dance album. They combine fame and infamy. And, most importantly, they are half-American. They have both been the constant prey of European paparazzi, and it is the European tabloids that provide Kilimnik's drawings with their semifactual captions.

In a sense, it is this predatory journalism that has replaced the mythic proportions of the Gothic existence: Lives are ruined in a single act. The unbelievable truth about Hugh Grant (another featured Kilimnik performer) bleeds into two postmodern portraits of Princess Diana, and with it tabloid's role as hostage-holder in the church confessional. The tabloid purports to tell the secret and when it is lucky, its prodding forces the celebrity to confess. Again, as in Gothic literature, the secret looms large, but with the tabloids and Kilimnik, all acts become both unspeakable and simultaneously divulged. Like

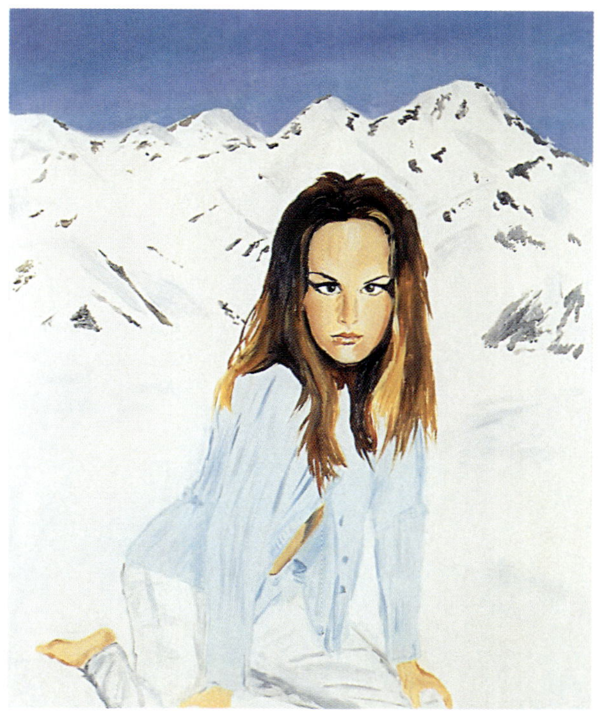

The Star and *The Sun*, Kilimnik loves to unveil society and celebrity; mentioning with admiration Monica Vitti's dyed hair and false eyelashes, repeating a cruel joke about a younger actress's inability to land a role.

If Gothic literature is tempered by winding plot-lines and locked doors, a labyrinth of probabilities characterized by the "Unspeakable, the unutterable horror,"[3] then Kilimnik's work revises not only the idea of the suppressed, but also the absence or veiling of narration. While there are any number of narrators in a Gothic tale or a Kilimnik work, the artist's handwriting and notations do much to reveal her desire to conflate the musings or accusations of others in the public sphere with her own.[4] Her intense printing, frantic, choppy, and at times dyslexic, is interspersed between and around bodies that may or may not be directly related; at times the text takes on the structure of a poetic stanza, at others entries from a diary. In the drawing THE FELLOWSHIP IS ALL (1994), a sullen-faced girl with one eye erased and the other blacked out becomes the unhappy anecdotist. "So I hoped he was going to cry. I did feel a little bad but he has been so mean to me—plus there he

was with Bianca and they were sharing their food—it was sickening." It is thus through her own handwriting that Kilimnik insinuates herself into the script, cast as the rival of Bianca Jagger. In a sense, she devises an alternative kind of autobiography where she is and is not revealed. Like a reluctant ghost writer, she retells someone else's story, but then can't resist dropping conflicted autobiographical hints, leaving her fingerprints. This subliminal form of biography enables masochism without the dreary blows of self-flagellation. The cruelty, the teasing, is almost always directed at those whom she admires. In the drawing BUBBLE GUM HABIT, the topic is the beloved Gia.[5] Drugs, AIDS, Studio 54, and Shopping are a few of the categories indexed in the tribute: "Call Marietta Plane Ticket…Get Heroin, Call Sandy, Buy Incense and Beautiful Rehab."

Kilimnik's snippets of text mimic her placement of objects across gallery floors in her "scatter" pieces, the seemingly unordered but, in fact, highly structured installations for which she is best known. The disturbing effects of these apparently strewn elements translates rather well into the two-dimension-

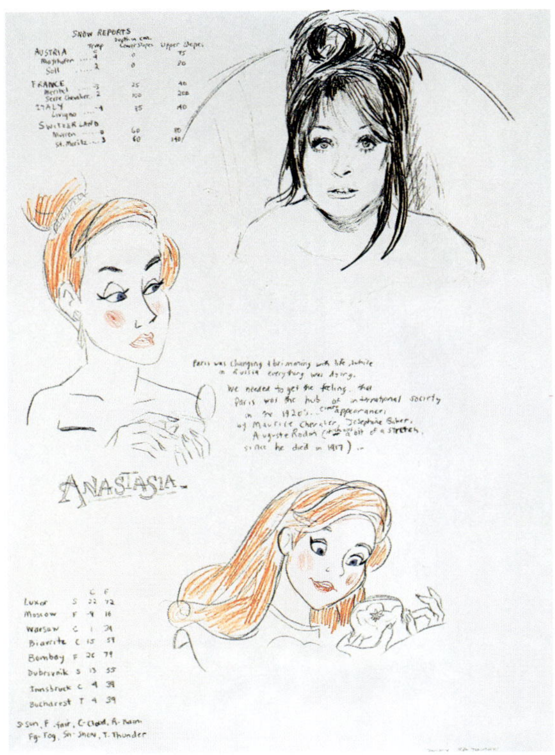

KAREN KILIMNIK, SNOW REPORTS, 1998,
crayon and pastel on paper, 35 x 23" /
SCHNEEBERICHTE, Kreide und Pastell auf Papier,
89 x 58,4 cm.

KAREN KILIMNIK, FAIRY FOOD ON STREET, 1993, color photograph / ELFENFUTTER AUF DER STRASSE, Farbphotographie.

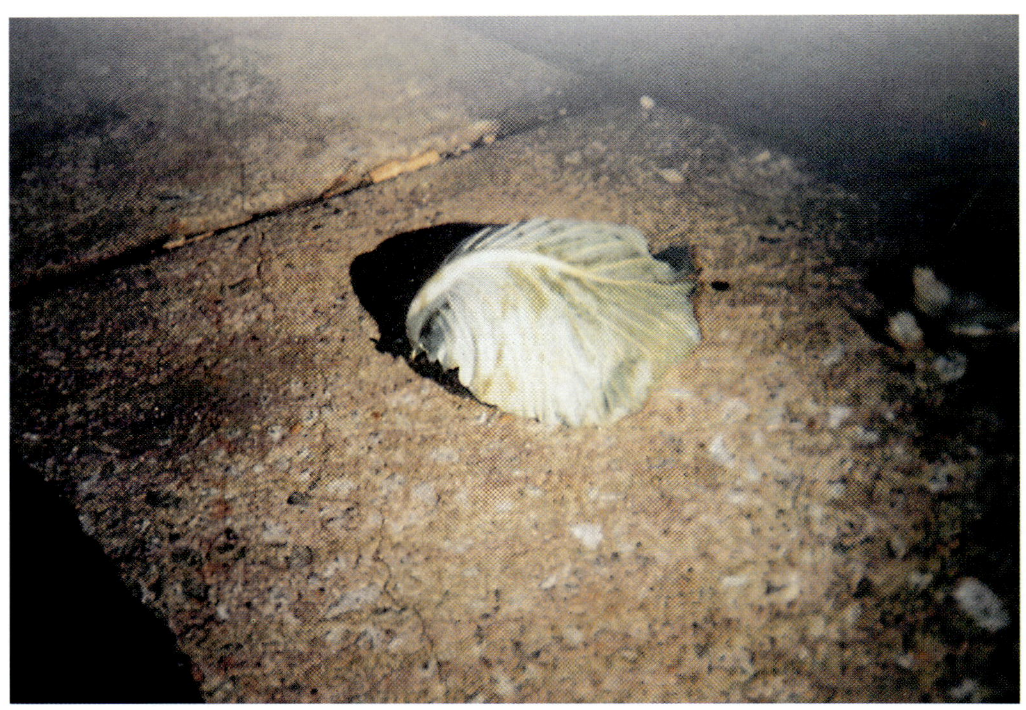

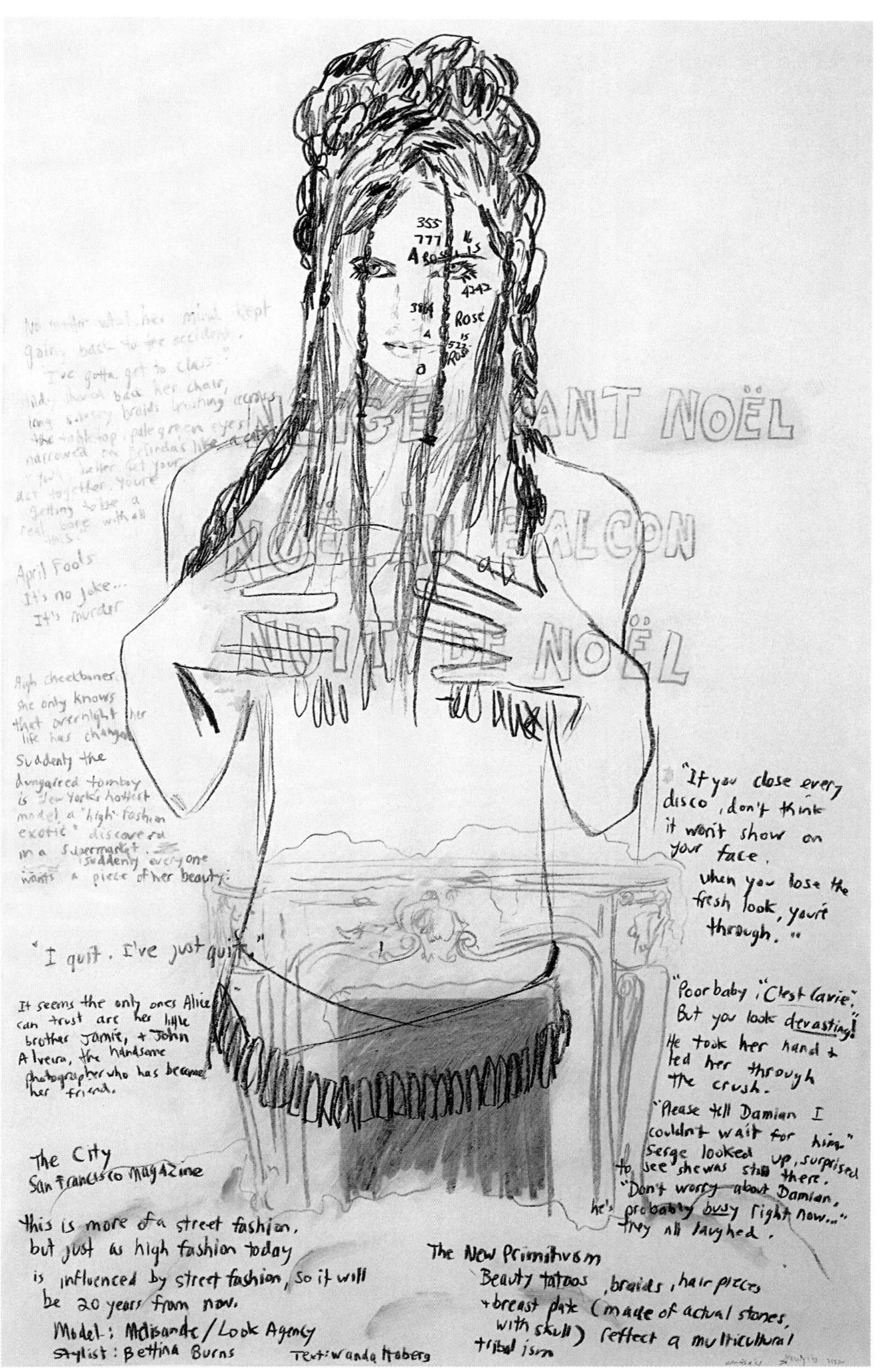

KAREN KILIMNIK, NUIT DE NOËL (THE NEW PRIMITIVISM), 1993, watercolor paint and crayon on paper, 35 x 22½ /
NUIT DE NOËL (DER NEUE PRIMITIVISMUS), Wasserfarbe, Pigment und Kreide auf Papier, 89 x 57 cm.

ality of drawing. She uses text in much the same way as she uses drops of blood or fire, to decorate and infuse. Like the tracks of crimson across the floor of the INSTITUT DE BEAUTÉ, the texts highlight her brutality at work, whether it occurs in a salon that gives dangerously close pedicures or in the revelations of the printed word. Every weakness is highlighted to show that Kilimnik has a fondness for those who have flaws.

In the Gothic, it is the uncovering of the secret and the subsequent confession that allows the protagonist to escape the uncanny. In literature, this might be a secret that frees a couple to unite or escape an underground prison; in Kilimnik's work, it is the static zone of the glossy fashion magazines that becomes the dungeon, albeit a sparkly one. A portrait of model Twiggy includes a telling pop quiz: *What are Twiggy's measurements? 29–20–26 or 31–22–32?* Above her head float names of dairy concoctions. Of course, Kilimnik is concerned with the issue of weight gain and loss, but at the same time she teases the slight figure with visions of whipping cream. When asked if it was fun to imitate tabloid gossip, she answers. "Well, I guess I wish I could be that funny." She is, when she teases Elizabeth Hurley, but quickly adds that she hopes Elizabeth isn't hurt by it. Sympathy abounds.

Karen Kilimnik takes a certain pleasure in repeating the nasty innuendo. It is her desire that we, as gallery visitors, revisit our own desire to know how embarrassed someone else is, to monitor our attention to being mean. The Fashion Magazine plays good sister to the Tabloids' bad sister. Cut up tear sheets with odd pull-quotes float like Gossip Magazine collages. Kilimnik amplifies tabloid accusations, taking on their tone as well as their front-page assemblage of assorted characters. Her particular brand of transgression, this urge to reflect the most banal characteristics of someone else's life probably originated in the cold-blooded JANE CREEP series. Begun in the late eighties, these unceremonious scrawls of text—remarkable next to the equally psychotic handwritten jokes of Richard Prince—are a template of things to come. Lore says that the anonymous Jane was a torturer from Kilimnik's highschool days. In a litany spanning some twenty-five drawings, Jane is transformed from victimizer to victim, in effect switching places with Kilimnik. From the overwhelmingly Gothic JANE FALLS ASLEEP AT AN UNDERTAKERS + IS MISTAKEN FOR THE NEXT CLIENT to the hilarious JANE HAS A LOUD VOICE AND NOBODY CAN STAND HER, Kilimnik delights in confessing her ungood intentions—I GIVE JANE A MAN-EATING PLANT AND TELL HER IT NEEDS TO BE WASHED BY HAND NEXT WEEK. The aggression directed at Jane is synonymous with tales of heavy metal boys, satanists, greasers, and losers who end up in the news because of botched suicide pacts and successful patricides.[6]

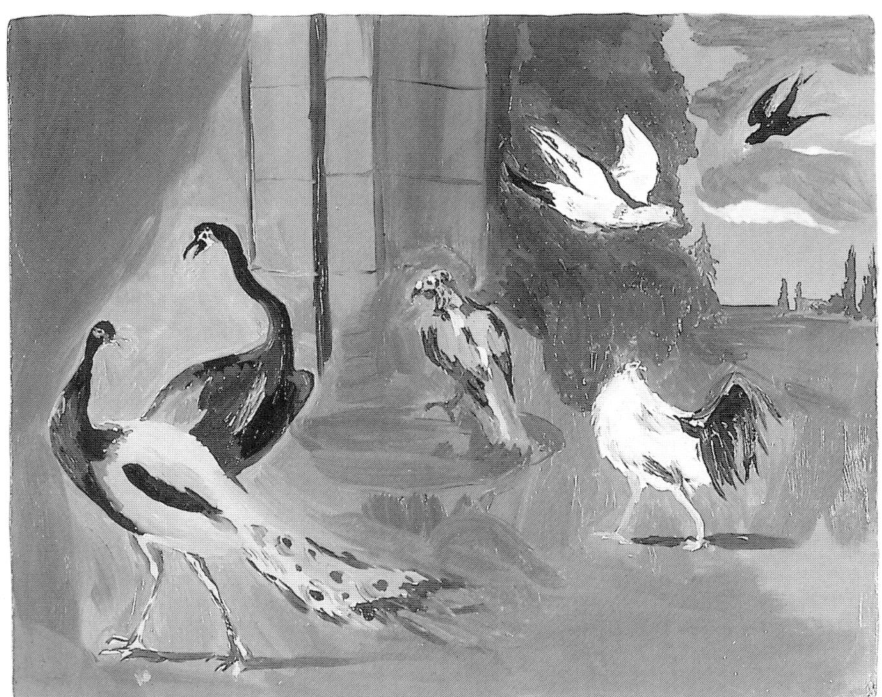

KAREN KILIMNIK, EXOTIC BIRDS I (AT BREAKFAST), 1996, 11 x 14" / EXOTISCHE VÖGEL I (BEIM FRÜHSTÜCK), 28 x 33,5 cm.

KAREN KILIMNIK, MY PETS—RALPH, 1997, oil on canvas, 20 x16" / MEINE SCHOSSTIERE – RALPH, Öl auf Leinwand, 51 x 41 cm.

Kilimnik writes like a kid copying rock lyrics onto notebooks and jeans: capital letters and the thrill of authoring, if only in dreams, such mantras as WE WILL, WE WILL, ROCK YOU. It is interesting to note that while Kilimnik's work is often described as girlish her posture seems quite unisexual, certainly crossing gender lines with regard to narration and action. Nowhere is this more apparent than in her compulsive use of arson. Fire, in her work, has usually been attributed to the feminine, to witchcraft, but the connection between boys and fire shouldn't be glossed over. Pyromania, or fire-setting, is generally diagnosed as a disorder affecting young boys. That it is a recurrent theme in Kilimnik's world suggests not only that the subject of many of her works is the little girl who covets the ballerina's body, but that little girl could also be a boy. This supposition would puncture the critiques that view the work as belonging exclusively to the feminine domain. While Kilimnik does investigate the construction of beauty complexes, she also reinvests her gender with less popular and gender-specific dysfunctions.

The castigation and rescue that reverberate simultaneously between text and body in Kilimnik's work create an odd and unsettling relationship to its subjects. Unlike other painters who focus on the well-known, the beautiful, and the dynamic between the famous and the secondary (Billy Sullivan's Johnny Depp and Skeet Ulrich, Elizabeth Peyton's Liam Gallagher and Jarvis Cocker), Kilimnik is less absorbed in their perfection. While Sullivan articulates an amused and enchanted cynicism and Peyton exercises the authentic doe eyes of fan, Kilimnik is a bit of a killer. She loves to love them but at times they seem to get on even her nerves. Each character, from fairy tale princesses and birds, to heiresses, orphans, and models, becomes a vessel for a broad mixture of self-doubt and conceit. They're so beautiful, she seems to say with some pause, as if talking about girls in her highschool, behind their backs, next to them in stalls they shared while they smoked cigarettes or made out. And yet, just when you're sure that the toes tracing with distraction at the caulk on the pink tiled floor are hers, you realise that she is far removed from any locale, social stratum or identity. Maybe she loves them but sometimes they are just an after-

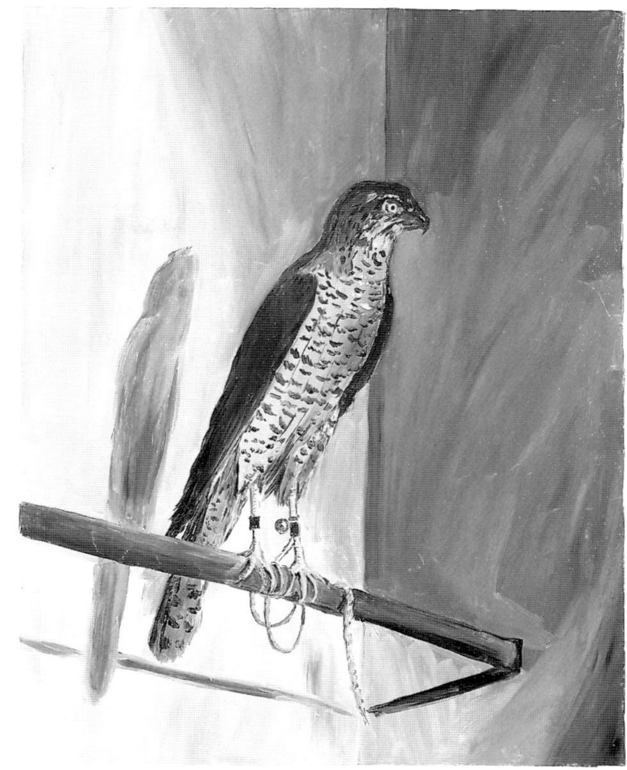

thought, a stroke of the brush through the long brown cartoon hair of Anastasia, or a notation that cuts sentimentality loose.

1) Eve Kosofsky Sedgwick, *The Coherence of Gothic Conventions* (New York and London: Methuen, 1980), p. 3.
2) When asked if the texts in her drawings were exclusively appropriated from articles, Kilimnik replied, "I'm not a really good person to ask, 'cause I will totally forget things and remember them later. But, it varies. Sometimes I'll write things and a lot of times I'll lift quotes that I find funny. Most of the time it's probably lifted quotes. With the earlier drawings it was my translation (when it was another language). The very early ones, before I barely knew any other languages, would be translated just for fun, kind of transposing the words, and what they sounded like, taking particular words and what they sounded like and turning them into something else, but I kind of knew." (From a conversation between the author and the artist in December 1997)
3) In Charles Robert Maturin's *Melmoth the Wanderer*, 1820, as cited by Sedgwick, p. 14.
4) Besides rewriting details, Kilimnik turns biographical studies into pseudo-autobiographies via her own hand.
5) The ill-fated Gia Carangi, a famous model who died penniless and homeless from drug-induced AIDS is Kilimnik's local obsession. Not only would Gia have been about the same age as Karen if she was alive today; they come from the same town, Philadelphia. Against the backdrop of the current widespread fixation with supermodels, Gia was recently the subject of a much-hyped American bestseller and, at the time of writing this essay, a movie made for television.
6) One need only look at her blood-splattered installations to see that this project goes beyond playing with ponies.

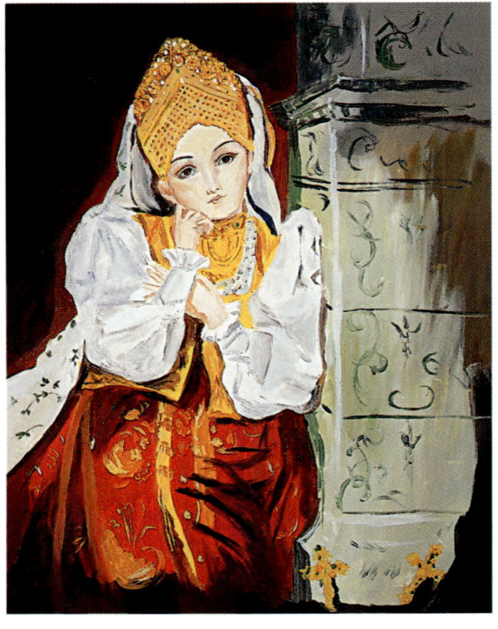

KAREN KILIMNIK, RUSSIAN ICON, 1998,
water-based oil on canvas, 20 x 16" /
RUSSISCHE IKONE, Emulsion auf Leinwand, 51 x 41 cm.

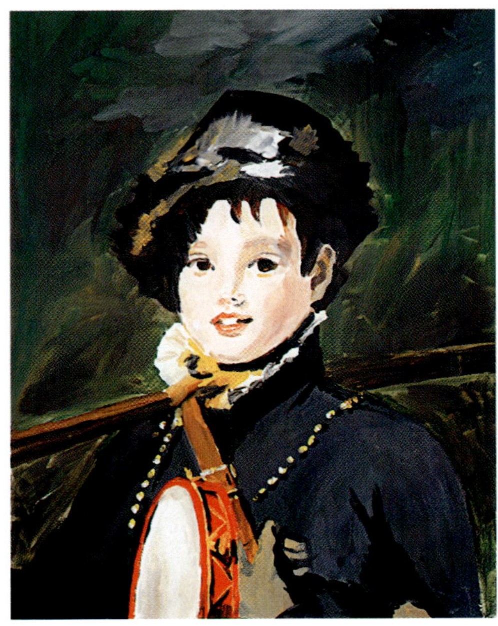

KAREN KILIMNIK, IAN PLAYING SOLDIER, 1997,
water-based oil on canvas, 20 x 16" /
IAN SPIELT SOLDAT, Emulsion auf Leinwand, 51 x 41 cm.

KAREN KILIMNIK, FROSTBITE IN THE TATAR ARMY, 1564,
WITH SNOWFLAKE. SNOWFLAKE, A MIRAGE OR WHITED OUT
SNOW, 1996, oil on canvas, 16 x 14" / FROSTBEULEN IN DER
TATARENARMEE, 1564, MIT SCHNEEFLOCKE. SCHNEEFLOCKE,
FATA MORGANA ODER AUSGESPARTER SCHNEE,
Öl auf Leinwand, 41 x 35,6 cm.

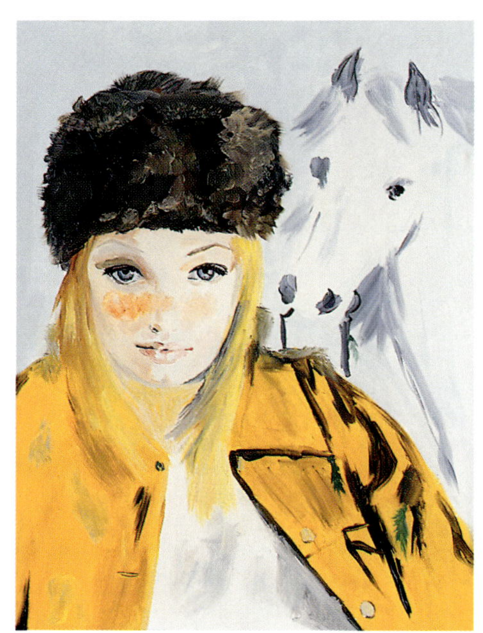

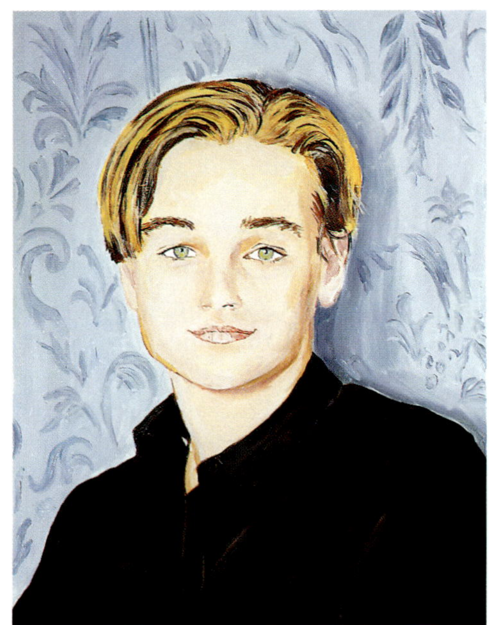

KAREN KILIMNIK, PRINCE DÉSIRÉE ON A BREAK FROM
SLEEPING BEAUTY OUT AT PETROSSIAN'S FOR DINNER, 1998,
water-based oil on canvas, 18 x 24" / PRINZ DÉSIRÉE BEURLAUBT
VON DORNRÖSCHEN IM PETROSSIAN ZUM ABENDESSEN,
Emulsion auf Leinwand, 46 x 61 cm.

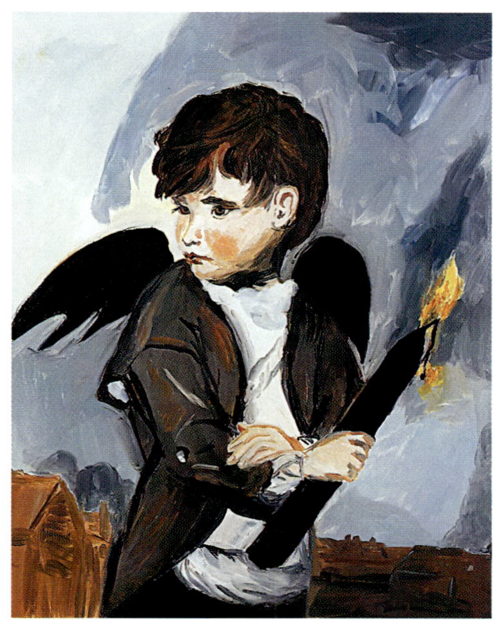

KAREN KILIMNIK, BABY, 1995, oil on canvas,
20 x 16" / Öl auf Leinwand, 51 x 41 cm.

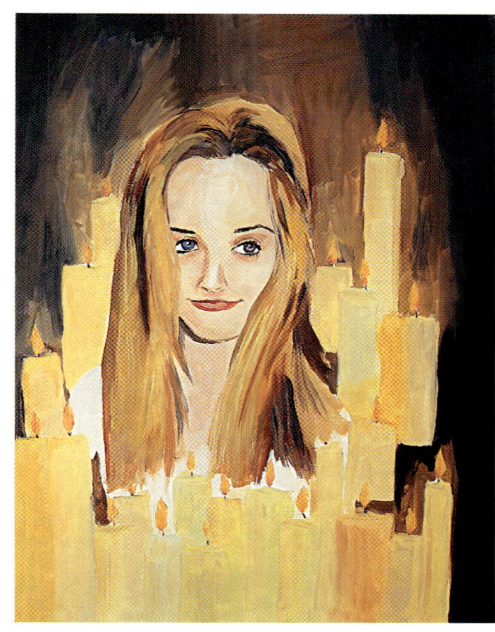

KAREN KILIMNIK, THE CRUSH, 1995, oil on canvas, 28 x 22" /
DER SCHWARM, 1995, Öl auf Leinwand, 71 x 56 cm.

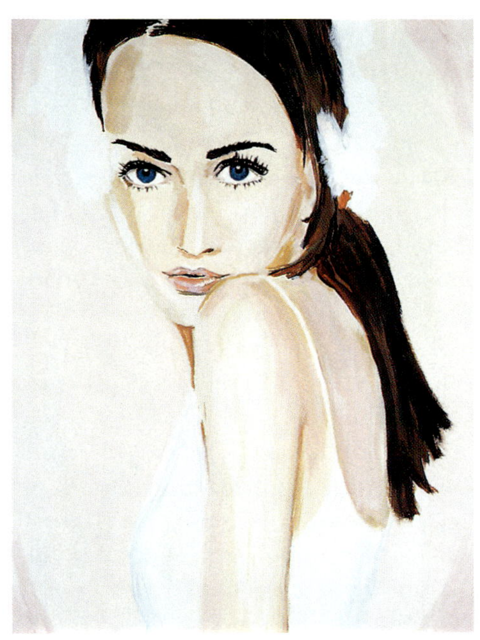

KAREN KILIMNIK, A SWAN BACKSTAGE AT THE BOLSHOI,
1996, oil on canvas, 16 x 14" / EIN SCHWAN HINTER DER BÜHNE
DES BOLSCHOITHEATERS, Öl auf Leinwand, 40,6 x 35,6 cm.

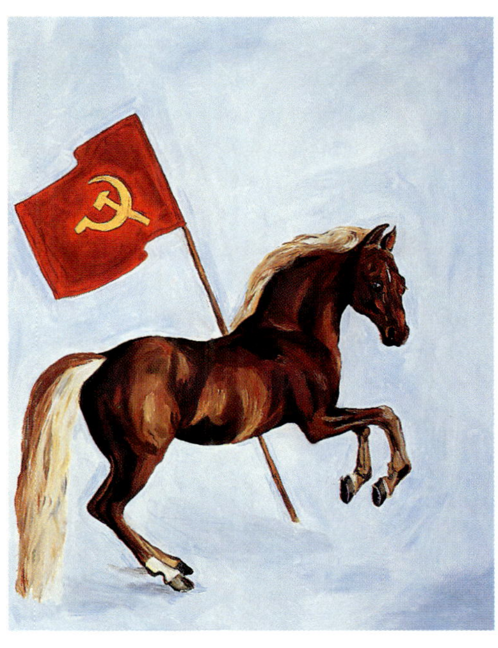

KAREN KILIMNIK, THE RED ARMY, 1998,
water-based oil on canvas, 20 x 16" /
DIE ROTE ARMEE, Emulsion auf Leinwand, 51 x 41 cm.

COLLIER SCHORR

Ich kann jede Art der Wahrnehmung jederzeit verändern.   Karen Kilimnik

Die Guten, die Bösen und die schrecklich Schönen

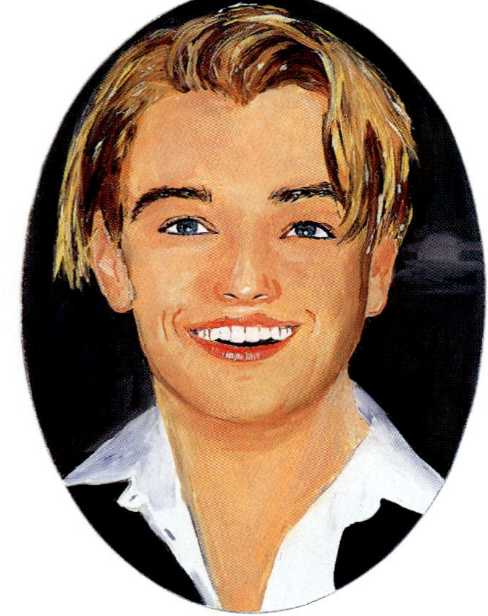

Das Wetter ist eine bestimmende Kraft in Karen Kilimniks Werk. Stürme und Buschfeuer. Die Folgen eines grösseren Hurrikans oder Tornados. Dunkelheit bricht herein, und es wird unheimlich; Dunstschleier muten im Mondlicht beinahe greifbar an. Ein Gebläse lässt Trockeneisnebel wallen. Ein Lagerfeuer zischt wie brennende Kerzen, als plötzlich Regentropfen fallen. All dies ist Stimmungsmusik. Orgelspiel von Vincent Price oder Lonely Widows. Led Zeppelin im Partykeller rückwärts gespielt. Im obersten Stock eines dunklen Hauses brennt in einem Fenster ein Licht. Doch hier geht es nicht um eine der Brontë-Schwestern, sondern um die jüngere Schwester, Prinzessin Stephanie. Manchmal geht sie aus und haut in einem Pariser Nachtklub auf den Putz, einer Disco mit Stroboskoplicht und Rennfahrern und Bodyguards im Überfluss. Manchmal eilt sie durch die engen, gewundenen Strassen Monacos, auf der Suche nach dem Geist ihrer Mutter. Und manchmal bleibt sie ganz einfach zu Hause und streift durch die endlosen Flure im Palast ihres Vaters. Sie ist eine traurige Prinzessin, wie die meisten, aber sie weiss auch, wie man sich amüsiert. Sie ist die Jüngste und das schwarze Schaf. Schlecht ist sie nicht, aber sie wird nie die gute Schwester sein.

Mitunter scheinen Kilimniks Werke überwältigend dramatisch und nostalgisch: Kerzen und Kandelaber schweben geisterhaft im Raum, Lichtstrahlen und gerötete Wangen werden durch kräftige Pastellstriche akzentuiert. Dann wieder sind sie ausgesprochen modern, durch und durch heutig und sarkastisch: Peinlich genau wird die Kleidung eines Models in allen Einzelheiten dokumentiert, ebenso wie Cindy Crawfords Geständnis, dass sie als Nachfolgerin des verstorbenen Starmodels Gia lanciert wurde. Das Spektrum ist breit: von Romanen, deren Helden Melmoth, Udolpho oder Ambrosio heissen, über Emily Brontës *Sturmhöhe*, Deborah Turbevilles Photos von Frauen im Nachtgewand, Andy Warhols *Frankenstein* und *Dracula*, Truman Capotes *Andere Stimmen, andere Räume* und Robert Smiths *The Cure* bis zu Models mit aufgeschminkten Augenringen, die im Schatten einer Gucci-Werbung herumtorkeln. Das ist nichts für schwache Nerven, sondern eher etwas für Leute, die begreifen, dass die Schande, das Böse und die Schuld ständig weiterentwickelt werden können,

---

COLLIER SCHORR ist Künstlerin und Amerika-Redaktorin der Kunstzeitschrift *Frieze*. Sie stellt in derselben Galerie wie Karen Kilimnik aus.

und die auch wissen, dass Anschuldigungen ein guter Nährboden für ein geschwächtes Selbstbewusstsein sind.

In WITCHCRAFT/THE CRAFT (Hexerei/Das Handwerk, 1995) hängt wiederum ein dunkler Himmel über einer Ansammlung von Kerzen, die ein Lagerfeuer darstellen sollen. Der Wind dreht, da ein gewaltiger Sturm im Anzug ist. Weshalb hätten die Camper sonst fliehen sollen? Weil sie den Geist eines Toten beschworen hatten? Wegen Sex? Vielleicht. Der Regen und die damit einhergehenden Gedanken an Düsterkeit, Donner und schützende Dunkelheit lösen vielerlei Assoziationen aus. Wenn Kilimnik auf einem Friedhof oder hinter einem Porträt von Prinzessin Diana schwarze Farbe verstreicht, verhüllt sie den grellen Schein der Modernität und kreiert eine Landschaft, in der die Romantik gedeihen kann. Besonders bemerkenswert ist, dass es ihr gelingt, ihren Werken etwas Zeitloses zu verleihen, obschon sie ständig mit Bildern der Popkultur arbeitet. Aber auch wenn sich Kilimnik einer aktuellen Ikonographie bedient – Kate Moss, Calvin Klein und Amber Valetta, Bulgari, Alicia Silverstone und Hugh Grant –, so sind es doch die Prinzipien des Schauerromans, die ihren Werken den expansiven Fluss verleihen. Im Roman hatte das Gruselige die Funktion, den Horizont über soziale Muster, rationale Entscheidungen und offiziell anerkannte Emotionen hinaus zu erweitern, mit einem Wort, den Realitätssinn und seine Auswirkung auf den Menschen auszudehnen.[1] Häuser gehen in Flammen auf oder, was seltsamer anmutet, Möbel brennen wie ein schmucker Kamin, der etwas ungünstig mitten im Raum plaziert ist. Fenster dienen dazu, Trennlinien zwischen Natur und Heim zu ziehen, die Dimension von Räumen zu verändern und ihre Existenz in Zweifel zu ziehen. Frauen sind oft dünn, die Stimmung melancholisch. In I'M NOT WHO YOU THINK I AM, AND I HATE YOU TOO (Ich bin nicht die, für die du mich hältst, und ausserdem hasse ich dich, 1994) gleitet einer geheimnisvollen Person eine Maske von der Nase und bringt sie zum Schweigen. Die meisten von Kilimniks Figuren scheinen irgendwo ausgeschnitten und zu Collagen verarbeitet worden zu sein, als Reisende zwischen verschiedenen Kontexten und Sprachen – Italienisch und Französisch, vor Übersetzungsfehlern nie gefeit.[2]

Kilimniks Zeichnungen sind merkwürdig transparent oder hohl; obschon ihre Motive nach Photos abgezeichnet sind, scheinen sie einfach durch die Bilder zu wandern, wobei die Hauptperson eines Bildes als Nebenfigur wieder in einem anderen auftauchen kann. Das soll nicht heissen, dass sie falsch wirken, sondern vielmehr, dass sie uns vor Augen führen, wie kurzlebig sowohl die rühmliche als auch die berüchtigte Berühmtheit ist. Als Einzelbilder vermitteln sie das Gefühl, man könne sie mit dem Finger durchbohren. Zusammen stellen sie, wie anatomische Auflegefolien in einem medizinischen Lehrbuch, ein komplexes Gebilde dar. Ausgeführt mit kräftigen Pastellstrichen und feineren, unruhigen Kreidestrichen, erscheinen die Zeichnungen vermeintlich ungeschickt im Gestus und zugleich boshaft konkret, was die schriftlichen Anmerkungen betrifft. Anders als die kleinformatigen viskosen Bilder, die im allgemeinen von einem einzigen Gedankenstrom und nur einem Hintergrund ausgehen, spielen Kilimniks Zeichnungen mit einer ganzen Palette von ständig wiederkehrenden und miteinander in Beziehung stehenden Themen: gefallene Idole, soziale Schichten, Karrierefrauen, öffentliches Scheitern. Immer wieder thematisiert wird die Geschwisterrivalität, vor allem jene zwischen Schwestern: Ob es um Cindy Crawford und ihren Doppelgänger-Geist Gia geht, um die Grimaldis, um Serena und Samantha Boardman, stets werden Unterscheidungen gemacht: «Stephanie ist blond, kleiner … Lisa ist ein Profimodel.»

In leiser Anlehnung an die Sehnsucht, die Maxim nach seiner Rebecca verspürt, entwickelt Kilimnik in ihrem neuesten Zeichnungsbuch einen perfekten Grusel-Plot: Es erscheinen sowohl der Geist der toten Schönheit, Gia Carangi, als auch die Anwärterin auf ihren Thron, Cindy Crawford. Ihr trockener Humor zeigt sich in Texten wie «… Tod am Donnerstag … Tod am Donnerstag, derselbe Club, der am Montag angesagt ist, ist am Donnerstag tot …», dann aber unterbricht Kilimnik das Orgelspiel, lässt die Geigenklänge verstummen, die Sehnsucht und unglückliche Liebe symbolisieren, und kommt unweigerlich auf die Dichotomie von innerem Drama und äusserer Handlung zurück. Eine Frau namens Harriet Neston starrt ins Leere, während ein Fenster, das möglicherweise eine böse Vorahnung

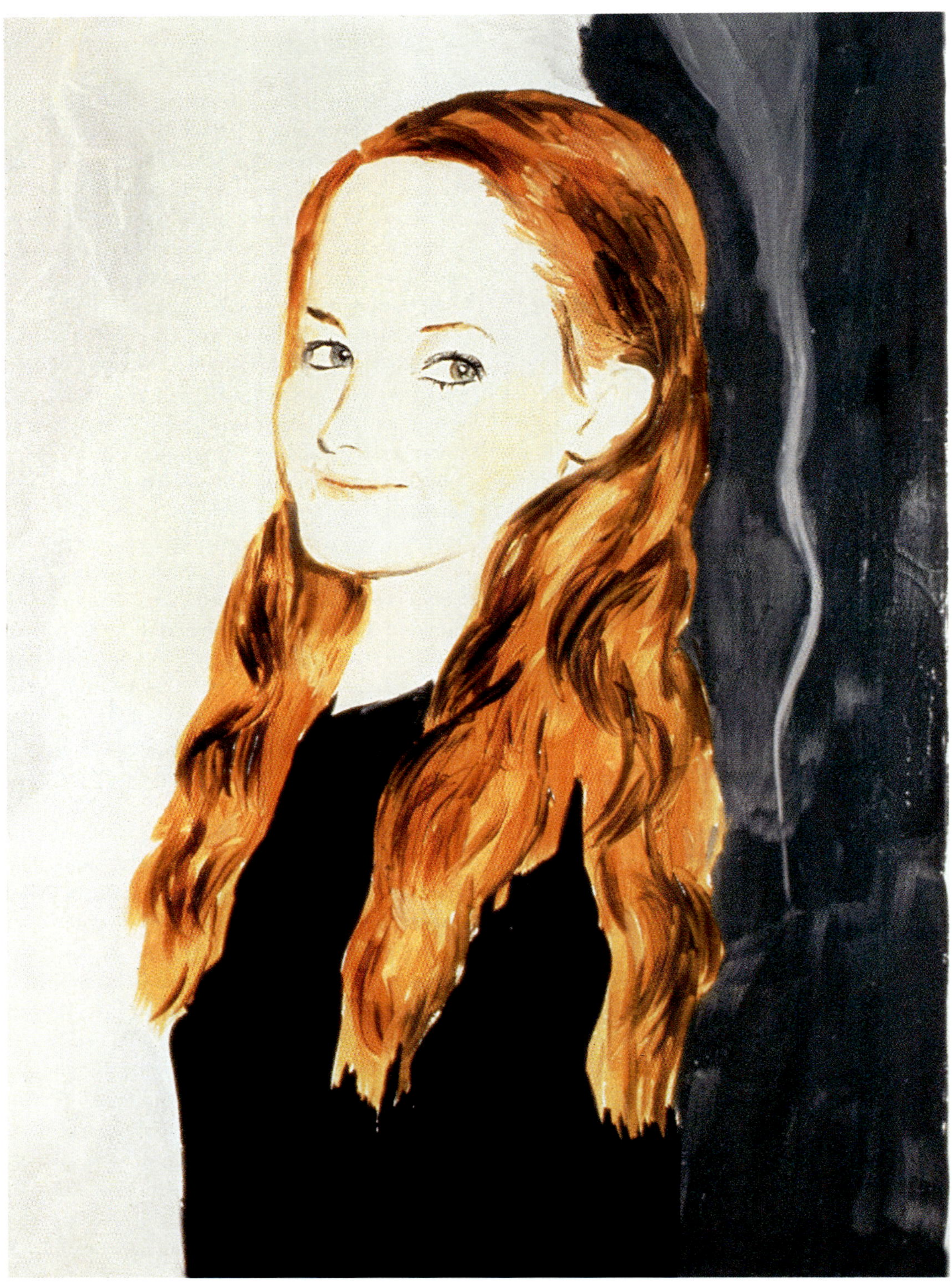

KAREN KILIMNIK, WITCHCRAFT, 1995,
oil on canvas, 16 x 12" / HEXEREI, Öl auf Leinwand, 41 x 30,5 cm.

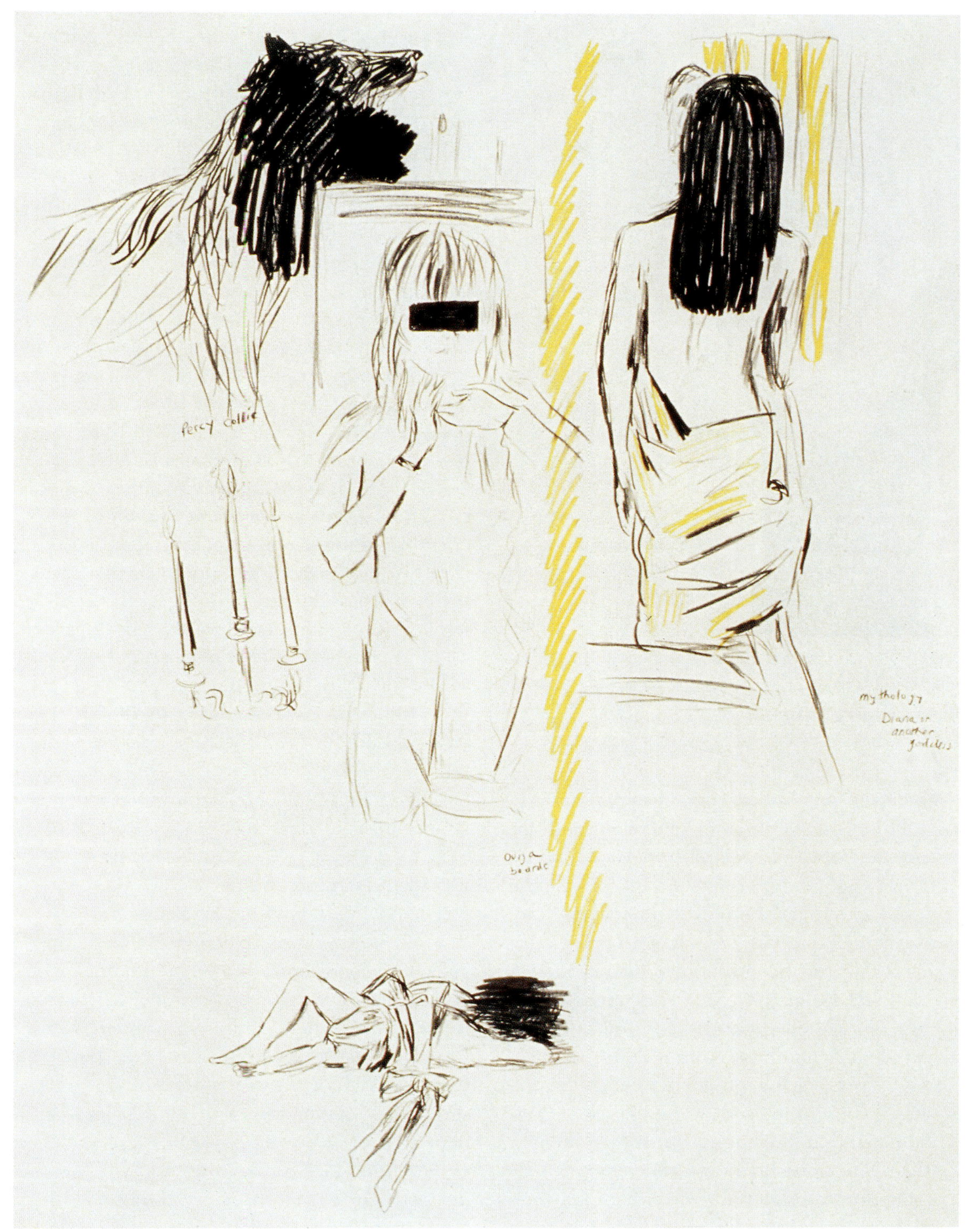

KAREN KILIMNIK, OUIJA BOARDS, 1987,
crayon on paper, 25½ x 20" / ALPHABETTAFELN, Kreide auf Papier, 64,8 x 51 cm.

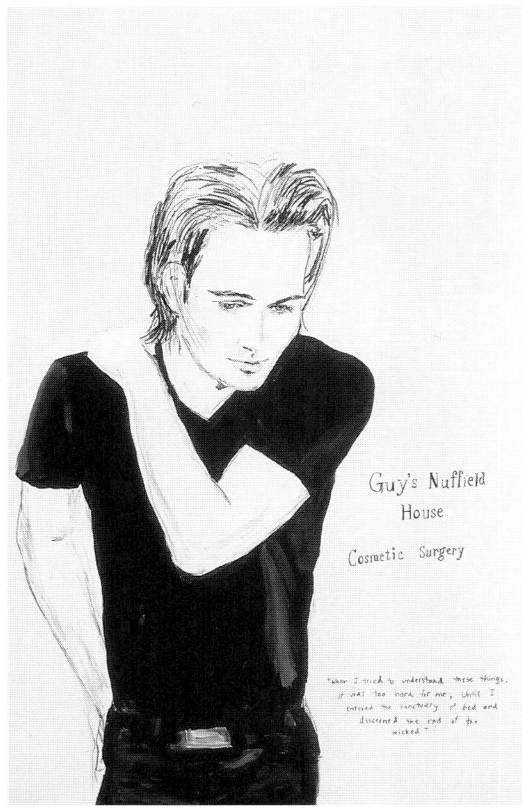

KAREN KILIMNIK, GUY'S NUFFIELD HOUSE/
COSMETIC SURGERY, 1996, china marker on paper, 40 x 26" /
GUYS HAUS IN NUFFIELD/SCHÖNHEITSCHIRURGIE,
Tuschestift auf Papier, 101,6 x 66 cm.

zeigt, ein eng umschlungenes Paar umrahmt. Gemäss Kilimnik ist Neston mit einem Freund aus Kindertagen verlobt (Heathcliff und Cathy lassen grüssen), und «sie musste wissen, was ihn beschäftigte, denn wieder einmal hatte Harriet das Gefühl, draussen zu stehen und bloss Zuschauerin zu sein…» An diese Idee wurde bei Kilimniks letzter Ausstellung in der 303 Gallery in New York angeknüpft: Zweimal die Woche, jeweils mittwochs und samstags, gingen vor dem Schaufenster der Galerie automatisch dichte Samtvorhänge nieder, welche die Besucher als Vorbereitung auf Kilimniks SLEEPING BEAUTY-Sound-and-Light-Show in Dunkelheit hüllten.

Kilimnik schlägt eine Brücke zwischen dem Schauerroman des neunzehnten und zwanzigsten Jahrhunderts und heutigen Grusel-Subkulturen, indem sie sowohl die Stimmung und das Dekor des ersteren als

auch den Klatsch und die Geschwätzigkeit der letzteren für ihre Werke nutzt. Wie James Purdy, der Meister des modernen Südstaaten-Schauerromans, setzt sie historische Manieriertheiten und Ausdrucksweisen nach modernen Prinzipien ein. In Purdys *In a Shallow Grave* (einem Stück über Gruseljargon) erhält sich ein bis zur Unkenntlichkeit verstümmelter Soldat dank der täglichen Liebkosungen eines Jungen am Leben, während er eine Epistel an seine längst verlorene Verlobte schreibt. Die Sprache bewegt sich zwischen Vergangenheit und Gegenwart hin und her, genauso wie die herrschenden Sitten. Auch Kilimnik verwendet gestelzte Dialoge: «…Das Herz des Hauses schlägt wärmer» oder «Harriet Nestons Verlobung mit ihrem Jugendfreund… schien ein natürliches, glückliches Ergebnis ihrer engen Freundschaft zu sein» oder «Als ich diese Dinge zu verstehen versuchte, war das zu schwierig für mich; bis ich bei Gott Zuflucht suchte und erkannte, dass das Böse ein Ende hatte» – vermischt mit umgangssprachlichen Wendungen wie «Wenn es wahr wäre, dass er (der Priester) sich für Strichjungen interessiert, hätte mir das bestimmt mal einer gesagt» oder «Ich hatte nie Probleme mit Drogen, nur mit Polizisten, und wenn du jede Disco schliesst, glaub bloss nicht, man wird es dir nicht ansehen.»

In Kilimniks Werken erscheint ein Zuhause gleich einer Anstalt als etwas, woraus man entweder flieht oder worin man einbricht. Es ist kaum je ein Ort familiärer Eintracht. Am akutesten gestaltet sich das Drama wohl in der Zeichnung HE ATTEMPTED TO FREE HER FROM THE COFFIN (THE [POUND] 50,000 BREAKFAST) (Er versuchte, sie aus dem Sarg zu befreien [Das 50 000-Pfund-Frühstück], 1984), in der sich ein androgynes Mädchen die Zehennägel lakkiert, umgeben von verschiedenen Ikonen wie einem Kalenderblatt von Donnerstag, dem 12., brennenden Kerzen und einem hufeisenförmigen Kranz. Das Drama liegt hier in Kilimniks Text: «Sein nächstes Geschwister, eine Schwester, starb, als er fünf war + er stand ihr so nahe, dass er sie an der Beerdigung aus dem Sarg zu befreien versuchte.» Das Mädchen, das einen Union-Jack-Anzug trägt und von einem Colonel aus dem 18. Jahrhundert abstammt, verkörpert eine wertvolle Dyade: Euroamerikanerin, altes versus neues Vermögen, Modeltätigkeit und königliche

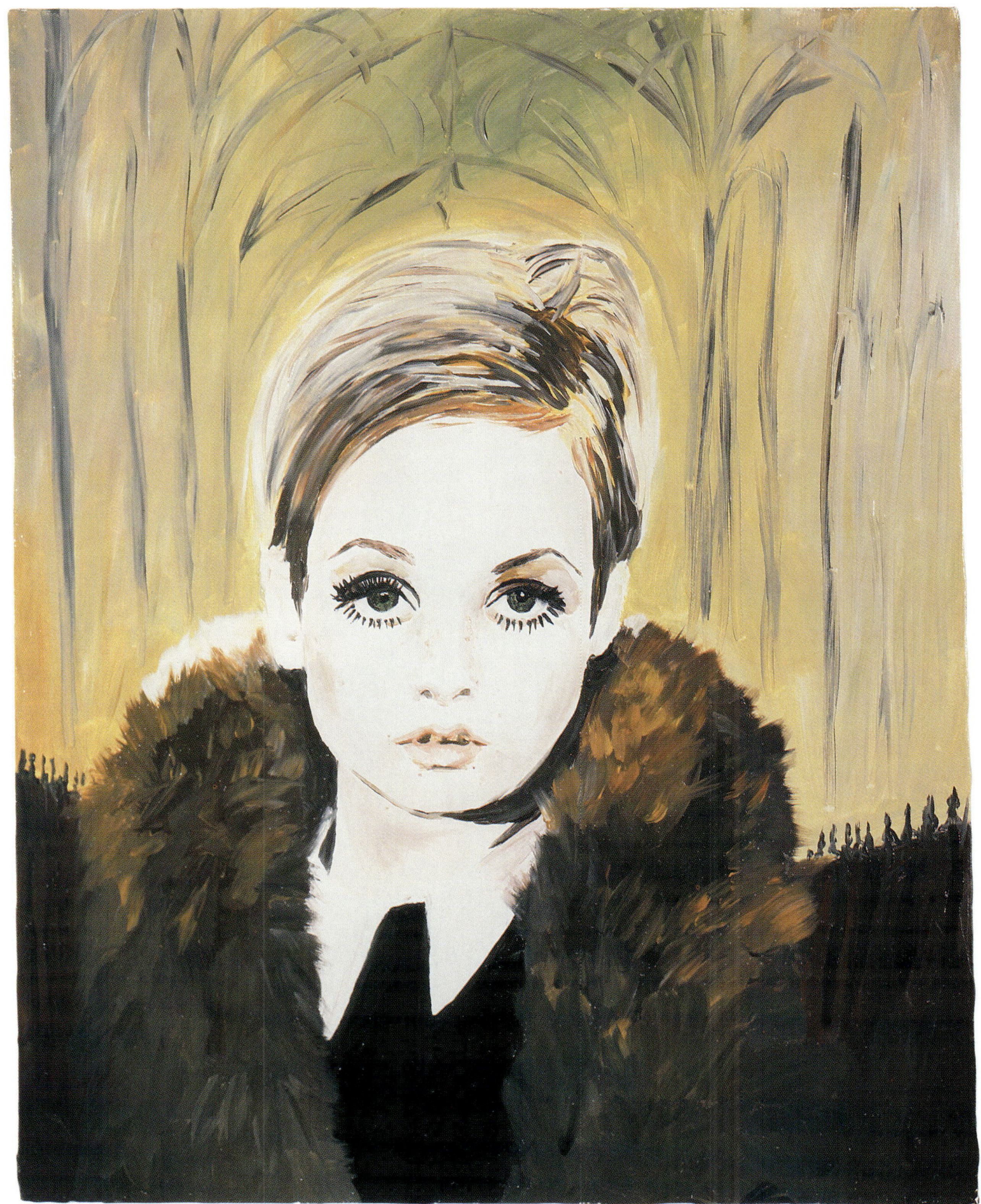

KAREN KILIMNIK, TWIGGY AT SCHOOL AT CAMBRIDGE, 1997, water-based oil on canvas, 20 x 16" / TWIGGY IN DER SCHULE IN CAMBRIDGE, Emulsion auf Leinwand, 51 x 41 cm.

KAREN KILIMNIK, THE FELLOWSHIP IS ALL, 1994, crayon and acrylic on paper, 39¹/₂ x 26" / DABEISEIN IST ALLES, Kreide und Acryl auf Papier, 100 x 66 cm.

Familie; Berühmtheit und Reichtum. In Königshäusern gibt es immer eine uneinnehmbare Festung, ein uneheliches Kind, eine eingesperrte Gemahlin, einen ungeratenen Spross oder einen Irren. In den Prinzessinnen Stephanie und Caroline von Monaco hat Kilimnik das ideale Paar gefunden, mit dem sie spielen kann. Die eine ist gut, die andere hat ein Dance-Album aufgenommen. In ihnen sind Ruhm und Unrühmlichkeit vereint. Und, was am wichtigsten scheint, sie sind halbe Amerikanerinnen. Sie sind beide ständig von europäischen Paparazzi belagert, und so sind es denn auch europäische Boulevardblätter, denen Kilimnik die nur zum Teil sachlichen Anmerkungen zu ihren Zeichnungen entnimmt.

In gewisser Weise hat der Sensationsjournalismus die mythischen Proportionen des Schauergenres übernommen: Ein Leben wird mit einer einzigen Tat ruiniert. Die unglaubliche Wahrheit über Hugh Grant (auch er gehört zu Kilimniks Sujets) sickert in zwei postmoderne Porträts von Prinzessin Diana, und damit auch die Rolle der Boulevardpresse als Geiselnehmerin im Beichtstuhl. Die Boulevardpresse gibt vor, ein Geheimnis an die Öffentlichkeit zu bringen, und wenn sie Glück hat, entlockt ihre Hartnäckigkeit dem Prominenten ein Geständnis. Wie im Schauerroman spielt das Geheimnis hier eine tragende Rolle, doch im Falle von Kilimnik und der Boulevardpresse sind alle Taten einerseits unbeschreiblich und werden andererseits der Öffentlichkeit preisgegeben. Wie *The Star* und *The Sun* liebt es Kilimnik, die Prominenz blosszustellen, indem sie bewundernd Monica Vittis gefärbte Haare und falsche Wimpern erwähnt oder einen boshaften Witz über eine jüngere Schauspielerin weitererzählt, die es nicht schafft, eine Rolle zu kriegen.

Während der Schauerroman durch gewundene Handlungsstränge und verschlossene Türen, durch ein Labyrinth von Wahrscheinlichkeiten, die «unbeschreiblichen, unsäglichen Horror»[3] in sich bergen, gewürzt wird, revidieren Kilimniks Arbeiten nicht bloss die Vorstellung des Verdrängten, sondern auch das Fehlen oder die Verschleierung von erzählerischen Elementen. Zwar gibt es in einer Gruselgeschichte oder einem Werk Kilimniks etliche Erzähler, doch die Handschrift und die Anmerkungen der Künstlerin offenbaren recht deutlich ihren

Wunsch, die Überlegungen und Anschuldigungen, die andere in der Öffentlichkeit äussern, mit ihren eigenen zu verschmelzen.[4] Ihre energische Schrift, hektisch, sprunghaft und mitunter unorthographisch, verteilt sich rund um Gestalten, die möglicherweise etwas miteinander zu tun haben – oder auch nicht; die Texte lesen sich manchmal wie eine Gedichtstrophe, dann wieder wie ein Tagebucheintrag. In der Zeichnung THE FELLOWSHIP IS ALL (Dabeisein ist alles, 1994) wird ein verdriesslich dreinblickendes Mädchen, deren eines Auge ausradiert und das andere schwarz übermalt ist, zur unglücklichen Anekdotenerzählerin. «Da hoffte ich, er würde in Tränen ausbrechen. Ich hatte ein bisschen ein schlechtes Gewissen, aber er war so gemein zu mir gewesen – und ausserdem sass er da mit Bianca, und die beiden fütterten einander –, es war zum Kotzen.» So schleicht sich Kilimnik durch ihre eigene Handschrift ins Drehbuch ein, in der Rolle der Rivalin von Bianca Jagger. Sie erfindet gewissermassen eine alternative Autobiographie, in der sie sich zugleich offenbart und versteckt hält. Als sei sie eine Ghostwriterin wider Willen, erzählt sie die Geschichte eines anderen Menschen nach, kann jedoch der Versuchung nicht widerstehen, durch widersprüchliche autobiographische Andeutungen ihre Fingerabdrücke zu hinterlassen. Diese unterschwellige Form der Biographie macht es möglich, sich einem Masochismus ohne die eintönigen Schläge der Selbstgeisselung hinzugeben. Grausamkeit und Spott sind fast immer gegen Leute gerichtet, die sie bewundert. In der Zeichnung BUBBLE GUM HABIT (Bubble-gum-Sucht) geht es um die geliebte Gia.[5] Drogen, Aids, Studio 54 und Einkaufen sind einige der Dinge, die in der Würdigung aufgelistet werden: «Marietta anrufen Flugticket … Heroin besorgen, Sandy anrufen, Weihrauch und schönen Entzug organisieren.»

Kilimniks Textfetzen finden eine Entsprechung in der Art, wie sie in ihren *Scattered art*-Werken Gegenstände auf dem Boden verteilt: in den scheinbar ungeordneten, doch in Wirklichkeit höchst strukturierten Installationen, für die sie hauptsächlich bekannt ist. Die beunruhigende Wirkung dieser scheinbar wahllos ausgestreuten Elemente lässt sich recht gut in die Zweidimensionalität der Zeichnungen übertragen. Kilimnik setzt Texte auf ganz ähnliche Weise ein wie

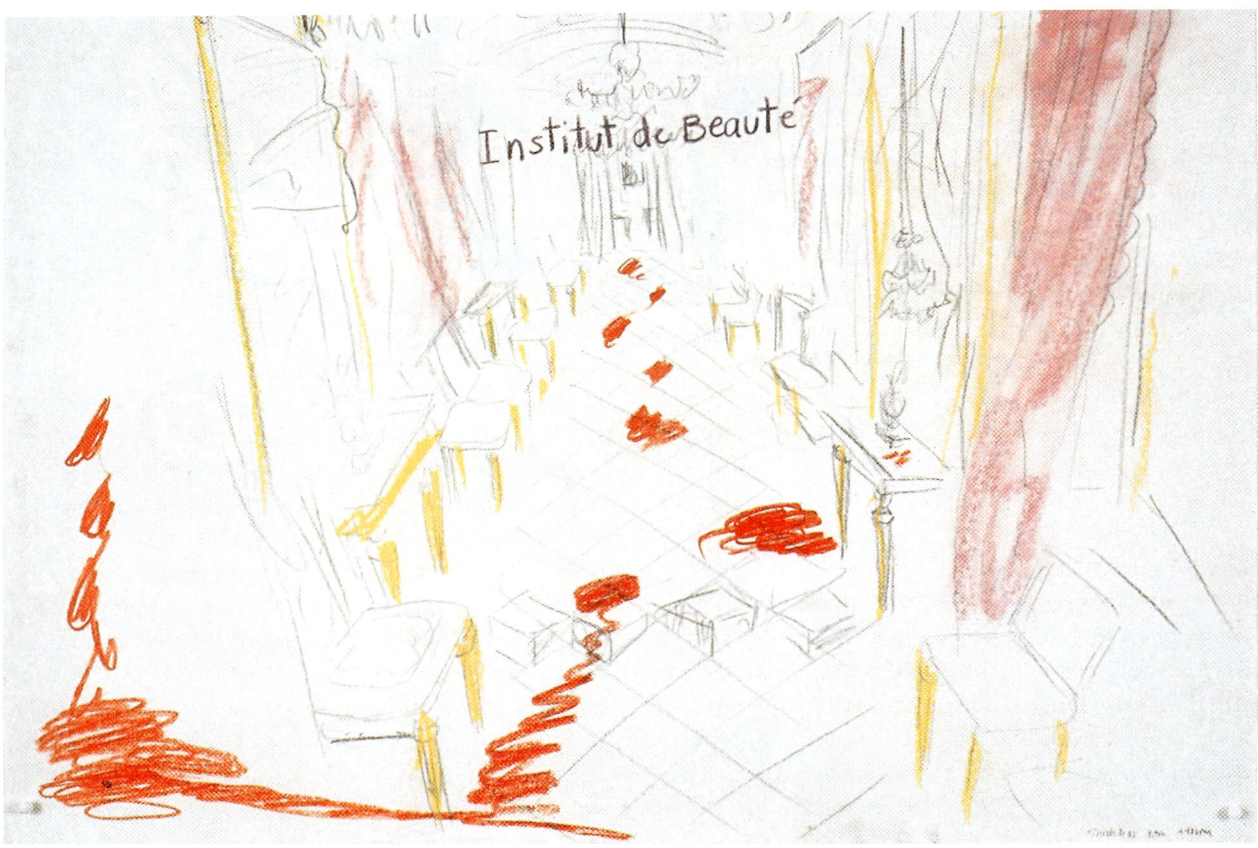

Blutstropfen oder Feuer, nämlich als Dekorationsmittel und zur Belebung. Wie die roten Spuren auf dem Boden des INSTITUT DE BEAUTÉ (Schönheitssalon) werfen auch die Texte ein Schlaglicht auf die Brutalität ihrer Arbeit, ob diese sich nun in einem Salon, der gefährlich gründliche Pediküren macht, oder in den Enthüllungen des geschriebenen Wortes zeigt. Kilimnik hebt jedermanns Schwächen hervor, um zu zeigen, dass sie Leute mag, die Fehler haben.

Im Schauergenre sind es die Enthüllung des Geheimnisses und das anschliessende Geständnis, die es dem Protagonisten ermöglichen, dem Unheimlichen zu entfliehen. In der Literatur ist das vielleicht ein Geheimnis, dessen Aufdeckung ein Paar zusammenführt oder ihm die Flucht aus einem Kellerverlies ermöglicht; in Kilimniks Werken ist es das statische Gebiet der Hochglanzmagazine, das zum dumpfen, wenn auch glitzernden Kerker wird. Ein Porträt des Models Twiggy enthält ein aufschlussreiches Popquiz: *Was sind Twiggys Masse: 29–20–26 oder 31–22–32?* Über ihrem Kopf schweben Namen von Milchprodukten. Natürlich beschäftigt Kilimnik das Problem der Gewichtszunahme und -abnahme, und gleichzeitig quält sie die schmächtige Gestalt mit Schlagsahne-Visionen. Auf die Frage, ob es Spass mache, Klatsch aus der Regenbogenpresse zu kolportieren, antwortet sie: «Na ja, ich glaube, ich wollte, ich könnte so amüsant sein.» Das ist sie, wenn sie sich etwa über Elizabeth Hurley lustig macht, doch sie fügt rasch hinzu, sie hoffe, Elizabeth sei deswegen nicht gekränkt. Ihr Mitgefühl ist grenzenlos.

Karen Kilimnik scheint es ein gewisses Vergnügen zu bereiten, boshafte Andeutungen zu wiederholen. Sie möchte, dass wir uns als Galeriebesucher mit unserem Wunsch auseinandersetzen, jemand anders in einer peinlichen Lage zu erleben, und versucht

KAREN KILIMNIK, INSTITUT DE BEAUTÉ, 1985,
crayon and pastel on paper, 17½ x 23¼" /
Kreide und Pastell auf Papier, 44,5 x 59 cm.

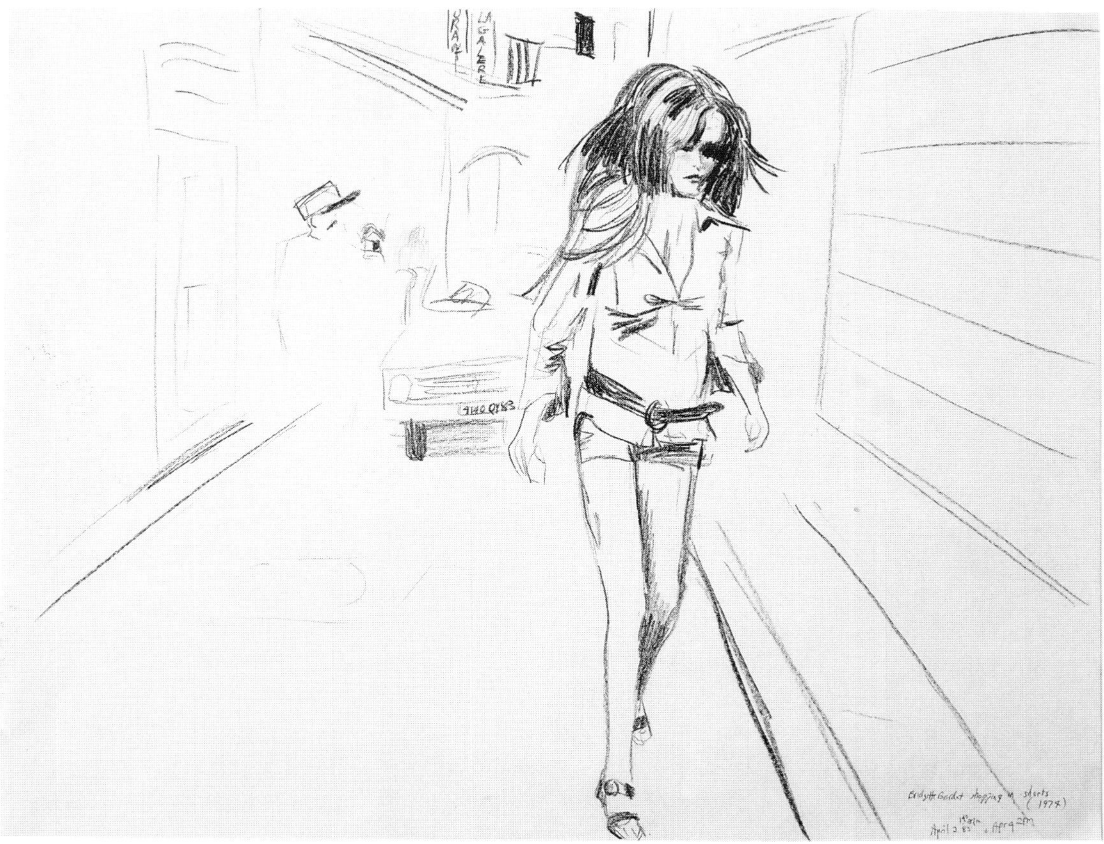

unsere Aufmerksamkeit auf alltägliche Gemeinheiten zu lenken. Die Modezeitschrift spielt die gute Schwester des bösen Boulevardblatts. Zerschnittene Seiten mit seltsamen Zitaten treiben dahin wie Klatschmagazin-Collagen. Kilimnik bläht die Anschuldigungen der Boulevardpresse auf, indem sie sowohl deren Ton als auch die Art der Titelblattgestaltung imitiert. Ihre besondere Art der Transgression, dieser Drang, die banalsten Einzelheiten des Lebens eines anderen Menschen festzuhalten, hat ihren Ursprung vermutlich in der kaltblütigen JANE CREEP-Serie. Begonnen Ende der 80er Jahre, sind diese unverblümt hingekritzelten Texte – den gleichermassen psychotischen handschriftlichen Witzen Richard Princes bemerkenswert ähnlich – ein Vorbote der späteren Werke. Angeblich ist die anonyme Jane ein Mädchen, das Kilimnik in der Highschool das Leben schwergemacht hat. In einer Litanei, die aus rund 25 Zeichnungen besteht, wird Jane von der Peinigerin zum Opfer und tauscht so effektiv mit

Kilimnik die Plätze. Vom überwältigend gruseligen JANE FALLS ASLEEP AT AN UNDERTAKERS + IS MISTAKEN FOR THE NEXT CLIENT (Jane schläft in einem Bestattungsinstitut ein und wird für die nächste Kundin gehalten) bis zum urkomischen JANE HAS A LOUD VOICE AND NOBODY CAN STAND HER (Jane hat eine laute Stimme und niemand kann sie ausstehen) macht sich Kilimnik ein Vergnügen daraus, ihre unguten Absichten zu beichten – I GIVE JANE A MAN-EATING PLANT AND TELL HER IT NEEDS TO BE WASHED BY HAND NEXT WEEK (Ich schenke Jane eine menschenfressende Pflanze und sage ihr, sie müsse nächste Woche von Hand gewaschen werden). Die gegen Jane gerichtete Aggressivität ist sinnver-

KAREN KILIMNIK, BRIGITTE BARDOT SHOPPING IN HER SHORTS, 1974, 1985, crayon on paper, 16 x 20" / BRIGITTE BARDOT AUF EINKAUFSTOUR IN SHORTS 1974, Kreide auf Papier, 41 x 51 cm.

wandt mit den Geschichten von Heavy metal-Jungs, Satansjüngern, Rockern und Verlierertypen, die wegen gescheiterten Selbstmordpakten und gelungenen Vatermorden in die Schlagzeilen geraten.[6] Kilimnik schreibt wie ein Teenager, der Songtexte auf Schulhefte und Jeans kopiert: Grossbuchstaben und der erregende Reiz, sich als Verfasserin von Mantras wie WE WILL, WE WILL, ROCK YOU zu wähnen. Obschon Kilimniks Kunst häufig als girlish bezeichnet wird, wirkt ihre Haltung ziemlich geschlechtsneutral und überschreitet in bezug auf Erzählgestus und Action eindeutig die Geschlechtergrenzen. Nirgends zeigt sich dies deutlicher als in ihrem exzessiven Gebrauch von Feuer. Dieses Feuer wird in ihren Werken zwar gemeinhin mit Weiblichkeit, mit Hexerei in Zusammenhang gebracht, aber die Verbindung zwischen Jungen und Feuer sollte nicht ausser acht gelassen werden. Pyromanie oder Brandstiftung wird im allgemeinen als Störung diagnostiziert, die bei kleinen Jungen auftritt. Dass sie in Kilimniks Welt ein ständig wiederkehrendes Thema ist, deutet darauf hin, dass es in vielen ihrer Arbeiten nicht nur um das kleine Mädchen geht, das sich den Körper einer Ballerina wünscht, sondern dass dieses kleine Mädchen auch ein Junge sein könnte. Diese Annahme würde jene Kritiker widerlegen, die ihre Werke ausschliesslich der weiblichen Domäne zuordnen. Während Kilimnik die Entstehung von Schönheitskomplexen erforscht, stattet sie ihr Geschlecht auch mit weniger weitverbreiteten und geschlechtsspezifischen Funktionsstörungen aus.

Züchtigung und Rettung, die in Kilimniks Werken gleichzeitig zwischen Text und Körper oszillieren, lassen eine merkwürdige, beunruhigende Beziehung zu ihren Sujets entstehen. Anders als andere Maler, die sich auf das Bekannte, das Schöne und die Dynamik zwischen Berühmtheit und Zweitrangigkeit konzentrieren (Billy Sullivans Johnny Depp und Skeet Ulrich, Elizabeth Peytons Liam Gallagher und Jarvis Cocker), ist Kilimnik weniger von deren Drang nach dem Perfekten gepackt. Während Sullivan einen amüsierten und entzückten Zynismus zum Ausdruck bringt und Peyton den authentischen Rehblick des Fans übt, ist Kilimnik eine ziemliche Spielverderberin. Sie liebt es, diese zu lieben, aber manchmal gehen sie sogar ihr auf die Nerven. Jede Figur, von Märchenprinzessin und Vögeln über Erbinnen, Waisen und Models, wird zum Träger einer deutlichen Mischung von Selbstzweifel und Dünkel. Sie sind so hübsch, scheint sie zu sagen, als spräche sie von den Mädchen in ihrer High-School, hinter deren Rücken oder neben ihnen auf der Toilette, wo sie mit Rauchen oder Knutschen beschäftigt sind. Dennoch, kaum ist man sich sicher, dass die Zehen, die selbstvergessen die Fugen der rosa Fussbodenfliesen nachzeichnen, die ihren sind, wird einem klar, dass Kilimnik weit entfernt ist von jeder Örtlichkeit, sozialen Schicht oder Identität. Vielleicht mag sie diese, aber manchmal sind sie nur ein Nachgedanke, ein Strich mit der Bürste durch das lange braune Cartoonhaar von Anastasia oder eine Notation, die sich vom Sentimentalen absetzt.

(Übersetzung: Irene Aeberli)

1) Eve Kosofsky Sedgwick, *The Coherence of Gothic Conventions*, Methuen, New York und London 1980, S. 3.
2) Auf die Frage, ob die Texte in ihren Zeichnungen ausschliesslich Zitate aus Artikeln sind, antwortete Kilimnik: «Darüber kann ich eigentlich wenig sagen, denn manchmal vergesse ich gewisse Dinge vollkommen und erinnere mich erst später daran. Aber es ist unterschiedlich. Manchmal schreibe ich selbst etwas, und oft kupfere ich Zitate ab, die ich lustig finde. Meist sind es wohl abgekupferte Zitate. Bei den frühen Zeichnungen habe ich sie übersetzt (wenn sie in einer Fremdsprache waren). Die allerersten, als ich noch kaum eine andere Sprache beherrschte, habe ich einfach aus Spass übersetzt, irgendwie transponierte ich die Wörter und ihren Klang, nahm zum Beispiel bestimmte Wörter und ihren Klang und verwandelte sie in etwas anderes, aber irgendwie habe ich es verstanden.» (Aus einem Gespräch zwischen der Autorin und der Künstlerin im Dezember 1997)

3) In Charles Robert Maturins *Melmoth the Wanderer*, 1820, zitiert in Sedgwick, S. 14.
4) Kilimnik gibt nicht nur Details wieder, sondern wandelt biographische Studien eigenhändig in Pseudo-Autobiographien um.
5) Die unglückselige Gia Carangi, ein berühmtes Model, ist Kilimniks Leidenschaft. Sie starb verarmt und obdachlos an Aids, das sie sich durch ihre Drogenabhängigkeit zugezogen hatte. Gia wäre, wenn sie noch leben würde, nicht nur ungefähr gleich alt wie Kilimnik, die beiden kommen auch aus derselben Stadt, aus Philadelphia. Im Zusammenhang mit der derzeit herrschenden Supermodel-Manie war Gia kürzlich Thema eines gross herausgebrachten amerikanischen Bestsellers und Fernsehfilms.
6) Man braucht sich bloss ihre blutverspritzten Installationen anzusehen, um zu erkennen, dass es in diesem Projekt nicht um harmlose Kinderspiele geht.

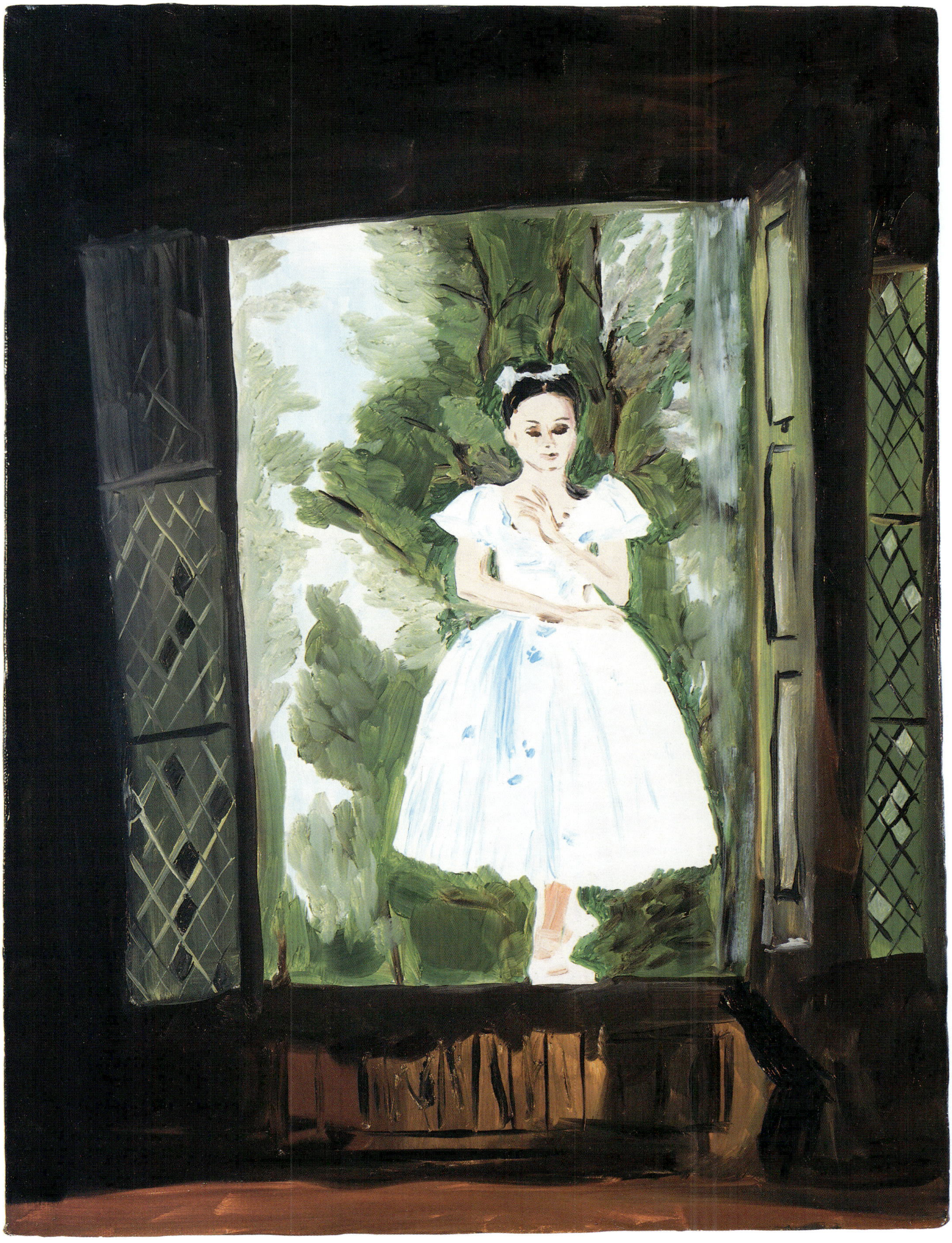

KAREN KILIMNIK, SYLPH, 1997, water-based oil on canvas, 18 x 14" / SYLPHIDE, Emulsion auf Leinwand, 45,7 x 35,6 cm.

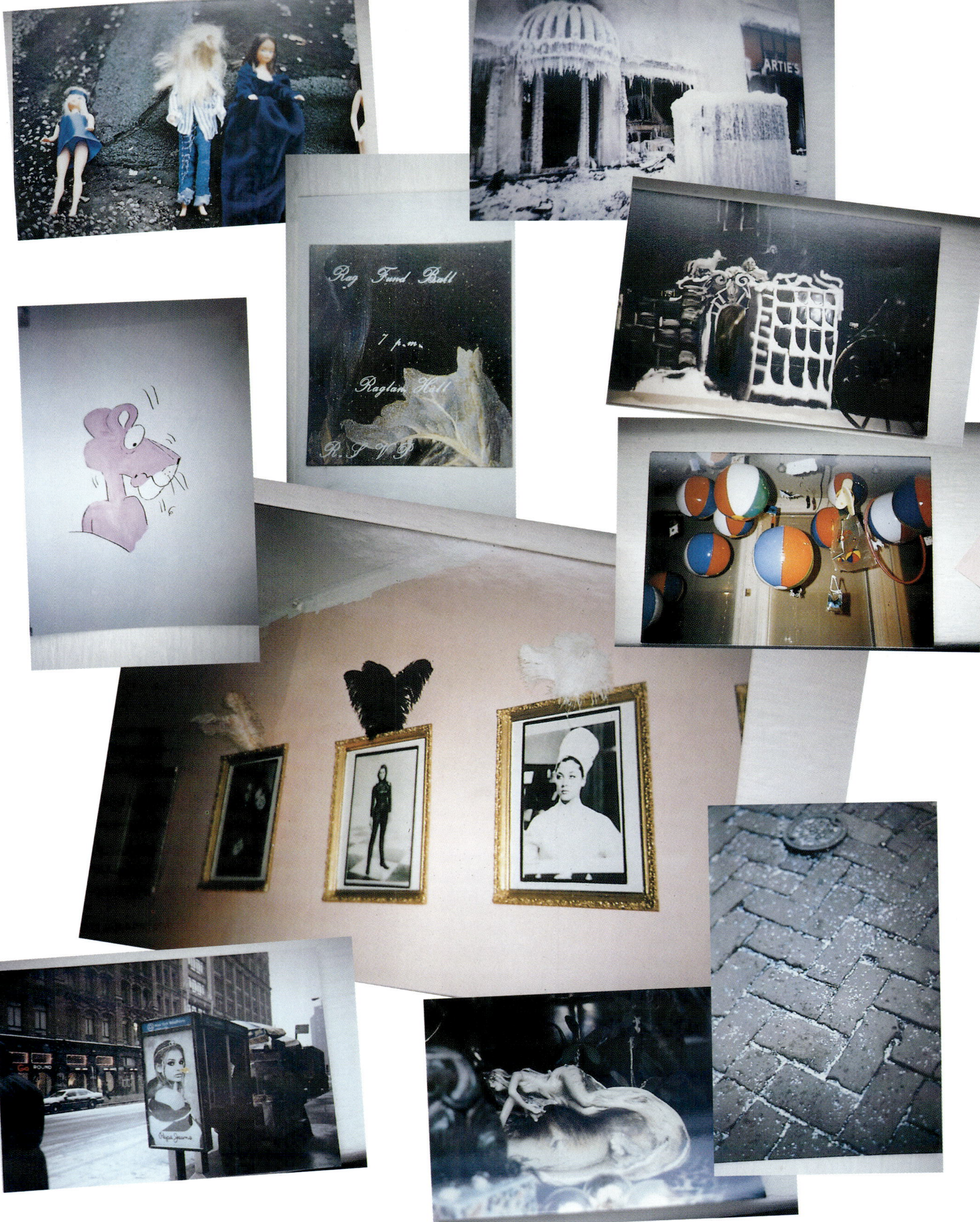
Rag Fund Ball
7 p.m.
Raglam Hall
R.S.V.P.

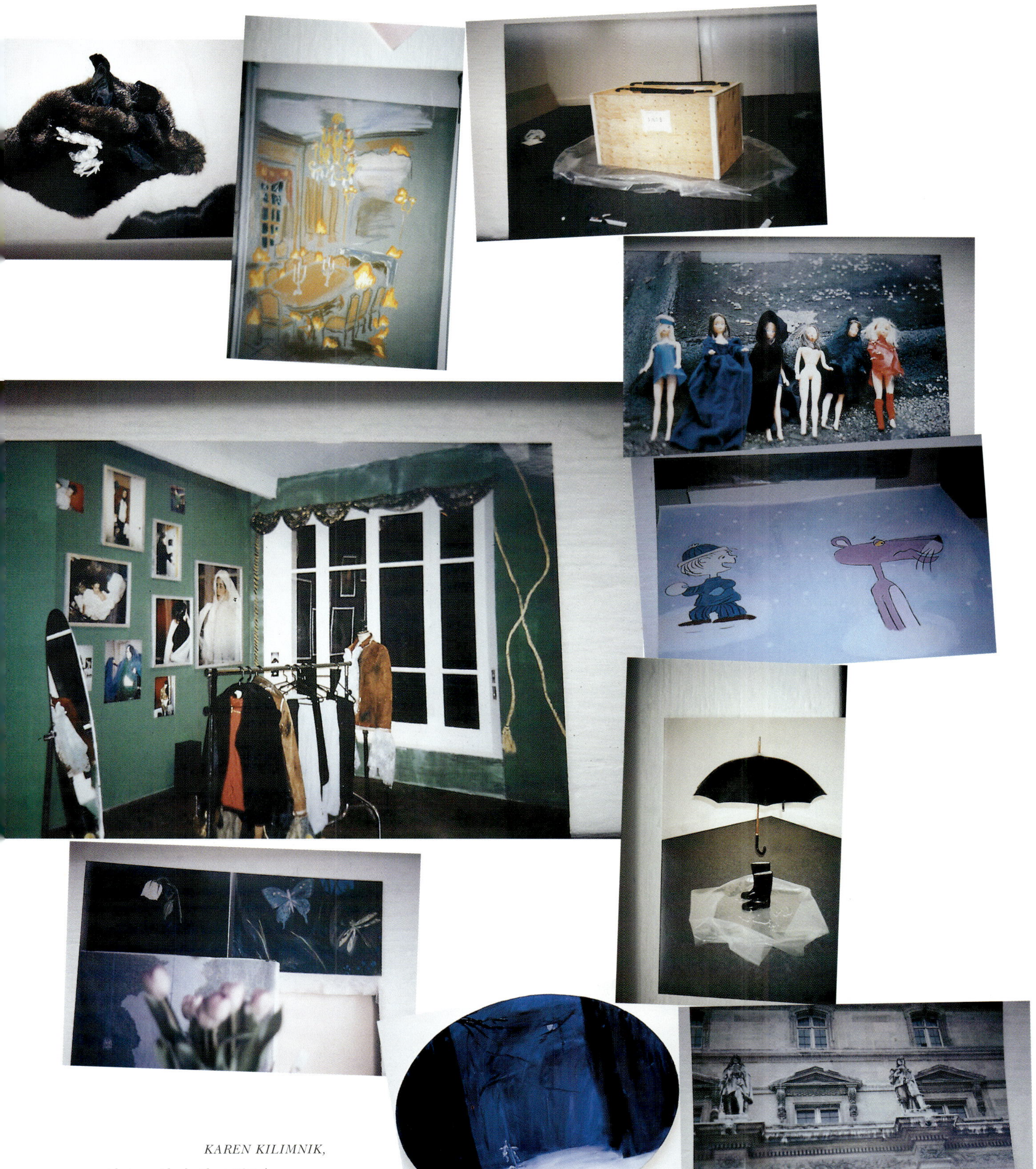

KAREN KILIMNIK,
photographs by the artist /
Photographien der Künstlerin.

Battles or the Art of War

BERNHARD BÜRGI

Gerne assoziiert man – wohl nicht nur in Europa – den Namen Karen Kilimnik zuallererst mit ihren Zeichnungen in schwarzer Wachskreide. Insbesondere skizzenhafte Umrisslinien und Schattierungen, die teilweise von dünner Acrylfarbe durchwirkt werden und an einen etwas verblichenen Modeillustrationsstil erinnern, kombinieren sich in einem Atemzug mit hingekritzelten Zitaten zwischen Klatsch, Schlagzeile und Tagebuchnotiz. Als Teil einer verwunschenen und fragilen Welt umkreisen sie durch Frauenpostillen, Fernsehen oder Modeanzeigen medial aufbereitete und seit Kindheit genährte Träume und Sehnsüchte. Dies geschieht mit einer obsessiven Hingabe, die sonst zu den Eigenheiten eines Teenagers gehört, der das Zimmer seiner Tagträume nicht verlassen will. Einerseits sind blonde Elfen Kilimniks Heldinnen, personifiziert durch Starmodels wie Twiggy oder Kate Moss, die ätherisch-leicht von Unschuld und Schönheit und zugleich von ihrer Anfälligkeit sprechen, andererseits durch Amazonen wie etwa Emma Peel von der in die Jahre gekommenen TV-Serie «The Avengers (Mit Schirm, Charme und Melone)», die von düsteren Phantasien, weiblicher Dominanz und Zerstörung zeugen. Berühmtheit, Schönheit und Macht müssen als Bruchstücke einer überzeichneten Realität aus zweiter Hand zusam-

---

BERNHARD BÜRGI ist Leiter der Kunsthalle Zürich. Er organisierte 1997 eine grosse Karen Kilimnik-Ausstellung.

mengetragen und gebannt werden, um an ihrem Glanz und Elend teilhaben zu können. Dabei verlieren Klischee und eigene Realität, Mädchenschlafzimmer und Mordschauplatz eine klar konturierte Gegensätzlichkeit, amalgamieren sich krude und zugleich mit Meisterschaft und Sensibilität. Zwischen femininer Romantik und Terror angelegt, ist es die unironische Wendung der schillernden Vorbilder hin zum Authentischen, die mit seltsamer Magie berührt und spürbar macht, was der mediale Schein an existentiellen Wünschen und Bedrohungen absorbiert.

In der Ölmalerei Kilimniks bildet weniger der Glamour der Mode ein Projektionsfeld als etwa die durch Bücher und Hefte popularisierte Tradition der englischen Landschaftsmalerei des späten achtzehnten Jahrhunderts, in die sich beispielsweise Szenen aus «Bewitched» einwirken können, einer von Karen Kilimniks TV-Lieblingssendungen. Farbgesättigt und süss-schauerlich umlodert Feuer die Fassade trauter Bürgerlichkeit. Obskures und Okkultes mischt sich mit Tierliebe und Naturgewalt, zum Beispiel in Form von sintflutartigen Regengüssen oder Blitzen.

Da die Ölmalerei in intimen Formaten in letzter Zeit Kilimniks bevorzugtes Ausdrucksmittel ist, gerieten ihre raumgreifenden Installationen wie beispielsweise THE HELLFIRE CLUB – EPISODE OF THE AVENGERS, mit denen sie Anfang der 90er Jahre in New York an die Öffentlichkeit trat und die als Inbegriff von «scatter art» umschrieben wurden, etwas in den Hintergrund. Und doch bringt Karen Kilimnik in Ausstellungen auch ihre Tafelbilder in unmittelbare Zusammenhänge mit dem Realraum. So scheinen sie etwa auf farbigen Wänden mit gemusterten Zier-

KAREN KILIMNIK, BATTLES OR THE ART OF WAR, 1991, mixed media installation, 303 Gallery, New York / SCHLACHTEN ODER DIE KUNST DER KRIEGSFÜHRUNG.

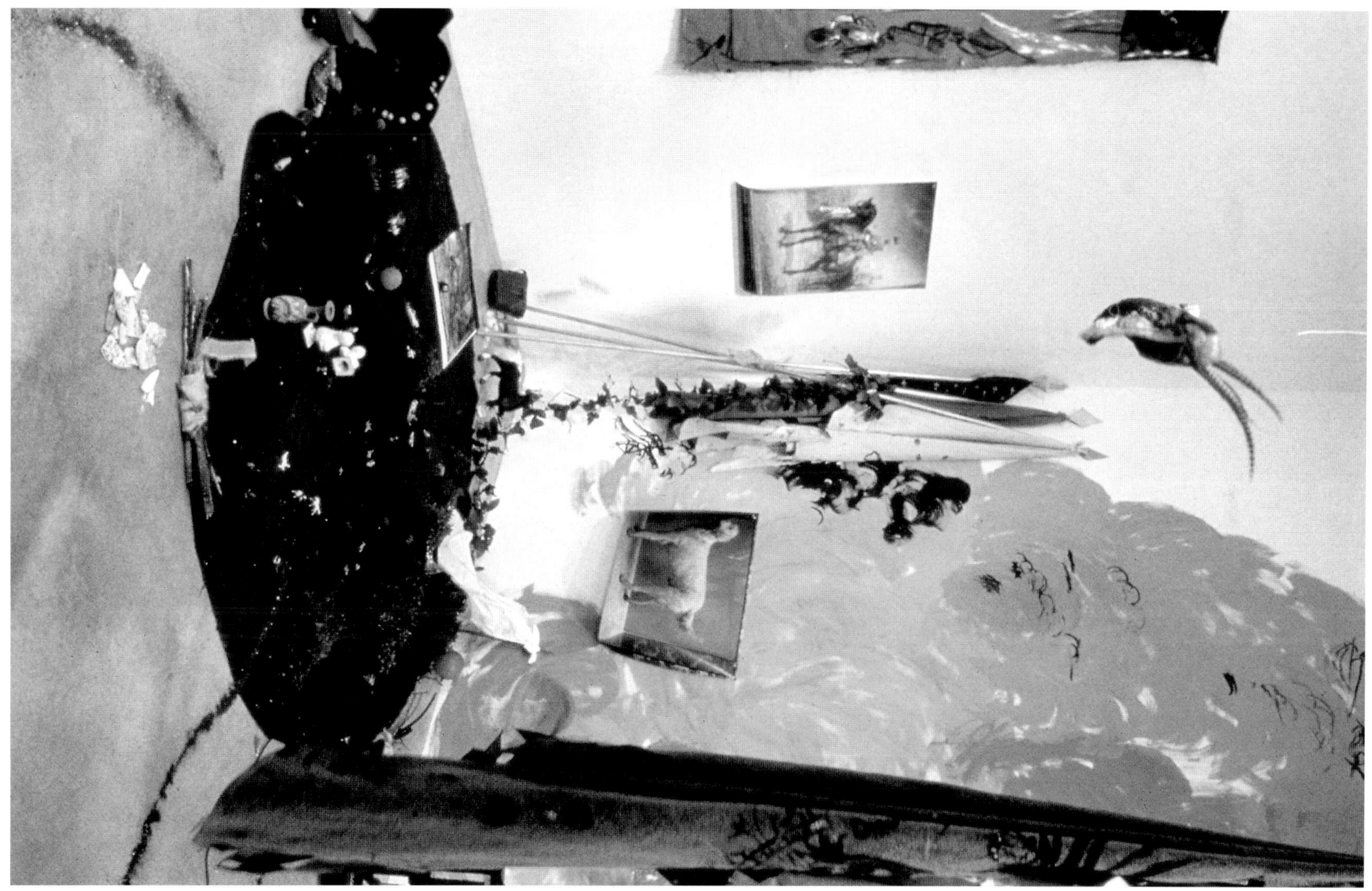

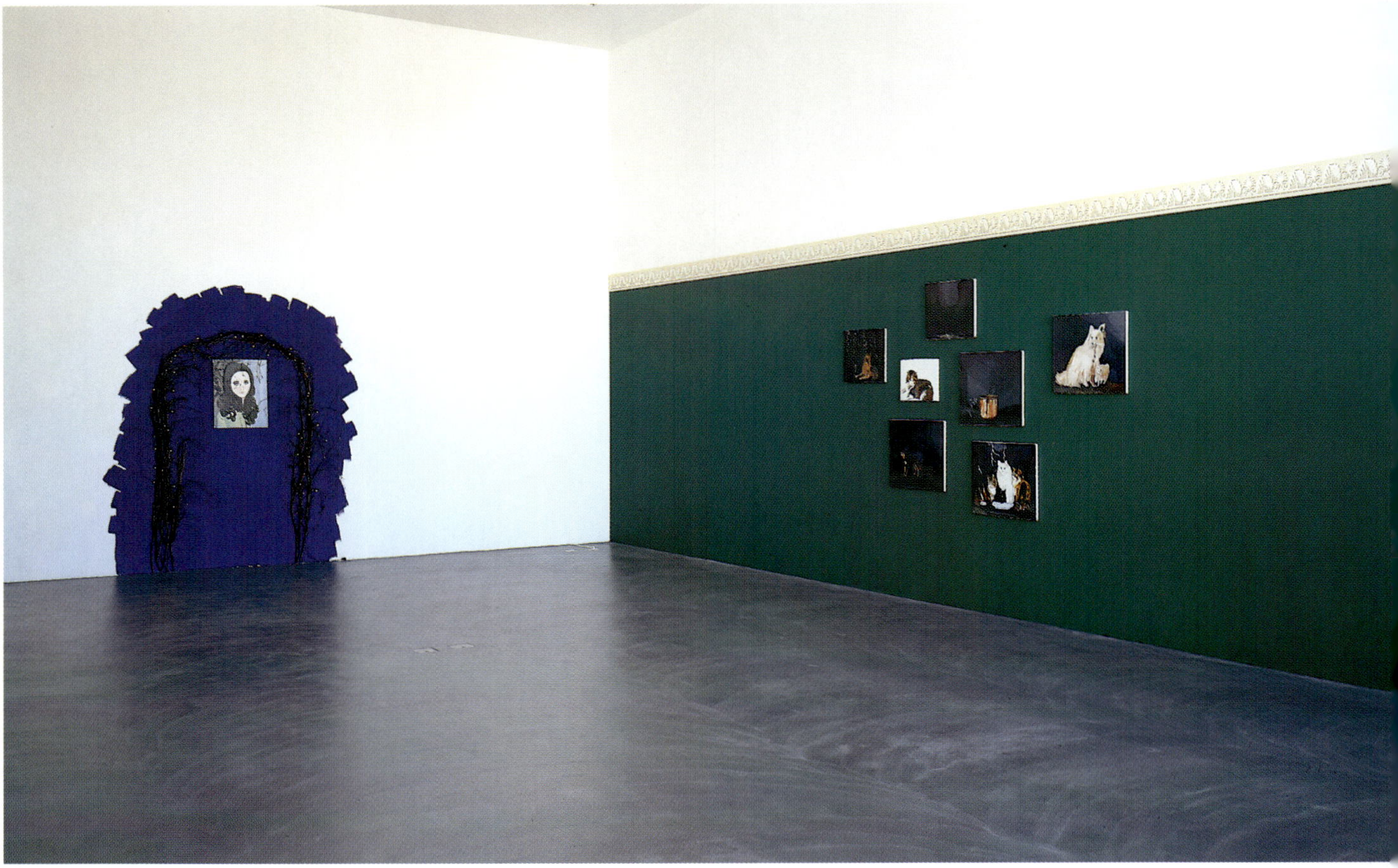

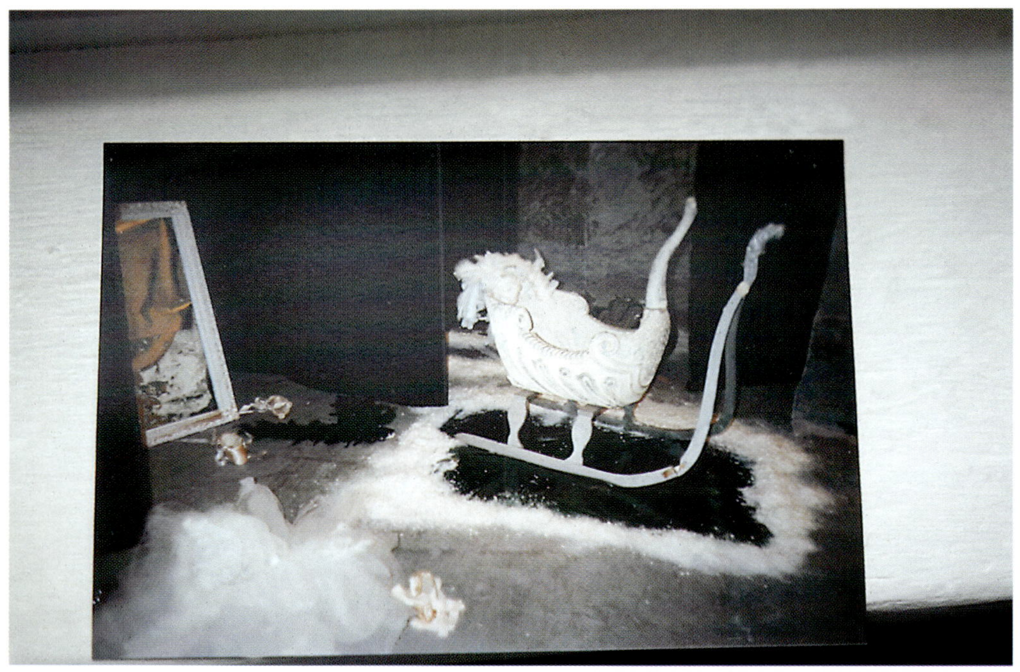

KAREN KILIMNIK, *exhibition view / Ausstellungsansicht, Kunsthalle Zürich 1997. (PHOTO: A. TROEHLER, ZÜRICH)*

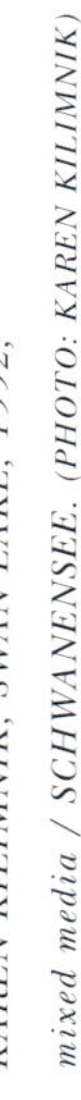

KAREN KILIMNIK, SWAN LAKE, 1992,
mixed media / SCHWANENSEE. (PHOTO: KAREN KILIMNIK)

leisten auf, die die Erinnerung an eine klassische Gemäldegalerie wachrufen, aber wiederum – durch eine für Karen Kilimnik bezeichnende Verschiebung der Konvention – in zentrischen Konstellationen angeordnet sind. Mittelpunkt eines solchen installativen Umgangs mit dem klassischen Tafelbild, dessen Eindringlichkeit immer auch der Charme der Trivialität anhaftet, bildet das Mädchenporträt ANGEL'S COUSIN FROM BLOOD ON SATAN'S CLAW MCMLXX, (Engel Verwandte aus Blut auf Satans Kralle MCMLXX, 1996) umrahmt von einem torartigen Kranz aus Lichtern und Zweigen auf violett wucherndem Grund.

In ihren Rauminszenierungen – jenem Teil ihres Werkes, der mir wesentlich, innovativ und doch zu wenig beachtet scheint – arbeitet Karen Kilimnik neben handgefertigten oder gemalten Elementen mit solchen aus der Alltags- und Populärkultur (Photokopien, Glitter, Kerzen, Verpackungen, Stoffe, Soundfragmente oder Nippes), bis hin zu wenig kostbaren oder nachempfundenen Relikten der Historie. Sie breiten sich auf dem Boden und an der Wand aus, vereinen und zerstreuen sich. Ist auch die jeweilige Konstellation von disparaten Teilen scheinbar instabil und am Rande bruchstückhafter Vereinzelung, evoziert sie in sozusagen traumatischer Verwandlung der gewöhnlichen Dinge eine unterschwellig verdichtete Atmosphäre, ohne einen bestimmten motivischen Ansatz erzählerisch aufzuschlüsseln.

BATTLES OR THE ART OF WAR (Schlachten oder die Kunst der Kriegsführung, 1991) bildet bei aller Offenheit seiner Anlage ein geschlossenes Environment, das in der Rekonstruktion in der Kunsthalle Zürich 1997 nur durch eine Tür betretbar war. Quelle der Inspiration war ein Raum im Blenheim Palace, voller Tapisserien, die sich nach allen Seiten und Zeiten auszubreiten scheinen, als ob sie von den Wänden treten und den Raum überschwemmen würden. Zwischen Bühnenbild und Filmset angelegt, wird man von künstlichen Nebelschwaden umstrichen, die sich in dem grau-hellblauen Gewölk einer Wandmalerei fortsetzen. Grelle Töne – ein hart geschnittenes Sampling in lausiger Qualität von Haydns sinfonischen Böllerschüssen bis zu New Wave – steigern lust- wie qualvoll die suggerierte Landschaftskulisse, in der ein Strauch auch Flora nahelegt. Eine Theaterkanone im Vordergrund, ein goldbeknöpftes Soldaten

wams, Kanonenkugeln aus Plastik, eine Feldtasche, ein Rebhuhn als Jagdtrophäe und selbstgefertigte Standarten, die sich frei im Raum bündeln oder sich von Plastikefeu umrankt an die Wand lehnen, schaffen pittoresk und doch etwas bedrohlich Allusionen an ein Schlachtenpanorama, in dem wir uns unmittelbar bewegen. Eine Art Gobelin an der Stirnwand, gehöht von Reitern, die das Kriegerische ins Rokokohaft-Tändelnde entspannen, entzaubert sich in der Nahsicht zur zerschlissenen und schmuddeligen Teppichmatte, besetzt mit ruppigen Farbschlieren, die man kaum als Peinture bezeichnen könnte. An die Wand gepinnte, teils verwackelte Schnappschüsse und Photokopien, so von einem Feldherrenporträt oder von Pferd und Hund Napoleons, die als ausgestopfte Reminiszenzen in Vitrinen des Kriegsmuseums in Paris zu finden sind, öffnen weitere Mikrokosmen, die mit den Spielzeug-Miniaturen korrespondieren, die am Boden auf einem zum Kreis drapierten, dunkelgrünen Tuch ausgebreitet sind. Man blickt von oben auf eine Kinderzimmerschlacht verschiedener Grössenverhältnisse herab. Sie ist ein Machtspiel, bei dem man schon früh und unbewusst nicht nur die militärische Attacke und Kriegskunst einübt. Wie der durchlässige Makrokosmos der Gesamtinstallation pendelt dieses Spiel zwischen Anarchie und Zucht und unterlegt dem Unausweichlichen und Schrecklichen der Kriegshysterie das Simulierte, Manipulierbare und Verlogene.

Sorgsam imitierte Disco-Kugeln, Glitterausschweifungen zu unseren Füssen und farbiges Licht lassen den historisierenden Schall und Kanonenrauch unter Umkehrung der Vorzeichen zum Sound und Nebel heutigen Nachtlebens werden. «Wo bin ich?» scheint als Frage bei allen Betrachtern im Raum zu hängen. Ein ambivalentes Schweben, das einen psychedelisch umfängt und vereinnahmt, eine Gratwanderung zwischen den Zeiten, den Stilen, den Grössenverhältnissen, ohne die Gefahren des Lächerlichen und Billigen zu scheuen. Lessings These der Einheit von Raum, Zeit und Handlung wird in dieser Beschwörung des Lebens und des Todes im Sauseschritt umgeworfen. Sie ist erschaffen aus lauter Nebensächlichkeiten, ist jederzeit zerlegbar und doch ein Kosmos von unumstösslicher künstlerischer Präzision.

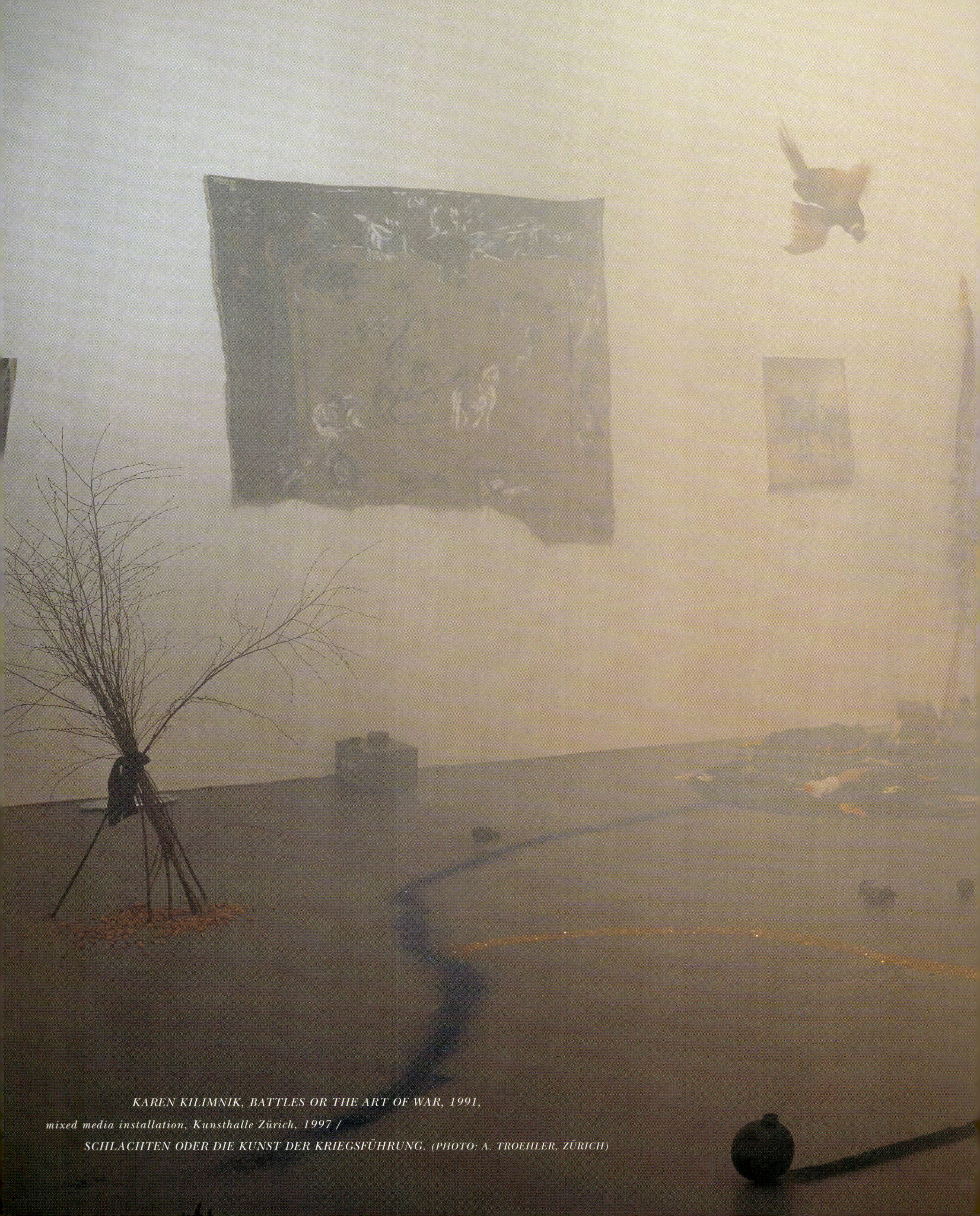

KAREN KILIMNIK, BATTLES OR THE ART OF WAR, 1991,
mixed media installation, Kunsthalle Zürich, 1997 /
SCHLACHTEN ODER DIE KUNST DER KRIEGSFÜHRUNG. (PHOTO: A. TROEHLER, ZÜRICH)

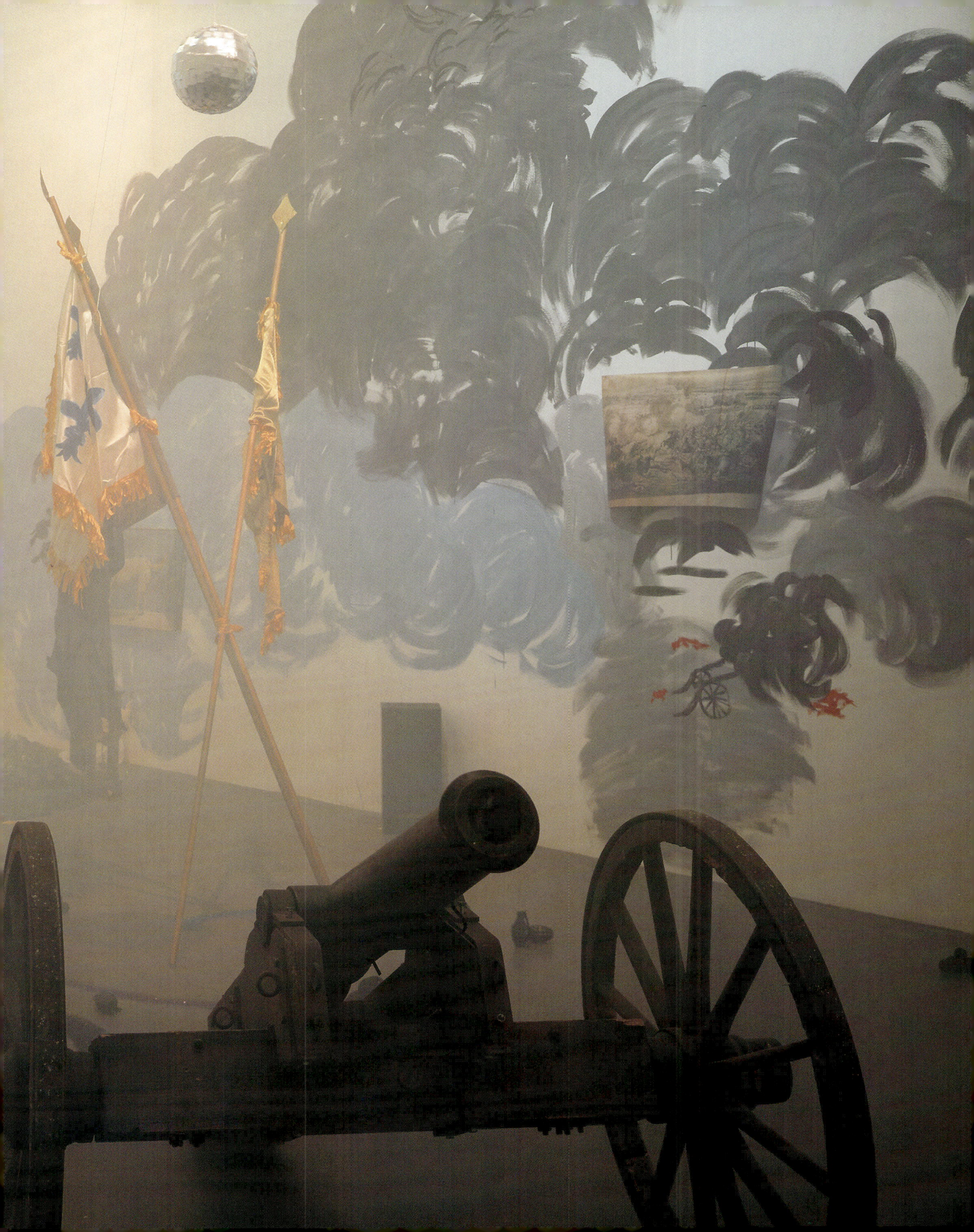

BERNHARD BÜRGI

Battles or the Art of War

Not only in Europe is there a tendency to associate the name Karen Kilimnik primarily with drawings done in black crayon. Their particularly sketchy contours and shading, partially worked over with a thin layer of acrylic and evoking a slightly jaded style of fashion illustration, are combined in one breath with scribbled quotations situated somewhere between gossip, headline, and diary. As part of an enchanted and fragile world, they circle around dreams and longings, nurtured since childhood and medially processed through women's mags, television or fashion ads. This is done with an obsessive devotion, ordinarily the preserve of teenagers unwilling to leave the rooms of their daydreams. On one hand, Kilimnik's heroines are blonde elves, personified by such super models as Twiggy or Kate Moss, whose ethereal lightness bespeaks not only innocence and beauty but vulnerability as well; on the other, they are amazons, like Emma Peel of the aging TV series, *The Avengers*, and, as such, embody a mix of dark fantasy, female dominance and destruction. Fame, beauty, and power must be garnered and transfixed as fragments of an overstated, secondhand reality in order to share in their glory and misery. In the process, cliché and personal reality, a girl's bedroom and the scene of the murder, lose their clearly contoured dis-

creteness in a crude amalgamation, effected with mastery and sensitivity. Suspended between feminine romanticism and terror, the deadpan shift of iridescent models towards authenticity shows a curious magic in revealing the extent to which the medial gloss absorbs existential wishes and threats.

The field on which Kilimnik projects her oil paintings has less to do with the glamorous world of fashion and more with the tradition of late eighteenth century landscape painting, popularized in books and magazines. This she interweaves, for example, with scenes from *Bewitched*, one of her favorite TV series. Saturated with color and a cloying horror, a fire may be seen eating away at the facade of familiar bourgeois respectability. The obscure and the occult blend with a love of animals and the forces of nature, such as torrential downpours or lightning.

Since oil paintings in intimate formats have become Kilimnik's preferred form of expression, she has focused less on large-scale installations, like THE HELLFIRE CLUB—EPISODE OF THE AVENGERS, seen in New York in the early nineties and described, at the time, as the quintessence of "scatter art." But the artist also relates her paintings directly to the real space of her exhibitions. They might appear on colored walls with patterned molding, evoking the classical painting gallery, except that the arrangement is centered in a characteristically Kilimnik-ian shift of viewing conventions. The installation-like approach

---

BERNHARD BÜRGI is the director of the Kunsthalle Zurich. In 1997 he organized a show of Karen Kilimnik's work.

to classical painting, itself of an urgency that flirts with the charm of triviality, might be heightened by framing a single painting, such as ANGEL'S COUSIN FROM BLOOD ON SATAN'S CLAW MCMLXX (1996), in a portal-like wreath of lights and twigs against a background of rampant purple.

In her installations—that aspect of her oeuvre which is, to my mind, essential, innovative, and underestimated—Karen Kilimnik works with handmade or painted elements but also with things drawn from daily life and popular culture (photocopies, glitter, candles, packaging, fabric, fragments of sound, and knickknacks), down to not particularly valuable or even faked remains of history. These elements are spread out on the walls and floors, where they are united and scattered. As precarious and on the verge of fragmented isolation as these configurations of disparate elements may seem, the so-to-speak traumatic transformation of ordinary things produces a condensed, atmospheric undercurrent without lending any specific motif a narrative thrust.

BATTLES OR THE ART OF WAR (1991), though entirely open-ended in intent, forms a closed environment, accessible only through one door, upon its

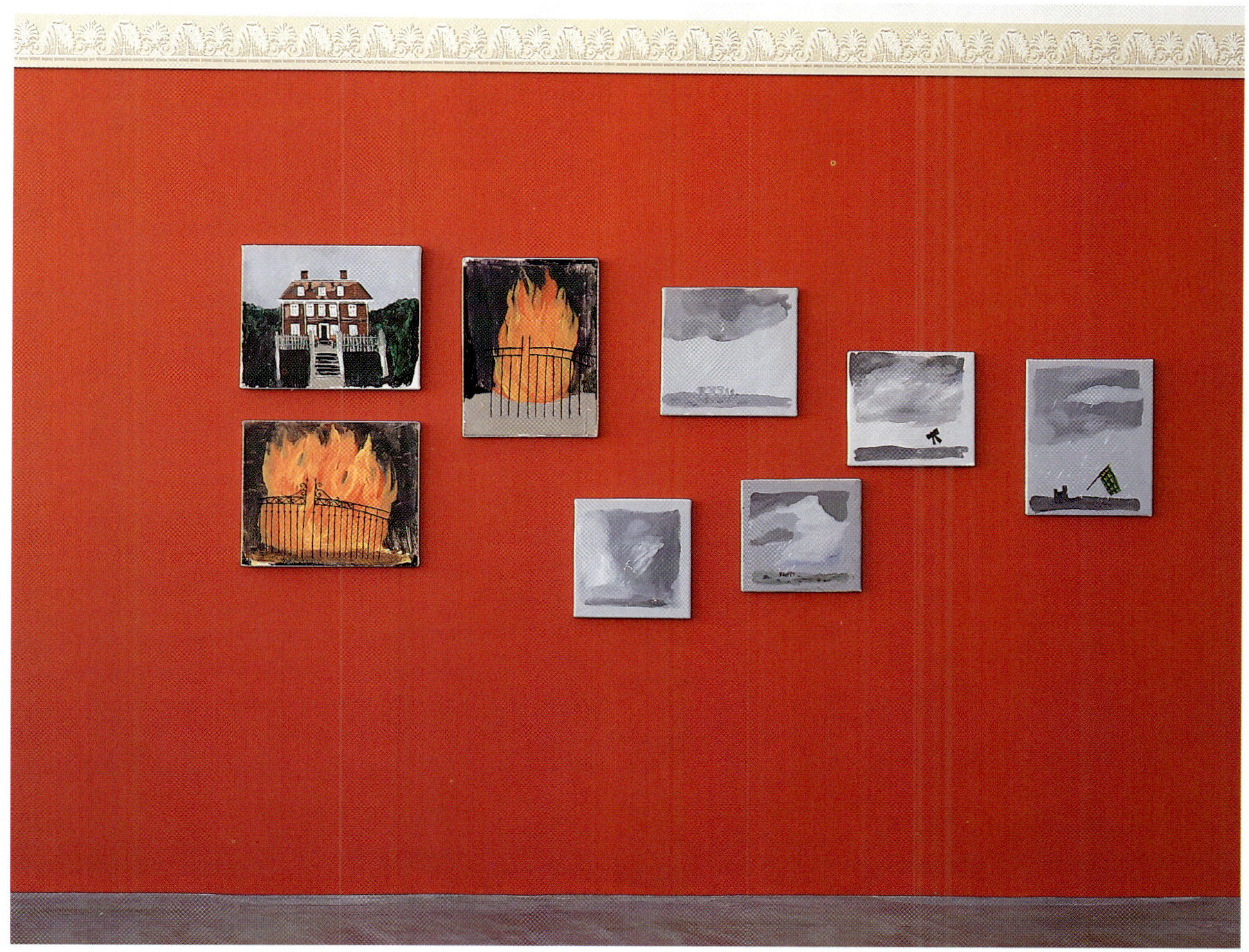

KAREN KILIMNIK, exhibition view / Ausstellungsansicht, Kunsthalle Zürich 1997.
(PHOTO: A. TROEHLER, ZÜRICH)

reconstruction in the Zurich Kunsthalle in 1997. It draws its inspiration from a room full of tapestries in Blenheim Palace, which seem to spread out in all directions and times, as if they were about to walk off the walls and flood the space. In a cross between stage and film set, wisps of artificial mist lick at our feet, lapping over into a grayish, light blue cover of clouds in a wall painting. Shrill sounds—a hard-cut sampling of lousy quality ranging from Haydn's symphonic gun salutes to new wave music—add both pain and pleasure to the suggested backdrop of a landscape in which an extra, a bunch of twigs, plays flora. A stage canon in the foreground, a gold-buttoned soldier's doublet, plastic canon balls, a field bag, a partridge as a hunting trophy, and self-made standards, suspended in the room or leaning against the wall with plastic ivy curling around them, all make for a picturesque but still slightly menacing allusion to a battle panorama—and we are in its midst. A kind of Gobelin on the front wall, heightened by riders who relax the belligerence of war to the point of rococo philandering, turns out—in close-up—to be a frayed and grimy mat, invaded with coarsely splattered pigment that could hardly be called peinture. Blurred snapshots and photocopies pinned to the wall, the portrait of a commander or of Napoleon's horse and dog, the latter found stuffed

and on display in Paris's war museum, reveal other microcosms that correspond with the toy miniatures spread out on the floor on a piece of dark green fabric laid out in a circle. One looks down at a pillow-fight battlefield of varying scales. In children's rooms, the power game, practiced at an early age, includes unconscious training in military attack and the martial arts. Like the permeable macrocosm of the installation as a whole, the miniature scene shuttles between anarchy and discipline, and colors the inevitability and horrors of war hysteria with simulation, manipulation, and hypocrisy.

Meticulously imitated disco globes, swathes of glitter at our feet, and colored lights convert the historicizing racket and canon smoke into the sound and mist of today's night life. Where am I? The question seems to be on the tip of every viewer's tongue. An ambivalent state of suspension surrounds and usurps us psychedelically, walking the line between times, styles, and scale without shying away from the risk of being ridiculous or cheap. Lessing's thesis of the unity of space, time, and action is overthrown in rapid strides by this invocation of life and death. It is an invocation that issues from a host of irrelevant items; it can be taken apart at any time; and yet it is a cosmos of precise artistic irrefutability.

(Translation: Catherine Schelbert)

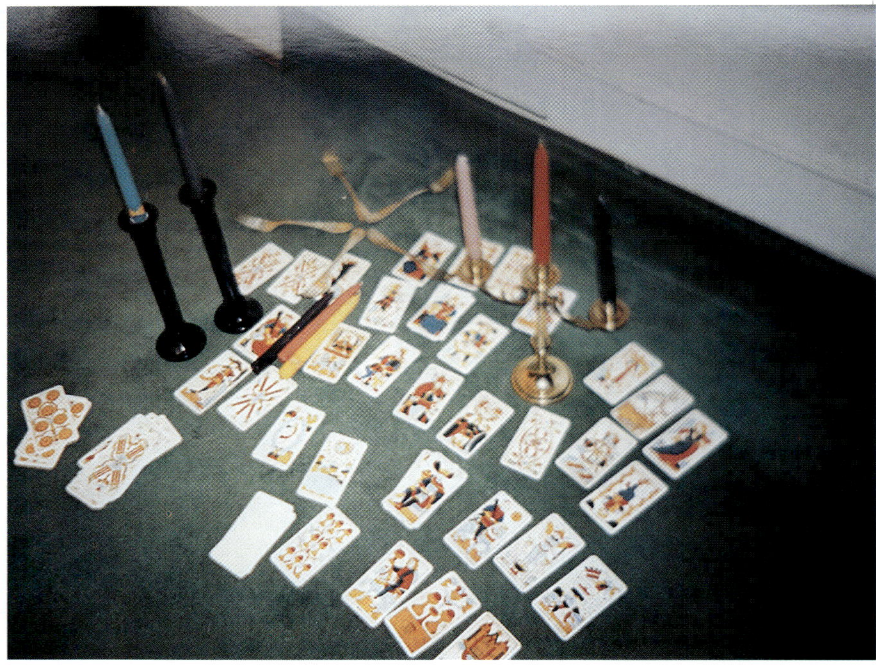

KAREN KILIMNIK,
TAROT CARDS IN TURIN, 1993,
tarot cards, candelabra, 2 candlesticks,
candles and 5 forks, installation at
Claudio Bottello, Turin, Italy /
TAROTKARTEN IN TURIN,
Tarotkarten, Kandelaber,
2 Kerzenständer, Kerzen und 5 Gabeln.
(PHOTO: KAREN KILIMNIK)

KAREN KILIMNIK, SWITZERLAND, THE PINK PANTHER & PETER SELLERS & BORIS & NATASHA IN SIBERIA, 1991, mixed media installation, 303 Gallery, New York /
DIE SCHWEIZ, DER ROSAROTE PANTHER & PETER SELLERS & BORIS & NATASCHA IN SIBIRIEN.

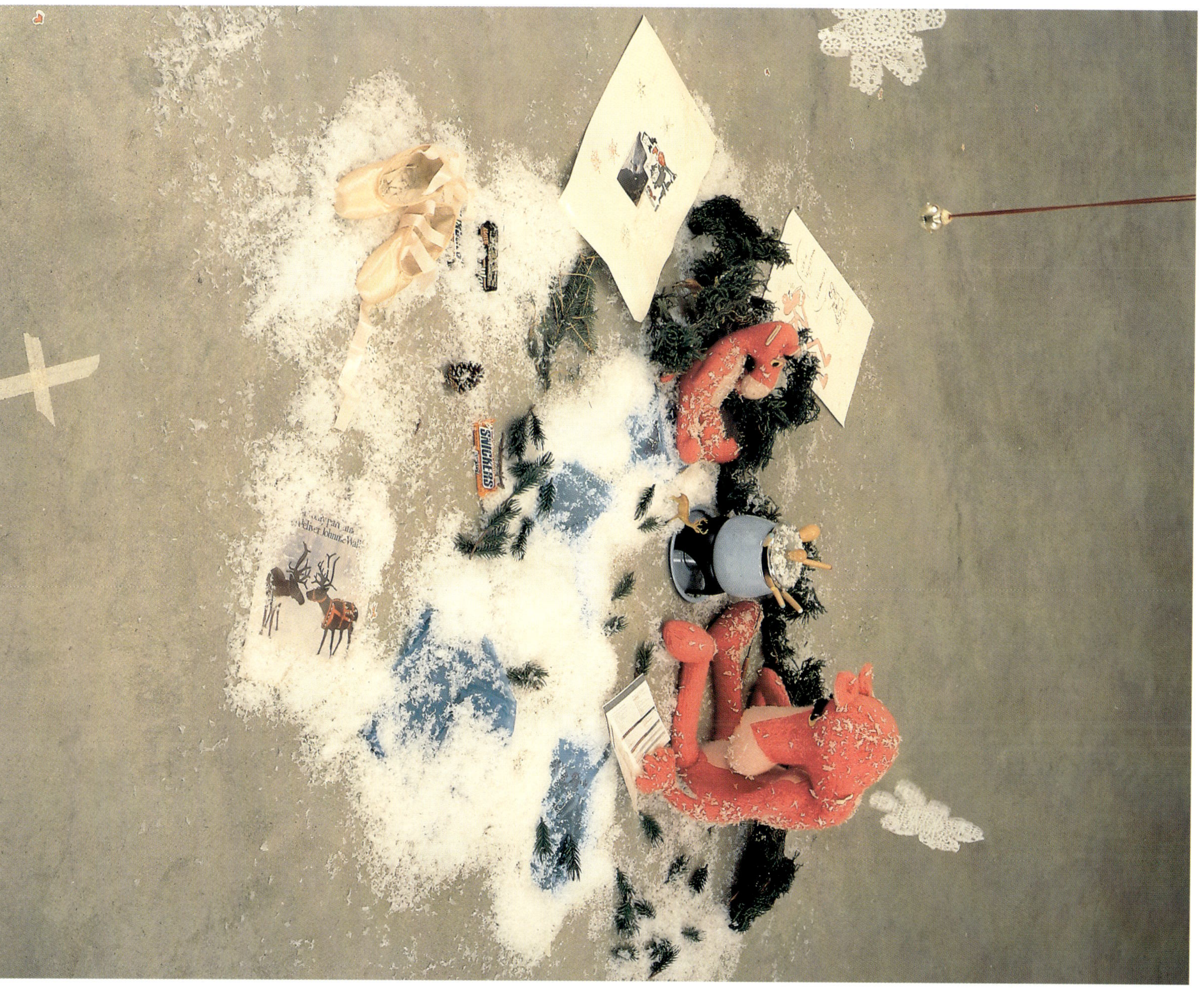

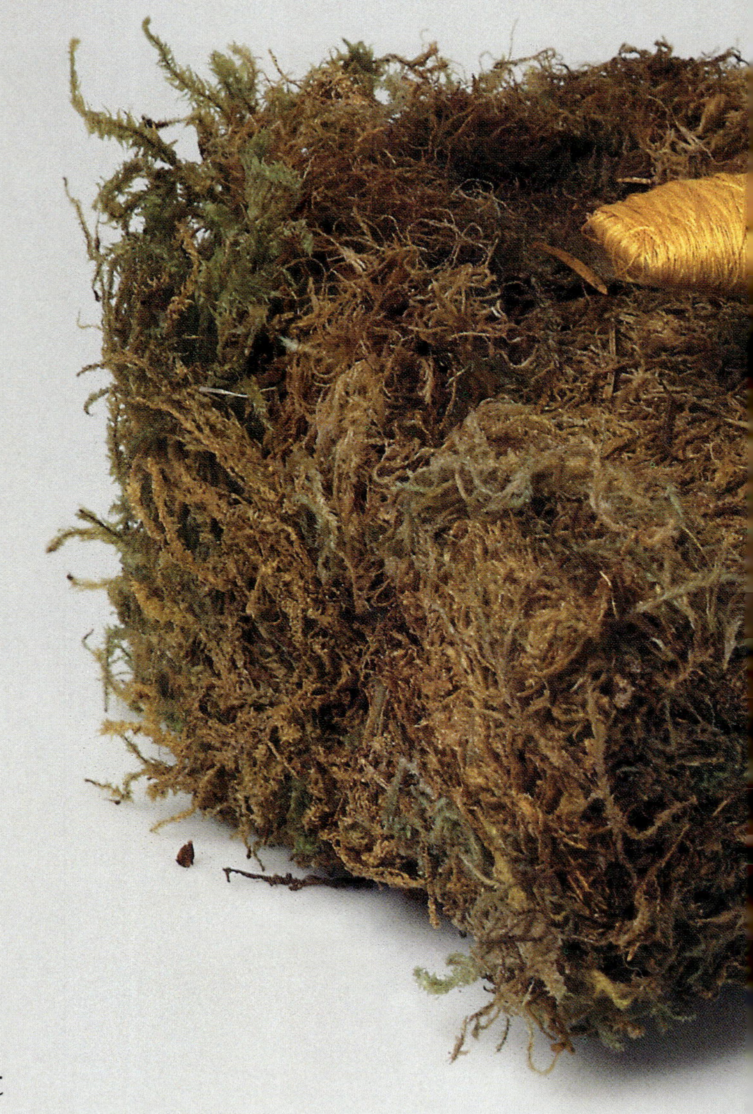

Edition for Parkett

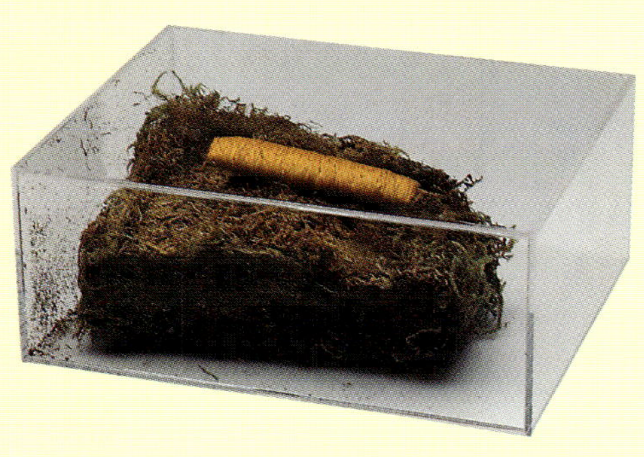

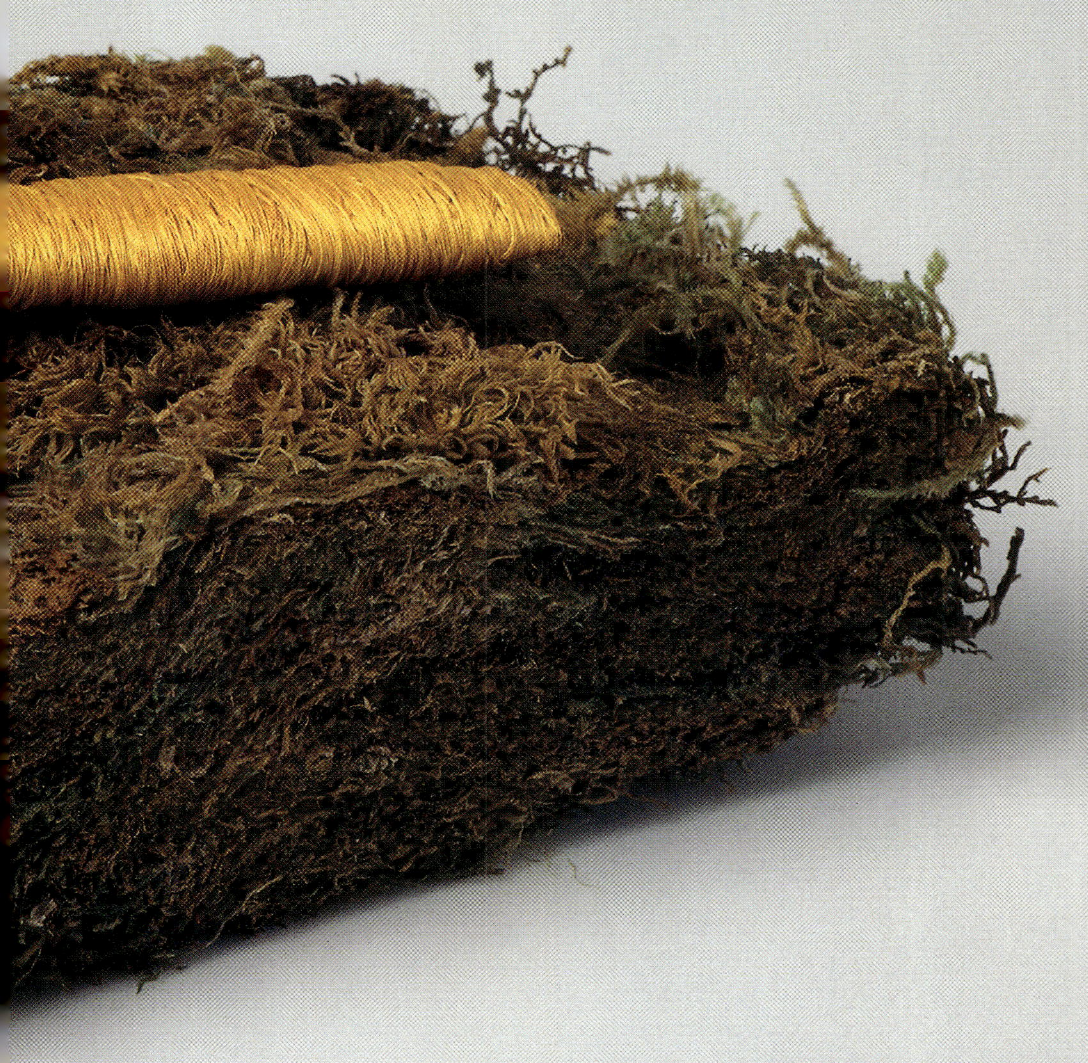

KAREN KILIMNIK

RAPUNZEL, 1998
Spindle of gold thread (hair) on bed of moss
(thread and moss are separately packaged to be assembled by the collector),
Plexiglas box, ca. 4 x 8 x 10".
Edition of 45, signed and numbered certificate with diagram by the artist.

Goldhaarspindel auf Moos gebettet
(separat verpackt, kann selbst arrangiert werden),
Plexiglasbox, ca. 10 x 20 x 25 cm.
Auflage: 45, signiertes und numeriertes Zertifikat mit Abbildung.

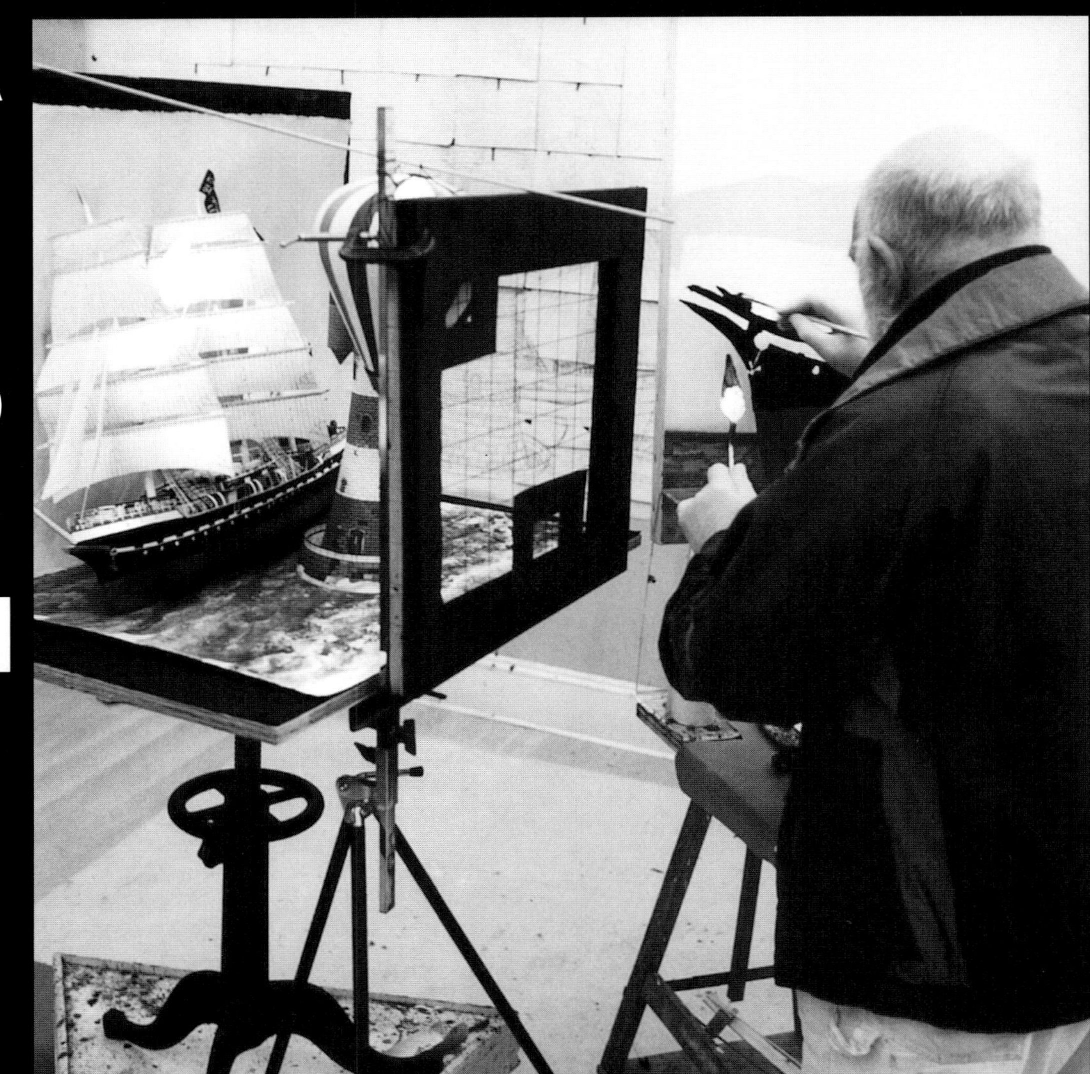

MORLEY
MALCOLM

ENRIQUE JUNCOSA

MALCOLM MORLEY ODER DIE MALEREI ALS ABENTEUER

«Als Pilot kam ich von der Strasse, hinter mir lag ein langer Wanderweg, ich war immer viel gewandert und fast immer mit dem Blick zum Boden. Ich war gefesselt von der Bewegung, vom Fliessen der Miniaturlandschaft. Von klein auf schien es mir beim Wandern und Betrachten des Bodens, dass jene Bewegung so aussah wie das, was man von einem Flugzeug aus sehen würde...» Daniele del Giudice[1]

Das Werk Malcolm Morleys hat sich stets dadurch ausgezeichnet, dass es ganz bewusst verschiedene Betrachtungsebenen nahelegt, ohne dabei jemals seine Interpretationsmöglichkeiten einzuschränken. Er ist ein Künstler mit makelloser Technik, gleichermassen fasziniert von den theoretischen wie von den praktischen Fragen, die von der Malerei aufgeworfen werden, aber ebenso offen für die Geschenke, die der Zufall feilhält, und natürlich für die Subjektivität der Betrachter. Seine jüngsten Werke sind Meisterstunden in Malerei und zugleich voller unlösbarer Rätsel, etwa vergleichbar mit unterbrochenen Schachpartien.

Nicht umsonst sah man bei seiner letzten Ausstellung in Paris[2] neben einigen Rittern in Rüstung und zu Pferd verschiedene Schiffsszenen, die von einem gemalten Schachbrett umrahmt waren. Auf diese Weise rief uns Morley die zweidimensionale Beschaffenheit der Malerei in Erinnerung – ein gängiges Thema in seinem Werk –, und zugleich betonen die Verweise auf dieses ursprünglich aus Adelskreisen stammende Spiel metaphorisch, dass die Intelligenz im ständigen Kampf gegen den Tod steht. Ein absurder Kampf, denn wir wissen ja, wie er ausgehen wird.

Das besondere Kennzeichen der Malerei Malcolm Morleys in den 90er Jahren ist die scharfe Abgrenzung der Konturen seiner Bildschöpfungen. Diese liegen zudem in reichhaltig und intensiv kolorierten Flächen, in denen Purpur-, Blau-, Orange-, Gelb- und Rottöne dominieren. Das Resultat – und das ist ebenfalls eine Konstante in seiner ganzen Produktion – erzählt uns von einer geistigen Wirklichkeit, die anders als die unsere ist und die uns sogar als Traumwelt vorkommen kann – sie erinnert uns unter anderem an das magische Leben

ENRIQUE JUNCOSA lebt in Barcelona. Er ist Dichter und ist als Kritiker für *El País* sowie als freier Kurator tätig.

67

der Spielzeuge –, auch wenn wir wissen, dass sie ursprünglich aus harmlosen dreidimensionalen Modellen und wunderschönen Aquarellen besteht.

Morleys künstlerische Laufbahn, eine Aufeinanderfolge wechselnder Stilrichtungen, hat jedenfalls bewiesen, dass für ihn der Stil nie Endzweck gewesen ist, sondern ein nützliches Mittel zur Entwicklung eines sowohl geistigen als auch biologischen Prozesses.[3] Wir dürfen diese Arbeiten deshalb nicht als blosse realistische Wahrscheinlichkeitsübungen verstehen. Sie sind vielmehr leidenschaftliche, malerische Manifeste, die uns mittels einer sehr persönlichen Bildgestaltung offene Metaphern oder zweideutige Allegorien nahelegen. Auf dem Wege fesselnder Bilder, die unsere Psyche stark anregen, bietet uns Morley eine eigentümliche Theorie der Wahrnehmung.

Unter den Themen jüngster Zeit sind besonders Wikingerschiffe, Walfänger und Renaissance-Galeonen zu erwähnen, mittelalterliche Ritter und Insignien, Schiffbruchszenen, Frachtschiffe und Hafenszenen, Flotten in der Dämmerung, unterschiedlichste Kriegsmalerei aus dem Ersten Weltkrieg oder zahlreiche Reiseskizzen – davon zuletzt Erinnerungen an eine Photosafari in Südafrika. All dies wird uns in unnatürlichen Farbgebungen dargeboten und in ausschweifenden Bildausschnitten, die manchmal auch um der Komposition willen gewaltig verzerrt sind.[4]

Letztendlich erhalten Morleys Malereien so einen dramatischen, mythischen oder orakelhaften Charakter. Die Titel einiger seiner jüngsten Werke, wie THE ORACLE (1992), ICARUS (1992), THE GUARDIAN OF THE DEEP (Der Hüter der Tiefe, 1993), KEEPERS OF THE LIGHTHOUSE (Leuchtturmwärter, 1994), TITAN (1994), THE FLIGHT OF ICARUS (Der Flug des Ikarus, 1995) oder DAEDALUS (1996) sind bezeichnend für die Suggestivwirkung seiner Bilder.[5] All dies erzählt uns auch – mit einem Sinn für Humor, der jedwede Prätention untergräbt – vom Leben und der Kunst als phantastische Heldenabenteuer.

Morleys Arbeitsmethode – er ist ein Künstler, der die feinsten Grade der Ironie herausarbeitet – ist von Besessenheit und peinlicher Genauigkeit bestimmt, fast wie das Sprechen eines Mantras. Die ersten Gemälde, mit denen er bekannt wurde, seine hyperrealistischen Ozeandampfer aus der Mitte der 60er Jahre, waren auf der Grundlage von Photographien entstanden, die er in Raster einteilte, um sie in vergrössertem Massstab so naturgetreu wie möglich abzubilden. Diese Werke sehen von weitem wie Photographien aus, doch aus der Nähe erweisen sie sich als malerisches Freudenbankett feiner dynamischer Pinselstriche.

Wie zu erwarten war, wurden diese Pinselstriche bald gröber und versahen seine späteren Bilder mit einer seltsamen und fesselnden inneren Dynamik, die Morley vom sogenannten Photorealismus distanzierte, jener Bewegung, der seine Arbeit in diesem Zeitraum zugeordnet wurde. Ausserdem errichtete Morley in den 70er Jahren eine Art *Tableaux vivants*, um sie als Modelle zu verwenden. Da es nicht möglich war, sie naturgetreu in zwei Dimensionen darzustellen, gelangte er unter anderem dazu, «die Rolle des Künstlers bei der Darstellung der Welt» zu thematisieren.[6] Jedenfalls trat Ende der 70er Jahre ein grundlegendes Ereignis in Morleys künstlerischer Laufbahn ein. Er begann mit einer gewaltigen Produktion von Aquarellen, die ihm von da an, wie bereits gesagt, als Vorlagen für seine Gemälde dienen sollten. Diese Arbeiten, die aus einer Mischung von Zufall und Kontrolle entstehen, drücken die

MALCOLM MORLEY, SS FRANCE, 1974, oil on canvas with objects on two panels, aluminum, 80½ x 60½ x 3" / Öl auf Leinwand mit Objekten auf zwei Tafeln, Aluminium, 205 x 154 x 7,6 cm.

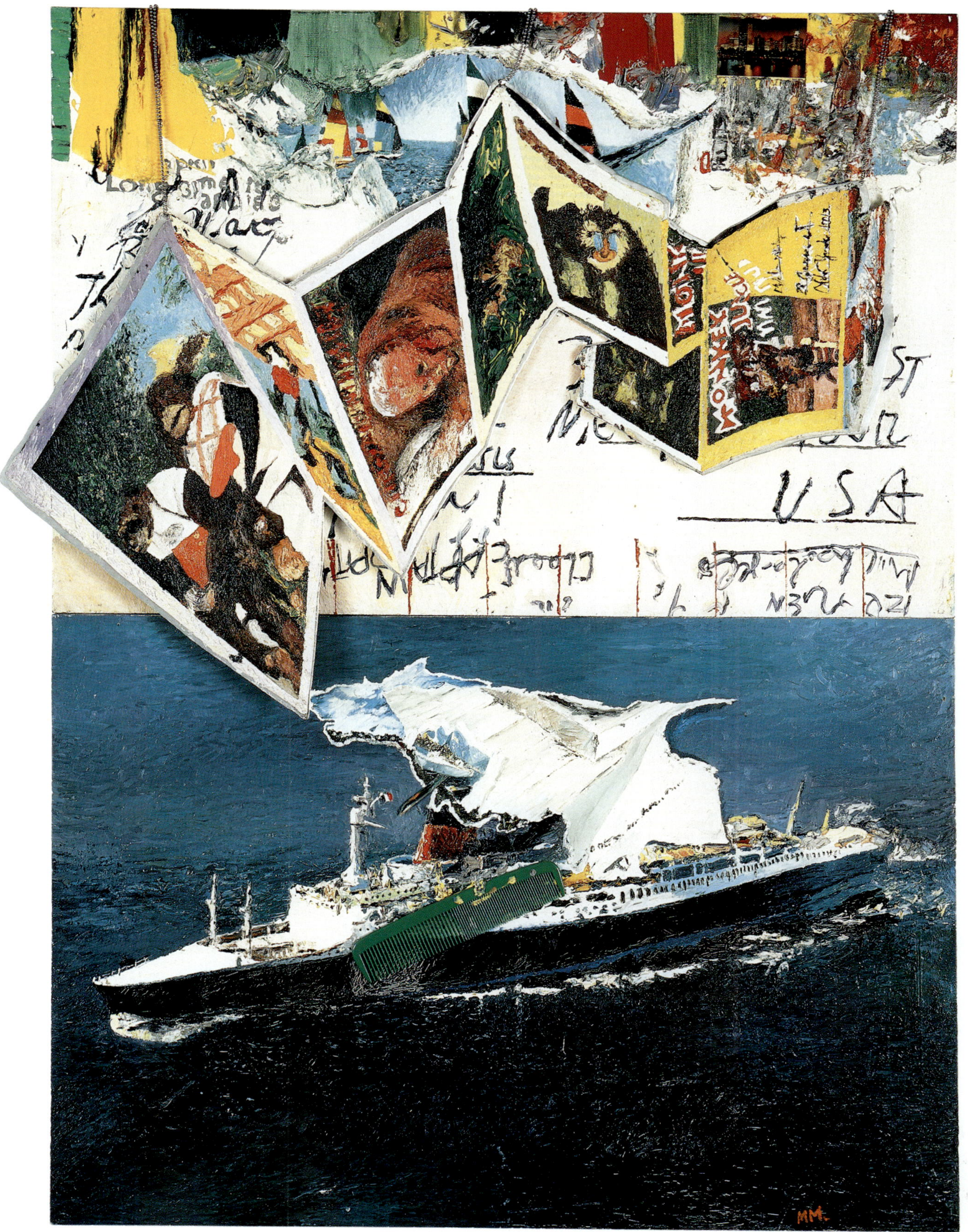

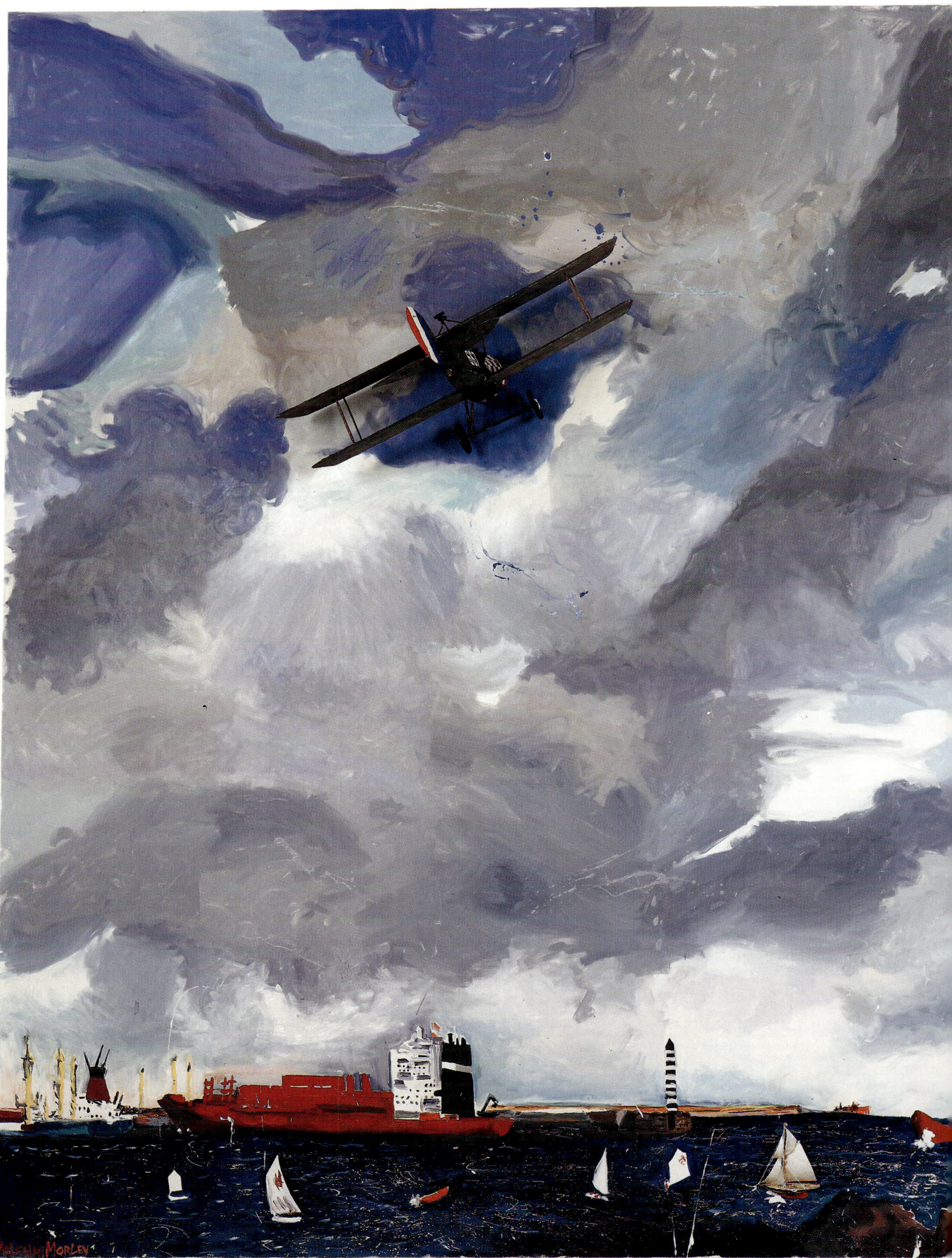

Malcolm Morley

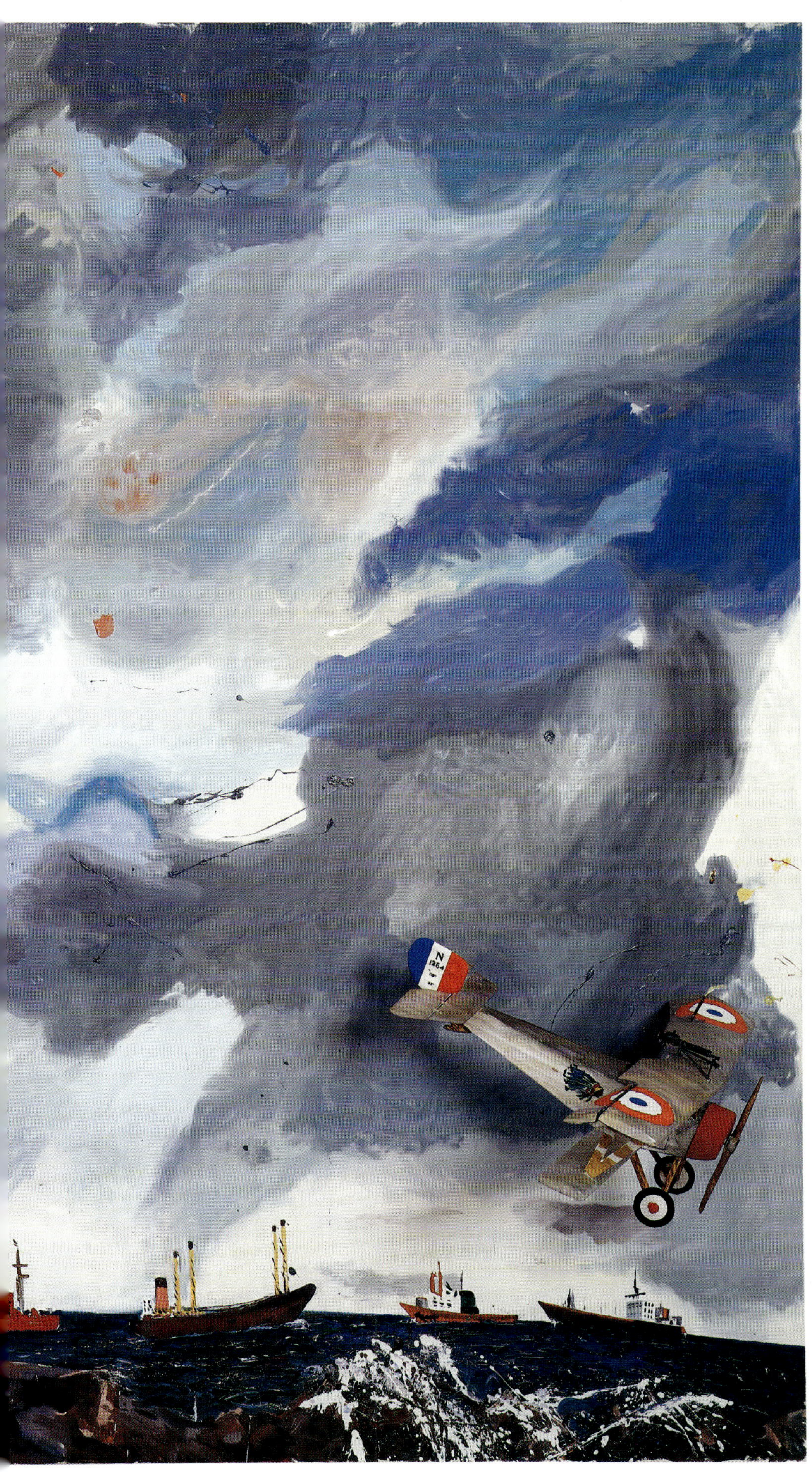

MALCOLM MORLEY,
ICARUS, 1993,
oil on canvas with airplanes
(1 rotating), 80 x 110" /
IKARUS,
Öl auf Leinwand mit Flugzeugen
(eines rotierend), 203 x 279,5 cm.
(PHOTO: DOROTHY ZEIDMAN)

MALCOLM MORLEY, THE FLIGHT OF ICARUS, 1995,
watercolor, paper, wood, metal frame, encaustic, 113 x 45 x 80" /
DER FLUG DES IKARUS, Wasserfarbe, Papier, Holz,
Metallrahmen, Enkaustik, 287 x 114,3 x 203,2 cm.

MALCOLM MORLEY, TITAN, 1994,
oil on canvas, 56 x 60" /
Öl auf Leinwand, 142 x 152,4 cm.

Wahrnehmungsvorgänge des Künstlers vor einer konkreten Wirklichkeit aus. Die genaue und methodische Übertragung seiner spontanen Bilder in grossformatige Malereien führte zu einem Expressionismus, der eigentlich gar keiner ist, wenn auch die sogenannten Neo-Expressionisten der 80er Jahre Morley nachdrücklich für sich beanspruchten.

Die Affinität Morleys zum Expressionismus stützt sich allein auf den malerischen Hochgenuss seiner Werke, der eigentlich das Ergebnis seiner analytischen und programmatischen Betrachtungsweise ist und sie eher zu den metalinguistischen Abstraktionen in Bezug bringt. Seine Malerei geht ausserdem über die rhythmische Sinnlichkeit der *All-over-Ästhetik* von Pollock oder de Kooning hinaus. Eine jede von Morleys quadratischen Einheiten ist wie ein kleines abstraktes Gemälde, das beim Zusammenfügen mit den anderen ein grosses vibrierendes, dramatisches und musikalisches Ganzes ergibt. Diese ganze dynamische Ebene bietet uns zudem eine dreidimensionale Illusion, die wir als eine Metapher für die Bedeutungsmacht der Malerei lesen können.

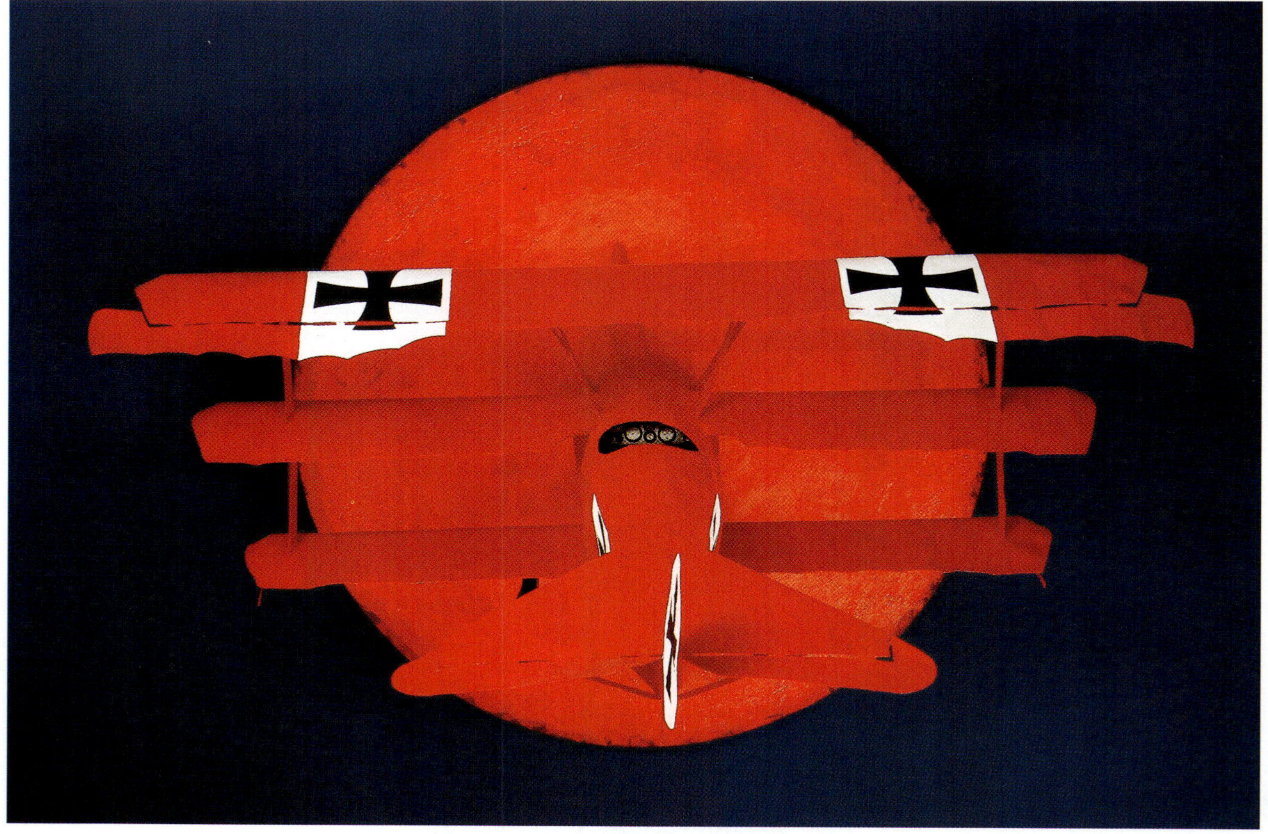

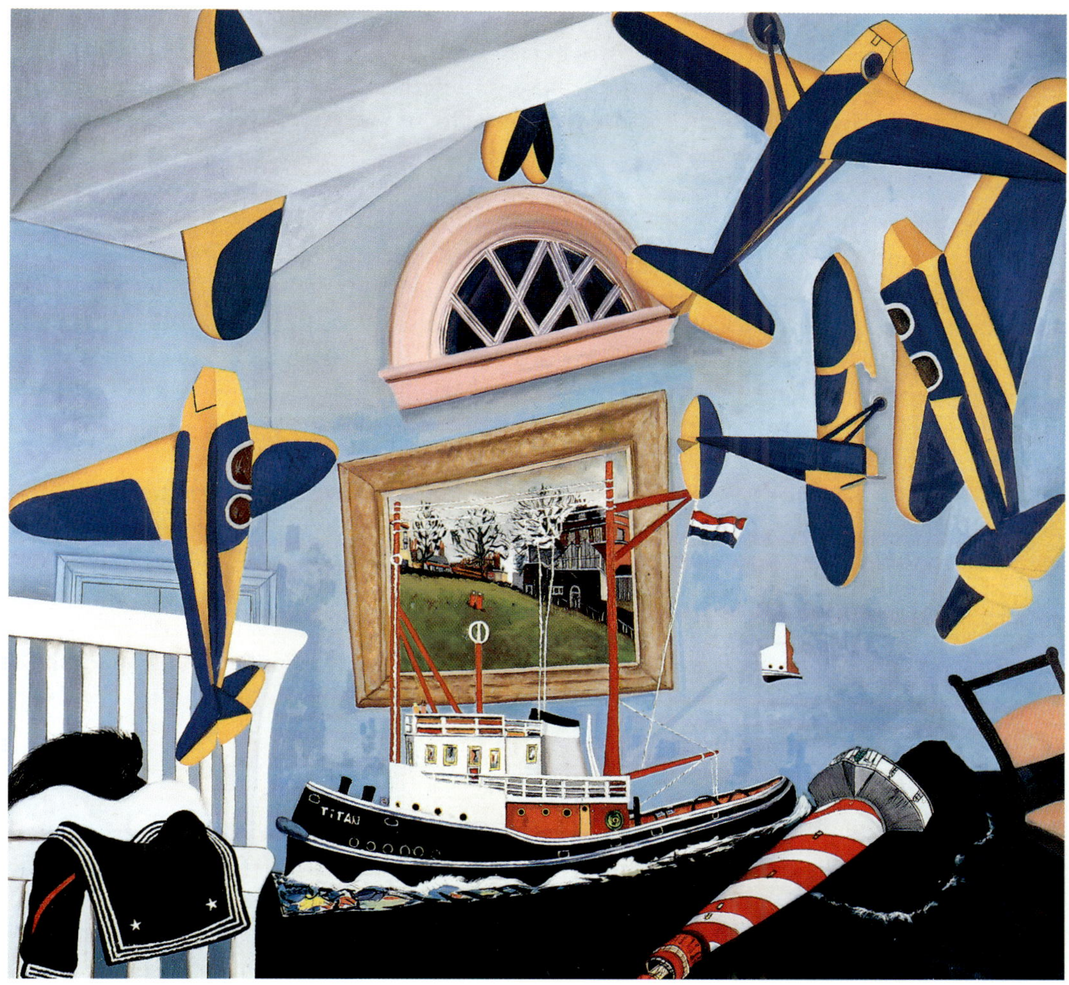

Tatsächlich ist Morley der grosse zeitgenössische Nachfolger von Cézanne. Schon 1980 sagte er uns: «Cézannes Erzfeind ist Clement Greenberg. ‹Befreien wir uns von der Illusion und bewahren wir die Flachheit.› Cézanne wäre über diese Idee entsetzt gewesen, weil er genau das Gegenteil glaubte – dass Malerei nicht dreidimensional genug sein kann. Und paradoxerweise erreicht man dies dadurch, dass man sie auf eine flache Ebene reduziert – paradoxerweise wird die Illusion um so stärker, je flächiger die Malerei ist. Aber das kann nur von einer besonderen Sensibilität oder Intelligenz, der des Malers, verstanden werden. Es ist sehr schwer, Illusion und Flachheit zu bewahren… gerade darin aber liegt Cézannes herausragendes Genie. Mir scheint, Cézanne ist für die Malerei, was Einstein für die Physik gewesen sein könnte, der Quantensprung in achthundert Jahren Renaissance-Raum.»[7]

Aber Morley setzt Cézanne nicht innerhalb der reduzierenden Formalistentradition fort, welche Greenberg im Kubismus beginnen und im Minimalismus enden lässt, sondern nimmt das malerische Lehrmaterial des Franzosen mit auf sein eigenes Aktionsfeld. Dabei tritt er ausserdem in den Dialog mit einigen späteren theoretischen Debatten, ausgelöst vom Surrealismus (Bild und Unterbewusstsein), dem Abstrakten Expressionismus (Bild und kreative Energie), dem Minimalismus (Einheit zwischen Konzept und Darstellung), der Pop-art (kritisches Potential der banalen Bilder) und dem postmodernen Pluralismus. Stets bleibt er auf der Suche nach höchstmöglicher Komplexität, ausgehend von einem Verständnis der Zweideutigkeit als bereicherndes Element.

Einige der jüngsten Werke Malcolm Morleys tragen dreidimensionale Zusätze (Flugzeuge, Fahnen, ...) und verweisen dadurch erneut auf die flache Beschaffenheit der Malerei. In Natura oder als Photographie von vorn gesehen, wirken diese Elemente flach, und die Gemälde sehen wie konventionelle Gemälde aus. Aus diesem Grund stellen diese Werke, wie Klaus Kertess treffend beschreibt, eine Serie aus realen und fiktiven Spielen und Aggressionen auf der Ebene der Malerei dar: «Der Maler ist wörtlich und bildlich ein ‹Pilot of planes›, ein ‹Pilot von Ebenen und von Flugzeugen›.»[8]

Einige Kritiker haben diese Gemälde ausserdem als postmoderne Allegorien der Fehlschläge der Moderne angesehen. Wir sehen Schiffe und Flugzeuge, die untergehen, abstürzen oder den Raum durchqueren und Unglücken ausweichen. Verschiedene Embleme (schwarze Kreuze, konzentrische Kreise...) verweisen uns auf eine umfassende heraldische Tradition, die mit Malewitsch beginnt und bis Stella, Johns oder Noland reicht. Die primitiven Fahrzeuge, die die Embleme zur Schau stellen, zerschellen als Metapher für die Niederlage der utopischen Ideale der Fläche, die in den 60er Jahren durch ihre formalistischen Dogmen und Reinheitsvorstellungen die Malerei beinahe vernichteten.

All diese Dinge geschehen in Bildern eigentümlicher Klarheit und von höchst intensivem Licht, die Morley vor allem dazu dienen, seine persönliche Welt voller Kindheitserinnerungen und Träume zu beschreiben. Sehr oft ist zitiert worden, wie in seiner Kindheit eine deutsche Bombe ein Modell seines Lieblingsbootes zerstörte, das im Fenster seiner Wohnung in London stand. Die Kunst Morleys bildet seitdem eine Art Wiedererlangung eines Abenteurerideals, das die Funktionalität kritisiert und dabei die Phantasie verteidigt. Seine Schiffe und Flugzeuge sind starke metaphorische Maschinen, auf denen wir die stürmischen Meere des Unglücks und der Logik durchqueren sollen. Morleys Triumph besteht darin, dass es ihm gelingt, Idee und Darstellung – seine eigene Weltsicht und seine Wahrnehmungsstruktur – in bestechend schönen und zudem sinnreichen Werken zu vereinen.

(Übersetzung aus dem Spanischen: Hans Bolt, UGZ)

1) Daniele del Giudice, in: *Staccando l'ombra da terra,* Giulio Einaudi editore, Turin 1994.
2) Galerie Daniel Templon, Paris 29. April–28. Mai 1997.
3) Siehe *Malcolm Morley on Painting,* im Katalog seiner Ausstellung in der Galerie Fabian Carlsson, London 1984, S. 13.
4) In einem Gespräch erinnerte mich Morley daran, wie Canaletto die städtische Struktur Venedigs zugunsten der Komposition seiner Gemälde verfälschte.
5) Die meisten dieser Gemälde sind im Ausstellungskatalog der Morley-Retrospektive in der «La Caixa»-Stiftung, Madrid 1995, wiedergegeben.
6) Michael Compton, *Malcolm Morley,* im Ausstellungskatalog der Morley-Retrospektive in der Whitechapel Art Gallery, London 1983, S. 14.
7) Nena Dimitrijevic, Interview mit Malcolm Morley, veröffentlicht in *Flash Art,* Nr. 142, Oktober 1988, S. 76.
8) Klaus Kertess, *On the High Sea and Seeing of Painting,* im Ausstellungskatalog der Morley-Retrospektive im Musée National d'Art Moderne, Centre Georges Pompidou, Paris 1993, S. 226.

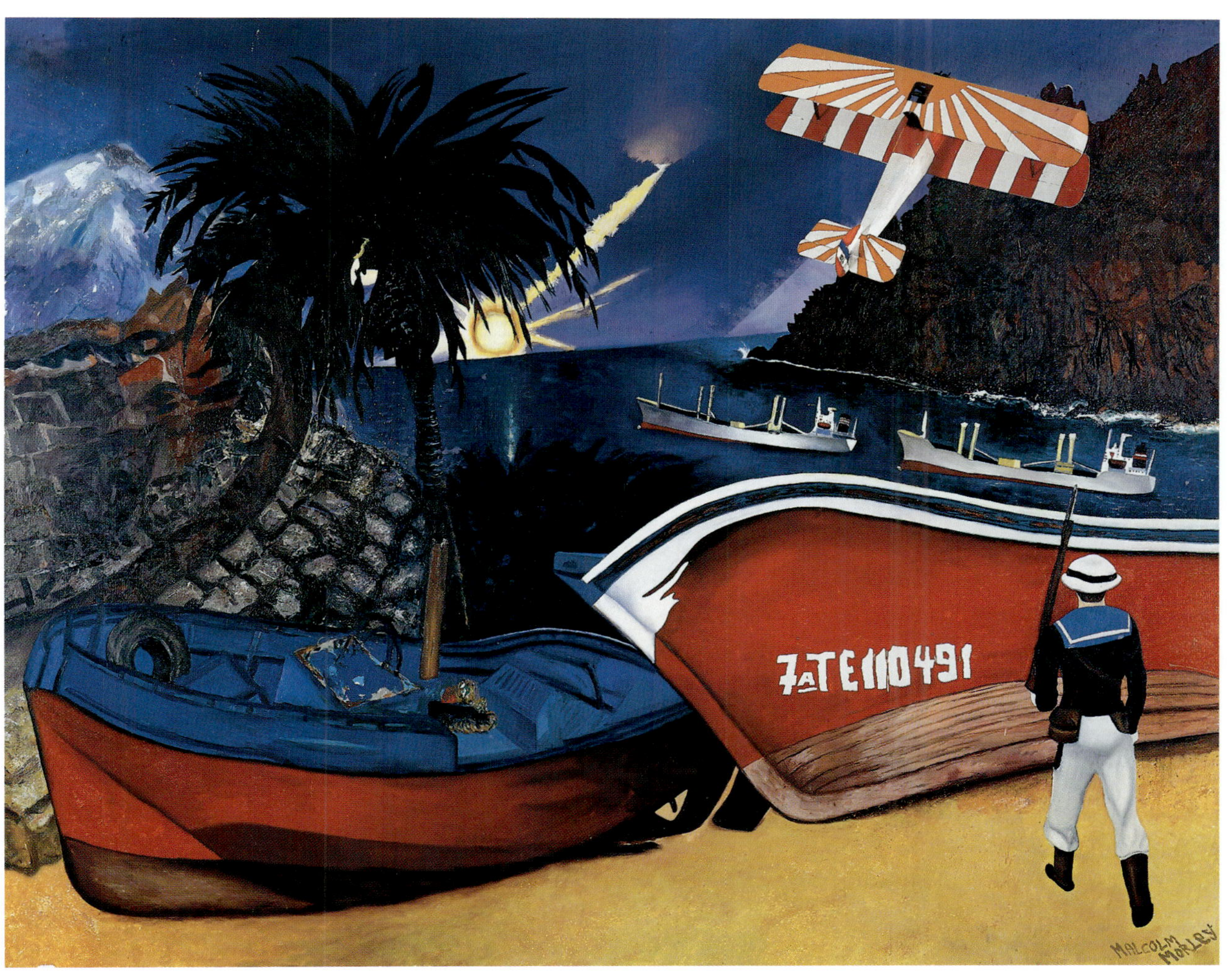

MALCOLM MORLEY, THE GUARDIAN OF THE DEEP, 1994,
oil, canvas, paper and wax encaustic plane, 78 x 100" /
DER HÜTER DER TIEFE,
Öl, Leinwand, Papier und Flugzeug in Enkaustik, 198 x 254 cm.

ENRIQUE JUNCOSA

MALCOLM MORLEY OR PAINTING AS ADVENTURE

I came from the street like a pilot. Behind me I had a long career as a walker; I'd always walked a lot, almost always staring at the ground. I was hypnotized by movement, by the flow of the landscape in miniature. From the time I was a small boy, whenever I walked and stared at the ground, I got the feeling that the motion looked like what you'd see from a plane. Daniele del Giudice[1]

It is characteristic of Malcolm Morley's work that it consciously suggests different levels of reading but never limits the possibilities of interpretation. An artist of impeccable technique, fascinated equally by the theoretical and practical issues painting arouses, but open as well to the gifts offered by chance and, of course, to the subjectivity of the spectators. His most recent work constitutes a lesson of pictorial mastery at the same time it presents unsolvable enigmas, something like interrupted games of chess.

It is not by chance that in the paintings included in his last Paris show[2] we see, in addition to knights in armor and horses, naval scenes framed by a painted chessboard. This was Morley's way of reminding us of the planar nature of painting—a recurrent theme in his work—at the same time metaphorically underscoring these references to the aristocratic origins of the game with the knowledge that our human intelligence is locked in a constant struggle against death, an absurd struggle since we know what its outcome will be.

During the nineties, Morley's painting has been characterized by the very precise delineation of his images. These images are located on surfaces of rich, intense color dominated by purples, blues, oranges, yellows, and reds. The result—and this too is a constant in all his production—speaks to us of a mental reality different from our own, a reality that may in fact seem oneiric. These works recall, among other things, the magic life of toys, even though we know that they begin with three-dimensional models or extremely beautiful watercolors.

1) Daniele del Giudice, *Despegando la sombra del suelo* (Barcelona: Anagrama, 1996), p. 37.
2) At Galerie Templon, Paris, 29 April–28 May 1997.

ENRIQUE JUNCOSA is a poet, an art critic of *El País* and a free-lance curator. He lives in Barcelona.

MALCOLM MORLEY, KEEPERS OF THE LIGHTHOUSE, 1994,
oil on canvas, 56 x 49” / LEUCHTURMWÄRTER, Öl auf Leinwand, 142 x 125 cm.

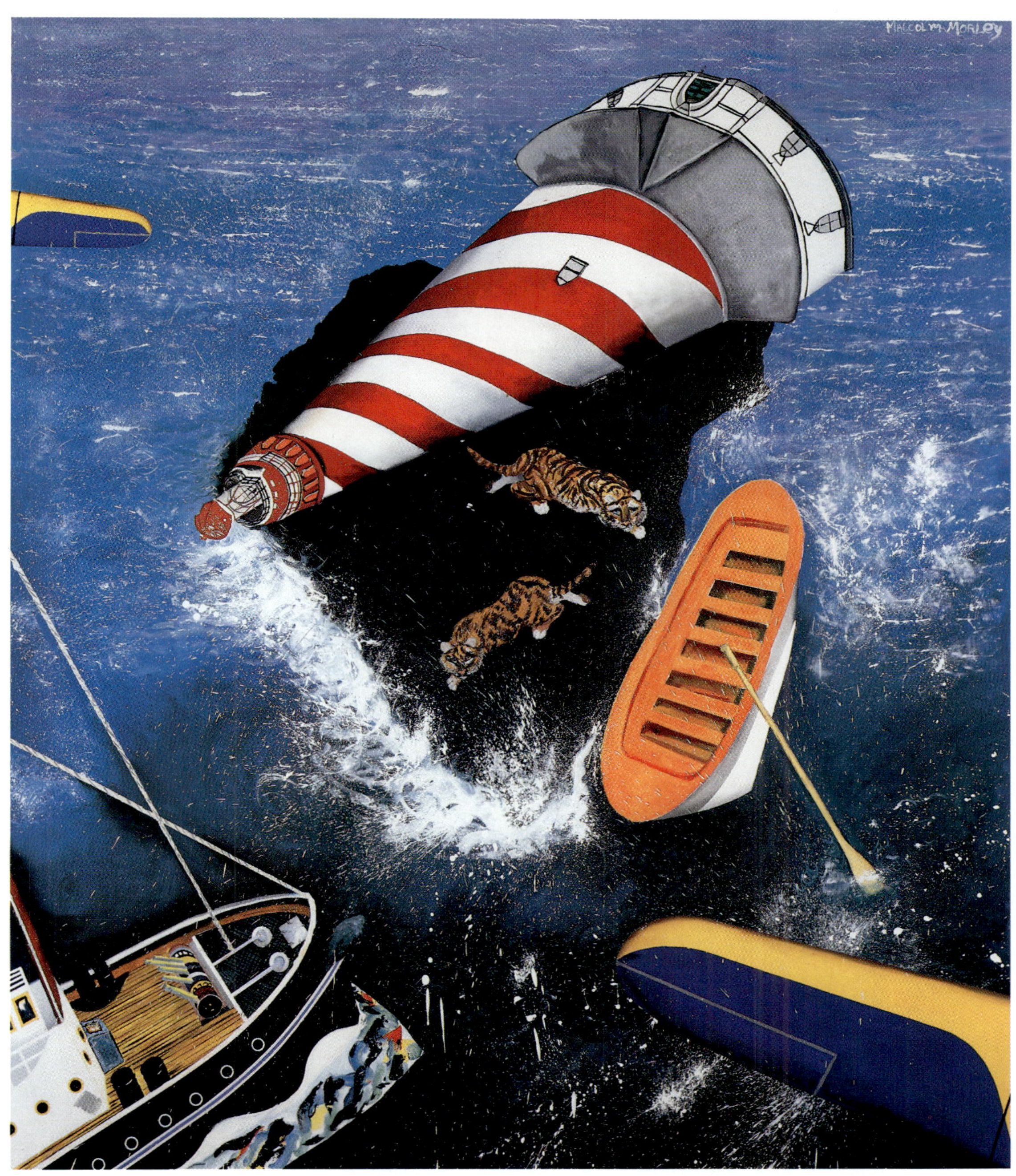

MALCOLM MORLEY, THE ORACLE, 1992, oil on linen, watercolor airplanes, goldleaf, 172 x 240" / DAS ORAKEL, Öl auf Leinen, Flugzeuge in Wasserfarbe, Blattgold, 437 x 610 cm.

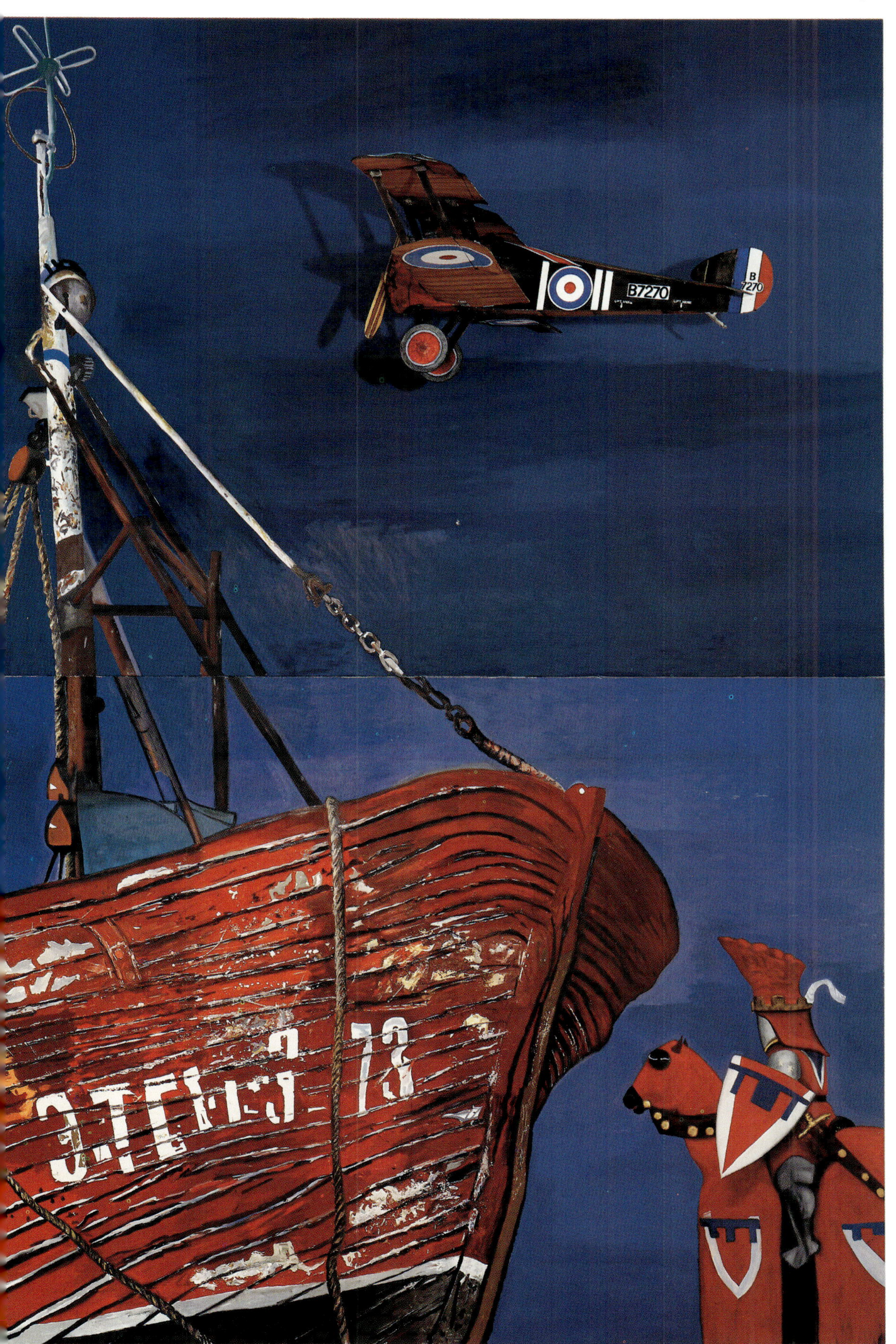

B7270
B 7270

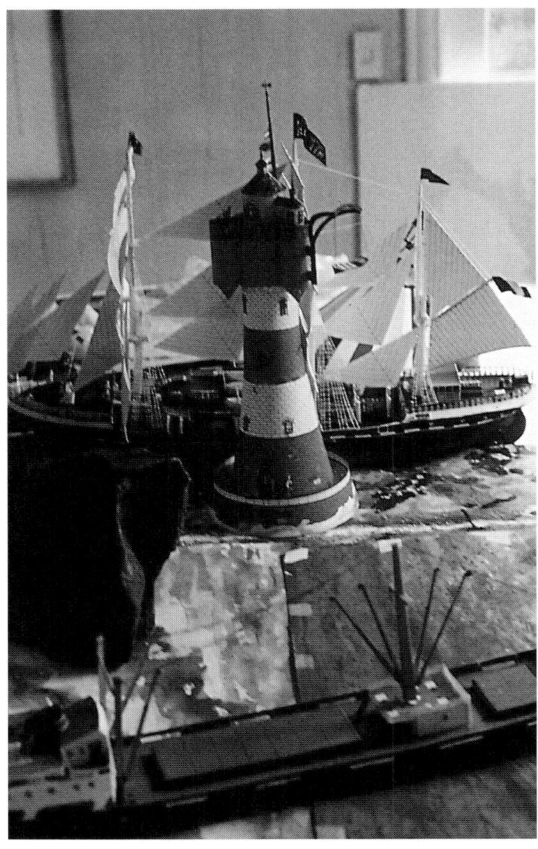

Studio of Malcolm Morley, 1995 / im Atelier.
(PHOTO: DANIEL MOSS)

Morley's artistic career, a succession of changing styles, demonstrates that for him style is never an end in itself but a means to the development of a process that is as spiritual as it is biological.[3] We should not take these works, then, to be mere exercises in realistic verisimilitude. Instead, they constitute impassioned pictorial manifestos that suggest, by means of a very personal iconography, open metaphors or ambiguous allegories. Morley offers us a particular theory of vision by using captivating images that powerfully excite our psyche.

Among the most frequent motifs in Morley's recent work are Viking ships and whales, Renaissance galleons, knights and medieval insignias, shipwrecks, cargo ships and ports, marine sunsets, the most diverse selection of World War I imagery, and numerous tourist notes—the most recent ones being souvenirs of a photographic safari in South Africa. All of these are presented to us in epic perspective—at times violently distorted for the sake of the composition[4]—and in nonnaturalistic colors.

Because of this, Morley's paintings acquire a dramatic and haunting mythic or oracular aura. The titles of some recent works like THE ORACLE (1992), ICARUS (1993), THE GUARDIAN OF THE DEEP (1993), KEEPERS OF THE LIGHTHOUSE (1994), TITAN (1994), THE FLIGHT OF

---

3) "Malcolm Morley on Painting," in: *Malcolm Morley,* ex. cat. (London: Fabian Carlsson Gallery, 1984), p. 13.
4) In a conversation, Morley reminded me of how Canaletto would alter the urban configuration of Venice to benefit the composition of his paintings.

ICARUS (1995), or DAEDALUS (1996) reveal the suggestive potential of his images.[5] Everything here also speaks to us with a sense of humor that undermines any possible pretentiousness, a sense of life and art as marvelous epic adventures.

Morley's work method—and he is an artist who cultivates the most refined ironies—is obsessive and scrupulous, almost mantra-like. The first paintings that brought him notoriety, his superrealist ocean-liners of the 1960s, derive from photographs that he divided in little squares so that he could copy them with the greatest possible accuracy. Seen from a distance, these works look like photographs, but close up they disclose themselves as jubilant pictorial feasts made up of tiny, dynamic brushstrokes.

As might be imagined, those brushstrokes quickly grew, imbuing Morley's later images with a strange internal and hallucinatory energy that distanced him from so-called photorealism, a movement with which his work was associated during that period. In the seventies, Morley also constructed something akin to *tableaux vivants* to use as models. The impossibility of representing them faithfully in two dimensions allowed him, among other things, to dramatize "the role of the artist representing the world."[6] At the end of the seventies, in any case, a fundamental change took place in Morley's artistic career. He embarked on what was to become a huge production of watercolors, which he used, as mentioned, as models for his paintings. These works, which derive from a mixture of chance and control, translate the processes of the artist's perception in the face of concrete reality. The minute, methodical translation of his spontaneous images into large-format paintings gave rise to an expressionism that in actuality is not expressionism, although Morley was claimed energetically by the so-called neo-expressionists of the eighties.

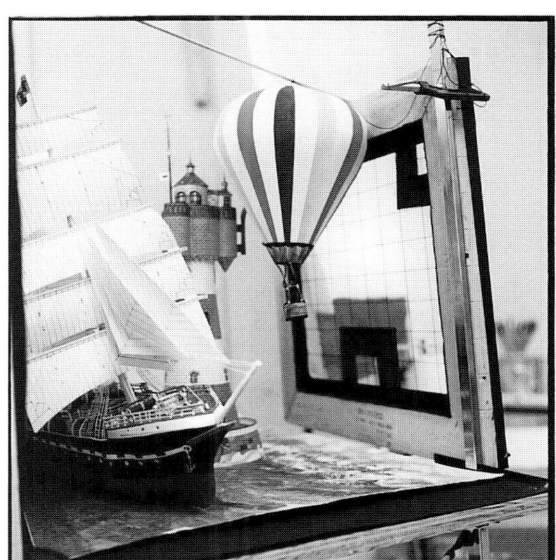

Morley's expressionist affinities only manifest themselves in what might be perceived as the "pictorial feast" of his work, in reality the fruit of an analytical and programmatic vision that brings them closer to metalinguistic abstractions. Besides, his paintings go beyond the rhythmic sensuality of the all-over aesthetics of Pollock or de Kooning. Each square unit in Morley is like a small abstract picture which, when joined to the others, forms a great, vibrant unity that is both dramatic and musical. This entire dynamic plane offers us as well an illusion of three-dimensionality that we can read as a metaphor for the signifying power of painting.

Morley, in point of fact, is the great contemporary link with Cézanne. In 1988 he said: "The arch-enemy of Cézanne is Clement Greenberg: 'Let's get rid of the illusion and keep the

5) Most of these paintings are reproduced in *Malcolm Morley 1965–1995* (Madrid: la Fundación "la Caixa," 1995).
6) Michael Compton, "Malcolm Morley," in: *Malcolm Morley* (London: Whitechapel Art Gallery, 1983), p. 14.

plane...' Cézanne would be horrified by this idea, because he believed just the opposite—that it cannot be three-dimensional enough. And the paradox is that you achieve this by restricting it to a flat plane. Paradoxically, the more you flatten it, the more illusion you get. But only a certain kind of sensitivity or intelligence—the painterly intelligence—can understand that. It is very hard to keep both the illusion and the plane simultaneously ... this was the incredible genius of Cézanne. For me Cézanne is to painting what Einstein may be to physics—the quantum leap in eight hundred years of Renaissance space."[7]

But Morley does not continue Cézanne's pictorial teachings within the formalist, reductive tradition that Greenberg's narrative initiates in cubism and ends with minimalism. Instead, he relocates them in his own terrain. In doing so, he also enters into a dialogue with some later theoretical debates aroused by surrealism: image and the subconscious, abstract expressionism; image and creative energy, minimalism; unity between concept and representation, pop art; potential criticism of banal images; and postmodern pluralism. He is always searching for maximum complexity and taking the point of view that considers ambiguity as something enriching.

Some of Malcolm Morley's most recent works—and, again, with reference to the planar condition of painting—have three-dimensional attachments, such as airplanes or flags. Seen frontally, in reality or in a photograph, these elements flatten out; the paintings seen in this way become conventional paintings. For this reason, these works constitute in Klaus Kertess's cogent description a series of games and aggressions, real and imagined, on the plane of painting: "The painter is literally and figuratively a pilot of planes."[8]

Some critics have also seen these paintings as postmodern allegories about the failures of modernity. We see ships and planes that sink, crash, or plough their way through space, dodging adversities. Different emblems—black crosses, concentric circles—return us to an entire heraldic tradition that begins with Malevich and reaches Stella, Johns, Noland. The primitive machines that bear them fall, a metaphor for the defeat of the utopian ideals of the plane that almost assassinated painting during the sixties with their formalist dogmas and purist pretensions.

All these things occur in images of peculiar clarity, of extremely intense light, that help Morley, above all, to depict his personal world, replete with childhood memories and dreams. It is often recalled that when he was a boy, a German bomb destroyed a model of his favorite ship, which he kept in the window of his London house. Ever since then, Morley's art has constituted a kind of recovery of an adventurous ideal that criticizes functionality in defense of imagination. His ships and airplanes constitute powerful metaphorical machines that invite us to sail the turbulent seas of adversity and logic. Morley's triumph derives from his having fused concept and representation—his particular vision of the world and his perceptual structure—in works of spectacular beauty that are also filled with meaning.

(Translation from the Spanish: Alfred MacAdam)

7) Nena Dimitrijevic, "Malcolm Morley," in: *Flash Art*, vol. 142 (October 1988), p. 76.
8) Klaus Kertess, "On the High Sea and Seeing of Painting," in: *Malcolm Morley* (Paris: Musée National d'Art Moderne, Centre Georges Pompidou, 1993), p. 226.

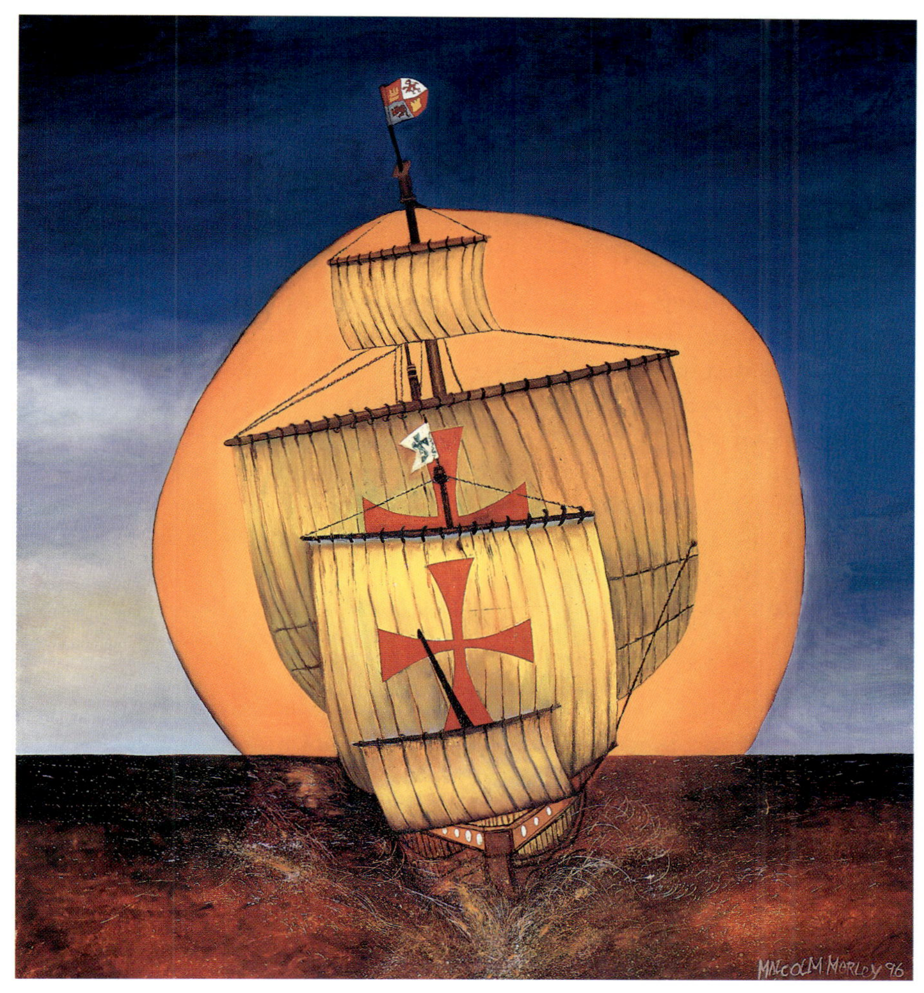

MALCOLM MORLEY, DAEDALUS, 1996,
oil on canvas, 60 x 56" / Öl auf Leinwand, 152,4 x 142,2 cm.
(PHOTO: ZINDMAN/FREMONT)

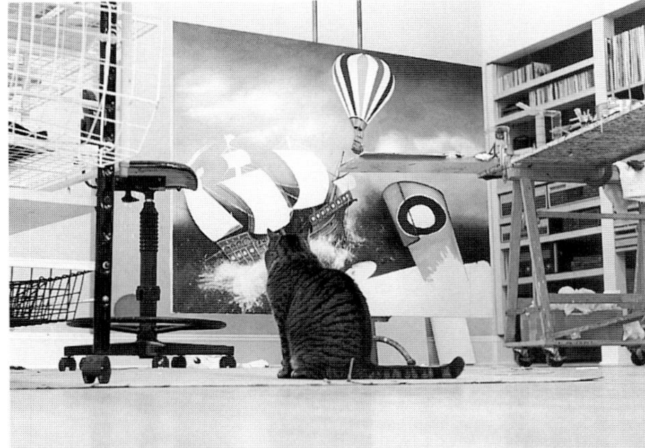

MALCOLM MORLEY

On Painting

The way in which I've made paintings over the years has been on grids: There's nothing very original about that; the Egyptians were using them. They used differently proportioned grids according to the various gods that they were depicting; so some were more square, others more rectangular. As far as my use of the grid is concerned, it's about the idea of making a painting by making little bits of things that add up to one single thing that appears to be intelligent. I've been reading *The Blind Watchmaker* by Richard Darkins, which is about the whole question of Darwin's idea that intelligence, or the source of life, comes from the classic concept of a supreme intelligence which trickles down from top to bottom. The other idea that is very current is that there really is no supreme intelligence but, rather, little bits of things that alone do not appear to be intelligent, but when you get a lot of them together they create what is described as intelligence.

With my painting, every bit is completed as it goes. I don't have to think about the whole; I can go around all day just thinking about a quarter tone of brown against a tone of red, very small without having the burden of the entire imagery upon me. This method also allows me to not be involved with the idea of gravity—of a top and bottom in terms of painting—because in order to get to it, I need to have the grid deadset in front of me. I can't have it lower because then the angle would be oblique and the image would be distorted. It always has to be straight in front of me. I have to keep moving the canvas so that it is always at shoulder level. This would allow me to paint the picture upside-down, for example, because here there really isn't any upside-down.

I've got this corresponding unit of what the information is through the model placed on the grid. It's like music, like notes, each note complete. Then there are spin-offs; for example, the tendency in painting is to go with gravity, but if you are painting the picture upside-down, and you turn it the other way up, then the brush strokes seem to be upbeat, not downbeat. That then creates an effect on the viewer. As far as the viewer is concerned, I am my own first viewer, both the doer and the viewer, just as the chef is his own first gourmet. I am the viewer who is impossible to satisfy. After all, we're all part of the same shebang. When you think about Greek art, very few of us know the names of Greek artists. You know what Greek art looks like, but you don't know anything more. Maybe in time, contemporary art will look like twentieth century art, but you might not think of individual artists; any member of the group that made that work would also be in some way reflecting the group, reflecting interaction on some level.

What is painterly? As Cézanne said, "I look for what is painterly in terms of my temperament." That's a beautiful idea, because one usually thinks of "painterly" in a very Germanic way as *malerisch*, that it should always be active paint and texture; that a smooth painting is not painterly. This is the association that I think people generally have. But it doesn't necessarily have to be like that.

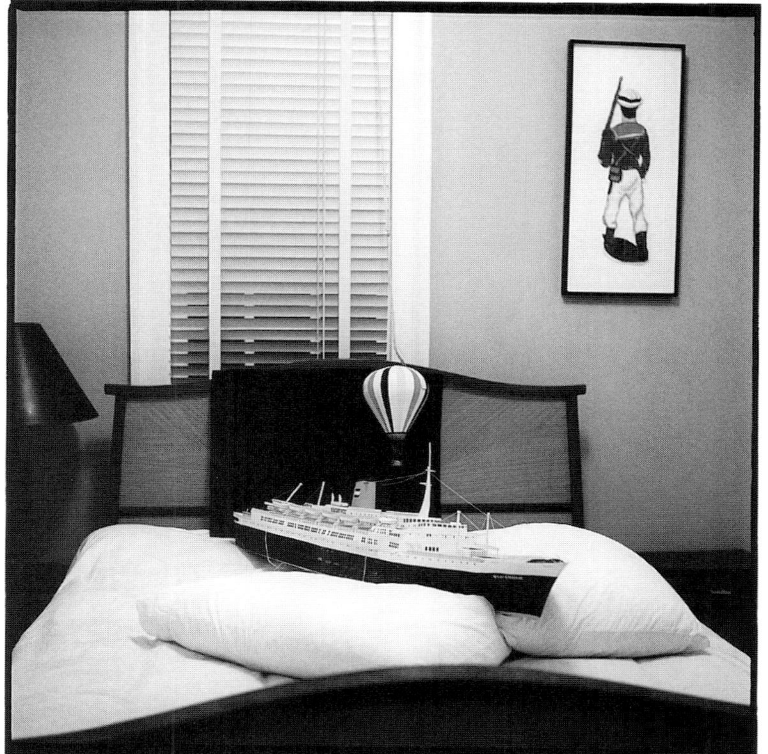

Studio views / im Atelier.

My paintings really come out of a tube of paint. I like to try to go with the process of paint itself without trying to put it through so many different stages that it hardly seems to be paint anymore. Up until the nineteenth century, painters had to make their paint as they painted. They had small amounts of powder and medium, and they made small amounts of paint at a time. A tube of paint probably has much more medium in it than early painters could ever mix into their paint. The idea of adding medium to a tube of paint is rather redundant. I started using pure paint from the tube. I wet the paint a little to move it because it's strong. Another thing about oil paint is that each tube is different. Some has a very strong foundation, some is very transparent, so you can build up a construction of actual paint itself based on the variety of foundation paint. For example, Naples Yellow has a lot of lead in it, and you can lay Orilian over the top because it's very transparent. So you have thin paint over thick paint, which creates an incredible sensation.

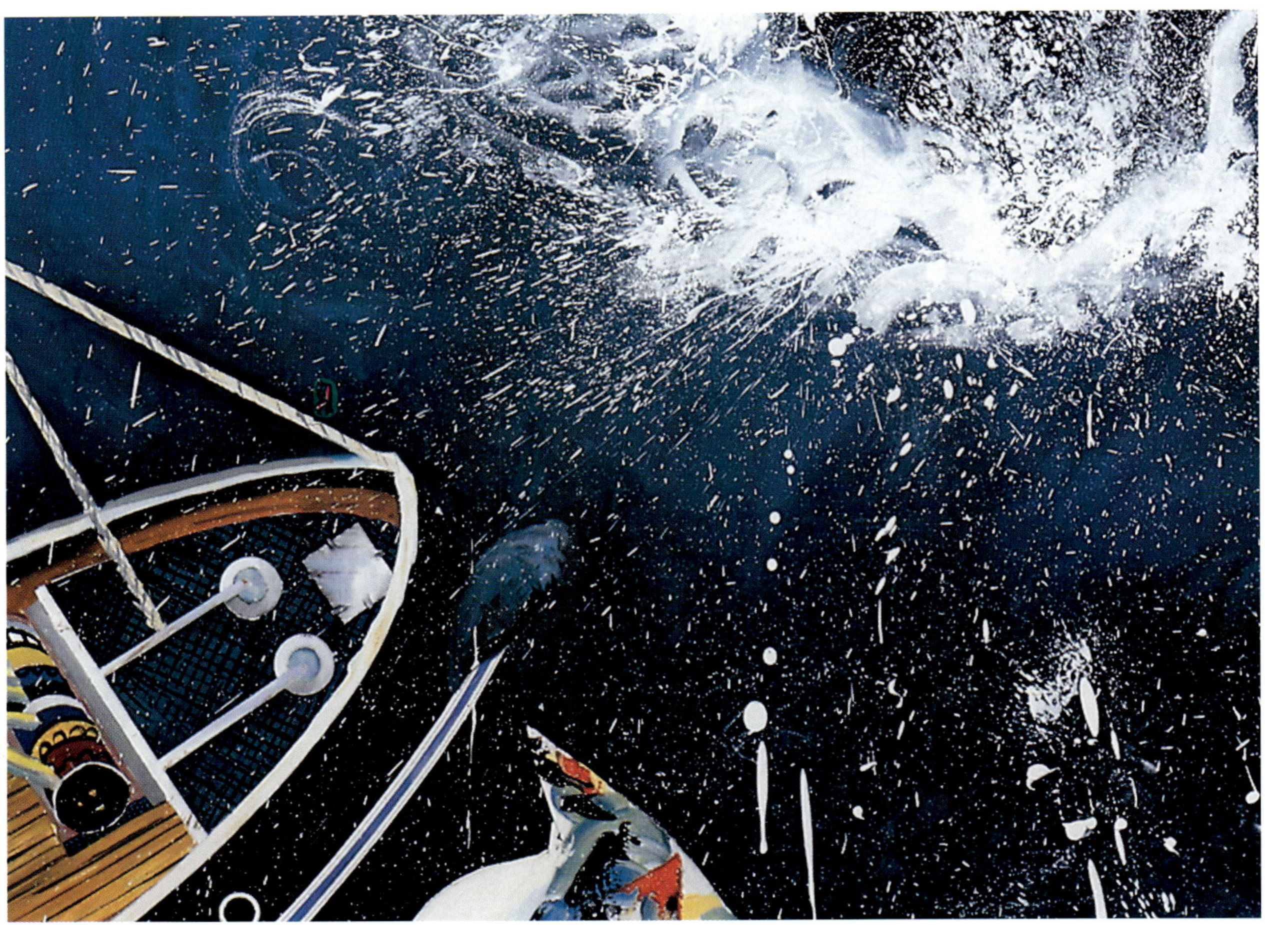

MALCOLM MORLEY, KEEPERS OF THE LIGHTHOUSE, 1994,
oil on canvas, detail / LEUCHTTURMWÄRTER, Öl auf Leinwand, Ausschnitt.

Über Malerei

Seit Jahren verwende ich beim Malen als Hilfsmittel der Übertragung den Raster. Daran ist an sich nichts Ungewöhnliches; schon die Ägypter benutzten unterschiedlich proportionierte Raster zur Darstellung ihrer verschiedenen Gottheiten; also waren einige quadratischer, andere rechteckiger. Mir geht es beim Gebrauch von Rastern darum, ein Bild aus kleinen Bruchstücken zu malen, die dann ein vernünftiges Ganzes ergeben. Ich habe Richard Darkins' *The Blind Watchmaker* gelesen, wo von Darwins Idee ausgehend untersucht wird, ob die Intelligenz oder Quelle des Lebens auf der klassischen Auffassung einer höchsten Intelligenz beruht, welche von oben nach unten rinnt. Eine andere sehr geläufige Idee ist, dass es überhaupt keine höchste

Intelligenz gibt, sondern vielmehr kleine Einheiten, die für sich genommen nicht intelligent erscheinen, sondern erst zusammen das ergeben, was man Intelligenz nennt.

In meinen Bildern ist jeder Teil für sich abgeschlossen. Ich muss nicht über das Ganze nachdenken. Ich kann mich den ganzen Tag frei bewegen und nur über eine Viertelnuance Braun in Verbindung zu einem Rot nachdenken, ohne die Last des ganzen Bildes auf mir zu spüren. Dank dieser Methode muss ich mich nicht um die Schwerkraft kümmern, weder darum, was oben ist, noch darum, was unten ist, denn ich habe den Raster absolut frontal vor mir. Ich kann ihn nicht tiefer ansetzen, sonst wäre der Winkel schief und das Bild verzerrt. Er muss immer direkt vor mir sein. Ich muss die Leinwand so bewegen, dass ich immer auf Schulterhöhe arbeiten kann. So könnte ich das Bild zum Beispiel auch umgekehrt malen, weil es hier überhaupt keine «richtige» Richtung gibt.

Ich erhalte die entsprechenden Einzelteile der eigentlichen Information durch das Übertragen des Modells auf dem Raster. Es ist wie Musik, wie Noten, wenn jede einzelne Note zur Vollendung beiträgt. Es gibt auch Begleiterscheinungen: Zum Beispiel spielt beim Malen tendenziell die Schwerkraft mit. Wenn man aber ein Bild auf dem Kopf malt und es anschliessend umdreht, scheinen die Pinselstriche aufwärts und nicht abwärts gerichtet. Dies wirkt dann anders auf den Betrachter. Was diesen betrifft: Ich bin mein eigener erster Betrachter – bin beides, der Ausführende und der Betrachtende, wie ein Küchenchef, der selber sein erster Feinschmecker ist. Ich bin der nie zufriedene Betrachter. Letztendlich sind wir alle Teil eines Ganzen. Denken wir an die Kunst der Griechen, so kennen die wenigsten die Namen griechischer Künstler. Man weiss, wie griechische Kunst aussieht, aber darüber hinaus weiss man nichts. Vielleicht wird zeitgenössische Kunst einmal einfach wie Kunst des zwanzigsten Jahrhunderts aussehen, und man wird vielleicht nicht an die individuellen Künstler denken; jedes Mitglied der Gruppe, die dieses Gesamtwerk schuf, würde in gewisser Weise die Gruppe spiegeln – deren Zusammenwirken sozusagen.

Was ist malerisch? Cézanne sagt, er sehe das Malerische entsprechend seinem Temperament. Das ist eine schöne Idee, weil man normalerweise bei *malerisch* an etwas sehr Germanisches denkt, daran dass Farbe und Textur sehr präsent sind, daran, dass ein ruhiges Bild nicht malerisch ist. Diese Assoziation haben die Menschen, glaube ich, normalerweise. Aber es muss nicht unbedingt so sein.

Meine Bilder kommen wirklich aus der Farbtube. Gerne versuche ich mich der Entwicklung der Farben anzupassen und sie nicht so stark zu mischen, dass zuletzt kaum noch Farbe übrigbleibt. Bis ins neunzehnte Jahrhundert stellten die Maler ihre Farben beim Malen her. Sie hatten nur eine geringe Menge an Pigmenten und Bindemitteln zur Verfügung, und sie rieben nur kleine Mengen gleichzeitig an. Eine Farbtube enthält wahrscheinlich viel mehr Bindemittel, als die Alten Meister je ihrer Farbe beimischen konnten. Die Idee, einer Farbtube Bindemittel hinzuzufügen, wäre ziemlich abwegig. Ich begann, die reine Farbe aus der Tube zu verwenden. Sie ist dick, also befeuchte ich sie etwas, um sie geschmeidig zu machen. Übrigens ist jede Tube Ölfarbe unterschiedlich. Einige Farben decken stärker, andere sind sehr transparent, und so kann man die eigentliche Farbe aus einer Variation an Deckkraft aufbauen. Antimongelb zum Beispiel ist sehr bleihaltig, man kann ein transparenteres Orilian hinzufügen. So erhält man eine dünne Farbschicht über einer opakeren, und das schafft eine ungeheure Wirkung.

(Übersetzung: Karin Klussmann)

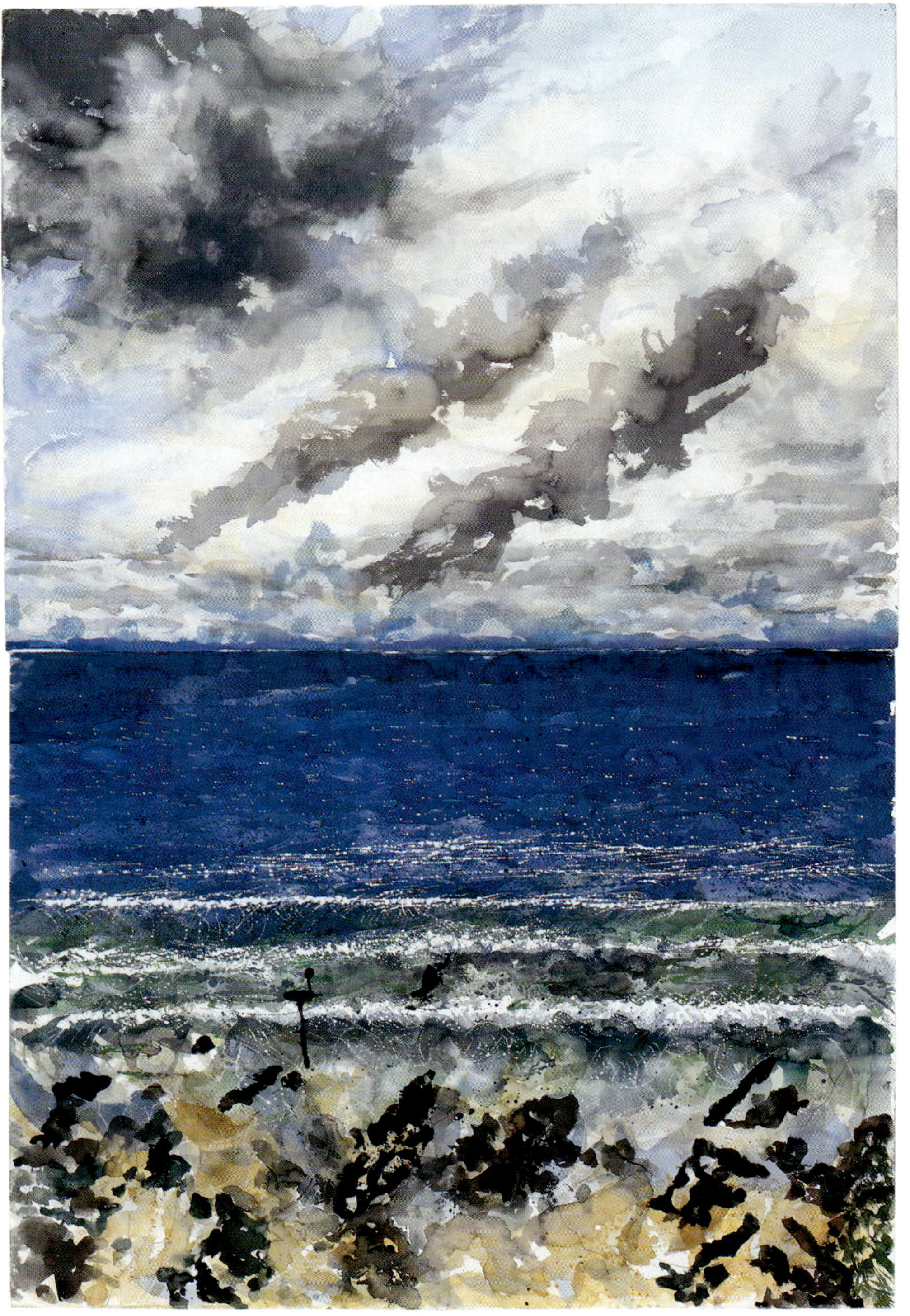

MALCOLM MORLEY, WAVES BREAKING ON ROCK—AZORES SKY, 1994, watercolor on paper, 43⅜ x 30¼" / WELLEN, DIE SICH AN FELSEN BRECHEN – AZORENHIMMEL, Wasserfarbe auf Papier, 110 x 77 cm.

JEAN-CLAUDE LEBENSZTEJN

Seasickness

How can someone with no home be homesick?

Deke Rivers (Elvis Presley) in *Loving You,* 1957[1]

Malcolm Morley, who cultivates a retired navy captain look, is seasick the way others are homesick. He's got—shall I call it—"thalassalgia" and, if he has nostalgia too, his returnland has to be an island, an islet even, with lots of open sea—a little piece of *terra firma,* provided it's no mainland. His islet can be a dog, for instance, his little black Pomeranian, Max. "Why don't you stay a little longer in Paris? We could have fun." "I miss my dog."

We were having dinner in one of those farcical, fancy Right Bank hotels, and I asked him if he ever gets seasick. "Sometimes," he said, "but I use ginger pills as medicine." "It's also an aphrodisiac." "Oh yes?" Patrick confirmed, and mentioned his craze for British chocolate gingers. I thought or said, "Ginger for seasickness, chocolate for lovesickness."

In these paintings, especially the ones with expanses of yellow paint, Morley has almost but not completely abandoned his traditional grid method. "The boat is painted after a model, the sea comes out of my head." Although he had done this occasionally in the past—UNTITLED SOUVENIRS, EUROPE (1973) is one

of his first ungridded works—he was rather reluctant until recently to paint without a grid. "Once in a while," he told Nena Dimitrijevic in 1988, "I try without a grid, and it's terrible, because there is no freedom. You can't let it go unless you have a structure. If there is a problem, I can isolate it into a smaller piece. Then, if that becomes too much of a problem, I can halve it. It is a great philosophy of life about problem-solving. To go for a deeper unexpectedness, I often tighten up the structure so no mistake can happen. This time, we cannot make a mistake. And then, this so-called 'mistake' occurs, but now it is much deeper. This is a way of discovering certain relationships, integrating the unconscious into the conscious, inviting it."[2] But what if the grid is abandoned? Does it or does it not mean abandoning the tightening of the problem, releasing the control, and therefore the relationship itself between the conscious and the unconscious? Morley, who is deeply interested in exploiting psychoanalysis in his painting process (especially the use of "mistakes"), does connect the figurative theme of the sea and the unconscious. He seemed curious when I mentioned Sándor Ferenczi's book *Thalassa,* which he did not know.

Why does the ocean or the sea make one seasick? Is not seasickness possibly like vertigo (Kant's *Anthropology* connects them), a longing for what makes you sick? What do you think, Malcolm? As in homesickness or lovesickness, there may be an element of deep ambivalence: the sea might make you sick because it's a sea-as-home sickness, an impossible, frustrated

JEAN-CLAUDE LEBENSZTEJN lives and teaches in Paris. His recent publications include *Les couilles de Cézanne, suivi de Persistance de la mémoire,* Paris, éditions Séguier, 1995, *De l'imitation dans les beaux-arts,* Paris, éditions Carré, 1996, *Le champ des morts (Fleurs de rêve I),* Paris, éditions du limon, 1997.

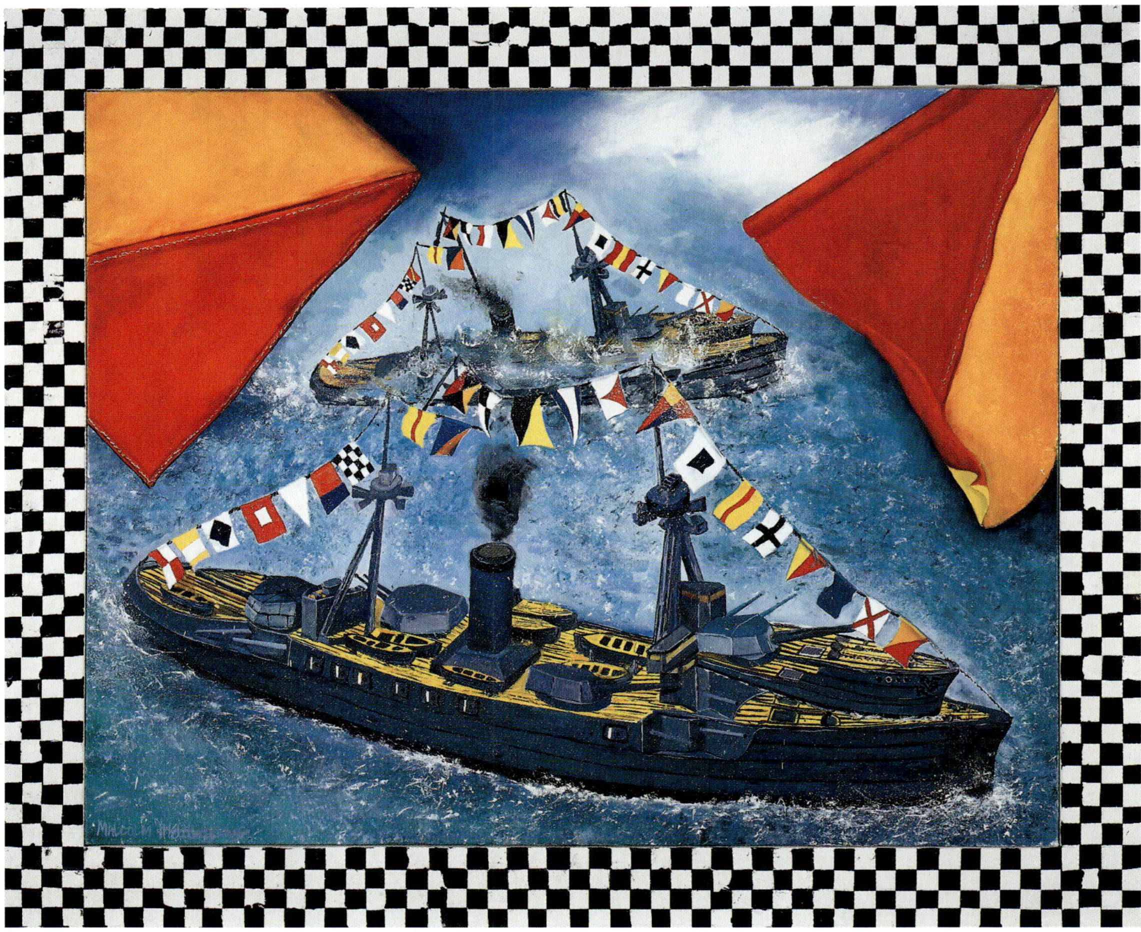

MALCOLM MORLEY, NAVY DAY, 1996, oil on linen, (painted frame attached), 43¼ x 42¼" (2 parts) /
TAG DER MARINE, Öl auf Leinen (mit bemaltem Rahmen), 109 x 107 cm (2-teilig). (PHOTO: DOROTHY ZEIDMAN)

or repressed desire to return there, what Ferenczi calls "thalassal regression… the idea of an urge to return to the ocean abandoned in primitive times." Coitus, he says, is a substitute for a desire to go back to the mother's womb as a substitute for the primal ocean since "the amniotic fluid figures the ocean 'introjected' into the maternal body." Therefore, "coitus is nothing else but the individual's freeing from a painful tension and simultaneously the fulfillment of the drive to return into the maternal body and into the ocean, model of all motherhood."

To grid the ocean would be like trying to hold it in a colander. Some of these paintings use a grid: THE LANDING (1996), for instance, is done after the watercolor WAVES BREAKING ON ROCKS—AZORES SKY (1994), painted on the spot on two separate sheets of paper, one for the sky, one for the sea and seashore. (In THE LANDING, the split horizon is translated into a hard edge obtained with masking paper: Close up, the blue sea looks like a layer in front of the sky, reminiscent of the sea-skin which Dalí as a six-year-old girl is delicately lifting in order to gaze at a sleeping dog, in his painting of 1950. And THE LANDING is signed twice: white on the sea, pink among the rocks.) But then the gridded squares are freely interpreted, especially in the richly textured blots at the bottom of the seashore. On the other hand, the more recent yellow paintings, such as BATTLE OF THE YELLOW SEA (1996), are not gridded[3]; the bright lemon-yellow color of these sea paintings

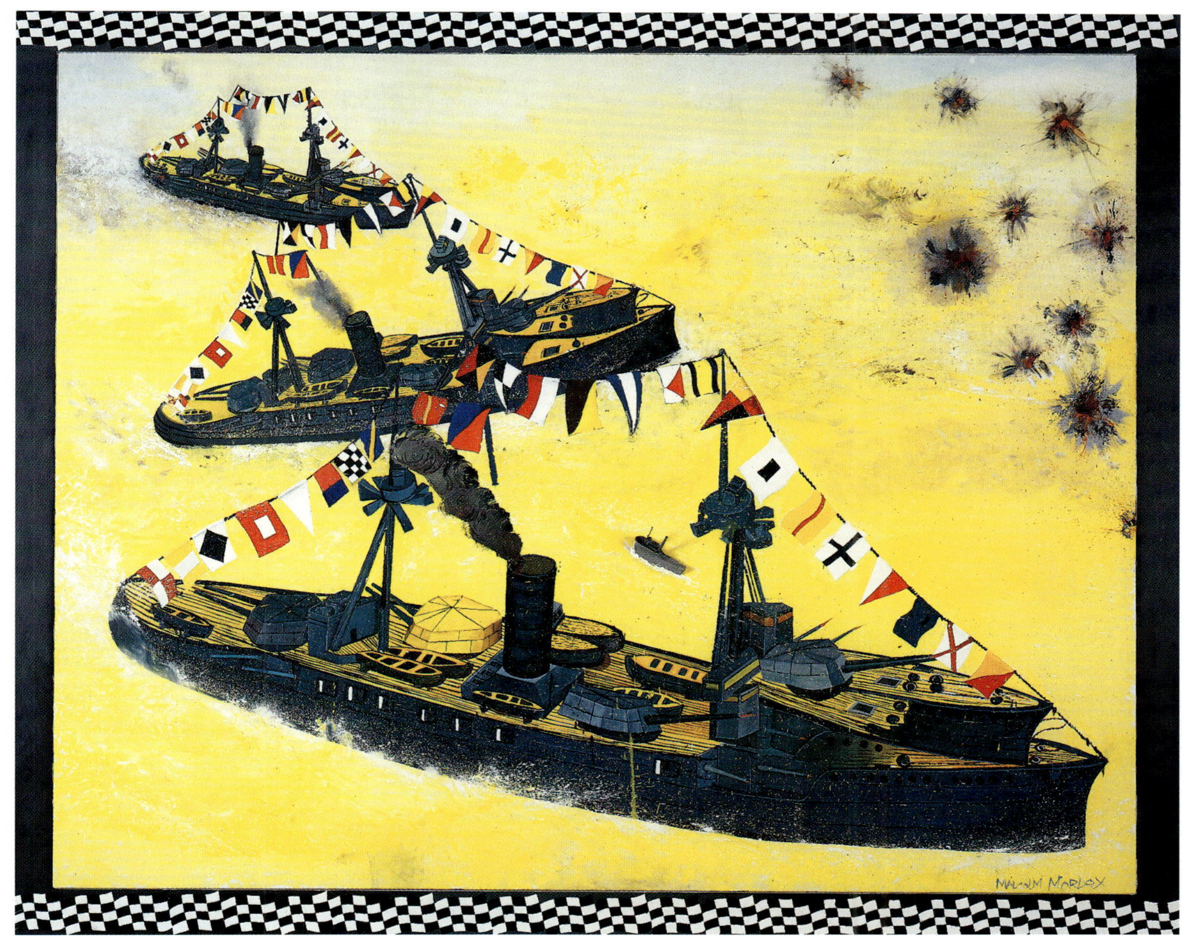

MALCOLM MORLEY, BATTLE OF THE YELLOW SEA, 1996, oil on linen (painted frame attached),
62¼ x 78¼"/ SCHLACHT AUF DEM GELBEN MEER, Öl auf Leinwand (mit bemaltem Rahmen), 158 x 199 cm. (PHOTO: DOROTHY ZEIDMAN)

affects the viewer in a strangely ambivalent way. What is that dense, opaque yellow fluid supposed to be? Just yellow? Or a visual rendering of the name "Yellow Sea" attached to that large gulf between Korea and China? Or does it suggest the same phantasy that was illustrated in 1907 in a Hungarian satirical magazine by an artist who signed "Bit"—you know, Malcolm, that "bite," pronounced "bit" or "beet," is French slang for cock—an eight-image story found by Ferenczi, studied by Otto Rank and incorporated by Freud into the 1914 edition of *The Interpretation of Dreams*? This "Dream of the French Nurse" shows, in the progressive manner of some Little Nemo comic strips, a nurse walking an infant who is expressing an urgent need, then peeing in a street corner, peeing

and peeing so much that the flow brings along a row boat, a gondola, a sailing ship and an ocean liner—until at last the nurse is awakened by the screams of the baby (looking younger than in the dream) who is in urgent need, or has already wet himself. But here, in BATTLE OF THE YELLOW SEA, that yellow sea hints at a female fluid, and the three-dimensional grey submarine-top emerging from the middle of it is conceived by the painter as the "man in the boat," a slang expression for an aroused clit. Morley seems to be using his unconscious, preconscious or conscious symbolism, and perhaps his knowledge of psychoanalytical literature, the way Renaissance and Baroque artists used iconological handbooks: Horapollo, Cartari, Valeriano or Ripa.

Malcolm Morley has always committed himself to childhood phantasies; is not infantile regression a small step in the long march of thalassal regression? His war games, toys, animals, his "childish" style of drawing, his Disneyland scenery are all part of the same nostalgic drive. Nostalgic-ironic drive: He is not simply submitting to these childish phantasies; he manipulates them the way he manipulates space, perspective, language, his "mistakes." Indeed, Morley is a master of pictorial manipulation: it is an essential component of his art. He likes to quote Jasper Johns's saying:

> *Take an object*
> *Do something to it*
> *Do something else to it*
> *"   "   " "*

Therefore, the yellow color can be sea (as in BATTLE OF THE YELLOW SEA), sky (as in MEDIEVAL WITH LEMON SKY), both, or neither: In THE RAIDER (1997)—and to a point in BATTLE… as well—the different perspectives of the ships in the same surface make it impossible to decide on the status of the yellow field turning greenish/bluish towards the top. And in M.V. PERCEPTION WITH CARGO OF PRIMARY COLORS AND BLACK AND WHITE (1997), the boat cleaves a narrow strip of blue and white water surrounded on three sides by an abstract expanse of yellow color. Morley has used masking paper (bits of *Yellow Pages* covers) to get a hard edge there and make the separation stronger, but he connects the yellow border with the blue water by splashing it with white "foam." (Perhaps the yellow cover of the *Yellow Pages* suggested the idea of these yellow sea pictures to him? No, he says over the phone, he just had a lot of yellow paint on top of his shelves, and didn't care for a blue ocean.) In the same painting, space is squeezed in many ways, and the cargo of dense, pure colors is inconsistently oriented: violet-green-orange upward, red-yellow-blue (a yellow redder than the lemon-yellow border) and black and white downward. One is reminded of the different directions of the thrones and altar in Giotto's VISION OF THE THRONES in Assisi. Morley's "perception" is indeed visionary.

Another kind of spatial manipulation occurs repeatedly in the two yellow battleship paintings and in one of the blue ones. Looking a little carefully at the dreadnought in THE RAIDER, at the two in NAVY DAY (1996) and at the three in BATTLE OF THE YELLOW SEA—all painted, apparently, after the same drawing, variously enlarged in the photocopy machine, and used as so many cartoons transferred through graphite paper onto the canvases—the smaller boat on top of the front of the ship exposes the same "mistake," a section which is both hull and deck. Already, in SS FRANCE (1974), there was a spatially impossible "fold" in the monkey-postcard foldout. The other blue battleship paintings BELOW THE WATER LINE (1997) and SPANISH DREADNOUGHT (1996) make another manipulation quite visible, an impossible unevenness in the deck of the ship. These spatial tricks convey the same effect as the multiplication of flags on the battleships sometimes engaged in various artillery exercises: Together with the painted frames, they contradict the function, the action, the consistency of space. These paintings are like so many exercises in making inconsistency consistent.

Painting itself becomes a big little game which the painter is playing the way he was—or is—playing with his war toys. This playful aspect is visible everywhere, and if many of these works remind the viewer of the late Malevich paintings with their pictorial density and their interplay of sometimes dissonant color patterns, there are niceties of detail one rarely finds in Malevich: the splashing of paint, the scraping of paint to denote spindrift in DAEDALUS (1996) or the seams of the flags in NAVY DAY, the painstaking brushing out of the brushstrokes in the skies, the painted frames, the trompe-l'oeil frame of MEDIEVAL LEMON WITH SKY (1996). Morley obviously enjoys the process of making his ocean waters alive through paint; he is deeply, seriously involved in his painting games, the way Bach was intricately involved in his play of constructing elaborate canonical works. The same seriousness, the same playfulness. A painting like DAEDALUS affects the viewer with a mixture of incongruity and evidence, kitsch and high art. Its huge, irregular sun, its color harmony of reddish purple, blue-violet, and orange for sea, sky, and boat/sun offer a combination that I can't recall having seen anywhere. The boat there is supposedly the Santa Maria, but she could be renamed the Devil-May-Care.

I must say—and this will condemn it to privacy—that this essay is the result of a private commission. As a rule I don't take orders, but this one is more like a game and a challenge. One evening, the day before his opening at the Galerie Templon last year, Malcolm Morley was recounting a discussion he had had many years ago with an artist. "Why don't you try using green?" he asked.

Lichtenstein responded, "Because I don't like to change my habits." In the mouth of the first painter, the reply of the second one sounded pretty much like a self-condemnation. What does it mean for an artist not to change his/her habits? I thought he was right of course, yet I, as the devil's advocate, protested. "But he did use green." "Not in the late sixties." "Yes, and in the early sixties too." "Well," he said, " I know Roy." "Do you want to bet?"

He didn't answer—his awfully rich dinner guest was shouting for attention with diamonds and a pair of *vaginae dentatae*—and he knew, perhaps, that offering a bet is rude, as Giovanni della Casa's book on manners had already reminded sixteenth-century readers. The day after, at the opening, I came with Lawrence Alloway's book on Lichtenstein in my bag.

"You've lost your bet," I said, showing the reproduction of TAKKA TAKKA (1962). He looked at the green foliage. "This is not green." "What is it then?" "It's grey-green." Lida looked. "It's green, Malcolm." "OK, what did we bet? Twenty dollars?" "We did not bet," I said, "but now you are condemned." "To what?" "You must paint a green painting. You can use all the greens you want, but you cannot use any other color. This is not for me, it's for yourself." "You are the devil. I'll do a painting that will make you seasick."

Usually I shy away from the art crowd because I cannot take the ego trip. Whatever is said and done, socially and often artistically, could be summed up in an endless me-me-me-me-me. To be in contact with artists, dealers, critics, and collectors means being forced to sip Tex Avery's Jumbo Gro: everyone—cat, mouse, dog, canary—tries to outgrow everyone else to absurdly cosmic proportions, a painful scene for me, especially when I can't be on top. However, suppressing the terrible tyrant "I" is like suppressing life itself, for life is as ridiculous as I is; therefore the only

way out is a way in, playing around with I as cats play with their tails. In a way, that is just what Morley does. I like his persona because he is not playing the ego game—or if he does, he does it in a supreme way which hides the game by performing it as a play. So I was not very surprised when, after returning to his island, he called to propose a deal. "I'll do a green painting, not a very big one, but something you can hang on your wall, and you'll write a text in English on the show at Templon, just for me." "But I can't write in English," I protested, "and I have no key to enter your paintings." "Perhaps there is no key—perhaps there is no door, and perhaps there is no wall." This reminded me of Kafka's tale, "Before the Law."

I did not say yes, but I could not say no. The idea of working in a language that I can't master on a resistant material, and especially through the demand of a painter I admire, was enough to paralyze me and to bind me—an offer so much in excess of my contribution, but then I also like the idea of a swap of incommensurable goods, where the monetary value of the things being traded is beside the point. It reminds me of Vasari's story of Pontormo refusing to work for Ottaviano the Magnificent, and trading some beautiful paintings with Rossino—not Rosso the painter who had been his coapprentice, but Rossino the mason who did some house repairs for him. Work for work, even though the paintings eventually made their way up to Ottaviano's house. Of course, Pontormo knew that trying to cross out the exchange value of art and replace it with a new scale of value was bound to fail with the astute Rossino. But I am not spendthrift enough to deprive myself of the riches of nonmonetary value. The problem is that it is as difficult to accept a token of generosity by which one is the profiteer as it is to refuse an act of generosity. That's the doublebinding cruelty of generosity.

As I was getting ready to leave the opening at Templon and waiting to say goodbye to Malcolm, he was talking to Bernard Blistène, who had hosted the show of his watercolors in Marseille. In front of his painting THE RAIDER, Malcolm was discussing the four figures in the boat at the top. "This is me as the captain, this is me as a sailor in a white beard, this is

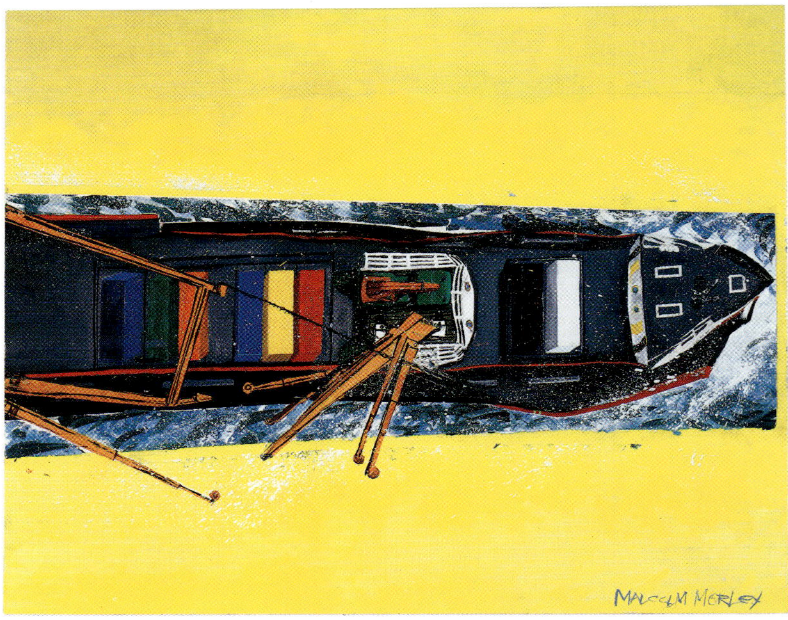

MALCOLM MORLEY, M.V. PERCEPTION WITH CARGO OF
PRIMARY COLORS AND BLACK AND WHITE, 1997,
*oil on linen, 28 x 36" / Die M.V. PERCEPTION MIT EINER
FRACHT VON GRUNDFARBEN UND SCHWARZ UND WEISS,
Öl auf Leinwand, 71 x 91 cm.*

me falling overboard. This (pointing to an athletic sailor in a singlet) is me when I was fourteen. I was a hustler then and one night I picked up an Arab with a prick like an olive. I was so disgusted that I ran away with his pants." Blistène was flabbergasted.

Morley is a great storyteller. Sometimes he makes them up, even those that sound really real, like the one of him in a shower hearing a voice saying, "You are not an oil painter! You are a turpentine painter!" "What? What?" That story he told his ex-dealer, Arnold Glimcher,[4] and he has repeated it on different occasions, including at his Templon opening. A little later, he confessed to me that he had made it up, but it's a lie that tells the truth—like the story he told Matthew Collings about the opera singer performing in Palma (writes Collings, but Malcolm may have said Parma), "where they really know their opera." After singing badly (he has a sore throat), the opera singer is called back for encore after encore. He thinks to himself, "This is funny, I thought they really knew their opera here." Finally he croaks,"I can't sing anymore!" And a voice from the back of

the theatre says, "You'll sing it till you learn it!"[5] A parable, of course, and parable is the same as parabola: To speak in parables is to unstraighten the line of meaning by squaring an element; by considering, for example, space as a function of time, as when Morley said to Anthony Haden-Guest, "I consider myself a post-American."[6] Morley is a parabolic artist.

1) *Loving You*, 1957; screenplay by Herbert Baker and Hal Kanter, directed by Hal Kanter.
2) Nena Dimitrijevic, "Malcolm Morley," *Flash Art* 142, 1988, pp. 76–80.
3) Except for MEDIEVAL WITH LEMON SKY, where Patrick Fischer pointed out that a wide, penciled grid is still visible. That painting, Morley said afterward, was done after a gridded image of a model.
4) "A Conversation: Malcolm Morley and Arnold Glimcher," in: *Malcolm Morley* (New York: Pace Gallery, 1988).
5) Matthew Collings, "Malcolm Morley," *Artscribe* 42, 1983, pp. 49–55.
6) Anthony Haden-Guest, "Malcolm Morley," *New York Magazine*, April 4, 1983, p. 37.

JEAN-CLAUDE LEBENSZTEJN

Seekrankheit

Wie kann jemand ohne Heimat Heimweh haben?
Deke Rivers (Elvis Presley) in *Loving You*, 1957[1]

Malcolm Morley, der den Stil eines Marineoffiziers im Ruhestand pflegt, hat Meerweh wie andere Heimweh haben. Er leidet sozusagen unter «Thalassalgie», und falls ihn auch Nostalgie plagt, so muss das Ziel seiner Sehnsucht eine Insel sein, vielleicht sogar nur ein Inselchen, mitten im offenen Meer – ein kleines Stück fester Boden, jedenfalls kein kontinentales Festland. Sein Inselchen kann zum Beispiel ein Hund sein wie Max, sein kleiner schwarzer Spitz. «Warum bleibst du nicht noch eine Weile in Paris? Wir könnten soviel Spass haben.» «Mein Hund fehlt mir.»

Wir sassen beim Abendessen in einem dieser unverschämt teuren Hotels am rechten Seineufer, und ich fragte ihn, ob er jeweils seekrank würde. «Manchmal», sagte er, «aber ich nehme Ingwerpillen dagegen.» «Das ist auch ein Aphrodisiakum.» «Ah ja?» Patrick bestätigte dies und sprach von seiner Schwäche für englische Ingwerschokolade; ich sagte oder dachte: «Ingwer gegen Seekrankheit, Schokolade gegen Liebeskummer.»

JEAN-CLAUDE LEBENSZTEJN lebt und lehrt in Paris. Zuletzt veröffentlichte er: *Les couilles de Cézanne und Persistance de la mémoire*, Editions Séguier, Paris 1995, *De l'imitation dans les beaux-arts*, Editions Carré, Paris 1996, und *Le champ des morts (Fleurs de rêve I)*, Editions du limon, Paris 1997.

In seinen neuen Bildern, besonders in jenen mit den grossen gelben Farbflächen, weicht Morley manchmal von seiner gewohnten Rastertechnik ab. «Das Schiff ist nach einem Modell gemalt, das Meer hatte ich im Kopf.» Obwohl er dies schon früher gelegentlich tat – UNTITLED SOUVENIRS, EUROPE (1973), war eine seiner ersten ohne Raster entstandenen Arbeiten –, hat Morley bis vor kurzem nur ungern auf einen Raster verzichtet. «Hin und wieder», erzählte er Nena Dimitrijevic 1988, «versuche ich es ohne Raster und es ist entsetzlich, weil dabei die Freiheit verlorengeht. Man kann nicht loslassen, wenn keine Struktur vorhanden ist. Taucht ein Problem auf, kann ich es auf kleinerem Raum eingrenzen, wird es wiederum zu schwierig, halbiere ich noch einmal. Das ist eine grossartige lebensphilosophische Strategie der Problemlösung. Um das Unerwartete auf einer tieferen Ebene zu erreichen, verdichte ich die Struktur oft, um Fehler möglichst auszuschliessen. Diesmal können wir gar keinen Fehler machen. Und dann passiert dieser sogenannte Fehler, aber nun ist er viel tiefer. So entdeckt man gewisse Beziehungen, indem man das Unbewusste ins Bewusste integriert, es einlädt oder herausfordert.»[2] Aber was, wenn man den Raster aufgibt? Heisst das die Zuspitzung des Problems aufgeben und mit der Kontrolle auch die

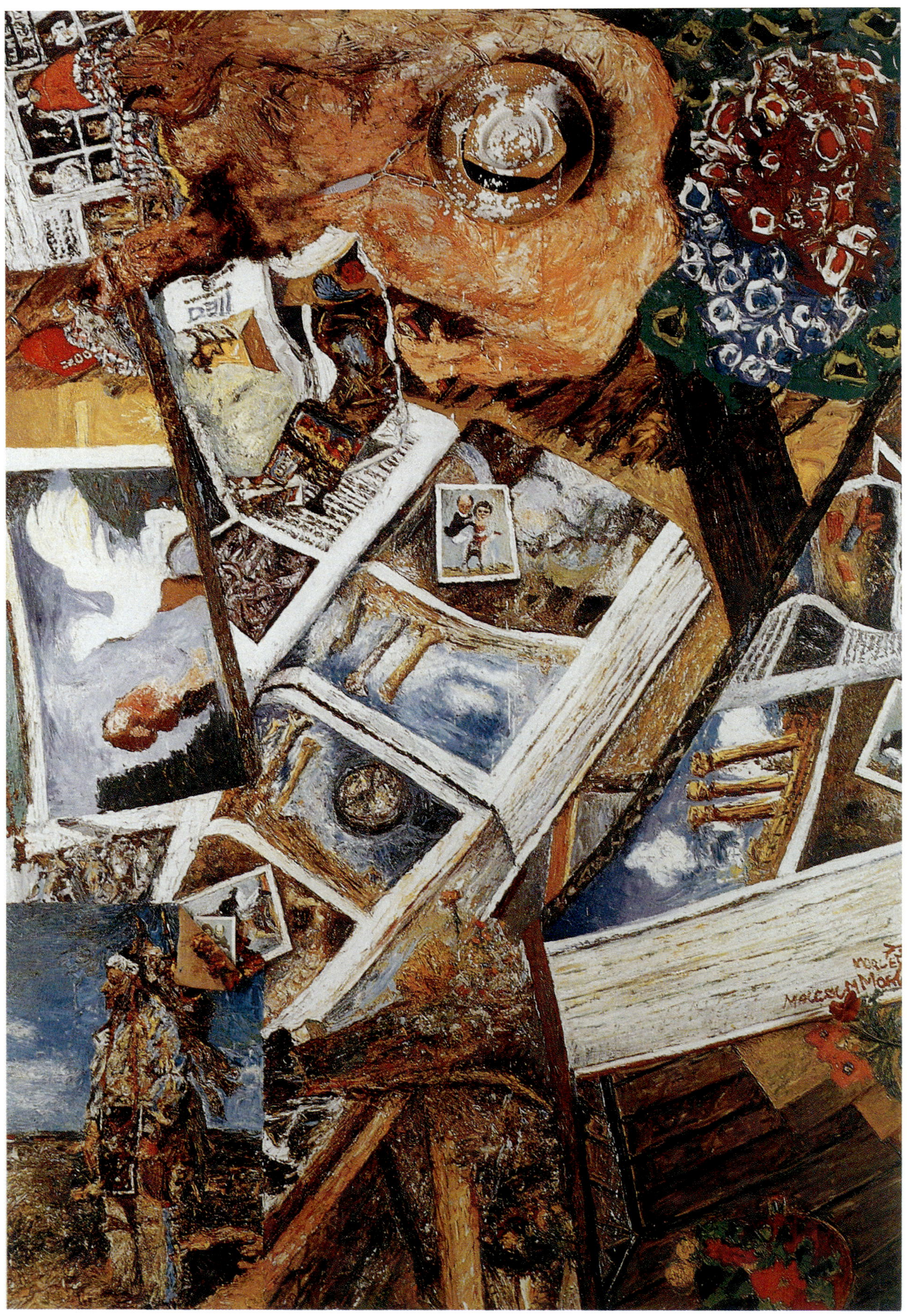

MALCOLM MORLEY, UNTITLED SOUVENIRS, EUROPE, 1973,
oil on canvas, 96¼ x 68¼"/
ANDENKEN OHNE TITEL, EUROPA,
Öl auf Leinwand 244,5 x 173,4 cm.

Beziehung zwischen Bewusstem und Unbewusstem fallenlassen, oder nicht? Morley, dem daran liegt, im Malprozess die Psychoanalyse zu nutzen (besonders im Umgang mit «Fehlern»), stellt eine Verbindung her zwischen dem Meer als figuratives Bildthema und dem Unbewussten. Er schien interessiert, als ich von Sándor Ferenczis Buch *Thalassa* sprach, das er nicht kannte.[3]

Warum macht uns der Ozean oder das Meer seekrank? Ist nicht vielleicht Seekrankheit wie Schwindel (Kants *Anthropologie* bringt beide miteinander in Verbindung) eine Sehnsucht nach etwas, was uns krank macht? Was meinst du, Malcolm? Wie Heimweh oder Liebeskummer könnte sie ein zutiefst ambivalentes Element enthalten: Das Meer macht uns vielleicht krank, weil Seekrankheit eine Art Heimweh ist, ein unmöglicher, enttäuschter oder unterdrückter Wunsch, dorthin zurückzukehren; Ferenczi nennt das den «thalassalen Regressionszug»: «das Streben nach der in der Urzeit verlassenen See-Existenz». Der Koitus, sagt Ferenczi, sei ein Ersatz für den Wunsch zur Rückkehr in den Mutterleib und dieser wiederum ein Ersatz für das Ur-Meer, denn das Fruchtwasser verkörpert den in den Mutterleib introjizierten Ozean. Demnach sei der Koitus nichts anderes als die Befreiung des Individuums von einer schmerzlichen Spannung und zugleich «die Befriedigung des Triebes nach Regression in den Mutterleib und in das Meer, das Vorbild aller Mütterlichkeit».

Das Meer einem Raster zu unterwerfen wäre, als wollte man es mit einem Sieb ausschöpfen. Manche dieser Bilder verwenden einen Raster: THE LANDING (Das Anlegen) etwa entstand nach dem Aquarell WAVES BREAKING ON ROCKS – AZORES SKY (Wel-

len, die sich an Felsen brechen – Azorenhimmel), das vor Ort auf zwei verschiedene Blätter gemalt wurde, der Himmel auf das eine, das Meer und die Küste auf das andere. (In THE LANDING wird die Horizontlinie mit Hilfe von Abdeckpapier zu einer scharfen Kante: Aus der Nähe wirkt das blaue Meer, als läge es wie eine Schicht vor dem Himmel, ähnlich der Meer-Haut, die Dalí als sechsjähriges Mädchen vorsichtig lüftet, um den darunter schlafenden Hund zu betrachten – in einem Bild Dalís aus dem Jahr 1950. THE LANDING ist zweimal signiert: weiss auf dem Meer und rosa zwischen den Felsen.) Allerdings sind die Rasterquadrate frei interpretiert, insbesondere an den stark strukturierten Stellen im unteren Teil der Küste. Andrerseits sind die neueren, gelben Bilder wie BATTLE OF THE YELLOW SEE (Schlacht auf dem Gelben Meer) nicht gerastert,[4] die helle zitronengelbe Farbe dieser Meerstücke berührt den Betrachter merkwürdig ambivalent. Was stellt diese dichte, undurchsichtige gelbe Flüssigkeit dar? Einfach Gelb? Oder eine bildliche Darstellung des Namens «Gelbes Meer», der den breiten Golf zwischen Korea und China bezeichnet? Oder spielt es mit derselben Phantasievorstellung, die ein Künstler unter dem Namen Bit 1907 in einer ungarischen satirischen Zeitschrift illustrierte? (Du weisst ja, Malcolm, dass «bite» ein französischer Slangausdruck für Schwanz ist.) Diese Erzählung in acht Bildern hat Ferenczi entdeckt, Otto Rank studierte sie und Freud nahm sie in seine 1914 erschienene Ausgabe der *Traumdeutung* auf. Dieser «Traum vom französischen Kindermädchen» zeigt in der aufgeschlossenen Manier einiger *Little Nemo*-Comics ein Kindermädchen, das ein Kind spazierenführt, welches dringend mal muss, das dann an eine Strassenecke pinkelt und pinkelt und pinkelt, bis auf dem Strom ein Ruderboot vorbeikommt, eine Gondel, ein Segelschiff und ein Ozeandampfer; schliesslich wacht das Kindermädchen durch das Geschrei des Kindes auf (das kleiner ist als im Traum), das dringend pinkeln muss oder sich bereits nass gemacht hat. Aber hier, in BATTLE OF THE YELLOW SEA, spielt das gelbe Meer auf eine weibliche Körperflüssigkeit an, und das dreidimensionale graue U-Boot, das in der Mitte auftaucht, sieht der Künstler als «Mann im Schiff», ein Slangwort für die erregte Klitoris. Morley scheint mit seinem unbewussten, vorbewussten und bewussten Symbolismus und vielleicht auch mit seiner Kenntnis der psychoanalytischen Literatur in gleicher Weise zu arbeiten wie die Künstler der Renaissance und des Barock mit ihren Handbüchern über Ikonologie, Horapollo, Cartari, Valeriano oder Ripa.

Malcolm Morley hat sich schon immer mit Kindheitsphantasien beschäftigt. Ist nicht die Regression in die Kindheit ein erster kleiner Schritt auf dem langen Weg zurück ins Meer? Seine Kriegsspiele, Spielzeuge, Tiere, seine kindliche Art zu zeichnen, seine Disneyland-Szenerien, alles ist Ausdruck desselben nostalgischen Hangs, besser: ironisch-nostalgischen Hangs. Denn er gibt nicht einfach diesen kindischen Phantasien nach; er verfremdet sie, wie er den Raum verfremdet, durch die Perspektive, die Sprache, durch seine «Fehler». Morley ist in der Tat ein Meister der Verfremdung mit malerischen Mitteln. Diese ist ein wesentlicher Bestandteil seiner Kunst. Er zitiert denn auch gern das folgende Wort von Jasper Johns:

Nimm einen Gegenstand
Bearbeite ihn
Bearbeite ihn nochmals anders
"   "   "   "

Die gelbe Farbe kann also Meer sein (wie in BATTLE OF THE YELLOW SEA), Himmel (wie in MEDIEVAL WITH LEMON SKY), aber auch beides oder keines von beiden, zum Beispiel in THE RAIDER (Der Zerstörer) und bis zu einem gewissen Grad auch in BATTLE..., wo die verschiedenen Perspektiven der Schiffe auf derselben Fläche es einem verunmöglichen, die Bedeutung des gelben Feldes zu bestimmen, das im oberen Teil ins Grünblaue übergeht. In M.V. PERCEPTION WITH CARGO OF PRIMARY COLORS AND BLACK AND WHITE durchpflügt das Schiff einen schmalen Streifen blauweissen Wassers, das auf drei Seiten von einem abstrakten Feld aus gelber Farbe umgeben ist. Morley hat Abdeckpapier verwendet (Streifen aus Umschlägen der *Los Angeles Yellow Pages*), um eine scharfe Kante zu haben und die Abgrenzung zu verstärken, aber er verbindet die gelbe Kante mit dem blauen Wasser, indem er sie mit weissen «Schaumspritzern» bekleckert. (Lieferte vielleicht das gelbe Umschlagpapier die Idee zu den gelben Meerbildern? Nein,

sagt Morley am Telephon, er habe einfach massenhaft gelbe Farbe zuvorderst auf seinen Gestellen gehabt und wollte nicht unbedingt ein blaues Meer.) Im gleichen Bild wird der Raum auf vielerlei Art strapaziert, und die Ladung satter, reiner Farben ist unregelmässig verteilt: Violett, Grün und Orange nach oben, Rot, Gelb, Blau (das Gelb ist rötlicher als das Zitronengelb am Rand) sowie Schwarz und Weiss nach unten. Man fühlt sich an die unterschiedliche Ausrichtung der Throne und des Altars in Giottos VISION DER THRONE in Assisi erinnert. Morleys Wahrnehmung ist im Grunde visionär.

In den beiden gelben und in einem der blauen Schlachtschiff-Bilder wird der Raum auf andere Art verfremdet. Schauen wir uns das Kriegsschiff in THE RAIDER (Der Zerstörer), die beiden in NAVY DAY (Tag der Marine) und die drei in BATTLE OF THE YELLOW SEA etwas genauer an. (Alle sind offenbar nach derselben Zeichnung entstanden, die mit dem Photokopierer unterschiedlich vergrössert und mit Kohlepapier auf die Leinwand übertragen wurde.) Das obere kleinere Boot vorn am Schiff weist immer denselben «Fehler» auf, einen Teil, der Rumpf und Deck zugleich ist. Schon in SS FRANCE (1974) gibt es eine räumlich unmögliche «Falte» in dem nur zum Schein ausklappbaren Postkartenteil. Die anderen blauen Bilder mit Kriegsschiffen (BELOW THE WATER LINE und SPANISH DREADNOUGHT) weisen eine andere Verfremdung auf, eine unmögliche Unebenheit im Deck des Schiffes. Diese räumlichen Spielereien laufen auf dasselbe hinaus wie die übertriebene Anzahl von Flaggen auf diesen Schiffen, die oft mit diversen Schiessübungen beschäftigt sind: Im Verein mit den bemalten Rahmen stellen sie die Funktion, die Wirkung und die Kontinuität des Raumes in Frage. Diese Bilder sind gleichsam Übungen darin, Unzusammenhängendes in Verbindung zu bringen.

Die Malerei selbst wird zu einem alles umfassenden kleinen Spiel, das der Künstler auf die gleiche Weise spielt, wie er mit seinen Kriegsspielzeugen spielte (oder spielt). Diesen spielerischen Aspekt erkennt man überall, und obwohl viele dieser Arbeiten an den späten Malewitsch erinnern wegen ihrer malerischen Dichte und dem Wechselspiel von manchmal dissonanten Farbmustern, enthalten sie schöne

Details, wie sie bei Malewitsch kaum vorkommen: das Verspritzen oder das Wegkratzen von Farbe zum Andeuten von Gischt in DAEDALUS oder von Falten in den Flaggen in NAVY DAY, das minuziöse Vertreiben der Pinselspuren am Himmel, die bemalten Rahmen, oder der Trompe-l'œil-Rahmen von MEDIEVAL WITH LEMON SKY. Morley geniesst es offensichtlich, seinen Meeresfluten mittels Farbe Leben zu verleihen; er ist zutiefst und ernsthaft an seinen Malspielen beteiligt, so wie Bach mit jeder Faser an seinen spielerischen Konstruktionen kompliziertester kirchlicher Partituren hing. Derselbe Ernst, dieselbe Spiellaune. Ein Bild wie DAEDALUS vermittelt dem Betrachter das gemischte Gefühl von Evidenz und Nicht-Zusammenpassen, von Kitsch und Kunst. Die riesige, unregelmässige Sonne; die farbliche Harmonie von rötlichem Lila, Blauviolett und Orange für Meer, Himmel, Schiff und Sonne ist eine Kombination, der ich nirgends sonst je begegnet bin. Das Schiff ist wahrscheinlich die *Santa Maria*, aber es könnte auch auf den Namen *Scher dich zum Teufel* umgetauft werden.

Ich muss sagen, dass dieser Text das Ergebnis eines privaten Auftrags ist (und das macht ihn notwendigerweise zu einer privaten Angelegenheit). Normalerweise schreibe ich nicht auf Befehl, aber diesmal war es mehr wie ein Spiel oder eine Herausforderung. Eines Abends, am Tag vor der Eröffnung seiner Ausstellung in der Galerie Templon in Paris, erzählte Malcolm Morley von einem Gespräch mit Roy Lichtenstein, vor vielen Jahren. «Warum versuchst du nicht einmal Grün zu verwenden?»

Lichtenstein antwortete: «Weil ich meine Gewohnheiten ungern verändere.» Aus dem Mund von Morley klang diese Antwort wie eine Art Todesurteil. Was heisst es für einen Künstler, seine Gewohnheiten nicht zu verändern? Insgeheim musste ich ihm natürlich recht geben, dennoch spielte ich den Advocatus Diaboli und widersprach:

«Aber er hat Grün verwendet.» «Nicht Ende der 60er Jahre.» «Doch, und Anfang der 60er Jahre ebenfalls.» «Nun», sagte er, «ich kenne Roy.» «Wollen wir wetten?»

Er antwortete nicht, und vielleicht war er sich bewusst, wie unhöflich die Aufforderung zum Wetten ist, was schon Giovanni della Casas Benimmbuch aus dem sechzehnten Jahrhundert seiner Leserschaft

vorhielt. Am Tag danach kam ich mit Lawrence Alloways Buch über Lichtenstein in der Tasche zur Ausstellungseröffnung. «Du hast die Wette verloren», sagte ich und hielt ihm die Reproduktion von TAKKA TAKKA (1962) unter die Nase. Er betrachtete das grüne Laub: «Das ist nicht grün.» «Sondern?» «Es ist graugrün.» Lida schaute ebenfalls: «Es ist grün, Malcolm.» «O.K., was haben wir gewettet? Zwanzig Dollar?» «Wir haben nicht gewettet», sagte ich, «aber du bist nun verurteilt.» «Wozu?» «Du musst ein grünes Bild malen. Du darfst alle Arten von Grün verwenden, aber keine andere Farbe. Und zwar nicht für mich, sondern für dich selbst.» «Du bist ein Teufel. Ich werde ein Bild malen, von dem du seekrank wirst.»

Meistens verdrücke ich mich aus dem Kunstklüngel, weil ich den Egotrip dort nicht aushalte. Das Unterdrücken des tyrannischen Ichs gleicht der Unterdrückung des Lebens selbst, denn das Leben ist ebenso lächerlich wie das Ich; der einzige Ausweg ist deshalb ein Weg hinein, indem man mit dem Ich herumspielt wie eine Katze mit ihrem Schwanz. Eigentlich tut Morley genau dies. Ich mag ihn, weil er nicht das Ego-Spiel spielt – und falls er es dennoch tut, dann ganz subtil, indem er vorgibt, Theater zu spielen. Die Überraschung war deshalb nicht allzu gross, als er mich nach der Rückkehr auf seine Insel anrief und mir einen Handel vorschlug: «Ich male ein grünes Bild, kein sehr grosses, aber eines, das du an die Wand hängen kannst, und du schreibst einen englischen Text über die Ausstellung bei Templon, nur für mich.» «Aber ich kann nicht englisch schreiben», protestierte ich, «und ich kann deine Bilder nicht entschlüsseln.» «Vielleicht gibt es da nichts zu entschlüsseln – vielleicht gibt es gar keinen Zugang und vielleicht auch kein Hindernis.» Das erinnerte mich an Kafkas Erzählung «Vor dem Gesetz».

Ich sagte weder zu, noch konnte ich nein sagen. Der Gedanke, in einer Sprache zu schreiben, die ich nicht wirklich beherrsche, über einen schwierigen Gegenstand und erst noch auf Wunsch eines Künstlers, den ich bewundere, wirkte ebenso lähmend wie verpflichtend. Die Grosszügigkeit des Angebots schien mir in keinem Verhältnis zu meinem Beitrag zu stehen. Dann gefiel mir aber die Idee eines Austauschs von unbezahlbaren Gütern, bei dem es nicht um deren Geldwert geht. Ich erinnerte mich an die Geschichte Vasaris über Pontormo, der sich weigert, für Ottaviano Magnifico zu arbeiten, und einige schöne Bilder mit Rossino tauscht – nicht mit Rosso, dem Maler und ehemaligen Mitschüler, sondern mit Rossino, dem Maurer, der dafür einige Bauarbeiten für ihn erledigte. Arbeit für Arbeit, obwohl die Bilder schliesslich doch ihren Weg ins Haus von Ottaviano fanden. Natürlich wusste Pontormo, dass sein Versuch, den Tauschwert von Kunst zu umgehen und ihn durch eine neue Art von Wertmassstab zu ersetzen, zum Scheitern verurteilt war gegenüber dem geschäftstüchtigen Rossino. Aber ich bin nicht verschwenderisch genug, um auf Güter von nichtmonetärem Wert zu verzichten. Das Problem ist, dass es genauso schwierig ist, eine grosszügige Geste zu akzeptieren, wie eine solche jemandem zu verweigern. Das ist die doppelte Grausamkeit der Grosszügigkeit.

Als ich am Eröffnungsabend bei Templon drauf und dran war wegzugehen und darauf wartete, mich von Malcolm verabschieden zu können, sprach dieser gerade mit Bernard Blistène, der seine Aquarell-Ausstellung in Marseille organisierte. Sie standen vor seinem Bild THE RAIDER, und Malcolm erläuterte die vier Gestalten im Schiff oben auf dem Bild. «Das bin ich als Kapitän, das bin ich als Seebär mit weissem Bart, das bin ich, der über Bord geht, das hier (auf einen athletischen Matrosen im Unterleibchen zeigend) bin ich mit vierzehn Jahren. Damals war ich noch Strichjunge und eines Nachts las ich einen Araber auf, dessen Schwanz aussah wie eine Olive; ich

ekelte mich derart, dass ich samt seinen Hosen abhaute.» Blistène war wie vor den Kopf gestossen.

Morley ist ein grossartiger Geschichtenerzähler. Manchmal erfindet er sie, selbst jene, die wirklich echt tönen, wie jene über ihn selbst, wie er unter der Dusche steht und eine Stimme sagen hört: «Du bist kein Ölmaler! Du bist ein Terpentinmaler!» «Was? Was?» Diese Geschichte erzählte er seinem früheren Kunsthändler Arnold Glimcher,[5] und seither hat er sie bei verschiedenen Gelegenheiten wiederholt, auch an dem Abend bei Templon. Später hat er mir gestanden, dass er sie erfunden habe. Aber in der Lüge steckt ein Stück Wahrheit, auch in der Geschichte, die er Matthew Collings erzählte «über den Opernsänger, der in Palma auftrat (so schreibt Collings, wahrscheinlich hat Malcolm Parma gesagt), wo das Publikum sich in Sachen Oper wirklich auskennt. Nachdem er schlecht gesungen hat (er litt unter Halsweh), fordert das Publikum Zugabe um Zugabe, und er denkt: «Das ist ja merkwürdig, ich dachte, die verstehen was von Oper hier.» Schliesslich krächzt er: «Ich kann nicht mehr singen!» Und eine Stimme von den hinteren Plätzen ruft: «Und du wirst das singen, bis du es kannst!»[6] Natürlich eine Parabel. Eine Parabel ist auch eine mathematische Kurve: In Parabeln zu sprechen heisst, die gerade Bedeutung zu krümmen, indem man ein Element mit dem anderen quantitativ in Beziehung setzt, wie wenn man, zum Beispiel, den Raum als Funktion der Zeit betrachtet, oder wie wenn Morley zu Anthony Haden-Guest sagt: «Ich betrachte mich als Post-Amerikaner.»[7] Morley ist ein parabolischer Künstler.

(Übersetzung: Susanne Schmidt)

1) *Loving you*, 1957, Filmdrehbuch von Herbert Baker und Hal Kanter, unter der Regie von Hal Kanter.
2) Nena Dimitrijevic, «Malcolm Morley», *Flash Art* 142, Oktober 1988, S. 76–80.
3) Sándor Ferenczi, *Versuch einer Genitaltheorie (1924)*, in: ders., *Schriften zur Psychoanalyse*, Bd. 2, S. Fischer, Frankfurt am Main 1972; englisch unter dem Titel *Thalassa* erschienen.
4) Ausser MEDIEVAL WITH LEMON SKY. Patrick Fischer betonte, dass ein breiter Bleistiftraster noch sichtbar ist. Das Gemälde, sagte Morley später, entstand nach dem Rasterbild eines Modells.
5) «A conversation: Malcolm Morley and Arnold Glimcher», in: *Malcolm Morley*, Pace Gallery, New York 1988–89.
6) Matthew Collings, «Malcolm Morley», *Artscribe* 42, August 1983, S. 49–55.
7) Anthony Haden-Guest, «Malcolm Morley», *New York Magazine*, 4. April 1983 (Sonderheft «The British Are Here»), S. 37.

MALCOLM MORLEY, THE LANDING, 1996,
oil on linen, 80 x 54½" /
DAS ANLEGEN, Öl auf Leinen, 203 x 136 cm.

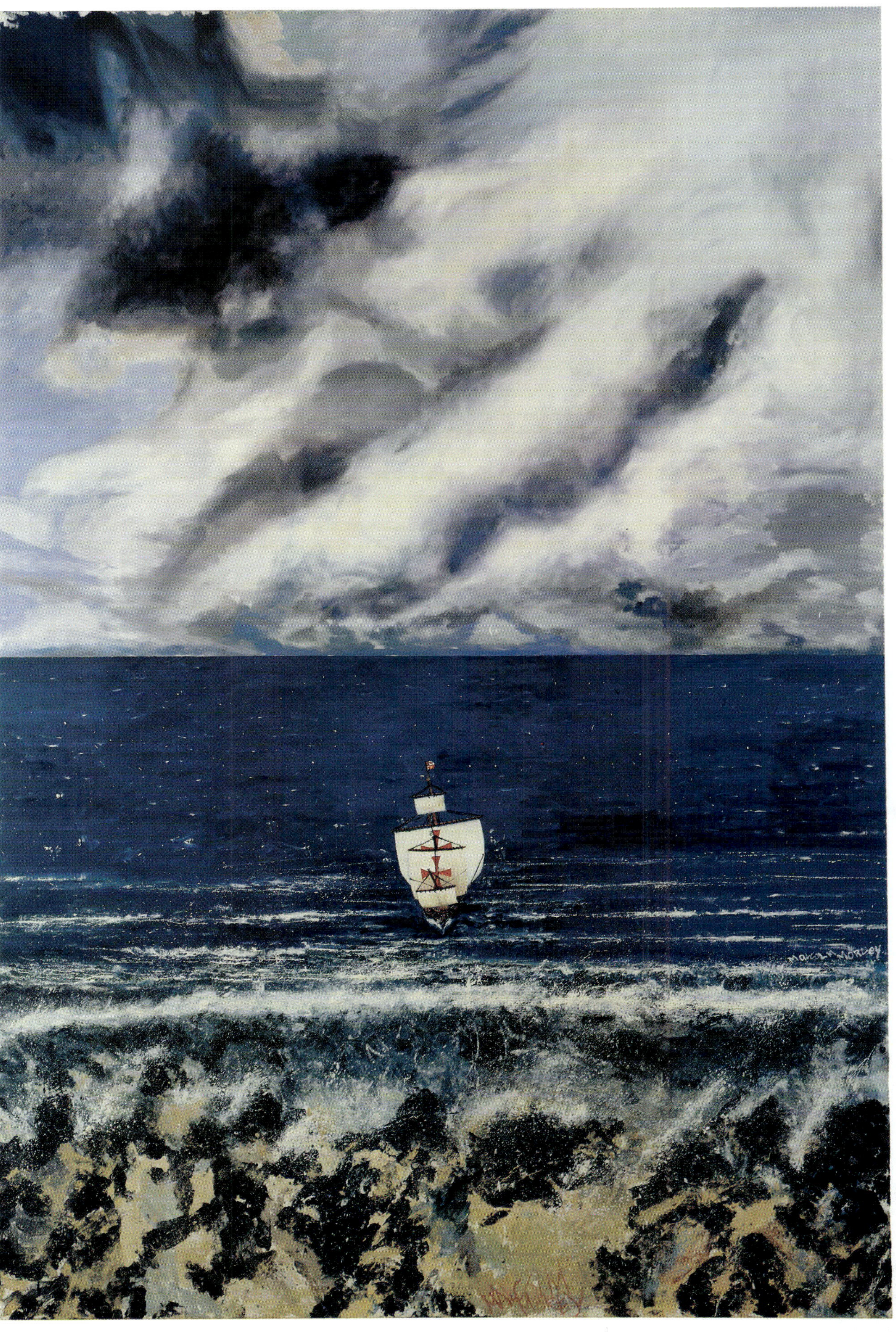

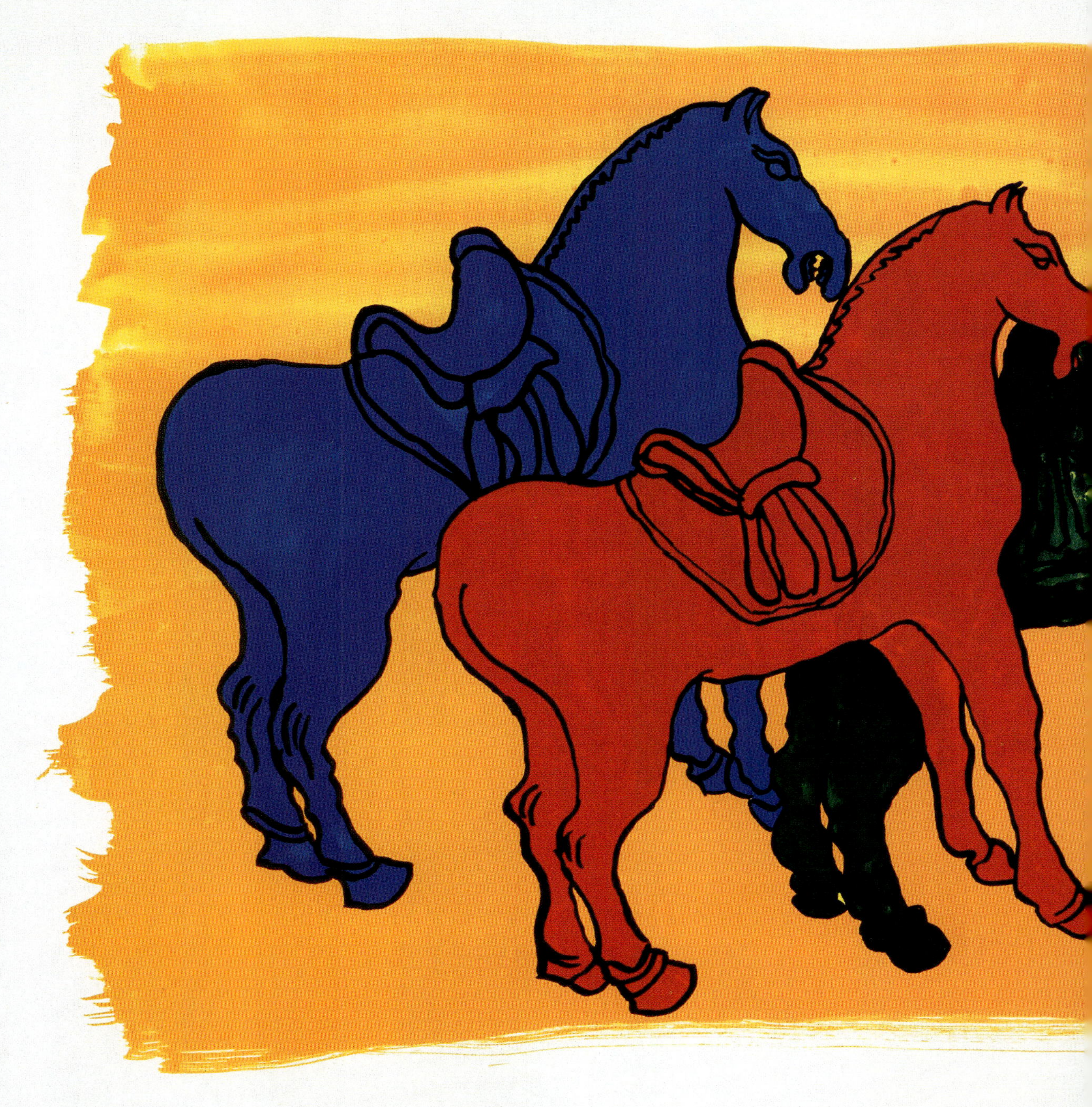

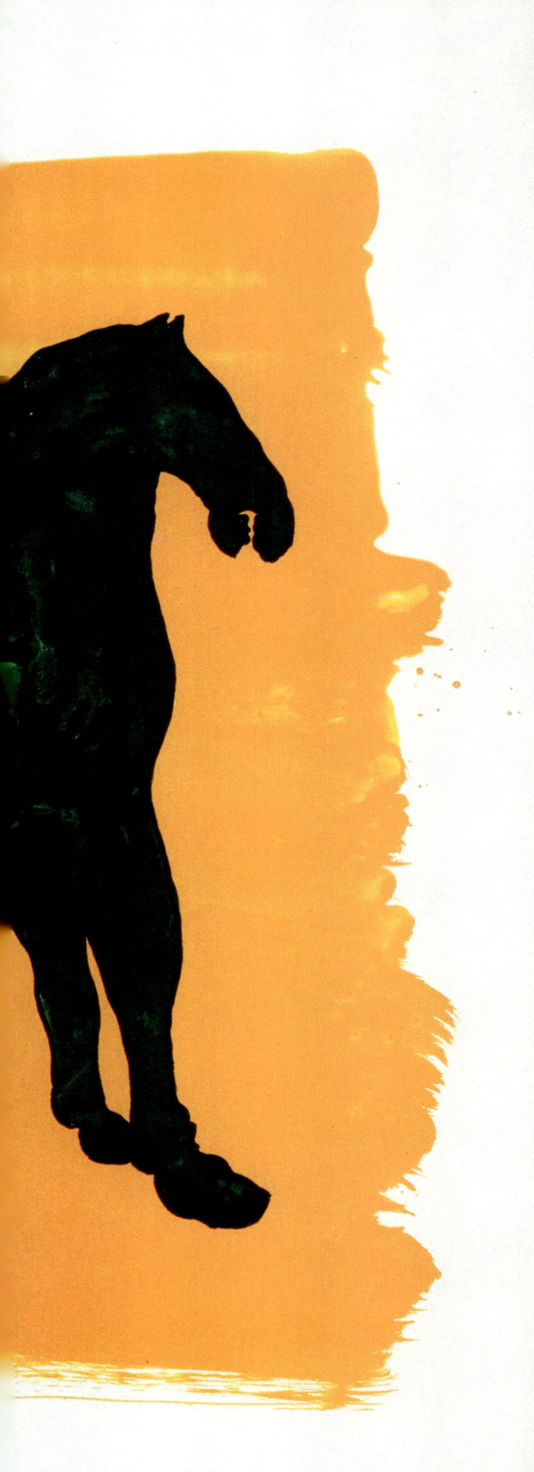

MALCOLM MORLEY

ANCIENT CHINESE HORSES, 1998
11-color lithograph, $23\frac{1}{4}$ x $33\frac{7}{8}$"
on Somerset soft white paper, $28\frac{3}{4}$ x 38".
Printed by Maurice Sanchez, Derrière l' Etoile Studio, New York.
Edition of 60, signed and numbered

ALTCHINESISCHE PFERDE, 1998
Lithographie (11 Farben), 59 x 86 cm, auf Somerset-Papier, 73 x 96,4 cm.
Gedruckt bei Maurice Sanchez, Derrière l'Etoile Studio, New York.
Auflage: 60, signiert und numeriert

Edition for Parkett

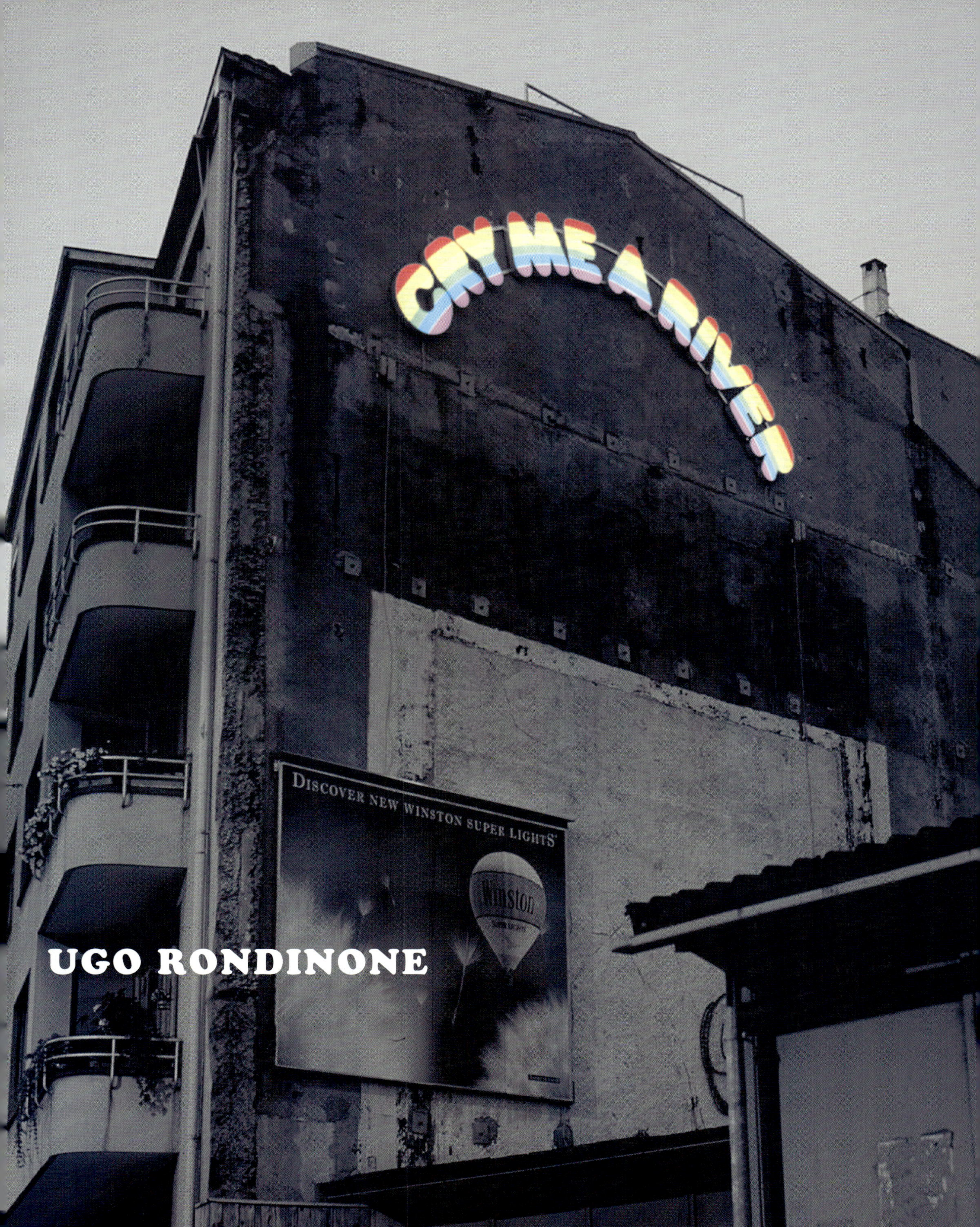

UGO RONDINONE

FRANCESCO BONAMI

UGO RONDINONE:
"Grounding"

In a famous parting speech for his friend Holly Martins (Joseph Cotten) in Carol Reed's film version of *The Third Man* (1949) by Graham Greene, Harry Lime (Orson Welles) looks cynically at history. "After all, it's not that awful. You know what the fellow said: For thirty years in Italy, under the Borgias, they had warfare, terror, murder, bloodshed; they produced Michelangelo, Leonardo da Vinci, and the Renaissance. In Switzerland they had brotherly love, five hundred years of democracy and peace, and what did that produce? The cuckoo clock. So long, Holly."

Ugo Rondinone is both Swiss and Italian, so he can claim to be both the cuckoo in the clock and Leonardo waiting for it to come out, measuring, like any other human being, the time left before he slips into the ground, into the nothingness from whence he departed. All of Rondinone's work focuses on a kind of inertia, and his figure lies in the contemporary world just as Orson Welles stood on a dark corner of postwar Vienna, fighting depression through hubris rather than practising "grounding," the procedure invented by the psychiatrist Alexander Lowen to fight clinical depression. "Grounding" is intended to help the patient feel his or her guts in the legs, to feel rooted again in the world. Yet Rondinone's approach to contemporary art is closer to Lowen's philosophy than to Welles's vision of omnipotence and

glory. His attitude is in sympathy with that of the cuckoo waiting for the door to open rather than with Leonardo's anxious expectation at the other side of the door of the bird's appearance. What does the cuckoo do when it's not yet time to come out? This is a question which belongs to Rondinone's meditation. The little bird, no matter how well it has been carved, always conveys a sense of melancholia for the time it wastes inside the clock. The cuckoo's melancholia is the awareness of knowing that it will never be better than an object because it is an object. The same awareness seems to reside in all of Rondinone's work, and in turn, we find the same melancholia and depression.

The artist talks about the sense of isolation that he craves and turns into a sort of aesthetic claustrophobia, which then devolves into a maze of signifiers of the most recent contemporary art and language. You may try to trace one of Rondinone's many quotations of other contemporary artists but you will fail, because he extracts them from a kind of mnemonic skin and dips them into an oneiric realm where clowns and targets, landscapes and photographs reappear with no direct relationship to the reality of daylight: They belong forever to the realm of darkness, yet they are neither gloomy nor gothic but simply evasive, floating between wakefulness and narcolepsy. Rondinone encloses his exhibitions in a barn-like structure which functions as his own cuckoo clock for sitting in, waiting for his time to be called.

FRANCESCO BONAMI is a writer and curator who lives in New York.

UGO RONDINONE, CRY ME A RIVER, 1997, Plexiglas, neon, 295¾ x 137¼" / 750 x 350 cm.

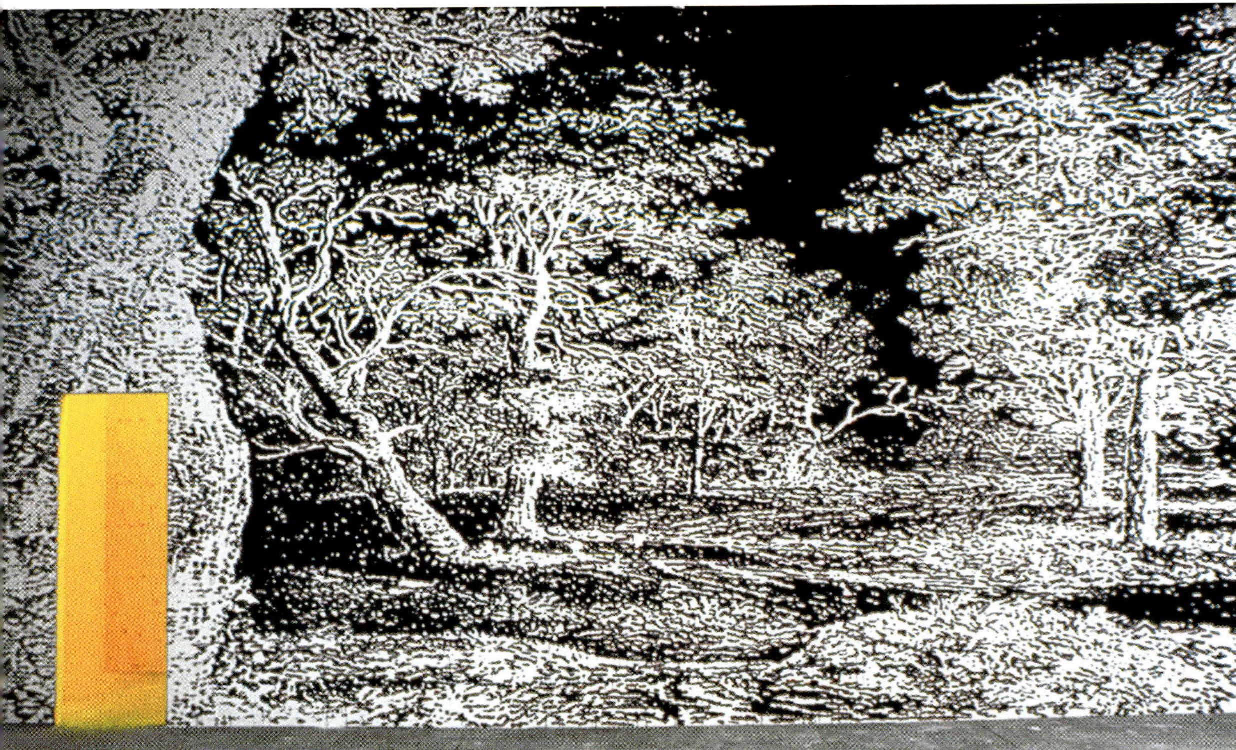

Rondinone often seems to refer to J. K. Huysmans's *A Rebours (Against Nature)*, in which the main character, Des Esseintes, isolates himself in a world of aesthetic and intellectual pleasures only to end up mentally deprived and deeply depressed, with no solution but to beg a certain god for help. This reference is not to be taken literally but as an example of how an individual can recede into a mental state of separation from the outside world yet still reflect and expand in his mind the landscape that he has rejected.

Rondinone's black-and-white or white-and-black landscapes point to this capacity to be alone in nature and to look at it from outside or inside, depending on whether the artist is impersonating the viewer or the object. The landscapes are originally small drawings on small pieces of paper. Later in the studio they are enlarged into ideal, life-size dimensions, just as the artist might abruptly enlarge his thoughts and memory to match them with what has been left behind, lost in the experience of time—the bird again, wasting his own time, sings inside.

In a way, Rondinone the cuckoo accepts the recurring delusion of a glorious exit that results in nothing but an entrance to another room slightly bigger but nevertheless oppressive as the clock we all inhabit. So landscapes are enlarged to create the illusion of turning them once again into a natural panorama, while they remain pictures, simulacra playing with night and day. Even the photo series I DON'T LIVE HERE ANYMORE, a self-portrait in which the artist's face replaces that of a female subject, reveals the trap into which the artist has fallen. In an episode of *The Twilight Zone* a boy possesses the evil power to make his wishes or thoughts come true, for example, erasing the mouth of his blabbering sister or turning himself into a cartoon character. Rondinone looks as though he's fallen into the same nightmare, an ineluctable wish; he falls out of one character into another, trying to remember who he is and how he might imagine himself back into his own body.

If Huysmans's hothouse novel makes one melancholic cornerstone to Rondinone's activity, Jon Krakauer's 1996 bestseller, *Into the Wild,* makes another,

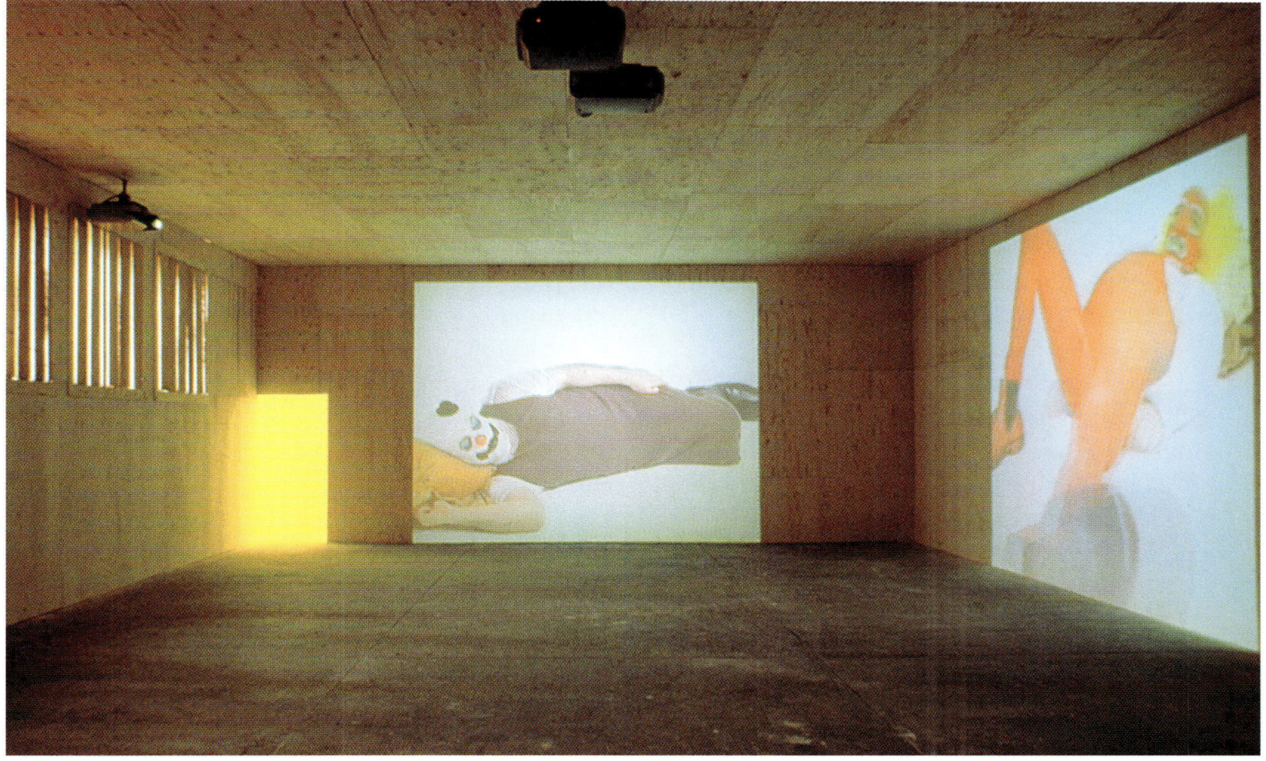

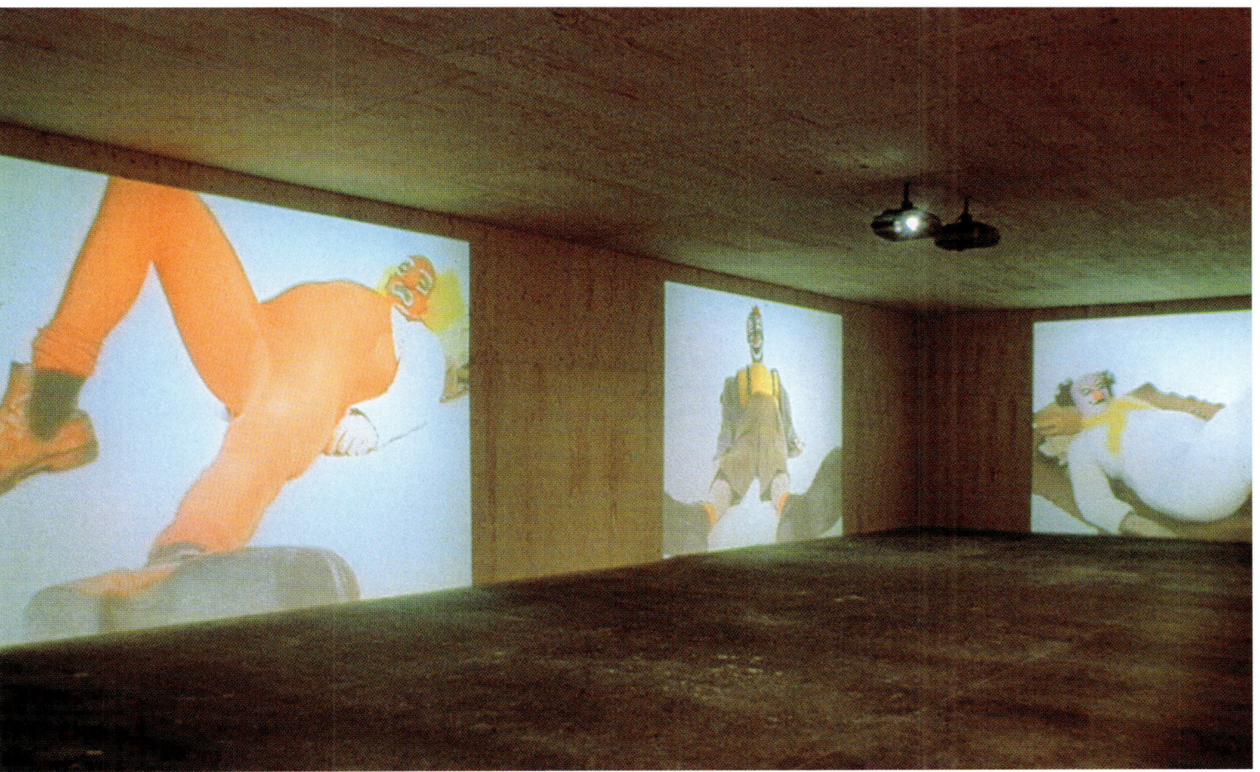

UGO RONDINONE, WHERE DO WE GO FROM HERE? 1997, installation view, 4 video projections, wood, sound / 4 Videoprojektionen, Holz, Sound.

this time from an external perspective. *Into the Wild* is the true story of Chris McCandless, a young man from a well-to-do family, who decided to abandon society to live in nature, in the wilds of Alaska. Four months later, a hunter found his decomposed body. He had died from starvation after one hundred and thirteen days of total isolation in an abandoned bus. Rondinone's targets and landscapes, clowns and self-portraits address the tension between total abandonment and activity. The tempting desire to get up and move, to exit the mind-clock and enter total, real isolation—to escape claustrophobia and embrace agoraphobia—constantly reappears. To accept a sense of abandonment is one way of getting back to the solidity and safety of the earth to renew the energy and strength of our being, which is the latent reality of Rondinone's vision: the desire to fall.

Into the Wild was suggested to me by the artist Charles Ray, which now brings me to consider that these two artists, like Huysmans and Krakauer, McCandless and Des Esseintes, enter different kinds of depth and isolation from the opposite ends of culture. Ray's NO (1992), a professional color photograph of a fiberglass dummy of the artist, is a disturbing coun-

terpoint to Rondinone's depressed figure, HEYDAY (1995). Ray's dummy is the inner fragility of the mind transformed into a sculptural object, abandoned in order to be fully represented. In the act, the sculptor succeeds in recovering from melancholy through the belief that he is better than the object, that he is superior to it. He plunges into the depths of the idea of himself, resulting in a useless simulacrum, yet one that is sufficiently different and imperfect to redeem the subject. McCandless saw himself as nature but discovered, tragically, that he was the imperfection, the difference. The Rondinone figure, a self-portrait, seated, abandoned against the wall of the gallery, is the subject which accepts the unavoidable destiny of becoming an object; it gives up the idea of being nature, or anything even close to it. He sits there, his gaze lost on the floor, all energy dispersed. He lies on the ground having given up the struggle against gravity, the instinct to do something. He is on the verge of depression, but might be ready to get up and fight back. Ideally, this is the real "grounding," the acceptance that sooner or later we have to give up touching the earth, being safe and healthy.

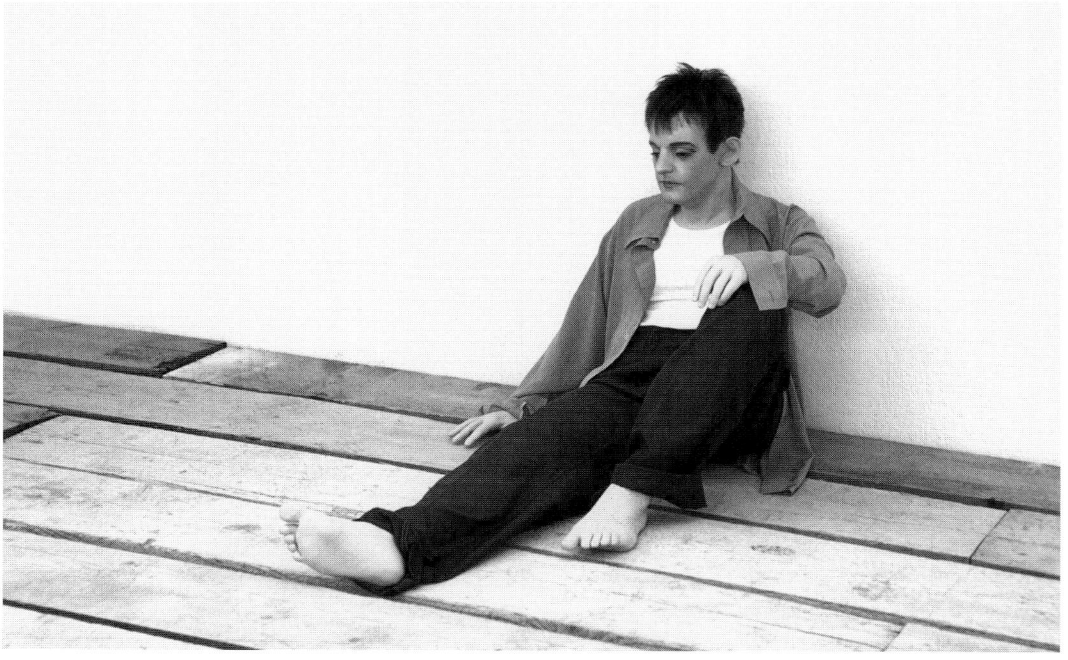

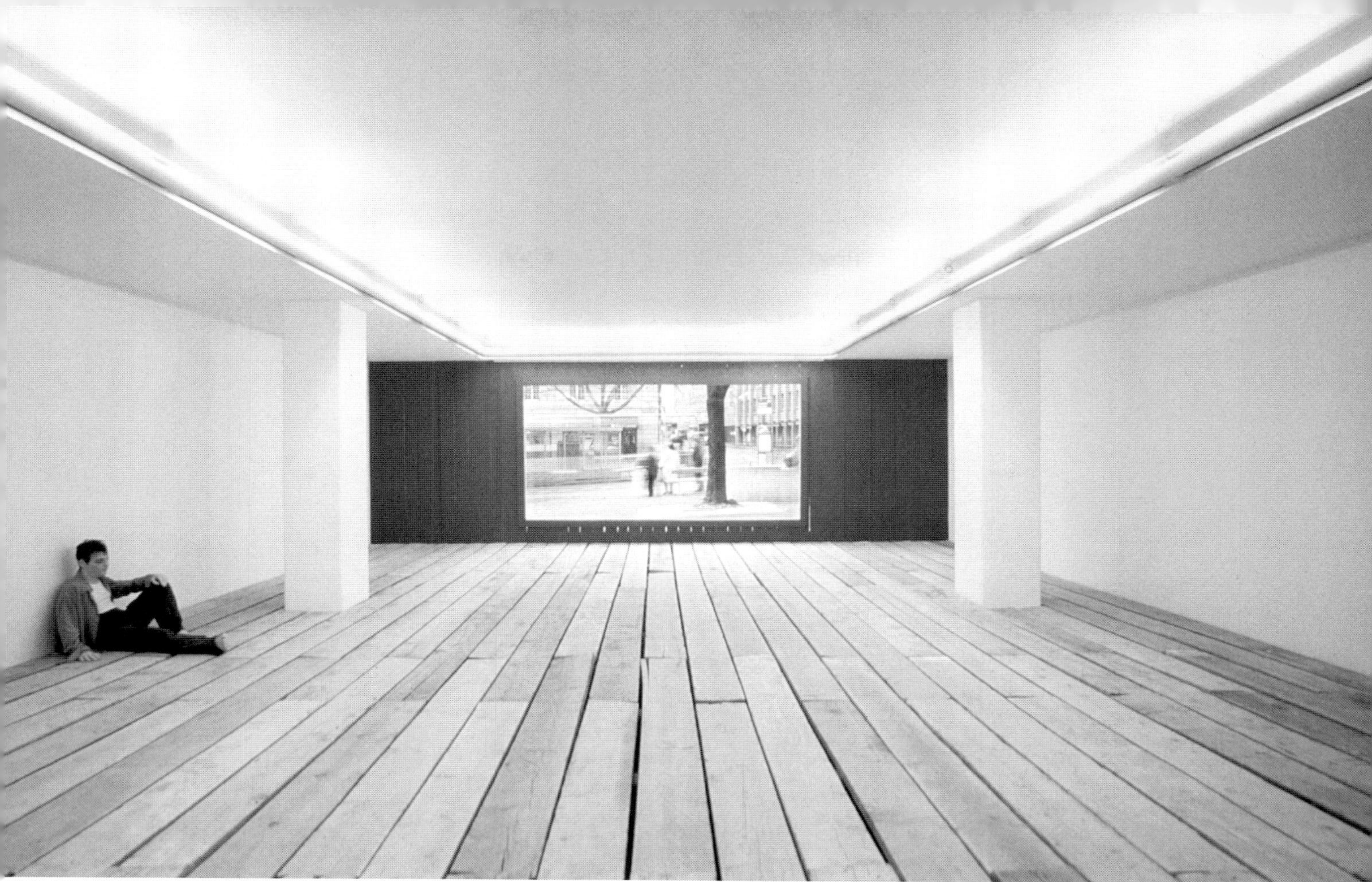

The installation of HEYDAY at the Galerie Walcheturm in Zurich may be Rondinone's most eloquent expression to date. The visitor, experiencing the space from one end of the installation, can see Rondinone's self-portrait slumped against the left wall on a rough wooden floor. At the back of the space on a black wall there is a projection. A projection? What projection? A tree, a bus stop, people walking by or waiting. In truth, it's not a projection at all, but the outside reality that the artist has framed and isolated. It is the landscape of the mind that won't disappear. The visitor passes the figure and moves slowly towards the outside, as in the final scene of Michelangelo Antonioni's *The Passenger* out into the world, into noise and life, away from existential malaise, to the oblivion of the man lying against the wall. At the bus stop across the street, a woman looks into the gallery window; the empty space lures her out of time and through the door of the cuckoo clock. She moves closer and closer, through the big glass, into the silent room, over the creaking planks. She moves closer to the figure, she looks at him. Maybe it breathes. Maybe not. Suddenly, she realizes that she is a visitor, the only one, and turns back to the window. Her bus passes by, she's too late, and she, too, slides down to the floor against the wall.

Ugo Rondinone's challenge is to push objects and subjects against each other, collapsing in exhaustion or levitating in meditation. He walks three hundred and sixty degrees within reality, sealing himself inside again and again, wrapping himself outside in a perpetually brief state of stillness, like Joyce's artist as a young man: "He would fall. He had not yet fallen but he would fall silently, in an instant. Not to fall was too hard, too hard; and he felt the silent lapse of his soul, as it would be at some instant to come, falling, falling, but not yet fallen, still unfallen, but about to fall."

FRANCESCO BONAMI

UGO RONDINONE:

«Erdung»

In einer berühmten Abschiedsrede für seinen Freund Holly Martins (Joseph Cotten) wirft Harry Lime in Carol Reeds Verfilmung von Graham Greenes Roman *Der dritte Mann* einen zynischen Blick auf die Geschichte. «Letztendlich ist es gar nicht so schrecklich. Du weisst, was der Bursche gesagt hat: Unter den Borgias gab's in Italien dreissig Jahre lang nur Krieg, Terror, Mord, Blutvergiessen, und doch brachten sie Michelangelo, Leonardo da Vinci und die Renaissance hervor. In der Schweiz hingegen herrschte fünfhundert Jahre lang brüderliches Einvernehmen, Demokratie und Frieden, und was brachten sie hervor? Die Kuckucksuhr. Bis dann, Holly.»

Ugo Rondinone ist beides, Schweizer und Italiener, und er kann deshalb auch von sich behaupten, beides zu sein: der Kuckuck in der Uhr und Leonardo, der darauf wartet, dass er herauskommt, während er, wie jedes andere menschliche Wesen, die Zeit abschätzt, die ihm bleibt, bevor er in die Erde, in das Nichts verschwindet, dem er entstammt. Rondinones gesamtes Werk befasst sich mit einer Art Regungslosigkeit, und seine Figur liegt in unserer Zeit in einer dunklen Ecke, so wie Orson Welles im Wien der Nachkriegsjahre stand als einer, der die De-

pression durch Hybris und nicht durch die Praxis der «Erdung» bekämpfte, jenes Verfahren, das der Psychiater Alexander Lowen bei klinischen Depressionen anwandte. «Erdung» bedeutet, dem Patienten das Gefühl zu vermitteln, seine Eingeweide in den Beinen zu spüren wie Wurzeln, die sich bewegen; das Individuum wieder auf die Erde zurückzubringen oder wörtlich an Boden gewinnen zu lassen. Und doch entspricht Rondinones Konzeption von zeitgenössischer Kunst eher Lowens Philosophie als Welles' Vision von Allmacht und Ruhm. Er sympathisiert eher mit dem Kuckuck, der darauf wartet, dass das Türchen aufgeht, als mit Leonardo, der auf der andern Seite des Türchens gespannt dem Erscheinen des Vogels entgegensieht. Was macht der Kuckuck, wenn er gerade nicht an der Reihe ist? Diese Frage gehört zu Rondinones Meditation. Der kleine Vogel kann noch so hübsch geschnitzt sein, aufgrund der Zeit, die er in der Uhr vergeudet, hat er immer etwas Melancholisches an sich. Die Melancholie des Kuckucks ist in dem Wissen begründet, dass er, weil er ein Ding ist, nie besser als ein Ding sein wird. Dieses Wissen scheint allen Arbeiten Rondinones innezuwohnen, und dementsprechend finden wir in ihnen dieselbe Melancholie und Niedergeschlagenheit.

Der Künstler spricht über das Gefühl der Isolation, nach dem er sich sehnt und das er in eine Art ästhetische Klaustrophobie verwandelt, aus der wiederum ein Labyrinth von Signifikanten der neuesten

---

FRANCESCO BONAMI ist Schriftsteller und Kurator mit Wohnsitz in New York. Er organisierte 1997 die Ausstellung «Truce, Site Santa Fe».

UGO RONDINONE, GONE WITH THE WIND, 1996, 32 plastic balls, tape recorder, burnt-in car paint, $19\frac{5}{8}$–$27\frac{1}{2}$" in diameter / VOM WINDE VERWEHT, 32 Kunststoffbälle, Tonbandgerät, eingebrannter Autolack, Durchmesser 50–70 cm

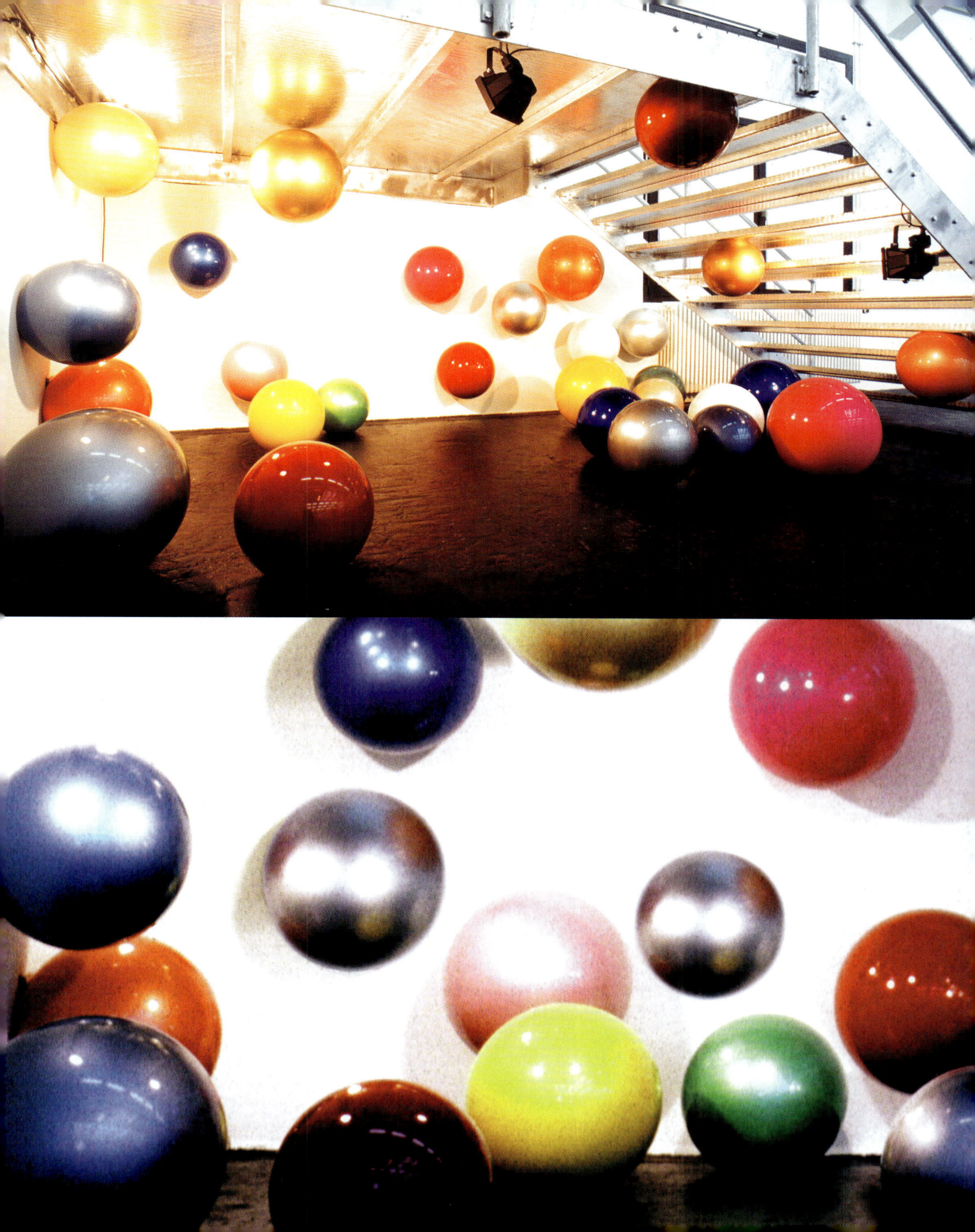

Kunst und Sprache wird. Man kann versuchen, einem von Rondinones zahllosen Zitaten anderer zeitgenössischer Künstler nachzugehen, es wird jedoch zu nichts führen, denn er entnimmt sie einer Art mnemonischer Haut und taucht sie in eine Traumsphäre, in der Clowns und Zielscheiben, Landschaften und Photographien ohne direkte Beziehung zur Realität des Tageslichtes auftauchen. Sie gehören für immer dem Dunkel an, doch sind sie weder düster noch gruselig, sondern eben nur schwer zu fassen, da sie zwischen Wachsein und Narkolepsie schwanken. Rondinone baut eine Art Scheune um seine Ausstellungen, die für ihn die Funktion einer Kuckucksuhr hat, in der er sitzt und wartet bis er aufgerufen wird.

Rondinone scheint häufig auf J. K. Huysmans' Roman *Gegen den Strich* anzuspielen, dessen Protagonist, Des Esseintes, sich in einer Welt des ästhetischen und intellektuellen Vergnügens isoliert, doch nur, um verstört und verzweifelt zu enden, ohne eine andere Lösung, als einen Gott um Hilfe anzuflehen. Dieser Bezug sollte nicht zu wörtlich genommen werden, sondern als ein Beispiel dafür, wie weit sich ein Individuum in einen geistigen Zustand der Trennung von der Aussenwelt zurückziehen kann und dennoch in seinem Kopf immer die Landschaft, der es entsagt hat, widerspiegelt und weiterentwickelt.

Rondinones Schwarzweiss- oder Weissschwarz-Landschaften illustrieren diese Fähigkeit, allein in der Natur zu sein und sie von innen oder von aussen betrachten zu können, je nachdem ob der Künstler den Betrachter oder das Objekt verkörpert. Die Landschaften sind ursprünglich kleine Zeichnungen auf einem Stückchen Papier. Erst später im Studio werden sie zu idealen, natürlichen Dimensionen vergrössert, so als wollte der Künstler abrupt seine Gedanken und sein Gedächtnis vergrössern, um sie dem, was zurückgelassen wurde, was in der Erfahrung der Zeit verlorenging, anzupassen – wiederum der Vogel, der seine Zeit vergeudet, der drinnen in der Uhr singt.

Wie der Kuckuck akzeptiert auch Rondinone den immer wiederkehrenden Trug eines grossartigen Abgangs, der nichts weiter als das Eintreten in einen anderen Raum bedeutet – einen etwas grösseren, aber trotzdem bedrückenden, so wie die Kuckucks-

uhr, die wir alle bewohnen. Landschaften werden so vergrössert, um wieder die Illusion eines echten Panoramas zu erzeugen, während sie Bilder bleiben, Scheinbilder, die mit Tag und Nacht spielen. Auch die Photoserie *I don't live here anymore* (ich wohne nicht mehr hier), ein Selbstporträt, in dem das Gesicht des Künstlers das eines weiblichen Sujets ersetzt, enthüllt die Falle, in die der Künstler geraten ist. In einer Episode aus *The Twilight Zone* besitzt ein Junge die verhängnisvolle Macht, seine Wünsche oder Gedanken wahr werden zu lassen, wie zum Beispiel den ständig plappernden Mund seiner Schwester auszuradieren oder sich in eine Trickfilmfigur zu verwandeln. Rondinone scheint demselben Alptraum zum Opfer gefallen zu sein, einem Wunsch, vor dem es kein Entrinnen gibt; er fällt von einem Charakter in den andern und versucht sich zu erinnern, wer er ist und wie er sich in seinen eigenen Körper zurückdenken könnte.

Ist Huysmans' Treibhausroman für Rondinones Schaffen ein melancholischer Eckpfeiler, so liefert Jon Krakauers 1996 erschienener Bestseller *In die Wildnis* einen weiteren, dieses Mal jedoch von einem Standpunkt ausserhalb. *In die Wildnis* ist die wahre Geschichte von Chris McCandless, einem jungen Mann aus einer wohlhabenden Familie, der beschloss, der Gesellschaft den Rücken zu kehren, um in der Natur zu leben, im tiefsten Alaska. Vier Monate später wurde sein verwester Körper von einem Jäger aufgefunden. Nach hundertdreizehn Tagen völliger Isolation in einem verlassenen Bus war er verhungert. Rondinones Zielscheiben und Landschaften, Clowns und Selbstporträts befassen sich mit der Spannung zwischen vollkommenem Aufgeben und aktivem Handeln. Der verführerische Wunsch, aufzustehen und sich zu bewegen, aus der geistigen Kuckucksuhr herauszutreten und sich in eine totale, echte Isolation zu begeben – der Klaustrophobie zu entkommen, um die Agoraphobie willkommen zu heissen –, taucht ständig auf. Das Loslassen zu akzeptieren ist ein Weg, um festen Boden und die Sicherheit der Erde wiederzugewinnen, um die Energie und Kraft unseres Seins zu erneuern, was die verborgene Realität von Rondinones Vision ist: der Wunsch zu fallen.

Auf das Buch *In die Wildnis* wurde ich durch den Künstler Charles Ray aufmerksam; davon ausgehend entwickelte ich dann die Theorie, dass Ray und Rondinone, ähnlich wie Huysmans und Krakauer, McCandless und Des Esseintes, von entgegengesetzten kulturellen Polen verschiedene Arten von Tiefen und Isolation ausloten. Rays NO (1992), ein professionelles Farbphoto von einer dem Künstler nachgebildeten Figur aus Fiberglas, ist ein beunruhigendes Gegenstück zu Rondinones bedrückter Figur HEYDAY (Überschwang), die in einer Installation der Galerie Walcheturm 1955 in Zürich gezeigt wurde. Rays Attrappe ist die zur Skulptur gewordene Gefährdung des Geistes, ein zum Zweck der Darstellung verlassenes Objekt. Der Glaube, besser als das Objekt zu sein, ihm überlegen zu sein, lässt den Bildhauer von seiner Melancholie genesen. Er taucht in die Tiefen der Vorstellung, die er von sich hat, und erschafft ein nutzloses Simulacrum, das jedoch genügend Unterschiede und Unvollkommenheiten aufweist, um das Sujet erlösen zu können. McCandless

betrachtete sich als Natur, musste aber die tragische Entdeckung machen, dass er das Unvollkommene, das Andersartige war. Die zusammengesunken gegen die Wand der Galerie gelehnte Rondinone-Figur, ein Selbstporträt, ist das Subjekt, das sich in sein unausweichliches Schicksal ergibt, Objekt zu werden; sie gibt die Vorstellung auf, Natur oder auch nur etwas ihr Verwandtes zu sein. Sie sitzt da, starrt verloren auf den Fussboden, matt, energielos. Sie liegt auf dem Boden und kämpft nicht mehr gegen die Schwerkraft, gegen den Instinkt an, etwas zu tun. Sie ist am Rande einer Depression, könnte aber auch jederzeit aufstehen und zurückschlagen. Idealerweise ist es das, was man unter «Erdung» versteht, das Hinnehmen der Tatsache, dass wir früher oder später nicht mehr die Erde berühren werden, nicht mehr sicher und gesund sein werden.

Die Installation HEYDAY ist vielleicht Rondinones expressivstes Werk bisher. Der Betrachter, der den

UGO RONDINONE, BONJOUR TRISTESSE, 1997,
2 part sculpture: polyester, cotton, 61½ x 30¾ x 17"; wood, loudspeaker, spot lights, sound, 197 x 118" /
2-teilige Skulptur: Polyester, Baumwolle, 156 x 78 x 43 cm; Holz, Lautsprecher, Scheinwerfer, Sound, 500 x 300 cm.

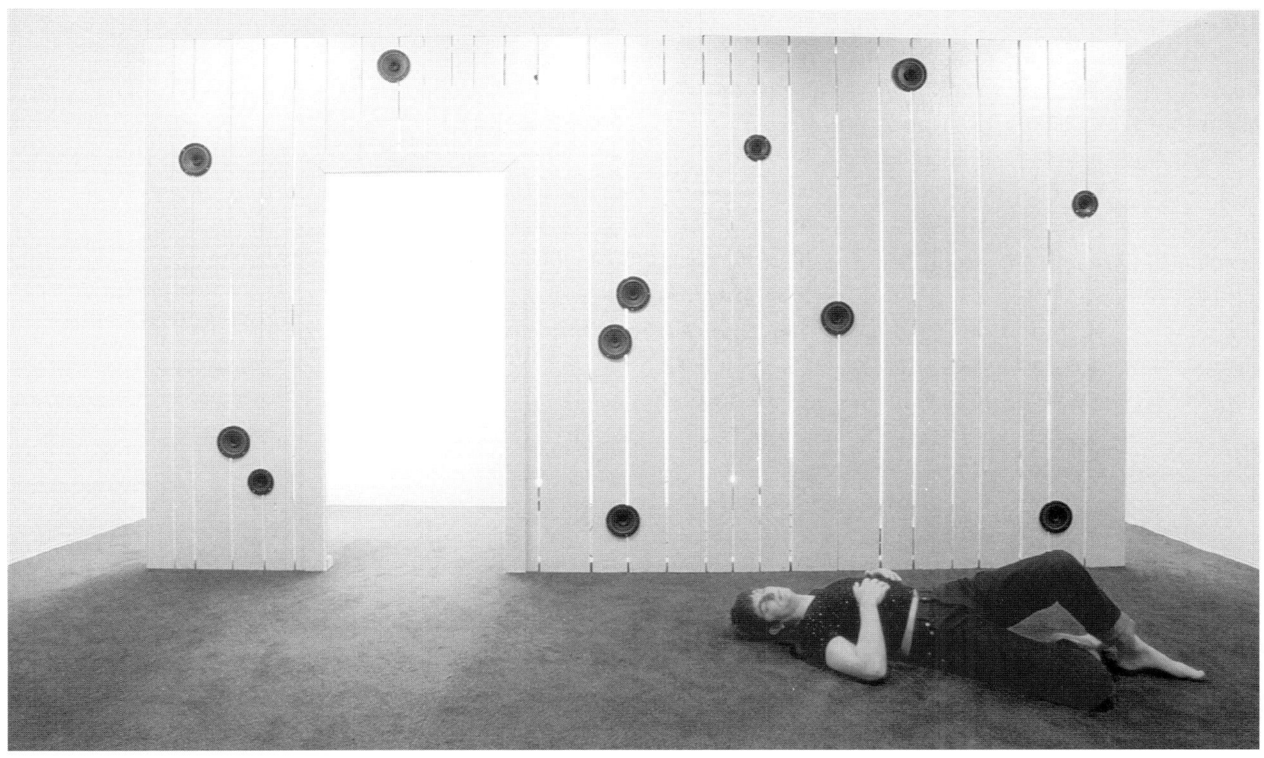

Raum von einem Ende der Installation her wahrnimmt, sieht Rondinones Selbstporträt, wie er auf einem rohen Holzboden in sich zusammengesackt gegen
die linke Wand lehnt. Im hinteren Teil des Raums
wird etwas auf eine schwarze Wand projiziert. Projiziert? Was wird projiziert? Ein Baum, eine Bushaltestelle, Leute, die vorbeigehen oder stehenbleiben. In
Wahrheit wird aber überhaupt nichts projiziert, es ist
vielmehr die Realität draussen vor dem Fenster, die
der Künstler gerahmt und isoliert hat. Es ist die geistige Landschaft, die nicht verschwinden will. Der
Besucher geht an der Figur vorbei und bewegt sich
langsam auf den Ausgang zu, wie in der letzten Szene
von Antonionis *Professione: Reporter*: hinaus in die
Welt, in den Lärm und das Leben, weg von dem existentiellen Unbehagen, den an der Wand liegenden
Mann aus dem Gedächtnis verbannend. An der Bushaltestelle auf der gegenüberliegenden Strassenseite
späht eine Frau in das Fenster der Galerie; der leere
Raum lockt sie aus der Zeit und durch die Tür der
Kuckucksuhr. Sie kommt näher und näher durch die
Glasfront in den schweigenden Raum, über die knarrenden Holzplanken. Sie nähert sich der Figur,
schaut sie an. Vielleicht atmet sie, vielleicht nicht.
Plötzlich wird ihr klar, dass sie eine Besucherin ist,
die einzige, und sie dreht sich zum Fenster um. Ihr
Bus fährt vorbei, sie hat ihn verpasst und rutscht
selbst mit dem Rücken zur Wand zu Boden.

Ugo Rondinones Herausforderung ist, Objekte
und Subjekte gegeneinander auszuspielen, wobei er
entweder erschöpft zusammenbricht oder meditierend abhebt. Er dreht einen 360-Grad-Kreis innerhalb der Realität, schliesst sich innerlich immer wieder hermetisch ab und hüllt sich äusserlich in einen
ewigen Moment der Stille, wie Joyces Künstler als
junger Mann: «Er würde fallen. Er war noch nicht
gefallen, aber er würde fallen, still, in einem Augenblick. Nicht zu fallen war zu schwer, zu schwer: und
er fühlte den stillen Sturz seiner Seele, der eines
kommenden Augenblicks geschähe, wie sie fiel, fiel
doch nicht gefallen war, noch ungefallen doch am
Fallen.»[1]   *(Übersetzung: Uta Goridis)*

[1] James Joyce, *Ein Porträt des Künstlers als junger Mann*, übersetzt von Klaus Reichert, in: Joyce, *Werke*, Bd. 2, Suhrkamp,
Frankfurt am Main 1972, S. 430.

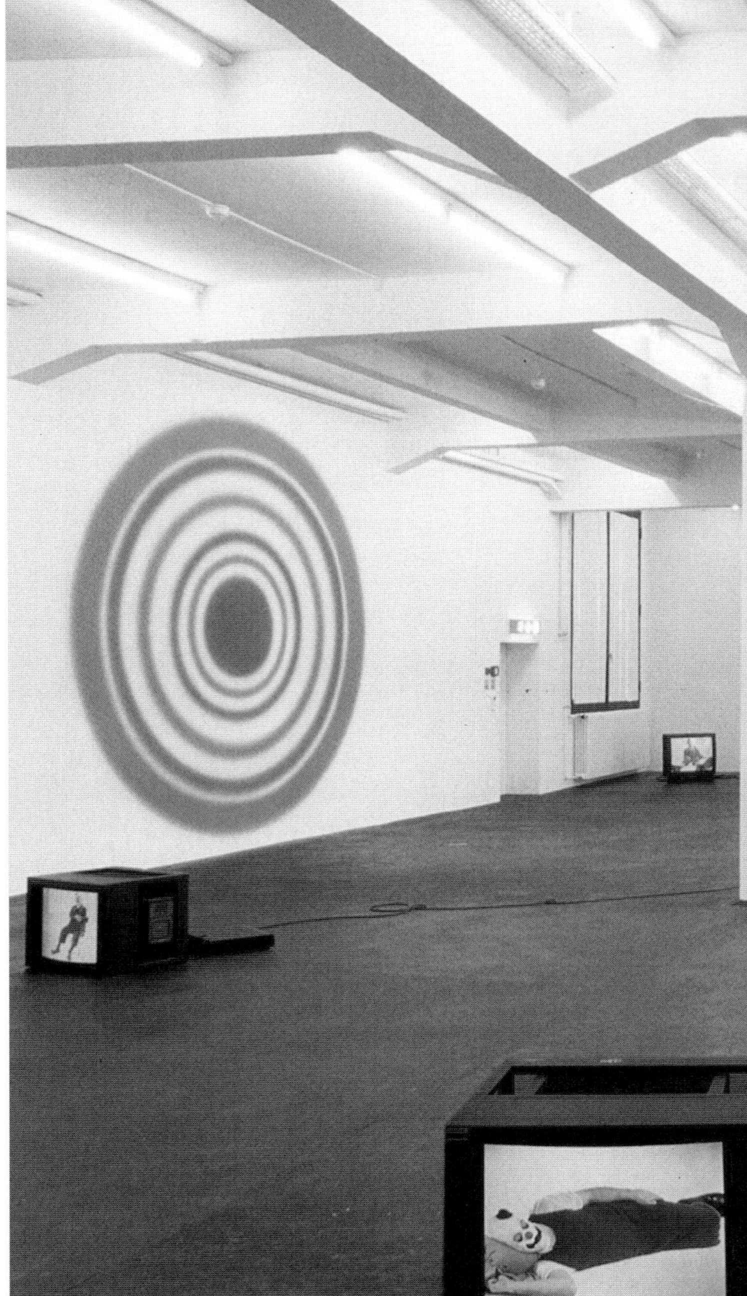

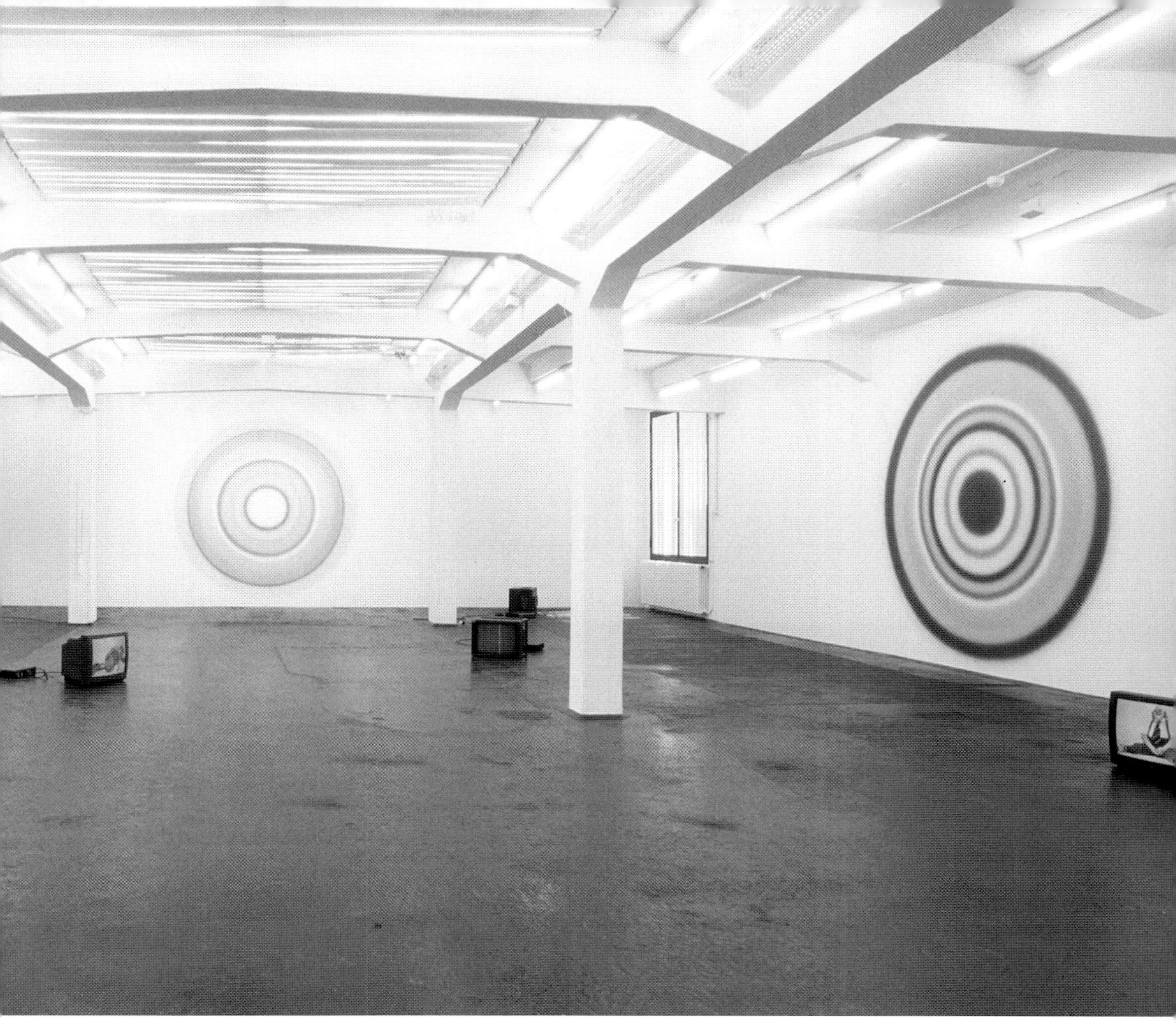

UGO RONDINONE, DOGDAYS ARE OVER, 1996, exhibition view /
DIE HUNDSTAGE SIND VORBEI, Ausstellungsansicht, Museum für Gegenwartskunst, Zürich.

JAN VERWOERT

«*Pictures came and*

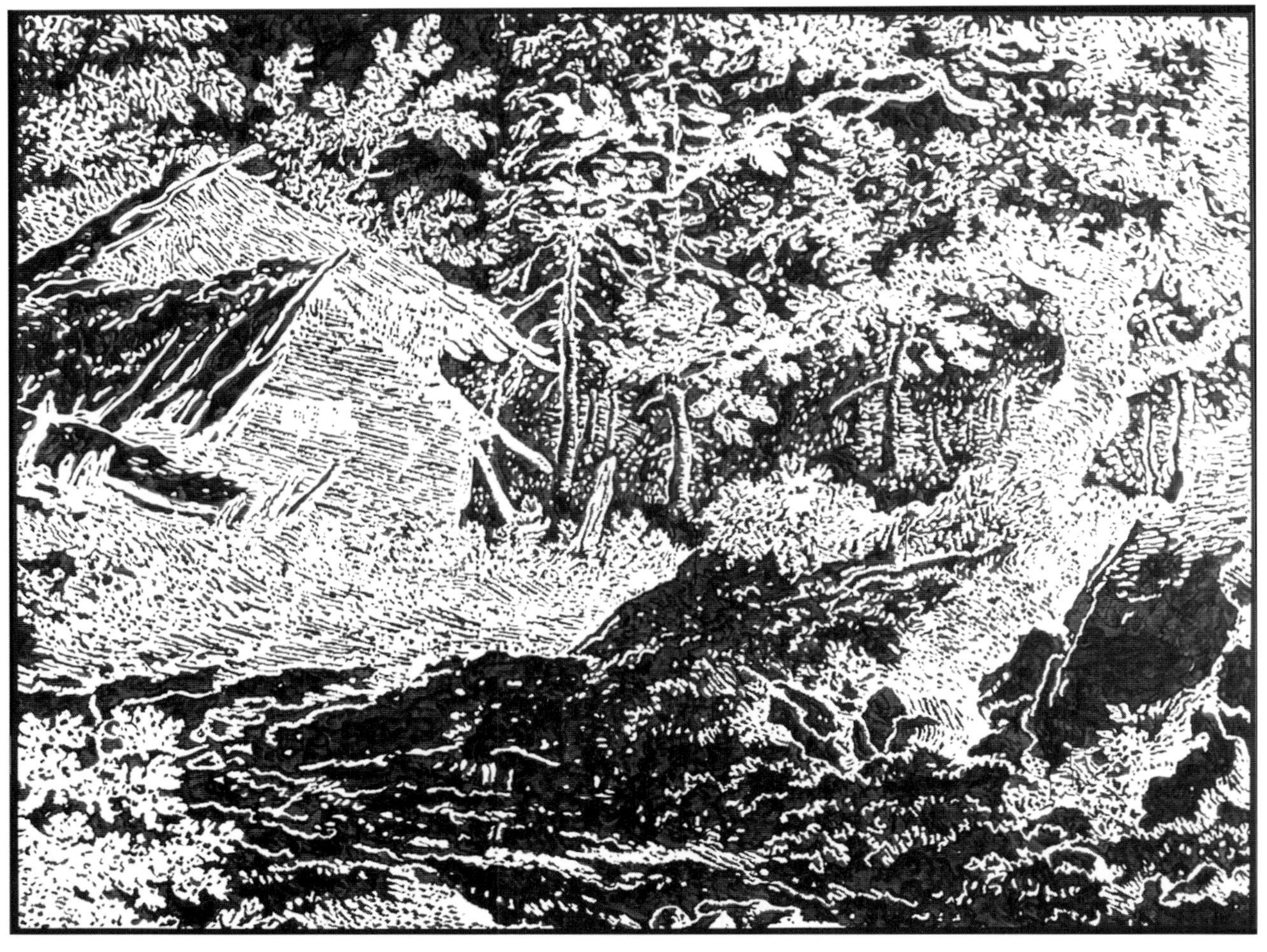

UGO RONDINONE, NO. 76, SIEBZEHNTERMAINEUNZEHNHUNDERTNEUNZIG, 1996,
Tusche auf Papier, 210 x 270 cm /
MAYSEVENTEENTHNINETEENHUNDREDNINETY, ink on paper, 82⅝ x 106¼".

broke my heart...» [1]

«If you don't want my love...»

Die Stimme schleppt sich müde von Ton zu Ton: zwei, drei Takte triste Countrymusik, mit der Ugo Rondinone seine Installation THE HEART IS A LONELY HUNTER (Das Herz ist ein einsamer Jäger) [2] unterlegt hat. Das kurze Sample tropft in Abständen, immer wieder und wieder, aus einem Dutzend Lautsprechern, die in verschiedener Höhe und Grösse in eine Bretterwand eingelassen sind. Jeder Ton klingt noch zäher und tiefer als im schon elend langsamen Original von *Souled American* – «If you don't want my l-o-o-o-v-e...» Was bleibt dem lonesome Cowboy, dessen Liebe verschmäht wird? Er reitet in den Sonnenuntergang und überlässt sich den endlosen Weiten der Prärie. Der Melancholiker der alten Welt dagegen sucht seine Einsamkeit in malerischen Waldlandschaften. In Waldlandschaften, wie sie die Zeichnungen zeigen, die die Installation in Szene setzt. Countrymusik und Waldidylle: Rondinone verschmilzt beide Genres und erzeugt so eine dichte Stimmung der Melancholie.

Die Zeichnungen sind grossformatig in Schwarzweiss mit Tusche ausgeführt, so grossformatig, dass der Breitwandeffekt einsetzt: Der Bildhorizont öffnet sich weit und zieht einen hinein in die dargestellte Landschaft, hinein in einsame Waldgegenden, die mal von einem Fluss, mal von einer Lichtung durchbrochen werden. Dem Szenarium entsprechend, wird man auf der Stelle melancholisch. Das gute, genussvoll traurige Gefühl vom Selbst stellt sich ein. Das Gefühl, das deshalb so genussvoll ist, weil es die Gewissheit verschafft, dass so schön traurig ausser einem selbst gerade unmöglich noch irgend jemand anders auf der Welt sein kann – die Gewissheit authentischer Individualität also.

Mit dem Gefühl kommt jedoch auch die Erinnerung daran, dass es immer solche Bilder waren, die einem diesen melancholischen Selbstgenuss vermittelt haben – und mit der Erinnerung kommt die Einsicht, dass so einsam die Waldidylle nicht ist, dass immer schon vor einem jemand da war: man selbst, früher, zwecks Selbstfindung mit wichtigem Blick und Goethes Werther in der Tasche, Werther mit Ossian an der Brust zum Ausheulen am Busen der Natur – letztendlich die ganze bürgerliche Kultur, die den trauten Birkenhain zum angestammten Exerzierplatz ihrer Innerlichkeitsrituale gemacht hat. Ist die Melancholie so vielleicht nur die klassische Technik der Bourgeoisie, aus Selbstmitleid ihr Selbstwertgefühl zu gewinnen? [3]

JAN VERWOERT ist Student der Kulturwissenschaft und Philosophie, freier Kritiker und Bassist bei Sexpop.

Die Motive, die Rondinone in seine Rauminstallationen einbringt, tragen ihre Geschichte mit: Sie provozieren eine Reflexion auf ihren Kontext, ihre Herkunft und Form. Eine Reflexion, die die vormals homogene Stimmung des Raums dekonstruiert. Dekonstruieren heisst jedoch immer zugleich Aufbrechen und Verklammern: Die Stimmung besteht als gebrochene weiter – denn die emotionale Identifikation mit den Motiven und die distanzierte Reflexion über sie bleiben, obwohl scheinbar unvereinbar dennoch immer vereint, nebeneinander bestehen. Die Arbeiten von Rondinone haben also eine zwiespältige Wirkung, sie involvieren in Authentizitätsgefühle und distanzieren zugleich von ihnen.

Angefangen mit dem Titel der Zeichnungen; er nennt nur ihre Datierung und verstärkt so als biographischer Index ihren Authentizitätsanspruch. Dass sich in der Zeichnung die Einheit von Ort, Zeit und Stimmung des Zeichners im Moment ihres Entstehens ausdrückt, dem schenkt man gerne Glauben – es kommt einem nur auch der Gedanke, dass die formale Gestaltung der Zeichnung diesen Anspruch eigentlich in Frage stellt. Denn in diesem Format kann niemand sie freihändig vor der Natur hingetuscht haben; der geduldig schwarz ausgepinselte Himmel verrät auch kein naturverbundenes Stürmen und Drängen, sondern eher die desengagierte Tätigkeit des Kopisten oder Plakatmalers. Man ist infolgedessen hin und her gerissen zwischen zwei Lesarten der Arbeit: Ist sie das authentische Zeugnis selbstversunkenen Zeichnens in der Natur, als das sie ihr Titel ausweist – oder das Genrezitat, die grossformatige Reproduktion einer konventionellen Vorlage, als die sie ihre Ausführung erscheinen lässt?

Für das Moment der Reproduktion spricht, dass die Zeichnungen im Negativ ausgeführt sind und dementsprechend wie Schablonen wirken. Für das Moment der Authentizität spricht, dass die graphische Qualität und Motivwahl der Tuschen die Aura altehrwürdiger Stiche evozieren, die Zeichnungen sich demzufolge als intime Projektionsflächen persönlicher Sehnsüchte anbieten. Schablone oder Stich? Öffentliches Medium oder private Devotionalie?

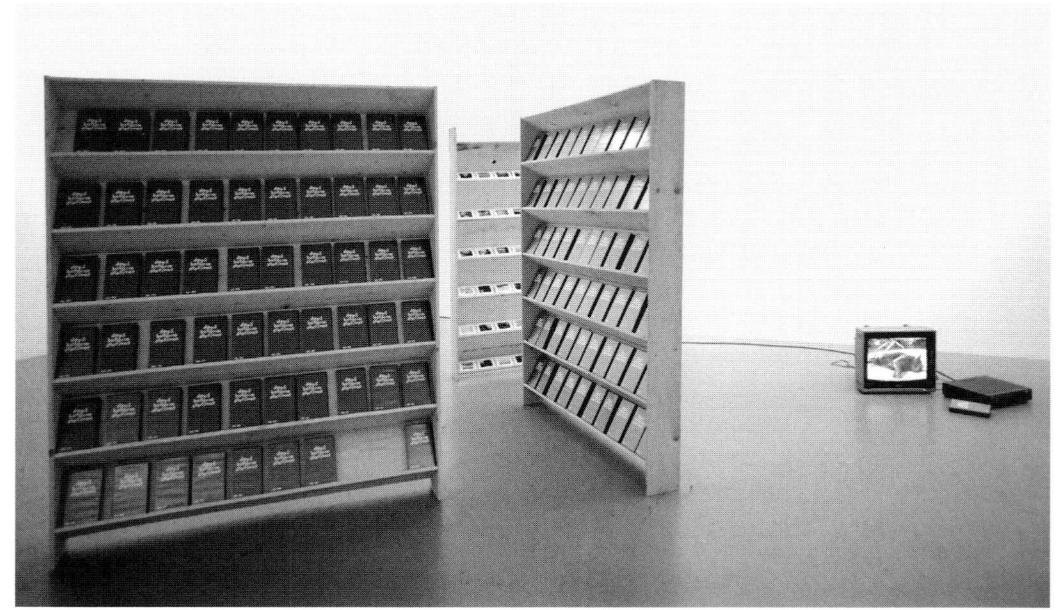

UGO RONDINONE, DAYS BETWEEN STATIONS, 1993–1997, 180 VHS PAL videos, 60 min. each, 3 wooden shelves, 90½ x 65¾ x 7⅞″ each, 180 video prints / TAGE ZWISCHEN STATIONEN, 180 VHS PAL Videos à 60 Min., 3 Tannenholzregale, je 203 x 167 x 20 cm, 180 Videoprints.

Die Installation umfasst noch weitere Elemente: Girlanden aus Zigaretten, die, auf Fäden aufgezogen, von der Decke hängen – und mehrere Displayregale mit Videobändern. Je nach Wahl können die Videos auf zwei Monitoren angeschaut werden, sie zeigen Alltagsszenen, aufgenommen mit statischer Kamera. Der stilvolle Solipsismus des einsam kettenrauchenden Westernhelden trifft auf die wohlige Desintegration des Hausmanns, der sich mit jedem Stück Aussenwelt, das er archiviert, mehr ins Reich seiner Heimvideothek zurückzieht. Beide kultivieren sie Genüsse, die man allein geniesst – in denen man sein Alleinsein geniesst. Ihre Welten grüssen sich in der intensiven Melancholie, die sie ausstrahlen. Sie treten auseinander beim Gedanken an ihre näheren Umstände: die grosse Weite von Marlboro-Country einerseits, die heimische Enge des Videoarchivs andererseits.

Durch die Kombination verschiedenster Motive der Melancholie – romantische Landschaften, schwermütige Countrymusik, Zigarettenkult, Videonirwana – baut Ugo Rondinone in THE HEART IS A LONELY HUNTER eine dichte Stimmung und starke Identifikationen mit den Ikonen und Praktiken melancholischen Selbstgenusses auf.

Zugleich jedoch legt er die formalen Implikationen und inhaltlichen Referenzen der Motive so an, dass die Bedingungen ihrer Vermittlung, ihre Abhängigkeit und Medialität einsichtig werden. Das Pendeln zwischen Identifikation und Distanznahme, in das man infolgedessen gerät, entspricht irgendwie den Schleifen, in denen die Countrymusik ein- und aussetzt. Die Pausen perforieren die Atmosphäre, jeder Einsatz erzeugt sie neu: Für einen Moment distanziert, versinkt man bald erneut in der Stimmung, um so genussvoller, weil es wider das bessere Wissen geschieht, dass das bessere Wissen einen wieder einholen wird – O.K., Cowboy, let's get lost…

«Dizzy – my head is spinning like a whirlpool…» [4]

Ein anderes Motiv, das Ugo Rondinone in Serie produziert, ist die Zielscheibe – grossformatige, konzentrisch angeordnete Kreise, in variierenden Bonbonfarben gesprayt. Die *Targets* funktionieren direkt: Die Sogwirkung der konzentrischen Komposition setzt ein, alles fängt an, sich zu drehen und groovy zu leuchten. Durch pulsierende Kreise induzierte Trancezustände sind jedem geläufig – die hypnotische Geometrie des Mandalas ist vertraut: Seit den 60er Jahren ist sie ein Popemblem für Psychedelik, für das Abtauchen im Sog der eigenen Psyche, für den Selbstgenuss durch Selbsthypnose. Unvermeidlich also schiesst das bessere Wissen um die Konventionalität der Targets mit dem von ihnen erzeugten Rauschgefühl zusammen. Rausch und Ernüchterung: *Ceci n'est pas une discothèque* – man steht in einer Galerie vor einem Schmuckstück aus Sprayfarbe und Leinwand.

Selbstgenuss durch Selbsthypnose, wie man ihn vom Tanzen kennt. Ernüchterung, wie sie einen nach dem Tanzen am Rand der Tanzfläche überkommt – wenn aus der Distanz besehen im exhibitionistischen Autismus der Tanzenden die peinliche Realität des eigenen Authentizitätsrauschs erkennbar wird. Auf einmal sind die Formen des eigenen Selbstgenusses so einfach zu durchschauen. Eine melancholische Selbstdistanz stellt sich ein, die jedoch nichts von Abgeklärtheit hat, denn selbstverständlich bleibt man bei dem, was einem das gute Gefühl vom Selbst gibt. Natürlich will und wird man sich weiterhin in Mandalas versenken und sich beim Tanzen authentisch fühlen. Davon handelt der Titel der Ausstellung, in der die Targets zuletzt zu sehen waren – «Still Smoking» [5] –, vom melancholischen Festhalten an Obsessionen, über deren Umstände und Motive man aufgeklärt ist.

«*Pictures came and broke my heart…*»

Freud beschreibt die Melancholie als das gespaltene Verhältnis, in dem ein Subjekt zum Gegenstand seiner Liebe steht, nachdem dieser ihm entzogen wurde.[6] Nach dem erlittenen Rückschlag probiert der Melancholiker zunächst zwar, sich aus seiner emotionalen Bindung zu lösen und Distanz zum verlorenen Objekt seiner Liebe zu gewinnen – es stellt sich jedoch bald heraus, dass er nicht von ihm lassen kann: Er ist hin- und hergerissen zwischen dem obsessiven Festhalten an der verlorenen Liebe und dem besseren Wissen um die Unwiederbringlichkeit ihres Verlusts. Er ist somit im selben Masse rational distanziert von seiner Liebe, wie er emotional in sie involviert bleibt. Dieser Zwiespalt begründet seine reflektierte Wehmut.

Es gibt die lange Rede von der Melancholie als Charakterzug des kontemplativen Menschen. Es gibt Bilder über die Melancholie. Und es gibt Bilder, zu denen man selbst in einem melancholischen Verhältnis steht. Letztere sind die Bilder, die man geliebt hat, weil man sich so mit ihnen identifizierte, dass man glaubte, dass sie einen selbst und nur einen selbst identifizierten – Bilder also, die man für den authentischen Ausdruck der eigenen Einzigartigkeit hielt, denen man deswegen glaubte, auf ewig treu zu bleiben. Eine Treue, die die Bilder brachen: Denn sie hatten vor und neben einem immer schon massenweise andere Liebhaber und stellten sich schliesslich als die Klischees einer Kultur heraus, die sich einen Spass daraus macht, einem für befristete Zeit das Gefühl zu vermitteln, zum Individuum auserkoren zu sein.

Diesen Bildern, den Medien der eigenen Individuation, bleibt man in Melancholie verbunden: Es ist weder möglich, das Bedürfnis nach einem authentischen Verhältnis zu ihnen aufzugeben, noch die enttäuschende Einsicht in ihre Promiskuität zu verwinden. Die Erinnerung an sie treibt einen um und zwingt dazu, den Konflikt mit ihnen immer wieder und wieder zu reinszenieren. Sei es, um den Bildern das Eingeständnis abzutrotzen, dass sie einem schliesslich noch einiges schulden, weil sie es waren, in die man seine Gefühle investiert hat – sei es, um den melancholischen Zwiespalt zwischen Identifikation und Distanznahme als ebendas Selbstgefühl auszuleben, in dem das über seine Bedingtheit aufgeklärte Subjekt sich auf seine je eigene Weise erfährt.

Was für ein Subjekt ist es genau, das sich im Zwiespalt dieser Melancholie konstituiert? Es handelt sich um eine Form der Subjektivität, die so als erstes der Dandy[7] verkörpert hat: Der Dandy ist ein Genussmensch; er lebt für die raffinierten Genüsse, die ihm erlesene ästhetische Erfahrungen vermitteln. Der Dandy ist zugleich aber auch ein reflexiv distanzierter Beobachter seiner selbst; er weiss nur allzu gut um das Vermittelte seiner Genüsse. Der *Spleen*, der den Dandy charakterisiert, ist ebendie Melancholie, die ihn befällt, wenn die Reflexion ihm schon im Moment des ästhetischen Genusses dessen Vermitteltheit vor Augen führt. Eine Melancholie, deren Ambivalenz und Dekadenz darin liegt, dass sie zutiefst in ebenden Genüssen schwelgt, deren Hinfälligkeit sie einsieht.

«*Dreaming of Me*»[8]

Der Spleen ist nun kein Privileg der Noblesse mehr. Selbstgenuss in den 90er Jahren ist immer leicht spleenig, denn die Popkultur hat ihre Kinder freigebig mit einer Diät aus Sentimentalität und Selbstreflexivität zu Dandys aufgezogen: Der Popdandy weiss um die ästhetischen Oberflächen, denen er seine Subjektivität verdankt, und er geniesst es, sie und sich zugleich ganz

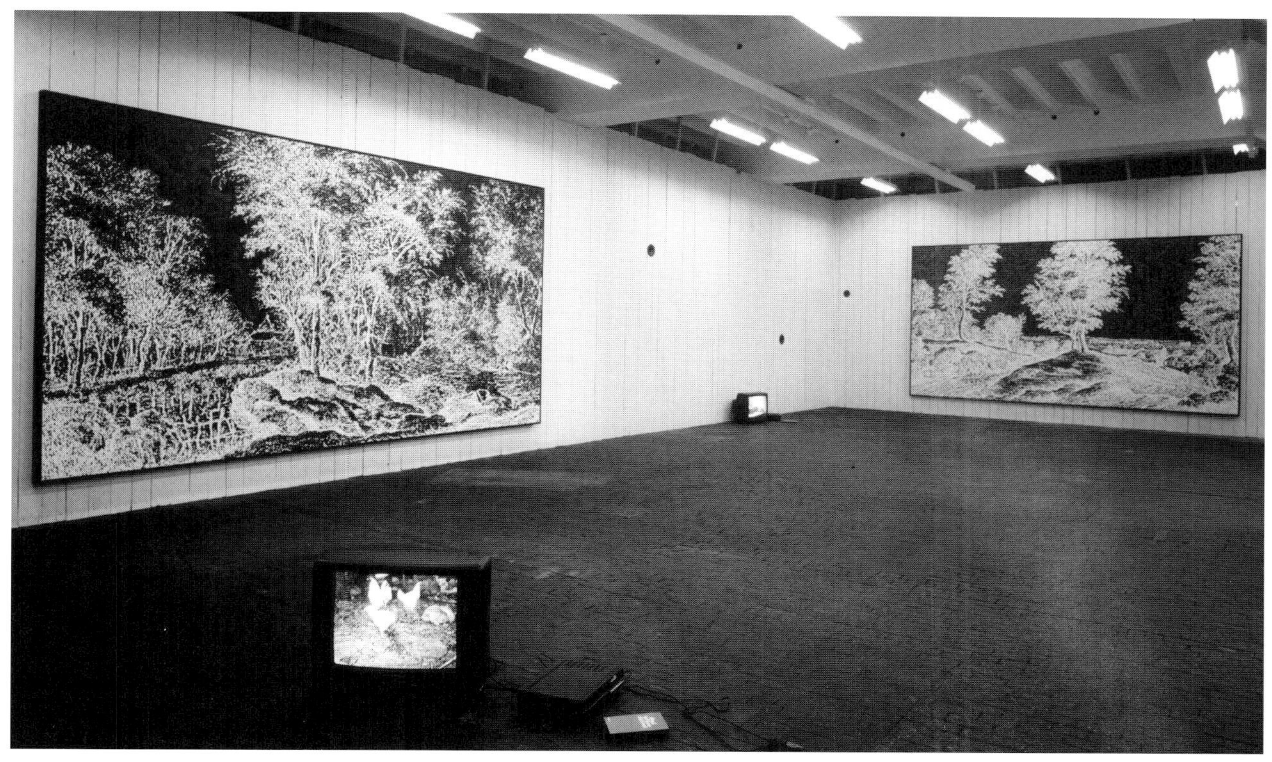

UGO RONDINONE, HEYDAY, 1995/96, installation views, Centre d'Art Contemporain, Genève / HÖHEPUNKT, Installationsansichten.

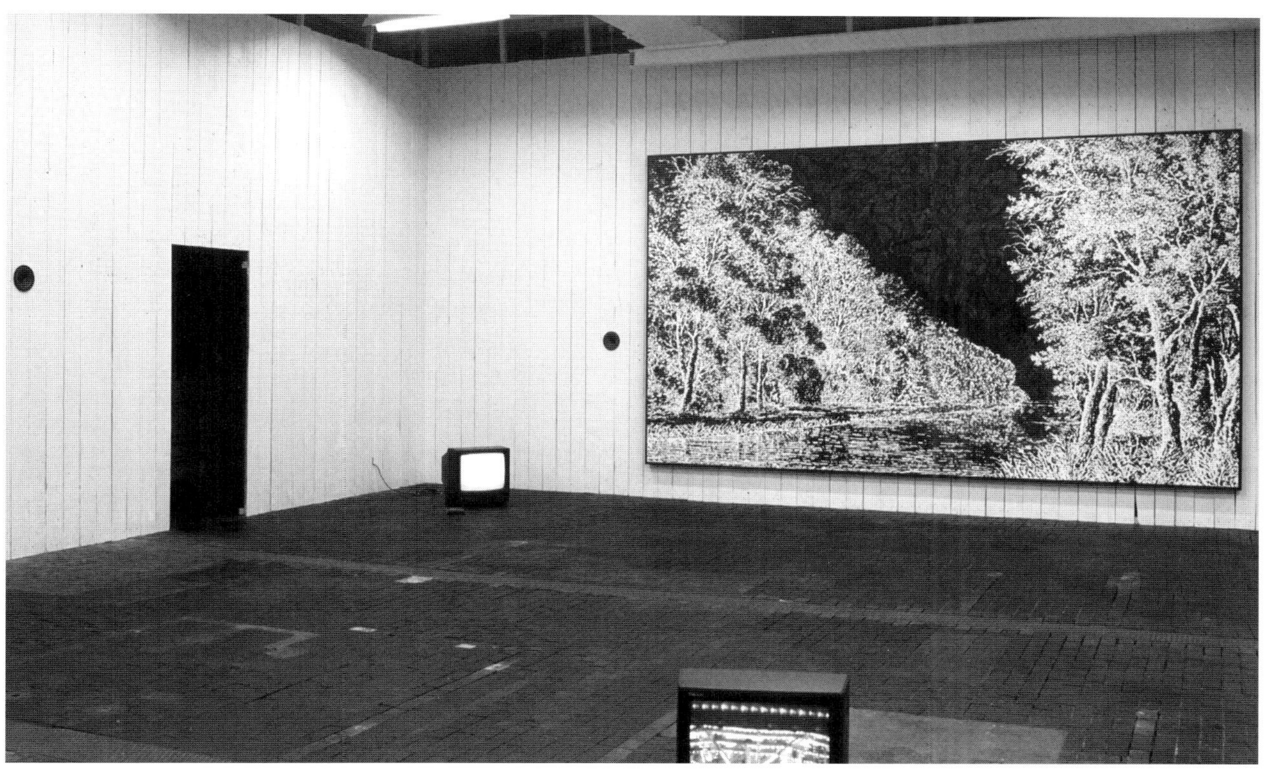

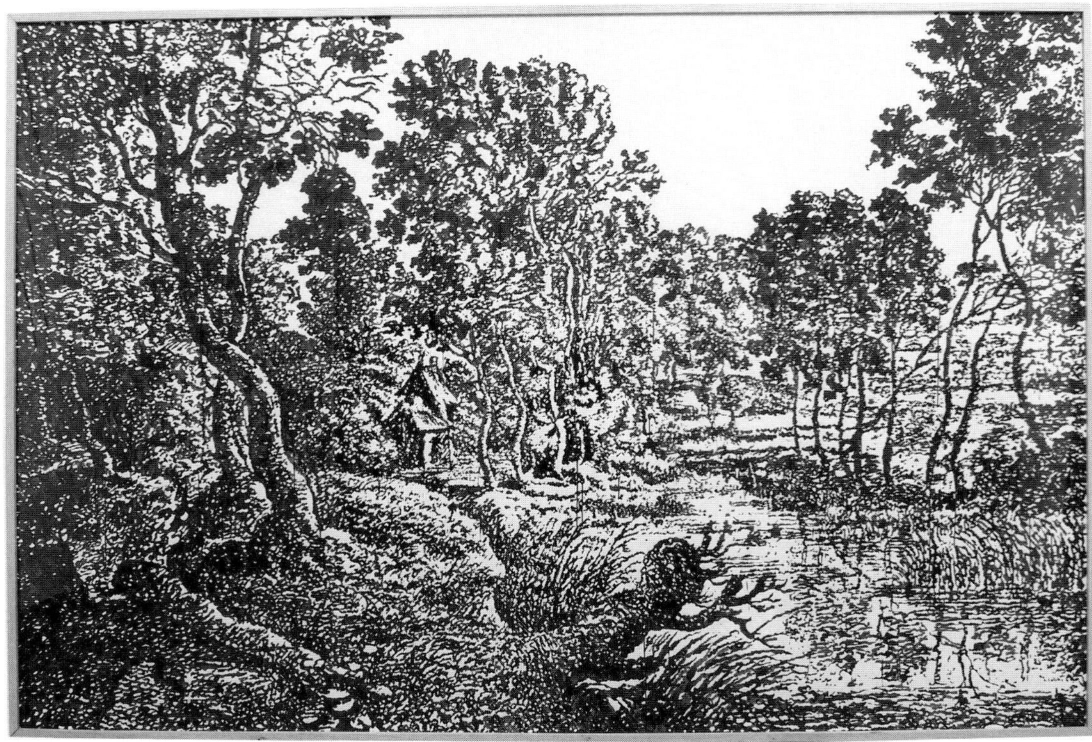

UGO RONDINONE, NO. 80, ACHTZEHNTERJUNINEUNZEHNHUNDERTSECHSUNDNEUNZIG, 1997,
Tusche auf Papier, 300 x 200 cm / JUNEEIGHTEENTHNINETEENHUNDREDNINETYSIX, ink on paper, 118⅛ x 78¾".

ernst und ganz ironisch aufzufassen. Seine Melancholie artikuliert sich in Campness, er zelebriert seine Sehnsüchte genussvoll in einem Mix aus überbordender Empathie und liebevoller Selbstironie. Der Schauplatz seiner Selbstinszenierung ist sein ästhetisches Universum, ein isolierter Raum, der gefüllt ist mit den Medien seiner Sehnsucht, mit den Bildern, der Musik, die er liebt.[9] Mit ihnen spielt er das Spiel von sentimentaler Identifikation und reflektierter Selbstdistanzierung, das ihn in den Genuss seines melancholisch gespaltenen Selbst bringt.

Solche Räume zu schaffen ist das Prinzip der Installationen von Ugo Rondinone. Jede Installation definiert einen *state of mind*, eine Befindlichkeit des dandyesken Subjekts. Jede Installation ist ein genau abgestimmtes Arrangement bestimmter Schlüsselmotive ästhetisch vermittelten Selbstgefühls – und kreiert so einen Schauplatz, auf dem der innere Konflikt mit den Bildern, Geschichten etc. ausgetragen wird, denen das dandyeske Selbst sich und seine Sehnsüchte verdankt.

Das Stilmittel, das Rondinone dabei wiederholt einsetzt, um die Stimmung melancholischer Selbstisolation und Introspektion zu erzeugen, ist die Wandverschalung aus Holzbohlen mit eingelassenen Lautsprechern. In seiner jüngsten Installation MOONLIGHT AND ASPIRIN[10] ist eine solche Verschalung an der Stirnwand des Galerieraums installiert. Symbolisch nach aussen abgeschottet, vermittelt der Raum ein Gefühl des Insichgekehrtseins. In die Holzwand ist zudem ein Fenster aus purpurnem Glas eingefügt: Das Tageslicht fällt veredelt herein, ästhetisiert und emotional eingefärbt – kein reales Licht mehr, sondern das *Virtual Light* subjektivierter Wahrnehmung. Assoziiert mit ihm tönt aus den Lautsprechern in Endlosschleife der melancholische Refrain «Everyday Sunshine... Everyday Sunshine...». Die Atmosphäre ist fürstlich, wohlig warm und trist.

In jedem der beiden Ausstellungsräume ist jeweils ein ganz in Tesapack eingewickelter Orangenbaum installiert, der an seinen Ästen kleine Lautsprechermembranen trägt. Die Verpflanzung der Bäume in den Innenraum hat ihnen die Züge des melancholischen Dandys aufgeprägt. Sein ästhetisch distanzierter Blick lässt sie einsam in ihrer Zeichenhaftigkeit erstarren, mumifiziert sie in Artifizialität. Seine empathische Phantasie hingegen erweckt sie zu virtuellen Gesprächspartnern seines inneren Monologs: Zeitversetzt und in grossen Abständen beginnen die Bäume zu erzählen. Unter dem einen Baum ist eine Shortstory von Bukowski, unter dem anderen eine von Carver zu hören.

Umgeben sind die Bäume von vier grossformatigen Schwarzweissphotos: Modeaufnahmen im Hard edge-Stil der Sixties, auf denen ein mondänes Model posiert, mal nackt, mal im kleinen Schwarzen, mal lasziv die Selbstgedrehte zuleckend und mal im Pelzchen gelangweilt auf der Ledercouch loungend. Die Photos erzählen den Traum des Dandys, wie das Model ganz und gar ästhetisch zu sein, den Traum vom Luxus des perfekten Körpers und der erhabenen Langeweile der perfekten Seele. Sein melancholischer Konflikt ist den Bildern eingeschrieben – Ugo Rondinone hat den weiblichen Modelkörpern sein Gesicht aufmontiert. Eine Identifikation, die zugleich möglich und unmöglich, zugleich überzeugend und komisch wirkt.

Zumal Rondinone eine Miene macht, die die Differenz zwischen Gesicht und Körper zugleich behauptet und abstreitet. Sein Blick ist souverän distanziert, als würde er seine absurde Physiognomie stoisch zur Kenntnis nehmen – und nonchalant, als würde er in aller Selbstverständlichkeit fragen: Ich bin's doch nur, ist was?

Ugo Rondinone handelt in seinen Installationen also von einer bestimmten Form des Selbstverhältnisses: von einem Selbstgenuss, der in der gebrochenen Identifikation mit den Motiven der eigenen Authentizitäts-Sehnsüchte entsteht – von einer Melancholie, in der sich die Lust an der eigenen Unmittelbarkeit mit dem Wissen um das Vermittelte dieses Selbstgefühls mischt – von der melancholischen Freude darüber, sich just in dem Moment in den eigenen Sehnsüchten wiederzuerkennen, wo sie einem im Genuss als vermittelte vor Augen treten.

1) The Buggles: «Video killed the Radio Star», 1979.

2) Die Installation war Teil der Ausstellung «Hip» im Museum für Gegenwartskunst Zürich (8.11.97–4.1.98).

3) So in etwa liesse sich zumindest Wolf Lepenies' Sicht der Dinge zusammenfassen, in: *Melancholie und Gesellschaft*, Suhrkamp, Frankfurt am Main 1969.

4) Aus einem Song von Tommy Roe: «Dizzy», 1969.

5) In der Galleria Raucci/Santamaria, Neapel (9.12.97–22.1.98). Die Targets sind hier kombiniert mit zwei Serien an die Wand gedübelter Lautsprecher, aus denen ein melancholisches Popsample kommt; der Refrain «Everyday Sunshine» in Endlosschleife. Die Fenster der Galerie sind blau verglast. Auf vier Monitoren läuft je ein Videoloop: ein Mann unter der Dusche, bekleidet; einer beim Stiefellecken; einer beim Verlassen eines Wohnblocks; ein nackter Torso, der sich langsam ins Bild, einen urbanen Nachthimmel, hebt und wieder absinkt. Die Stimmung im Raum ist ein Mix aus Obsessivität und Nüchternheit.

6) Sigmund Freud, «Trauer und Melancholie», in: *Gesammelte Schriften*, Bd. V., S. Fischer, London 1948, S. 535–553.

7) Ich benutze für den Dandy, seinem grammatikalischen Genus entsprechend, maskuline Pronomina. Das soll nicht heissen, dass der Sexus des leibhaftigen Dandys nur männlich sein kann. Die Figur des Dandys ist für beide Geschlechter zugänglich.

8) Depeche Mode: «Dreaming of Me», 1981.

9) Das Vorbild des Dandys, der aus dem Sozialen in eine private Welt aus subjektiv ästhetischen Bezügen flieht, ist Huysmans' Jean Floressas des Esseintes, in: *Gegen den Strich*, Frankfurt am Main 1972.

10) Galleria Bonomo, Rom (3.12.97–30.1.98).

JAN VERWOERT

"*Pictures came and*

"*If you don't want my love…*"

The voice drags wearily from note to note in two or three measures of dismal country music accompanying Ugo Rondinone's installation, THE HEART IS A LONELY HUNTER.[2] The brief sample dribbles over and over again at intervals out of a dozen speakers of various sizes, inserted at different heights into wooden planking. Every note sounds even more drawn-out and deeper than the original from Souled American, which is already infinitely prolonged: "If you don't want my l-o-o-o-v-e…" There's only one thing for the lonesome cowboy and his unrequited love to do. They ride off into the sunset vanishing into the endless expanses of the prairie. Not so the melancholic of the Old World. He vanishes into the loneliness of picturesque, wooded landscapes, such as those shown in the drawings which form the backdrop for the installation. Country music and sylvan idyll: Rondinone blends the two genres and creates a taut mood of melancholy.

The pictures are large-format, black-and-white drawings in ink, so large that the wide-screen effect sets in: The horizon opens out and you are drawn into the depicted landscape, into lonely forests broken only by the occasional stream or clearing. The scenario instantly fills you with melancholy. That good, pleasurably mournful feeling of the self sets in—pleasurable, because it gives you the certainty that no one else on earth could possibly feel as poignantly sad at this moment; the certainty, in other words, of authentic individuality.

But the feeling also reminds us that images of this kind have always been the source of such pleasurably self-indulgent melancholy, and the reminder goes hand in hand with the insight that the sylvan idyll is not that isolated after all, that someone else has inevitably been there before: we ourselves, long ago—for the purpose of "finding ourselves," with soulful gaze and Goethe's *Young Werther* tucked into a coat pocket, Werther hugging his cherished Ossian and sobbing his heart out at the bosom of nature—and ultimately the whole of bourgeois society, having turned the birch copse into the regulation stomping grounds of self-searching rituals. Is perhaps melancholy simply the classical technique of the bourgeoisie for gleaning self-esteem out of self-pity?[3]

The motifs of Udo Rondinone's installations bring their own history along. They compel us to reflect on their context, provenance, and form: reflection that deconstructs the once homogeneous atmosphere of the space. But deconstruction means both breaking down and tighten-

---

JAN VERWOERT is a student of art history and philosophy, a free-lance critic, and bass-player for Sexpop.

broke my heart..."[1)]

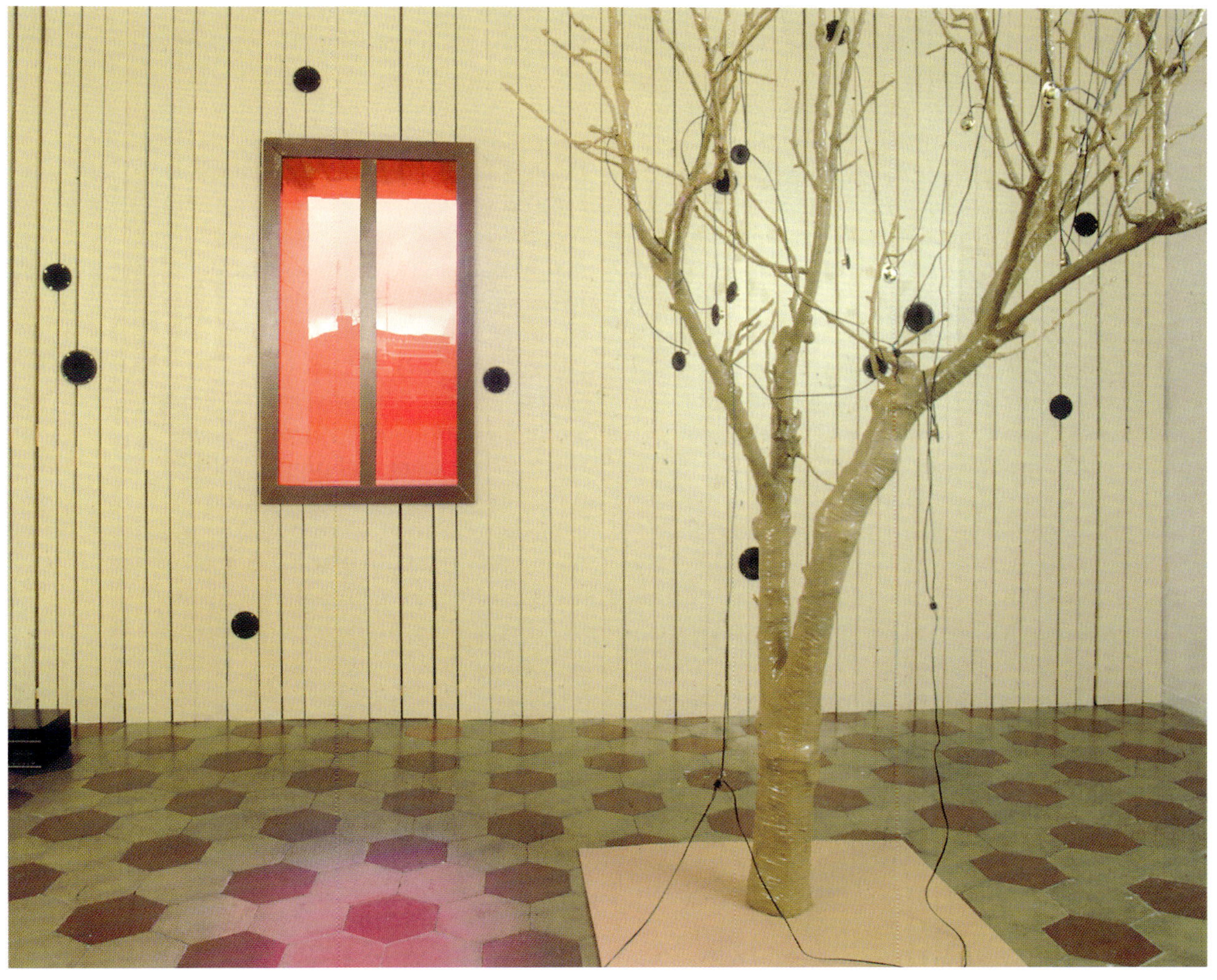

ing up. The mood, though broken, is sustained because emotional identification with the motifs and detached reflection on them remain united side by side despite the appearance of disunity. Rondinone's works have an ambivalent effect by simultaneously encouraging and alienating feelings of authenticity.

To begin with, take the titles of the drawings: Rondinone merely dates them—a biographical index that heightens their claim to authenticity. The fact that the drawings express unity of time, place, and the artist's mood at the moment of their making is perfectly credible, but then the thought comes to mind that the formal composition of the drawing actually undermines this claim. Given the format, they couldn't possibly have been inked freehand *en plein air*. Nor does the sky, patiently filled in with black brushstrokes, reveal an impassioned closeness to nature; it is more like the disinterested product of the copyist or poster artist. We are thus torn between two readings: Does the work bear authentic witness to self-absorbed depiction in nature, as indicated by the title, or does it borrow genre painting in the large-format reproduction of a conventional model, as implied by its execution?

The reading as reproduction is supported by the fact that the drawings are executed in the negative and therefore resemble templates. The reading as authenticity is supported by the fact that the graphic quality and choice of motif evoke the aura of venerable etchings; the drawings could then be said to comport themselves like intimate projected planes of personal longings. Template or etching? Public medium or private devotional?

Other elements flesh out the installation: garlands of cigarettes strung across the ceiling and several shelves of videos. Videos can be chosen and watched on two monitors. They show scenes of everyday life, shot with a stationary camera. The refined solipsism of a lonesome, chain-smoking westerner is juxtaposed with the cozy disintegration of the househusband, whose retreat into the empire of his personal video library intensifies with every piece of outside world that he files away. Both cultivate pleasures that are enjoyed alone, that enhance the enjoyment of being alone. Their worlds make contact in the intensity of a shared melancholy; they diverge at the thought of their specific circumstances: the great wide world of Marlboro country versus the snug confines of the domestic video archives.

In Ugo Rondinone's THE HEART IS A LONELY HUNTER the combined but diverse motifs of melancholy—romantic landscapes, nostalgic country music, the cigarette cult, video nirvana—generate a dense atmosphere and compelling identification with the icons and practice of self-indulgent melancholy pleasures. But the formal implications and contextual references of the motifs are designed to lay open the conditions of their mediation: their conditionality and mediacy. Our consequent wavering between identification and detachment might be compared to the on-and-off of the loops in Rondinone's country music sample. The pauses perforate the atmosphere, which is regenerated with every new entry. Disengaged for a moment, you sink into the mood again all the more pleasurably because it happens against your better judgment that your better judgment will catch up with you again—OK cowboy, let's get lost...

"Dizzy—my head is spinning like a whirlpool..."[4]

Another motif that Ugo Rondinone produces serially is the target—large-format, concentric circles sprayed in a variety of candy colors. The impact of the targets is immediate: the pull of the concentric composition takes effect; everything begins to spin with a groovy luminosity. The trance-like states induced by the pulsating circles are familiar. So is the hypnotic geometry of the mandala, the sixties' pop emblem of psychedelia, of plunging into the maelstrom of one's own psyche, of the self-indulgent pleasure of self-hypnosis. Predictably, our better judgment of the target's conventions collides with the rapture of intoxication. Getting high and coming down: *ceci n'est pas une discothèque*, but rather a gallery with a decorative piece of lacquered canvas mounted on the wall.

Self-indulgence through self-hypnosis, the feeling is familiar from dancing. So is coming down afterwards, standing at the edge of the dance floor where the autistic exhibitionism of the dancers, now seen from a distance, confronts us with the embarrassing reality of having been stoned on authenticity. Suddenly it is so easy to see through the outgrowths of our own self-indulgence. However, there is nothing limpid about the resulting melancholy self-detachment since we naturally stick to the things that flatter the ego. Of course, we want to and will continue to immerse ourselves in mandalas and to feel authentic when we dance. The title of the exhibition in which the targets were most recently seen—"Still Smoking"[5]—addresses this attitude—the melancholy attachment to obsessions about whose circumstances and motives we are all too well informed.

"Pictures came and broke my heart..."

Freud describes melancholy as the ambivalent relationship of the subject to the object of his love, upon having been deprived of it.[6] Having suffered defeat, the melancholic seeks to sever his emotional ties and to liberate himself from the lost object of his desires, only to discover that he cannot let go. He is torn between obsessively clinging to his lost love and the better judgment that the loss is irrevocable. He is, thus, as rationally detached from his love as he is emotionally involved. This ambivalence underlies his contemplative melancholy.

There is a lot of talk about melancholy being the trait of contemplative people. There are pictures of melancholy. And there are pictures with which we have a melancholy relationship. The latter are pictures we once loved because of our profound identification with them in the belief that they identified our singular selves. We thought these pictures were the authentic expression of our own uniqueness and therefore swore eternal allegiance to them. But they betrayed us because they already had masses of other lovers before and beside us, ultimately proving to be the clichés of a culture that enjoys deluding us into thinking, for a time, that we are among those chosen to be individuals.

The melancholy ties to these pictures, the media of our own individuation, do not fade. We can neither relinquish the need to have an authentic relationship with them, nor can we master our disappointment at their promiscuity. Their memory is harrowing and forces us to relive the

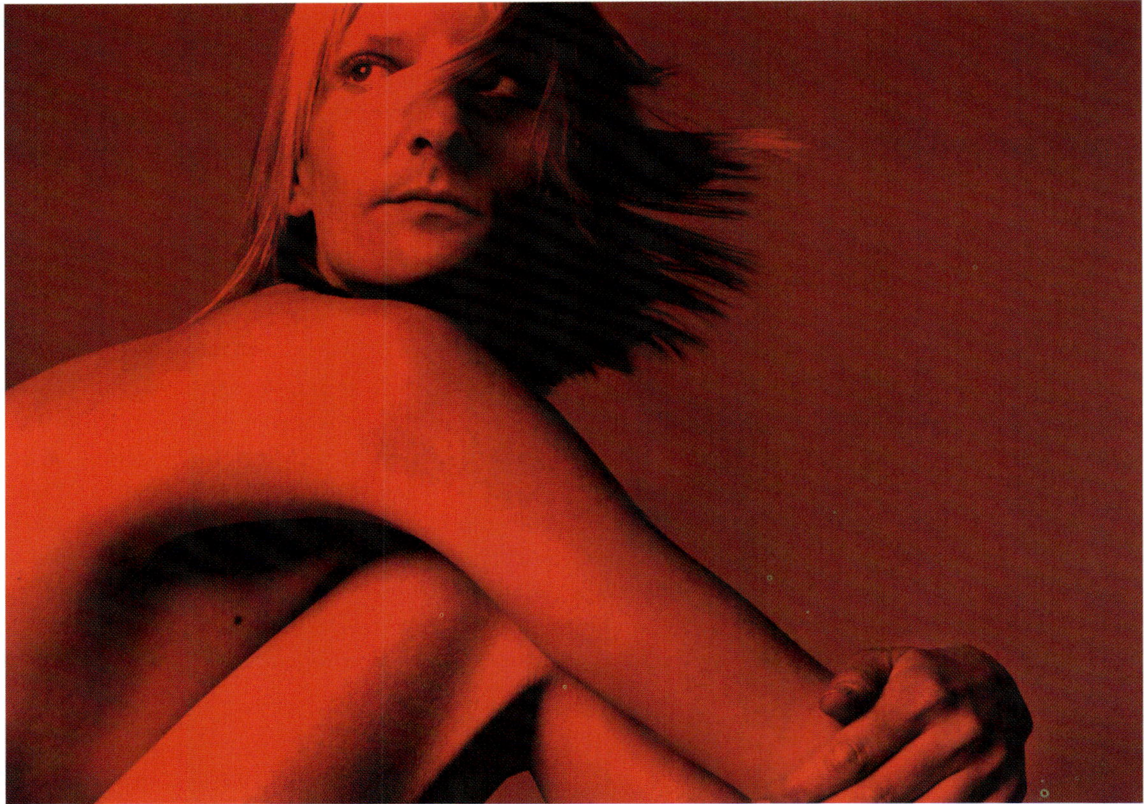

conflict over and over again: be it to make them admit that they do owe us something after all, since we gave them so much of our emotional selves; be it to act out the melancholy ambivalence between identification and detachment, as precisely that feeling of the self through which subjects can experience themselves in the knowledge of their own conditionality.

Exactly what is the nature of subjects that constitute themselves in the ambivalence of this melancholy? It is a form of subjectivity that was originally embodied by the dandy.[7] The dandy is a hedonist. He lives for the refined pleasures that obtain in highly select aesthetic experiences. At the same time, the dandy is a reflexive, detached observer of himself. He knows perfectly well that his pleasures are mediated. The "spleen" that characterizes the dandy is that self-same melancholy that befalls him when aesthetic pleasure is adulterated by cognizance of its mediacy. The ambivalence and decadence of this melancholy lie in the fact that it indulges in those very pleasures whose vanity it cannot deny.

"Dreaming of Me" [8]

The "spleen" is no longer an upper class privilege. Self-indulgence in the nineties is always on the verge of eccentricity because popular culture has raised her children as dandies on a bountiful diet of sentimentality and self-reflexivity: The Pop dandy is aware of the aesthetic surfaces

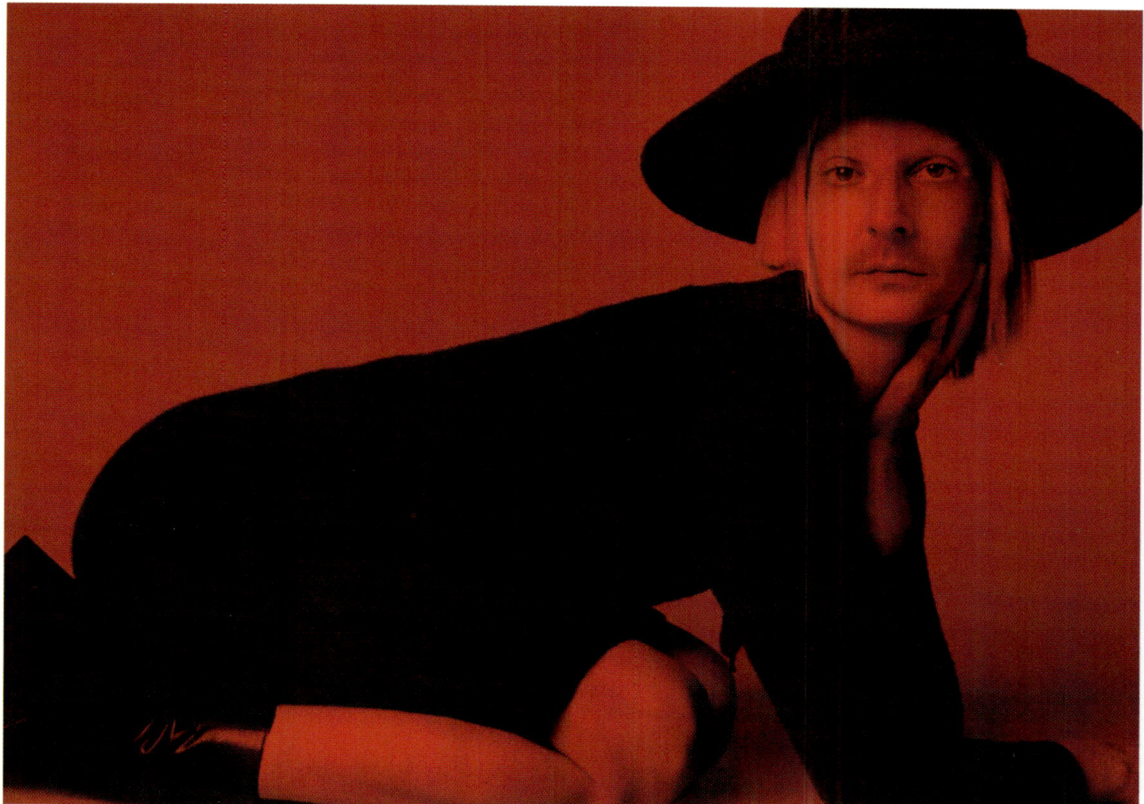

to which he owes his subjectivity and enjoys taking both serious and ironic stabs at it and himself. His melancholy is articulated in camp; he celebrates his longings in a lusty mix of excessive empathy and affectionate self-irony. He acts out his life in a self-devised aesthetic universe, an isolated space that is filled with the media of his longing, with the pictures and the music that he loves.[9] There he plays a game of sentimental identification and contemplative self-detachment that allows him to enjoy his melancholy split ego.

The creation of such spaces is the principle underlying Ugo Rondinone's installations. Each installation defines a dandyesque state of mind. Each installation precisely matches and arranges certain key motifs of aesthetically mediated self-assurance; it creates an arena in which the inner conflict is acted out through pictures and stories, which are the source of the dandyesque self and its longings.

The stylistic device that Rondinone repeatedly marshals in order to generate a mood of melancholy self-isolation and introspection consists of loudspeakers inserted into wooden planking. In his most recent installation, MOONLIGHT AND ASPIRIN,[10] he mounts the boarding on the front wall of the gallery space. Symbolically cut off from the outside world, the room conveys a feeling of being introspectively turned in on oneself. In addition, a window with purple glazing, which is set into the planking, refines, aestheticizes, and emotionally colors the incoming daylight; it is no longer real light but the "virtual light" of subjective perception. In keeping with this illumination, a melancholy refrain sounds from the loudspeakers in a continuous loop "Everyday Sunshine… Everyday Sunshine…" The atmosphere is royal, cozily warm, and dreary.

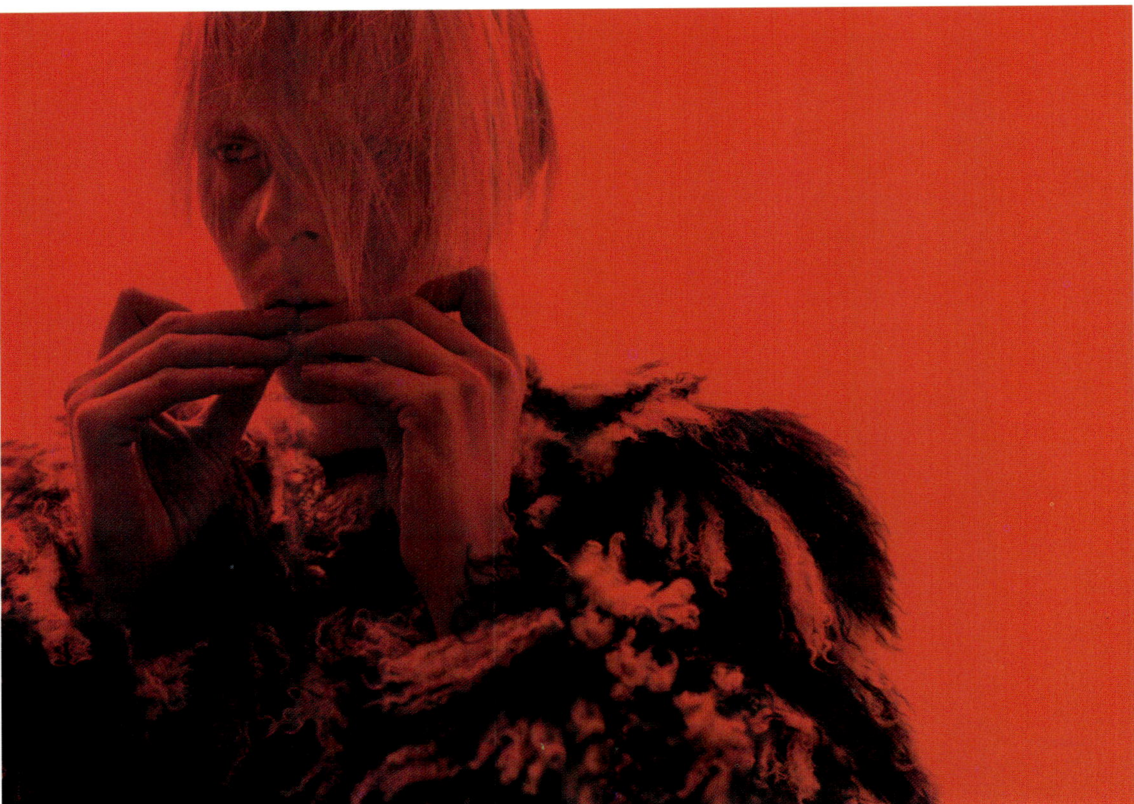

Two completely taped-up orange trees, placed in each of the exhibition spaces, have little speaker membranes attached to their branches. By moving the trees inside, Rondinone imposes upon them the traits of the melancholy dandy. His aesthetically detached gaze freezes them into the loneliness of their emblematic existence and mummifies them in artificiality. His empathetic imagination, on the other hand, arouses them and turns them into virtual partners of his inner monologue: at staggered times and great intervals, the trees begin to talk. Under one tree we hear a short story by Bukowski; under the other one by Carver.

The trees are surrounded by four large-format black-and-white photographs: fashion shots in hard-edged sixties style in which a chic model poses for the camera, sometimes in the nude, sometimes in a little black shift, sometimes lasciviously licking at a hand-rolled cigarette, or dressed in furs and lounging, utterly blasé, on a leather couch. The photographs recount the dandy's dream of an impeccably aesthetic model, the luxurious dream of the perfect body and the lofty boredom of the perfect soul. The melancholy conflict is inscribed in the pictures, for Ugo Rondinone has mounted his own face on the body of the woman model—an identification that is both possible and impossible, both convincing and funny.

…especially since Rondinone makes a face that at once asserts and denies the difference between face and body. His gaze is superior, detached, as if in stoic acceptance of his absurd physiognomy—and casual as if he were merely asking: It's only me, and so?

Ugo Rondinone's installations thus take a specific approach to the relationship with the self: They deal with the self-indulgence that arises through a broken identification with the motives

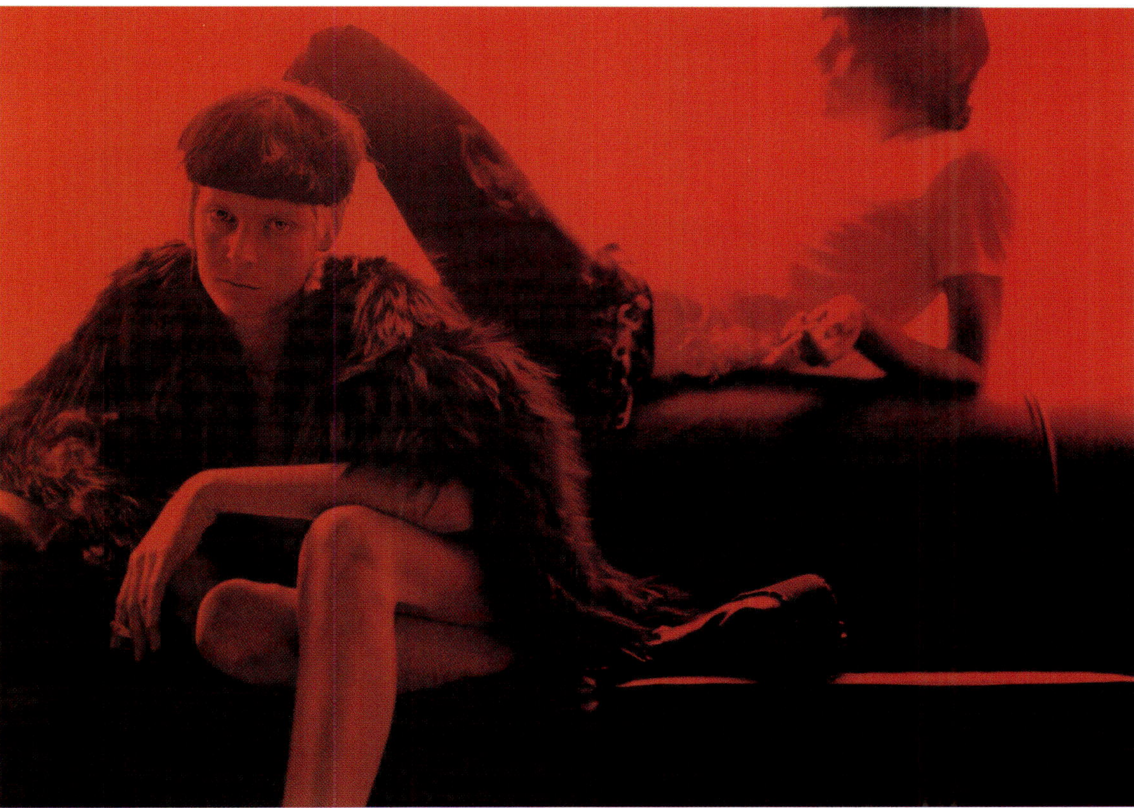

of one's own yearnings for authenticity; with a melancholy in which the pleasure of one's own immediacy is adulterated by the knowledge that these feelings are mediated; with the melancholy joy of recognizing oneself in one's own yearnings at the very moment of their obviously mediated pleasure.

(Translation: Catherine Schelbert)

1) The Buggles: "Video killed the Radio Star," 1979.
2) The installation was part of the exhibition "Hip" at the Zurich Museum of Contemporary Art (8 November 97–4 January 98).
3) That would at least sum up Wolf Lepenies's view of things, in: *Melancholie und Gesellschaft*, Frankfurt/M.: Suhrkamp, 1996.
4) Tommy Roe: "Dizzy," 1969.
5) At the Galleria Raucci/Santamari, Naples (9 September 97–22 January 98). Here the targets were combined with two series of speakers doweled to the wall, playing a melancholy pop sample: the refrain "Everday Sunshine" in a loop. The windows of the gallery had blue glazing. Four different video loops were running in four monitors: a fully-dressed man in the shower; a man licking boots; a man leaving an apartment building; a naked torso, slowly rising and dropping out of a picture of an urban sky at night. The mood in the room is a mix of obsessiveness and sobriety.
6) Sigmund Freud, "Trauer und Melancholie," in: *Gesammelte Schriften V* (London, 1948), pp. 535–553.
7) I use the masculine pronoun in speaking of a dandy but that does not mean that a dandy is necessarily male. The figure of the dandy is accessible to both genders.
8) Depeche Mode: "Dreaming of Me," 1981.
9) The model of a dandy who escapes from society into a private world of subjective aesthetic relations is J.-K. Huysmans' Jean Floressas des Esseintes, in: *A Rebours/Against Nature* (Paris: Groves & Michaux, 1926).
10) Galleria Bonomo, Rome (3 December 97–30 January 98).

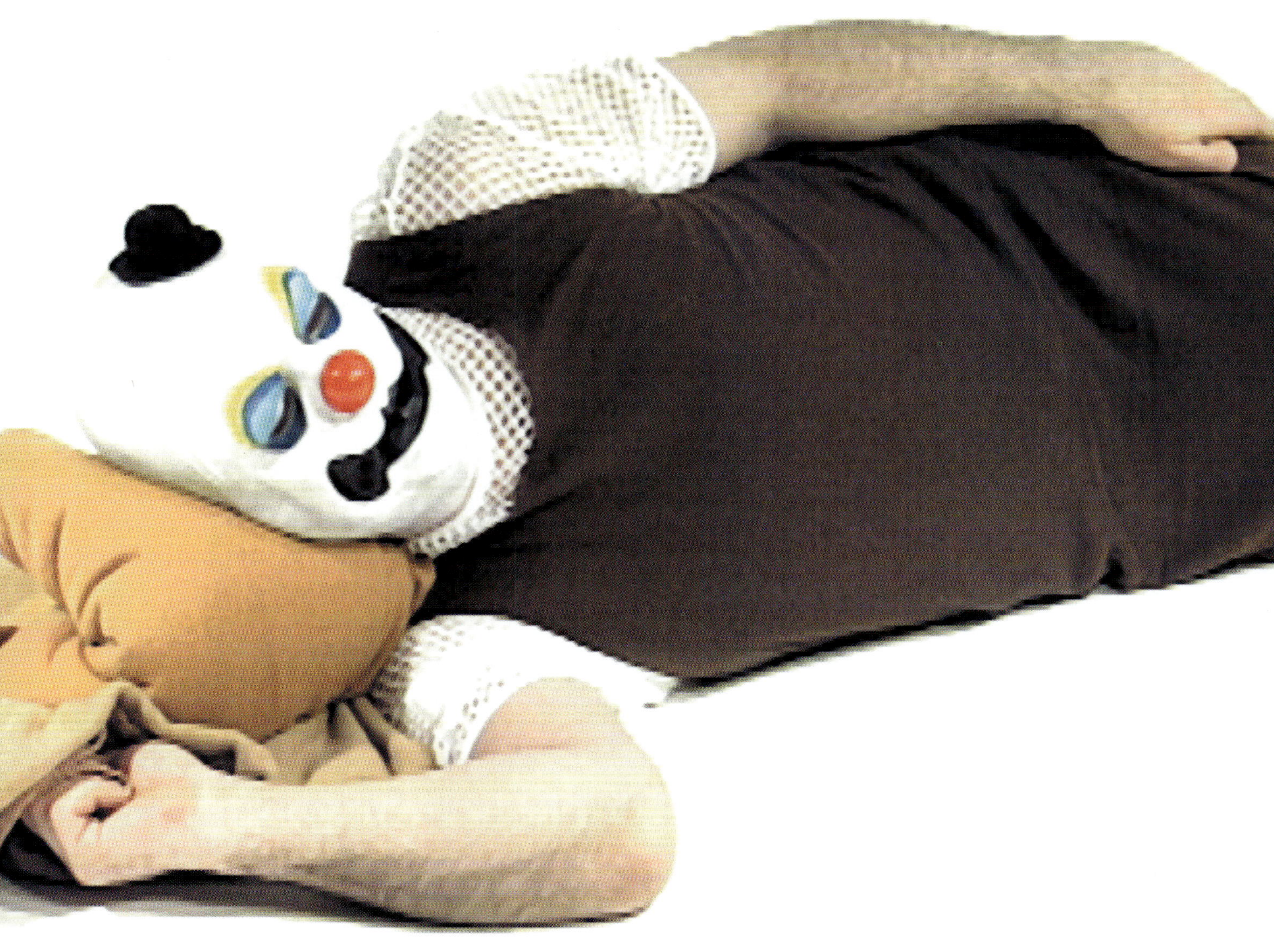

UGO RONDINONE, DOGDAYS ARE OVER, 1995, *video still / DIE HUNDSTAGE SIND VORBEI, Videostill.*

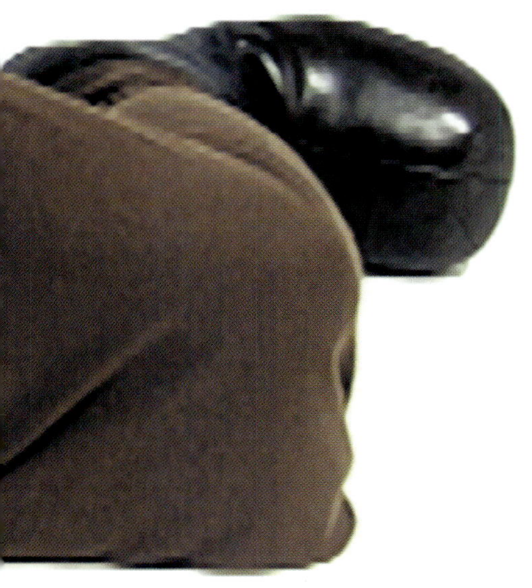

Against Nature

LAURA HOPTMAN

On a rough-hewn boarded floor in an empty gallery, a young man, looking very much like the artist Ugo Rondinone, slumps against a wall, still and waxen, staring without seeing. Through a large picture window that dominates the end of the room and gives onto a busy street, passersby glance in periodically. The figure's desperation is palpable. The figure is a dummy.

This installation by Rondinone, at the Galerie Walcheturm in Zurich in 1995, is a complex comparative reflection on the conflict between the real and the artificial, and the artist's role as the mediating force between the two. As such it can serve as a frame for various projects he has embarked upon over the last several years.

Oscar Wilde wrote proudly about himself that "Whatever I touched I made beautiful in a new mode of beauty: I treated art as the supreme reality and life as a mere mode of fiction."[1] For Wilde, quotidian experience was vastly overrated; life in real time was tawdry, boring, and, more often than not, without pleasure. Art was there to redress this situation either by masking life's ugly vicissitudes, or simply by replacing them with something more agreeable. Given contemporary art's grail-like search for an authentic experience that we very rationally understand does not exist, the notion that its success can be measured by its level of artifice might seem to some to be a gross cynicism. However, the hard-line view that a work of art's achievement can be measured in direct proportion to its closeness to reality, or to the revelation of some sublimated aspect of it, does not take into account what Wilde knew to be the case—that in masquerade there is pleasure, in artifice there is delight, and in falseness there is revelation of certain truths.

In Rondinone's installation, nature and artifice are not interchangeable; rather, they serve as one another's foil. Carefully framing the view of the busy street by masking all the architectural details of the window and wall under a neutral black drop, Rondinone presents real life in real time as if it were a film, videotape, or even a photograph. On the other hand,

---

LAURA HOPTMAN is a curator of contemporary drawing at The Museum of Modern Art, New York City.

the life-size, stuffed Ugo-dummy looks like the real thing to spectators both inside and outside the gallery space. In a memorable description of Beau Brummell, William Hazlitt reported that the eponymous dandy was so excessively statuesque when in company that he resembled a still life.[2] In a pose readily identifiable from nineteenth-century romantic painting as that of the melancholy and contemplative artist, Rondinone's stuffed surrogate oscillates between living thing and art object. More than a still life, the mannequin is a kind of *trompe l'oeil*, marvelous first for its resemblance to life, and doubly so for its virtuoso artificiality. Rather than mourning the impossibility of capturing genuine experience, both the window and the sculpture bid it farewell with a flourish.

Rondinone's TARGET paintings (1993–1997) seem at first to be straight appropriations of American Pop, color-field, and hard-edge abstraction. In fact, these works are less copies than giddy impersonations their irony and impurity coming through their deceptively simple surfaces like a five o'clock shadow on a drag queen. Slightly blurred and clearly vibrating as if electric, these Kenneth-Nolands-on-parade jiggle and cavort. Wearing what can only be described as the costume of high modernist abstraction, they reveal their decorative quality and their humor with the false coyness of a coquette lifting her petticoat to a customer. In this, they are exemplary of a pattern of subversive celebration of the ersatz that culminates in Rondinone's series of large color photos entitled I DON'T LIVE HERE ANYMORE (1995). In these works, the facial features of provocatively posed female models are digitally replaced by Rondinone's clearly male ones. The results are at first startling in their infelicity. They are neither technologically produced transgenderings, nor seamless transvestitisms because we never lose the sense that Rondinone is wearing these bodies as if they were costumes. However, the artist's features are not so ill-fitting as to spoil the models' erotic pull. Recalling the cross-dressing surrealist photographer Claude Cahun's pronouncement *"sous ce masque un autre masque,"*[3] beneath the clearly masculine characteristics lurks a kind of femininity, false, but no less intentional for that fact. As Pierre-André Lienhard so perceptively

observes, for Rondinone, "It is no longer a question of *being* the story he enacts, but of *acting* out the story he is."[4] The pleasure in these works is in the masquerade, and behind the painted faces, Rondinone's magnetic eyes, wistful and furtive, guilty and defiant, communicate nothing less.

That all gender is drag is almost a Lacanian truism, but the implication of that notion—that nature itself can be artificial—is rarely addressed. Rondinone does so in an ongoing series of India-ink wall drawings that take as their subject pastoral alpine landscapes. These romantic views of lush forests dotted with humble cottages and well-worn paths fall squarely within the tradition of the early nineteenth-century German *Wandermaler,* or itinerant painter.[5] Rondinone explains that these large but highly detailed works are taken from sketches he has made directly from nature during walks through the Swiss countryside. Compelling in their studied specificity, the wall drawings have been praised for their authenticity.[6] They are, however, quite simply a lie, as these views do not exist except as drawings. This is not to contradict Rondinone's explanation that his motifs come from the observation of nature nor to criticize the works themselves. In fact, as the artist quite clearly recognizes, it is in their falseness that their strength lies. Despite their source in plein-air sketches, these works are scrupulously realistic renderings, not of a specific landscape, but of the landscape in art. Rendered in grisaille, and carefully numbered and dated to the day not when the scene was purportedly captured in a preparatory drawing, but when it was inked on a wall, there is no mistaking them for a window onto the world at large. That Rondinone actually cut an interior doorway (leading to another gallery space) through one of his landscape murals at Le Consortium in Dijon in 1997 only reinforces this notion.

Walking in the Italian countryside with the critic Wladimiro Greco almost forty years ago, the conceptual artist and clown Piero Manzoni is reported to have complained about the triteness of the excessively scenic landscape, claiming that the locale had been painted so many times that even the grazing sheep comported themselves "by instinct" in a self-consciously picturesque manner.[7] In this curious story, nature not only cannot help but succumb to artifice, it is also instinctively aware of its own artificiality. By trying to re-represent nature, then, visual art is doubly false. For Manzoni, the only reality that art could represent was its own as an object in the world, no more, no less. His infamous MERDA D'ARTISTA, both the ultimate product of the artist and the constitutive example of what is in the world, is his most ironic example. In its reliance on illusion, Rondinone's oeuvre is the antipode to Manzoni's, but it is no less dedicated to the view that the sin is not in the lie, but in the pretense that the lie is the truth. DAYS BETWEEN STATIONS, a collection of more than 120 hour-long videotapes that record random periods of everyday reality with a stationary camera in real time, is a kind of inversion of the incontrovertible can of shit. By the very virtue of having been recorded, these tapes are unredeemably self-conscious and ultimately false specimens of "canned" reality. Displayed in sealed boxes and identified by the place and date of their production, they are as much a product of the artist as Manzoni's shit.

The clown is an appropriate, if almost inevitable, masquerade for Rondinone. Clowns of all sorts have appeared so frequently in his work on and off over

UGO RONDINONE, DOGDAYS ARE OVER, 1995, *video still / DIE HUNDSTAGE SIND VORBEI, Videostill.*

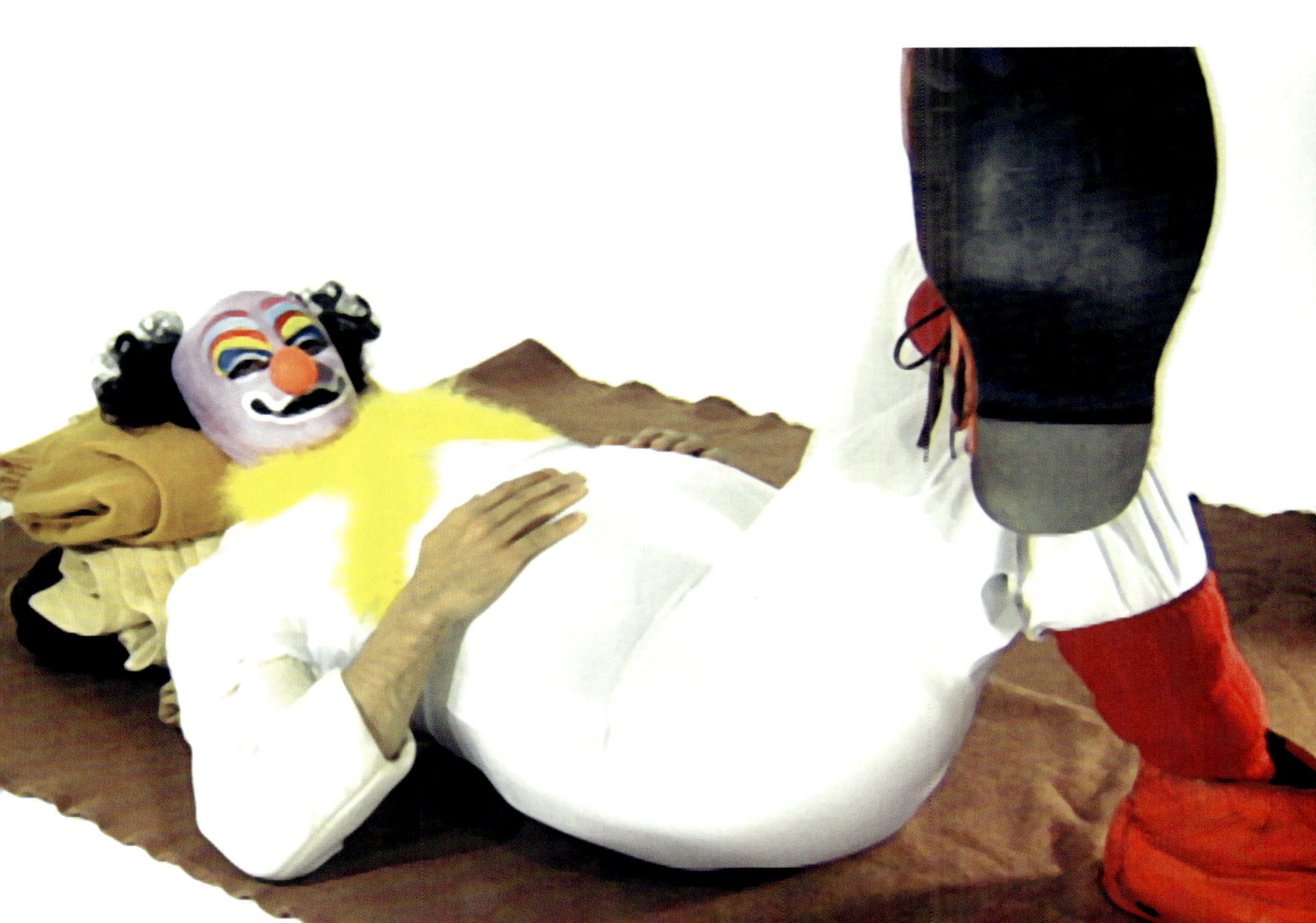

the past several years that they have become, in a sense, his signature. The clown, along with the dandy and the sexual masquerader, are all of a type, occupying a peculiar, intermediary space. From the great Italian *buffone* Totò, who claimed that "one can't be a true comic, without having made war on life,"[8] to Søren Kierkegaard, who wrote that an ironist must live as a "stranger and an alien"[9] divorced from actuality and indifferent to existence, it is evident that these characters hover somehow outside daily life "in an ambivalent position between fiction and reality."[10] And so they should, as their purpose is not to participate in quotidian life, but to caricature it—to render it completely artificial. In an echo of Wilde, the more skillfully this is done, the closer it gets to the truth.

Reminiscent of the Ugo-dummy in Rondinone's Zurich installation, the clowns appearing in the artist's most recent large-scale video projections are completely passive. In WHERE DO WE GO FROM HERE? (1996), a multiclown, multichannel video installation, the enormous figures projected on the wall do not attempt to entertain. Instead, they snooze peacefully, moving rarely and only to find a more comfortable position. In their indolence they conform to the description of Arlecchino the dandified clown of the *commedia dell'arte*... "idle, resistant to interpretation and to causal forces that interpretation tries so busily to control."[11]

Rondinone's idle clowns know (because, of course, they have read their Kierkegaard) that "the immediately real situation is the unreal situation; behind this there appears a new situation which is no less false, and so forth."[12] Action, then, is uncalled for, because the only necessity is pure display. It is enough that they are there in their heavy greasepaint, funny wigs, and outlandish clothes, because they embody in one image a seemingly paradoxical truth—one that Rondinone, in his many guises, has been telling us all along. That is, that the artificial, if it remains gloriously true to its artificiality, can in fact, be as real as it gets.

1) Oscar Wilde, *De Profundis*, in: *Complete Works of Oscar Wilde* (New York: Harper & Row, 1989), pp. 873–957, p. 912.
2) As quoted by Carter Ratcliff, "Dandyism and Abstraction in a Universe Defined by Newton," *Artforum* (December, 1988), pp. 82–89, p. 83.
3) Christoph Doswald, "Oh Dandy, Oh Dandy," in: *Ugo Rondinone: Where Do We Go From Here?* 23rd International Biennale of São Paulo (Bern: Swiss Federal Office of Culture, 1996), unpaginated.
4) David Allen Mellor, "Beaton's Beauties," as noted by Jennifer Blessing, in: *Rrose is a Rrose, is a Rrose is a Rrose: Gender, Performance and Photography* (New York: Guggenheim Museum, 1997), footnote, p. 116.
5) Paolo Colombo, "Autobiography of Contradiction," in: *Heyday*, Centre d'Art Contemporain, Geneva, and Museum für Gegenwartskunst, Zürich (Zurich: Memory/Cage Editions, 1996).
6) Ibid.
7) Wladimiro Greco, *Un Romano a Milano* (Rome: Editrice Omnia, 1960), p. 105. The Italian text reads: "*Gita in Brianza con il pittore astrattista Manzoni. 'Vedi quella contadina che fa il pan all'aperto, mi dice indicando un' aia, sai che sarebbe piaciuta a Segantini. E falsa, falsa, come quelle pecore lassù.' 'Passi per la contadina, gli faccio, ma le pecore certo ignorano di essere mai state dipinte.' 'Lo so ma fingono lo stesso, per istinto, risponde lui.*"
8) Tullio Mazoni and Paolo Vecchi, "*Degneri e scostumati commedia, satira e farsa nel cinema sonor italiano,*" from: *Commedia all'Italiana: Angolazzioni contracampi*, Riccardo Napolitano, ed. (Milan: Gangemi Editore, 1986), pp. 75–87, p. 78.
9) Søren Kierkegaard, *Either/Or*, quoted by Josiah Thompson, "The Master of Irony," in: *Kierkegaard: A Collection of Critical Essays*, edited by Josiah Thompson (Garden City, New York: Anchor Books, 1972), pp. 101–163, p. 118.
10) Pierre-André Lienhard, "Portraits of the Artist as a Clown: From Flight to Immobility," in: *Ugo Rondinone: Where Do We Go From Here?*
11) Carter Ratcliff, p. 86.
12) Søren Kierkegaard, in: Josiah Thompson, "The Master of Irony," p. 138.

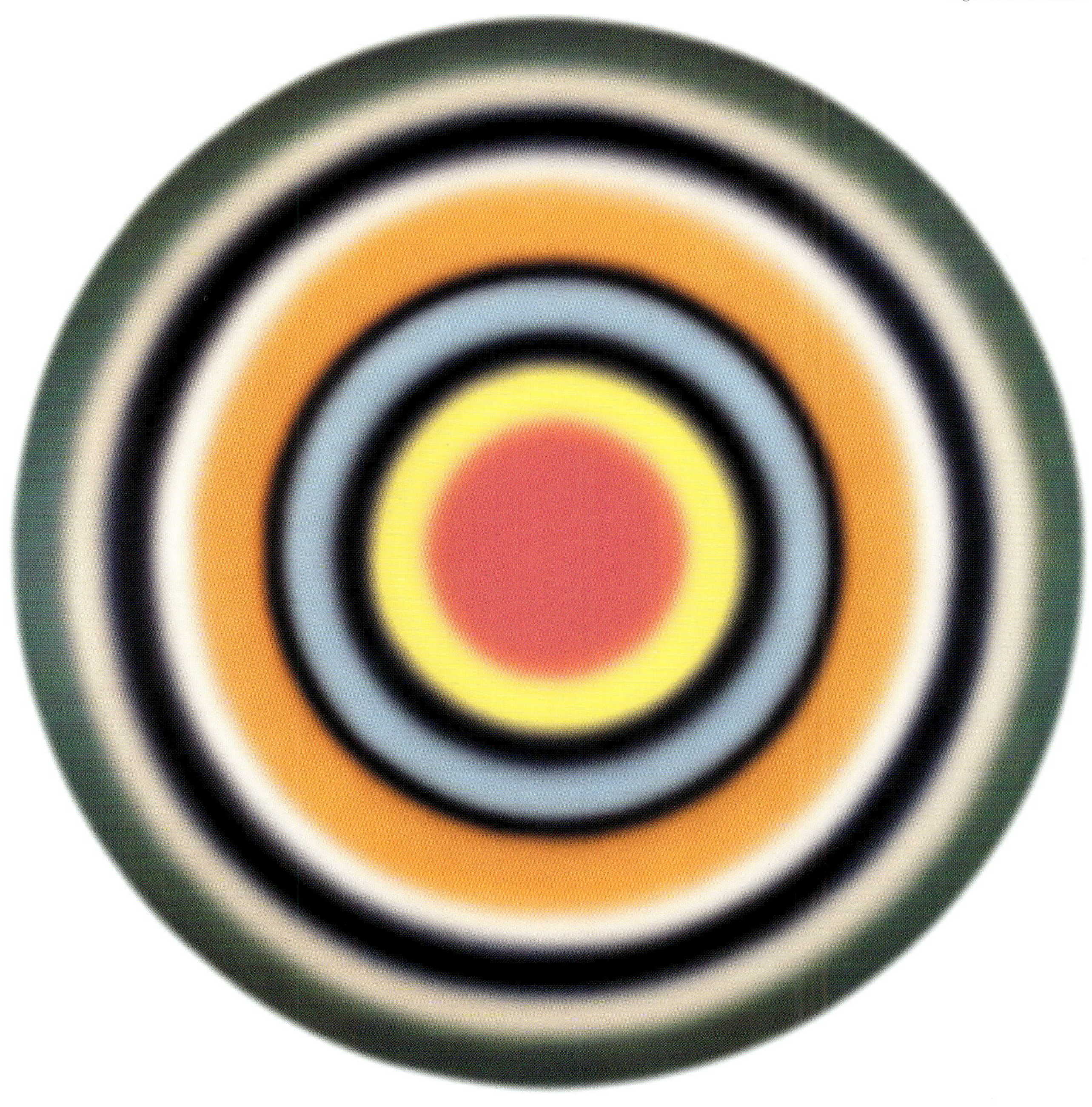

UGO RONDINONE, NO. 85, ACHTZEHNTEROKTOBERNEUNZEHNHUNDERTSECHSUNDNEUNZIG, 1997,
Acryl auf Leinwand, Durchmesser 220 cm /
OCTOBEREIGHTEENTHNINETEENHUNDREDNINETYSIX, acrylic on canvas, 86⅝" in diameter.

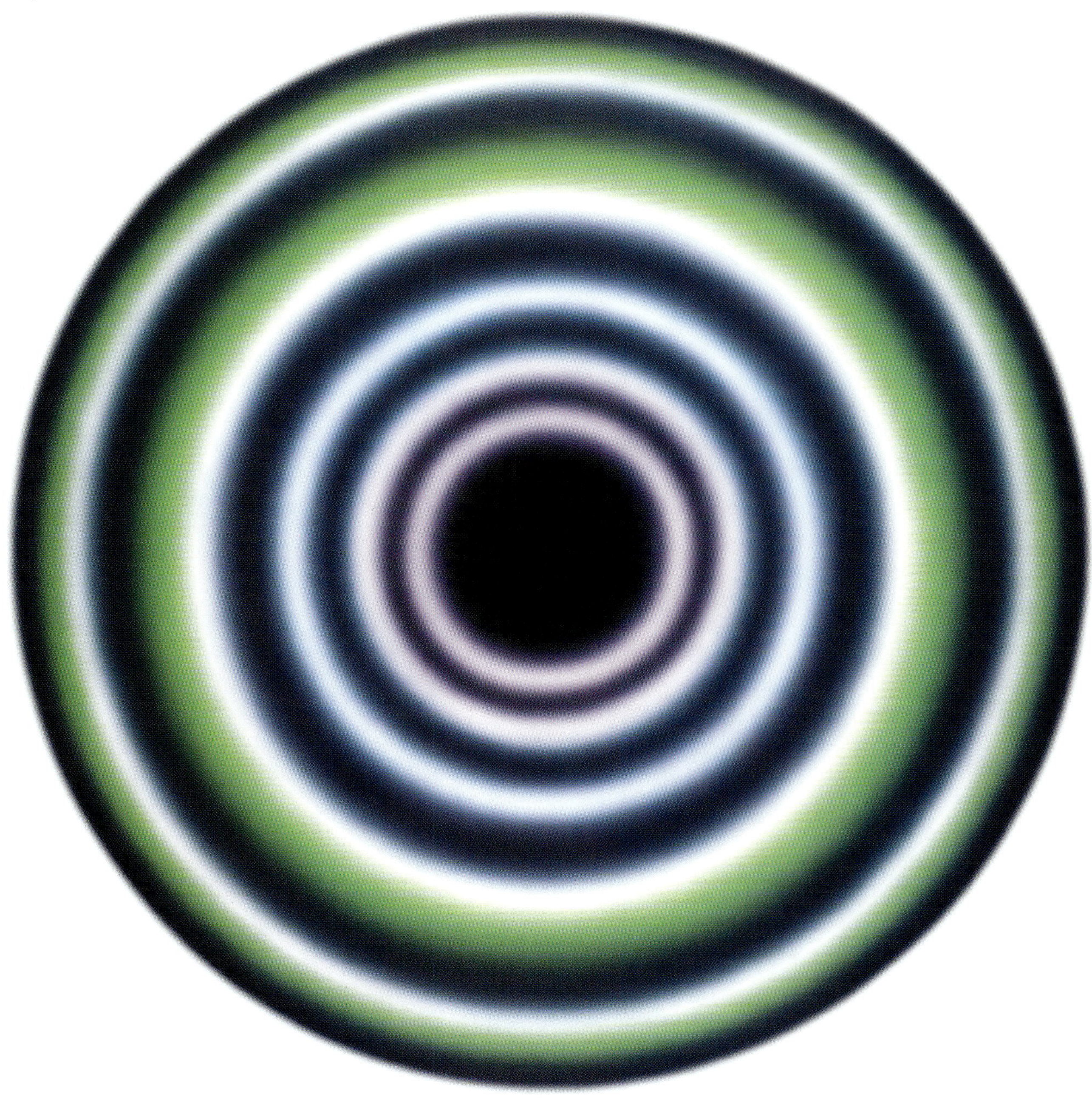

UGO RONDINONE, NO. 92, SIEBTERJULINEUNZEHNHUNDERTSIEBENUNDNEUNZIG, 1997,
Acryl auf Leinwand, Durchmesser 220 cm /
JULYSEVENTHNINETEENHUNDREDNINETYSEVEN, acrylic on canvas, 86⅝" in diameter.

Wider die Natur

LAURA HOPTMAN

Auf dem rohen Holzfussboden einer leeren Galerie sitzt ein in sich zusammengesunkener junger Mann, der grosse Ähnlichkeit mit dem Künstler Ugo Rondinone aufweist, mit dem Rücken gegen eine Wand gelehnt, starr, wächsern, blicklos. Durch ein grosses Aussichtsfenster, welches das andere Ende des Raums beherrscht und auf eine belebte Strasse hinausgeht, blicken hin und wieder Passanten herein. Die Verzweiflung der Figur ist spürbar. Es handelt sich um eine Puppe.

Die 1995 in der Zürcher Galerie Walcheturm gezeigte Installation Rondinones ist eine komplexe, komparative Betrachtung über den Konflikt zwischen Realem und Artifiziellem und über die Rolle des Künstlers als vermittelnde Instanz zwischen beiden. Als solche kann sie auch als Bezugsrahmen für andere Projekte dienen, auf die sich Rondinone in den letzten Jahren eingelassen hat.

Oscar Wilde rühmte sich: «...was immer ich anfasste, wurde durch mich schön in einer neuen Art Schönheit. In der Kunst sah ich die höchste Form der Realität, im Leben nur eine Spielart des Romans.»[1] Wilde war der Meinung, dass die alltägliche

Erfahrung gewaltig überschätzt wurde; das Leben in Echtzeit erschien ihm öde, langweilig und gewöhnlich ohne den geringsten Reiz. Die Kunst war dazu da, dem abzuhelfen, indem sie die unangenehmen Wechselfälle des Lebens maskierte oder einfach durch etwas Erfreulicheres ersetzte. Angesichts der modernen Gralsuche nach der authentischen Erfahrung, die es, wie wir sehr wohl wissen, gar nicht geben kann, mag die Behauptung, das Artifizielle sei ein Gradmesser für ihren Erfolg, von manchen als grober Zynismus aufgefasst werden. Doch die strenge Ansicht, dass die Vollkommenheit eines Kunstwerkes daran gemessen werden kann, wie sehr es sich der Wirklichkeit oder der Enthüllung eines sublimierten Aspektes dieser Wirklichkeit annähert, lässt ausser acht, was Wilde bereits erkannt hatte – dass nämlich Maskerade Spass macht, das Artifizielle Entzücken hervorruft und das Falsche gewisse Wahrheiten in sich birgt.

In Rondinones Installation sind das Natürliche und das Artifizielle nicht austauschbar, vielmehr dienen sie einander als Kontrast. Indem er alle architektonischen Details des Fensters und der Wand unter einem neutralen, schwarzen Vorhang verbirgt, zeigt Rondinone echtes Leben in Echtzeit, als wäre es ein Film, ein Video oder sogar ein Photo. Ande-

LAURA HOPTMAN ist Kuratorin für zeitgenössische Zeichnung am Museum of Modern Art in New York.

rerseits wirkt die lebensgrosse Ugo-Puppe für die Betrachter draussen wie drinnen verblüffend lebendig. In einer denkwürdigen Beschreibung von Beau Brummell berichtet William Hazlitt, dass der Ur-Dandy in Gesellschaft so statuesk wirkte, dass man ihn für ein Stilleben halten konnte.[2] In einer Pose, die sich leicht aus der romantischen Malerei des neunzehnten Jahrhunderts als jene der Melancholie und des sinnenden Künstlers erschliessen lässt, oszilliert Rondinones ausgestopftes Surrogat zwischen lebendigem Wesen und Kunstobjekt. Die Puppe ist weniger ein Stilleben als eine Art Trompe-l'œil, verblüffend lebensecht, und das um so mehr, weil so virtuos artifiziell. Statt die Unmöglichkeit, echte Erfahrung festzuhalten, zu betrauern, lassen das Fenster wie auch die Skulptur diese mit einem Tusch hinter sich.

Rondinones TARGET-Bilder (1993–97) scheinen auf den ersten Blick direkte Appropriationen von Pop, Colorfield und Hard edge Abstraction zu sein. Tatsächlich sind diese Arbeiten aber weniger Kopien als übermütige Travestien, deren Ironie und Unvollkommenheit durch täuschend einfache Oberflächen durchschimmern, so etwa der nachmittägliche Bartschatten einer Drag Queen. Leicht verschwommen und so vibrierend, als wären sie elektrisch aufgeladen, kommen diese Kenneth-Nolands-Kapriolen taumelnd angetanzt, Clowns, die sich in Szene setzen. Im Gewand der hochmodernistischen Abstraktion daher kommend, enthüllen seine Arbeiten ihre dekorative Qualität und ihren Humor mit der falschen Schamhaftigkeit einer Kokotte, die für einen Kunden den Rock lüftet. Darin sind sie exemplarisch für eine subversive Glorifizierung des Ersatzes, die in Rondinones Serie grosser Farbphotographien I DON'T LIVE HERE ANYMORE (Ich wohne nicht mehr hier) kulminiert. Mit Hilfe digitaler Manipulation wurden in diesen Arbeiten die Gesichtszüge aufreizender weiblicher Modelle durch Rondinones offenkundig männliche Züge ersetzt. Das Ergebnis erscheint auf den ersten Blick völlig missglückt. Es sind weder technologisch perfekte Beispiele von Transsexualität noch nahtlose Travestien, da wir nie das Gefühl loswerden, dass Rondinone diese Körper wie Kostüme trägt. Doch sind die Züge des Künstlers nicht so unpassend, dass sie die eroti-

sche Ausstrahlung der Modelle zunichte machen würden. Entsprechend der Erklärung der surrealistischen, häufig in Kleidern des anderen Geschlechts auftretenden Photographin Claude Cahun: «unter dieser Maske eine andere Maske»[3], lugt auch unter den eindeutig männlichen Charakteristika eine Art von Weiblichkeit hervor, falsch, aber deswegen nicht weniger beabsichtigt. Pierre-André Lienhards passender Kommentar zu Rondinone lautet: «Es ist nicht mehr die Frage, die Geschichte zu *sein*, die er spielt, sondern die Geschichte zu *spielen*, die er ist.»[4] Das Vergnügen, das diese Arbeiten bereiten, entspringt der Maskerade, und die magnetischen Augen Rondinones hinter den geschminkten Gesichtern, melancholisch und verstohlen, schuldig und herausfordernd, vermitteln genau das.

Dass alles Geschlechtsspezifische Travestie ist, könnte beinahe eine Lacansche Binsenweisheit sein, doch was diese Vorstellung beinhaltet – dass Natur auch künstlich sein kann –, wird selten angesprochen. Rondinone tut es in einer fortlaufenden Serie von Wandtuschzeichnungen, die pastorale Landschaften zum Thema haben. Diese romantischen Ansichten von dichten Wäldern mit vereinzelten Weilern und ausgetretenen Pfaden gehören eindeutig der Tradition der deutschen Wandermaler des frühen 19. Jahrhunderts an.[5] Rondinone erklärt, dass diese riesigen, aber sorgfältig ausgearbeiteten Bilder nach Skizzen ausgeführt worden seien, die er auf seinen Wanderungen durch die Schweiz angefertigt habe. Die durch ihre ausgeklügelte Detailtreue überzeugenden Wandmalereien wurden wegen ihrer «Authentizität» gepriesen.[6] Doch sind sie schlicht und einfach eine Lüge, da es solche Ansichten überhaupt nicht gibt oder nur als Zeichnungen. Dies steht nicht im Widerspruch zu Rondinones Erklärung, seine Motive würden der Betrachtung der Natur entspringen, und es ist auch keine Kritik an seinen Arbeiten. Denn wie der Künstler selbst zugibt, liegt ihre Stärke gerade in ihrer Unwahrheit. Trotz ihres Ursprungs in Pleinairskizzen sind diese Arbeiten realistische Wiedergaben, nicht einer spezifischen Landschaft, sondern der Landschaft in der Kunst. Grau in Grau und peinlich genau durchnumeriert und mit dem Datum versehen, an dem die Szene angeblich in einer vorbereitenden Zeichnung festge-

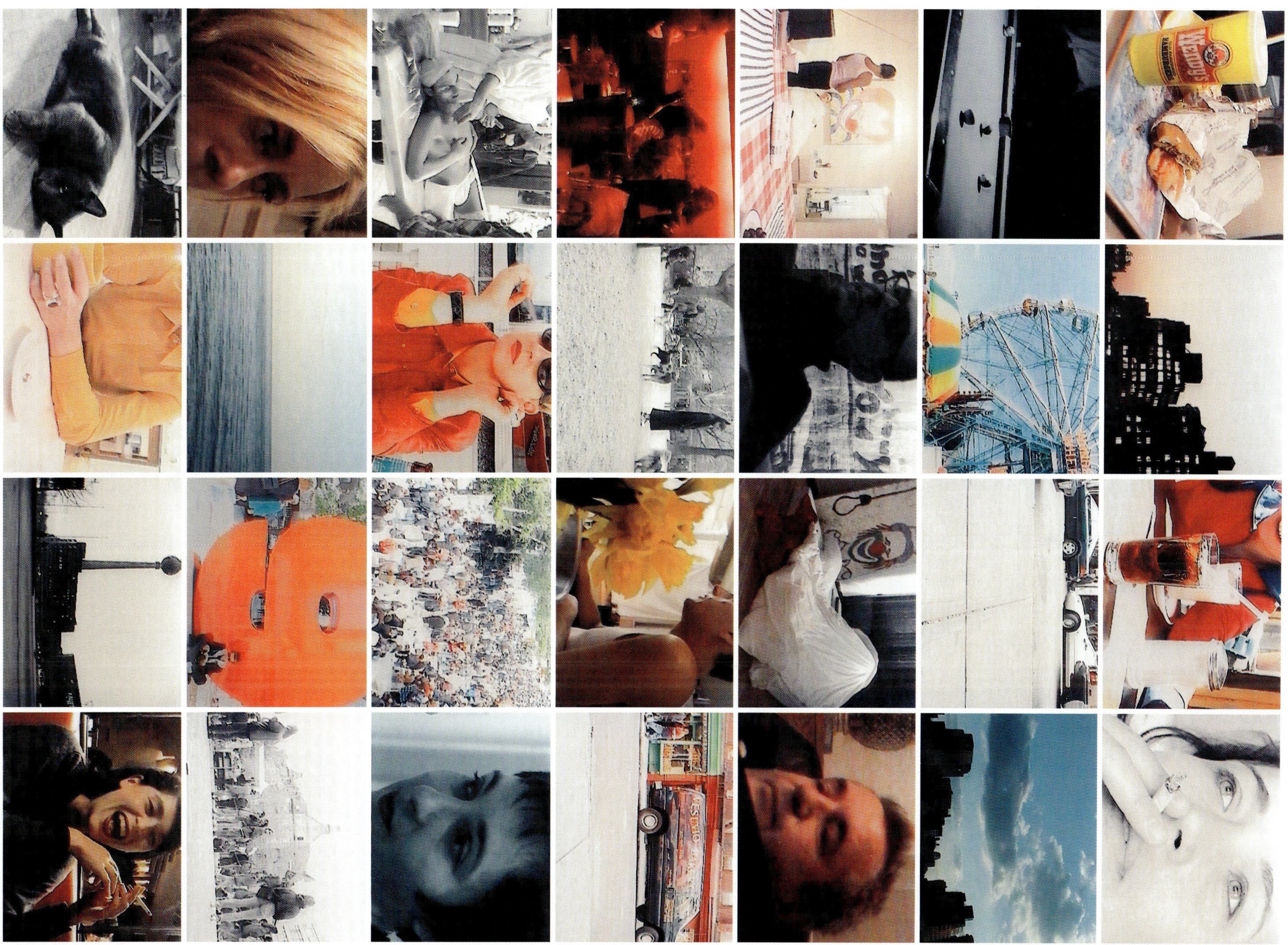

UGO RONDINONE, DAYS BETWEEN STATIONS, 1993–1997–, 180 VHS PAL videos, 60 min. each, stills / TAGE ZWISCHEN STATIONEN, 180 Videos zu je 60 Min., Stills.

halten wurde, können sie jedoch auf keinen Fall für ein Fenster zur Welt gelten, wenn er sie auf die Wand tuscht. Dass Rondinone tatsächlich in einer seiner in Dijon ausgestellten Wandmalereien (Le Consortium, 1997) eine Tür (die zu einem anderen Galerieraum führte) herausbrechen liess, untermauert diese These.

Als er vor beinahe vierzig Jahren mit dem Kritiker Wladimiro Greco auf dem Land spazieren ging, soll sich der Konzeptkünstler und Clown Piero Manzoni über die Banalität der pittoresken italienischen Landschaft beklagt haben, darüber, dass diese Szenen schon so oft gemalt worden seien, dass selbst die Schafe auf der Weide «instinktiv» posieren würden.[7] In dieser kuriosen Geschichte bleibt der Natur gar nichts anderes übrig, als sich dem Artifiziellen zu beugen und sich dabei instinktiv ihrer eigenen Künstlichkeit bewusst zu sein. Wenn die bildende Kunst versucht, Natur darzustellen, ist sie also doppelt

unwahr. Für Manzoni war die einzige Realität, die Kunst darstellen kann, ihre eigene als einen Gegenstand in der Welt, nicht mehr und nicht weniger. Sein ironischstes Beispiel ist seine berüchtigte MERDA D'ARTISTA (Künstlerscheisse), das elementarste Produkt des Künstlers und gleichzeitig das grundlegendste Beispiel für alles, was in der Welt ist. Indem es auf der Illusion aufbaut, ist das Werk Rondinones dem Manzonis diametral entgegengesetzt, trotzdem verteidigt es die Ansicht, dass nicht die Lüge eine Sünde ist, sondern die Behauptung, die Lüge sei Wahrheit. DAYS BETWEEN STATIONS (Tage zwischen Stationen), das aus mehr als 120 Stunden Videobändern besteht, auf denen willkürlich ausgewählte Phasen alltäglicher Realität mit einer festmontierten Kamera in Echtzeit aufgezeichnet wurden, ist eine Art Inversion der für sich stehenden Büchse mit Scheisse. Dadurch, dass sie aufgenommen wurden,

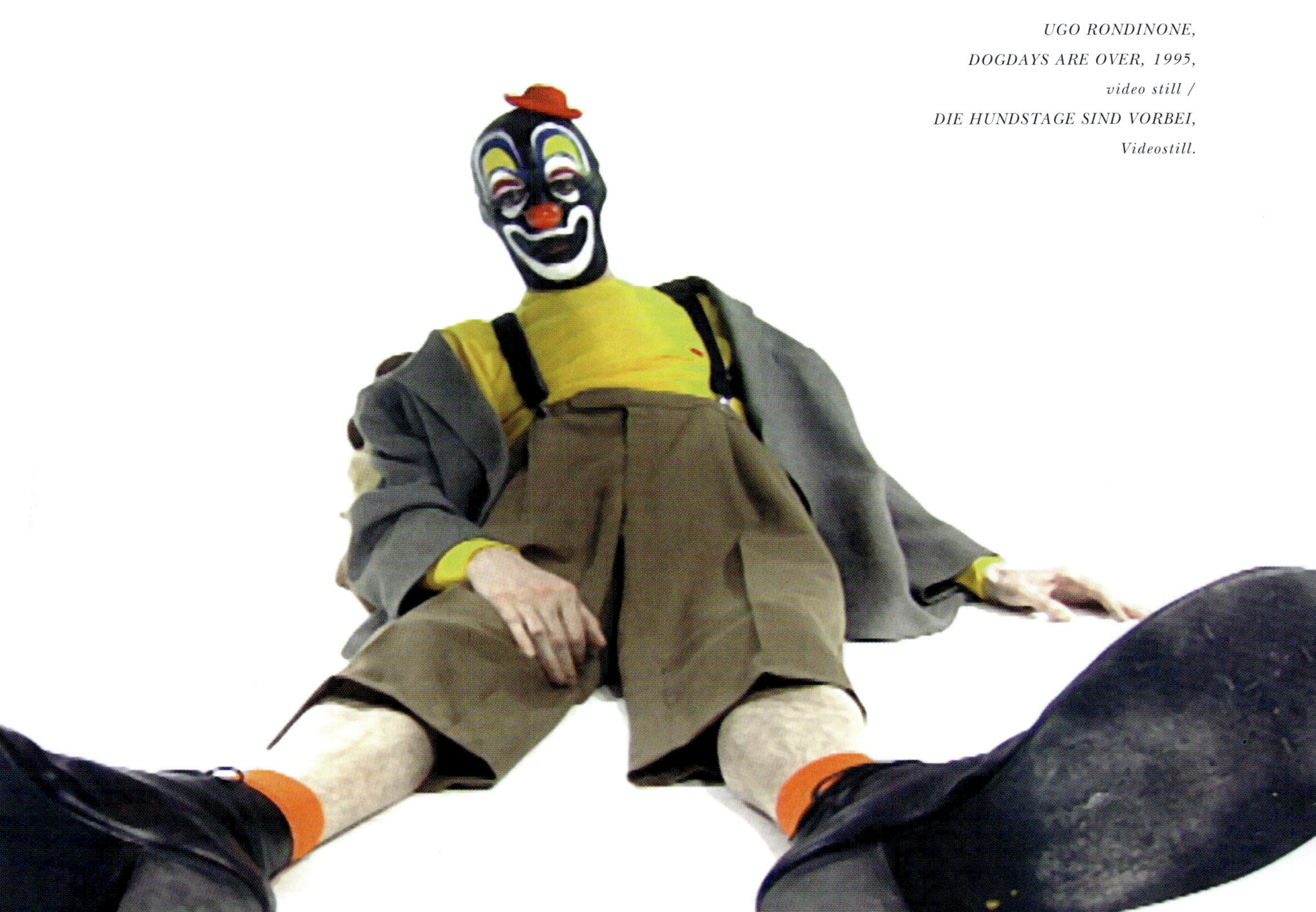

UGO RONDINONE,
DOGDAYS ARE OVER, 1995,
video still /
DIE HUNDSTAGE SIND VORBEI,
Videostill.

sind diese Videobänder notgedrungen bewusste und letztendlich falsche Beispiele einer «konservierten» Realität. In ihren versiegelten Behältern mit dem Ort und dem Datum ihrer Entstehung sind sie ebensosehr ein Produkt des Künstlers wie Manzonis Ausscheidung.

Der Clown ist für Rondinone eine passende, ja beinahe unumgängliche Maskerade. So tauchten in den letzten Jahren immer wieder Clowns unterschiedlichster Provenienz in seinen Werken auf, und sie sind gewissermassen schon zu seinem Markenzeichen geworden. Der Clown, der Dandy und der Transvestit gehören einem Typus an, der einen besonderen Platz d a z w i s c h e n beansprucht. Von dem grossen italienischen *buffone* Totò, der behauptete, dass «man kein echter Komiker sein könne, ohne gegen das Leben gekämpft zu haben»[8], bis zu Sören Kierkegaard, der schrieb, dass ein Ironiker als Fremder und Ausländer leben müsse; abgeschnitten von der Aktualität und gleichgültig gegenüber dem Leben, sieht man diese Charaktere irgendwie ausserhalb des täglichen Lebens, in einer ambivalenten Situation zwischen Fiktion und Realität[9]. Und das muss auch so sein, denn es ist nicht ihre Absicht, am täglichen Leben teilzunehmen, sondern es zu überzeichnen – es vollständig artifiziell werden zu lassen. Und wie schon Wilde meinte, kommt man um so näher an die Wahrheit heran, je geschickter man dabei zu Werke geht.

Ähnlich wie die Ugo-Puppe in Rondinones Zürcher Installation sind die Clowns in den jüngsten, grossformatigen Videoprojektionen des Künstlers vollständig passiv. In WHERE DO WE GO FROM HERE (Wohin gehen wir von hier aus, 1996), einer mit vielen Clowns bevölkerten und aus diversen Kanälen kommenden Video-Installation, unternehmen die riesigen, auf die Wand projizierten Figuren nicht den geringsten Versuch, uns zu unterhalten. Statt dessen schlummern sie friedlich in einer Ecke und bewegen sich nur, um eine bequemere Stellung einzunehmen. In ihrer Trägheit entsprechen sie der Beschreibung Arlecchinos, dem dandyfizierten Clown der Commedia dell'arte... «...müssig, sich jeder Deutung und kausalen Kräften entziehend, die die Deutung so verzweifelt in den Griff zu bekommen versucht».[10]

Da sie natürlich ihren Kierkegaard gelesen haben, wissen Rondinones träge Clowns, dass die unmittelbar reale Situation die unwirkliche Situation ist, hinter der eine neue, nicht weniger falsche Situation auftaucht, und so weiter.[11] Aktion ist also unerwünscht, wichtig ist nur das Zeigen. Es reicht, dass sie da sind, mit ihrer dicken Schminke, ihren komischen Perücken und merkwürdigen Kleidern, denn sie verkörpern in einem einzigen Bild eine scheinbar paradoxe Wahrheit, eine, die Rondinone uns mit seinen diversen Maskeraden schon die ganze Zeit über verkündet hat, dass nämlich das Artifizielle, wenn es der Künstlichkeit treu bleibt, in der Tat so real ist wie überhaupt nur möglich.

(Übersetzung: Uta Goridis)

1) Oscar Wilde, *De Profundis*, übersetzt von H. Soellner, O. Hauser, M. Jakob, Diogenes Verlag, Zürich 1987, S. 90/91.
2) Carter Ratcliff, in: «Dandyism and Abstraction in a Universe Defined by Newton», *Artforum*, Dezember 1988, S. 82–89, S. 83.
3) Christoph Doswald, «Oh Dandy, Oh Dandy», in: *Ugo Rondinone: Where Do We Go From Here?* 23. Internationale Biennale von São Paulo, Schweiz. Bundesamt für Kultur und Lars Müller Verlag, Baden 1996, nicht paginiert.
4) David Allen Mellor, «Beaton's Beauties», zitiert von Jennifer Blessing, in: *Rrose is a Rrose, is a Rrose is a Rrose: Gender, Performance and Photography* (New York: Guggenheim Museum, 1997), Fussnote, S. 116.
5) Paolo Colombo, «Autobiographie des Widerspruchs» in: *Heyday*, Centre d'Art Contemporain, Genf, und Museum für Gegenwartskunst, Zürich, Memory/Cage Editions, Zürich 1996.
6) Ebenda.
7) Wladimiro Greco, *Un Romano a Milano*, Editrice Omnia, Rom 1960, S. 105. Im italienischen Text heisst es: «*Gita in Brianza con il pittore astrattista Manzoni. ‹Vedi quella contadina che fa il pan all'aperto, mi dice indicando un' aia, sai che sarebbe piaciuta a Segantini. E falsa, falsa, come quelle pecore lassù.› ‹Passi per la contadina, gli faccio, ma le pecore certo ignorano di essere mai state dipinte.› ‹Lo so ma fingono lo stesso, per istinto›, risponde lui.*»
8) Tullio Mazoni und Paolo Vecchi, «Degneri e scostumati commedia, satira e farsa nel cinema sonor italiano», aus: *Commedia all'Italiana: Angolazzioni contracampi*, Riccardo Napolitano, ed. Gangemi Editore, Milano 1986, S. 75–87, S. 78.
9) Pierre-André Lienhard, «Portraits des Künstlers als Clown: zwischen Aufstieg und Bewegungslosigkeit», in: *Ugo Rondinone: Where Do We Go From Here?* (vgl. Anm. 3).
10) Carter Ratcliff, S. 86.
11) Sören Kierkegaard laut Josiah Thompson, «The Master of Irony», in: ders. (Hrsg.), *Kierkegaard: A Collection of Critical Essays*, Anchor Books, Garden City, New York 1972, S. 118 und 138.

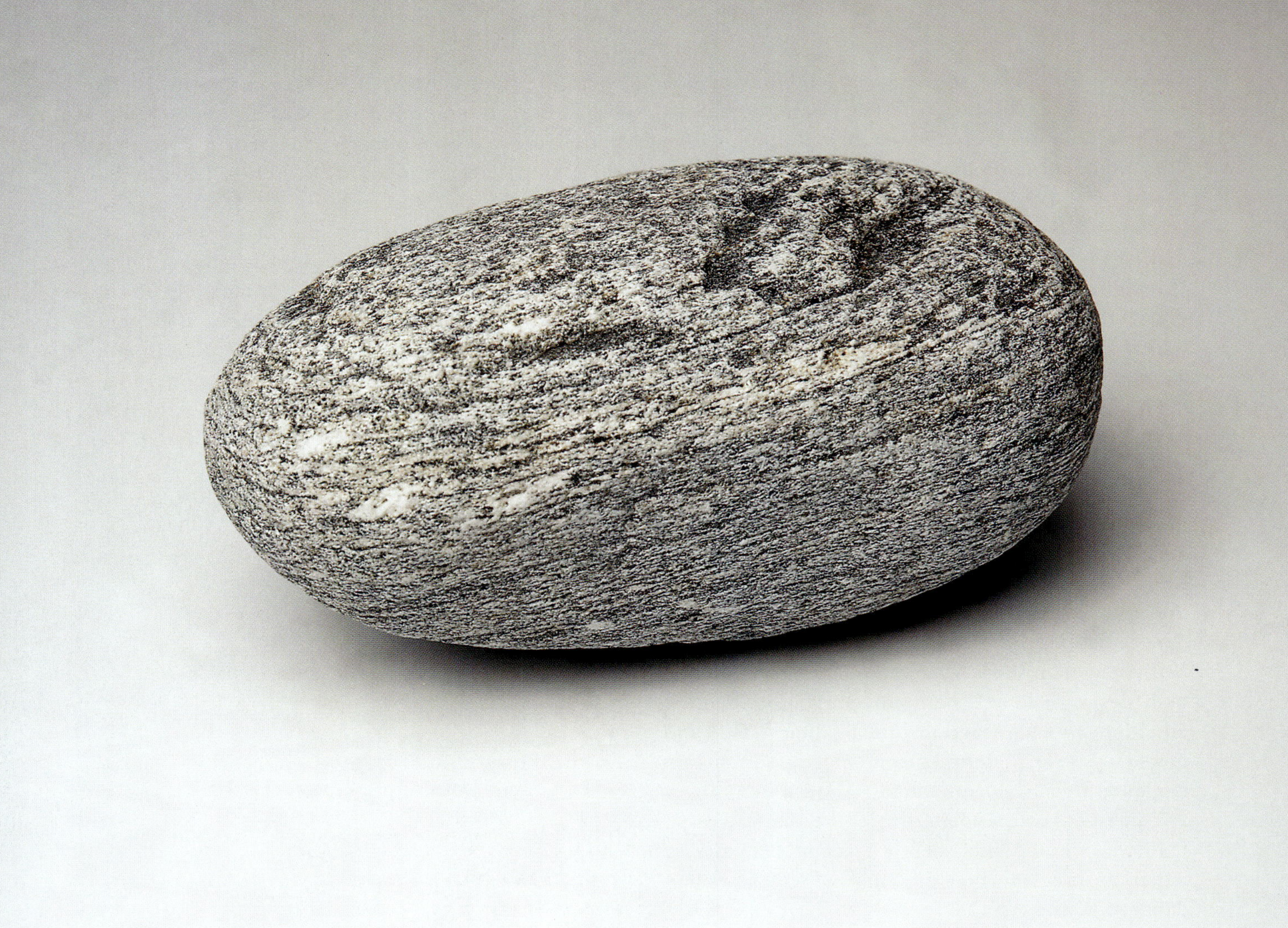

Edition for Parkett

UGO RONDINONE

ALLE AUGENBLICKE HÖREN HIER AUF UND GEMEINSAM WERDEN WIR ZU JEDER ERINNERUNG, DIE ES JEMALS GEGEBEN HAT, 1998
Stein aus dem Maggiatal, ca. 30 x 20 x 10 cm, Gewicht ca. 7 bis10 kg,
Polaroidaufnahme des Steins durch den Künstler.
Auflage: 50, signiert und numeriert

ALL MOMENTS STOP HERE AND TOGETHER WE BECOME EVERY MEMORY THAT HAS EVER BEEN, 1998
Stone from the Valle Maggia (Ticino, Switzerland).
Approximate size 12 x 8 x 4", approximate weight 14 to 20 lbs., Polaroid photo of the stone by the artist.
Edition of 50, signed and numbered

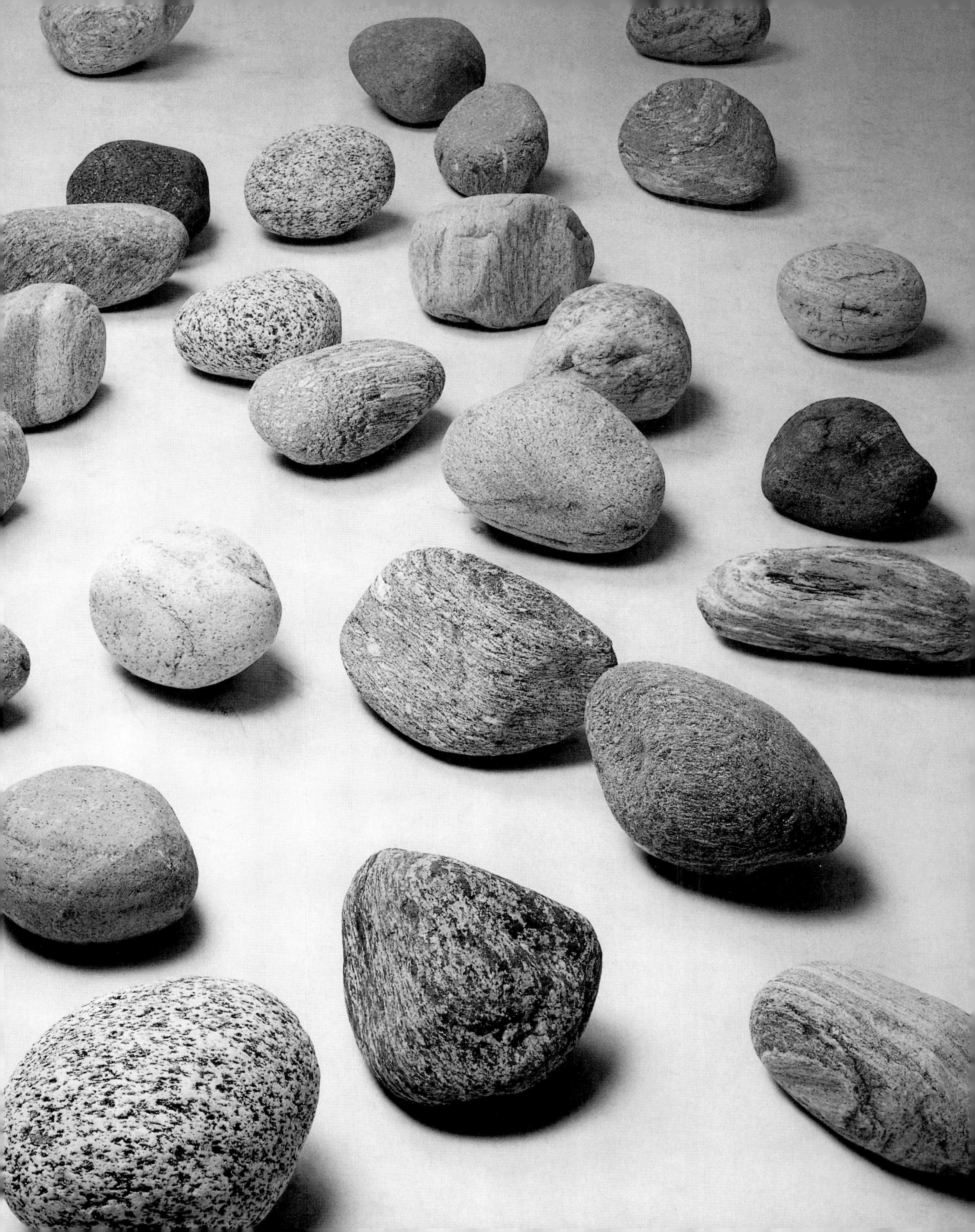

The Sound Wah-Wah: of Crying or the Sound of an Electric Guitar

GILDA WILLIAMS

There's a teach-yourself page on the Internet called "Easy Air-Guitar,"[1] featuring lessons by one R. "Bud" Philson, self-proclaimed the world's most accomplished air-guitar player, who performs a Pete Townsend-style high kick while playing his famous invisible Fender Stratocaster. The air-guitar (a nonexistent instrument which you strum at groin-level with your right hand while fingering imaginary chords with your left) is the most democratic musical instrument ever invented, requiring no skill, practice or investment of any kind. It is the easily ridiculed, rarely documented subject of Gillian Wearing's 1994–1995 video (SLIGHT REPRISE). Here on the big screen we watch the obviously pleasurable, virtuosic air-guitar playing of young men and women whom the artist found through a classified advertisement. Dabblers in this musical subculture, like poachers, they claim the assets of others as their own.

(SLIGHT REPRISE) is fascinating, witty, and emblematic of many of the themes in Wearing's seven-year oeuvre: The ambiguous relationship between an artist and her subject; the cataloguing of urban uniforms and masks in the presentation of the self; the affirmation of abject desire and behaviour as a depictable aesthetic subject; and mass culture as a metaphor for democracy. Added to this is Wearing's nonjudgmental, unaggressive personality, in which an openly voyeuristic curiosity combines with a finely

tuned sensibility for the undercurrents of contemporary culture to tease out of virtual strangers their most idiosyncratic sides. The crux of Wearing's work lies in the following statement, in which she explains the nature of her curiosity: "People get all nervous when you stick a camera up their noses. They want to look their best or come across as being witty and clever, rather than just being themselves, which is far more interesting."[2] Whether in (SLIGHT REPRISE), or the series SIGNS THAT SAY WHAT YOU WANT THEM TO SAY AND NOT SIGNS THAT SAY WHAT SOMEONE ELSE WANTS YOU TO SAY (1992–1993) (where she photographed passersby holding placards on which each wrote a message) or CONFESS ALL ON VIDEO. DON'T WORRY YOU WILL BE IN DISGUISE. INTRIGUED? CALL GILLIAN (1994) (where she videotaped masked adults baring the deepest secrets of their lives), the fundamental miracle in her work is her ability to get people to betray their most biting reality.

Perhaps Wearing's subjects comply not only because she carves out a space for potentially "abject" desires, but also because she offers the opportunity to gratify them. Thus her work meets with a sort of covert appreciation. The imposing, wall-sized video projection of (SLIGHT REPRISE), for example, pro-

GILDA WILLIAMS is an art critic and commissioning editor for contemporary art at Phaidon Press in London.

vides the bedroom rockstars with a moment to be larger than life. It becomes, moreover, an analogy of masturbation as the riff builds to a crescendo and the "guitarist" turns to vocals, dropping his instrument to cup a microphone to his mouth in the heat of the moment while his backup player bobs orgasmically to the music. In this it resembles Bruce Nauman's CLOWN TORTURE (1987), in which abject, private behaviour is made public on a large-screen video. Likewise, in the video WESTERN SECURITY, Wearing films wannabe cowboys (who, she discovered, gather regularly in a South London pub) fulfilling their fantasies of being wild west outlaws by acting out a *High Noon*-style shoot-out in the empty Hayward Gallery. In particular, SIGNS... gave hundreds of randomly selected

group portrait: The assumed identity of these urban cowboys rests solely in their checked shirts, bandannas, and Buffalo Bill-style moustaches. Without the uniform, they are a bunch of high-spirited Englishmen and -women engaged in typical pub behaviour, not remotely connected to anything west of Heathrow! Wearing's most literal homage to the importance of uniform is SIXTY-MINUTES SILENCE (1996), in which she convinced twenty-six men and women dressed in police uniform to sit still for a whole hour in a videotaped group portrait. What appears at first to be an innocuous memento of the Policemen's Ball gradually devolves into a symphony of twitching and nervous coughing; the crescendo of unease builds until, finally, the sitters are figuratively

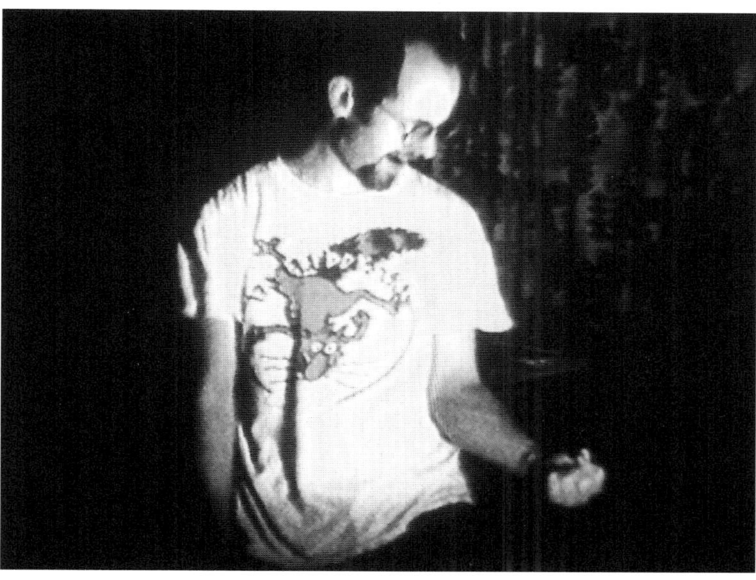

GILLIAN WEARING,
(SLIGHT REPRISE), 1995,
17 min. video projection, /
(LEICHTE WIEDERAUFNAHME),
Videoprojektion.

individuals the occasion to say what's on their minds, no matter how contradictory or disturbing that might be, like the pleasant young man in a neatly tailored suit whose sign reads "I'M DESPERATE."

Key to (SLIGHT REPRISE) and to Wearing's work in general is her attention to clothing and appearance. "Everybody wears a uniform," Frank Zappa once observed[3] and we are all masters at recognising the dress codes that, particularly for subcultural groups, constitute a nonnegotiable passport. In THE REGULATOR'S VISION (1995–1996), the complementary piece to WESTERN SECURITY, the same gunslinger group is seen joking and drinking together in a noisy

stripped of their uniforms becoming as uncomfortable as any civilian would be when placed under observation.

The most extreme form of uniform, the mask, is another common motif in Wearing's work, becoming a true *commedia dell'arte* in this context. The mask acts as a foil for her concern for the connection or rather disjunction between image and concept. In CONFESS ALL..., gag-shop masks of George Bush and Neil Kinnock are the indispensable fronts that allow the wearers to feel comfortable enough to volunteer the darker secrets of their lives, like the man who admits to sleeping with a prostitute, or another who reveals that he loves making obscene phone calls. In one of her most beautiful videos, HOMAGE TO THE WOMAN WITH THE BANDAGED FACE WHO I SAW YESTERDAY DOWN WALWORTH ROAD (1995), Wearing tells the story of an anonymous, conventionally dressed woman with an unforgettable blank, plaster-white, bandaged face whom she saw walking in the street, transforming it into a sort of urban myth. The striking image of the bandaged woman as she walked down Walworth Road trying to maintain her self-possession moved Wearing to assume the same identity

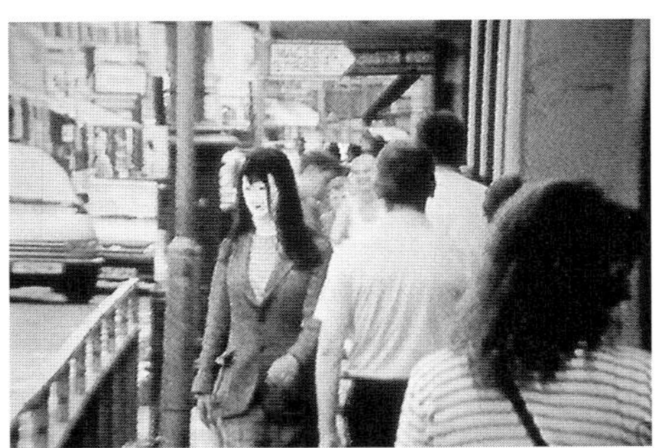

GILLIAN WEARING, HOMAGE TO THE WOMAN WITH THE BANDAGED FACE WHO I SAW YESTERDAY DOWN WALWORTH ROAD, 1995, 7 min. video projection / HOMMAGE AN DIE FRAU MIT DEM VERBUNDENEN GESICHT, DIE ICH GESTERN AUF DER WALWORTH ROAD SAH, Videoprojektion.

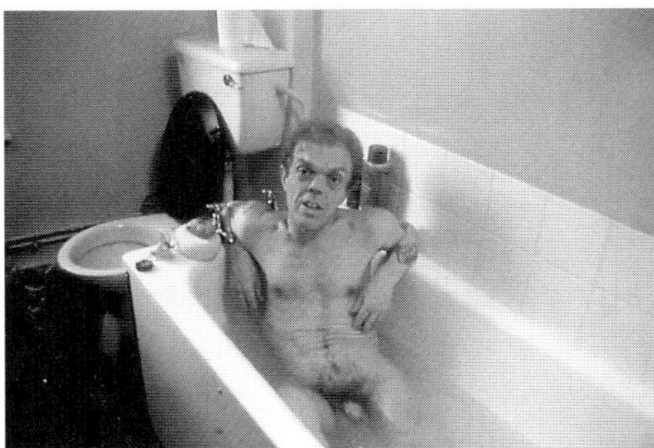

in public with a mummylike disguise punctured by two spooky eyeholes. As Wearing's thoughts of fear and bewilderment appear silently on the screen, "I was incredibly nervous... I was tormented about adverse reactions to my appearance... I felt dejected," it becomes apparent that, like her other sub-

jects, the artist feels uncommonly free to communicate her thoughts when protected by a mask.

A self-confessed TV addict, Gillian Wearing first took a video camera in hand in 1990. Her plan was to follow what she'd enjoyed in seventies television, particularly fly-on-the-wall documentary, where the apparent lack of stylistic intervention lends the work a veneer of authorless credibility intended to encourage the audience's voyeuristic response. In Wearing's work, the seemingly casual presentation belies the instinctively effective yet formal decisions that account for much of the work's appeal. Art-historical predecessors range from August Sander, with his systematic portraiture of all members of society and their professions, to Diane Arbus, with her unflinching, nonjudgmental perceptions of unconventional and disturbing subjects.

It is evident that Wearing is intrigued by subcultures. Sharing nineteenth-century French literary fascination with the demimonde, she has found a way to represent her own contemporary subjects without pity or moralism. Baudelaire, a great observer of the underbelly of modern life, once said, "The life of our city is rich in poetic and marvellous subjects... but we do not notice it." The main character, a detective, in Edgar Allan Poe's short story "The Man of the Crowd," (1850),[4] describes in detail every "suspect" he observes in a London crowd, particularly its most unremarkable members. It is a kind of prephotographic, literary parallel to Wearing's project. Like Poe and other flaneur-realists such as Balzac, Baudelaire, and Zola, Wearing's urban an-

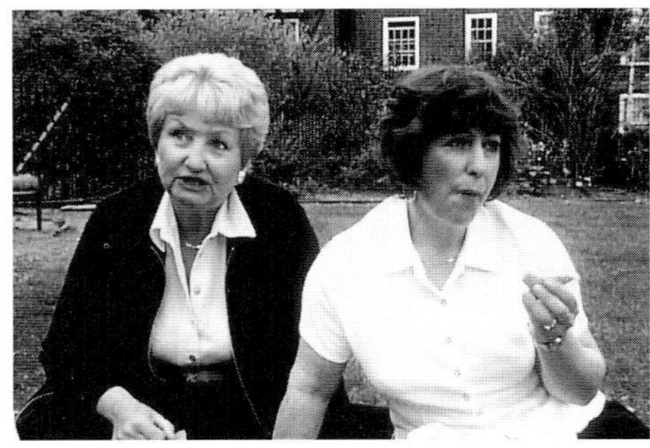

148

thropology relies on the backdrop of a big, crowded city. What distinguishes Wearing's work from these earlier portrayals of society, however, is the specifically late twentieth-century preoccupation with the consumer-based construction of one's physical image in the determination of identity.

In her most recent video work, 10–16 (1997), the mask has been enlarged to conceal the whole body, as adult actors lip-synch the words of children. This is certainly Wearing's most complex and formally daring work to date, as if, after having exhausted her research into how thought and personal image are performed and distorted in daily life, she has now set out to construct them for herself, concentrating on the perplexing contradictions that she has unearthed so many times before.

10–16 presents seven short vignettes, each based on the audiotaped monologues of a different child or adolescent, one from each year between the ages of ten and sixteen. Each voice is synchronized with the image of an adult mouthing the youngster's words: The acting and dubbing techniques are so seamless that one's attention is riveted. The first speaker, a ten-year-old "masked" as a balding, pudgy dreamer,

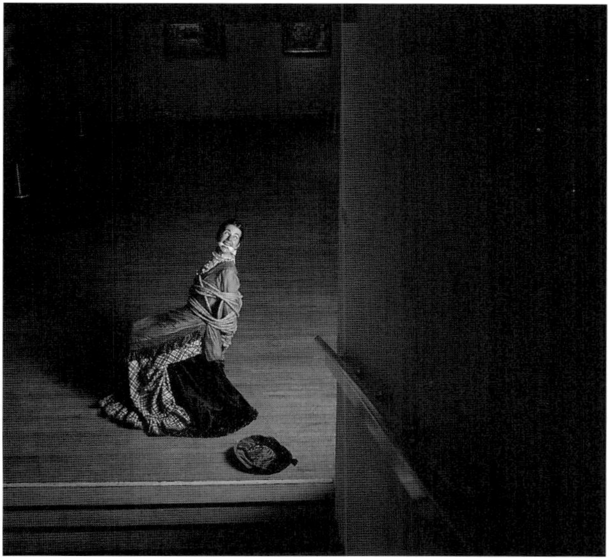

tells of his escape into a tree house, looking from high in the branches over his neighbours' distant gardens, playing make-believe characters. The world here is a wondrous and infinite place, truly "joyful," to use the kid's own vocabulary. Further on, older kids discuss their growing awareness of social constraints, their discovery of opinions (pronouncing harsh judgements on abortion, lesbian love, and so on) until finally, in the last scene, a sixteen-year-old (lip-synched by an unassuming, elderly gentleman) focuses all his worldly attention on to (what else?) his penis, his sexual confusion, and anxieties. Collectively, the children's words remind us of the rapid demise of innocence in early adolescence, and of the subsequent descent into self-doubting consciousness which persists into adulthood. Presented to us through these dubbed performances, the voices are jarring and unplaceable. Once again Wearing has invented a device to make us listen, just as she has coaxed so many to respond to her promptings.

Ultimately, Wearing's work is unnerving because she forces the viewer into the position of voyeur; we never asked to crawl inside anyone's mind, yet we're transported there nonetheless. The frame of her work is always provided by the formal limitations of the video screen and photographic print, never by the nature or motives behind her inquiry, which remain ambiguous as does our own curiosity in them. In the final scene of 10–16, Wearing is seen from the back, facing her subject, listening just like the rest of us in the audience who are watching the performance and each other. Once again, in the litany of a very young man's insecurities, all the potentially detrimental, random combinations of one individual's body, family, and education are laid bare unapologetically; Wearing convinces us that in presenting humankind to us raw, we can all empathise along with her.

1) Easy Air-Guitar @http:/www.digitalrag.com/mirror/air/air.
2) Gillian Wearing interviewed by Gregor Muir, "Sign Language," *Dazed and Confused*, no. 25 (London, 1996) p. 55. Italics mine.
3) Frank Zappa "Quote of the Day" @http://www.fwi.uva.nl/ ~heederik/zappa/index/quote/gopher.
4) Paul Claydon, "Botanizing on the Asphalt: Walter Benjamin and the City," *Inventory*, vol. 1 (London, 1996), pp. 41–42 in reference to Edgar Allan Poe, "The Man of the Crowd" (1850), reprinted in: *The Complete Tales & Poems of Edgar Allan Poe*, (New York: Random House, 1975), pp. 475–81.

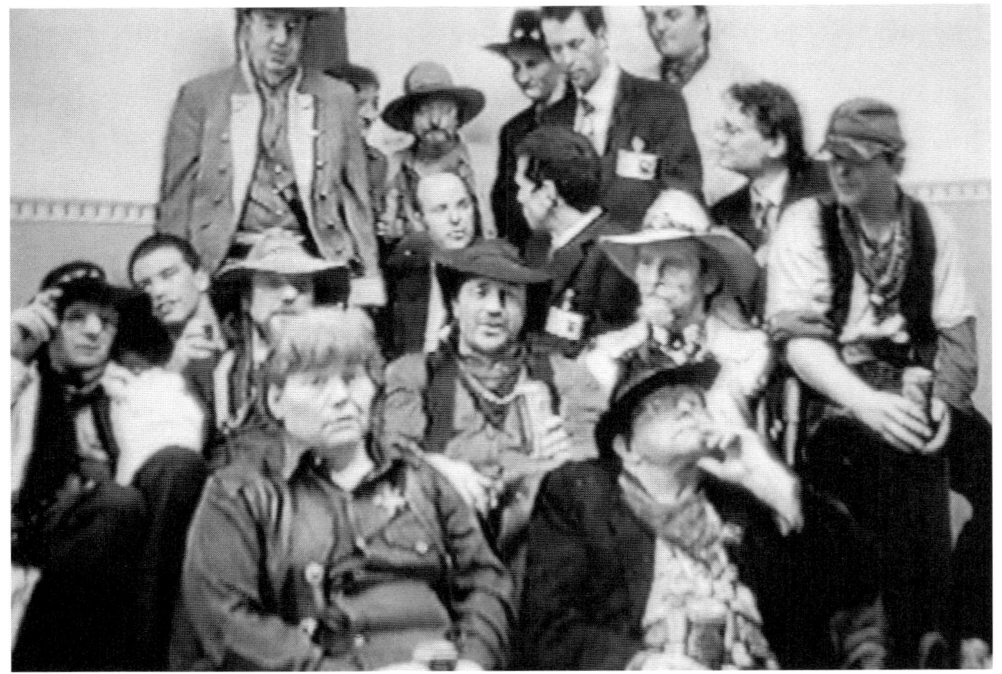

GILLIAN WEARING, THE REGULATOR'S VISION, 1996, 7 min. video projection and 17 min. video for monitor / DIE VISION DES ORDNUNGSHÜTERS, 7 Min. Videoprojektion und 17 Min. Bildschirmvideo.

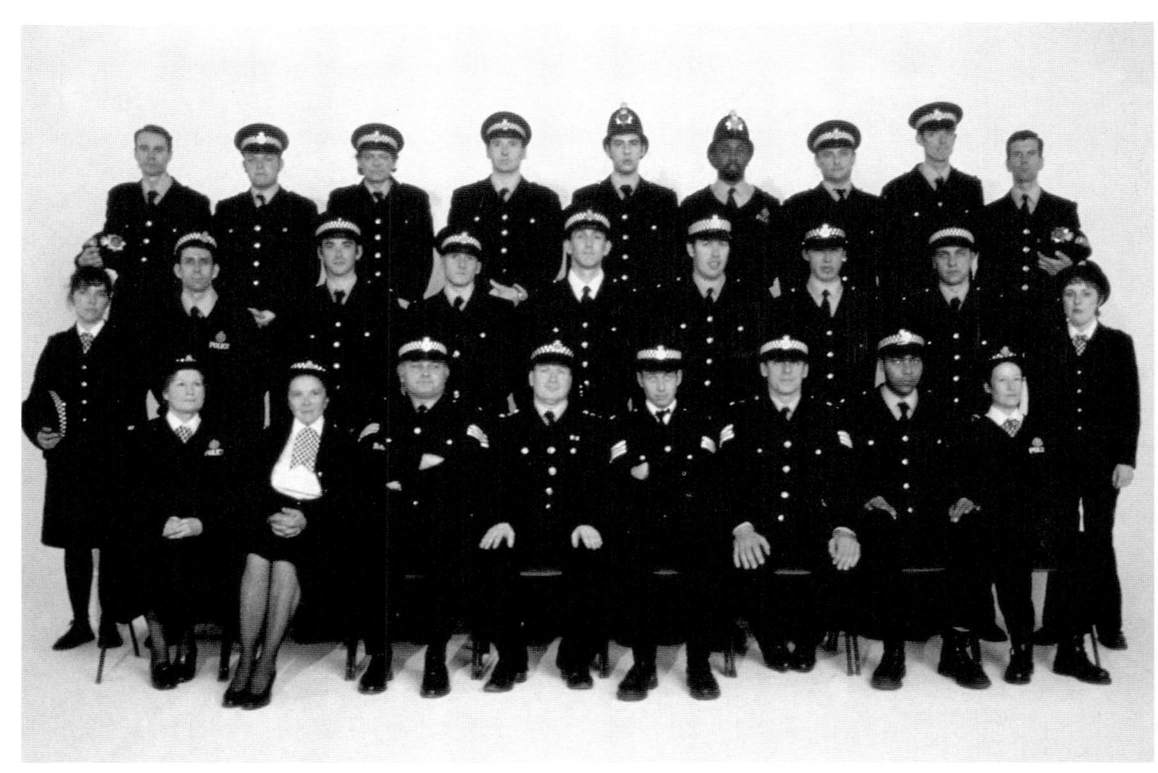

GILLIAN WEARING, SIXTY MINUTES SILENCE, 1996, 60 min. video projection / SECHZIG MINUTEN SCHWEIGEN, 60 Min. Videoprojektion.

(ALL PHOTOS: MAUREEN PALEY INTERIM ART)

Wäää-wäää: Jammerlaute Klänge einer oder die elektrischen Gitarre

GILDA WILLIAMS

Im Internet gibt es eine Selbstunterricht-Page namens «Easy Air-Guitar»[1] mit Übungsanleitungen von einem gewissen R. «Bud» Philson, der Welt bestem Luftgitarrenspieler, der auf seiner weltberühmten unsichtbaren Fender Stratocaster ein Meisterstückchen à la Pete Townsend zum besten gibt. Die Luftgitarre (ein nicht existentes Instrument, dessen Saiten man mit der rechten Hand auf Leistenhöhe anschlägt, während man mit den Fingern der linken imaginäre Akkorde bildet) ist das demokratischste Instrument, das je erfunden wurde: Sie erfordert keinerlei Geschick, keinerlei Übung und keinerlei Investition. Ebendiese Luftgitarre ist der nur allzu leicht zu belächelnde, selten dokumentierte Gegenstand von Gillian Wearings Videoarbeit (SLIGHT REPRISE) (leichte Wiederaufnahme) von 1994/95. Auf Grossprojektionen sehen wir dem offensichtlich vergnüglichen, virtuosen Luftgitarrenspiel junger Männer und Frauen zu, die die Künstlerin über eine Kleinanzeige gefunden hat – Dilettanten in dieser musikalischen Subkultur, die, Wilddieben gleich, die Leistung anderer als die ihre ausgeben.

(SLIGHT REPRISE) ist faszinierend, witzig und vereint in exemplarischer Form viele der Themen von Wearings Schaffen aus sieben Jahren: das zwiespältige

Verhältnis zwischen einer Künstlerin und ihrem Gegenstand, die Katalogisierung städtischer Uniformen und Masken in der Darstellung der eigenen Person, die Bejahung anstössigen Verlangens und Verhaltens als ein legitimer Gegenstand der Kunst und die Massenkultur als eine Metapher der Demokratie. Hinzu kommt Wearings mit Urteilen zurückhaltende, unaggressive Persönlichkeit, in der sich eine unverhohlen voyeuristische Neugier mit einem feinen Gespür für die untergründigen Tendenzen zeitgenössischer Kultur verbindet, um praktisch virtuellen Leuten ihre jeweils idiosynkratische Seite zu entlocken. Die Crux in Wearings Werk findet sich in folgender Aussage angedeutet, in der sie die Art ihrer Neugier erläutert. «Leute werden ganz nervös, wenn man ihnen eine Kamera vor die Nase hält. Sie wollen möglichst gut aussehen oder möchten als besonders witzig und gescheit rüberkommen, statt einfach nur sie selbst zu sein, was wesentlich interessanter ist.»[2] Ob in (SLIGHT REPRISE) oder in der Serie SIGNS THAT SAY WHAT YOU WANT THEM TO SAY AND NOT SIGNS THAT SAY WHAT SOMEONE ELSE WANTS YOU TO SAY (Tafeln, die sagen, was du sie sagen lassen möchtest, und nicht Tafeln, die sagen, was jemand anderer möchte, dass du sagst, 1992/93) – für die sie Passanten photographierte, die eine Tafel in der Hand hielten, auf die sie eine Mitteilung ihrer Wahl geschrieben hatten – oder in der Arbeit CONFESS ALL ON VIDEO. DON'T WORRY, YOU WILL BE IN DISGUISE. INTRIGUED? CALL GILLIAN (Beichten Sie alles auf Video. Keine Sorge, Sie bleiben unerkannt. Interessiert? Melden Sie sich bei Gillian, 1994) – bei der sie

---

GILDA WILLIAMS ist Kunstkritikerin und Lektorin für zeitgenössische Kunst beim Verlag Phaidon Press in London.

vermummte Erwachsene beim Beichten der tiefsten Geheimnisse ihres gequälten Lebens auf Video aufnahm: Das eigentliche Wunder in ihrem Werk ist ihre Fähigkeit, Leute dazu zu bringen, ihre schmerzhafteste Realität zu offenbaren.

Vielleicht sind die Personen, die in Wearings Werk auftreten, nicht nur deshalb gewillt mitzumachen, weil die Künstlerin einen Freiraum für potentiell anstössige Begierden schafft, sondern auch weil sie eine Gelegenheit zur Befriedigung derselben anbietet. Aus diesem Grund trifft ihr Werk auf eine Art unausgesprochener Anerkennung. Die imposante, wandfüllende Videoprojektion von (SLIGHT REPRISE) zum Beispiel gewährt den Schlafzimmerrockstars einen Augenblick, um über sich hinauszuwachsen. Das Ganze wird zudem zu einer Analogie der Selbstbefriedigung, wenn der Riff zum Crescendo anschwillt und der «Gitarrist» sich aufs Singen verlegt und sein Instrument fallenlässt, um im Überschwang des Augenblicks mit der Hand ein Mikrophon vor seinem Mund zu bilden, während sich sein Hintermann orgastisch zur Musik hin und her bewegt. Darin steht es Bruce Naumans CLOWN TORTURE (Clownfolter, 1987) nahe, einem Werk, in dem schamlos anstössiges privates Verhalten in Grossprojektionen der Öffentlichkeit vorgeführt wird. In vergleichbarer Weise filmt Wearing in der Videoarbeit WESTERN SECURITY Möchtegerncowboys (die sich, wie sie herausgefunden hat, regelmässig in einem Pub im Süden Londons treffen) beim Ausleben ihrer Phantasien, indem sie in der leer geräumten Hayward Gallery als Wildwestbanditen ein Pistolenduell à la *High Noon* inszenieren. Insbesondere die Serie SIGNS... gab Hunderten von zufällig ausgewählten Personen die Gelegenheit, endlich auszusprechen, was ihnen wirklich auf der Seele liegt, und sei dies auch noch so widersprüchlich oder verstörend, wie im Falle jenes freundlichen jungen Mannes im Massanzug, auf dessen Plakat I'M DESPERATE (Ich bin verzweifelt) geschrieben steht.

Der Schlüssel zu (SLIGHT REPRISE) und Wearings Werk im allgemeinen ist die Aufmerksamkeit, die sie der Kleidung und dem Aussehen entgegenbringt. «Jeder trägt eine Uniform», hat Frank Zappa einmal festgestellt,[3] und wir sind alle Experten im Erkennen der Kleiderkodes, die, insbesondere für Grup-

pen der Subkultur, ein unübertragbares Dokument der Identität darstellen. In THE REGULATOR'S VISION (1995/96), dem Pendant zu WESTERN SECURITY, sehen wir die gleiche Gruppe von Revolverhelden in einem lärmenden Gruppenporträt beim gemeinschaftlichen Trinken und Scherzen: Die angenommene Identität dieser Stadtcowboys stützt sich lediglich auf ihre karierten Hemden, bunten Halstücher und Schnurrbärte à la Buffalo Bill. Ohne diese Uniform sind sie ein Haufen lustiger englischer Männer und Frauen, die sich typischem Pubverhalten hingeben, das nicht im entferntesten mit irgend etwas westlich vom Londoner Flughafen Heathrow zu tun hat! Wearings unverhohlenste Huldigung an die Bedeutung von Uniformen ist SIXTY MINUTES SILENCE (Sechzig Minuten Schweigen, 1996), ein Werk, bei dem sie sechsundzwanzig uniformierte Polizisten und Polizistinnen dazu überredete, für ein auf Video aufgezeichnetes Gruppenbild eine ganze Stunde lang stillzusitzen. Was zunächst als eine harmlose Erinnerung an den Polizistenball daherkommt, geht allmählich in eine Symphonie des Zuckens und nervösen Hüstelns über: Das Crescendo des Unbehagens steigert sich, bis die Porträtierten schliesslich im übertragenen Sinn ihrer Uniformen entledigt sind und sich ebenso unwohl in ihrer Haut fühlen wie jeder andere, der unter Beobachtung steht.

Die extremste Form, die eine Uniform annehmen kann, die Maske, ist ein weiteres regelmässig wiederkehrendes Motiv in Wearings Werk, das in diesem Zusammenhang zu einer richtigen Commedia dell'arte wird. Die Maske fungiert als Folie für ihre Beschäftigung mit dem Zusammenhang – oder besser: dem Bruch – zwischen Bild und Vorstellung. In CONFESS ALL... bilden Faschingsmasken von George Bush und Neil Kinnock die unverzichtbare Fassade, die es der Person dahinter ermöglicht, sich sicher genug zu fühlen, um freiwillig die dunkleren Geheimnisse ihres Lebens preiszugeben, wie etwa der Mann, der bekennt, dass er mit einer Prostituierten ins Bett geht, oder ein anderer, der gesteht, dass er gerne obszöne Telefonanrufe macht. In einer ihrer schönsten Videoarbeiten HOMAGE TO THE WOMAN WITH THE BANDAGED FACE WHO I SAW YESTERDAY DOWN WALWORTH ROAD (Hommage an die Frau mit dem verbundenen Gesicht, die ich gestern auf der Walworth Road sah, 1995) erzählt Wearing die Geschichte von einer namenlosen, konventionell gekleideten Frau mit einem unvergesslich leeren, gipsweissen, bandagierten Gesicht, die sie auf der Strasse gehen sah, und überhöht sie zu einer Art Grossstadtmythos. Das frappierende Bild der Frau mit dem Verband, die beim Gehen auf der Walworth Road bemüht war, Haltung zu bewahren, bewog Wearing, die gleiche Identität anzunehmen und sich verkleidet wie eine Mumie mit zwei gespenstischen Löchern an der Stelle der Augen in die Öffentlichkeit zu begeben. Wenn Wearings von Angst und Verwirrung erfüllte Gedanken stumm auf der Projektionswand erscheinen – «Ich war unglaublich nervös… Mich quälte der Gedanke an mögliche negative Reaktionen auf meine Erscheinung… Ich war deprimiert» –, wird augenscheinlich, dass die Künstlerin ebenso wie die anderen Personen in ihrem Werk uns ihre Gedanken nur mitteilen kann, wenn sie durch eine Maske geschützt ist.

Gillian Wearing, die zugibt, fernsehsüchtig zu sein, nahm 1990 zum ersten Mal eine Videokamera in die Hand. Sie gedachte dem nachzueifern, was ihr im Fernsehen der 70er Jahre gefallen hatte, insbesondere die scheinbar spontanen und völlig anspruchslosen Dokumentarsendungen, bei denen der offensicht-

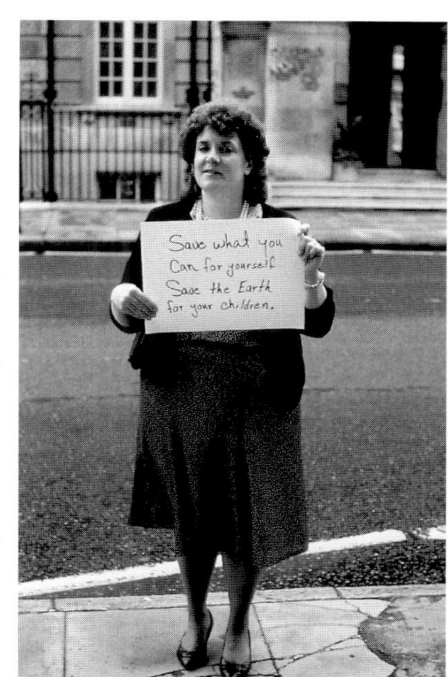

GILLIAN WEARING, SIGNS THAT SAY WHAT YOU WANT THEM TO SAY AND NOT SIGNS THAT SAY WHAT SOMEONE ELSE WANTS YOU TO SAY, 1992/93, c-prints, 15¾ x 11⁴⁄₅" / TAFELN, DIE SAGEN, WAS DU SIE SAGEN LASSEN MÖCHTEST, UND NICHT TAFELN, DIE SAGEN WAS JEMAND ANDERER MÖCHTE, DASS DU SAGST, C-Prints, 40 x 30 cm.

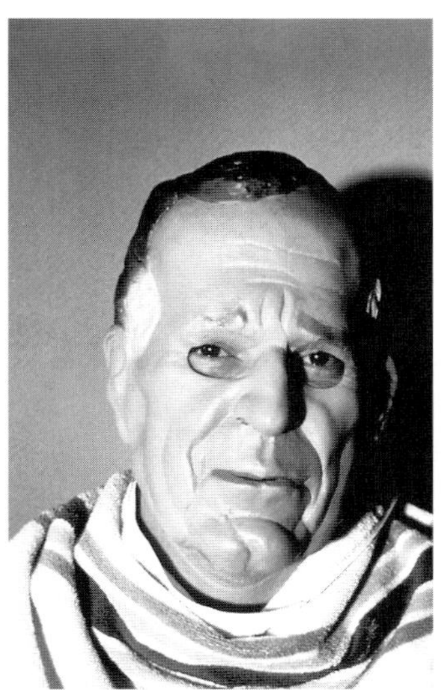

GILLIAN WEARING, CONFESS ALL ON VIDEO. DON'T WORRY YOU WILL BE IN DISGUISE. INTRIGUED? CALL GILLIAN, 1994, 30 min. video.

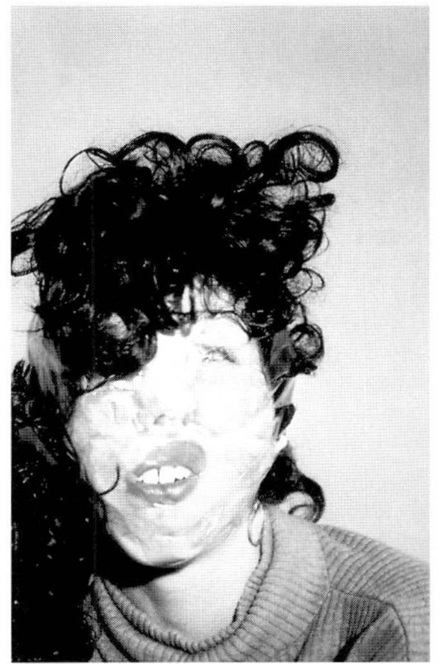

GILLIAN WEARING, BEICHTEN SIE ALLES AUF VIDEO. KEINE SORGE, SIE BLEIBEN UNERKANNT. INTERESSIERT? MELDEN SIE SICH BEI GILLIAN, 1994, 30 Min. Video.

liche Verzicht auf stilistische Eingriffe dem Werk einen Anstrich urheberloser Glaubwürdigkeit verleiht, in der Absicht, den voyeuristischen Impuls des Publikums anzustacheln. In Wearings Werk täuscht die scheinbar beiläufige Art der Darstellung über die instinktiv effektvollen, gleichwohl aber formalen Entscheidungen hinweg, denen vor allem die Wirkung ihrer Arbeiten zuzuschreiben ist. Die kunsthistorischen Vorläufer reichen von August Sander mit seiner systematischen Porträtierung von Vertretern aller Gesellschaftsbereiche und ihren Berufen bis hin zu Diane Arbus mit ihren unerschrockenen, urteilsfreien Beobachtungen ausgefallener und beunruhigender Sujets.

Wearing ist offensichtlich fasziniert von Formen der Subkultur. Getrieben von einem ähnlichen Interesse wie dem, das französische Dichter des 19. Jahrhunderts der Demimonde entgegenbrachten, hat sie eine Methode entwickelt, entsprechende Sujets ihrer eigenen Epoche ohne Mitleid oder Moralismus darzustellen. Baudelaire, ein anderer grosser Beobachter der Niederungen des modernen Alltags, hat einmal gesagt: «Das Leben unserer Stadt ist reich an poetischen und wunderbaren Themen … wir nehmen sie nur nicht wahr.» Die Hauptfigur in Edgar Allan Poes Kurzgeschichte *Der Mann der Menge* (1850) beschreibt detailliert jeden «Verdächtigen», den er in einer Menschenmenge in London beobachtet, und zwar insbesondere die unscheinbarsten unter ihnen[4]. Es ist dies gewissermassen eine vorphotographische, literarische Entsprechung zu Wearings Projekt. Wie Poe und andere dem Realismus verpflichtete Flaneure (Balzac, Baudelaire, Zola) ist Wearings Anthropologie auf den Kontext einer überfüllten Grossstadt angewiesen. Was Wearings Werk von jenen früheren Gesellschaftsporträts jedoch scharf unterscheidet, ist der für das späte zwanzigste Jahrhundert typische Vorrang, der der konsumbegründeten Konstruktion der äusseren Erscheinung bei der Bestimmung der Identität zugewiesen wird.

In ihrer jüngsten Videoarbeit 10–16 (1997) wurde die Verkleidung auf den ganzen Körper ausgedehnt: Sie zeigt erwachsene Schauspieler, die die im Playback zu hörenden Worte von Kindern mit den Lippen nachformen. Es ist dies zweifellos Wearings bislang vielschichtigste und formal kühnste Arbeit, so, als ob – nachdem ihre Erforschungen darüber, wie das Denken und die Selbstdarstellung im täglichen Leben sich manifestieren und verzerren, ausgeschöpft sind – sie sich vorgenommen hat, diese jetzt für sich zu konstruieren, wobei sie sich auf die verblüffenden Widersprüche konzentriert, die sie schon oft zutage gefördert hat.

Die Arbeit 10–16 präsentiert sieben kurze Vignetten, denen jeweils der auf Tonband aufgenommene Monolog eines Kindes oder Heranwachsenden zugrunde liegt. Die Kinder sind im Alter von zehn bis sechzehn Jahren, jede Altersstufe ist einmal vertreten. Die jeweilige Stimme wird synchronisiert mit dem Bild eines Erwachsenen, der die Worte des Jugendlichen spricht: Man ist fasziniert von der nahtlosen Ausgefeiltheit der Schauspiel- und Synchrontechnik. Der erste Sprecher, ein Zehnjähriger in der «Verkleidung» eines beleibten Träumers mit Halbglatze, erzählt von seiner Flucht in ein Baumhaus: wie er von hoch oben im Geäst über die fernen Gärten seiner Nachbarn hinausblickt und erfundene Figuren spielt. Die Welt ist hier ein wunderbarer, unbegrenzter Ort, im wahrsten Sinne des Wortes «voller Freude», wie es der Knabe selbst ausdrückt. Später diskutieren ältere Kinder über ihr zunehmendes Gewahrwerden sozialer Zwänge sowie über ihr verstärktes Bekenntnis zu Meinungen (in Form von

scharfen Verurteilungen etwa der Abtreibung und lesbischen Liebe), bis schliesslich in der letzten Szene ein Sechzehnjähriger (dargestellt von einem unscheinbaren, ältlichen Herrn) all sein weltliches Sinnen auf – was sonst – seinen Penis, seine sexuelle Verwirrung und dazugehörige Ängste richtet. Zusammengenommen erinnern uns die Worte der Kinder an den rapiden Wegfall der Unschuld in der frühen Adoleszenz und das Versinken in ein von Selbstzweifeln geplagtes Bewusstsein, das sich bis ins Erwachsenenalter hinein hält. Weil sie in dieser Playbackform vorgeführt werden, wirken die Stimmen auf uns dissonant und nicht zuweisbar: Wearing hat aufs neue eine Methode erfunden, uns zum Zuhören zu bringen, so, wie sie schon so viele vorher zu einer Reaktion auf ihr Werk gezwungen hat.

Letztlich ist Wearings Werk entnervend, weil sie den Betrachter in die Lage des Voyeurs drängt: Wir hatten nie darum gebeten, in jemandes Seelenleben einzudringen, und dennoch werden wir hineinversetzt. Die Grenzen werden ihrem Werk immer durch die formalen Beschränkungen der Videoprojektion und des photographischen Abzuges gesetzt, nie durch die Art ihrer Nachforschung oder die Motive dahinter, die verschwommen bleiben – ebenso wie unser Interesse an ihnen. In der Schlussszene von 10–16 ist Wearing von hinten zu sehen: Der dargestellten Person zugewandt, hört sie ihr zu, genauso wie wir im Publikum, die wir die Vorstellung und uns gegenseitig anschauen. Noch einmal werden in der Litanei der Unsicherheiten eines Jünglings all die potentiell misslichen Zufallskombinationen von Parametern wie Körper, Familie und Ausbildung einer Person schonungslos offengelegt: Indem sie uns die Menschheit ungeschminkt vor Augen führt, überzeugt uns Wearing davon, dass wir alle unter ihrer Anleitung der Einfühlung fähig sind.

(Übersetzung: Bram Opstelten)

1) Easy Air-Guitar @http://www.digitalrag.com/mirror/air/air.
2) Gillian Wearing im Gespräch mit Gregor Muir, «Sign Language», in: *Dazed and Confused* Nr. 25, London 1996, S. 55.
3) Frank Zappa Quote of the Day, @http://www.fwli.uva.nl/~heederik/zappa/index/quote/gopher.
4) Ich beziehe mich hier auf den ausgezeichneten Aufsatz von Paul Claydon, «Botanizing on the Asphalt: Walter Benjamin and the City», in: *Inventory* Nr. 1/2, London 1996, S. 41–42.

INSERT THOMAS BAYRLE

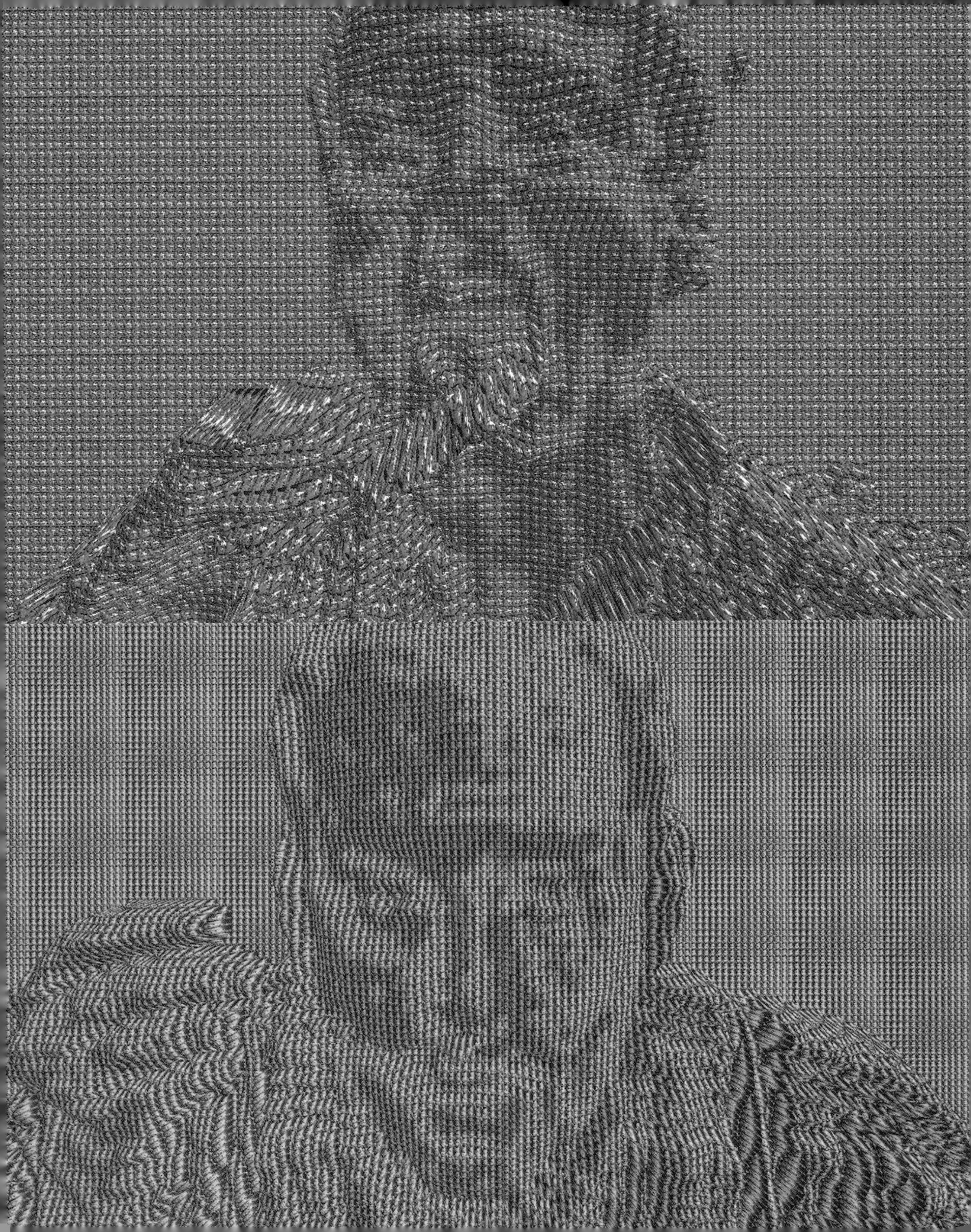

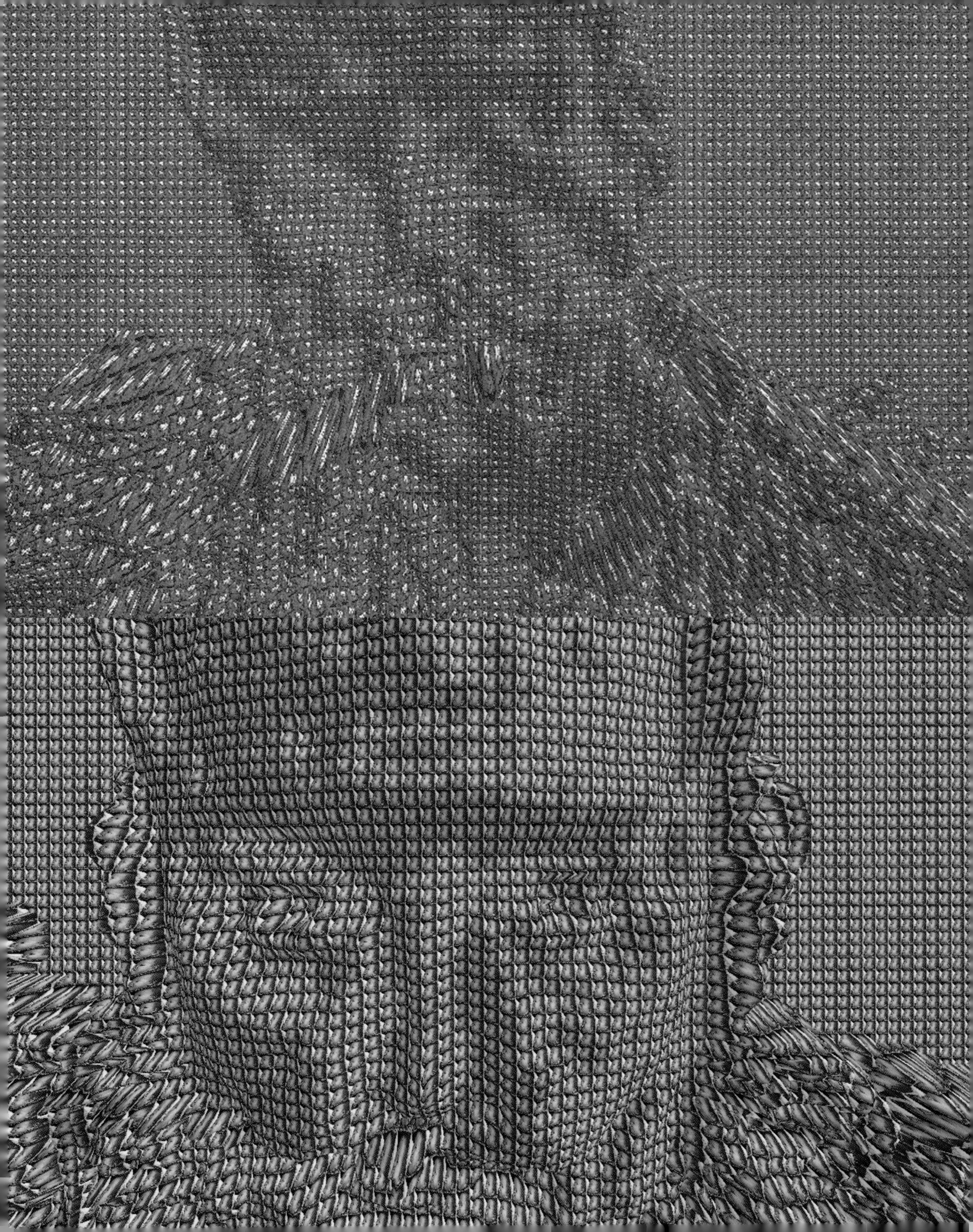

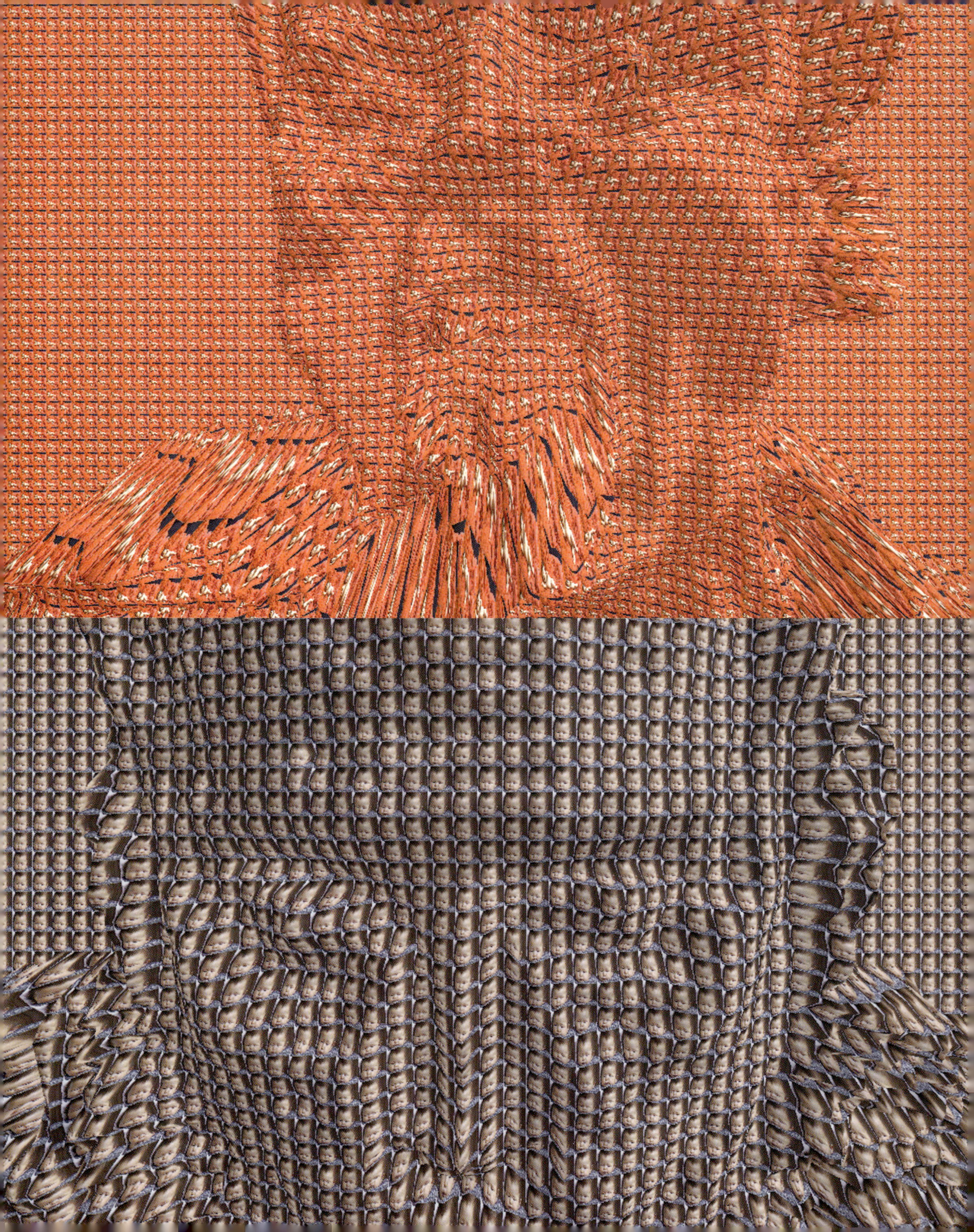

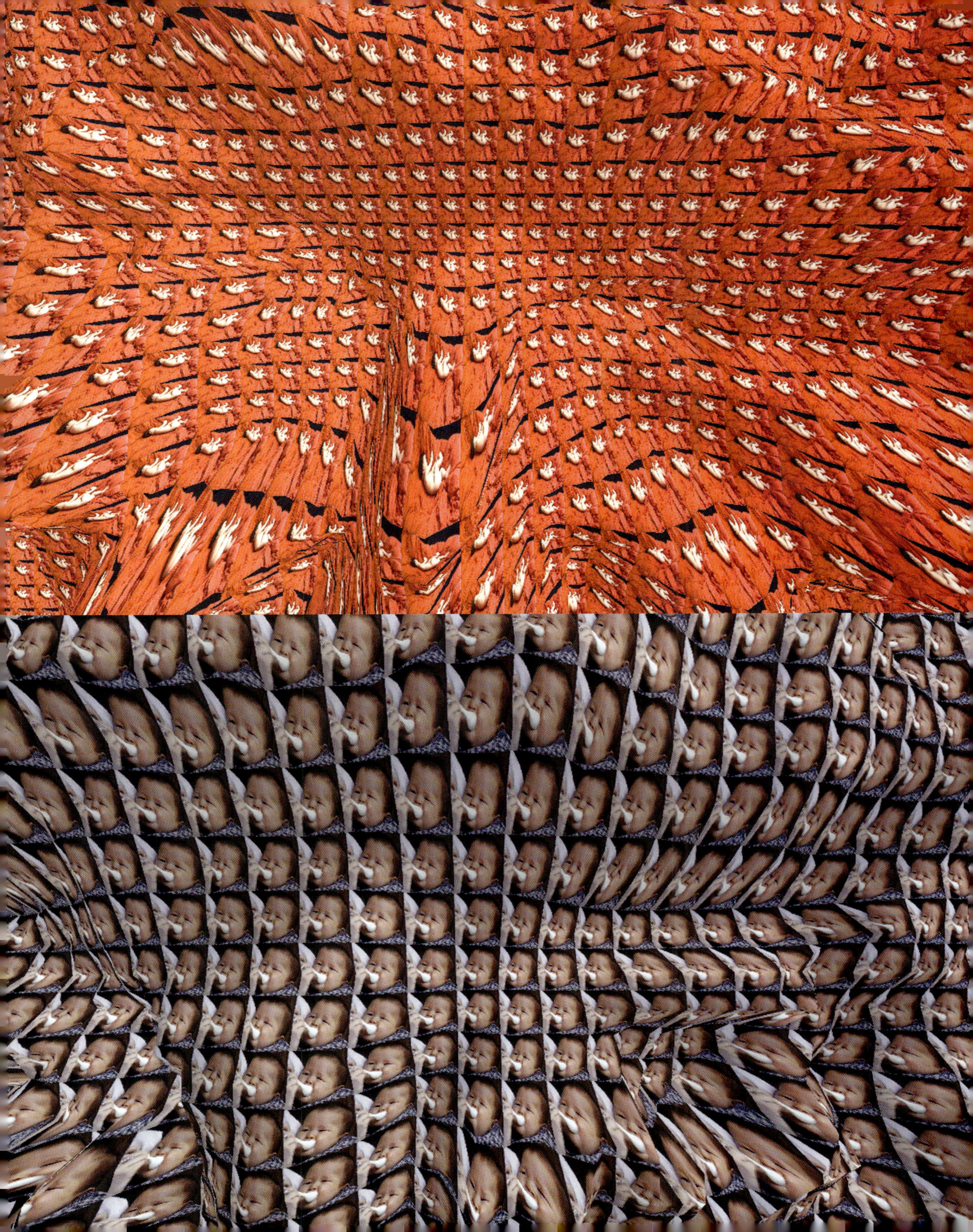

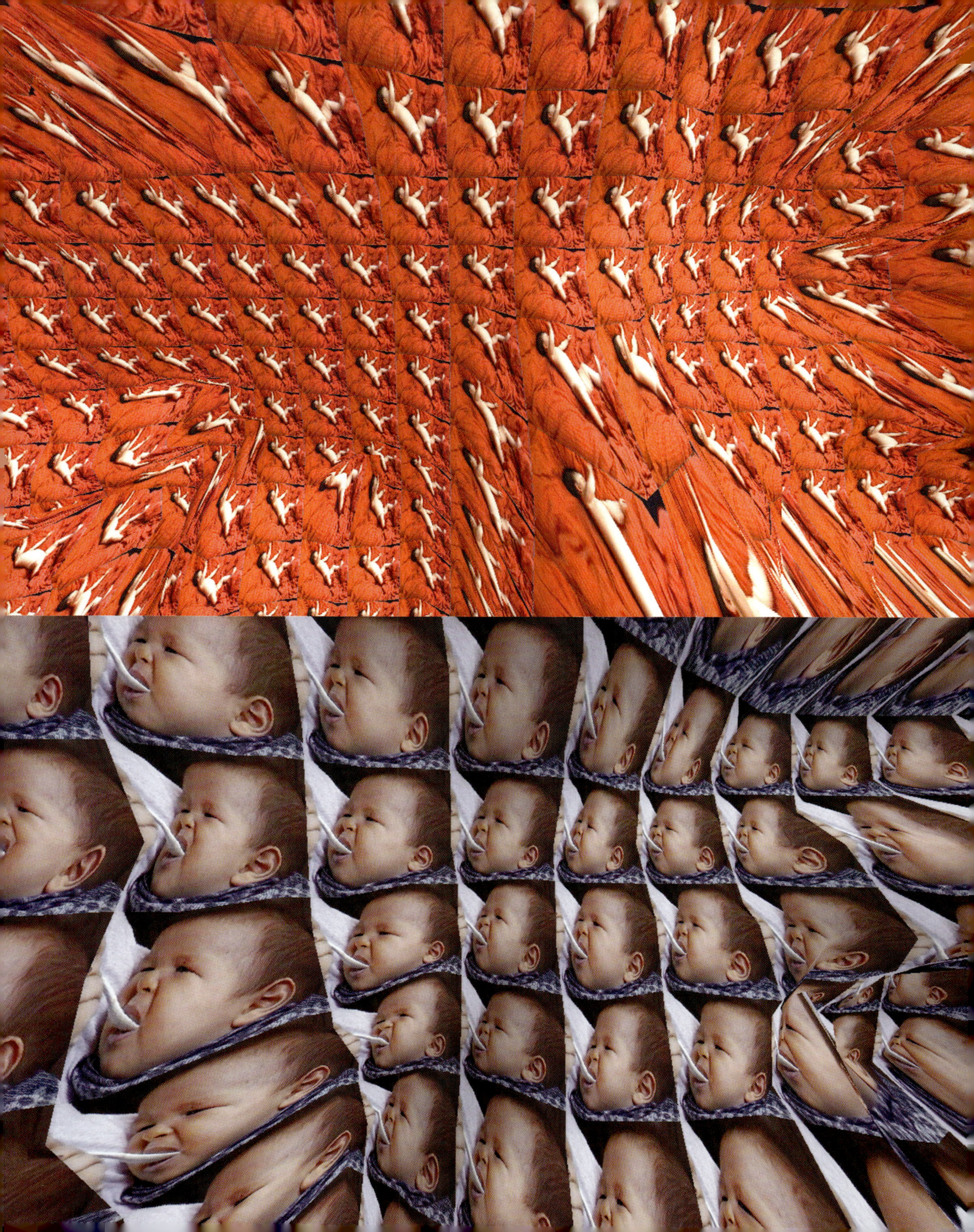

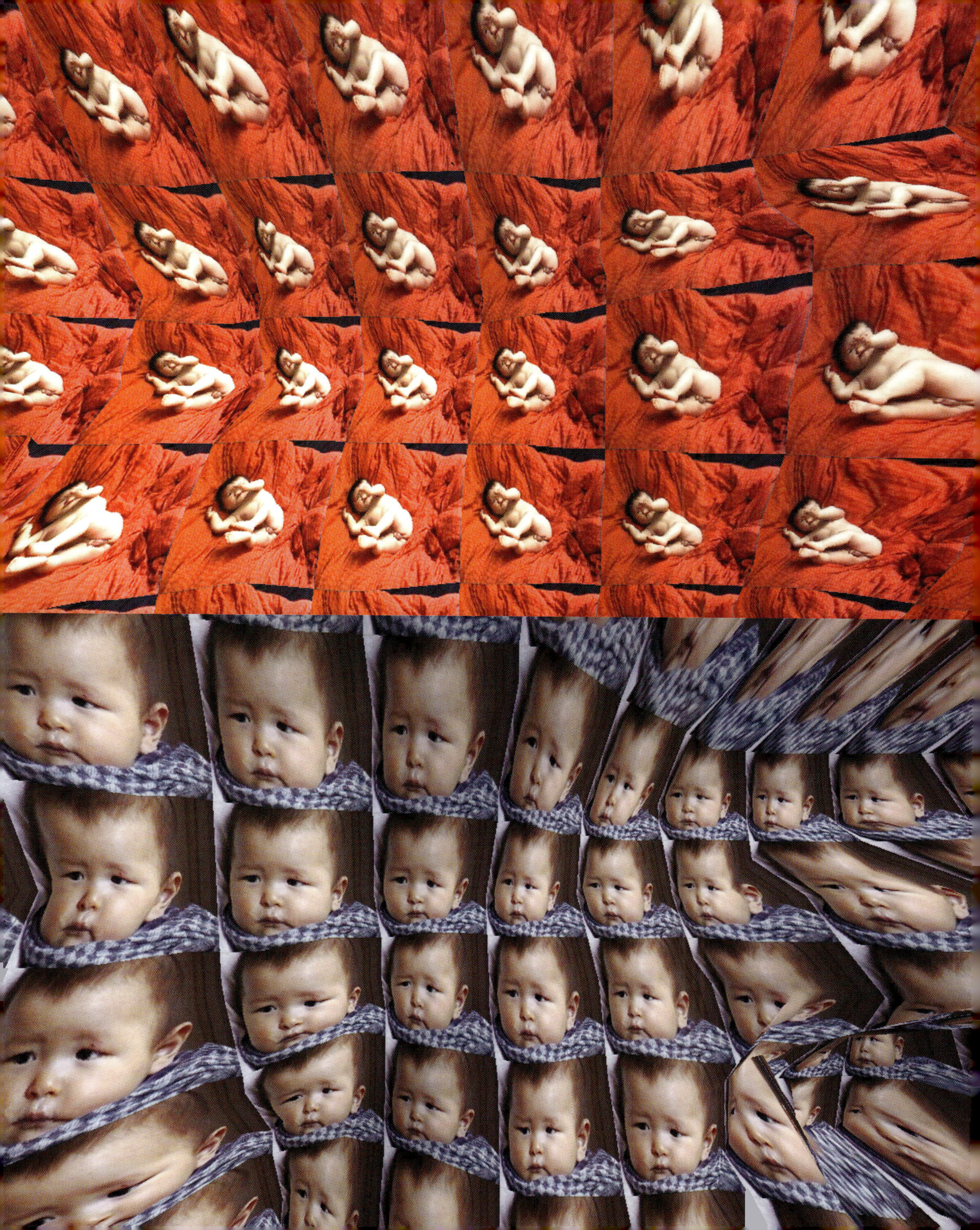

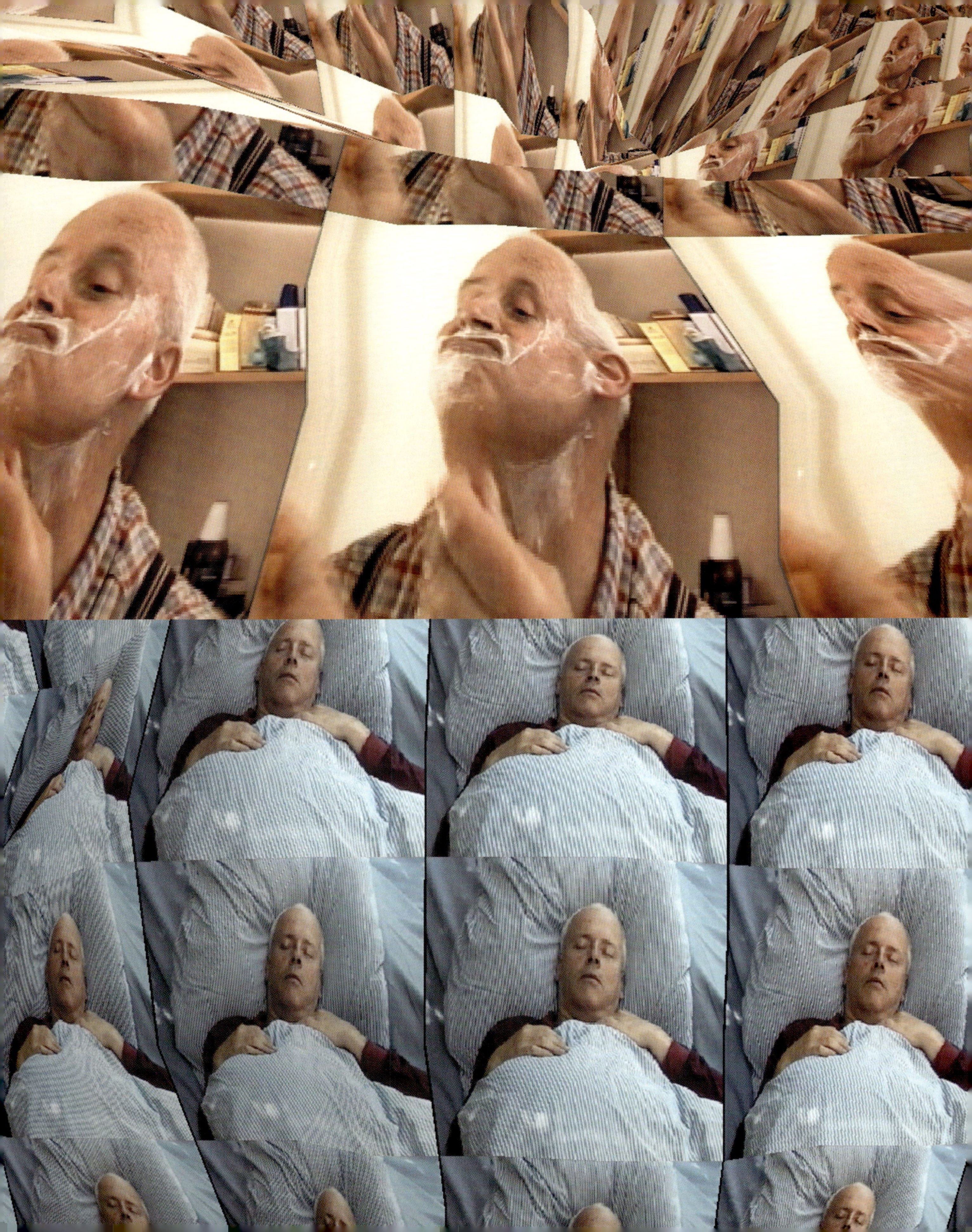

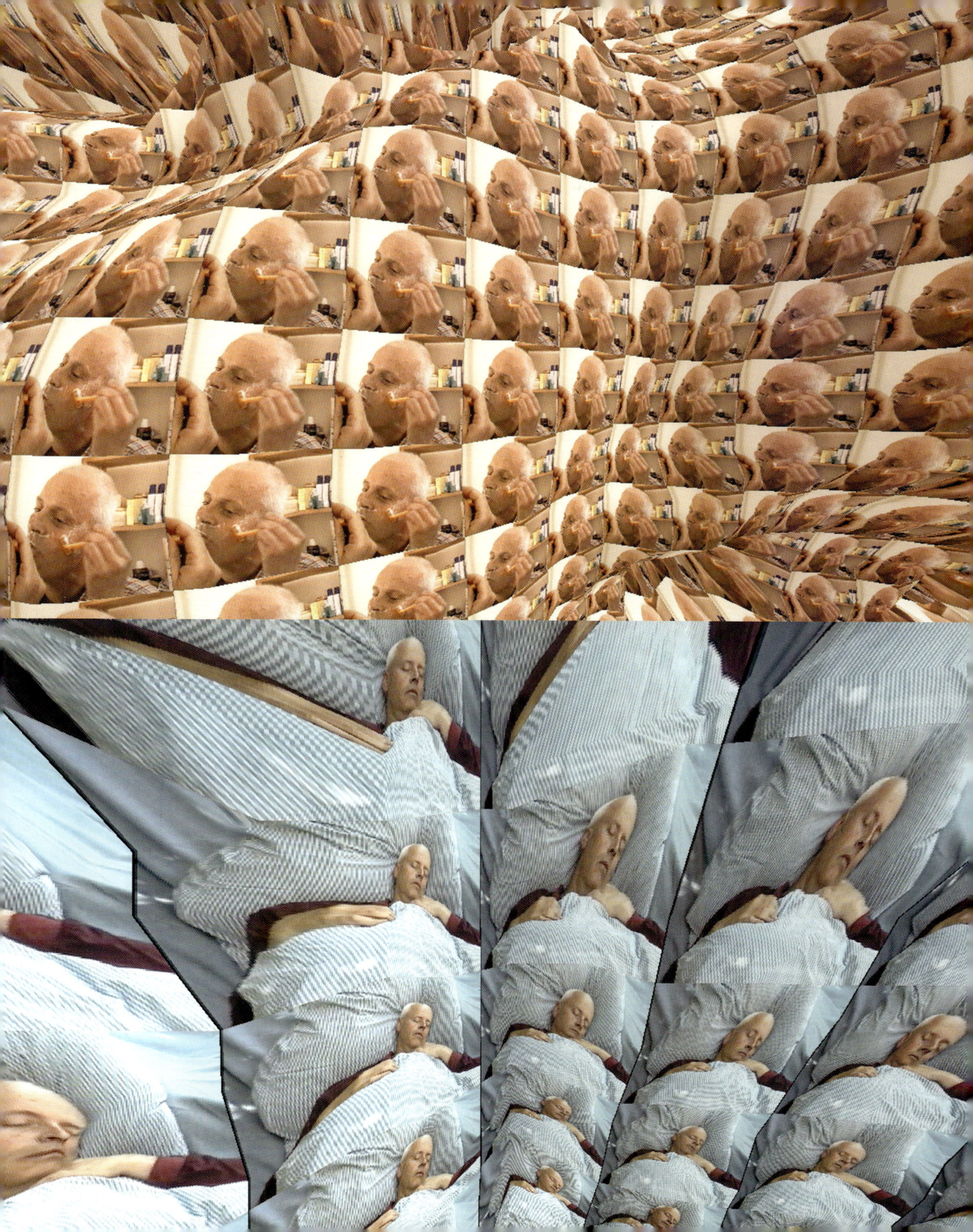

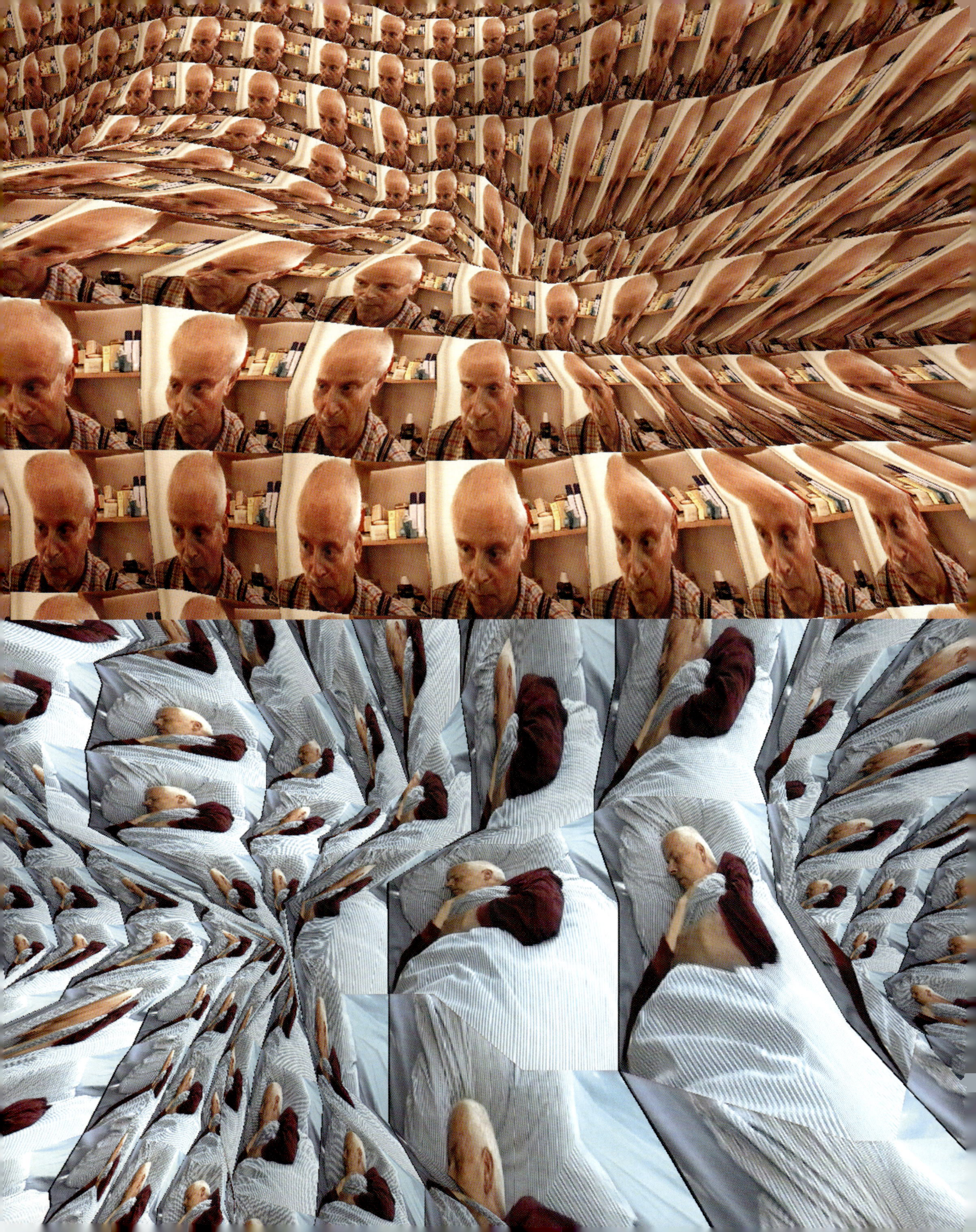

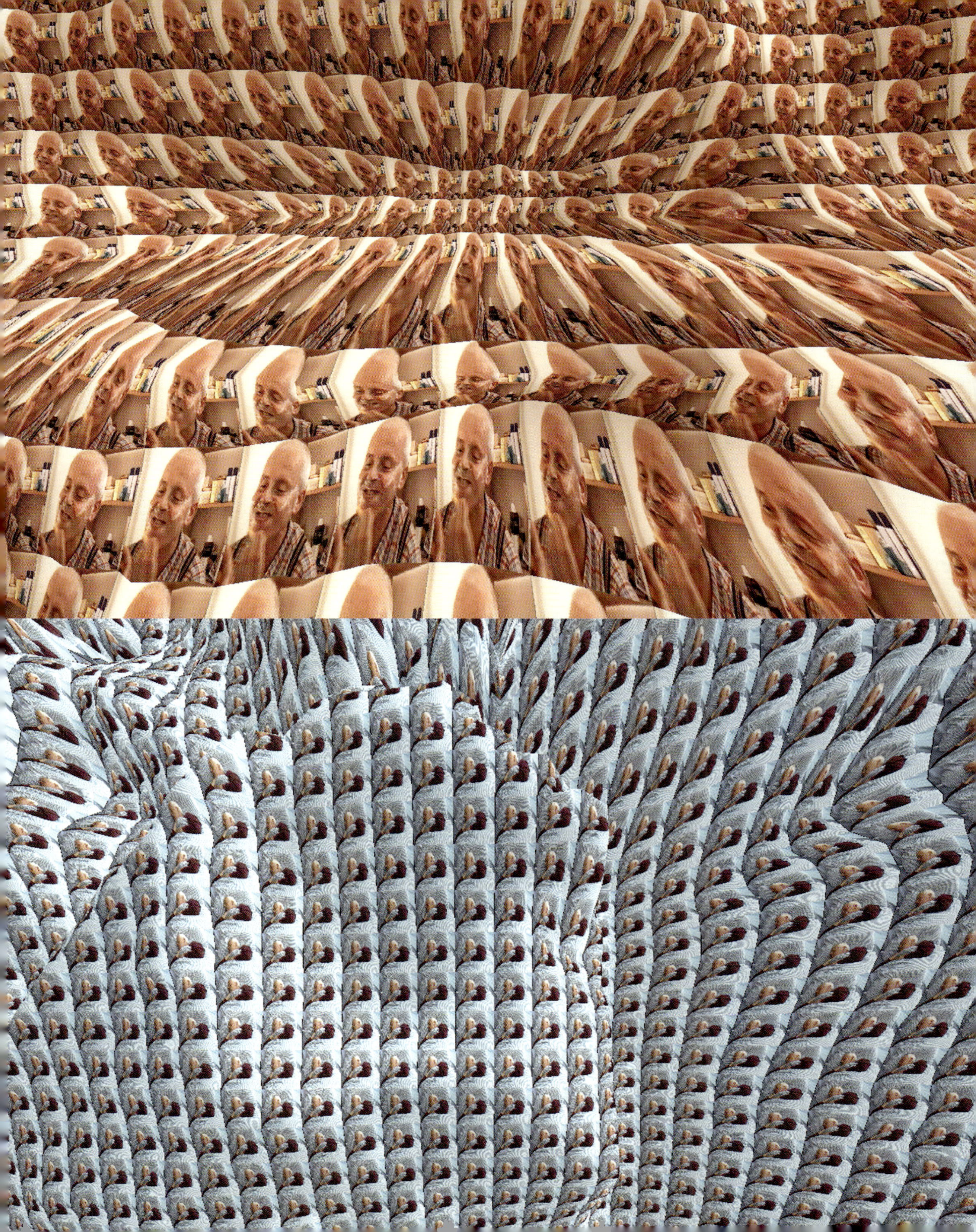

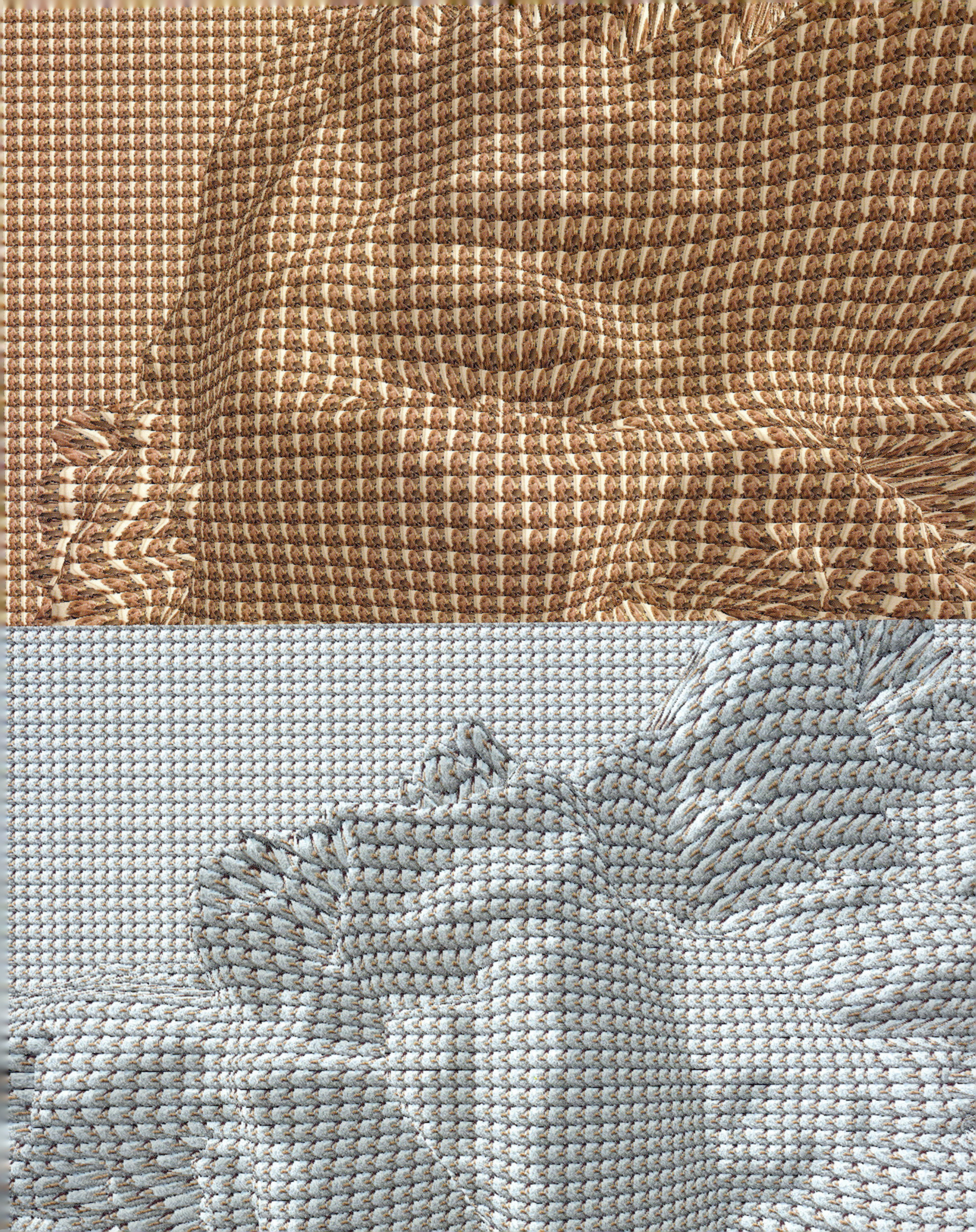

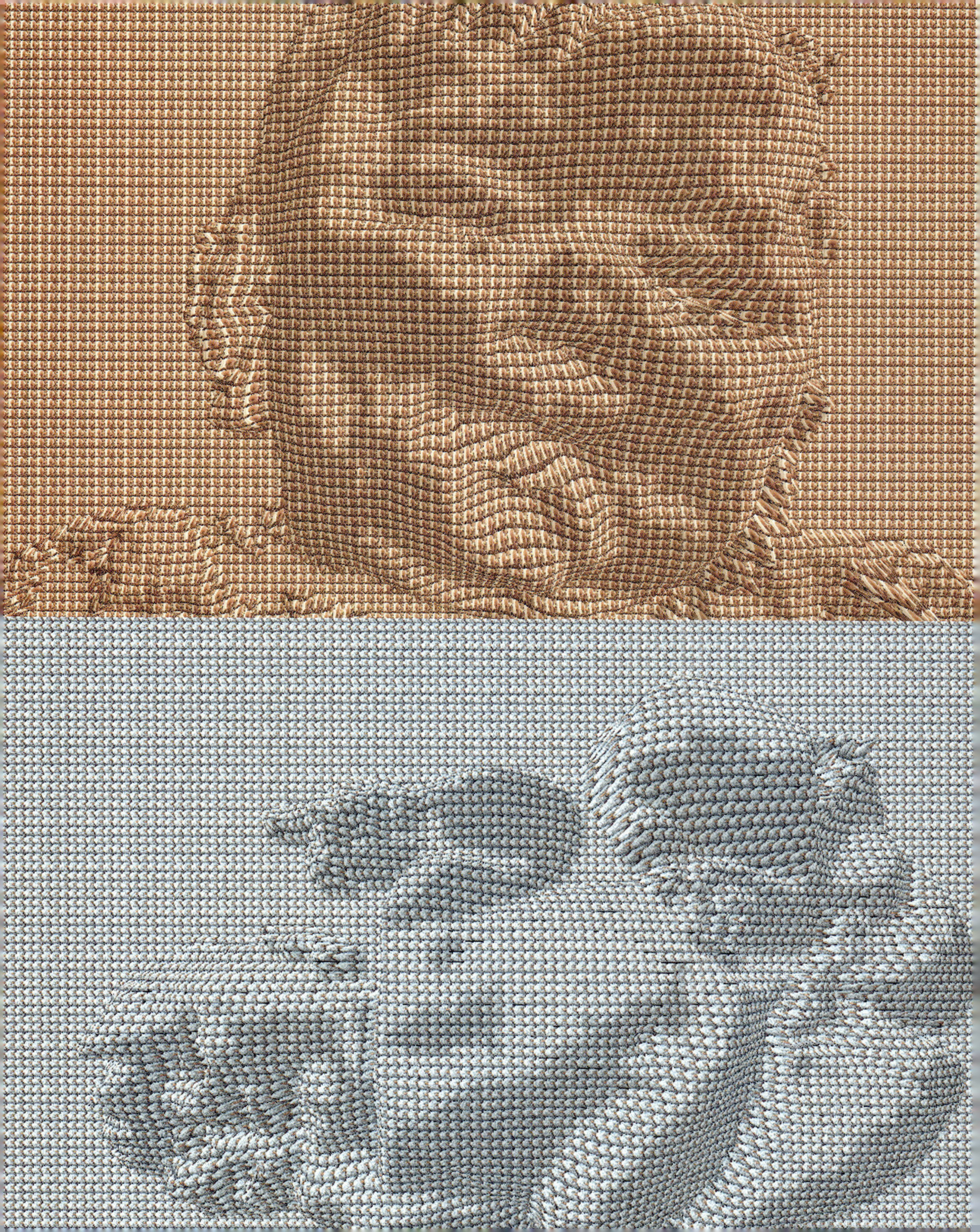

THOMAS BAYRLE, INSERT FOR PARKETT 1998,
Stills aus *b (alt)*, Computeranimation 1997 (6 Min. Video),
mit Hilfe von Kobe Matthys und Helke Bayrle.

Scenario—an outline of the plot

of a dramatic work, giving the particulars

of scenes, characters, etc.

ROBERT GRESKOVIC

Invisible Scenario

What seems fine to me, what I would like to do, is to write a book on nothing, a book without any extraneous support which would sustain itself by the inner force of its style as the world, without being held up, riding through space, a book which would be almost devoid of subject, or at least in which the subject would be invisible, if that were possible. Gustave Flaubert, 1852 [1]

Before Merce Cunningham's SCENARIO (1997)—a choreographic spectacle with no scenario for fifteen dancers with setting and costumes by Rei Kawakubo and score by Takehisa Kosugi—the history of dance theater had a kind of precedent in Oscar Schlemmer's 1922 *Triadisches Ballett (Triadic Ballet)*. The Stuttgart-born painter and Bauhaus teacher who became fascinated with theater had devised a non-ballet for figurine-like characters dressed in body-distorting costumes. Padded, molded and metalworked costume details made the dancers puppet-like. A pivotal figure, *Der Abstrakte (The Abstract*, performed by Schlemmer himself) took the form of a wildly asymmetrical personage, exemplifying the principle of disequilibrium. But for all his anomalies—mismatched legs, an un-evenly masked head sheared up the middle, contrastingly prehensile "hands," one like a pointy bell-clapper, the other like a baseball bat—Mr. Abstract cut a dapper figure with his human frame still recognizably intact. Even his fellow players, some who looked like squat chess pieces and others seemingly dressed in slinkies, revealed the essential outline of their human physicality. In an age when things mechanistic and the industrial were being canonized as ideal, the human form beneath Schlemmer's fanciful, geometric figures was intentional: "Not machine, not abstract—always man!" [2]

In our postmodern age, we have some apt words from Cunningham: "And though dancing appeals through the eye to the mind, the mind instantly rejects its meaning unless the meaning is betrayed immediately by the action. The mind is not convinced by kinetics alone, the meaning must be clear, or the language familiar and readily accessible. But clarity is the lowest form of poetry, and language, like all else in our lives, is always changing." And from Kawakubo: "I want to rethink the body, so the body and the dress become one. The idea is, no references. Today there are so many trends yet everything looks the same. It's our job to question convention."

When Cunningham's lithe and expert dancers enter Kawakubo's bright, bleached arena defined by

ROBERT GRESKOVIC is a freelance writer and dance critic. His book, *Ballet 101* will be published by Hyperion this spring.

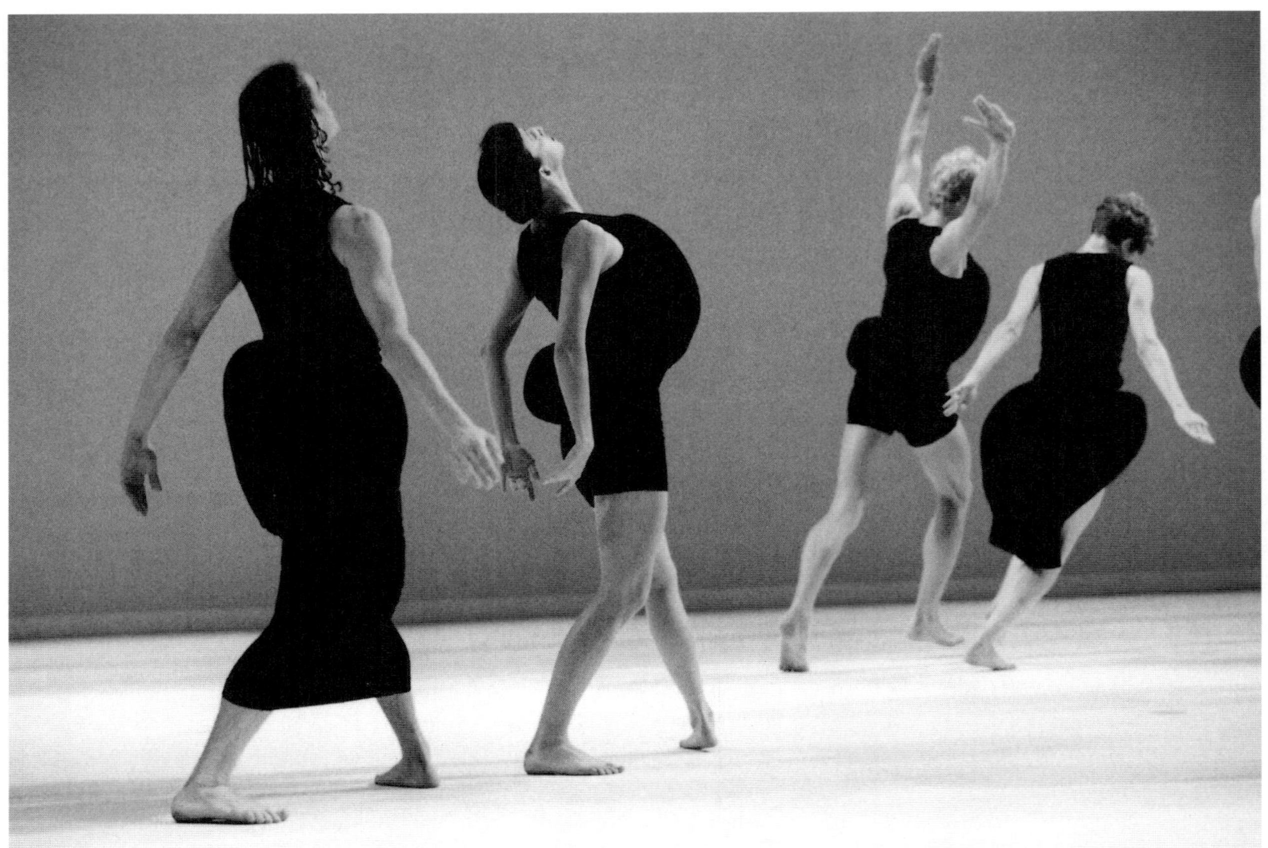

naked fluorescent light on white floor and sides, and background of taut, cream scrim, they pace, bolt, gesture, and pick their way with naked limbs working out of artfully blobular bodies. If we didn't know better from Cunningham's career-long insistence on lean and lithe dancers with necks so supple and articulate that they function like a fifth limb, we might think he'd gone extra-inclusional, going beyond multibody type and multigenerational personnel into a realm best termed "multideformational." In one sense the dancers of SCENARIO remain men and women, in another, not. They appear altogether grotesque, whimsical, absurd, off-putting, amazing.

During more than fifty years of dance-making, Cunningham has bodied forth with related events, mostly in collaboration with Robert Rauschen-berg: In 1958, for ANTIC MEET, the dancer/choreographer performed with a bentwood chair strapped to his back, which he described "like a large mosquito that won't go away"; in 1977, for TRAVELOGUE, company member Robert Kovitsch danced, somewhat hyperactively, with strings of tin cans attached to his legs like cowboy chaps. Like Schlemmer's oddly formed costumes, previous eccentric costuming for Cunningham's dances stopped short of thoroughly deforming the body, or of somehow competing with it. The basic dancer's figure remained more or less in clear view.

Enter Kawakubo's recent fashion experiments and statements in her Spring/Summer 1997 collection—"Body meets dress, dress meets body/body becomes dress, dress becomes body"—and Cunningham's SCENARIO becomes a brave new world. Down-filled pads variously attached to the dancers' torsos—some as plump as sofa bolsters, some like bulging fanny packs, others shaped like wading-pool inner tubes—act to distend stretch-fabric garments cut like clinging sleeveless sheaths, sarongs, straight skirts, or biker shorts. At the beginning of SCENARIO, Kawakubo's creations work their strangeness in a mix of gigantic turquoise gingham checks and clear periwinkle awning stripes; the patterning extra-dramatizes the topology of the swollen distortions. Subsequently, the undaunted, limber dancers with bulbous bodies change color. Patterns give way to black hole black, so that their bare limbs act as if they emanate from silhouette ink blobs. Into the arms and manipulations of a quartet of such black-clad men, Cunningham has

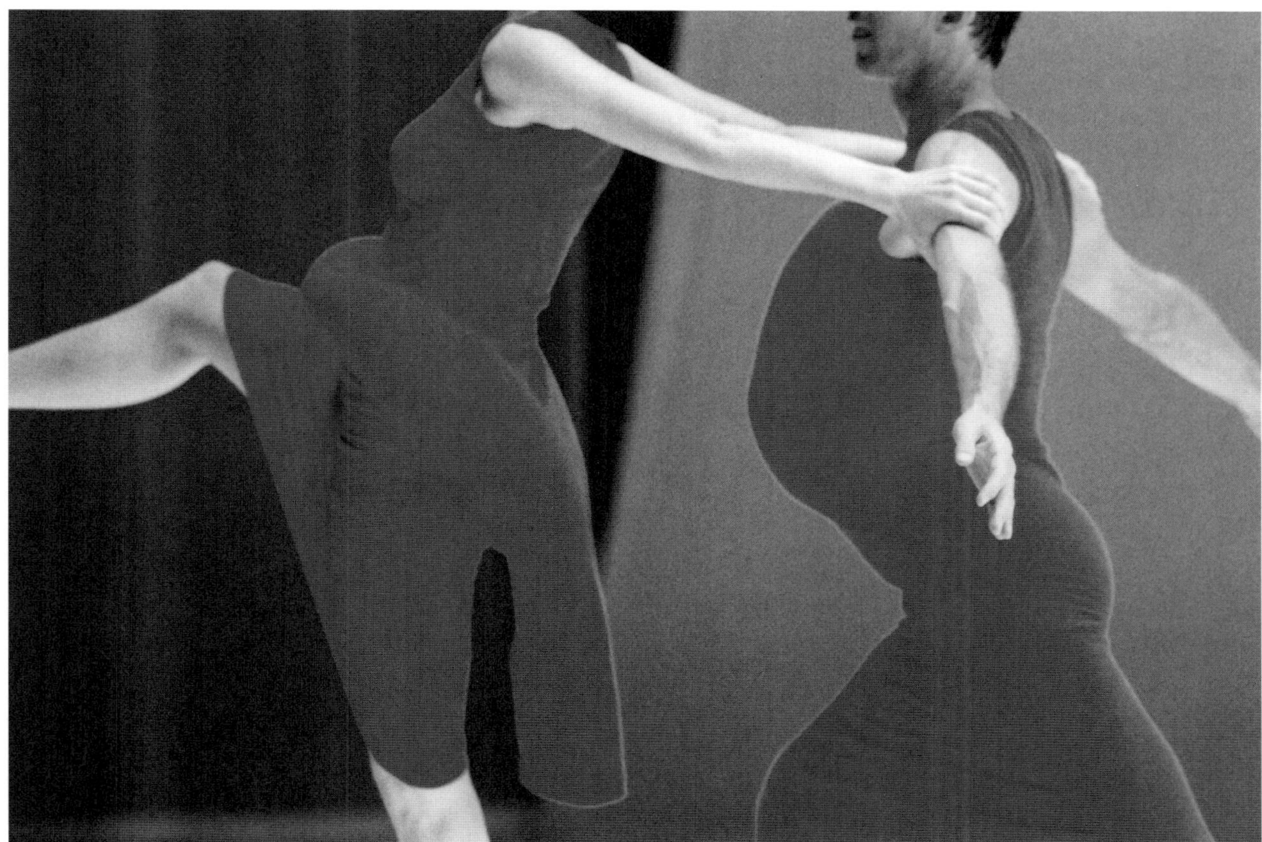

dancer Jeannie Steele passed around, swaddled like a bloated mummy in finely gathered scarlet. Red, the hue of valentine hearts and healthy blood, colors the final set of costumes and the closing segment of SCENARIO. The white lighting doesn't vary, and the dancing pays no particular heed to the segmenting defined by the costume changes. The solo, duet, and group work that make up the grand choreographic plan remain filled with the complexities and unpredictabilities of accent that Cunningham so loves to explore, particularly of late in combinations inspired by working with computer-generated dance figures.

To preempt the might of Kawakubo's harumphing deformations, Cunningham noted that the sights outside the windows of the studio in which SCENARIO was created included that of a pedestrian with a big parka and backpack expanding his body silhouette. Further observations about the world of SCENARIO keep surfacing during the play of poetically marvelous movement from dancers sporting unpredictable blobs, paunches, humps, and other sundry growths from their persons. What constitutes traditional curvaceousness? When are rich, protruding curves from a woman's torso not erotic, or anti-erotic? What about the sometimes fashionable notion of men "showing it"? When is a bulge from a male torso's midsection not provocative or lewd? What about the "pouter-pigeon silhouette" that so captivated poet/critic Edwin Denby in his 1959 writing about the Bolshoi Ballet's Galina Ulanova, where the puffed-up torso is about as fulsome as the real bird's? What about Hugo's Quasimodo sil-

houette, recently reintroduced to the world by Disney, where that hunchback sits on a willowy dancer? The nonexistent scenario of SCENARIO answers nothing for us while it floats on a stream of beguiling questions.

1) Gustave Flaubert in a letter to Louise Colet (January 16, 1852).
2) Quote by Oscar Schlemmer in: Arnold Lehman and Brenda Richardson, eds., *Oscar Schlemmer* (exhibition catalogue) (The Baltimore Museum of Art, 1986), p. 132, excerpted from Schlemmer's diaries (February, 1922), collected in: *The Letters and Diaries of Oscar Schlemmer*, selected and edited by Tut Schlemmer, trans. Krishna Winston (Wesleyan University Press, 1972).

ROBERT GRESKOVIC

Szenario – Skizze des Handlungsablaufs

eines dramatischen Werks, die Angaben über

die Szenenfolge, die auftretenden Personen etc. enthält.

Unsichtbares Szenario

Was mir schön vorkommt, was ich machen möchte, das ist ein Buch über nichts, ein Buch, das an nichts Äusserem hängt, das sich durch die innere Kraft seines Stils von selbst hält, so wie sich die Erde, ohne gestützt zu werden, in der Luft hält, ein Buch, das fast kein Thema hätte, oder in dem das Thema beinahe unsichtbar wäre, wenn das möglich ist. Gustave Flaubert, 1852[1]

SCENARIO (1997), Merce Cunninghams choreographisches Spektakel ohne Szenario für 15 Tänzer, mit Kostümen und Bühnenbild von Rei Kawakubo und Musik von Takehisa Kosugi, hat in der Geschichte des Tanztheaters in Oskar Schlemmers 1922 uraufgeführtem *Triadischem Ballett* eine Art Vorläufer. Der theaterbegeisterte Stuttgarter Maler und Bauhaus-Lehrer hatte ein ungewöhnliches Ballett für figurinenhafte Gestalten geschaffen, deren Kostüme ihre Körper verfremdeten. Polsterungen, Modellierungen und Metallgebilde verwandelten die Tänzer in marionettenhafte Spielzeuge oder Puppen. Eine zentrale Figur, *Der Abstrakte* (von Schlemmer selbst dargestellt), verkörperte das Prinzip des Ungleichgewichts und war vollkommen asymmetrisch gestaltet. Doch trotz aller Absonderlichkeiten und der nicht zueinander passenden Körperteile (verschiedenartige Beine, einen nur zum Teil maskierten, in der Mitte hochgeschorenen Kopf, unterschiedlich greiffähige «Hände», die eine wie ein Glockenklöppel, die andere wie ein Baseballschläger geformt) war Herr Abstrakt ein schmuckes Geschöpf, dessen Körper wohl umgewandelt, aber immer noch als menschliche Gestalt erkennbar war. Selbst jene Darsteller, die wie gedrungene Schachfiguren aussahen oder Kostüme trugen, die aus Sprungfedern zu bestehen schienen, offenbarten eindeutig ihre menschliche Körperform. Schlemmer liess in seinem Kommentar zu einem Zeitalter, das alles Mechanistische und Industrielle glorifizierte, die menschliche Gestalt unter den phantastischen, geometrischen Kostümen ganz bewusst erkennbar bleiben: «Nicht Maschine, nicht abstrakt – immer der Mensch!»[2]

In unserem postmodernen Zeitalter haben wir treffende Worte von Cunningham: «Und obwohl der Tanz den Geist durch das Auge anspricht, verweigert sich der Geist der Bedeutung, wenn diese nicht unmittelbar durch die Handlung offenbar wird. Kinetik allein vermag den Geist nicht zu überzeugen, die Bedeutung eines Tanzes muss klar sein, seine Sprache vertraut und leicht fassbar. Doch Klarheit ist die einfachste Form der Poesie, und die Sprache verändert sich ständig, wie alles andere in unserem Leben.» Und von Kawakubo: «Ich möchte den Körper neu erfinden, so dass Körper und Bekleidung eins werden. Es geht darum, ohne Referenzen auszukommen. Heutzutage gibt es so viele Trends, und doch sieht alles gleich aus. Es ist unsere Aufgabe, Konventionen in Frage zu stellen.»

Wenn Cunninghams graziöse und routinierte Tänzer Kawakubos helle, ausgeblichene Arena betreten, die durch nacktes Neonlicht auf weissem Boden und einen Hintergrund und Seitenwände aus straffem, cremefarbenem Stoff definiert ist, schreiten, flitzen, gestikulieren und suchen sie ihren Weg mit nackten Gliedmassen, die aus listig aufgeblähten Leibern herauswachsen. Wüssten wir nicht, dass Cunningham seit jeher grossen Wert auf

ROBERT GRESKOVIC ist freischaffender Publizist und Balletkritiker. Sein Buch *Ballet 101* erscheint dieses Frühjahr bei Hyperion.

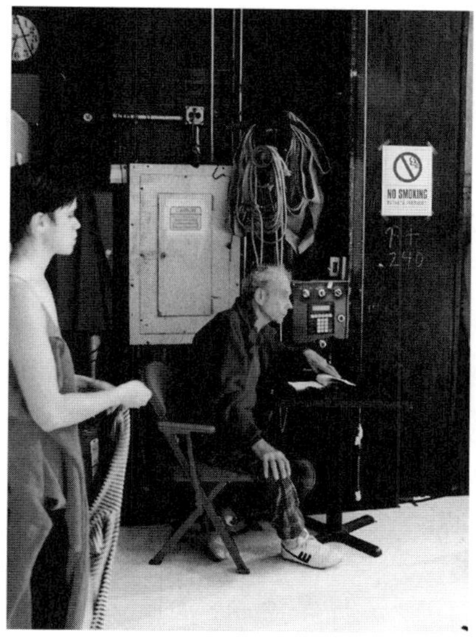

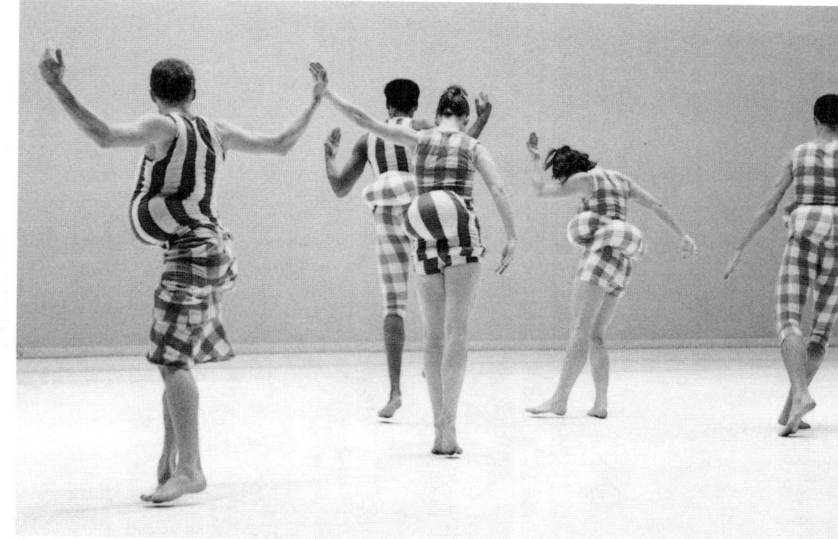

dünne und geschmeidige Tänzer legt, deren Hälse so biegsam sind, dass sie wie ein fünftes Körperglied funktionieren, glaubten wir vermutlich, er wolle zu viele Dinge einbeziehen und habe sich über die Wahl von vielfältigen Körpertypen und Darstellern verschiedenen Alters hinaus in einen Bereich hineinbewegt, der wohl am treffendsten als «multi-deformierbar» bezeichnet werden kann. Einerseits bleiben die in SCENARIO mitwirkenden Tänzer Männer und Frauen, andererseits aber auch nicht. Sie erscheinen ganz und gar grotesk, kurios, absurd, abstossend und verblüffend.

Während mehr als fünfzig Jahren choreographischen Schaffens hat Cunningham immer wieder verwandte Events gestaltet, meist in Zusammenarbeit mit Robert Rauschenberg: So 1958, als der Tänzer-Choreograph in ANTIC MEET (Groteske Begegnung) mit einem auf den Rücken geschnallten Wiener Stuhl auftrat und ihn als «riesige Stechmücke, die einfach nicht weggeht» bezeichnete; oder 1977 in TRAVELOGUE (Reisebericht), als das Ensemblemitglied

Robert Kovitsch mit Blechdosen die – ähnlich der Fransendekoration eines Cowboys – an einer Schnur an seinen Beinen festgebunden waren, hyperaktiv einen Tanz vorführte. Genau wie Schlemmers bizarr geformte Kostüme gingen die bisherigen exzentrischen Kostümierungen für Cunninghams Ballette niemals soweit, den Körper gänzlich zu deformieren oder irgendwie mit ihm in Konkurrenz zu treten. Die eigentliche Gestalt der Tänzer war stets mehr oder weniger klar erkennbar.

Lässt man sich auf Kawakubos neueste Modeexperimente und die Aussagen ein, die sie in ihrer Frühling-Sommer-Kollektion 1997 macht, formuliert als «Körper trifft Kleid, Kleid trifft Körper/Körper wird Kleid, Kleid wird Körper», so wird Cunninghams SCENARIO zu einer «schönen neuen Welt». Über daunengefüllte Polster, die da und dort am Körper der Tänzer befestigt sind, manche dick wie Sofakissen, andere modelliert wie pralle Pobacken, wieder andere geformt wie die wulstigen Luftkammern eines Kinderplanschbeckens, spannen sich die Kleidungsstücke aus

Stretchgewebe, geschnitten wie ärmellose, enganliegende Futteralkleider, Sarongs, gerade Röcke oder Bikerhosen. Zu Beginn des Stücks zeigt sich die Exzentrik von Kawakubos Kreationen in einer Mischung aus riesigen, blaugrünen Gingham-Karos und klaren, veilchenblauen Markisen-Streifen, wobei die Muster der Topologie der aufgeblähten Verformungen noch eine zusätzliche Dramatik verleihen. Später wechseln die unerschrockenen, gelenkigen Tänzer mit den knolligen Leibern die Farbe. Tiefstes Schwarz löst die Muster ab, so schwarz dass die nackten Gliedmassen der Tänzer sich bewegen, als würden sie aus Tintenklecksen wachsen, die nur aus Umrissen bestehen. In die Arme und unter der Führung eines Quartetts solch schwarzgekleideter Männer lässt Cunningham die Tänzerin Jeannie Steele hineingehen, die einer aufgeblasenen Mumie gleich in fein gekräuselte, scharlachrote Tücher gewickelt ist. Rot, die Farbe von Valentinsherzen und gesundem Blut, gibt bei der letzten Kostümserie und im Schlussab-

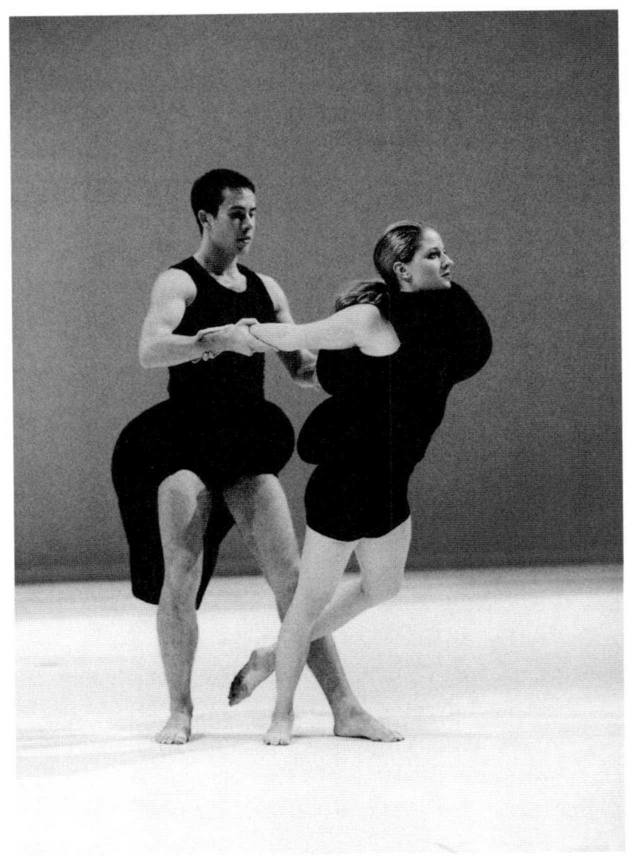

CUNNINGHAM DANCE FOUNDATION, COMME DES GARÇON COLLABORATION, 1997.

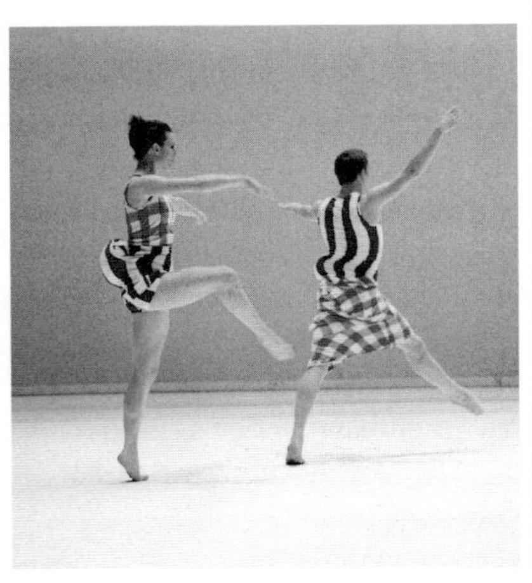

Kawakubos eindrücklichen und krassen Deformationen – durch die Fenster des Studios, in dem SCENARIO entstand, unter anderem einen Passanten erblickte, der eine voluminöse Parka und einen Rucksack trug, die seine Silhouette aufblähten. Weitere Gedanken zur Welt von SCENARIO tauchen auf, wenn man den wunderbar poetischen Bewegungen zusieht, die von Tänzern ausgeführt werden, deren Körper alle möglichen bizarren Wülste, Rundungen, Buckel und andere Wucherungen aufweisen. Was macht traditionellen Kurvenreichtum aus? Wann sind üppige, ausladende Rundungen eines weiblichen Oberkörpers nicht erotisch oder gar anti-erotisch? Was hat es mit der Gewohnheit mancher Männer, ihn zur Schau zu stellen, auf sich? Wann wird eine Wölbung in der Mittelgegend eines Männerkörpers nicht als provozierend oder anstössig empfunden? Was ist mit der «Kropftauben-Silhouette», die den Dichter und Kritiker Edwin Denby 1959 so beeindruckte, als er über die Bolschoi-Tänzerin Galina Ulanowa schrieb, deren Oberkörper aufgeplustert war wie bei einem richtigen Vogel? Was geschieht mit der Silhouette von Victor Hugos Quasimodo, die uns dank Disney seit kurzem wieder vertraut ist, wenn der Buckel auf dem Rücken eines biegsamen Tänzers sitzt? Das nichtvorhandene Szenario von SCENARIO liefert uns keine Antworten, sondern wirft eine Flut faszinierender Fragen auf. *(Übersetzung: Irene Aeberli)*

schnitt von SCENARIO den Ton an. Die weisse Beleuchtung bleibt unverändert, und die Choreographie macht keine besonderen Zugeständnisse an die Gliederung des Stücks, die sich aus dem Wechsel der Kostüme ergibt. Die Soli, Duette und Gruppenparts, aus denen sich das grosse choreographische Konzept zusammensetzt, sind nach wie vor von der Komplexität und den unvorhersehbaren Akzenten durchdrungen, die Cunningham so gerne erforscht, vor allem in jüngster Zeit in Kombinationen, die von der Arbeit mit computergenerierten Tanzfiguren inspiriert sind.

Cunningham hielt fest, dass man – gleichsam als Vorankündigung von

1) Gustave Flaubert in einem Brief an Louise Colet vom 16. Januar 1852. Aus: Gustave Flaubert, *Die Briefe an Louise Colet*, Haffmans Verlag, Zürich 1995, S. 357.
2) Zitat aus Schlemmers Tagebüchern (Februar 1922), gesammelt in: Oskar Schlemmer, *Briefe und Tagebücher*, herausgegeben von Tut Schlemmer, Hatje, Stuttgart 1977, S. 56.

CUMULUS

From America (and Africa)

IN EVERY EDITION OF PARKETT, TWO CUMULUS CLOUDS, ONE FROM AMERICA, THE OTHER FROM EUROPE, FLOAT OUT TO AN INTERESTED PUBLIC. THEY CONVEY INDIVIDUAL OPINIONS, ASSESSMENTS, AND MEMORABLE ENCOUNTERS—AS ENTIRELY PERSONAL PRESENTATIONS OF PROFESSIONAL ISSUES.

OUR CONTRIBUTORS TO THIS ISSUE ARE HAMZA WALKER, AN ARTIST, WRITER, AND CURATOR AT THE RENAISSANCE SOCIETY IN CHICAGO, AND ROMAN KURZMEYER, CURATOR OF THE PROJEKTRAUM AT THE KUNSTHALLE BERN.

HAMZA WALKER

South Africa

Although South Africa has eleven official languages, its style of journalism is clearly modeled on the British tabloid. The day I departed from Johannesburg, there were posters for the daily paper advertising an article on the Biennale which read THE BIENNALE: IS IT ALL A SCAM? Press of this order certainly was not going to help an exhibition which, rumor had it, was thrown into fiscal crisis when the city, one week before the opening, withdrew a large amount of promised support. Under these circumstances, it was a miracle that the exhibition was happening at all. Given that the Johannesburg Biennale was problematic for the right reasons, its most pressing need is that it be insured of happening again.

I was somewhat taken aback by Johannesburg's familiarity. On the way to the hotel from the airport, a gentleman from France, after hearing me declare a mild disbelief at being in Africa, said that I must remember that South Africa isn't really Africa. This would haunt me throughout the trip. I found it bothersome because I knew what he meant and I didn't want to admit it to myself. Johannesburg's coming of age is marked by a renegade urban sprawl. Since the bus driver took me to the wrong Holiday Inn, I got to see Sandton, one in a string of white suburban communities on the city's rapidly developing edges. It didn't take long to realize that the city was undergoing white flight. Nice suburban homes… homes with walls… walls with razor wire. A downtown which everyone (everyone I came into contact with thus far being white) said to avoid at all cost. No one had heard of the Biennale, "the big art show" in layman's terms. Nor did they seem to hear me when I told them it was taking place downtown. Without missing a beat, they continued to warn me of the horror of the inner city, "the drugs, the car jackings, the senseless brutality." What they said of the city and what I saw of the suburbs amounted to a Neo-Detroit circa 1969. I was well aware of the arrogance in projecting my experiences on to South Africa, but I was unaware of its use as a crutch necessary in replacing the mythic with a more sociological scale.

I arrived on Yom Kippur and the night spots which had been recommended by the hotel staff were closed. It was also the night Michael Jackson, or "Jacko" as he was referred to in the tabloids, was performing at the stadium. Lucas 23, my cab driver, kindly offered his services free of charge for the remainder of my stay if I could score him two tickets. We were in Rosebank, a happenin' nightspot, and the only place open was a gay nightclub. All of the nauseating feelgood associations I have with the international symbol for gaypride were quickly dispelled by a pro-death penalty sticker on the cigarette machine. Despite the irony in its placement, I had a hard time reconciling the sticker with the rainbow windsocks dangling overhead.

These experiences did little to change the symbolic order of my expectations for the Biennale, which actually grew as I headed into the notorious downtown for the opening of the exhibition. While it would be impossible for an exhibition held in a context as socially and politically charged as South Africa to avoid being critical of existing international art exhibitions, how and to what extent would it participate in the development of a cultural gulf stream of sorts, a force which hints at an homogenized set of art practices expanded to a global level? Or would the exhibition exercise a sensitivity towards its context that would keep such critical terms as margins and center from collapsing under the rhetoric of globalism?

"The Biennale is an announcement that South Africa is opening itself up to the world." This noble sentiment, expressed at a press tour by Okwui Enwezor, the exhibition's head curator, laid bare the project's ambitions. By bringing the flow of global cultural goods through Johannesburg, South Africans would have the opportunity to plug into a larger dialogue, to declare their cosmopolitanism. Between the lines, however, this international welcome read as an urban redevelopment scheme for the world to witness. By holding the exhibition in a disused downtown power plant whose architectural twin incidentally contained a

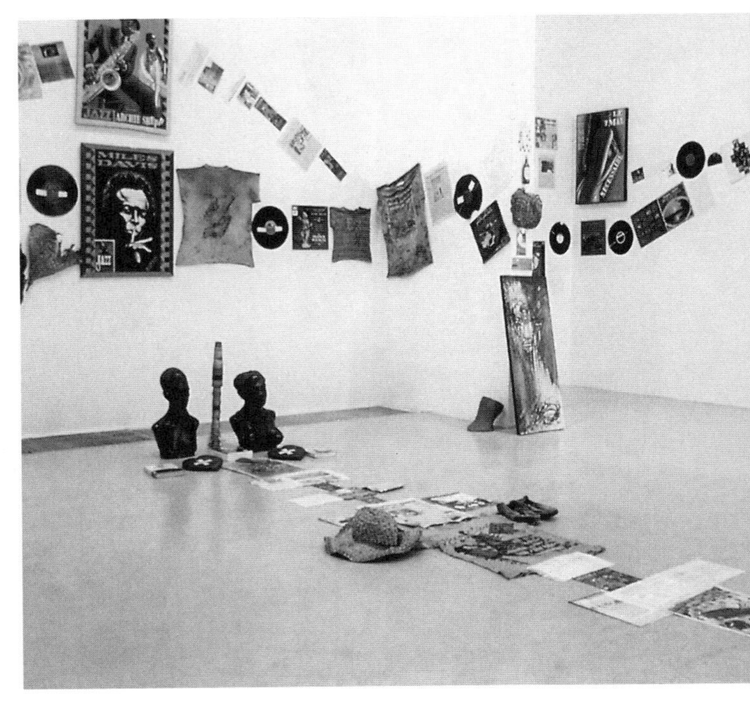

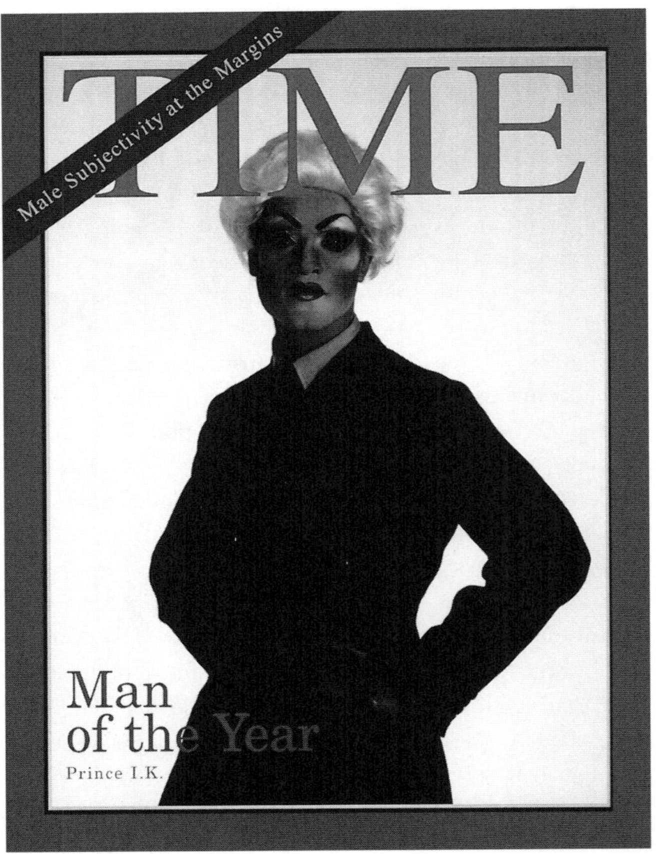

IKE UDE, MAN OF THE YEAR, 1997, from the "HE" series.

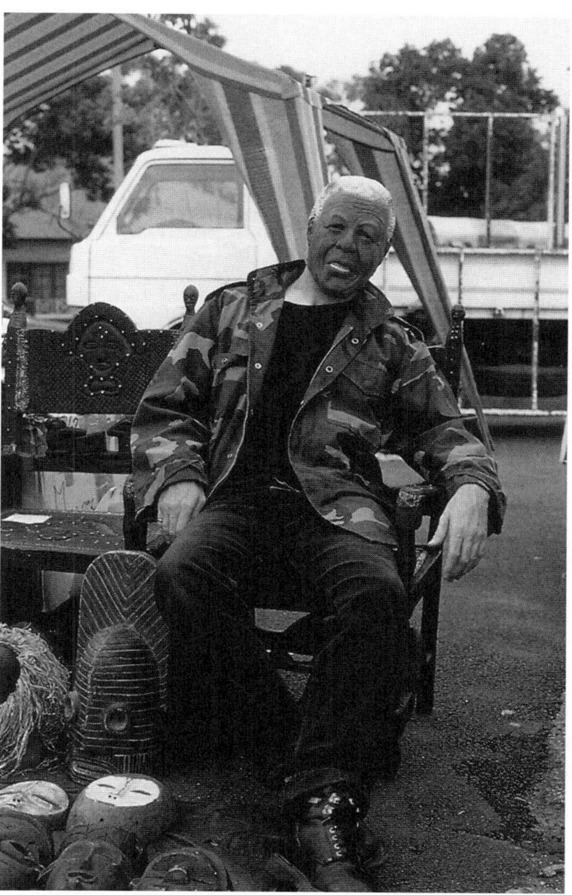

KENDELL GEERS, T.W. (MASK), 1996 / T.W. (MASKE).

PAT MAUTLOA, SHACK, 1997, construction / HÜTTE.

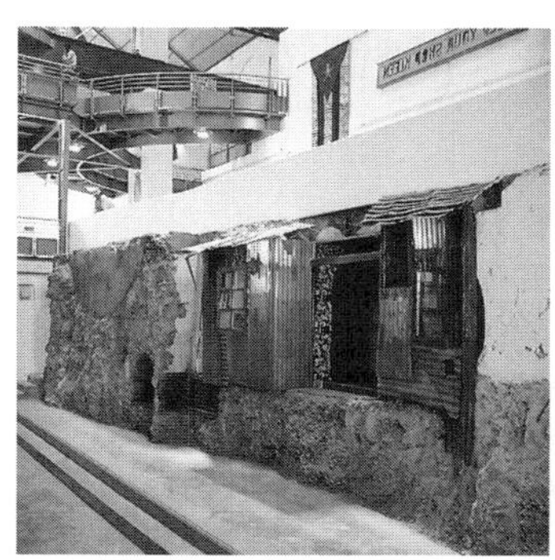

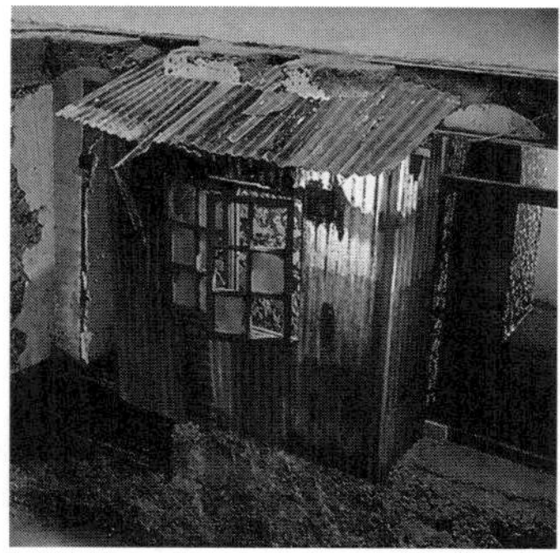

shanty town, one got the sense that culture was being used as a carrot to help spur interest in a decaying metropolitan area. While Hans Haacke's flag piece and William Kentridge's stunning animated video work, *Ubu Tells the Truth*, were quite successful in engaging South Africa's politically mythic context, engaging the immediate downtown context proved to be beyond the exhibition's grasp. Ike Ude's exercise in unbridled narcissism, a public work consisting of a poster plastered around the city announcing him as Time Magazine's Man of the Year was simply no match for the tabloid advertisements covering *Jacko's* every move.

Enwezor abandoned the model of the national pavilion in favor of an international grabbag spread over six separate components, whose curators included Colin Richards, Kellie Jones, Gerardo Mosquera, Hou Hanru, and Yu Yeon Kim. The consequences of Enwezor's decision to forsake the national pavilion, however, far from addressing, let alone resolving, the dilemma of nationalism, actually affirmed the existing mechanics of globalization as they have already been absorbed into the art market. The Biennale's six components, two of which took place in Capetown, were grouped under the title "Trade Routes: History and Geography." As this title suggests, the national pavilion would have been problematic simply because of the exhibition's overwhelming number of émigré artists; artists who, born in one country, ultimately came to reside in a cosmopolitan center following their training in a western art school. While on one level, this diasporic phenomenon may seem to counter the failure of the National Pavilion, the question it raises, but in no way resolves, is who, then, does the artist represent? If this question were put in anecdotal form it would be as follows: Does the most famous Siamese artist live in Siam? No. She lives in New York along with the rest of the world's most famous artists. It was actually the curatorial zeal that gathered together a reputable and worthy list of international cultural vagrants that kept the exhibition from feeling rooted in its context. Two of the most successful works in the exhibition, one by Pierre Huyghe and the other by Suchan Kinoshita, acknowledged the condition of vagrancy inherent in the act of cultural translation as it applies to both the artistic producer and product. The subtle casting changes in Pierre Huyghe's piece which featured three simultaneous projections of the 1920s version of *Titanic* filmed in three different languages, exposed the degree of cultural specificity behind even the most stock cinematic stereotypes. Kinoshita's video piece, experienced remotely through a telescope and headphones from an architectural structure suitable for a single person, featured the artist in a comically desperate attempt to translate into English different stories being told to her simultaneously by her Japanese mother and her Norwegian father, each speaking in their native languages at the same time in a different ear: the artist as a multilingual muse, good only as a conduit for fragmentation.

The exhibition, like any of its size, had its share of winners and losers. The symbolic dimension of the Biennale, however, remained elusive as the experience devolved into varying degrees of appreciation for individual works. As a result, I looked to the panel discussions to address issues relevant to an undertaking of the Biennale's scope in sites such as Johannesburg. This proved to be a disaster. The opening panel was entitled "Cultures in Diaspora," featuring Howardena Pindell, Meena Alexander, Gerardo Mosquera, and Sarat Maharaj. Pindell's incredibly drab critique of Kara Walker and Michael Ray Charles, which is in no way supported by a critical reading of either artist's work, quickly became an attempt to establish a good-versus-bad black artistic canon. Her failure to address a spectrum of cultural production in the African-American community, some naughty and some nice, from Walker to Martin Puryear, makes her scheme far too simplistic to address the deeper complexities of how work such as Walker's functions at a post-civil rights moment. While the content of Alexander's poetry may address the way traditonal non-western art forms must negotiate modernity, its form felt static and its theatrical presentation was painfully sweet. Mosquera's references to Afro-Latin hybridity were dated celebrations of diversity and Maharaj's talk, which held the most promise since it sought to address temporally blurred geographies and histories as a high, low and postmodernist phenomenon, was beleaguered with unforgiving technical problems. In the end, any real and immediate stakes as they related to the topic of globalism, cosmopolitanism and/or nationalism would have been better addressed if we had held hands and sung "Kumbaya." There was no intellectual fire in the room about the world-that-is, nor the world-to-be, just tepid words and slides of so-so art. My expectations were overbearing. I flew standby on the next flight to Capetown.

The rental car agent had every right to feel confident in handing me the keys. He heard me request the maximum amount of insurance. Not only was I driving on the left side of the road, I had to learn how to shift with my left hand. Each time I mistook third for first gear, the passenger cabin would flood with gasoline fumes. Had I been unable to get my shift together, I would have entered what is probably one of the most scenic parts of the world nauseous and intoxicated. The landscape surrounding Capetown ranging from Stellenbosch to the Cape of Good Hope is damn near Wagnerian. What were originally two days in wine country turned into four. Johannesburg seemed about as far away as Detroit. I wondered if my thoughts about the exhibition were rash and if there were alternatives. I wondered to what extent the Biennale reflected the terms on which South Africa was to open up, if in fact these terms were not identical to the rhetoric of cultural tourism and economic trickle-down. I wondered while I laughed. I wondered while I cried. I wondered while I drank.

South Africa's relative isolation from broader cultural developments would lead one to believe that there is a desire to belong to a cultural gulf stream. Yet, in a way which lacks the relative social and political neutrality of, say, Kassel, the presence of such a stream runs the risk of becoming a form of cultural tourism, or worse, cultural imperialism. Who owns the Johannesburg Biennale? The residents of Johannesburg or the international art community? Although I would hope it is a healthy mixture of both, for all the goodwill of the international community, winning local support at both the political and community level is imperative to ensure the possibility of such an event, let alone its success in any way, shape or form. South Africa is a new nation state strained for resources which it desperately needs to make good on collective hopes. It would be naive to imagine that the exhibitions are exempt from the pressures of a painfully new New World. But these are precisely the pressures which can shape a new event.

I returned to Johannesburg to see Soweto. Tumi, a young artist and curator, took the day to show me around. No sooner had he mentioned the random police checks and corruption in the ranks than a cop pulled us over. The officer was black. He wanted to check the serial number, call it in, see if the car was stolen. Tumi gave him lots of paper. They were too far away for me to discern which of the eleven official languages they were speaking, whether it was Xhosa, Zulu, or Afrikaans. It didn't matter. Thoroughly annoyed driver, assinine officer: the scenario is universal. The cop left us alone. Soweto is located about thirty miles outside of Johannesburg. From a lookout tower in Oppenheim Park we surveyed a good portion of the townships. Tumi

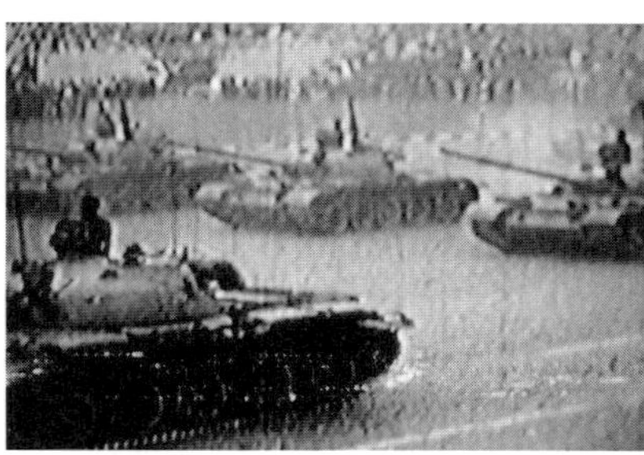

SALEM MEKOURIA,
YE WONZ MAIBEL (DELUGE), 1996,
16mm film to video / 16mm-Film auf Video.

pointed and with each settling of the index finger came a tale. He then took me to another exhibition he had curated. It was an exhibition of photos taken during the 1986 student uprising and it was held in cargo trailers situated on the site where the first student was killed. School had just let out and the streets were filled with children in their uniforms. This forced my imagination to do work for which it had little enthusiasm. There were five trailers, four of them containing artwork, and the fifth a gift shop with T-shirts and Mandela paraphernalia, a reminder that the sto-

ry has a successful outcome: Freedom. Now what? Time for faith to be tested.

Although I did not attend the first Biennale, I heard that this one was somewhat conservative by comparison. Given that its ambitions were focused on putting the event on the global map, it did not seem to ask the more crucial question of what will set it apart from other international exhibitions. The fact that South Africa is a charged context makes it a rich context. It is not simply in theory but in practice that the Johannesburg Biennale represents a chance to reinvigorate the model of the international exhibition and combat the rather dreary state of our political imaginations. Assembling a roster of artists from around the world does not make an international spectacle, especially when the circulation of artists becomes the status quo. Although the proliferation of international exhibitions would appear to make the task of curating easier, cultural vagrancy actually presents the new challenge of giving roots to events occurring in the cultural gulf stream.

Auch wenn Südafrika elf offizielle Sprachen kennt, steht dort beim journalistischen Stil offensichtlich die britische Boulevardpresse Pate. Am Tag meiner Abreise aus Johannesburg waren in der Stadt Plakate für die lokale Tageszeitung angeschlagen, die mit einem Artikel über die Biennale unter der Überschrift THE BIENNALE: IS IT ALL A SCAM? (Die Biennale: ein einziger Schwindel?) warben. Eine Presse dieser Art war gewiss nicht hilfreich für eine Ausstellung, die Gerüchten zufolge in eine Finanzkrise gestürzt wurde, als die

HAMZA WALKER

Südafrika

Stadt eine Woche vor der Eröffnung zugesagte Fördermittel von beträchtlicher Höhe zurückzog. Unter diesen Umständen war es ein Wunder, dass die Ausstellung überhaupt stattfand. Da die Biennale von Johannesburg aus guten Gründen problematisch war,

braucht sie nichts dringlicher als die Versicherung, dass sie wieder stattfinden wird.

Ich war ein wenig überrascht, wie vertraut Johannesburg wirkte. Als ich auf dem Weg vom Flughafen zum Hotel der Empfindung Ausdruck verlieh, nicht richtig glauben zu können, dass ich in Afrika sei, meinte ein Herr aus Frankreich, ich solle bedenken, dass Südafrika nicht wirklich Afrika sei. Dies sollte mich während meiner Reise nicht mehr loslassen. Es ärgerte mich, weil ich wusste, was er meinte, und ich es mir selbst nicht eingestehen wollte. Der Reifeprozess Johannesburgs ist gekennzeichnet durch die ungezügelte Ausbreitung des Stadtgebiets. Da mich der Busfahrer zum falschen *Holiday Inn* fuhr, bekam ich Sandton zu sehen, ein Glied in einer Kette weisser Vorstadtgemeinden an dem in rasantem Tempo erschlossenen Stadtrand. Man brauchte nicht lange, um einzusehen, dass die Stadt eine weisse Flucht erlebte. Hübsche Vorstadthäuser... Häuser mit Mauern drum herum... Mauern mit Stacheldraht. Ein Stadtzentrum, das ich, wie mir jeder sagte (wobei jeder, dem ich bis dahin begegnet war, weiss war), unbedingt meiden sollte. Keiner hatte etwas von der Biennale, von der, für Laien verständlich ausgedrückt, «grossen Kunstausstellung», gehört. Und es schien, als hörte man mich gar nicht, wenn ich sagte, dass sie im Stadtzentrum veranstaltet wurde. Ohne Atempause fuhr man fort, mich vor den Schrecken der zentrumsnahen Wohnviertel zu warnen, vor den «Drogen, den Autoentführungen, der sinnlosen Brutalität». Was andere über die Stadt erzählten und was ich von den Vorstädten sah, lief hinaus auf eine Neuauflage von Detroit um 1969. Ich war mir der Anmassung, die in der Projektion meiner Erfahrungen auf Südafrika lag, durchaus bewusst, was ich jedoch nicht wusste war, dass diese Projektion tatsächlich als Krücke zu gebrauchen war, um anstelle der mythischen einen eher soziologischen Massstab anlegen zu können.

Als ich ankam, war gerade Jom Kippur, und die Nachtklubs, die mir die Leute vom Hotel empfohlen hatten, waren geschlossen. Ausserdem trat an jenem Abend Michael Jackson, oder «Jacko», wie er in den Boulevardblättern genannt wird, im Stadion auf. Lucas 23, mein Taxifahrer, bot mir freundlicherweise für meinen weiteren Verbleib kostenlos seine Dienste an, falls ich ihm zwei Eintrittskarten verschaffen könnte. Wir befanden uns in Rosebank, einem Amüsierviertel, und das einzige Lokal, das geöffnet war, war ein Schwulennachtklub. All die übel aufstossenden wohligen Gefühle, die das internationale Symbol der Schwulenbewegung in mir auszulösen pflegt, verflogen sogleich, als ich auf dem Zigarettenautomaten einen Aufkleber erblickte, der für die Todesstrafe warb. Trotz der Ironie, die in dem Ort seiner Anbringung lag, fiel es mir schwer, den Aufkleber mit den regenbogenfarbenen Windsäcken über meinem Kopf in Einklang zu bringen.

Diese Erlebnisse änderten wenig an der symbolischen Ordnung meiner Erwartungen an die Biennale, die sogar noch stiegen, als ich schliesslich zur Eröffnung der Ausstellung in das berüchtigte Stadtzentrum fuhr. Während eine Ausstellung in einem sozial und politisch derart spannungsgeladenen Kontext wie Südafrika sich unmöglich einer Kritik an bestehenden internationalen Kunstausstellungen würde enthalten können, fragte ich mich, auf welche Weise und inwiefern sie ihrerseits zur Entwicklung einer Art kulturellen Golfstroms beitragen würde, einer Kraft, die auf eine vereinheitlichte, auf globale Ebene ausgedehnte Kunstpraxis hinausläuft. Oder würde die Ausstellung eine Sensibilität für ihren Kontext an den Tag legen, die verhinderte, dass kritische Begriffe wie Peripherie und Mitte unter der Rhetorik des Globalen begraben würden?

«Die Biennale setzt ein Signal, dass Südafrika sich der Welt öffnet.» Dieser hehre Gedanke, den Okwui Enwezor, der leitende Kurator der Ausstellung, bei einem Presserundgang äusserte, offenbarte die Ziele des Projekts. Indem man den Fluss globaler kultureller Güter durch Johannesburg leitete, würde den Südafrikanern die Gelegenheit geboten, sich in einen übergreifenden Dialog einzuklinken und ihren Kosmopolitismus zu beweisen. Genauer besehen, hatte dieser internationale Empfang freilich eher etwas von einer Präsentation eines Stadtsanierungsplans, zu der die Welt als Zeuge eingeladen war. Da die Ausstellung in einem stillgelegten Kraftwerk veranstaltet wurde, in dessen Zwillingsbau im übrigen eine Barackensiedlung untergebracht war, konnte man sich des Eindrucks nicht erwehren, dass die Kultur als Köder benutzt wurde, um das Interesse an einer heruntergekommenen Grossstadtgegend anzufachen. Während sich Hans Haackes Flaggenarbeit und das grossartige Zeichentrickvideo *Ubu Tells the Truth* (Ubu erzählt die Wahrheit) von William Kentridge in durchaus gelungener Weise mit Südafrikas politisch mythischem Kontext auseinandersetzten, überstieg eine Auseinandersetzung mit dem unmittelbaren innerstädtischen Kontext offenbar den geistigen Horizont der Ausstellung. Ike Udes Übung in ungezügeltem Narzissmus, eine Arbeit im öffentlichen Raum, bestehend aus einem im ganzen Stadtgebiet angeschlagenen Plakat, das ihn als den vom US-Nachrichtenmagazin *Time* ausgerufenen «Mann des Jahres» darstellte, konnte einfach nicht mithalten mit den Werbeplakaten für die Boulevardblätter, die über jeden einzelnen Schritt *Jackos* berichteten.

Enwezor verzichtete auf das Prinzip der nationalen Pavillons zugunsten einer internationalen Wundertüte bestehend aus sechs voneinander unabhängigen Teilen, für die als Kuratoren Colin Richards, Kellie Jones, Gerardo Mosquera, Hou Hanru und Yu Yeon Kim fungierten. Die Folge von Enwezors Entscheidung, auf nationale Pavillons zu verzichten, war freilich keineswegs, dass etwa das Dilemma des Nationalismus angesprochen, geschweige denn gelöst wurde, sondern vielmehr eine Bekräftigung der bestehenden Mechanismen der Globalisierung, wie sie bereits in den Kunstmarkt Eingang gefunden haben. Die sechs Teilausstellungen der Biennale, von denen zwei in Kapstadt stattfanden, wurden zusammengefasst unter dem Titel «Handelsrouten: Geschichte und Geographie». Wie dieser Titel andeutet, wäre das Prinzip des nationalen Pavillons schon allein wegen der überwältigenden Anzahl von Exilkünstlern problematisch gewesen, das heisst von Künstlern, die ihre ursprüngliche Heimat verlassen und sich nach dem Kunststudium im Westen schliesslich in einem kosmopolitischen Zentrum niedergelassen hatten. Während es auf einer Ebene den Anschein haben mag, als würde dieses diasporaähnliche Phänomen dem Fehlen des Nationalen Pavillons etwas anderes entgegensetzen, besteht das Dilemma, das es aufwirft, aber keineswegs löst, in der Frage, wen der Künstler denn nun vertritt. In eine anekdotische Form gekleidet, würde sich dieses Dilemma wie folgt darstellen: Lebt der/die berühmteste siamesische KünstlerIn in Siam? Nein, sie lebt in New York zusammen mit all den anderen

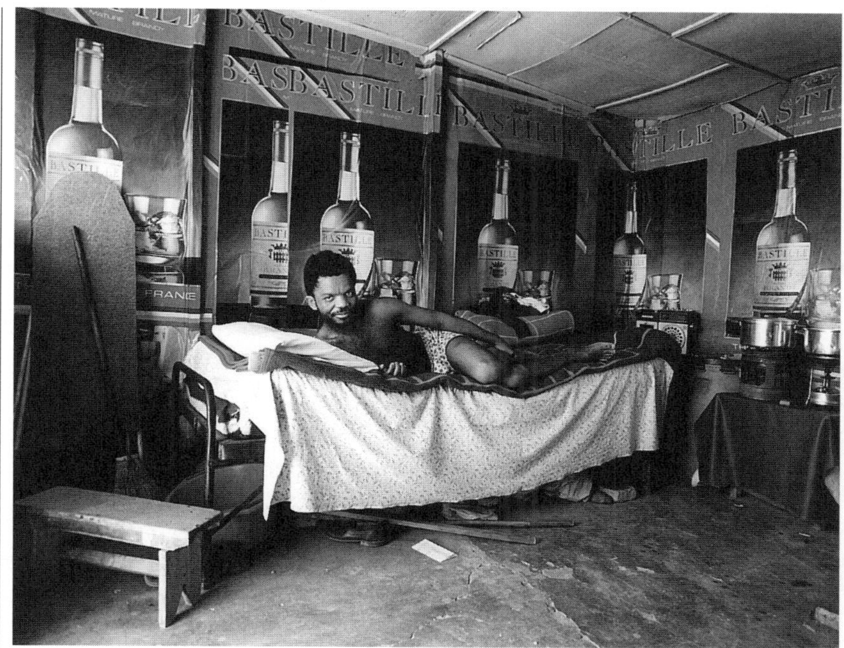

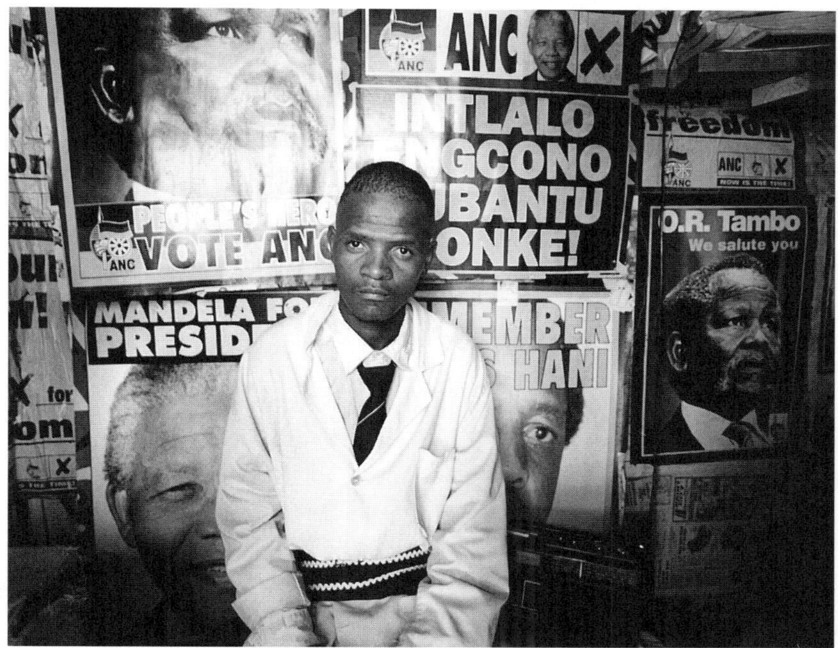

berühmtesten KünstlerInnen der Welt. Tatsächlich war es der kuratorische Eifer, mit dem ein renommiertes, prestigeträchtiges Aufgebot internationaler kultureller Nomaden zusammengetragen wurde, der eine Verwurzelung der Ausstellung in ihrem Kontext verhinderte. Zwei der gelungensten Werke in der Ausstellung, eines von Pierre Huyghe und das andere von Suchan Kinoshita, bestätigten den Zustand der Unstetheit, die, auf den Akt der kulturellen Übersetzung bezogen, sowohl den künstlerischen Produzenten wie dem künstlerischen Produkt innewohnt. Die subtilen Rollenwechsel in Pierre Huyghes Arbeit, die drei simultane Projektionen der in den 20er Jahren gedrehten Version von *Titanic* in drei verschiedenen Sprachfassungen zeigte, deckten das Mass der kulturellen Spezifität sogar hinter den grössten filmischen Klischees auf. Kinoshitas Videoarbeit, die man aus der Entfernung über ein Teleskop und Kopfhörer von einer auf jeweils eine Person zugeschnittenen Konstruktion aus erlebte, zeigte die Künstlerin bei dem verzweifelten und zugleich nicht der Komik entbehrenden Versuch, verschiedene Geschichten, die ihr ihre japanische Mutter und ihr norwegischer Vater in deren jeweiliger Muttersprache gleichzeitig jeweils in ein anderes Ohr erzählten, ins Englische zu übersetzen. Die Künstlerin als multilinguale Muse, geeignet nur als ein Medium der Fragmentierung.

Die Ausstellung hatte wie jede Schau dieser Grössenordnung ihr Kontingent an Gewinnern und Verlierern. Die symbolische Dimension der Biennale jedoch blieb ungreifbar, da das Ausstellungserlebnis abglitt in eine mehr oder weniger positive Würdigung einzelner Arbeiten. So erhoffte ich mir von den Podiumsdiskussionen, dass zumindest sie Fragen ansprechen würden, die für ein Projekt von der Grössenordnung der Biennale in einer Stadt wie Johannesburg von Bedeutung waren. Dies erwies sich als glatter Reinfall. Das erste Podiumsgespräch stand unter dem Motto «Kulturen in der Diaspora», und die Diskussionsteilnehmer waren Howardena Pindell, Meena Alexander, Gerardo Mosquera und Sarat Maharaj. Pindells unglaublich geistlose Kritik an Kara Walker und Michael Ray Charles, die in keiner Weise durch eine eingehende Auseinandersetzung mit dem Werk der beiden Künstler gestützt wird, verkam schnell zu einem Versuch, einen Kanon guter gegen einen solchen schlechter schwarzer Kunst abzugrenzen. Die Ausblendung einer ganzen Bandbreite teils provokanten, teils entgegenkommenden kulturellen Schaffens in der afroamerikanischen Szene von Walker bis Martin Puryear machte ihr Schema viel zu simplifizierend, als dass es den tieferen Komplexitäten von einem Œuvre wie dem Kara Walkers zum Zeitpunkt der Nach-Bürgerrechtsbewegung Rechnung tragen könnte. Der Inhalt von Alexanders Poesie möchte zwar erörtern, wie sich traditionelle nichtwestliche Kunstformen mit der Moderne auseinanderzusetzen hätten, doch von der Form her wirkt sie statisch, und ihre theatralische Präsentation war von einer peinlichen Süsslichkeit. Was Mosquera über afrolateinamerikanische Vermischung zu sagen hatte, war eine altbackene Verklärung der Vielfalt, und Maharajs Vortrag, der am vielversprechendsten war, weil er zeitlich verwischte Geographien und Geschichten als Phänomen von High, Low und Postmoderne behandelte, wurde von unerbittlichen technischen Problemen heimgesucht. Am Ende wäre eher etwas von wirklicher, unmittelbarer Relevanz zum Thema Globalisierung und Kosmopolitismus beziehungsweise Nationalismus herausgekommen, wenn wir alle Händchen gehalten und «Kumbaya» gesungen hätten. Es gab im Saal keine intellektuelle Begeisterung, weder über die bestehende noch über eine zukünftige Welt, sondern nur lauwarme Worte und Dias von eher mässiger Kunst. Ich hatte meine Erwartungen zu hoch geschraubt. Ich flog mit dem nächstbesten Flugzeug, in dem noch ein Platz frei war, nach Kapstadt.

Der Vertreter der Mietwagenfirma hatte, als er mir die Autoschlüssel übergab, allen Grund zur Zuversicht. Ich hatte ihn um die maximale Versicherungssumme gebeten. Schliesslich fuhr ich nicht nur auf der linken Strassenseite, ich musste auch lernen, mit meiner linken Hand zu schalten. Jedesmal, wenn ich den dritten mit dem ersten Gang verwechselte, strömte Benzindunst ins Wageninnere. Wäre ich des Problems nicht Herr geworden, so hätte ich eine der wohl schönsten Gegenden der Welt kotzenderweise und völlig benebelt erreicht. Die Landschaft um Kapstadt, von Stellenbosch bis zum Kap der Guten Hoffnung, kommt einer Wagnerschen Szenerie verdammt nahe. Aus ursprünglich zwei Tagen im Weinbaugebiet wurden schliesslich vier. Johannesburg schien ungefähr so weit weg wie Detroit. Ich fragte mich, ob meine Überlegungen über die Ausstellung voreilig und ob vielleicht andere Einschätzungen denkbar waren. Ich fragte mich, inwiefern die Biennale die Rahmenbedingungen widerspiegelte, unter denen sich die Öffnung Südafrikas vollziehen würde, ob diese Rahmenbedingungen nicht im Grunde identisch waren mit der Rhetorik des Kulturtourismus und des wirtschaftlichen Sickereffekts. Ich wunderte mich, während ich lachte. Ich wunderte mich, während ich weinte. Ich wunderte mich, während ich trank.

Die weitgehende Ausgrenzung Südafrikas von den übergreifenden kulturellen Entwicklungen liesse vermuten, dass nunmehr das Bedürfnis da ist, Teil eines kulturellen Golfstroms zu sein. Doch auf eine Art und Weise, wie sie im gesellschaftlich und politisch eher neutralen Rahmen etwa von Kassel undenkbar wäre, birgt das Vorhandensein eines solchen Stroms die Gefahr, dass dabei am Ende eine Form von Kulturtourismus oder, schlimmer noch, kulturellem Imperialismus herauskommt. Wem gehört die Biennale von Johannesburg? Den Einwohnern von Johannesburg oder der internationalen Kunstszene? Wie ich hoffen würde, einer gesunden Mischung aus beiden. Doch bei allem guten Willen der internationalen Szene ist es, um sicherzustellen, dass eine Veranstaltung wie diese überhaupt stattfinden, geschweige denn in irgendeiner Form oder Ausgestaltung ein Erfolg werden kann, unbedingt erforderlich, lokale Unterstützung zu gewinnen. Südafrika ist ein neuer Nationalstaat, der nach Ressourcen giert, derer er dringend bedarf, um die kollektiven Hoffnungen nicht zu enttäuschen. Es wäre naiv zu glauben, dass Ausstellungen von den Zwängen einer schmerzhaft neuen Neuen Welt befreit wären. Zugleich aber sind es genau diese Zwänge, die einem neuen Ereignis ein spezifisches Gepräge verleihen können.

Ich kehrte nach Johannesburg zurück, um mir Soweto anzusehen. Tumi, ein junger Künstler und Ausstellungsmacher, nahm sich den Tag frei, um mich herumzuführen. Kaum hatte er die willkürlichen Polizeikontrollen und die Korruption in den Reihen der Gesetzeshüter erwähnt, wurden wir schon von einem Bullen an den Strassenrand dirigiert. Es war ein schwarzer Polizist.

Er wollte die Seriennummer des Autos kontrollieren, sie abrufen und überprüfen, ob der Wagen gestohlen war. Tumi übergab ihm jede Menge Dokumente. Die beiden waren zu weit weg, um auszumachen, in welcher der elf offiziellen Sprachen sie sich unterhielten, ob in Xhosa, Zulu oder Afrikaans. Es spielte keine Rolle. Ein völlig verärgerter Autofahrer, ein dämlicher Polizist, das Szenario ist überall gleich. Der Bulle liess uns laufen. Soweto ist etwa fünfzig Kilometer südwestlich von Johannesburg gelegen. Von einem Aussichtsturm im Oppenheim Park konnten wir einen Grossteil der Townships überblicken. Tumi zeigte mit dem Finger auf diese und jene Stelle, und jedesmal, wenn der Zeigefinger wieder sank, folgte eine Geschichte. Anschliessend führte er mich zu einer Ausstellung, die er ebenfalls organisiert hatte. Es war eine Ausstellung von Photos, die während des Schüleraufstandes 1986 aufgenommen worden waren, und sie war untergebracht in LKW-Anhängern, die man an der Stelle aufgestellt hatte, wo seinerzeit der erste Schüler getötet worden war. Die Schule war gerade aus, und die Strassen füllten sich mit Kindern in ihren Schuluniformen. Dies zwang mich, mir Dinge vorzustellen, für die ich mich nur wenig erwärmen konnte. Es gab fünf LKW-Anhänger, von denen vier Kunst beherbergten, während im fünften ein Laden untergebracht war, in dem T-Shirts und Mandela-Memorabilien verkauft wurden – eine Erinnerung an den guten Ausgang der Geschichte: Freiheit. Was nun? Zeit, die Erwartungen einer Prüfung zu unterziehen.

Obgleich ich die erste Biennale nicht gesehen hatte, hatte ich mir sagen lassen, dass die jetzige etwas reaktionär war. Da man darauf aus war, die Veranstaltung auf die Weltkarte zu bringen, hatte man offenbar vergessen, sich die wichtigere Frage zu stellen, wodurch sie sich von anderen internationalen Ausstellungen unterscheiden sollte. Südafrika bietet aufgrund der Spannungen, die in dem Land herrschen, einen ergiebigen Kontext. Die Biennale von Johannesburg stellt nicht nur in der Theorie, sondern gerade auch in der Praxis eine Chance dar, dem Prinzip der internationalen Ausstellung neues Leben einzuhauchen und dem ziemlich tristen Zustand unserer politischen Imagination entgegenzutreten. Ein Aufgebot von Künstlern aus aller Welt zusammenzutragen macht noch kein internationales Spektakel aus, zumal nicht, wenn der weltumspannende Schaulauf der Künstler zum Status quo wird. Obgleich die rapide Zunahme internationaler Ausstellungen die Aufgabe des Ausstellungsmachers zu erleichtern scheint, stellt das kulturelle Nomadentum uns tatsächlich vor die neue Herausforderung, Veranstaltungen, die sich im Rahmen des kulturellen Golfstroms bewegen, Wurzeln zu verleihen.

(Übersetzung: Bram Opstelten)

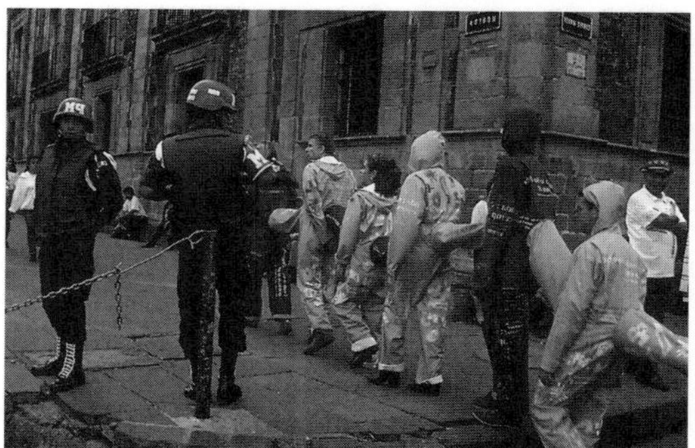

LUCY ORTA, COLLECTIVE WEAR, 1996, microporous polyester, silk-screen print, social links / KOLLEKTIVKLEIDUNG, atmungsaktiver Polyester, Siebdruck, Gesellschaftsglieder.

CUMULUS

Aus Europa (und Asien)

IN JEDER AUSGABE VON PARKETT PEILT EINE CUMULUS-WOLKE AUS AMERIKA UND EINE AUS EUROPA DIE INTERESSIERTEN KUNSTFREUNDE AN. SIE TRÄGT PERSÖNLICHE RÜCKBLICKE, BEURTEILUNGEN UND DENK- WÜRDIGE BEGEGNUNGEN MIT SICH – ALS JEWEILS GANZ EIGENE DAR- STELLUNG EINER BERUFSMÄSSIGEN AUSEINANDERSETZUNG.

IN DIESEM HEFT ÄUSSERN SICH ROMAN KURZMEYER, LEITER DES PROJEKT- RAUMS IN DER KUNSTHALLE BERN, UND HAMZA WALKER, KÜNSTLER, SCHRIFT- STELLER UND KURATOR DER RENAISSANCE SOCIETY IN CHICAGO.

ZWEI REISEN NACH SÜDKOREA

ROMAN KURZMEYER

Die Orient-Sehnsucht ist fester Bestandteil europäischer Geschichte. Spätestens seit dem 19. Jahrhundert gibt es ein spezifisches, immer wieder aktualisiertes Interesse für Asien. Davon zeugen nicht nur die Bestände der völkerkundlichen Sammlungen und deren Einfluss auf die ästhetischen Debatten in Europa, sondern auch die asiatischen Gesellschaften zur Erforschung der Kulturen Asiens, die schon zu Beginn des vergangenen Jahrhunderts in den europäischen Hauptstädten ins Leben gerufen wurden.

Nach den christlichen Zeichen zu schliessen, auf die ich in Südkorea überall traf, erfasste der französische Philosoph und Historiker Michel Foucault den Zivilisationsprozess äusserst präzise, als er 1969 in einem Gespräch mit Paolo Caruso zwar anerkannte, dass sich die westliche Kultur empfänglich für fremdes Denken zeige, zugleich aber auch betonte, in Wirklichkeit würde die gesamte Welt zunehmend verwestlichen.[1]

Nach Masakazu Yamazaki war es die duale Struktur von religiöser Herrschaft (Christentum) und Sprache (Latein), die die Ausbreitung der westlichen Zivilisation ermöglichte. «Im Gegensatz dazu», so die These des Autors, «hat es in Asien nie einen vergleichbaren über-ethnischen Zivilisationsrahmen gegeben. Ohne jede Erfahrung in politischer Einigung, wie es sie im römischen Imperium gab, haben die Asiaten keine gemeinsame Tradition in bezug auf Sprache, Währung, Gesetze, Verkehrswege oder architektonische Stile gehabt. Bei Abwesenheit jedes übergreifenden (wenn auch lockeren) religiösen Rahmens wie dem des Christentums haben Konfuzianismus, Buddhismus, Taoismus, Islam und eine Vielzahl von einheimischen Religionen immer gleichzeitig nebeneinander (und gegeneinander) gestanden.»[2] Bezeichnend dafür ist auch, dass es in Asien weder ein gemeinsames Schriftsystem noch gemeinsame Ursprungsmythen gibt.

In Korea heisst es, das koreanische Volk sei im Jahre 2333 v. Chr. aus der Verbindung von einem Sohn des Himmels mit einer in eine Frau verwandelten Bärin hervorgegangen. Der Mythos besagt, dass eine Bärin und ein Tiger den Himmel baten, er möge sie in Menschen verwandeln. Der Himmel hörte das Flehen der Tiere und gebot dem Tiger und der Bärin, 60 Tage das Sonnenlicht zu meiden und bei Wasser, Knoblauch und Beifuss zu fasten. Die Tiere taten, wie ihnen aufgetragen, aber nur die geduldigere Bärin hielt durch und verwandelte sich nach Ablauf der Frist in jene junge Frau, in die sich der Himmelssohn verliebte.

Dies vorausgeschickt, vermag es nicht zu überraschen, dass Yongwoo Lee, der 1995 mit der Durchführung

Die Königsgräber von Kyongju /
The Royal Tumuli of Kyongju.

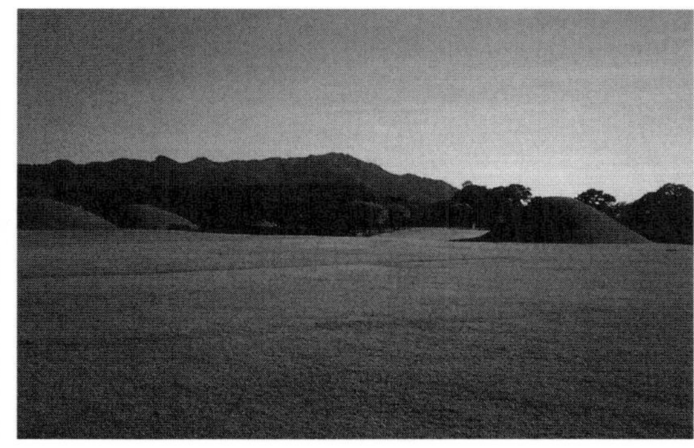

«Art as Witness» versuchte aufzuzeigen, wie im zwanzigsten Jahrhundert Künstler auf geschichtliche Veränderungen reagierten. «The Spirit of Kwangju Resistance in May» versammelte Arbeiten, die sich mit dem schon erwähnten Massaker vom Mai 1980 beschäftigten. «InfoART» widmete sich dem Thema Kunst und Neue Medien. «Eastern Spirit and Ink Painting» war der Geschichte und Gegenwart der orientalischen Malerei gewidmet. Schliesslich ermöglichte «Korea Contemporary Art» dem Publikum einen Einblick in das zeitgenössische Kunstschaffen Südkoreas. Wie sich bald zeigen sollte, war die Biennale von Yong-

lek, Wan-Kyung Sung, Bernard Marcadé) vorbereitete Biennale, die nahtlos an Venedig, Kassel und Lyon anschloss. Gegensätzlicher hätten die Konzepte der beiden bisherigen Biennalen nicht sein können, obwohl der Titel der zweiten Biennale «Unmapping the Earth» dies nicht erwarten liess. Während Yongwoo Lee nicht müde wurde zu betonen, die Biennale müsse in ihrer Konzeption unverwechselbar sein und auf ästhetischem Gebiet helfen, die globale Neuordnung (verstanden als weltweite Solidargemeinschaft) durchzusetzen, sieht Young-chul Lee die Biennale von Kwangju als Schwesterunternehmen zu den grossen Westausstel-

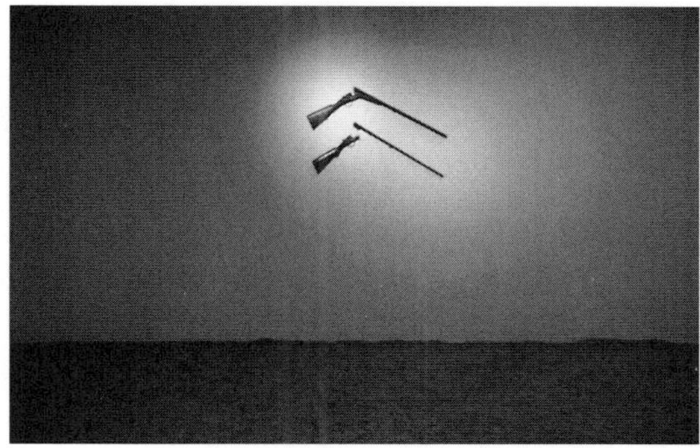

ABSOLUTNO ART ASSOCIATION
(Yugoslavia), PRElom /BREAKing, 1995,
Kwangju Biennale, 1997.

der ersten Biennale von Kwangju beauftragt war, die Kunst Asiens nicht im Zentrum der Ausstellung sehen wollte. Kwangju, die im Südwesten der Halbinsel gelegene Hauptstadt der Provinz Chollanam-do, ist die sechstgrösste Stadt Südkoreas. Die 1995 erstmals eröffnete Biennale wurde in Erinnerung an die blutige Niederschlagung der Demokratiebewegung in Kwangju durch das Militär im Mai 1980 ins Leben gerufen. Neben der Hauptausstellung, die in einem eigens dafür erstellten Gebäude in der Nähe des City Art Museums unter dem Titel «Beyond the Borders» gezeigt wurde, fanden verschiedene Sonderausstellungen statt.

woo Lee in Korea unter Fachleuten äusserst umstritten, obwohl die Ausstellung sehr gut besucht war. Yongwoo Lee handelte sich den Vorwurf ein, eine «Dritte-Welt»-Ausstellung organisiert zu haben, weil er paritätisch Kunst aus allen Erdteilen ausstellte. Die Ausstellung wurde kritisiert, weil diese die Realität des einzelnen Werks und dessen Kontext über die ästhetischen Debatten der westlichen Welt stellte.

Young-chul Lee, der in den Vereinigten Staaten ausgebildete künstlerische Direktor der zweiten Biennale 1997, entschied sich hingegen für eine von erfahrenen Kuratoren (Harald Szeemann, Kyong Park, Richard Kosha-

lungen. Die Akzente sind dennoch andere, etwa dann, wenn zivilisatorische Themen im Mittelpunkt stehen. Es ist nicht verwunderlich, dass die letzte Biennale in diesem Bereich viel aktueller war als Kassel. Deutlich wurde dies insbesondere in der von Kyong Park zusammengestellten Abteilung *«Space & Fire: The Architecture of a New Geography».* Dies liegt ganz einfach daran, dass die Zivilisationsdynamik in Ostasien eine ganz andere Kraft entwickelte als in Europa.

Südkorea, das noch in den 60er Jahren ein Pro-Kopf-Bruttosozialprodukt hatte, das dem Ghanas (230 US-Dollar) entsprach, ist heute eine der wichtigsten Industrienationen der Welt. Zusammen mit Singapur, Hongkong und Taiwan bildet das Land die Gruppe der «Newly Industrialized Countries» (NICs), die alle seit vielen Jahren ein aggressives und exportgetriebenes industrielles Wirtschaftswachstum verfolgen. Die schnelle Veränderung der bäuerlich geprägten Länder in Industrienationen war nur um den Preis einschneidender gesellschaftlicher Veränderungen zu haben, die wegen des raschen Vollzugs für die einzelnen viel deutlicher spürbar waren als im Westen. Die koreanische Wirtschaft wird von einigen wenigen Industriekonglomeraten («chaebol») kontrolliert, von deren Schwächung und deren Öffnung für westliche Investoren der Internationale Währungsfonds (IWF) jüngst sein Engagement zur Behebung der Finanzkrise abhängig machte. Diese Konglomerate sind in verschiedenen Wirtschaftssektoren tätig und übernehmen auch Aufgaben, die im Westen traditionellerweise zu denjenigen der öffentlichen Hand zählen. Zur Samsung Corporation etwa, neben Hyundai, Lucky-Goldstar und Daewoo eines der vier grössten Industriekonglomerate, gehört auch eine wichtige Tageszeitung und das Ho-Am Art Museum in Seoul, dessen Sammlung westlicher Kunst des zwanzigsten Jahrhunderts von ausserordentlicher Qualität ist. Diese enge Verflechtung von Wirtschaft, Kultur und Politik ist typisch für die Tigerstaaten und bildete nicht nur die Basis für den wirtschaftlichen Aufstieg, sondern ist wegen der systembedingten Korruptionsanfälligkeit auch deren Achillesferse.

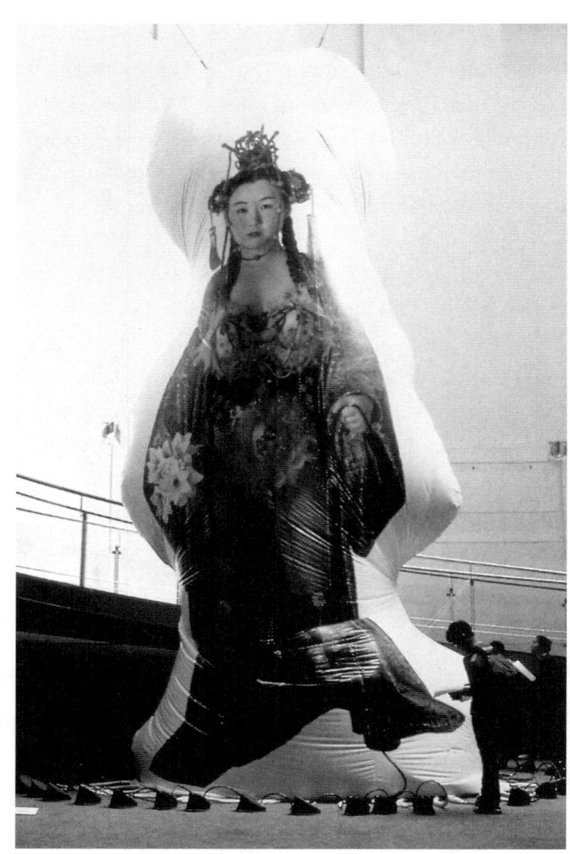

Aus der in Südkorea starken konfuzianischen Tradition des Respekts vor Gelehrsamkeit erklärt sich vielleicht auch der gute Bildungsstandard. Neben der hohen privaten Sparquote und dem starken Staat ist die konsequente Bildungspolitik einer der zentralen Faktoren, die trotz der momentanen Wirtschaftskrise die Chancen Koreas, auf Dauer zum wirtschaftlich prosperierenden Teil der Welt zu gehören, intakt halten (dies im Gegensatz zu den Staaten Afrikas und Lateinamerikas).

Auf meinen beiden Reisen durch das gebirgige, ausserhalb der grossen Städte noch immer sehr agrarische Land, von Seoul über Kwangju nach Taegu sowie über Kwangju zu der alten Königsstadt Kyongju im Süden des Landes, besuchte ich neben der Bien-

nale auch Künstlerinnen und Künstler. Dabei hat mich insbesondere jene Generation beeindruckt, die vor der allmählichen Öffnung des Landes nach dem Koreakrieg (1950–1953) geboren wurde. Die Werke von Se-Ok Suh und Hyong-Keun Yun, um nur zwei Künstler beim Namen zu nennen, die ich näher kennenlernte, stehen beide für die Überlieferung orientalischer Techniken, für koreanische Gelehrsamkeit und die fruchtbare Aneignung der westlichen Moderne.

Der 1928 in Chung-Puk geborene und heute in Seoul lebende Maler Hyong-Keun Yun verbrachte ausser einem kurzen Aufenthalt in Paris in den Jahren 1980–82 sein ganzes bisheriges Leben in Korea, wo er heute zu den bedeutendsten Künstlern des Landes gezählt wird. Hyong-Keun Yun malt mit

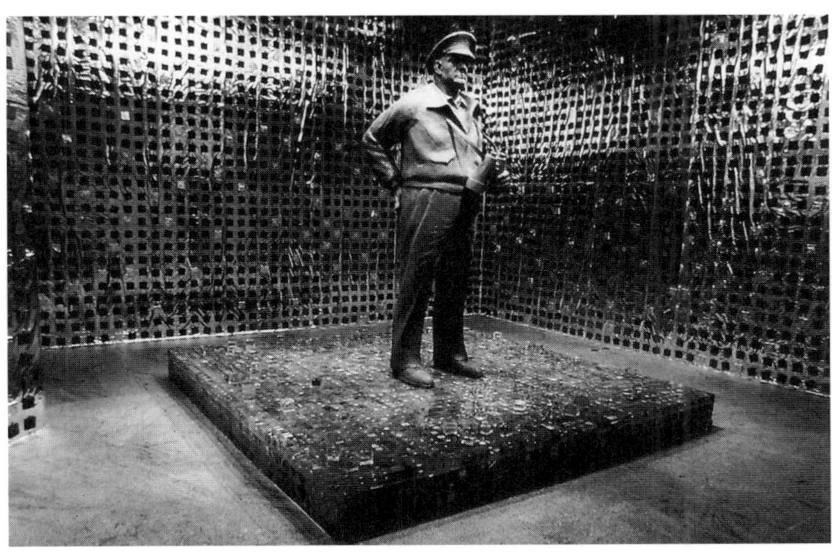

dünner Ölfarbe auf Papier und Leinwand. Er beschränkt sich seit den späten 70er Jahren auf das Malen von dunklen Farbfeldern. Die Farbe wird immer auf ungrundierte Leinwand oder weiches, saugfähiges Papier aufgetragen, so dass Öl und Pigmente sich trennen und unscharfe Ränder von unvorhersehbarem Verlauf bilden. Die Figur ist für Hyong-Keun Yun Ausdruck des Lebendigen schlechthin. Ihre Farbe ist diejenige von Erz und Erde, weil er mit seiner Malerei daran erinnern will, dass es nur eine Frage der Zeit ist, bis alles auf Erden, sowohl der Stoff wie die Bedeutung, die dem Stofflichen zugesprochen wurde, wieder zu Staub zerfallen ist. Seine Kunst ist Ausdruck der Suche nach Harmonie, Einfachheit und Unerfahrenheit und darin am Naturkreislauf orientiert. Einfachheit erreicht er durch einen strengen Bildaufbau. Der Unerfahrenheit, Versprechen noch nicht gelebter Gegenwart, gibt er Raum, indem er auf die rohe Leinwand malt, was den Farbverläufen eine eigene, unvorhersehbare Dynamik verleiht.

Der Naturbezug bei Hyong-Keun Yun und der Körperbezug bei Se-Ok Suh erinnern an den in Korea allgemein bewusst positiven, sinnlichen Bezug zu Nahrung und Körper, der vielleicht mentalitätsgeschichtlich zu erklären wäre. Sogar aus dem Schaffen von Nam June Paik, dem in Europa und den Vereinigten Staaten berühmt gewordenen Pionier der Video- und Multimedia-Kunst, ist der Körper nicht wegzudenken. Auffallend ist auch, dass eine junge Künstlerin wie Bul Lee, die sich explizit mit neuen Technologien und virtuellen Realitäten beschäftigt, die umfassende Thematisierung des Kreatürlichen nicht preisgibt. Das Spannungsfeld, in dem Bul Lee arbeitet, ist jenes zwischen Natur, Kultur und den durch Wissenschaft und Technik geschaffenen materiellen und sozialen Lebensbedingungen. Einige ihrer Arbeiten entwerfen ein Bild vom Menschen, wie es vielleicht bestimmte Tiere von uns haben. Ihre neuen Plastiken dagegen sind Hybride, die uns an die entfesselte Kunst der Biotechnologie erinnern.

1) Paolo Caruso, «Gespräch mit Michel Foucault», in: Michel Foucault, *Von der Subversion des Wissens,* Suhrkamp, Frankfurt am Main 1978, S. 7–31.
2) Masakazu Yamazaki, «Die Geburt einer ostasiatischen Zivilisation?», in: *Merkur,* Nr. 3, 1996, S. 263–264.

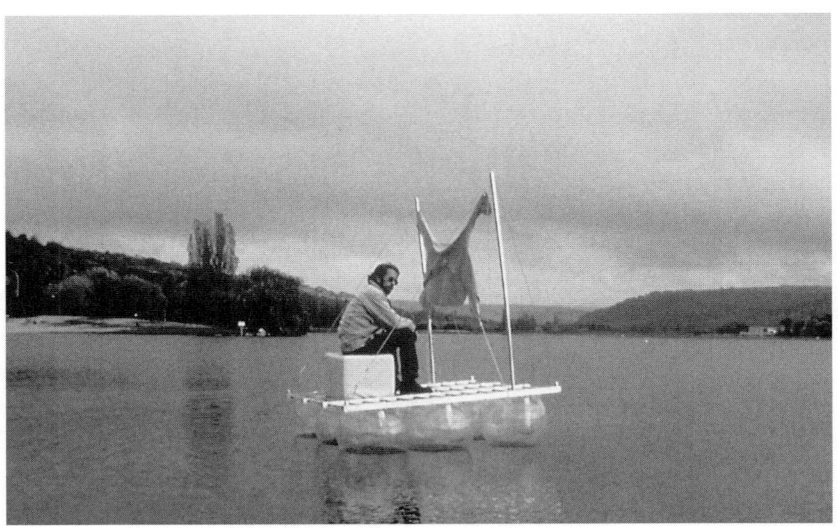

TWO JOURNEYS TO SOUTH KOREA

ROMAN KURZMEYER

Dreams of the Orient have long haunted Europe. Ever since the early nineteenth century, Asia in particular has continued to arouse active interest: witness not only the holdings of various ethnological collections and the influence these have exercised on aesthetic discourse in Europe, but also the many Asiatic societies for the appreciation of Asian culture that were already being founded in the major towns and cities of Europe at the beginning of the last century.

Judging by the signs of Christianity that I came across all over South Korea, the French philosopher and historian, Michel Foucault, in conversation with Paolo Caruso in 1969, was wholly accurate in his assessment of the process of civilization: whilst recognizing that western culture is clearly open to 'foreign' thinking, Foucault was also at pains to point out that in reality the entire world is becoming increasingly westernized.[1]

According to Masakazu Yamazaki, western civilization owes its progress to a dual structure of religious control (Christianity) and language (Latin). "In contrast to this," Yamazaki argues, "in Asia there has never been a comparable supra-ethnic framework of civilization. Without the experience of political unity that prevailed during the Roman Empire, Asian peoples had no shared tradition in matters of language, currency, laws, routes of communication, and architecture. In the absence of any all-embracing (even if loosely structured) religious framework such as that of Christianity, religions in Asia—Confucianism, Buddhism, Taoism, Islam, and a plethora of indigenous religions—have always stood shoulder-to-shoulder (or face-to-face)."[2] The fact that Asian peoples share neither a common calligraphy nor the same creation myths is ample evidence of this.

In Korea it is said that the Korean people came into being in the year 2333 B.C., born of a union between the son of a heavenly king and a she-bear transformed into a woman. Legend has it that a she-bear and a tiger asked the heavenly king to turn them into human beings. He listened to the animals' pleas and commanded the tiger and the she-bear to avoid the light of the sun for sixty days and to consume

KCHO (ALEXIS LEIVA, Cuba), PARA OLVIDAR / TO FORGET,
boat, 50,000 empty bottles, winner of the main prize at the 1995 Kwangju Biennale /
ZUM VERGESSEN, Boot, 50 000 leere Flaschen,
Gewinner des grossen Preises der Kwangju Biennale 1995.

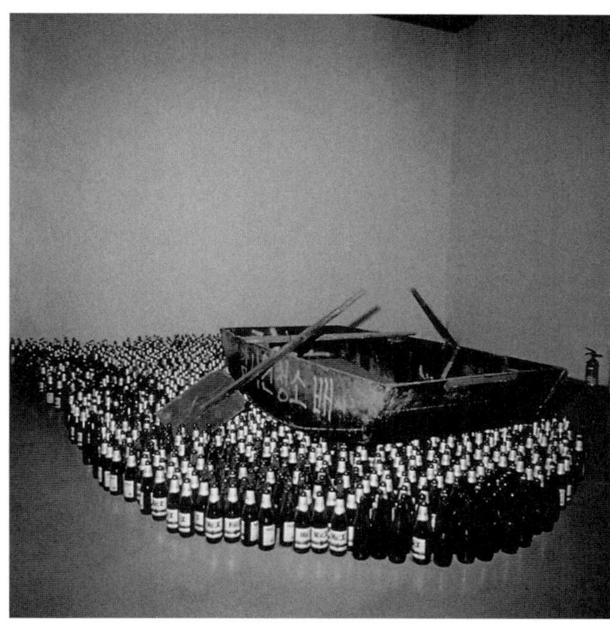

nothing but water, garlic and mugwort. Both animals tried to do as they had been bidden, but only the patient she-bear was able to stay the course and, when the allotted time had passed, she turned into the young woman who was to win the heavenly prince's heart.

In view of this, it is hardly surprising that in 1995, when Yongwoo Lee was appointed director of the First Korean Biennale, he was not interested in focusing specifically on Asian art. Kwangju, situated in the southwest of the peninsula and the capital of Chollanam-do Province, is the sixth largest town in South Korea. The Biennale was established in memory of the bloody suppression of the democratic movement in 1980 by the militia in Kwangju. Besides the main exhibition, "Beyond the Borders," which was shown in a spe-cially constructed building near the City Art Museum, there were other thematic exhibitions. "Art as Witness" sought to show how artists in the twentieth century have reacted to historical change; "The Spirit of Kwangju Resistance in May" brought together works that dealt specifically with the massacre of May 1980; "InfoART" was devoted to art and the new media; "Eastern Spirit and Ink Painting" traced the history of oriental painting to the present day; and, finally, "Korean Contemporary Art" gave the public an insight into contemporary artistic activity in Korea. However, all too soon it became clear that the critical response to Yongwoo Lee's Korean Biennale was extremely mixed, although visitor-numbers to the exhibitions were high. Yongwoo Lee found himself accused of having or-ganized a "third world" exhibition because he had shown art from all corners of the earth on an equal footing. The exhibition was also criticized for placing the reality of individual works and their context above the aesthetic debates of the western world.

For the Second Biennale in 1997, the artistic director Young-chul Lee, who had trained in the United States, chose experienced curators (Harald Szeemann, Kyong Park, Richard Koshalek, Wan-Kyung Sung, and Bernard Marcadé) who constructed a project that fitted in seamlessly with Venice, Kassel and Lyon. The concepts of the two Biennales so far could hardly have been more different, although the title of the second, "Unmapping the Earth," gave little hint of this. While Yongwoo Lee was tireless in his insistence that the Biennale must be utterly distinctive and play its part in establishing the new world order (of global solidarity) in aesthetic matters, Young-chul Lee saw the Kwangju Biennale as a sister to the major exhibitions of the west, only with a different accent—particularly when the focus is on questions of civilization. Small wonder, then, that in this respect the second Biennale was rather more up-to-date than Kassel. This was particularly so in the case of the exhibition, "Space & Fire: the Architecture of a New Geography," curated by Kyong Park—the reason being that civilization in the Asian-Pacific area has in fact developed a dynamic unlike anything in Europe.

In the sixties South Korea had a per capita gross national product equivalent to that of Ghana (230 US dollars). Today it is one of the most important industrialized nations in the world. Along with Singapore, Hong Kong, and Taiwan it is a member of the group known as the "Newly Industrialized Nations" (NICs) who have, for many years now, been pursuing an aggressive course of export-driven industrial economic growth. The rapid transformation of largely peasant economies into industrialized nations has only been bought at the price of far-reaching social changes, which are much more noticeable to individuals there than to their counterparts in the west, due to the sheer speed of the changes. The Korean economy is controlled by a small number of conglomerates ("chaebols") and it was only on condition that these would be opened up and somewhat weakened that the International Monetary Fund (IMF) agreed to step in during the recent financial crisis. These conglomerates operate in various sections of the economy and fulfill certain functions that are normally the responsibility of government or other public bodies in the west. Samsung, for example—one of the largest industrial conglomerates, on a par with Hyundai, Lucky-Goldstar, and Daewoo—also owns a leading daily newspaper and the Ho-Am Museum in Seoul, which has an outstanding collection of 20th century western art. This close interrelationship of economics, culture, and politics is typical for the Tiger States and has not only been the basis of their economic upsurge but has also proved to be their Achilles' heel in that the system itself is patently susceptible to corruption.

The traditional Confucian respect for learning that still holds good in Korea may explain the country's exceptional levels of education and culture. Besides the high rate of personal savings and the strength of the state itself, Korea's effective cultural politics form a major plank of the country's hope, despite the current economic crisis, of retaining its place in the prosperous half of the world, unlike the countries of Africa and Latin America.

On my two trips outside the major cities through mountainous, still very agrarian countryside from Seoul via Kwangju to Taegu, and from Kwangju to the old royal city of Kyongju in the south, I left the Biennale behind me and visited a number of artists. I was particularly impressed by those born before the country gradually opened up after the Korean War (1950–1953). Works by Se-Ok Suh and Hyong-Keun Yun for example—to name but two of the artists I got to know more closely—combine oriental techniques with Korean learning and productive awareness of western modernism.

Hyong-Keun Yun is a painter who was born in 1928 in Chung-Puk and is now resident in Seoul. Apart from a short stay in Paris between 1980 and 1982, he has spent all his life in Korea and is today recognized as one of the most important artists in the country. Hyong-Keun Yun paints with thin oils on paper or canvas. Since the late seventies he has limited himself to dark color-fields. He only ever uses unprimed canvases or soft, absorbent paper so that the paint and the pigments he applies separate and develop unpredictable, imprecise edges. For Hyong-Keun Yun, the figure is the ultimate expression of all living things. He colors it in the tones of iron ore and earth in order to remind us, through his painting, that it is only a question of time before everything on earth—all things material as well as the meanings attributed to them—returns to dust. Hyong-Keun Yun's art is an expression of the search for harmony, simplicity, and inexperience and, as such, is oriented towards the rhythms of nature. He achieves simplicity by means of stringent pictorial structures, which leave room for inexperience and the promise of an as yet unlived present.

The closeness to nature in Hyong-Keun Yun's work and Se-Ok Suh's interest in the human form reflect the consciously positive sensual relationship that Koreans generally have to food and the human body. Even the work of Nam June Paik—who made his name in Europe and the USA as a pioneer of video and multimedia art—is inconceivable without the human body. And it is striking that the young artist, Bul Lee, who works explicitly with new technologies and virtual realities, has not relinquished the animate world as an intrinsic part of her own work. Bul Lee addresses the tensions that exist between nature, culture, and the material and social conditions created by science and technology. In some of her works she has shown human beings as certain animals perhaps see us, while her latest sculptures are clearly hybrids—calling to mind the genie of biotechnology that has now been let loose on the world.

1) Paolo Caruso, "Gespräch mit Michel Foucault," in: Michel Foucault, *Von der Subversion des Wissens* (Frankfurt am Main: Suhrkamp, 1978), pp. 7–31.
2) Masakazu Yamazaki, "Die Geburt einer ostasiatischen Zivilisation?" in: *Merkur*, no. 3 (1996), pp. 263–4.

(Translation: Fiona Elliott)

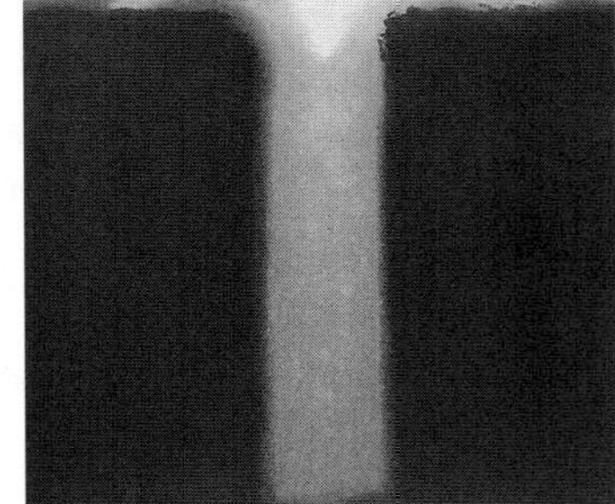

*HYONG-KEUN YUN, UMBER-BLUE, 1974, oil on cloth, 25⅝ x 31½",
Kwangju Biennale, 1997 / UMBRA-BLAU,
Öl auf Tuch, 65 x 80 cm.*

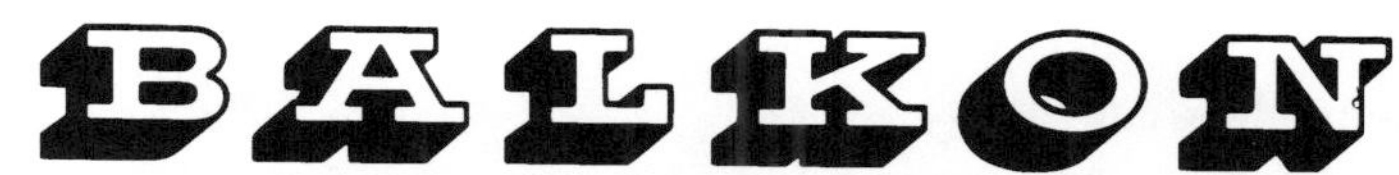

Impossible Weavings

Waimiri Atoroari Warma Kaha, a woven bracelet without beginning or end wraps itself around my wrist. The dryness of the loft air breaks it open and I begin

writing is a weaving of broken fragments

each letter a lost thread

Tara, the master of the impossible task, is invoked by a thread mansion of thought, a mandala constructed with threads.

"A mandala contains the architecture of the world," they say,

the word *contain* is to stretch with (a string), and *architecture* is the weaving of a first beginning, *arche.*

To think is to spin, to let it hang from a thread, *pendere, pensare, pesar*

(the first image of sadness, pesar comes from the measuring
act: to weigh)

The unspun wool, a ball of fleece, contains the energy of the cosmos.

A cloud of cosmic gas begins to rotate, matter coheres and a galaxy is born.

Playing with fleece, the hand begins to spin.

Thumb forward, it spins to the right. Thumb back, it spins to the left.

The energy flows down the hand like water in the irrigation canal.

Handspun, the thought of the hand.

Doing and undoing in place.

Only a tension keeps the thread from becoming undone.

A fiber of two strands (spun left and right) pulling against each other to make one.

Before spinning, the Mixtecos live with the fleece for many days and speak to it, "to impregnate it with thought."
This is called: "the first caress."

The unformed transformed

Fleece in rainbows

Fleece in love

Streaming down the alpaca's ears, the dyed fleece increases the fertility of the herd

by acknowledging the source,
the energy that runs through their wool.

CECILIA VICUÑA is an artist and poet from Chile living in New York. Her most recent book is *QUIPOem/The Precarious Art & Poetry of Cecilia Vicuña,* Wesleyan University Press (Middletown, CT).

In the Andes they say "the rainbow has a motor," each tone becoming the next out of love. Blue in love with green, green with yellow, and so on.

"A color gradation is an effort of light to reach shadow, its other side... Each tone becoming the other out of love"

An ethical code derived from the behavior of light:

to search for a common ground.

Green Tara and Pacha Tira. Tibetan and Andean concepts entwined.

Tara, the force of compassion, enlightened consciousness, is also "An Emerald Mountain Clothed in Rainbows."

The image of the Dalai Lama in rainbows over Lhasa, crushed and forbidden by the invaders.

Aymara men forbidden to wear their textiles since the rebellion of 1780. The women continue to weave K'isa gradations "to change perception imperceptibly."

Oh débiles, oh suaves ofendidos que
os eleváis, hacéis y llenáis de
poderosos débiles el mundo   – César Vallejo[1]

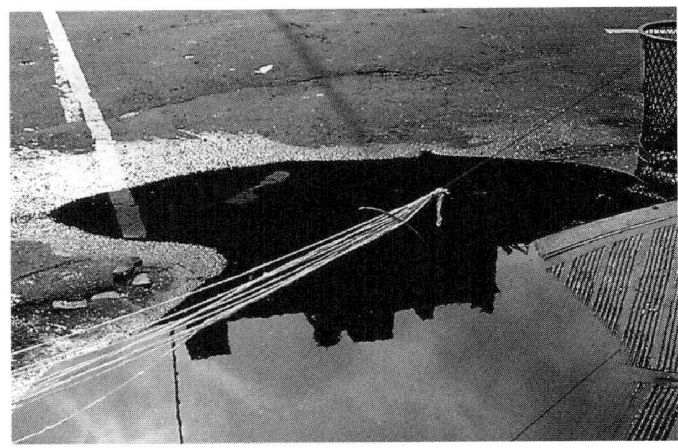

CECILIA VICUÑA,
A LOOM ON HUDSON STREET, 1993, New York /
EIN WEBSTUHL AN DER HUDSON STREET.

IM pulse of the POSSIBLE

to weave is to cross,

and across dimensions they went by spinning the impossibly small and the impossibly large.

Spinning the impossibly short vicuña's hair, hummingbird feathers, and bat skins

they spoke to the gods.

The art was to spin, the weaving almost an afterthought.

A dwelling in tension (intention)

A balance between

being and not.

A thread around a Brahmin's neck in Benares, a Brazilian wrist or an Irish grave

speaks across.

Worn to pieces or interred with the dead, burnt or torn apart by the wind, it dissolves and returns to the world.

Miniature garments placed at the top of the Aconcagua (Inca).

Nets of human hair (sixty-nine heads of human hair), forty miles wide across the valley (Mogollón).

Minute baskets, not half an inch across (Pima).

Shawls so fine the whole cloth could pass through a ring (India).

Rings of human hair, the warp and weft of the ancestors (Europe).

To inscribe the thread in its web.

A weaving not for daily life but for life itself.

A double act performed for the gods and for daily life at once.

A powerful and dangerous act, a distant echo of other processes.

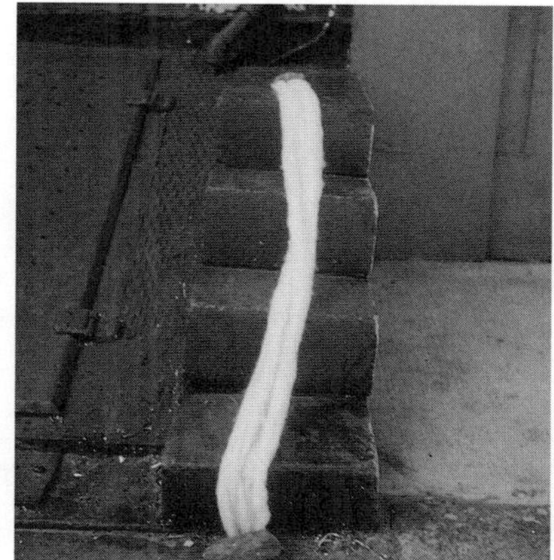

CECILIA VICUÑA, WHITE HAIR ON WHITE STREET, 1994,
in situ, New York / WEISSES HAAR AN DER WHITE STREET.
(PHOTO: CÉSAR PATERNOSTO)

In Lewa weaving is forbidden:

    Invisible threads attach the island to the bottom of the sea and to the highest layer of the sky. Weaving would weaken the warp and break the thread, and the island would sink to the bottom of the sea.

In Rari, two towns are superimposed, the "real" one with its road, gardens, and mud houses, and the other: the woven world hanging from threads, minute creatures and gardens woven in horsehair. The hair brought by the invader, transformed.

The thread pushed into non threadness—comes alive.

The Ceq'e lines,
    not a line, but a gaze, a weaving of gazes, sight lines radiating from Cuzco. A quipu calendar of virtual threads.

    A measure of heaven and of themselves.

    A weaving that is not.

Weaving the landscape into invisible lines, the singers of the Dreamtime walked about singing the world into existence.

Each song a line of two words,
a foot fall,
a foot print that is not.

Fertilizing the earth
    "as a kind of musical sperm,"
"sacred bloody baloney"
    Bruce Chatwin says.

In the Huitoto dance of death a group of women dance naked with their arms braided in a line, forming an edge, a selvage. Their thighs aligned form a weaving alive, their painted bodies one design.

CECILIA VICUÑA, THE BRAIN, 1997,
wool fleece, shells / DAS HIRN, Wollvlies, Muscheln.
(PHOTO: CÉSAR PATERNOSTO)

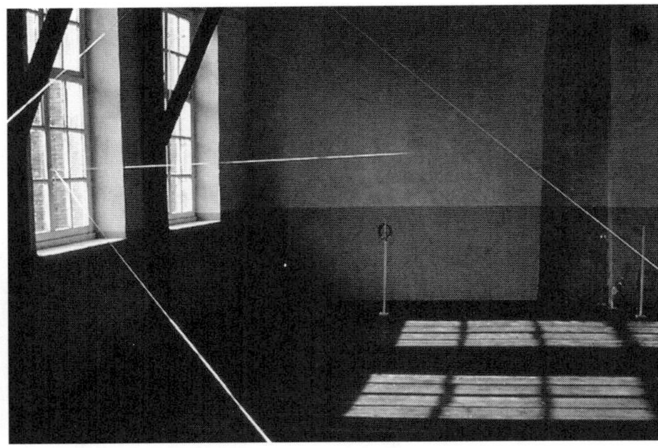

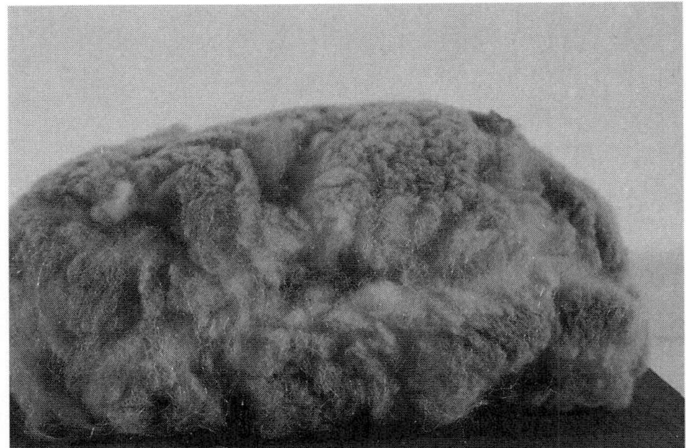

CECILIA VICUÑA, HILUMBRES ALLQA, 1994,
drawing with light, installation view at Beguinage de Kortrijk,
Belgium / Lichtzeichnung.

Below / unten: CECILIA VICUÑA, YELLOW THREAD, 1997,
New York / GELBER FADEN. (PHOTO: MIGUEL SAYAGO)

The thread is their blood passing from one to the next, from the old to the young.

In lake Titicaca, three girls play with a long, white loop of thread. Two girls create tension by holding it on their waists, as if their bodies were a loom. The third girl enters the loop and moves as in a trance, singing and laughing, creating geometric shapes as she pulls and swirls inside the thread.

Sitting by the fire, the Mbuti weave the shadows against the trees by rearranging the logs.

In New York, the cars weave sounds, criss-crossing the grid of the dark night streets.

The blood of ancient images runs through our words.

Perhaps our brokenness is a revelatory form of union.

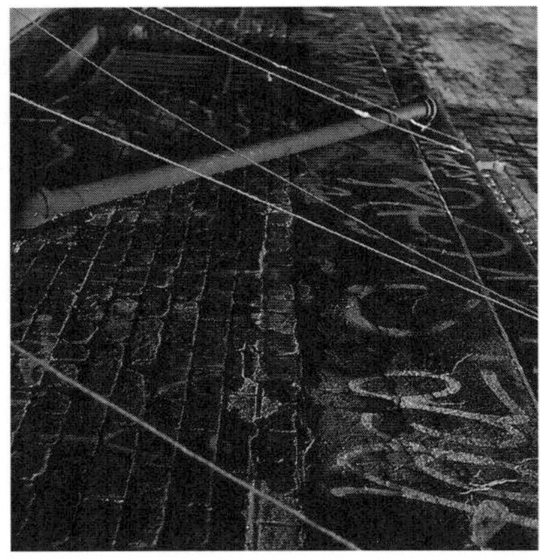

> _O water-coloured fleece_
> _…_
> _Thinner you grow, less knowable,_
> _finer._
> _Finer: a thread by which_
> _it wants to be lowered, the star_ — Paul Celan[2]

Special thanks to Andrés & Vanessa Moraga and to Lois Martin.

---

1) "Oh you weak ones, oh you gentle ones, offended ones who/Raise yourselves, create yourselves, and fill/the world with the powerful weak ones" (Translation: Alfred MacAdam).
2) From two poems of Paul Celan. _Poems of Paul Celan_, translated by Michael Hamburger (New York: Persea Books, 1972).

Unmögliches Gewebe CECILIA VICUÑA

Waimiri Atroari Warma Kaha, ein gewobenes Band ohne Anfang und Ende windet sich um mein Handgelenk. Die trockene Luft im Loft bricht es auf und ich beginne

Schreiben ist ein Verweben von Bruchstücken

                    jeder Brief ein verlorener Faden

Tara, der Meister der unlösbaren Aufgabe, wird angerufen durch das Spinnen eines Gedankengebäudes, eines Faden-Mandala.

«Ein Mandala enthält die Architektur der Welt», sagt man,
das englische Wort *contain* meint auch spannen (einer Schnur), und Architektur ist das erste, ursprüngliche Gewebe, *arche.*

Denken heisst spinnen, etwas an einem Faden hängen lassen, *pendere, pensare, pesar*

                (das Urbild der Traurigkeit, *pesar,* kommt vom Messen des Gewichtes: wiegen)

Die ungesponnene Wolle, ein weicher Vliesball, enthält die Energie des Kosmos.

Eine Wolke kosmischer Gase beginnt sich zu drehen, die Materie klumpt zusammen, und eine Galaxie entsteht.

Im Spiel mit der Wolle beginnt die Hand zu spinnen.

Ist der Daumen vorn, spinnt sie rechtsherum. Ist der Daumen hinten, spinnt sie linksherum.

Die Energie fliesst durch die Hand wie Wasser im Bewässerungskanal.

Handgesponnen, der Gedanke der Hand.

Erzeugen und auflösen zugleich.

Nur die Spannung verhindert, dass der Faden sich auflöst.

Ein Faden aus zwei Fasern (links- und rechtsherum gesponnen), die sich umeinander winden und eins werden.

Bevor sie mit dem Spinnen beginnen, sind die Mixteken tagelang mit dem Wollvlies zusammen und reden unablässig auf es ein, «um es mit Gedanken zu sättigen».
Sie nennen das: «die erste Liebkosung».

Die Umwandlung des Ungestalteten

Vlies in Regenbögen

Vlies und Liebe

Die Ohren des Alpaka umfliessend steigert das gefärbte Vlies die Fruchtbarkeit der Herde, eine Würdigung des
               Ursprungs, der Energie, die in der Wolle fliesst.

CECILIA VICUÑA lebt in New York und Santiago de Chile. Kürzlich erschienen ist ihr Buch *QUIPOem/The Precarious Art & Poetry of Cecilia Vicuña,* Wesleyan University Press, Middletown, CT 1997.

In den Anden sagt man: «Der Regenbogen hat einen Motor», da jeder Farbton sich aus Liebe in den nächsten verwandelt.

«Eine Farbabstufung ist der Versuch des Lichts, den Schatten zu erreichen, die andere Seite seiner selbst... jeder Farbton verliebt in den nächsten übergehend»

Eine Regel der Ethik, die vom Verhalten des Lichts hergeleitet wird:
die Suche nach dem Gemeinsamen.

Green Tara und Pacha Tira. Miteinander verflochtene Begriffe aus den Anden und aus Tibet.

Tara, die Macht des Mitgefühls, erleuchtetes Bewusstsein, ist auch «ein Smaragdberg im Regenbogenkleid».

Das Bild des Dalai Lama inmitten von Regenbogen über Lhasa, zerstört und verboten von der chinesischen Besatzung.

Aymara-Männer, denen es seit dem Aufstand von 1780 verboten ist, ihre traditionellen Textilien zu tragen. Die Frauen weben nach wie vor K'isa-Farbtöne, «um die Wahrnehmung unmerklich zu verändern».

«Oh débiles, oh suaves ofendidos
que os eleváis, hacéis y llenáis
de poderosos débiles el mundo»   – César Vallejo[1]

ImPuls des (Un-)Möglichen
weben heisst kreuzen,
und sie durchkreuzten Dimensionen, das unmöglich Kleine mit dem unmöglich Grossen verspinnend.

Indem sie das unmöglich kurze Haar des Vikunja ebenso zu Fäden spannen wie Kolibrifedern und Fledermaushäute,
sprachen sie zu den Göttern.

Die Kunst, auf die es ankam, war das Spinnen, das Weben war eher ein nachträglicher Einfall.

Ein bewusstes Leben in Spannung

Auf der Schwelle zwischen
Sein und Nichtsein.

Ein Band um den Hals eines Brahmanen in Benares, um ein Handgelenk in Brasilien oder in einem Grab in Irland
spricht mit dem anderen.

Bis zum Zerfall abgenützt oder mit den Toten begraben, verbrannt oder vom Wind zerfetzt löst es sich auf und kehrt in die Welt zurück.

Miniaturkleider auf der Spitze des Aconcagua (Inka).

Netze aus menschlichem Haar (das Haar von 69 Köpfen), 65 Kilometer lang quer durch das Tal (Mogollón).

Winzige Körbe mit weniger als 13 Millimeter Durchmesser (Pima).

Schals, so fein gesponnen, dass sie durch einen Fingerring gezogen werden könnten (Indien).

Ringe aus Menschenhaar, Kette und Schuss der Vorfahren (Europa).

Den Faden in sein Gewebe einschreiben.
Ein Gewebe nicht fürs tägliche Leben, sondern für das Leben selbst.

Eine doppelt wirksame Handlung: für die Götter und für das tägliche Leben zugleich.

Eine starke und gefährliche Handlung, fernes Echo anderer Prozesse.

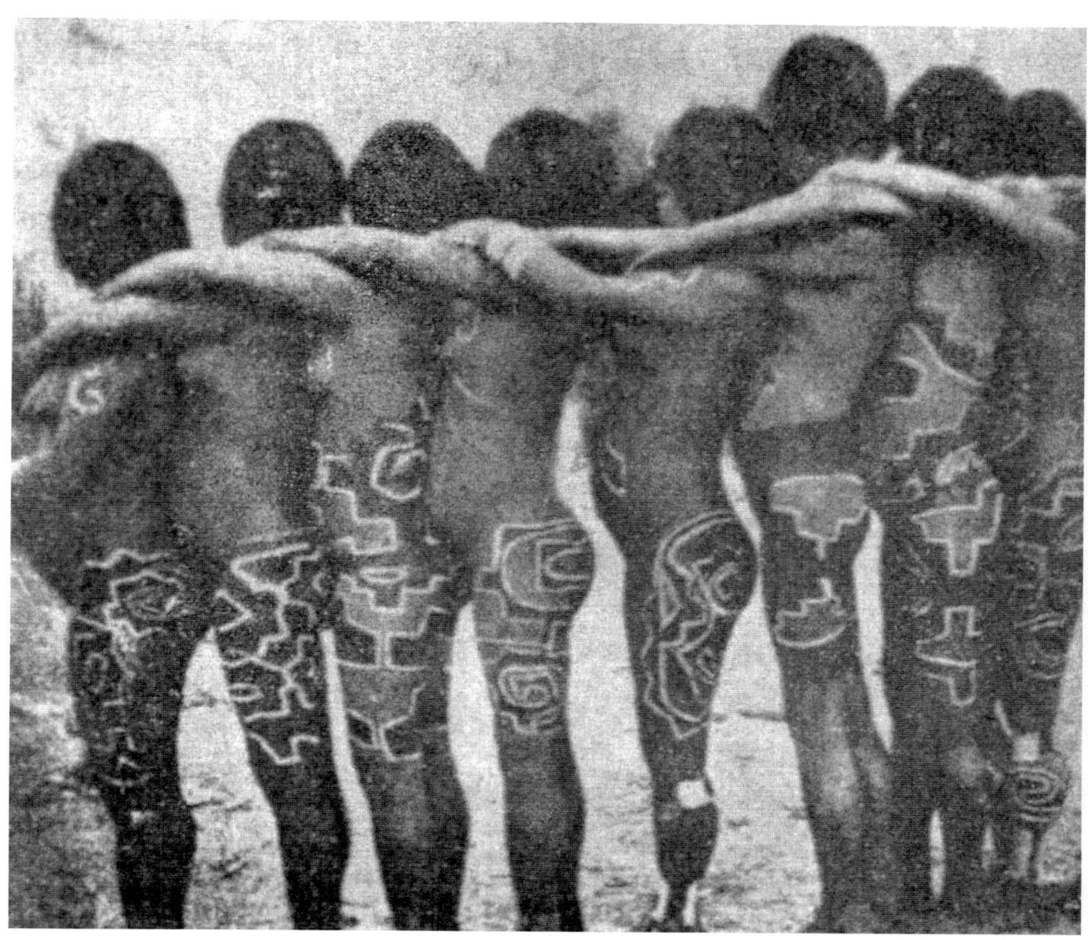

In Lewa ist das Weben verboten:

Unsichtbare Fäden befestigen die Insel am Grund des Meeres und an der höchsten Himmelskuppel. Das Weben würde den Kettfaden schwächen und das Band zerstören, und die Insel würde im Meer versinken.

In Rari liegen zwei Dörfer übereinander, das «wirkliche» mit seiner Strasse, seinen Gärten und Lehmhäusern und das andere: eine gewobene Welt, die an Fäden hängt, winzige Wesen und Gärten aus Rosshaar. Eine Verwandlung des Haares, welches die Besatzer mitbrachten.

Der ins Nichtfadenartige getriebene Faden erwacht zum Leben.

Die Ceq'e-Linien,

       keine Linie, sondern ein Blick, ein Geflecht von Blicken, Blickrichtungen ausgehend

von Cuzco. Ein Quipu-Kalender aus virtuellen Fäden.

       Ein Mass des Himmels und ihrer selbst.

       Ein Gewebe, das nicht ist.

Die Landschaft in unsichtbaren Linien webend, wanderten die Sänger der Traumzeit herum und sangen die Welt ins Dasein.

Jedes Lied eine Zeile aus zwei Wörtern,
ein Schreiten,
ein Fussabdruck, der nicht ist.

Die Erde befruchtend

       «wie eine Art musikalischer Samen»,
«heilig verdammt unsinnig»,

       sagt Bruce Chatwin.

Im Huitoto-Totentanz tanzt eine Gruppe von nackten Frauen, die Arme in einer Reihe ineinander verschränkt, sie bilden eine Grenze, einen Saum. Ihre Hüften reihen sich aneinander, ein lebendiges Gewebe, und ihre bemalten Körper bilden ein zusammenhängendes Muster.

Der Faden ist hier das Blutsband, das eine mit der anderen verbindet, die Alten mit den Jungen.

Am Titicacasee spielen drei Mädchen mit einer langen weissen Schlinge. Zwei Mädchen tragen die Schlinge um ihre Taillen und spannen sie, als wären ihre Körper ein Webstuhl. Das dritte Mädchen steigt in die Schlinge und bewegt sich wie in Trance, sie singt und lacht und erzeugt geometrische Muster, indem sie innerhalb der Schlinge am Band zieht und herumwirbelt.

Wenn die Mbuti am Feuer sitzen, weben sie Schatten auf die Bäume, indem sie unentwegt die Holzscheite im Feuer herumschieben.

In New York weben die Autos Geräusche kreuz und quer ins Netz der dunklen, nächtlichen Strassen.

Das Blut uralter Bilder strömt durch unsere Worte.

Vielleicht ist unser Gebrochensein eine Spiegelung der Einheit.

       O wasserfarbenes Vlies
       (...)
       Dünner wirst du, unkenntlicher, feiner!
       Feiner: ein Faden,
       an dem er herabwill, der Stern [2]

Mein besonderer Dank gilt Andrés & Vanessa Moraga und Lois Martin.

       (Übersetzung: Susanne Schmidt)

1) «O Ihr Schwachen, o Ihr Sanften, Ihr Verletzten, erhebet und erschaffet Euch und füllt die Welt mit mächtigen Schwachen.»
2) Aus den Gedichten «Die letzte Fahne» und «Sprich auch du», in: Paul Celan, *Gedichte I,* Suhrkamp, Frankfurt 1975, S. 23 bzw. 135.

Garderobe
'gär-ˌdrōb

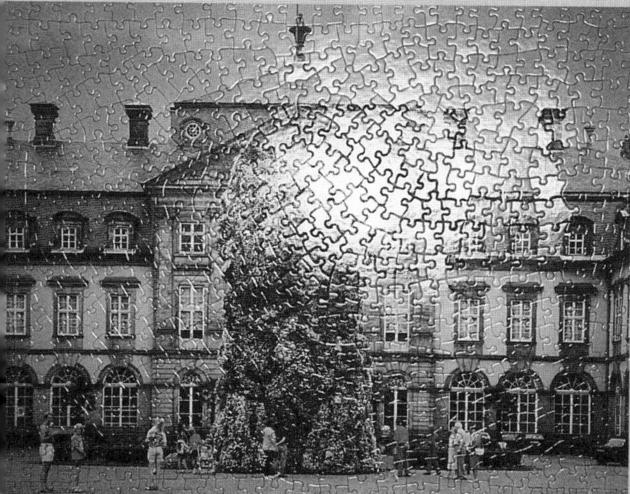

Des Rätsels Lösung /
Answer to our question in Garderobe 50/51:

Es ist Jeff Koons' Werk PUPPY, 1992 (Arolsen), das auf dem Puzzle abgebildet ist. Leider ist das Puzzle, das vom San Francisco Museum of Modern Art herausgegeben wurde, nicht mehr lieferbar; PUPPY war auf Seite 83 in Parkett Nr. 50/51 abgebildet. /
The work of art depicted on the jigsaw puzzle is none other than Jeff Koons's PUPPY, 1992 (Arolsen, Germany). Unfortunately, the puzzle, issued by the San Francisco Museum of Modern Art, is no longer available, but Koons's PUPPY is reproduced in Parkett 50/51, p. 83.

Das Jahresabonnement geht an / The one year gift subscription goes to: Mr. Edward Casaubon of Lowick Manor, Middlemarch, England. Congratulations!

Sommerakademie Salzburg 1998:
20. Juli – 22. August
NEU: MODEDESIGN!
Erstmals wird an der Sommerakademie Salzburg auch eine Klasse für Modedesign geführt.
Anmeldefrist: 15. April bis 15. Juni
Informationen dazu und zum übrigen Angebot der Sommerakademie sind erhältlich bei folgender Adresse:
Internationale Sommerakademie für Bildende Kunst, Postfach 18, A-5010 Salzburg, Tel. ++43-662-842113 und 843727;
Fax ++43-662-849638
E-mail: SoAk.Salzburg@magnet.at
Homepage: http://www.land-sbg.gv.at/sommer-akademie

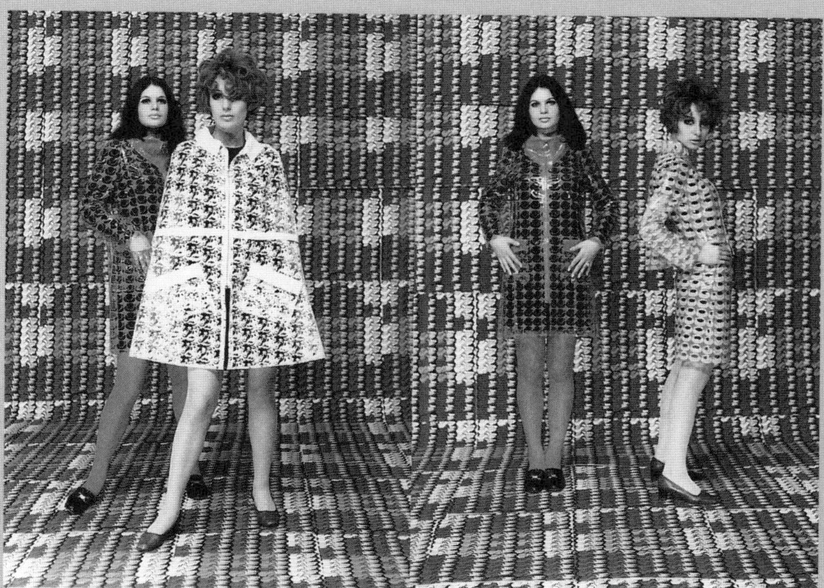

THOMAS BAYRLE, MÄNTEL VOR SCHUHRASTER, 1967
Passen diese Mäntel nicht wunderbar in unsere Garderobe? Sie zeigen überdies, dass Thomas Bayrle, der im Insert dieser Nummer tief in die Welt des Rasters eintaucht, schon in den 60er Jahren – ganz ohne Computer – seinen Rasterträumen nachhing.
COATS AGAINST A GRID OF SHOES, 1967
Just the thing for an "exchange of commodities" past and present, especially since Thomas Bayrle toyed with the notion of grid-like patterns long before he plunged into the world of the computergenerated grid (see this issue's INSERT)

SUBSCRIBE TO THE BEST BOOK SERIES WITH CONTEMPORARY ARTISTS.

ABONNIEREN SIE DIE BESTE BUCHREIHE MIT GEGENWARTSKÜNSTLERN.

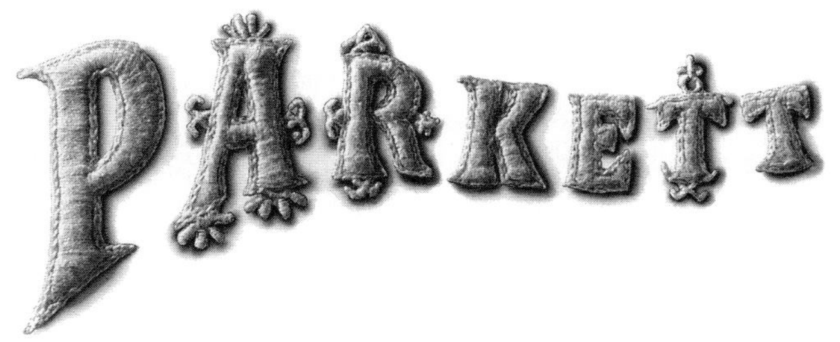

THE PARKETT SERIES WITH CONTEMPORARY ARTISTS
DIE PARKETT-REIHE MIT GEGENWARTSKÜNSTLERN

Bitte benützen Sie die Bestellkarte, die diesem Band beiliegt, und schicken Sie diese an folgende Adresse:
Please use the order form enclosed in this issue and send it to the following address:

PARKETT, Quellenstr. 27, CH-8005 Zürich,
Tel. 41-1-271 81 40, Fax 41-1-272 43 01

PARKETT, 155 Avenue of the Americas, 2nd floor
New York, NY 10013
phone (212) 673 2660, fax (212) 271 0704

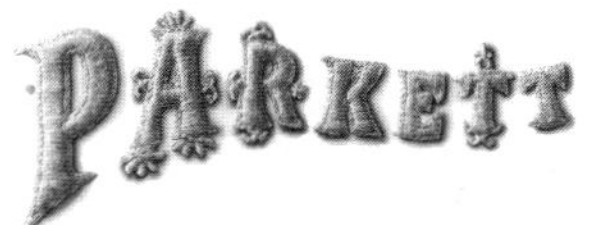

The PARKETT Series is created in collaboration with artists, who contribute an original work available exclusively to the subscribers in the form of a signed limited SPECIAL EDITION. The available works are also reproduced in each PARKETT issue.

Each SPECIAL EDITION is available by order from any one of our offices in New York or Zurich. Just fill in the details below and send this card to the office nearest you. Once your order has been processed, you will be issued with an invoice and your personal edition number. Upon receipt of payment, you will receive the SPECIAL EDITION. (Please note that supply is subject to availability. PARKETT does not assume responsibility for any delays in production of SPECIAL EDITIONS. Postage is not included.)

■ As a subscriber to PARKETT, I would like to order the following Special Edition(s), signed and numbered by the artist.

PARKETT No.	ARTIST		NAME:
PARKETT No.	ARTIST		ADDRESS:
PARKETT No.	ARTIST		CITY:
PARKETT No.	ARTIST		STATE/ZIP:
PARKETT No.	ARTIST		COUNTRY:
PARKETT No.	ARTIST		PHONE:

■ I have indicated my way of payment on the reverse side of this form.

Send this form to the PARKETT office nearest you:

PARKETT PUBLISHERS   155 AV. OF THE AMERICAS   NEW YORK, NY 10013   PHONE (212) 673-2660   FAX (212) 271-0704

PARKETT VERLAG   QUELLENSTRASSE 27   CH-8005 ZÜRICH   TELEFON +41-1-271 81 40   FAX +41-1-272 43 01

PARKETT VERLAG   TANNENWALDALLEE 17   D-61348 BAD HOMBURG   FAX 06172-937 444

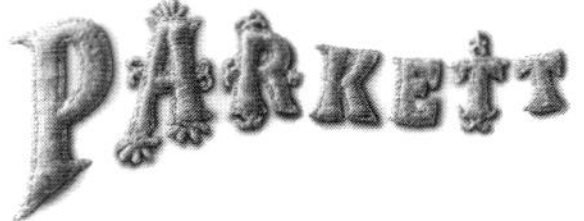

KÜNSTLEREDITIONEN FÜR PARKETT-ABONNENTEN — 52

Die PARKETT-Buchreihe entsteht in Zusammenarbeit mit Künstlern, die eigens für die Abonnenten einen Originalbeitrag in Form einer limitierten und signierten EDITION gestalten. Diese Editionen sind auch in der Zeitschrift abgebildet und können mit dieser Bestellkarte in jedem unserer Büros in Zürich, Frankfurt oder New York bestellt werden. Sie erhalten dann Ihre persönliche Editionsnummer und eine Rechnung. Sobald wir Ihre Zahlung erhalten haben, schicken wir Ihnen Ihre Edition(en). (Lieferung nur solange vorrätig. PARKETT übernimmt keine Verantwortung für allfällige Verzögerungen bei der Herstellung der Vorzugsausgaben. Versandkosten zuzüglich.)

■ Ich bin PARKETT-Abonnent(in) und bestelle folgende EDITION(EN), numeriert und vom Künstler signiert:

PARKETT Nr.	KÜNSTLER/IN		NAME:
PARKETT Nr.	KÜNSTLER/IN		STRASSE:
PARKETT Nr.	KÜNSTLER/IN		PLZ/STADT:
PARKETT Nr.	KÜNSTLER/IN		LAND:
PARKETT Nr.	KÜNSTLER/IN		TEL.:

■ Meine Zahlungsweise habe ich auf der Rückseite angegeben.

Senden Sie die Bestellkarte an das PARKETT-Büro in Ihrer Nähe:

PARKETT VERLAG   QUELLENSTRASSE 27   CH-8005 ZÜRICH   TELEFON +41-1-271 81 40   FAX +41-1-272 43 01

PARKETT VERLAG   TANNENWALDALLEE 17   D-61348 BAD HOMBURG   FAX 06172-937 444

PARKETT PUBLISHERS   155 AV. OF THE AMERICAS   NEW YORK, NY 10013   PHONE (212) 673-2660   FAX (212) 271-0704

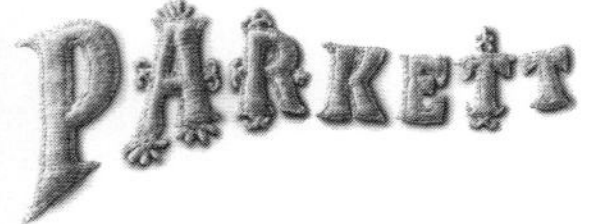

SUBSCRIBE, COMPLETE OR SEND A GIFT SUBSCRIPTION TO THE BEST BOOK SERIES ON CONTEMPORARY ARTISTS

- [ ] I subscribe to the PARKETT series
  - [ ] for 1 year (3 issues) at US$ 80 (USA/Canada), SFr. 118.– (Europe), SFr. 140.– (Rest of the world).
  - [ ] for 2 years (6 issues) at US$ 145 (USA/Canada), SFr. 215.– (Europe), SFr. 265.– (Rest of the world).
  - [ ] for 1 year (3 issues) at a 20% student discount (US$ 65 for USA/ Canada, SFr. 95.– for Europe). A copy of my student ID is enclosed.

- [ ] Send a gift subscription in my name
  - [ ] for 1 year (3 issues) at US$ 80 (USA/Canada), SFr. 118.– (Europe), SFr. 140.– (Rest of the world).
  - [ ] for 2 years (6 issues) at US$ 145 (USA/Canada), SFr. 215.– (Europe), SFr. 265.– (Rest of the world).
  A gift card in my name will be sent to the recipient.

Postage included. All prices subject to change.

- [ ] I wish to complete my PARKETT collection and order the following issue no(s): ___________

  at SFr. 43.– each (up to no 43: SFr. 30.–; no. 44–48: SFr. 39.–), postage not included. Within the USA & Canada $ 32 (up to no. 43: $ 19.50; no. 44–48: $ 29), add postage: $ 5 (USA), $ 10 (Canada). (Sold out: No. 1–10, 13, 16, 19, 27, 29–31, 35)

- [ ] I wish to order the catalog raisonné of all PARKETT Artists' Editions from 1984–95 (SILENT & VIOLENT, 183 pages of which 144 in color, text by Susan Tallman, short artists' biographies) for Sfr. 49.– (USA: $ 39), excl. postage.

- [ ] I wish to order ___________ copies of the set of 36 postcards featuring PARKETT Artists' Editions for Sfr. 19.– (USA: $ 16) per set, excl. postage.

NAME: ___________

ADDRESS: ___________

CITY: ___________

STATE/ZIP: ___________

COUNTRY: ___________

TEL.: ___________   FAX: ___________

GIFT RECIPIENT: ___________

ADDRESS: ___________

CITY: ___________

STATE/ZIP: ___________

COUNTRY: ___________

- [ ] Charge my Visa Card   [ ] Mastercard   [ ] AMEX

Card No. ___________   Expiration date ___________

- [ ] Payment enclosed (US check or money order)

DATE ___________

SIGNATURE ___________

Send this form to the PARKETT office nearest you:

PARKETT PUBLISHERS   155 AV. OF THE AMERICAS   NEW YORK, NY 10013   PHONE (212) 673-2660   FAX (212) 271-0704

PARKETT VERLAG   QUELLENSTRASSE 27   CH-8005 ZÜRICH   TELEFON +41-1-271 81 40   FAX +41-1-272 43 01

PARKETT VERLAG   TANNENWALDALLEE 17   D-61348 BAD HOMBURG   FAX 06172-937 444

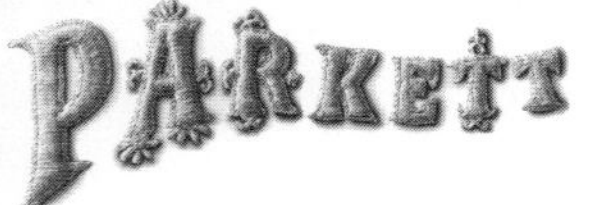

ABONNIEREN, VERVOLLSTÄNDIGEN ODER VERSCHENKEN SIE DIE UMFASSENDSTE BUCHREIHE ÜBER GEGENWARTSKÜNSTLER

- [ ] Ich abonniere die PARKETT-Reihe
  - [ ] für 1 Jahr (3 Ausgaben) zu: DM 130.– (BRD), SFr. 108.– (Schweiz), SFr. 118.– (übriges Europa).
  - [ ] für 2 Jahre (6 Ausgaben) zu: DM 238.– (BRD), SFr. 190.– (Schweiz), SFr. 215.– (übriges Europa).
  - [ ] für 1 Jahr (3 Ausgaben) mit 20% Studentenermässigung (BRD: DM 104.–/Schweiz: SFr. 87.–/Europa: SFr. 95.–). Eine Kopie meines Studentenausweises lege ich bei.

- [ ] Ich verschenke ein PARKETT-Abonnement
  - [ ] für 1 Jahr (3 Ausgaben) zu: DM 130.– (BRD), SFr. 108.– (Schweiz), SFr. 118.– (übriges Europa).
  - [ ] für 2 Jahre (6 Ausgaben) zu: DM 238.– (BRD), SFr. 190.– (Schweiz), SFr. 215.– (übriges Europa). Das Geschenk-Abo mit einer Geschenkkarte wird in meinem Namen versandt.

Preise einschliesslich Versandkosten. Preisänderungen vorbehalten.

- [ ] Ich möchte meine PARKETT-Sammlung vervollständigen und bestelle die folgende(n) noch erhältliche(n) Ausgabe(n) Nr. ___________ zu je DM 49.–/SFr. 43.– (bis Nr. 43: DM 35.–/SFr. 30.–; Nr. 44–48: DM 45.–/ SFr. 39.–, zzgl. Versandkosten (vergriffen: Nr. 1–10, 13, 16, 19, 27, 29–31, 35)

- [ ] Ich bestelle das Werkverzeichnis der PARKETT-Künstlereditionen von 1984–95 (SILENT & VIOLENT, 183 S., davon 144 farbig, Text von Susan Tallman, Kurzbiographien der Künstler) für DM 60.–/SFr. 49.– zzgl. Versandkosten.

- [ ] Ich bestelle ___________ Ex. des Postkarten-Sets mit 36 PARKETT-Künstlereditionen zum Preis von DM 23.–/SFr. 19.– pro Set, zzgl. Versandkosten.

NAME: ___________

STRASSE: ___________

PLZ/STADT: ___________

LAND: ___________

TEL.: ___________   FAX: ___________

BESCHENKTE(R): ___________

STRASSE: ___________

PLZ/STADT: ___________

LAND: ___________

- [ ] Ich zahle mit Visa   [ ] Eurocard/Mastercard   [ ] Amex

Karten Nr. ___________   Gültig bis ___________

- [ ] Mein Scheck über SFr./DM ___________ liegt bei.

DATUM ___________

UNTERSCHRIFT ___________

Senden Sie die Bestellkarte an das PARKETT-Büro in Ihrer Nähe:

PARKETT VERLAG   QUELLENSTRASSE 27   CH-8005 ZÜRICH   TELEFON +41-1-271 81 40   FAX +41-1-272 43 01

PARKETT VERLAG   TANNENWALDALLEE 17   D-61348 BAD HOMBURG   FAX 06172-937 444

PARKETT PUBLISHERS   155 AV. OF THE AMERICAS   NEW YORK, NY 10013   PHONE (212) 673-2660   FAX (212) 271-0704

MATTHEW BARNEY
SARAH LUCAS
ROMAN SIGNER
BRYSON, ONFRAY, SEWARD, GOODEVE,
SALTZ, VAN ADRICHEM, SCHORR, FREEDMAN,
JOUANNAIS, BITTERLI, DOSWALD,
VIEWING, WECHSLER, DELAND
INSERT: **ELLIOTT PUCKETTE**
HEIDI GILPIN: **WILLIAM FORSYTHE**
ROBYN McKENZIE: **GEOFF LOWE**
MICHAEL TARANTINO: **CHANTAL AKERMAN**
CUMULUS: McEVILLEY, WAKEFIELD

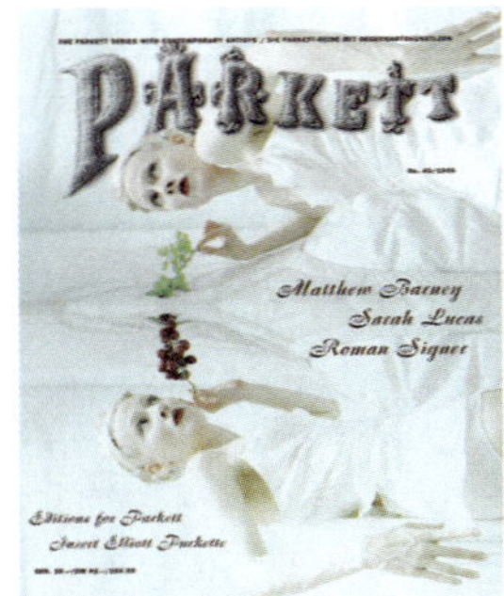

No. 45 - ISBN 3-907509-95-1

VIJA CELMINS
ANDREAS GURSKY
RIRKRIT TIRAVANIJA
PRINCENTHAL, LEWIS, SILVERTHORNE
SHIFF, CRIQUI, BURCKHARDT, WAKEFIELD
SCHORR, MELO, GILLICK, FLOOD, STEINER
INSERT: **HANS DANUSER**
LES INFOS: LIAM GILLICK & DOUGLAS GORDON
LYNNE COOKE, DAVID DEITCHER
DANIEL KURJAKOVIC: **MARIE JOSÉ BURKI**
NAN GOLDIN: **PETER HUJAR**
NOEMI SMOLIK: **ANDREAS SLOMINSKI**
JASON SIMON: **MARK DION**
LUK LAMBRECHT: **MARK LUYTEN**

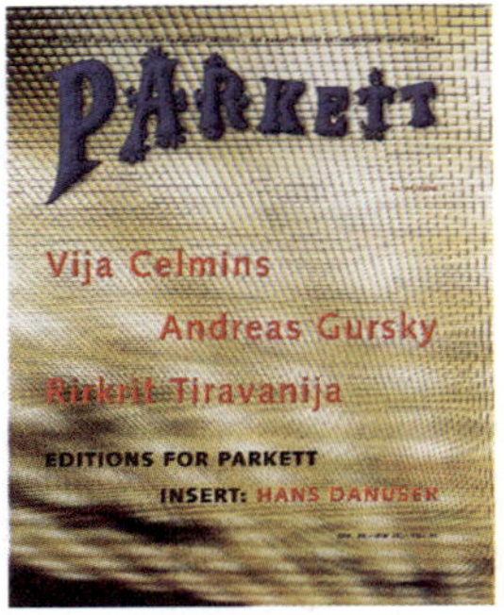

No. 44 - ISBN 3-907509-94-3

JUAN MUÑOZ
SUSAN ROTHENBERG
LYNNE COOKE, ALEXANDRE MELO
JAMES LINGWOOD, GAVIN BRYARS
ROBERT CREELEY, INGRID SCHAFFNER
JEAN-CHRISTOPHE AMMANN
MARK STEVENS, JOAN SIMON
INSERT: **ROBERT SMITHSON**
NEVILLE WAKEFIELD
MICHELLE NICOL: **CARSTEN HÖLLER**
HANS-ULRICH OBRIST: **FABRICE HYBERT**

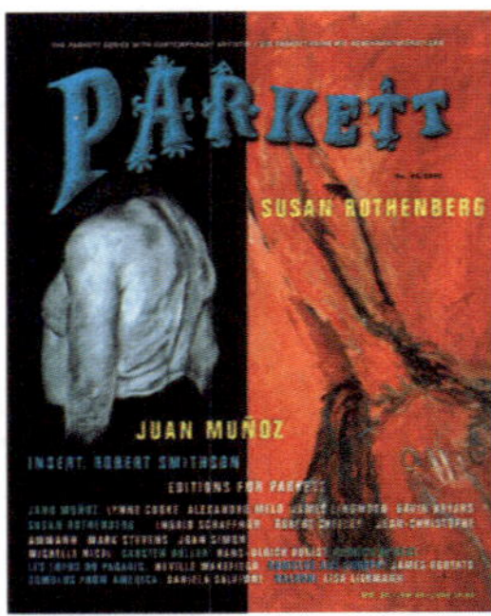

No. 43 - ISBN 3-907509-93-5

LAWRENCE WEINER
RACHEL WHITEREAD
BROOKS ADAMS, FRANCES RICHARD
DIETER SCHWARZ, DANIELA SALVIONI
ED LEFFINGWELL, LANE RELYEA
NEVILLE WAKEFIELD, RUDOLF SCHMITZ
TREVOR FAIRBROTHER, SIMON WATNEY
INSERT: **NAN GOLDIN**
VINCE LEO: **ROBERT FRANK**
CLAUDE RITSCHARD: **MARKUS RAETZ**

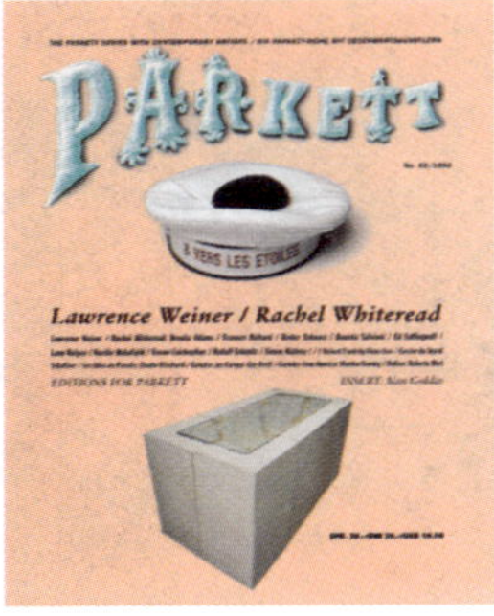

No. 42 - ISBN 3-907509-92-7

FRANCESCO CLEMENTE
GÜNTHER FÖRG
PETER FISCHLI / DAVID WEISS
DAMIEN HIRST
JENNY HOLZER
REBECCA HORN
SIGMAR POLKE
HOLLAND COTTER, BORIS GROYS
MAX WECHSLER, DAVID RIMANELLI
JOAN SIMON, GORDON BURN
GILBERT LASCAULT, WERNER SPIES
BICE CURIGER, JEFF PERRONE
G. ROGER DENSON, VIK MUNIZ
DAVE HICKEY

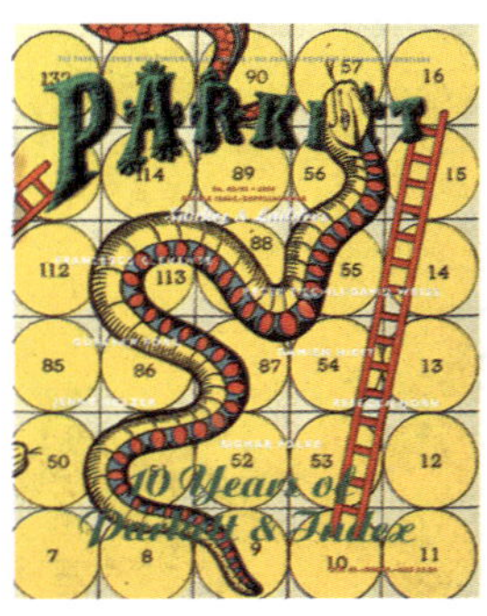

40/41 - ISBN 3-907509-90-0

FELIX GONZALEZ-TORRES
WOLFGANG LAIB
NANCY SPECTOR, SIMON WATNEY,
SUSAN TALLMAN, DIDIER SEMIN,
CLARE FARROW, JEAN-MARC AVRILLA,
THOMAS McEVILLEY
CLAUDE GINTZ: **GABRIEL OROZCO**
WALTER GRASSKAMP: **AXEL KASSEBÖHMER**
NEVILLE WAKEFIELD: **MATTHEW BARNEY**
INSERT: **RONI HORN**
LES INFOS DU PARADIS: **BURT BARR**
CUMULUS: **MEYER VAISMAN**

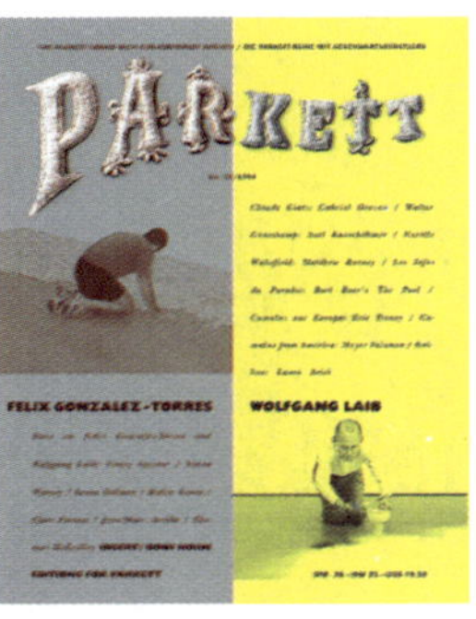

No. 39 - ISBN 3-907509-89-7

ROSS BLECKNER
MARLENE DUMAS
EDMUND WHITE, SIMON WATNEY
JOSE LUIS BREA, MARINA WARNER
ANNA TILROE, INGRID SCHAFFNER
ULRICH LOOCK
INSERT: **RUDI MOLACEK**
HARTMUT BÖHME
MAX WECHSLER: **ADRIAN SCHIESS**
DORIS VON DRATHEN:
RACHEL WHITEREAD

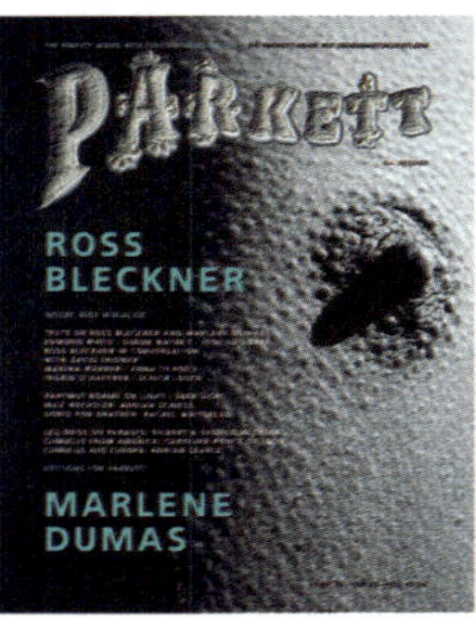

No. 38 - ISBN 3-907509-88-9

CHARLES RAY
FRANZ WEST
KLAUS KERTESS, CHRISTOPHER KNIGHT
PETER SCHJELDAHL, ROBERT STORR
JAN AVGIKOS, AXEL HUBER
MARTIN PRINZHORN, ELISABETH
SCHLEBRÜGGE, HARALD SZEEMANN,
DENYS ZACHAROPOULOS
INSERT: **PIPILOTTI RIST**
JEAN BAUDRILLARD
HANS RUDOLF REUST: **LUC TUYMANS**
PARKETT INQUIRY:
CHERCHEZ LA FEMME PEINTRE!

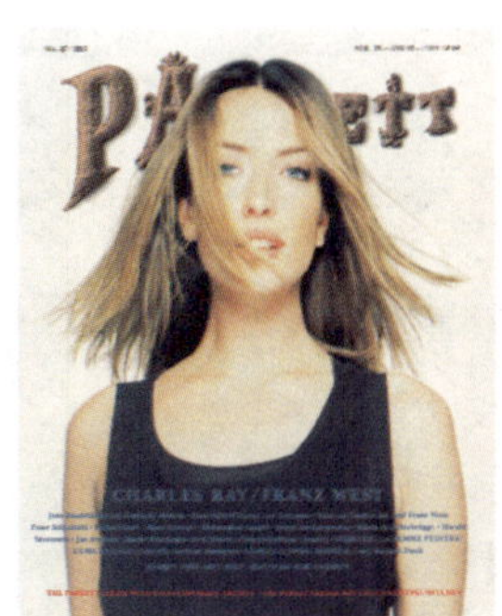

No. 37 - ISBN 3-907509-87-0

STEPHAN BALKENHOL
SOPHIE CALLE
NEAL BENEZRA, VIK MUNIZ, MAX KATZ
JEAN-CHRISTOPHE AMMANN
LUC SANTE, JOSEPH GRIGELY
PATRICK FREY, ROBERT BECK
INSERT: **RICHMOND BURTON**
URSULA PANHANS-BÜHLER: **EVA HESSE**
DOUGLAS BLAU: **JON KESSLER**
KIRBY GOOKIN: **LIZ LARNER**
LÁSZLÓ FÖLDÉNYI:
RUDOLF SCHWARZKOGLER

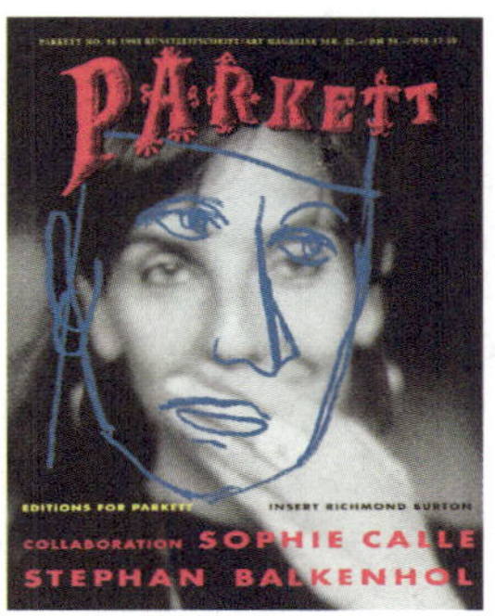

No. 36 - ISBN 3-907509-86-2

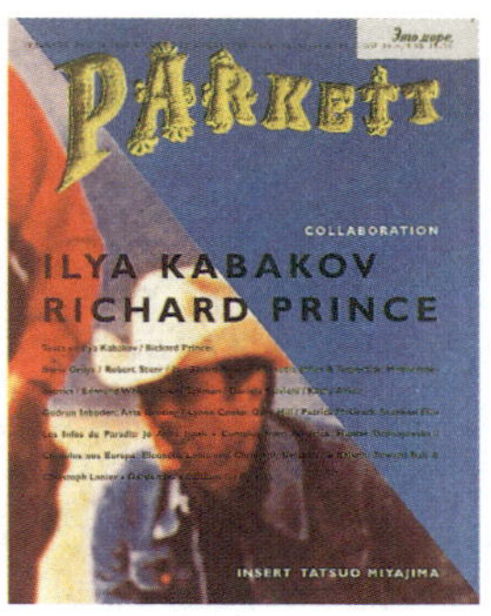

ILYA KABAKOV
RICHARD PRINCE
BORIS GROYS, ROBERT STORR
JAN THORN-PRIKKER
CLAUDIA JOLLES, EDMUND WHITE
SUSAN TALLMAN, DANIELA
SALVIONI, KATHY ACKER
INSERT: **TATSUO MIYAJIMA**
GUDRUN INBODEN: **ASTA GRÖTING**
LYNNE COOKE: **GARY HILL**
PATRICK McGRATH: **STEPHEN ELLIS**

No. 34 - ISBN 3-907509-84-6

ROSEMARIE TROCKEL
CHRISTOPHER WOOL
VERONIQUE BACCHETTA,
BARRETT WATTEN,
ANNE WAGNER, JIM LEWIS,
GREIL MARCUS, JEFF PERRONE,
DIEDRICH DIEDERICHSEN
INSERT: **ADRIAN SCHIESS**
MARINA WARNER: **PENIS PLENTY**
G. ROGER DENSON:
DENNIS OPPENHEIM
CAMIEL VAN WINKEL

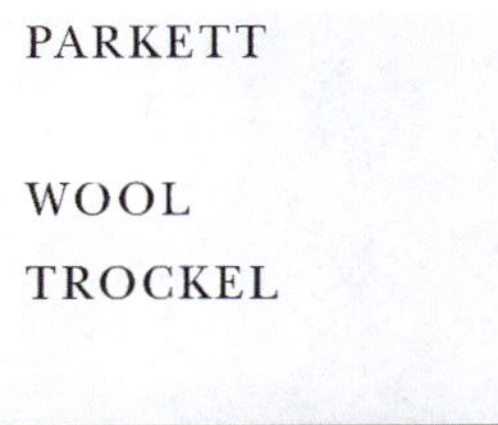

No. 33 - ISBN 3-907509-83-3

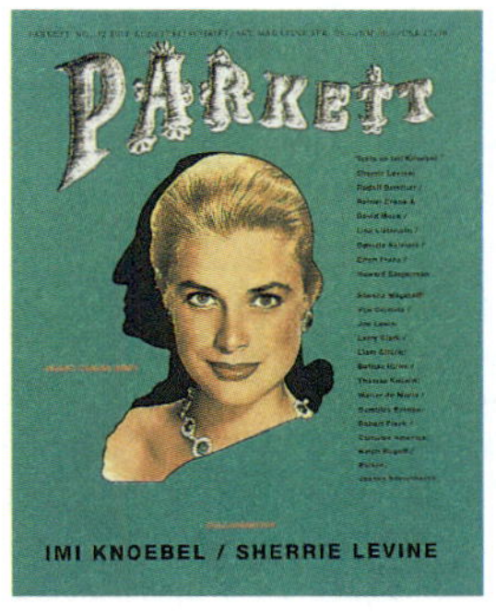

No. 32 - ISBN 3-907509-82-X

IMI KNOEBEL
SHERRIE LEVINE
RUDOLF BUMILLER
RAINER CRONE/DAVID MOOS
LISA LIEBMANN, DANIELA SALVIONI
ERICH FRANZ, HOWARD SINGERMANN
INSERT: **DAMIEN HIRST**
SHEENA WAGSTAFF: **VIJA CELMINS**
JIM LEWIS: **LARRY CLARK**
LIAM GILLICK: **BETHAN HUWS**
THOMAS KELLEIN: **WALTER DE MARIA**

FRANZ GERTSCH
THOMAS RUFF
HELMUT FRIEDEL, ULRICH LOOCK
I. MICHAEL DANOFF, AMEI WALLACH
RAINER MICHAEL MASON
MARC FREIDUS, JÖRG JOHNEN
TREVOR FAIRBROTHER/NORMAN BRYSON
INSERT: **LIZ LARNER**
JAMES LEWIS: **RICHARD PRINCE**
DAVID HICKEY:
THE INVISIBLE DRAGON/
DER UNSICHTBARE DRACHEN
PAUL TAYLOR: **JAMES ROSENQUIST**

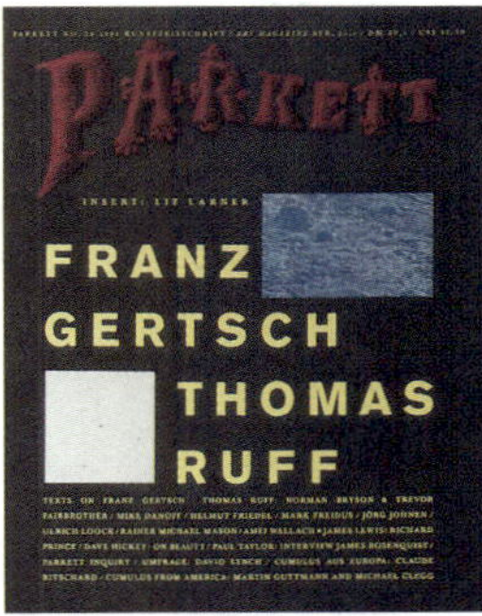

No. 28 - ISBN 3-907509-78-1

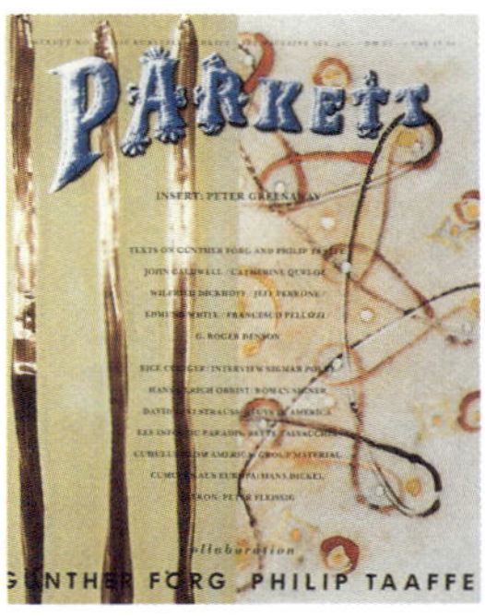

No. 26 - ISBN 3-907509-76-5

GÜNTHER FÖRG
PHILIP TAAFFE
JOHN CALDWELL, CATHERINE QUELOZ
WILFRIED DICKHOFF
JEFF PERRONE, EDMUND WHITE
FRANCESCO PELLIZZI
G. ROGER DENSON
INSERT: **PETER GREENAWAY**
BICE CURIGER: **SIGMAR POLKE**
HANS-ULRICH OBRIST:
ROMAN SIGNER
DAVID LEVI STRAUSS:
JOSEPH BEUYS

KATHARINA FRITSCH
JAMES TURRELL
GARY GARRELS
JULIAN HEYNEN, DAN CAMERON,
JEAN-CHRISTOPHE AMMANN,
DAVE HICKEY, RICHARD FLOOD &
CARL STIGLIANO, TED CASTLE
INSERT: **BEAT STREULI**
PATRICK FREY:
JEAN-FRÉDÉRIC SCHNYDER
DIETER SCHWARZ: **JAMES COLEMAN**
LYNNE COOKE:
RICHARD HAMILTON

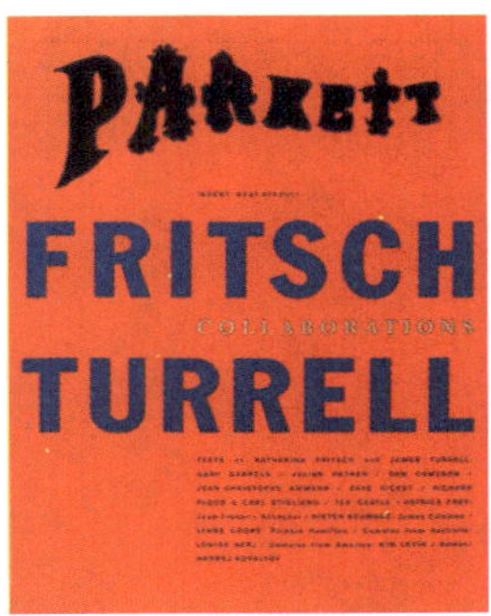

No. 25 - ISBN 3-907509-75-7

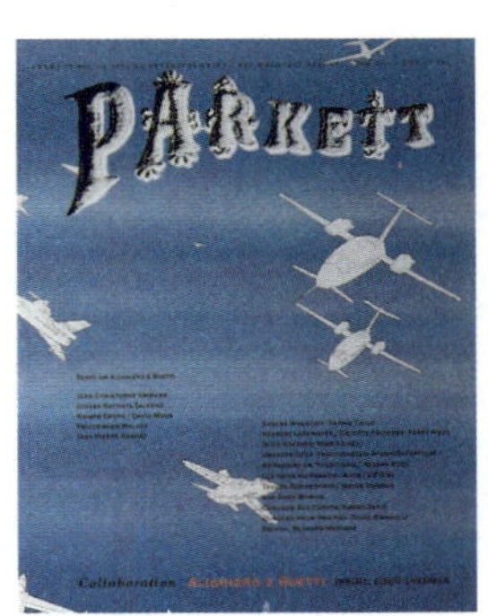

No. 24 - ISBN 3-907509-74-9

ALIGHIERO E BOETTI
JEAN-CHRISTOPHE AMMANN
GIOVAN BATTISTA SALERNO
RAINER CRONE & DAVID MOOS
FRIEDEMANN MALSCH
JEAN-PIERRE BORDAZ
ALAIN CUEFF
INSERT: **CINDY SHERMAN**
SHEENA WAGSTAFF:
SOPHIE CALLE
HERBERT LACHMEYER/
BRIGITTE FELDERER: **FRANZ WEST**
JUTTA KOETHER: **MIKE KELLEY**

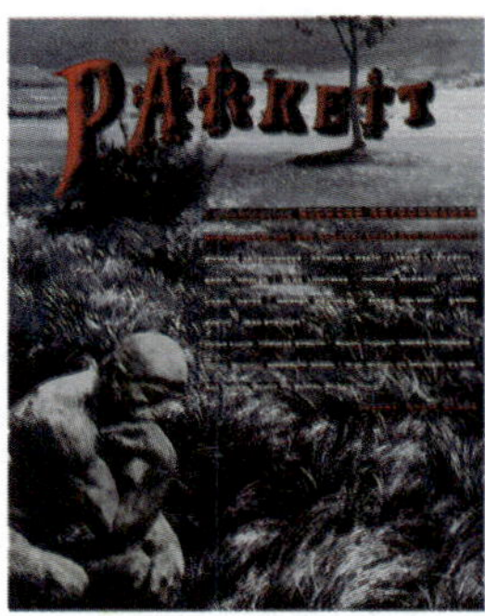

RICHARD ARTSCHWAGER
ARTHUR C. DANTO, GEORG KOHLER,
MARIO A. ORLANDO, JOYCE
CAROL OATES, WERNER OECHSLIN,
ALAN LIGHTMAN, PATRICK
McGRATH, DANIEL SOUTIF,
LASZLO F. FÖLDENYI, JEAN STROUSE
INSERT: **DAVID BYRNE**
RENATE PUVOGEL: **ANDRÉ THOMKINS**
ULRICH LOOCK: **THOMAS STRUTH**
NANCY SPECTOR: **MEREDITH MONK**

No. 23 - ISBN 3-907509-73-0

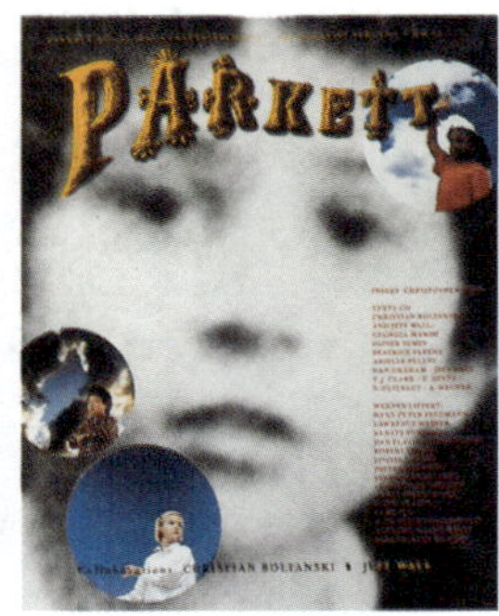

**CHRISTIAN BOLTANSKI
JEFF WALL**
DIDIER SEMIN, GEORGIA MARSH
BÉATRICE PARENT, DAN GRAHAM
JEFF WALL, ARIELLE PÉLENC
INSERT: **CHRISTOPHER WOOL**
DIETER KOEPPLIN:
STEPHAN BALKENHOL
RENATE PUVOGEL:
DAN FLAVIN, DONALD JUDD
WERNER LIPPERT: **VARIOUS SMALL
FIRES IN THE GUTENBERG GALAXY**

No. 22 - ISBN 3-907509-72-2

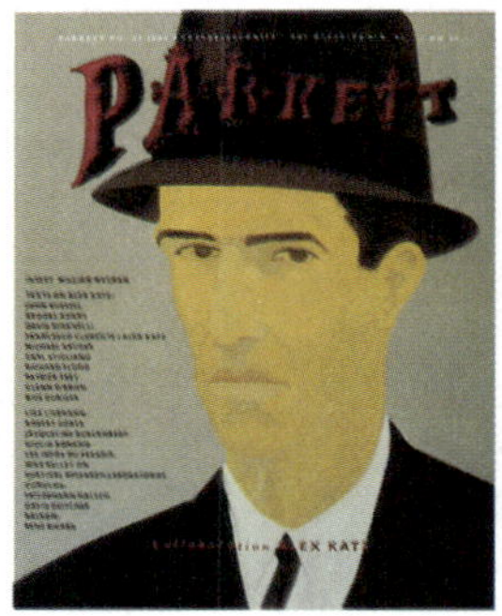

ALEX KATZ
JOHN RUSSELL, BROOKS ADAMS,
DAVID RIMANELLI, FRANCESCO
CLEMENTE, MICHAEL KRÜGER,
RICHARD FLOOD, PATRICK FREY,
CARL STIGLIANO, BICE CURIGER,
GLENN O'BRIEN
INSERT: **WILLIAM WEGMAN**
LISA LIEBMAN: **ROBERT GOBER**
JACQUELINE BURCKHARDT:
GIULIO ROMANO

No. 21 - ISBN 3-907509-71-4

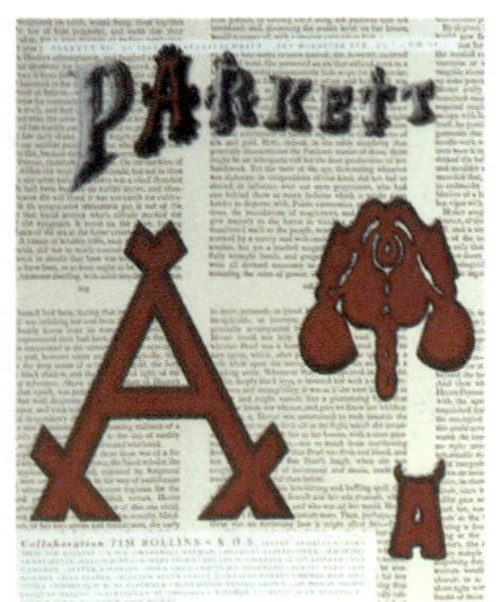

TIM ROLLINS + K.O.S.
MARSHALL BERMAN
TREVOR FAIRBROTHER
STATEMENTS, DIALOGUE 5
INSERT: **ANDREAS GURSKY**
MICHAEL NASH: **BILL VIOLA**
STEPHEN ELLIS: **ROSS BLECKNER**
KLAUS KERTESS: **TRISHA BROWN**

No. 20 - ISBN 3-907509-70-6

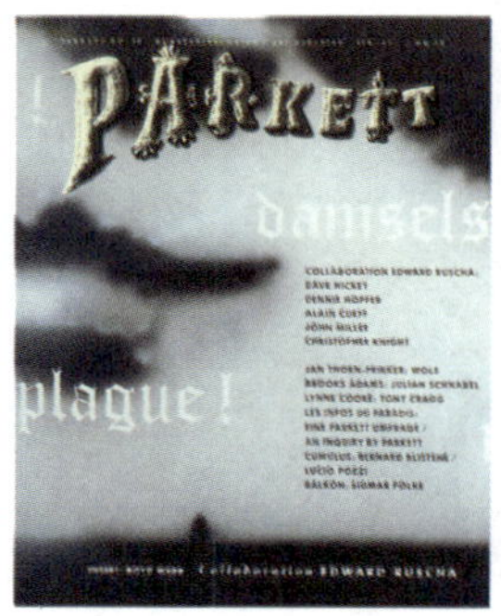

EDWARD RUSCHA
DAVE HICKEY, DENNIS HOPPER
ALAIN CUEFF, JOHN MILLER
CHRISTOPHER KNIGHT
INSERT: **BOYD WEBB**
JAN THORN-PRIKKER: **WOLS**
LYNNE COOKE: **TONY CRAGG**
BROOKE ADAMS: **JULIAN SCHNABEL**
DER KÜNSTLER ALS EXEM-
PLARISCH LEIDENDER?
EINE UMFRAGE / THE ARTIST AS A
MODEL SUFFERER? AN INQUIRY

No. 18 - ISBN 3-907509-68-4

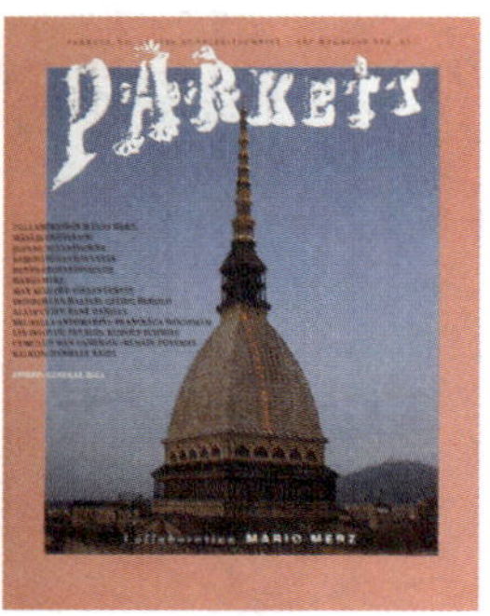

MARIO MERZ
MARLIS GRÜTERICH, JEANNE
SILVERTHORNE, DEMOSTHENES
DAVVETAS, HARALD SZEEMANN,
DENYS ZACHAROPOULOS
INSERT: **GENERAL IDEA**
MAX KOZLOFF: **GILLES PERESS**
FRIEDEMANN MALSCH:
GEORG HEROLD
BRUNELLA ANTOMARINI:
FRANCESCA WOODMAN

No. 15 - ISBN 3-907509-65-X

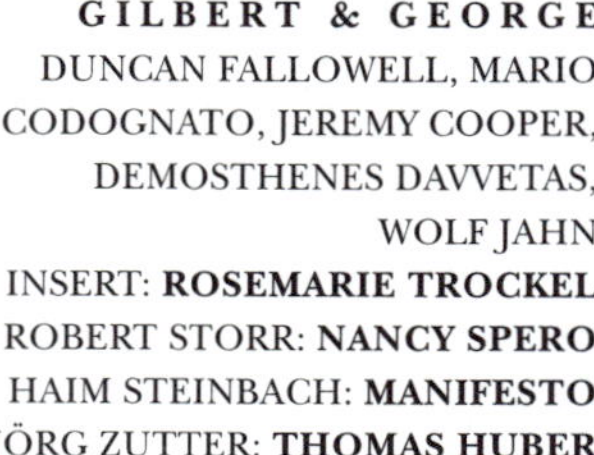
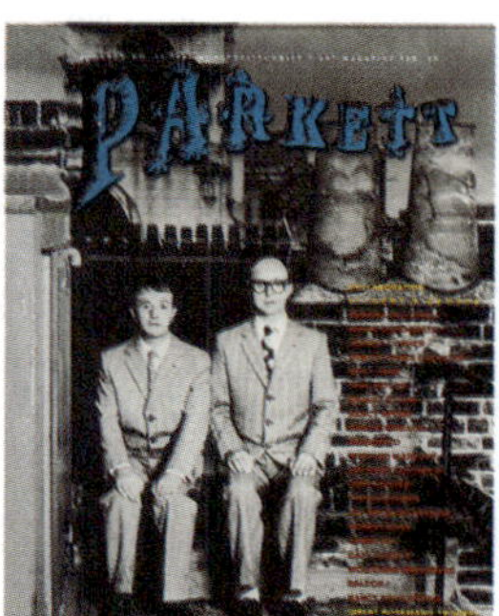

GILBERT & GEORGE
DUNCAN FALLOWELL, MARIO
CODOGNATO, JEREMY COOPER,
DEMOSTHENES DAVVETAS,
WOLF JAHN
INSERT: **ROSEMARIE TROCKEL**
ROBERT STORR: **NANCY SPERO**
HAIM STEINBACH: **MANIFESTO**
JÖRG ZUTTER: **THOMAS HUBER**

No. 14 - ISBN 3-907509-64-1

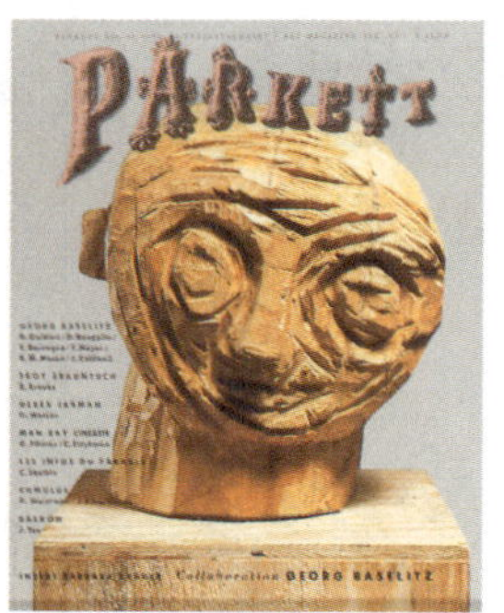

GEORG BASELITZ
REMO GUIDIERI, DIETER
KOEPPLIN, ERIC DARRAGON,
RAINER MICHAEL MASON, FRANZ
MEYER, JOHN CALDWELL
INSERT: **BARBARA KRUGER**
GRAY WATSON: **DEREK JARMAN**
CAROL SQUIERS:
PHOTO OPPORTUNITY
ROSETTA BROOKS:
TROY BRAUNTUCH

No. 11 - ISBN 3-907509-61-7

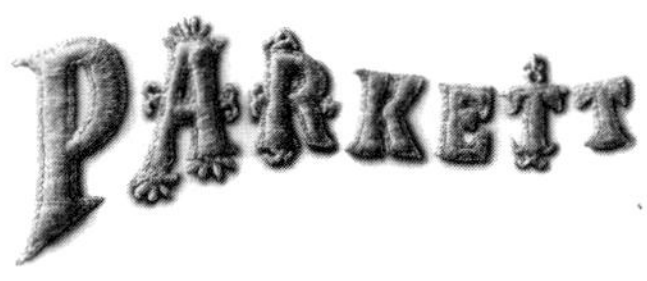

ARTISTS' MONOGRAPHS & EDITIONS / KÜNSTLERMONOGRAPHIEN & EDITIONEN,

Laurie Anderson, vol. 49	m	e	**Sherrie Levine**, vol. 32	m	
John Armleder, vol. 50/51	m	e	**Sarah Lucas**, vol. 45	m	e
Richard Artschwager, vol. 23, vol. 46	m		**Brice Marden**, vol. 7		
John Baldessari, vol. 29			**Mario Merz**, vol. 15	m	
Stephan Balkenhol, vol. 36	m	e	**Malcolm Morley**, vol. 52	m	e
Matthew Barney, vol. 45	m		**Juan Muñoz**, vol. 43	m	
Georg Baselitz, vol. 11	m		**Jean-Luc Mylayne**, vol. 50/51	m	e
Ross Bleckner, vol. 38	m		**Cady Noland**, vol. 46	m	e
Alighiero e Boetti, vol. 24	m	e	**Bruce Nauman**, vol. 10		
Christian Boltanski, vol. 22	m		**Meret Oppenheim**, vol. 4		
Louise Bourgeois, vol. 27			**Gabriel Orozco**, vol. 48	m	
Sophie Calle, vol. 36	m	e	**Tony Oursler**, vol. 47	m	
Vija Celmins, vol. 44	m		**Raymond Pettibon**, vol. 47	m	e
Francesco Clemente, vol. 9 & 40/41	m	e	**Sigmar Polke**, vol. 2, 30 & 40/41	m	e
Enzo Cucchi, vol. 1			**Richard Prince**, vol. 34	m	e
Martin Disler, vol. 3			**Markus Raetz**, vol.8		
Marlene Dumas, vol. 38	m		**Charles Ray**, vol. 37	m	
Eric Fischl, vol. 5			**Gerhard Richter**, vol. 35		
Peter Fischli/David Weiss, vol.17, 40/41	m		**Pipilotti Rist**, vol. 48	m	
Günther Förg, vol. 26 & 40/41	m		**Tim Rollins & K.O.S.**, vol. 20	m	
Katharina Fritsch, vol. 25	m	e	**Ugo Rondinone**, vol 52	m	e
Franz Gertsch, vol. 28	m	e	**Susan Rothenberg**, vol. 43	m	e
Gilbert & George, vol. 14	m		**Thomas Ruff**, vol. 28	m	e
Robert Gober, vol. 27			**Ed Ruscha**, vol. 18	m	
Felix Gonzalez-Torres, vol. 39	m		**Thomas Schütte**, vol. 47	m	e
Douglas Gordon, vol. 49	m	e	**Cindy Sherman**, vol. 29		e
Andreas Gursky, vol. 44	m		**Roman Signer**, vol. 45	m	e
David Hammons, vol. 31		e	**Thomas Struth**, vol. 50/51	m	
Damien Hirst, vol. 40/41	m		**Hiroshi Sugimoto**, vol. 46	m	
Jenny Holzer, vol. 40/41	m		**Philip Taaffe**, vol. 26	m	
Rebecca Horn, vol. 13 & 40/41	m		**Rirkrit Tiravanija**, vol. 44	m	e
Gary Hume, vol. 48	m	e	**Rosemarie Trockel**, vol. 33	m	e
Ilya Kabakov, vol. 34	m		**James Turrell**, vol. 25	m	e
Alex Katz, vol. 21	m	e	**Jeff Wall**, vol. 22 & 49	m	
Mike Kelley, vol. 31			**Andy Warhol**, vol. 12		
Karen Kilimnik, vol 52	m	e	**Lawrence Weiner**, vol. 42	m	e
Martin Kippenberger, vol. 19			**Franz West**, vol. 37	m	e
Imi Knoebel, vol. 32	m		**Rachel Whiteread**, vol. 42	m	
Jeff Koons, vol. 19, vol. 50/51	m	e	**Sue Williams**, vol 50/51	m	e
Jannis Kounellis, vol. 6			**Robert Wilson**, vol. 16		e
Wolfgang Laib, vol. 39	m	e	**Christopher Wool**, vol. 33	m	

m = available monograph
e = available edition
Delivery subject to availability at time of order

m = erhältliche Monographie
e = erhältliche Edition
Lieferung solange Vorrat

vol.	Collaboration		
52	Karen Kilimnik	m	e
	Malcolm Morley	m	e
	Ugo Rondinone	m	e
50/51	John Armleder	m	e
	Jeff Koons	m	e
	Jean-Luc Mylayne	m	e
	Thomas Struth	m	
	Sue Williams	m	e
49	Laurie Anderson	m	e
	Douglas Gordon	m	e
	Jeff Wall	m	
48	Gary Hume	m	e
	Gabriel Orozco	m	
	Pipilotti Rist	m	
47	Tony Oursler	m	
	Raymond Pettibon	m	e
	Thomas Schütte	m	e
46	Richard Artschwager	m	
	Cady Noland	m	e
	Hiroshi Sugimoto	m	
45	Matthew Barney	m	
	Sarah Lucas	m	e
	Roman Signer	m	e
44	Vija Celmins	m	
	Andreas Gursky	m	
	Rirkrit Tiravanija	m	e
43	Juan Muñoz	m	e
	Susan Rothenberg	m	e
42	Lawrence Weiner	m	e
	Rachel Whiteread	m	
40/41	Francesco Clemente	m	e
	Peter Fischli/David Weiss	m	
	Günther Förg	m	
	Damien Hirst	m	
	Jenny Holzer	m	
	Rebecca Horn	m	
	Sigmar Polke	m	e
39	Felix Gonzalez-Torres	m	
	Wolfgang Laib	m	e
38	Ross Bleckner	m	
	Marlene Dumas	m	
37	Charles Ray	m	
	Franz West	m	e
36	Stephan Balkenhol	m	e
	Sophie Calle	m	e

vol.	Collaboration		
35	Gerhard Richter		
34	Ilya Kabakov	m	
	Richard Prince	m	e
33	Rosemarie Trockel	m	e
	Christopher Wool	m	
32	Imi Knoebel		
	Sherrie Levine		
31	David Hammons		e
	Mike Kelley		
30	Sigmar Polke		
29	John Baldessari		
	Cindy Sherman		e
28	Franz Gertsch	m	e
	Thomas Ruff	m	e
27	Louise Bourgeois		
	Robert Gober		
26	Günther Förg	m	
	Philip Taaffe	m	
25	Katharina Fritsch	m	e
	James Turrell	m	e
24	Alighiero e Boetti	m	e
23	Richard Artschwager	m	
22	Christian Boltanski	m	
	Jeff Wall	m	
21	Alex Katz	m	e
20	Tim Rollins + K.O.S.	m	
19	Martin Kippenberger		
	Jeff Koons		
18	Ed Ruscha	m	
17	Peter Fischli/David Weiss		
16	Robert Wilson		
15,	Mario Merz	m	
14	Gilbert & George	m	
13	Rebecca Horn		
12	Andy Warhol		
11	Georg Baselitz	m	
10	Bruce Nauman		
9	Francesco Clemente		
8	Markus Raetz		
7	Brice Marden		
6	Jannis Kounellis		
5	Eric Fischl		
4	Meret Oppenheim		
3	Martin Disler		
2	Sigmar Polke		
1	Enzo Cucchi		

m = available monograph
e = available edition
Delivery subject to availability at time of order

m = erhältliche Monographie
e = erhältliche Edition
Lieferung solange Vorrat

EDITIONS FOR PARKETT

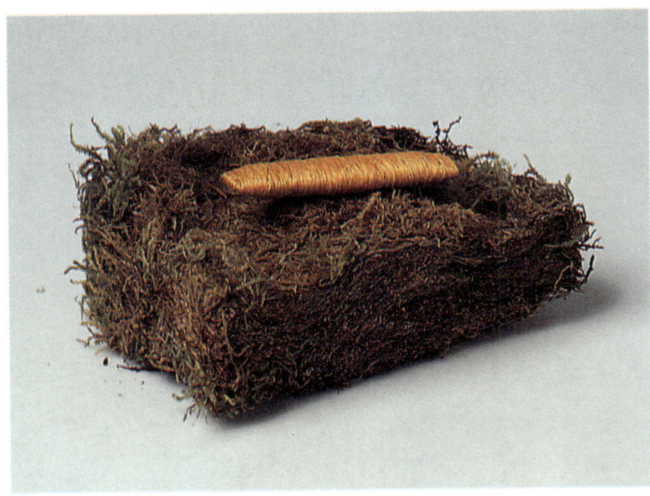

PARKETT 52

KAREN KILIMNIK
RAPUNZEL, 1998

Spindle of gold thread (hair) on bed of moss
(thread and moss are separately packaged to be assembled by the
collector), Plexiglas box, ca. 4 x 8 x 10".
Edition of 50, signed and numbered certificate
with diagram by the artist. **$ 550**

Goldhaarspindel auf Moos gebettet (separat verpackt, kann selbst
arrangiert werden), Plexiglasbox, ca. 10 x 20 x 25 cm.
Auflage: 50, signiertes und numeriertes Zertifikat
mit Abbildung. **sFr. 850.–**

PARKETT 52

MALCOLM MORLEY
ANCIENT CHINESE HORSES, 1998
11-color lithograph, 23¼ x 33⅞"
on Somerset soft white paper, 28¾ x 38".
Printed by Maurice Sanchez,
Derrière l' Etoile Studio, New York.
Edition of 60, signed and numbered, **$ 1400**

ALTCHINESISCHE PFERDE, 1998
Lithographie (11 Farben), 59 x 86 cm,
auf Somerset-Papier, 73 x 96,4 cm.
Gedruckt bei Maurice Sanchez,
Derrière l'Etoile Studio, New York.
Auflage: 60, signiert und numeriert,
sFr. 1900.–

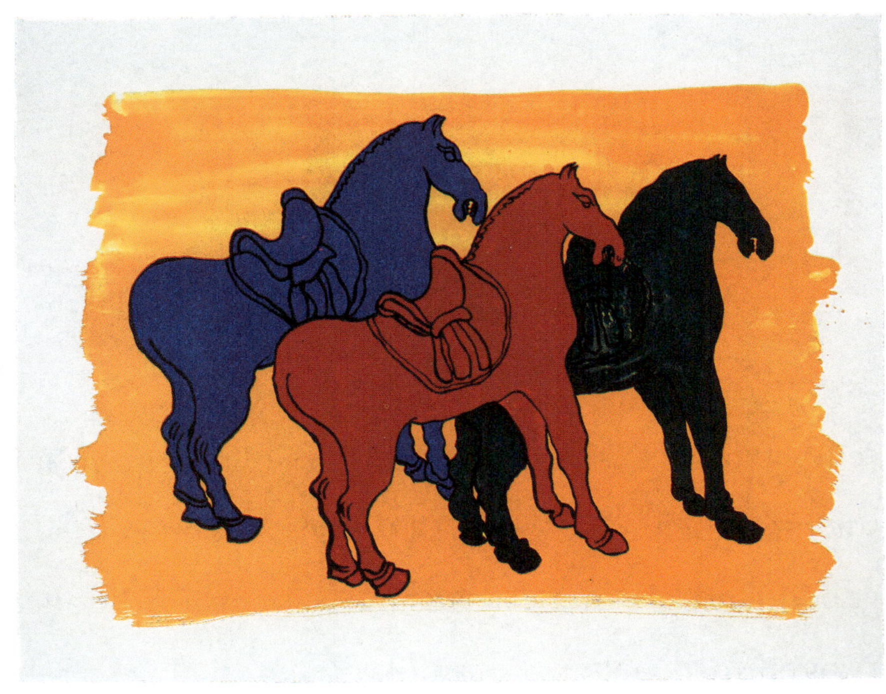

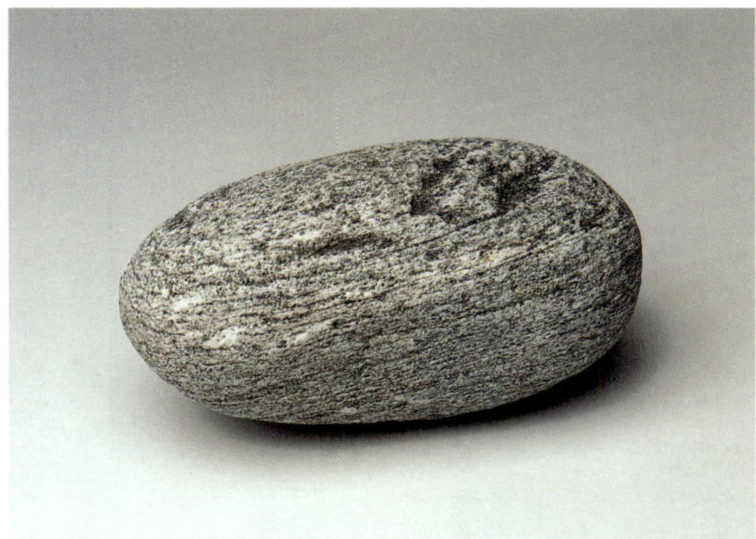

UGO RONDINONE
**ALLE AUGENBLICKE HÖREN HIER
AUF UND GEMEINSAM WERDEN WIR ZU
JEDER ERINNERUNG, DIE ES JEMALS
GEGEBEN HAT, 1998**
Stein aus dem Maggiatal,
ca. 30 x 20 x 10 cm, Gewicht ca. 7 bis 10 kg,
Polaroidaufnahme des Steins durch den Künstler.
Auflage: 50, signiert und numeriert, **sFr. 750.–**

**ALL MOMENTS STOP HERE AND
TOGETHER WE BECOME EVERY MEMORY
THAT HAS EVER BEEN, 1998**
Stone from the Valle Maggia
(Ticino, Switzerland).
Approximate size 12 x 8 x 4",
approximate weight 14 to 20 lbs.,
Polaroid photo of the stone by the artist.
Edition of 50, signed and numbered, **$ 500**

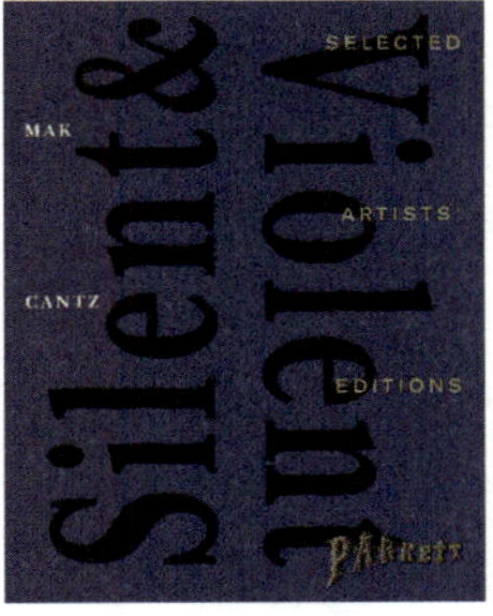

SILENT & VIOLENT
CATALOG RAISONNÉ OF ALL PARKETT ARTISTS' EDITIONS
from No. 1–44, 183 pages, 144 in color
text by Susan Tallmann, short biographies of all artists

WERKVERZEICHNIS ALLER PARKETT-KÜNSTLER-EDITIONEN
von Nr. 1–44, 183 Seiten, davon 144 in Farbe
Text von Susan Tallmann, Kurzbiographien der Künstler

sFr. 49.– / $ 39

ISBN 3-89322-796-3 (engl.), ISBN 3-89322-787-3 (dt.)

PARKETT-POSTCARD SET
featuring 36 artists' editions made for Parkett

PARKETT-POSTKARTEN-SET
mit 36 Editionen, die von Künstlern für
Parkett geschaffen wurden.

sFr. 19.– / $ 16

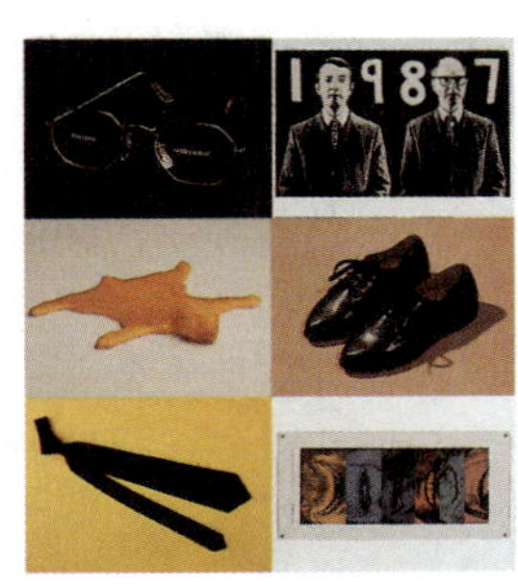

AUSKUNFT UND ABONNEMENTS / *INFORMATION AND SUBSCRIPTIONS:*

PARKETT VERLAG AG, QUELLENSTRASSE 27, CH-8005 ZÜRICH, TEL. 01/271 81 40, FAX 272 43 01; TANNENWALDALLEE 17, D-61348 BAD HOMBURG, FAX 06172/937 444

PARKETT, 155 AVENUE OF THE AMERICAS, 2ND FLOOR, NEW YORK, N.Y. 10013, PHONE (212) 673-2660, FAX 271-0704

SCHWEIZ

VERTRIEB
B + I BUCH UND INFORMATION AG
OBFELDERSTR. 35
8910 AFFOLTERN A. A.

BASEL
BUCHHANDLUNG STAMPA, SPALENBERG 2
BÜCHERSTAND STAMPA, KUNSTHALLE BASEL
W. JAEGGI AG, FREIESTR. 32

BERN
HANS HUBER AG, MARKTGASSE 59
BUCHHANDLUNG SCHERZ, MARKTGASSE 25
BUCHHANDLUNG STAUFFACHER, NEUENGASSE 25
BUCHHANDLUNG STAUFFACHER
IM KUNSTMUSEUM BERN, HODLERSTR.12

GENÈVE
LIBRAIRIE DESCOMBES, 6, RUE DU VIEUX-COLLÈGE
LIBRAIRIE PAYOT, 5, RUE DE CHANTEPOULET
LIBRAIRIE WEBER, 13, RUE DE MONTHOUX

LAUSANNE
LIBRAIRE BERNARD LETU,
MUSÉE D'ART CONTEMPORAIN
LIBRAIRIE PAYOT, 1, RUE DE BOURG

SCHAFFHAUSEN
BÜCHER-FASS, WEBERGASSE 13

ST. GALLEN
BUCHHANDLUNG COMEDIA, KATHARINENGASSE 20

ZÜRICH
BUCHHANDLUNG ZUM ELSÄSSER, LIMMATQUAI 18
BUCHHANDLUNG CALLIGRAMME, HÄRINGSTR. 4
SCALO BOOKS & LOOKS, WEINBERGSTRASSE 22 A
HEINIMANN & CO, KIRCHGASSE 17
BUCHHANDLUNG HOWEG, WAFFENPLATZSTR. 1
BUCHHANDLUNG KRAUTHAMMER, OBERE ZÄUNE 24
KUNSTKIOSK, LIMMATQUAI 31/HELMHAUS
ORELL FÜSSLI, FÜSSLISTR. 4
SEC 52, JOSEFSTR. 52

DEUTSCHLAND

VERTRIEB
VERSANDSERVICE RAINER PAPP
ANNA-VANDENHOECK-RING 36
37081 GÖTTINGEN

BERLIN
BÜCHERBOGEN, AM SAVIGNYPLATZ
GALERIE 2000, KNESEBECKSTR. 56–58
WASMUTH GmbH & CO., HORDENBERGSTR. 9A
WERNER GmbH, EHRENBERGSTR. 29

BONN
CARL KAYSER, POSTSTR. 16
GALERIE PUDELKO, HEINRICH-VON-KLEIST-STR.

BREMEN
ANTIQUARIAT, BEIM STEINERNEN KREUZ 1
JOHS. STORM, LANGENSTR. 10
KUNSTBUCH, SPITZENKIEL 16/17
B. SIEBRECHT, PANORAMA, VOR DEM STEINTOR 136
KUNST UND BUCH,
AM NEUEN MUSEUM, WESERBURG, TEERHOF 20

BREMERHAVEN
KABINETT FÜR AKTUELLE KUNST, KARLSBURG 4

DÜSSELDORF
M. + R. FRICKE, POSTSTR. 3
WALTHER KÖNIG, HEINRICH-HEINE-ALLEE 15
MÜLLER & TILLMANNS, NEUSTR. 38

FRANKFURT
HUGENDUBEL, STEINWEG 12
KARL MARX BUCHHANDLUNG, JORDANSTR. 11
PETER NAACHER, SCHWEIZERSTR. 57
SCHUMANN & COBET, BÖRSENSTR. 2–4
WALTHER KÖNIG, DOMSTR. 6

HAMBURG
H. VON DER HÖH, GROSSE BLEICHEN 21
SAUTTER UND LACKMANN
ADMIRALITÄTSSTRASSE 71/72
PPS, FELDSTR./ HOCHHAUS

HANNOVER
BUCHHANDLUNG IM SPRENGELMUSEUM
KURT-SCHWITTERS-PLATZ

HEIDELBERG
KUNSTHANDLUNG W. WELKER, HAUPTSTR. 106

KARLSRUHE
KUNSTBUCHHANDLUNG JUST, WALDSTR. 85

KIEL
GALERIE + EDITION KOCH, HOLSTENTÖRNPASSAGE

KÖLN
WALTHER KÖNIG, EHRENSTR. 4

MÜNCHEN
ILKA KÖNIG, AM KOSTTOR 1
H. GOLZ, TÜRKENSTR. 54
L. WERNER, RESIDENZSTR. 18
INT. BAHNHOFSBUCHHANDLUNG, BAHNHOFSPLATZ 2
MAX SUSSMANN GmbH, ARNULFSTR. 1/II
BASIS ANTIQUARIAT, ADALBERTSTR. 43

MÜNSTER
HEINRICH POERTGEN
HERDERSCHE BUCHHANDLUNG, HÖLTENWEG 51

NÜRNBERG
HEINRICH HUGENDUBEL, LUDWIGSPLATZ 1

OSNABRÜCK
H. TH. WENNER GmbH, GROSSE-STR. 69

REUTLINGEN
FETZER BUCH, WEINGÄRTNERSTR. 7

SAARBRÜCKEN
BOCK & SEIP, FUTTERSTR. 2

STUTTGART
WENDELIN NIEDLICH, SCHMALESTR. 9
GALERIE VALENTIEN, KÖNIGSBAU

TÜBINGEN
HUGO FRICK, NAUKLERSTR. 7

ULM
BUCHHANDLUNG UND GALERIE HOLM
HAFENBAD 11

ÖSTERREICH

GRAZ
BUCHHANDLUNG GALERIE
VERLAG DROSCHL, BISCHOFPLATZ 1

INNSBRUCK
PARNASS, SPECKBACHERSTR. 21
WAGNERSCHE UNIVERSITÄTSBUCHHANDLUNG
MUSEUMSTR. 4

LINZ
ALEX STELZER, HAUPTPLATZ 17

WIEN
JUDITH ORTNER, SONNENFELSGASSE 8
SHAKESPEARE & COMPANY
BOOKSELLERS, STEINGASSE 2

HOLLAND

DISTRIBUTION
IDEA BOOKS, NIEUWE HERENGRACHT 11
1011 RK AMSTERDAM

AMSTERDAM
ART BOOK, PRINSENGRACHT 645
ATHENAEUM NIEUWSCENTRUM, SPUI 14–16
MENEER KEES, PC HOOFSTRAAT 64-66
NIJHOF & LEE, STAALSTRAAT 13 A
PREMSELA, VAN BAERLESTRAAT 78
VERBEELDING, UTRECHTSESTRAAT 40

ARNHEM
HIJMAN, GROTE OORD 15
ARNHEMS GEMEENTEMUSEUM, UTRECHTSEWEG 87

BREDA
VAN KEMENADE & HOLLAERS, GINNEKENWEG 330

DORDRECHT
BENGEL, VOORSTRAAT 283

EINDHOVEN
MOTTA BERGSTRAAT 35
VAN ABBEMUSEUM, BILDERDIJKLAAN 10

ENSCHEDE
BROEKHUIS, MARKTSTRAAT 12

GRONINGEN
SCHOLTENS/WRISTERS, GULDENSTRAAT 20

HENGELO
BROEKHUIS, ENSCHEDESTRAAT 19

LEIDEN
GINSBERG, BREESTRAAT 127

MAASTRICHT
TRIBUNE, KAPOENSTRAAT 8
VELDEKE, KLEINE STAAT 14

ROTTERDAM
DONNER, LIJNBAAN 150
VAN GENNEP, OUDE BINNENWEG 131B

THE HAGUE
ULYSSES, DENNEWEG 108

TILBURG
DE PONT STICHTING, WILHELMINAPARK 1

UTRECHT
CENTRAAL MUSEUM, AGNIETENSTRAAT 1

BELGIQUE

ANTWERPEN
BRAMANTE, KOEPORTBRUG 4
F.N.A.C. GROENPLAATS
LANDSCHAP, WIJNGAARDSTRAAT 12
STANDAARD, HUIDEVETTERSTRAAT 57

BRUXELLES
PEINTURE FRAÎCHE, 10 RUE DU TABELLION
POST-SCRIPTUM, 37 RUE DES ÉPERONNIERS
TROPISMES, GALERIE DES PRINCES 11

GENT
COPYRIGHT JAKOBIJNENSTRAAT 8
INTELLECT, KALANDESTRAAT 1
KORTRIJK
THEORIA, ONZE LIEVE VROUWESTRAAT 22

LUXEMBOURG
LUXEMBOURG
CASINO LUXEMBOURG A.S.B.L.
FORUM D'ART CONTEMPORAIN
41, RUE DE NOTRE-DAME

ESPAÑA
BARCELONA
1+1 ART BOOKS, CENTRE CULTURAL DE LA
FUNDACIÒ CAIXA, PASSEIG DE SANT JOAN 108
LAIE LLIBRERIA
PAU CLARIS 85
MADRID
CENTRO REINA SOFIA, STA. ISABEL 52

FRANCE
AIX-EN-PROVENCE
LIBRAIRIE VENTS DU SUD, 7, RUE MARÉCHAL FOCH
BORDEAUX
LIBRAIRIE DU MUSÉE CAPC, ENTREPÔT LAINÉ
LIBRAIRIE MOLLAT, 9–15, VITAL CARLES
LYON
LIBRAIRIE LE RÉVERBÈRE, 4, RUE NEUVE
PARIS
LA HUNE, 170 BLVD ST-GERMAIN
«FLAMMARION 4», CENTRE GEORGES POMPIDOU
PLATEAU BEAUBOURG
LIBRAIRIE DU MUSEE D'ART MODERNE
9, RUE FERRIÈRE
GALERIE NATIONALE DU JEU DE PAUME
PLACE DE LA CONCORDE
TOULOUSE
LIBRAIRIE OMBRES BLANCHES, 50, RUE GAMBETTA

ISRAEL
TEL AVIV
BOOKWORM, 30 BASEL ST.

ITALIA
MILANO
A&M BOOKSTORE, VIA PLINIO 15
MILANO LIBRI, VIA G. VERDI 2
MODENA
LOGOS IMPEX
VIA CURTATONA, 5/F, 41010 SAN DAMASO/MODENA
ROMA
FELTRINELLI, VIA DEL BABUINO 41
GALLERIA PRIMO PIANO, VIA PANISPERNA 203

PORTUGAL
LISBOA
COMICOS ESPAÇO INTER-MEDIA
RUA TENENTE RAUL CASCAIS 1B

SVERIGE
STOCKHOLM
BOK & BILD, KULTURHUSET, SERGELSTORG 3
NORDENFLYCHTSVÄGEN 70

GREAT BRITAIN
DISTRIBUTOR
CENTRAL BOOKS, 99, WALLIS RD. LONDON E9 5LN
LONDON
HAYWARD GALLERY BOOKSHOP, SOUTH BANK
ICA BOOKSHOP, NASH HOUSE
12, CARLTON HOUSE TERRACE
LIBERTY, BOOK DEPT., 210 REGENT STREET

USA
DISTRIBUTOR
D. A. P. (DISTRIBUTED ART PUBLISHERS)
155 AVENUE OF THE AMERICAS, 2ND FLOOR,
NEW YORK, NY 10013
ANN ARBOR, MI
MAIN STREET NEWS, 220 S. MAIN
AUSTIN, TX
BOOK PEOPLE, 603 N. LAMAR
BERKELEY, CA
CODY'S BOOKS, 2454 TELEGRAPH AVENUE
UNIVERSITY ART MUSEUM, 2625 DURANT AVENUE
BOSTON, MA
MIT PRESS BOOKSTORE, 292 MAIN STREET,
CAMBRIDGE, MA 02142
TRIDENT BOOKSELLERS, 338 NEWBURY STREET
BUFFALO, NY
TALKING LEAVES, 3158 MAIN STREET
CHICAGO, IL
THE ART INSTITUTE OF CHICAGO,
104 EAST CHICAGO AVENUE
MUSEUM OF CONTEMPORARY ART
220 EAST CHICAGO AVENUE
COLUMBUS, OH
WEXNER CENTER, 30 W. 15TH AVENUE
DALLAS, TX
MCKINNEY AVENUE CONTEMPORY
3120 MCKINNEY AVENUE
HOUSTON, TX
BRAZOS BOOK STORE, 2421 BISSONNET
CONTEMPORARY ARTS MUSEUM SHOP
5216 MONTROSE AVENUE
MENIL COLLECTION BOOKSTORE, 1520 SUL ROSS
KANSAS CITY, MO
WHISTLER'S BOOKS, 427 WESTPORT ROAD
LOS ANGELES
BOOKSOUP, 8818 SUNSET BOULEVARD
MUSEUM OF CONTEMPORARY ART, 250 S. GRAND
UCLA/ARMAND HAMMER MUSEUM OF ART
10899 WILSHIRE BOULEVARD
MIAMI, FL
BOOKS & BOOKS, 296 ARAGON AVENUE,
CORAL GABLES, FL 33134
MOCA MUSEUM SHOP, 770 N.E. 125TH STREET
NORTH MIAMI, FL 33161
MINNEAPOLIS
WALKER ART CENTER, VINELAND PLACE
NEW YORK
BOOKS AND COMPANY, 939 MADISON AVENUE
GUGGENHEIM MUSEUM, 575 BROADWAY
RIZZOLI BOOKSTORES, 300 PARK AVENUE SOUTH
SAINT MARKS BOOKSHOP, 31 THIRD AVENUE
OAKLAND, CA
DIESEL, A BOOKSTORE, 5433 COLLEGE AVENUE
OMAHA, NE
JOSELYN ART MUSEUM, 2200 DODGE STREET
PHILADELPHIA, PA
WATERSTONE'S BOOKSELLERS, 2191 HORNIG ROAD
PITTSBURGH, PA
CARNEGIE INSTITUTE, 4400 FORBES AVENUE

PORTLAND, OR
POWELL'S BOOKS, 7 NW 9TH STREET
PROVIDENCE, NY
ACCIDENT OR DESIGN, 128 N. MAIN STREET
RHODE ISLAND SCHOOL OF DESIGN
30 N. MAIN STREET
SAN FRANCISCO, CA
CITY LIGHTS BOOKSHOP, 261 COLUMBUS AVENUE
JACK HANLEY GALLERY, 41 GRANT AVENUE
MUSEUMBOOKS SFMOMA, 151 3RD ST., 1ST FLOOR
ST. LOUIS, MO
LEFT BANK BOOKS, 399 NORTH EUCLID
SANTA MONICA, CA
ARCANA, 1229 3RD ST. PROMENADE
MIDNIGHT SPECIAL BOOKSTORE
1318 3RD ST. PROMENADE
SEATTLE, WA
UNIVERSITY BOOK STORE
4326 UNIVERSITY AVENUE
WASHINGTON, D.C.
FRANZ BADER BOOKSTORE, 1911 "I" STREET, NW
NATIONAL GALLERY OF ART
6TH & CONSTITUTION AVENUE, NW

CANADA
CALGARY
TREPANIER BAER GALLERY, 999 8TH STREET
MONTREAL
ARTEXTE, 3575 ST. LAURENT
TORONTO
ART METROPOLE, 788 KING STREET WEST
ART GALLERY OF ONTARIO, BOOKSTORE
317 DUNDAS ST. WEST
EDWARDS BOOKS & ART, 356 QUEEN ST. WEST
DAVID MIRVISH BOOKS ON ART, 596 MARKHAM ST.
VANCOUVER
ART GALLERY STORE, 750 HORNBY ST.

AUSTRALIA
DISTRIBUTORS
MANIC EX-POSEUR, WORLD TRADE CENTER
MELBOURNE 3005
THE ARTS BOOKSHOP, 1067 HIGH STREET
ARMADALE, VICTORIA 3143
VICTORIA
HARTWIGS BOOKSHOP
245 BRUNSWICK STR., VICTORIA 3182

NEW ZEALAND
DISTRIBUTOR
PROPAGANDA, 44 COLLEGE HILL, AUCKLAND

HONG KONG
PUBLISHERS MARKETING LTD.
TUNG ON BUILDING, 171, PRINCE EDWARD ROAD
KOWLOON
TAI YIP ART BOOK CENTRE
HONG KONG MUSEUM OF ART
TSIM SHA TSUI, KOWLOON

JAPAN
TOKIO
EUROPA ART GmbH, KAMIOGI 4-16-4, SUGINAMI-KU
ON SUNDAYS, 3-7-6 JUNGUMAE, SHIBUYA-KU
AOYAMA BOOKCENTER, ROPPONGI STORE
MINATO-KU
HAKUO TRADING COMPANY
KOJIMACHI SHINE BLD., 8F, CHIYODA-KU
SANSEIDO BOOKSTORE, 7-11-8 KOHAKU, ADACHI-KU
MY BOOK SERVICE, AOI BLD. 5-8, SARUGAKU-CHO

E X H I B I T I O N S

E X H I B I T I O N S

ANNEMARIE VERNA	Neptunstrasse 42	DONALD JUDD (1928–1994)	**April/Mai**
	8032 Zürich	JAMES BISHOP	**Mai/Juni**
	Tel. 01 262 38 20	RICHARD TUTTLE	**Juli/September**
		ART 29'98, HALLE 202/D19	**10.6.–15.6.98**
JAMILEH WEBER	Waldmannstrasse 6	BASELITZ, DE MARIA, HERDEG, JAHANGUIR,	
	8001 Zürich	LEE, LICHTENSTEIN, MARDEN, POTTORF	
	Tel. 01 252 10 66	RAUSCHENBERG, SCULLY, SERRA, SHAPIRO	
GALERIE	Gen. Guisan-Quai 32	ILONA RUEGG	**23.3.–10.5.98**
WEISSES SCHLOSS	8002 Zürich	RICHARD WENTWORTH	**24.5.–12.7.98**
	Tel. 01 202 00 46		

BERN

GALERIE	Lorrainestrasse 19	GÄSTE / GUESTS 6	
ERIKA + OTTO	Postfach 323	TRAVELING WITHOUT MOVING	
FRIEDRICH	3013 Bern	BURKI – NÄPFLIN – OPIE – SANTORO	
	Tel. 031 331 33 30	DANIEL KURJAKOVIC, KURATOR	**8.5.–4.7.98**
		ART 29'98, HALLE 214/B25	**10.6.–15.6.98**

GENÈVE

DANIEL VARENNE	8, rue Toepffer	PAINTINGS AND DRAWINGS	
	1206 Genève	19TH AND 20TH CENTURY	
	Tel. 022 789 16 75		

ST. GALLEN

WILMA LOCK	Schmidgasse 15	JÜRGEN PARTENHEIMER	
	9000 St. Gallen	NEUE ZEICHNUNGEN	**21.5.–12.7.98**
	Tel. 071 222 62 52	SOMMERPAUSE	**13.7.–1.9.98**
		ERWIN WURM	**6.9.–25.10.98**

Anish Kapoor

April – May

Richard Prince

June – July

BARBARA GLADSTONE GALLERY

515 West 24th Street
New York, New York 10011
Telephone 212 206 9300
Fax 212 206 9301

MALCOLM MORLEY

is represented by

SPERONE WESTWATER
New York

JEAN-MARC BUSTAMANTE

JANUARY - FEBRUARY 1998

FRANZ ERHARD WALTHER

MARCH - APRIL 1998

GERWALD ROCKENSCHAUB

JUNE - JULY 1998

VERA MUNRO

Galerie · Heilwigstraße 64 · 20249 Hamburg · Tel. 040/484552 - 474746 · Fax 472550

DOUG AITKEN

ALEX BAG

THOMAS DEMAND

HANS-PETER FELDMANN

MAUREEN GALLACE

RODNEY GRAHAM

MARTIN HONERT

KAREN KILIMNIK

ELKE KRYSTUFEK

LIZ LARNER

DANIEL OATES

KRISTIN OPPENHEIM

ROBERT PRUITT

THOMAS RUFF

COLLIER SCHORR

SUE WILLIAMS

JANE AND LOUISE WILSON

303GALLERY

525 WEST 22ND STREET NEW YORK 10011
TEL 212 255 1121 FAX 212 255 0024

23 May to 25 July 1998

2nd floor

DIETER ROTH

GALERIE HAUSER & WIRTH

Limmatstrasse 270 CH-8005 Zürich Tel +41 1 446 80 50 Fax +41 1 446 80 55 e-mail: info@ghw.ch
Gallery Hours: Tue-Fri 12-6pm Sat 11am-4pm

Art Chicago 8 to 12 May 1998   **Art Basel 10 to 15 June 1998**

23 May to 25 July 1998

1st floor

Dieter Roth

Galerie Hauser & Wirth 2 ▶
Director: Eva Presenhuber

Limmatstrasse 270, CH-8005 Zürich, T: +41-1-446 80 60, F: +41-1-446 80 65, e-mail: ghwzurich2@access.ch
Gallery Hours: Tue - Fri 12am-6pm, Sat 11am-4pm

Ugo Rondinone

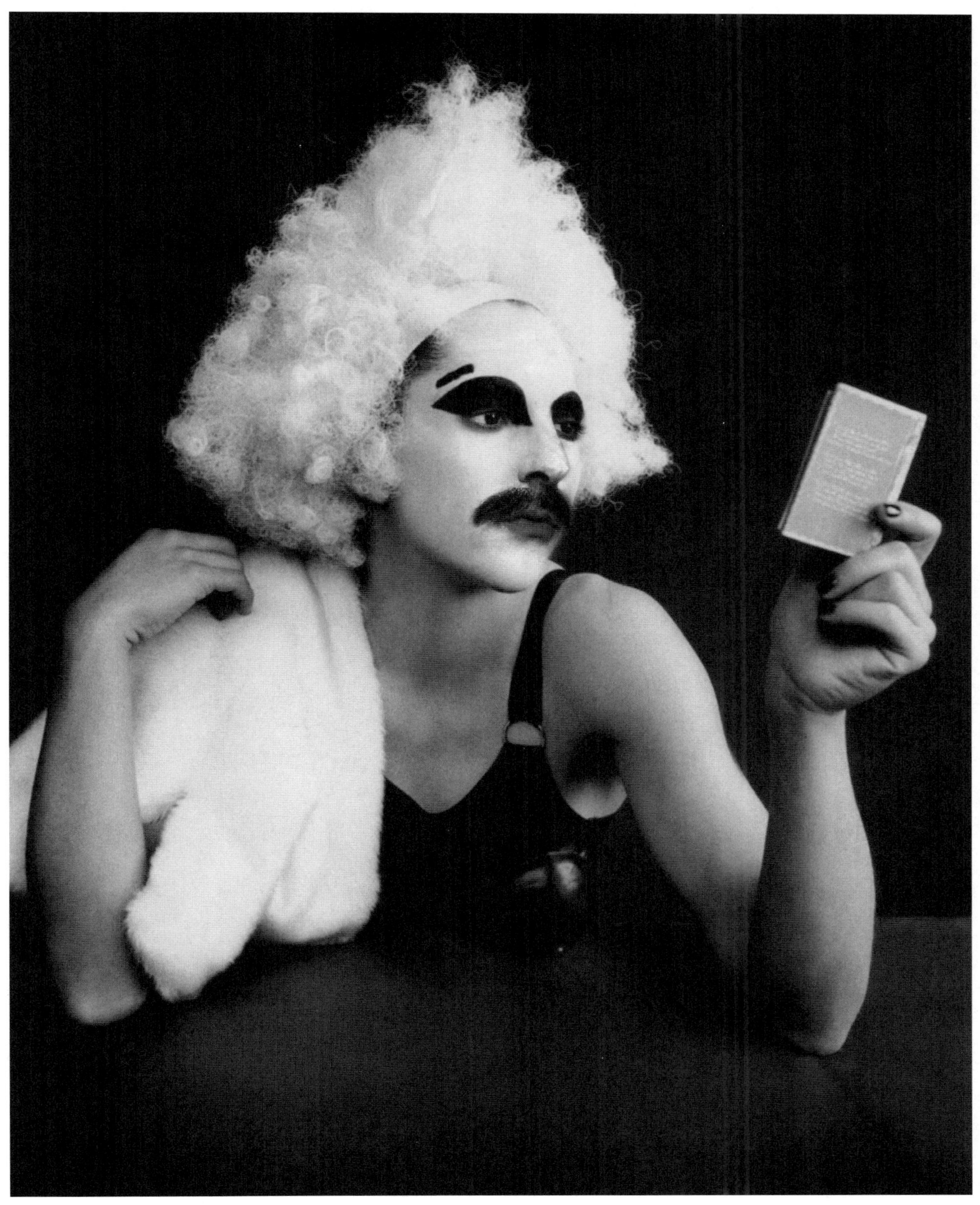

Spring

Ellsworth Kelly   **523 West 24th Street**

522 West 22nd Street

Summer

Joseph Grigely

Ugo Rondinone

Millie Wilson   **523 West 24th Street**

Matthew Marks Gallery

New York

JEAN BERNIER
51 MARASLI STR., GR–106 76 ATHENS, GREECE
TEL. 723 56 57   FAX 722 61 89

ERIC POITEVIN
MAY – JUNE 1998

ART 1998 CHICAGO
MAY 8 – MAY 12, 1998
BOOTH NO: C 228

AND

ART 29'98, BASEL
JUNE 10 – JUNE 15, 1998
BOOTH NO: 212/B9, TEL. +41 79 200 41 62

REBECCA HORN

MAY 5 – JUNE 13

MONIKA SPRÜTH GALERIE

ANDREAS SCHULZE
WALTER DAHN

Mai – July 98

ASTRID KLEIN
JENNY HOLZER

September – October 98

PETER FISCHLI
DAVID WEISS

November – December 98

MONIKA SPRÜTH GALERIE · WORMSER STR. 23 · D-50677 KÖLN · 02 21 - 38 04 15 FAX 38 04 17

PETER BLUM

April – May

HELMUT FEDERLE

Panthera Nigra

June – July

YAYOI KUSAMA

Works from the 50's

BLUMARTS INC.
99 Wooster Street
New York, N.Y. 10012
Tel (212) 343-0441
Fax (212) 343-0523

MAI 36 GALERIE

FRANZ ACKERMANN

IAN ANÜLL

JOHN BALDESSARI

STEPHAN BALKENHOL

MATTHEW BENEDICT

TROY BRAUNTUCH

ANKE DOBERAUER

PIA FRIES

ULRICH GÖRLICH

ANDREAS GURSKY

ANDREA KNOBLOCH

LES LEVINE

MATT MULLICAN

CHRISTOPH RÜTIMANN

THOMAS RUFF

LAWRENCE WEINER

RÉMY ZAUGG

HARALD F. MÜLLER
MAY 15 – JUNE 20

SUMMER SHOW
JUNE 25 – JULY 25

JÖRG SASSE
AUGUST 22 – OCTOBER 10

Rämistrasse 37, CH-8001 Zürich, Tel. 01 261 68 80, Fax 261 68 81

Jean-Marc **BUSTAMANTE**

Andreas **GURSKY**

Mike **KELLEY**

Tony **OURSLER**

Cindy **SHERMAN**

Adriana **VAREJAO**

Carroll **DUNHAM**

Wim **DELVOYE**

Juan **MUNOZ**

Karen **KILIMNIK**

Alain **SECHAS**

Franz **WEST**

Sue **WILLIAMS**

Christopher **WOOL**

Galerie Ghislaine Hussenot

5bis, rue des Haudriettes, 75003 Paris
Tél. 48 87 60 81, Fax 48 87 05 01

SEAN KELLY

43 MERCER STREET
NEW YORK   NY   10013
TELEPHONE 212 343-2405
FAX 212 343-2604

Chantal Akerman

Selfportrait/Autobiography

a work in progress

May 1 - June 13, 1998

We are delighted to announce the

representation of the Estate of

Gordon Matta-Clark

Michelangelo Pistoletto
Segno Arte Unlimited

25 APRIL – 30 MAY 1998

Mitja Tušek
no doupt

4 JUNE – 4 JULY 1998

Summer show

JULY – AUGUST 1998

Xavier Hufkens

Sint-Jorisstraat 6–8 rue Saint-Georges

Brussel 1050 Bruxelles

TEL. 32 (0)2 646 63 30 – FAX 32 (0)2 646 93 42

Open Tuesday to Saturday, noon to 6 pm

GALERIA ■ HELGA DE ALVEAR

DOCTOR FOURQUET, 12 28012 MADRID TEL.: (34) 91-468 05 06 FAX: (34) 91-467 51 34

DANIEL CANOGAR

DARIO CORBEIRA

SALOME CUESTA

CHRISTINE DAVIS

JOAN FONTCUBERTA

KAZUO KATASE

IMI KNOEBEL

JOSE MALDONADO

SHIRO MATSUI

MITSUO MIURA

MABEL PALACIN

JESUS PALOMINO

THOMAS RUFF

KARIN SANDER

EULALIA VALLDOSERA

JAVIER VALLHONRAT

JOSEPH MARIONI

Paintings

June 6–July 25, 1998

ART 29'98 Basel – 214.D12   – ARTISTS OF THE GALLERY
ART SCULPTURE Basel   – BEAT ZODERER

June 10–15, 1998

Galerie Mark Müller
Gessnerallee 36
CH-8001 Zürich
Tel. 01 211 81 55
Fax 01 211 82 20

MAI - JULI

DARA BIRNBAUM

ROBERT CAHEN

BRIAN ENO

GARY HILL

BILL SEAMAN

TRABANT

A - 1040 WIEN SCHLEIFMÜHLGASSE 13 TEL / FAX 0043 1 272 21 79

Castello di Rivara Center of Contemporary Art

23 May 1998–31 July 1998

ANKE DOBERAUER

paintings

BORIS MICHAÏLOV

photography

Castello di Rivara I-10080 Rivara/To t/f 0124 31122 sat–sun 14.30–19.00 (and by appointment)

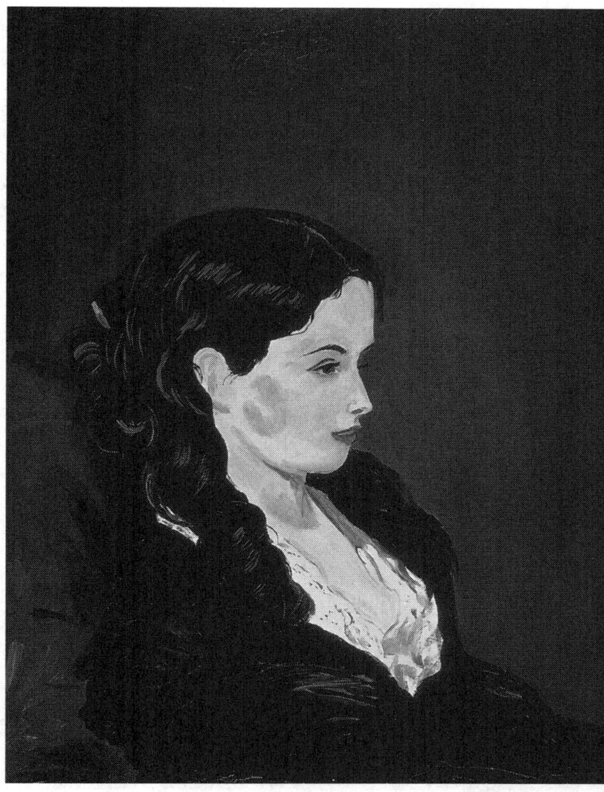

Karen Kilimnik

emily tsingou gallery

10 Charles II Street London SW1Y 4AA Tues – Sat 10–6pm
Tel 0171 839 5320 Fax 0171 839 5321

gallery bob van orsouw   zurich   switzerland
phone +41-1-273 11 00   fax +41-1-273 11 02

march 28
until
may 23 1998

callum innes

may 30
until
july 11 1998

fabrice gygi

KUNST MUSEUM LUZERN

Zwischen Raum 96-99

4. April bis 17. Mai 1998
Thomas Struth / Klaus vom Bruch
Photographie & Video

23. und 24. Mai 1998
KÖRPER: Tanz / Performance
Programm auf Anfrage

3. Juni bis 14. Juli 1998
AUSGANG
Höhere Fachklasse für Freie Kunst HFG, Schule für Gestaltung Luzern

27. Juni bis 9. August 1998
Hannah Villiger
Skulptur 1995-1997

Tribschenstrasse 61, CH-6005 Luzern, Telefon 041-410 90 40, Fax 041-410 90 92

Mittwoch 12.00 bis 20.00 Uhr, Donnerstag bis Sonntag 12.00 bis 17.00 Uhr
Montag und Dienstag geschlossen
e-mail: kunstmuseum@centralnet.ch; http://www.centralnet.ch/kultur/kunstmuseum

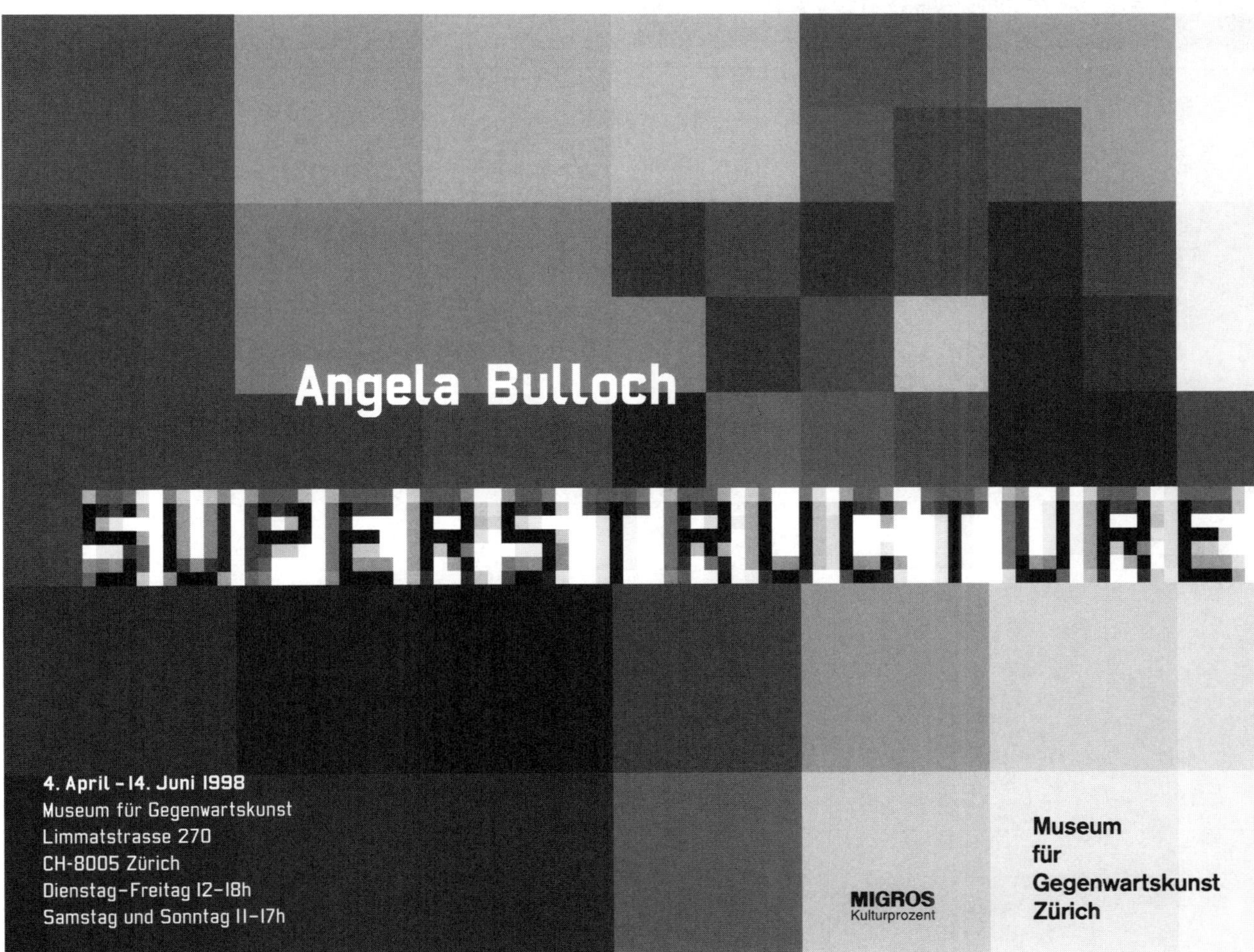

MUSEUM MODERNER KUNST STIFTUNG LUDWIG WIEN

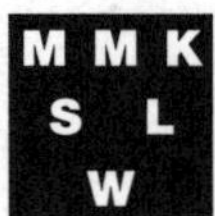
M M K
S L
W

Skulptur im Licht der Fotografie

26. 6. – 20. 9. 1998

Palais Liechtenstein
Fürstengasse 1 · 1090 Wien

Arte Povera
Die Sammlung Goetz

19. 6. – 30. 8. 1998

20er Haus
Arsenalstraße 1 · 1030 Wien

Mehr Informationen über diese   Ausstellungen finden Sie im Internet!
Internet: http://www.MMKSLW.or.at/MMKSLW/   E-mail: museum@MMKSLW.or.at

steirischer herbst 98
26. September – 26. Oktober

*steirischer herbst, Sackstraße 17/I, A-8010 Graz, Austria, Tel.: +43 316 82 30 07
Fax: +43 316 83 57 88, http: //www.stherbst.at, e-mail: stherbst@ping.at*

28 JUNE – 11 OCTOBER 1998
info: Manifesta 2 • B.P. 345 • L-2013 Luxembourg tel: (+352) 22 50 45 fax: (+352) 22 95 95 e-mail: manifesta2@ci.culture.lu http://www.men.lu/manifesta2/manifesta2.html
Manifesta 2
Biennale européenne d'art contemporain / European Biennial of Contemporary Art / Luxembourg
Selected Artists
Eija-Liisa Ahtila
Kutluğ Ataman
Orla Barry
Emese Benczúr
Christine Borland
Eriks Božis
Maurizio Cattelan
Alicia Framis
Dora Garcia
Dr Galentin Gatev
Dominique Gonzalez-Foerster
Felix Gonzalez-Torres
Carsten Höller
Pierre Huyghe
Sanja Iveković
Inessa Josing
Krištof Kintera
Elke Krystufek
Peter Land
Maria Lindberg
Michel Majerus
Bjarne Melgaard
Deimantas Narkevičius
Fanni Niemi-Junkola
Honoré d'O
Boris Ondreička
Tanja Ostojić
Franz Pomassl
Marko Peljhan
Dan Perjovschi
Antoine Prum
Tobias Rehberger
Jeroen de Rijke / Willem de Rooij
Bojan Šarčević
Eran Schaerf
Tilo Schulz
Nebojša Šerić Šoba
Ann-Sofi Sidén
Andreas Slominski
Sean Snyder
Apolonija Šušteršič
Sarah Sze
Bert Theis
Piotr Uklański
Gitte Villesen
Richard Wright
Curators
Robert Fleck – Maria Lind – Barbara Vanderlinden

musée art contemporain lyon
Robert Irwin
June 17 - September 13, 1998
Robert Morris
June 17 - September 13, 1998
Poèmes à petite vitesse
June 17 - September 13, 1998
Musée d'Art Contemporain de Lyon 81, quai Charles de Gaulle - 69006 Lyon - France
tél (00 33)4 72 69 17 17, fax (00 33)4 72 69 17 00

Kunsthalle
Basel

Tobias Rehberger - Dan Peterman
16. Mai - 30. August 1998

Mona Hatoum
6. Juni - 16. August 1998

Kunsthalle Basel, Steinenberg 7, CH-4051 Basel, Telefon 061/272 48 33, Fax 061/272 48 26
Öffnungszeiten: Dienstag – Sonntag 11–17 Uhr, Mittwoch 11 – 20.30 Uhr, Montag geschlossen. Führungen: Sonntag 11 Uhr

The Magazine of Digital Arts

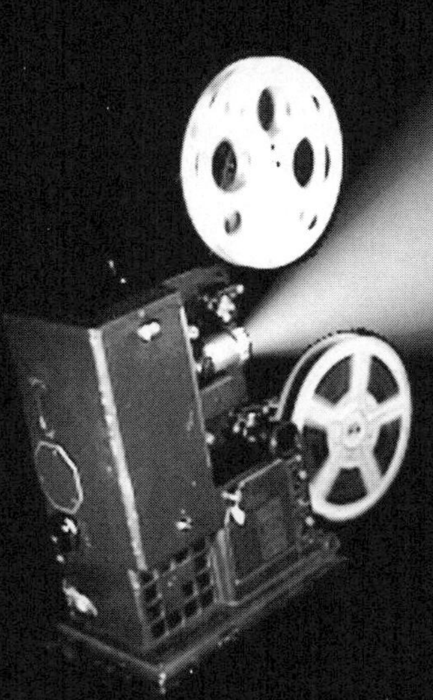

*...a new bimonthly ground breaking publication,
providing a cutting-edge perspective
on the rapidly evolving area of digital technology in the art world.*

Subscribe Now !

1 Year U.S. Subscription $34.95 / 2 Years $59.95 / Foreign Subscriptions add $28 per year

Tel. 212 988 5959   Fax 212 988 6107   info@artbyteonline.com   www.artbyteonline.com

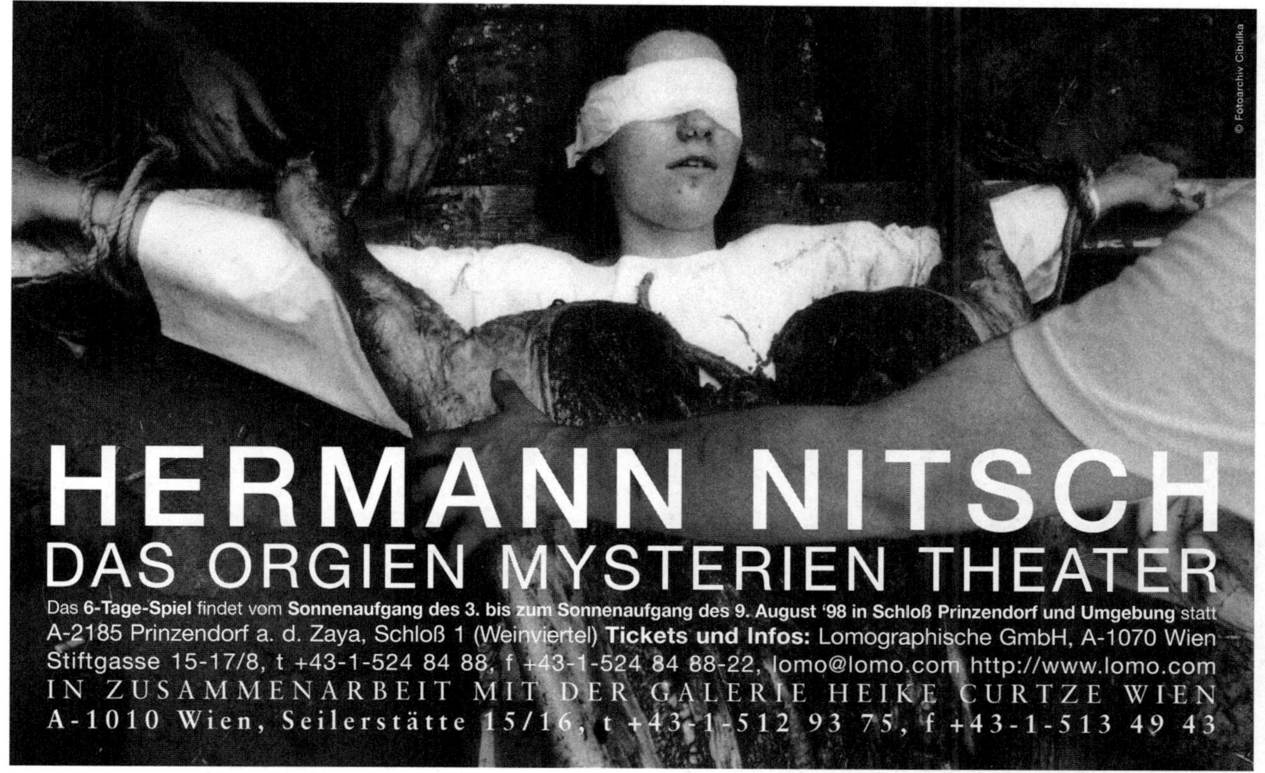
© Fotoarchiv Cibulka
HERMANN NITSCH
DAS ORGIEN MYSTERIEN THEATER
Das 6-Tage-Spiel findet vom Sonnenaufgang des 3. bis zum Sonnenaufgang des 9. August '98 in Schloß Prinzendorf und Umgebung statt
A-2185 Prinzendorf a. d. Zaya, Schloß 1 (Weinviertel) Tickets und Infos: Lomographische GmbH, A-1070 Wien
Stiftgasse 15-17/8, t +43-1-524 84 88, f +43-1-524 84 88-22, lomo@lomo.com http://www.lomo.com
IN ZUSAMMENARBEIT MIT DER GALERIE HEIKE CURTZE WIEN
A-1010 Wien, Seilerstätte 15/16, t +43-1-512 93 75, f +43-1-513 49 43

MODELLE.

Tom Burr
Christine & Irene Hohenbüchler
Florian Pumhösl
Andrea Zittel

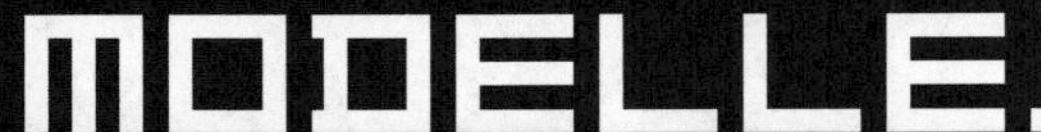

Eine Ausstellung der
Österreichischen Galerie Belvedere
im Atelier im Augarten

Atelier im Augarten
Scherzergasse 1a
A-1020 Wien

9. Juli bis 11. Oktober 1998

Information
+43.1.79557.113
E-mail: presse@belvedere.at

HANDBUCH DER EDITIONEN

Das jährlich erscheinende Nachschlagewerk
zeitgenössischer multiplizierter Kunst

Band 1 1989-94 ISBN 3-928330-07-X, DM 44,--
Band 2 1994-95 ISBN 3-928330-08-X, DM 44,--
Band 3 1995-96 ISBN 3-928330-11-X, DM 44,--
Band 4 1996-97 ISBN 3-928330-17-9, DM 58,--
Band 5 1997-1998 und Nachträge, DM 58,-- inkl. **CD-ROM**
Band 1 - 5, ISBN 3-928330-24-1

Jeder Band und die CD-ROM umfassen:

- Register der eingetragenen Editionen mit je einer
Farbabbildung und allen relevanten Angaben zu Titel, Technik,
Material, Auflage etc., alphabetisch nach Künstlernamen
sortiert

- Register der eintragenden europäischen Editeure mit
Anschriften

- Register der Künstler mit Kurzbiographien sowie der
Drucker

- Glossar mit den wichtigsten Fachbegriffen in deutsch,
englisch, französisch, italienisch und spanisch

- Branchenverzeichnis, alphabetisch nach Sparten sortiert

- separate Preisliste der abgebildeten Editionen, ab Band 2

Die Bände 1-5 im Format von je 29,7 x 14 cm mit
Fadenbindung und festem Einband umfassen ca. 3600 farbige
Abbildungen von über 1000 Künstlern
und etwa 400 Editeuren

Das Handbuch der Editionen erscheint in Zusammenarbeit
mit dem Bundesverband Deutscher Kunstverleger e.V.
und mit freundlicher Unterstützung durch die
Firma RÖMERTURM, Frechen

Galerie Depelmann Edition · Verlag GmbH
Walsroder Straße 305, D - 30855 Langenhagen
Telefon 0049-(0)511-73 36 93, Fax 0049-(0)511-72 36 29
E-mail: depelmann@T-online.de

DERRIERE L'ETOILE STUDIOS

CONTRACT PRINTERS OF LITHOGRAPHS

WOODBLOCKS, LINOCUTS AND MONOTYPES

MAURICE SANCHEZ

DERRIERE L'ETOILE STUDIOS

225 VARICK STREET, NEW YORK CITY,

NEW YORK 10014

212-229-2255/FX 212-807-1948

E-MAIL DLE STUDIO@AOL.COM

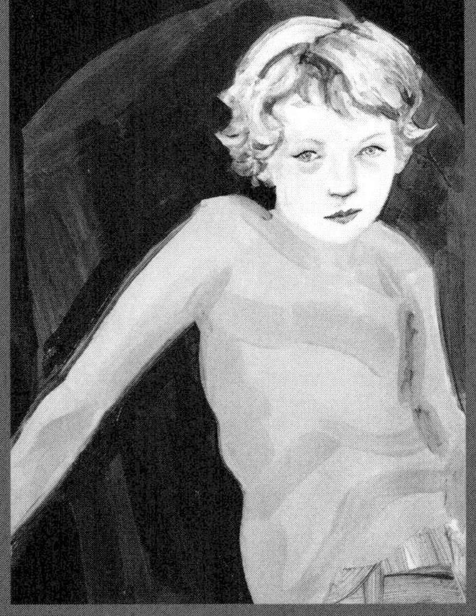

Elizabeth Peyton

bis 9. August 1998

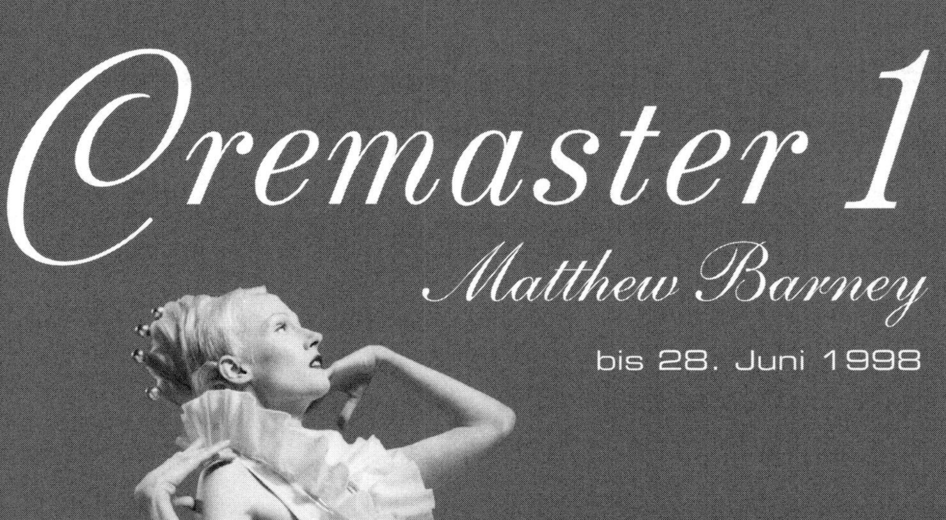

Cremaster 1
Matthew Barney
bis 28. Juni 1998

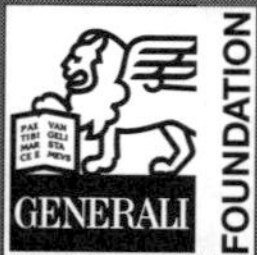

Generali Foundation
Wiedner Hauptstraße 15
A-1040 Wien

Telefon (+43 1) 504 98 80
Fax (+43 1) 504 98 83

e-mail: found_office@ea-generali.com
http://www.gfound.or.at

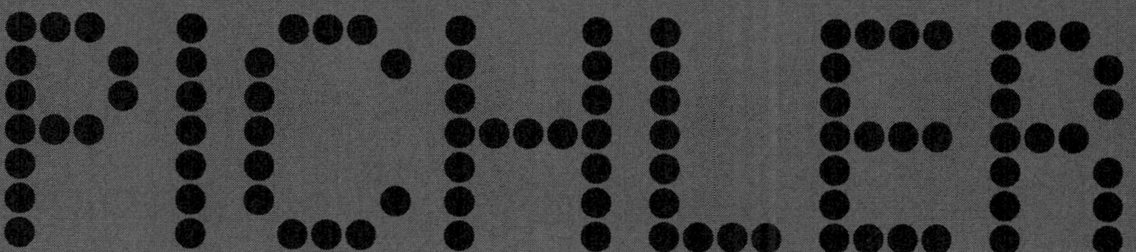

PICHLER

Prototypen 1966–69
15. Mai–9. August 1998

Katalog erhältlich

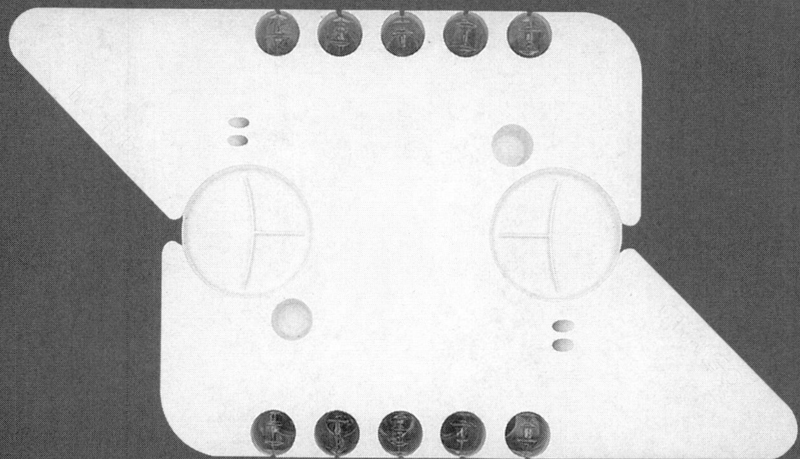

unterstützt von

Ü INTERUNFALL
der Qualitätsversicherung

↳↳ ↳↳↳. ..freie sicht aufs.mittelmeer...

↳junge schweizer kunst..., mit gästen....
.......................und gastmahl..:...

↳...↳kunsthaus:zürich....□. ....._ ......

↳5.juni bis 30.august'98.↳........ ..→..

↳kunsthaus zürich, heimplatz 1, 8001 zürich ↳↳↳↳ di-do 10-21h, fr-so 10-17h, 1.august geschlossen

↳ein kultur-engagement der CREDIT SUISSE PRIVATE BANKING

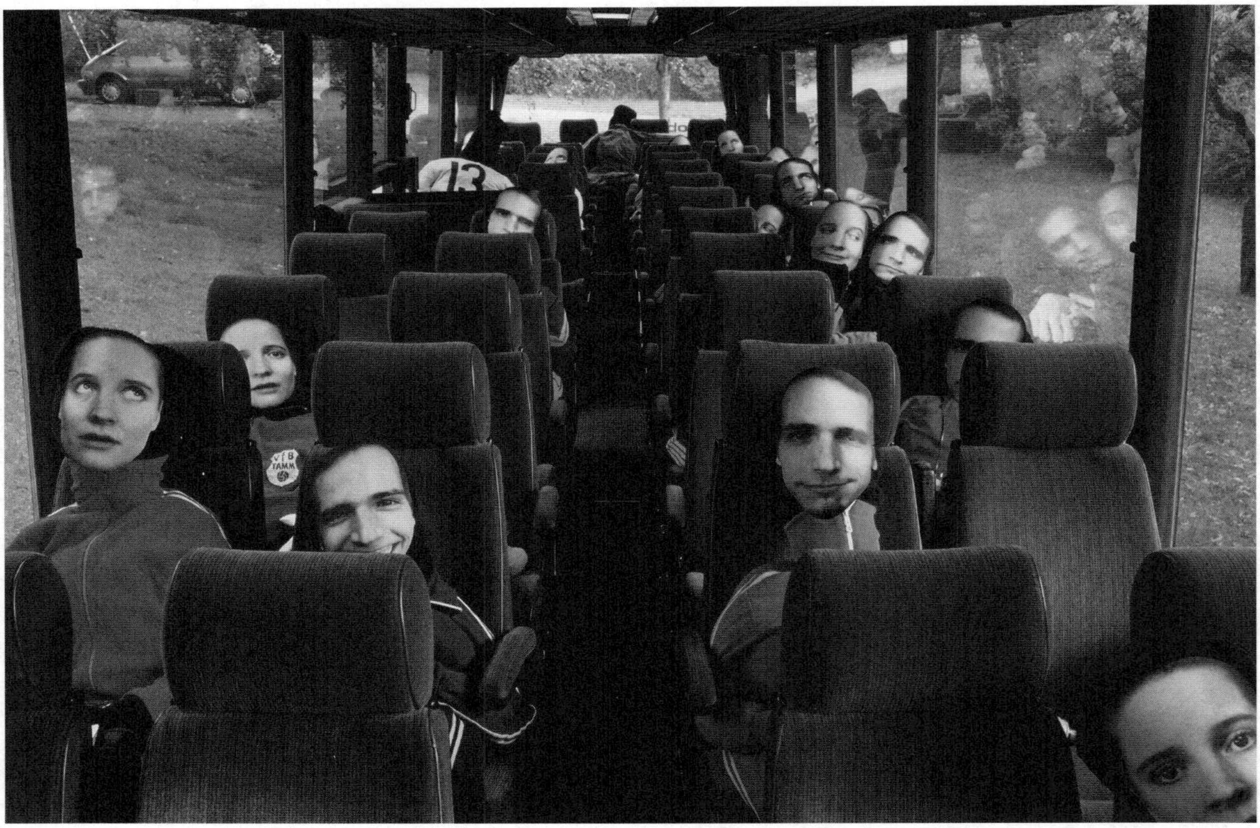

April-May 1998

MOSHE KUPFERMAN: WORK DIARY
SCREENPRINTS 1996-1998

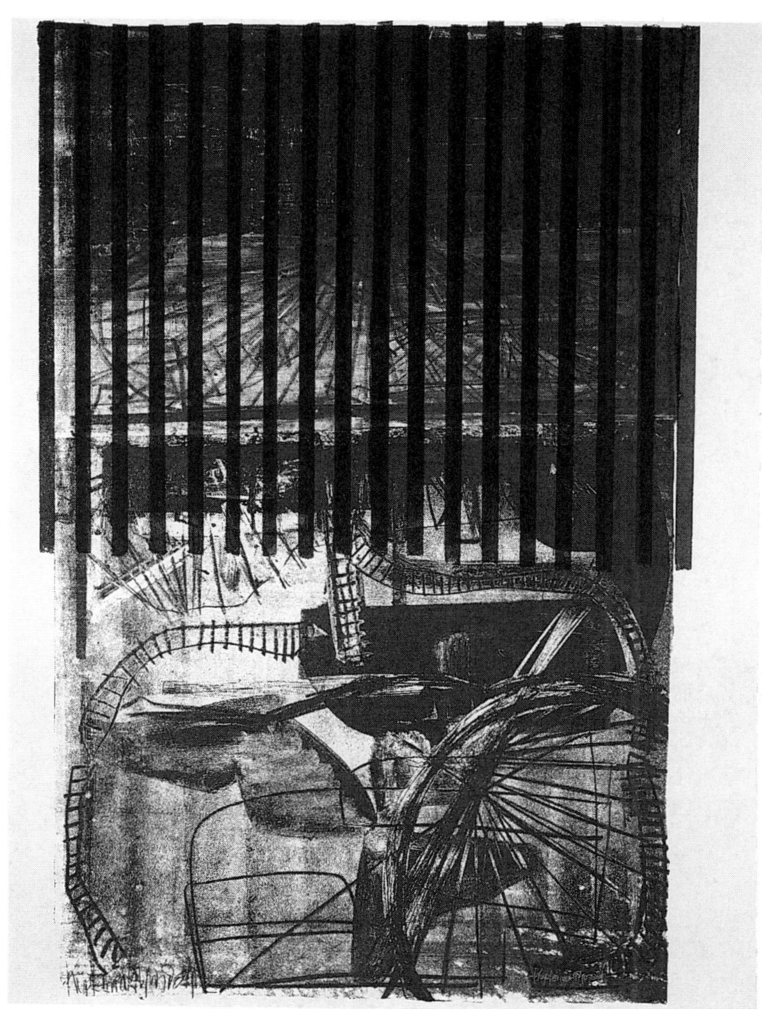

Screenprint, 1997, 168 x 127.5 cm, edition of 55

Catalogue available:

HAR-EL PRINTERS & PUBLISHERS
Jaffa Port, P.O.B. 8053, Jaffa 61081, Israel
tel: 972-3-6816834 fax: 972-3-6813563

e-mail: shai_h@netvision.net.il

website: www.interart.co.il/harel

10-13 septiembre
september

vernissage 9
[expo guadalajara]

expoarte guadalajara 98

VII feria internacional de arte contemporáneo
VII international contemporary art fair

VII foro internacional de teoría sobre arte contemporáneo
las letras del arte
VII international forum on contemporary art theory
art and textuality

farco a.c. - expoarte - fitac
av. juárez 385-103, 44100 guadalajara, jalisco, méxico
tel [523] 613 9866, 613 5834 fax [523] 658 2144
e.mail: exartgdl@vianet.com.mx

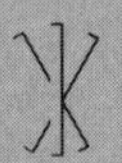

Der internationale Kunstmarkt führender Galerien
1. Okt.
ar.t..
.fo
bis 4. Okt.
rum
ber.li
1998
n
Infoline: + 49 - (0)30 - 88 55 16 46
unterstützt durch
BANK
GESELLSCHAFT
BERLIN
EUROPEAN GALLERIES.
Messe Berlin

June 10 - 14, 1998
opening hours: 1 - 9 pm
opening reception: Thuesday June 9, 4 - 10 pm
Werkraum Warteck pp, Burgweg 15, CH-4058 Basel, 0041 61 692 20 21
main sponsor: E. Gutzwiller & Cie, Banquiers, Basel

LISTE 98
THE YOUNG ART FAIR IN BASEL

AUSTRIA: Hoffmann & Senn, Vienna; Krobath Wimmer, Vienna; Raum Aktueller Kunst, Vienna. BELGIUM: Annette De Keyser, Antwerp; Mot & Van den Boogaard, Brussels. CZECH REBUBLIC: MXM, Prague. DENMARK: Stalke, Copenhagen; Nils Stark, Copenhagen; Nicolai Wallner, Copenhagen. FRANCE: Chez Valentin, Paris; Praz-Delavallade, Paris; Michel Rein, Tours. GERMANY: Paula Böttcher, Berlin; Contemporary Fine Arts, Berlin; Eigen + Art, Berlin; Meyer Riegger, Karlsruhe. GREAT BRITAIN: The Agency, London; Hales, London; Andrew Mummery, London; Anthony Wilkinson, London. GREECE: Ice Box, Athens. HOLLAND: de Expeditie, Amsterdam; Slewe, Amsterdam; Fons Welters, Amsterdam. ITALY: The Box, Torino. JAPAN: Tomio Kojama, Tokyo. NORWAY: c/o-Atle Gerhardsen, Oslo. RUSSIA: Aidan, Moscow. SPAIN: Emilio Navarro, Madrid. SWITZERLAND: Peter Kilchmann, Zürich; Francesca Pia, Bern, Walcheturm, Zürich. USA: Jack Hanley, San Francisco; Thomas Healy, New York; Casey Kaplan, New York; Lombard - Freid, New York.   (as of March 98)

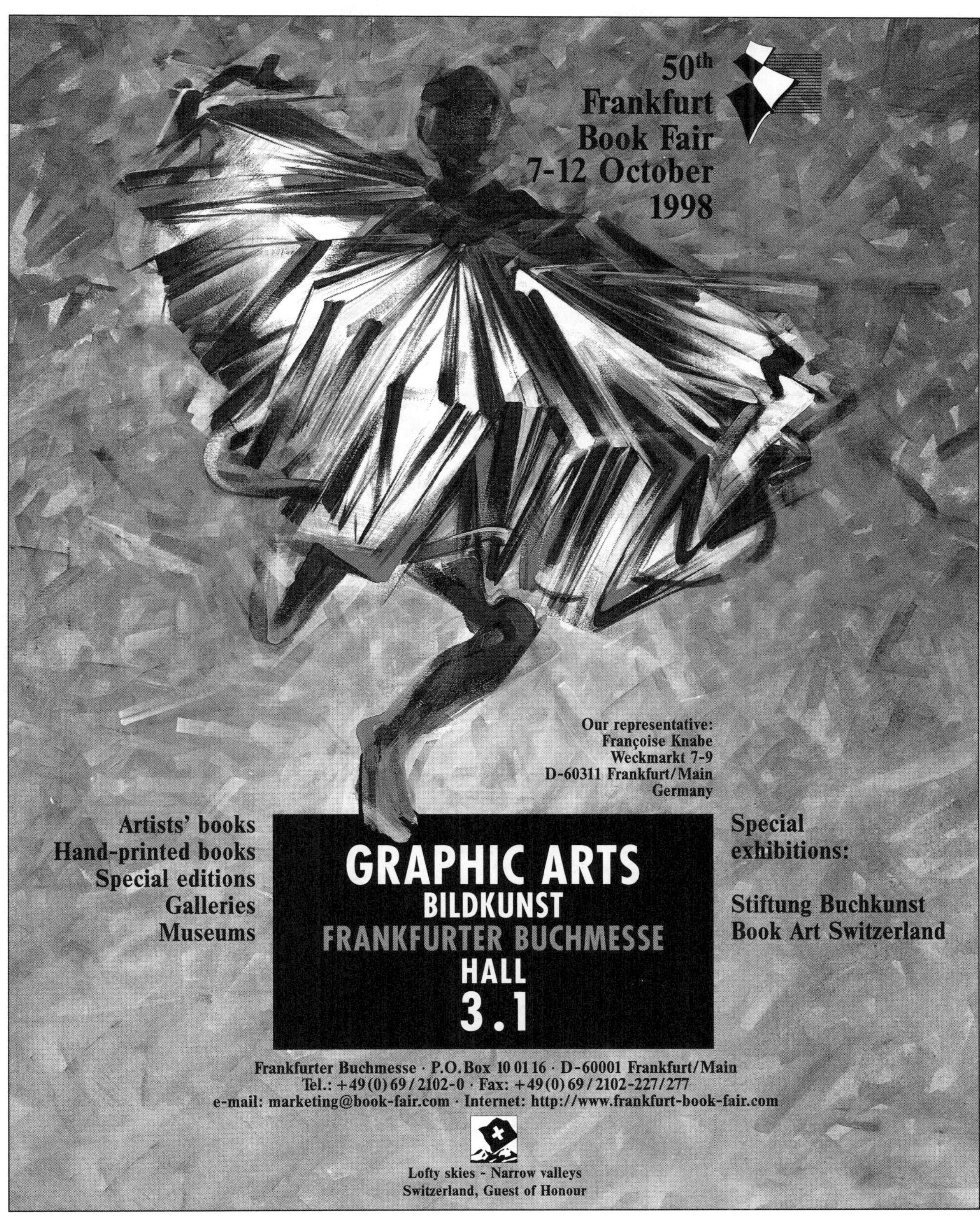50th
Frankfurt
Book Fair
7-12 October
1998

Our representative:
Françoise Knabe
Weckmarkt 7-9
D-60311 Frankfurt/Main
Germany

Artists' books
Hand-printed books
Special editions
Galleries
Museums

Special
exhibitions:

Stiftung Buchkunst
Book Art Switzerland

GRAPHIC ARTS
BILDKUNST
FRANKFURTER BUCHMESSE
HALL
3.1

Frankfurter Buchmesse · P.O. Box 10 01 16 · D-60001 Frankfurt/Main
Tel.: +49 (0) 69 / 2102-0 · Fax: +49 (0) 69 / 2102-227/277
e-mail: marketing@book-fair.com · Internet: http://www.frankfurt-book-fair.com

Lofty skies - Narrow valleys
Switzerland, Guest of Honour

FIAC
25th
7 - 12 October '98
Espace Eiffel-Branly · Paris
Country of honour: Austria

Every day from 12pm to 8pm
Late evening on Thursday 8 October from 12pm to 10pm
Saturday and Sunday from 10am to 8pm
Monday 12 October from 12pm to 6pm

Reed OIP. 11, rue du Colonel Pierre Avia. BP 571. 75726 Paris cedex 15. France.
Tel. 33 (0) 1 41 90 47 80. Fax 33 (0) 1 41 90 47 89.

ART 29'98 THE INTERNATIONAL ART FAIR • DIE INTERNATIONALE KUNSTMESSE • LE SALON INTERNATIONAL D'ART •
LA MOSTRA INTERNAZIONALE D'ARTE • A GALLERY NEW ORLEANS • ACA MÜNCHEN/NEW YORK • ACADEMIA SALZBURG •
ACHENBACH DÜSSELDORF • AIR DE PARIS PARIS • AIZPURU MADRID • ALEXANDER NEW YORK • DE ALVEAR MADRID •
AMMANN ZÜRICH • ANALIX GENÈVE • ANDRÉHN SCHIPTJENKO STOCKHOLM • ANGLES SANTA MONICA • ARCHIVES PARIS •
ARION PRESS SAN FRANCISCO • ARNDT & PARTNER BERLIN • ARSFUTURA ZÜRICH • ART CONCEPT PARIS • ART & PUBLIC GENÈVE •
ARTELIER GRAZ • ARTIACO POZZUOLI • VON BARTHA BASEL • BERNIER ATHENS • BEYELER BASEL • BISCHOFBERGER ZÜRICH •
BLAU MÜNCHEN • BLOOM AMSTERDAM • BLU MILANO • BLUM NEW YORK • BRACHOT BRUXELLES • BRANDSTRÖM STOCKHOLM •
BRANDSTETTER & WYSS ZÜRICH • BROWNSTONE, CORRÉARD & CIE. PARIS • BRUSBERG BERLIN •
BUCHMANN BASEL/KÖLN • BUGDAHN UND KAIMER DÜSSELDORF • C & M NEW YORK • CAMARGO VILAÇA SÃO PAULO •
CAMPANA KÖLN • CANNAVIELLO MILANO • CANUS LA COLLE SUR LOUP • CAPITAIN KÖLN • CARRÉ PARIS •
CARZANIGA & UEKER BASEL • CASOLI MILANO • CATS BRUXELLES • CHOMETTE PARIS • CLAIREFONTAINE LUXEMBOURG •
CONTINUA SAN GIMINIANO • CORKIN TORONTO • COTTIER SYDNEY • CRISTEA LONDON • CROUSEL PARIS • D'ASCANIO ROMA •
D'OFFAY LONDON • DABBENI LUGANO • DANZIGER NEW YORK • DE CARDENAS MILANO • DE CARLO MILANO • DENISE RENÉ PARIS •
DETTERER FRANKFURT • DEWEER OTEGEM • DI MEO PARIS • VAN DIETEN – D'EENDT AMSTERDAM • DITESHEIM NEUCHÂTEL •
DU JOUR PARIS • DURAND-DESSERT PARIS • ECART GENÈVE • EDICIONS T BARCELONA • ENTWISTLE LONDON • FANAL BASEL •
FARBER TRETS • FIEDLER KÖLN • FISCHER DÜSSELDORF • FRANCK & SCHULTE BERLIN • STEPHEN FRIEDMAN LONDON •
FRIEDRICH BERN • FRITH STREET LONDON • GAGOSIAN NEW YORK • GALERIE 1900-2000 PARIS • GALERIE DE FRANCE PARIS •
GALLIANI GENOVA • GAN TOKYO • GANA SEOUL • GASSER & GRUNERT KÖLN • GAVIN BROWN'S ENTERPRISE NEW YORK •
GEBAUER BERLIN • VAN GELDER AMSTERDAM • GEMINI LOS ANGELES • GENILLARD LONDON • GIAN FERRARI MILANO •
GIMPEL FILS LONDON • GMURZYNSKA KÖLN • GONZALEZ MADRID • GOODMAN NEW YORK/PARIS • GRÄSSLIN FRANKFURT •
GRAY CHICAGO • GREVE KÖLN/PARIS/MILANO • HAAS & FUCHS BERLIN • HACHMEISTER MÜNSTER •
HAMMELEHLE & AHRENS STUTTGART • HAUSER UND WIRTH ZÜRICH • HENGESBACH/RAUME WUPPERTAL • HETZLER BERLIN •
HILGER WIEN • HOFFMANN FRIEDBERG • HOHENTHAL UND BERGEN BERLIN • HOLTMANN KÖLN • HOSS PARIS •
HUSSENOT PARIS • HUTTON NEW YORK • HYUNDAI SEOUL • INTERIM ART LONDON • INVERNIZZI MILANO • ITEM PARIS •
JABLONKA KÖLN • JACOBSON LONDON • JANSSEN BRUXELLES • JONES IRVINE • JOPLING/WHITE CUBE LONDON •
JUDA LONDON • KALMAN LONDON • KAMAKURA TOKYO • KAUFMANN BASEL • KERLIN DUBLIN • KICKEN KÖLN •
KLOSTERFELDE HAMBURG/BERLIN • KLUSER MÜNCHEN • KNUST MÜNCHEN •
VAN DER KOELEN MAINZ • KÖNIG WIEN • KRAUS NEW YORK • KRINZINGER WIEN •
KROHN BADENWEILER • KRUGIER GENÈVE/NEW YORK • KUKJE SEOUL •
KULLI ST. GALLEN • L. A. FRANKFURT • LA CITTA VERONA •
LAAGE-SALOMON PARIS • LAHUMIERE PARIS • LAMBERT PARIS •
LANDAU MONTREAL • LEBON PARIS • LELONG ZÜRICH/PARIS/NEW YORK •
LIMMER KÖLN • LINDER BASEL • LINTEL MÜNCHEN •
LISSON LONDON • LITTMANN BASEL • LIVING STONE DEN HAAG •
LOCKS PHILADELPHIA • LÖHRL MÖNCHENGLADBACH •
LORENZO MADRID • LUDORFF DÜSSELDORF •
LUNN NEW YORK • M BOCHUM BOCHUM • MÄDER BASEL •
MAI 36 ZÜRICH • MAGERS/SPRUTH KÖLN • MARCH VALENCIA •
MARCOS ZARAGOZA • MARESCALCHI BOLOGNA/MONACO •
MARKS NEW YORK • MARLBOROUGH ZÜRICH/LONDON/NEW YORK •
MASOERO TORINO • MATHES NEW YORK • MAYER DÜSSELDORF •
MCKEE NEW YORK • MEERT RIHOUX BRUXELLES •
MEIER SAN FRANCISCO • MEILE LUZERN •
METRO PICTURES NEW YORK • MEYER-ELLINGER FRANKFURT •
MININI BRESCIA • MIRO LONDON • MODULO LISBOA •
MÜLLER ZÜRICH • MUNRO HAMBURG •
NÄCHST ST. STEPHAN WIEN • NAGEL KÖLN •
NEU BERLIN • NEUGERRIEMSCHNEIDER BERLIN •
NEW ART CENTRE SALISBURY • NIEMANN BERLIN •
NOIRE TORINO • NORDENHAKE STOCKHOLM •
NOTHELFER BERLIN • ORANGERIE-REINZ KÖLN •
OXLEY9 SYDNEY • PACE NEW YORK • PACEWILDENSTEIN NEW YORK •
PAILHAS MARSEILLE • PAPILLON PARIS • PARAGON LONDON •
PARK RYU SOOK SEOUL • PAULI LAUSANNE • PERSANO TORINO •
PETZEL NEW YORK • PHOTO & CO. TORINO • PHOTOLOGY MILANO •
PICARON PARIS • PICCADILLY LONDON • PRATS BARCELONA •
PRODUZENTENGALERIE HAMBURG • PUDELKO BONN •
PUTMAN S.D.O.P.M. PARIS • RAFFAELLI TRENTO •
RECKERMANN KÖLN • REYNOLDS LONDON • RICKE KÖLN •
RIVERHOUSE CLARK • RIZZO PARIS • RÖNTGEN TOKYO •
ROPAC SALZBURG/PARIS • ROSEN NEW YORK • ROTHE FRANKFURT •
RUBIN ZÜRICH • S65 AALST • SAMUEL PARIS • SCHEIBLER KÖLN •
SCHIPPER & KROME BERLIN • SCHLEGL ZÜRICH •
SCHOELLER DÜSSELDORF • DELLO SCUDO VERONA •
SEYDOUX PARIS • SFEIR - SEMLER HAMBURG • SHEEHAN NEW YORK •
SIKKEMA NEW YORK • SKARSTEDT NEW YORK • SKOPIA GENÈVE •
SOLLERTIS TOULOUSE • SPERONE ROMA/NEW YORK •
SPRINGER UND WINKLER BERLIN • STÄHLI ZÜRICH •
STAMPA BASEL • STARK NEW YORK • STEIN MILANO •
STEINEK WIEN • ZUR STOCKEREGG ZÜRICH • STOLZ KÖLN •
STRELOW DÜSSELDORF • SZWAJCER ANTWERPEN •
TANIT MÜNCHEN • TAUBERT DÜSSELDORF • TEGA MILANO •
TEMPLON PARIS • THOMAN INNSBRUCK • THOMAS MÜNCHEN •
THORENS BASEL • TORCH AMSTERDAM • TRIEBOLD BASEL •
TRISORIO NAPOLI • TSCHUDI GLARUS • UTERMANN DORTMUND •
VALLOIS PARIS • VAN ORSOUW ZÜRICH • VARENNE GENÈVE •
VERNA ZÜRICH • WACK KAISERSLAUTERN • WADDINGTON LONDON •
WADDINGTON THEO LONDON • WEBER JAMILEH ZÜRICH •
WEISS BERLIN • WERNER NEW YORK/KÖLN • WINTER WIEN •
WITTROCK DÜSSELDORF • WOOLWORTH PARIS •
YOUNG SEATTLE • ZENO X ANTWERPEN •
ZIEGLER ZÜRICH. (UPDATED: 19 MARCH 1998)
New: Art Sculpture Basel

Basel 10.–15.6.1998

**Art 29'98, Messe Basel, P.O.Box, CH-4021 Basel, Tel. +41 61 686 20 20,
Fax +41 61 686 26 86, e-mail: art@messebasel.ch Internet: www.art.ch**

The catalogue will appear in May 1998.
Reservations: Tel. +49 89 12 69 90 46
or Fax +49 89 12 69 90 11
USA: Toll Free 800 581 4839

sponsored by 

Messe Basel.

STHLM
Art Fair
10–14
MARCH-99

The 19th
Stockholm
Art Fair
Sollentuna
10–14 March 1999

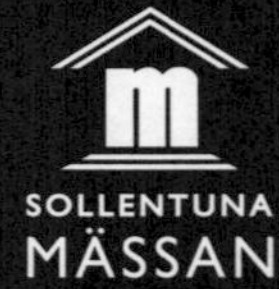

STOCKHOLM ART FAIR, PO BOX 174, SE-191 23 SOLLENTUNA, SWEDEN, TEL +46 8 92 59 00, FAX + 46 8 92 97 74, www.sollfair.se/artfair

A printing collaboration
for 12 years and
42 Parkett issues:

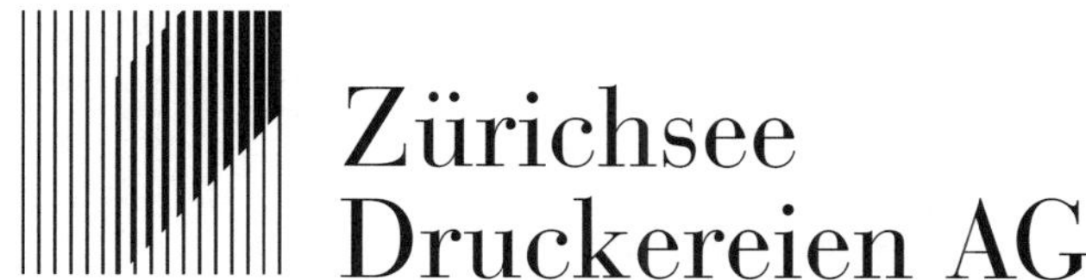

For an estimate of your next printing project please contact:
Zürichsee Druckereien AG, Seestrasse 86, 8712 Stäfa,
Telefon +41-1-928 53 03, Fax +41-1-928 53 10

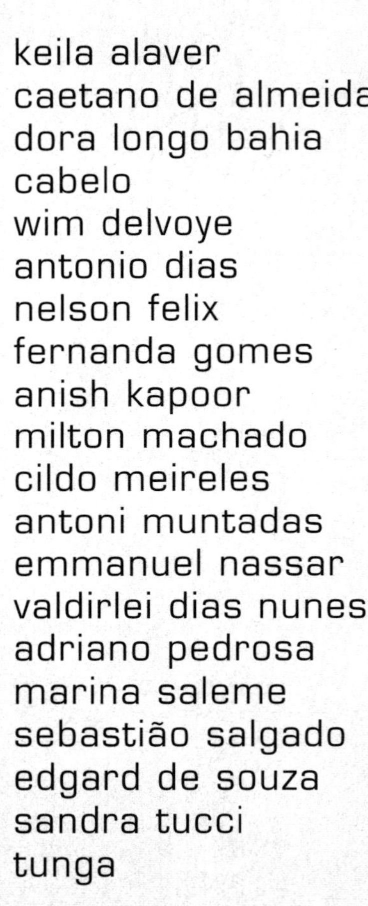

keila alaver
caetano de almeida
dora longo bahia
cabelo
wim delvoye
antonio dias
nelson felix
fernanda gomes
anish kapoor
milton machado
cildo meireles
antoni muntadas
emmanuel nassar
valdirlei dias nunes
adriano pedrosa
marina saleme
sebastião salgado
edgard de souza
sandra tucci
tunga

Edgard de Souza, 1997

GALERIA LUISA STRINA
R. Padre João Manoel 974 A São Paulo SP 01411-000 Brasil
tel 55 11 2802471 fax 30646391 gstrina@totalnet.com.br

SOL LEWITT: WALL PIECES
DRAWINGS 1972-1998 AND MAQUETTES FOR LARGE SCALE STRUCTURES
21 MAY - 4 JULY
LISSON
52-54 Bell Street London NW1 5DA Tel: 0171 724 2739 Fax: 0171 724 7124 E-mail: contact@lisson.co.uk

Ross Sinclair
9 April-16 May

Don't Look Now What moves in the late 90s
29 May-4 July

GALERIE WALCHETURM Claudia Spinelli
Walchestrasse 6 · 8035 Zürich · Switzerland · Phone +41 1 252 10 96 · Fax +41 1 252 10 97 · e-mail: walcheturm@access.ch
Tuesday - Friday 2 to 6 pm · Saturday 12 am to 4 pm

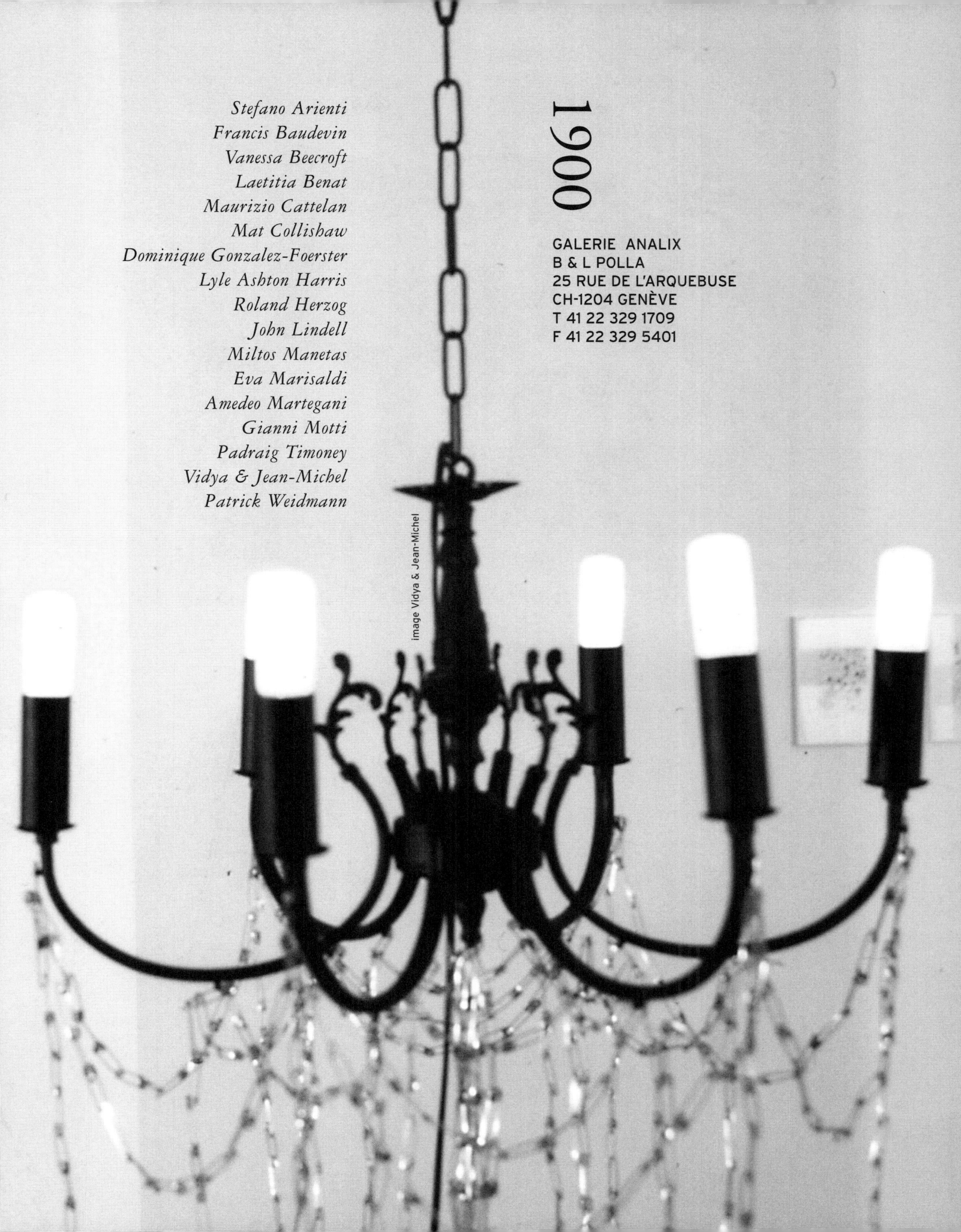

Stefano Arienti
Francis Baudevin
Vanessa Beecroft
Laetitia Benat
Maurizio Cattelan
Mat Collishaw
Dominique Gonzalez-Foerster
Lyle Ashton Harris
Roland Herzog
John Lindell
Miltos Manetas
Eva Marisaldi
Amedeo Martegani
Gianni Motti
Padraig Timoney
Vidya & Jean-Michel
Patrick Weidmann

1900

GALERIE ANALIX
B & L POLLA
25 RUE DE L'ARQUEBUSE
CH-1204 GENÈVE
T 41 22 329 1709
F 41 22 329 5401

image Vidya & Jean-Michel

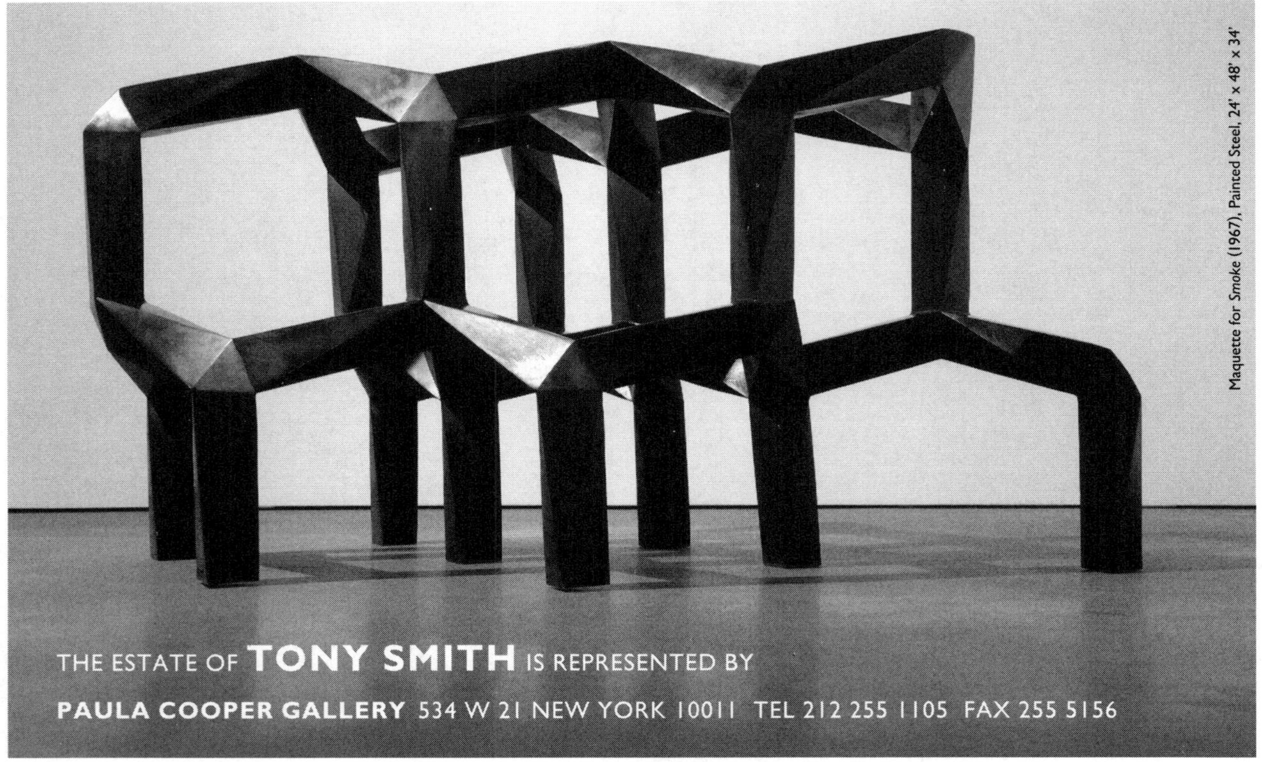

Robert Gober • Zoe Leonard • Michael Hurson • Carl Andre • Julian Lethbridge • John Baldessari Lorna Simpson • David Hammons • Christopher Williams • Adrian Piper • Felix Gonzalez-Torres Andrea Zittel • Rirkrit Tiravanija • Richard Long • Tseng Kwong Chi • Roni Horn • Ken Lum Ellsworth Kelly • Yayoi Kusama • Martin Kippenberger • Sherrie Levine • Jonathan Borofsky Jennifer Bartlett • Robert Gober • Zoe Leonard • Michael Hurson • Carl Andre • Julian Lethbridge John Baldessari • Lorna Simpson • David Hammons • Christopher Williams • Adrian Piper • Felix Gonzalez-Torres • Andrea Zittel • Rirkrit Tiravanija • Richard Long • Tseng Kwong Chi • Roni Horn Ken Lum • Ellsworth Kelly • Yayoi Kusama • Martin Kippenberger • Sherrie Levine • Jonathan Borofsky • Jennifer Bartlett • Robert Gober • Zoe Leonard • Michael Hurson • Carl Andre • Julian Lethbridge • John Baldessari • Lorna Simpson • David Hammons • Christopher Williams • Adrian Piper • Felix Gonzalez-Torres • Andrea Zittel • Rirkrit Tiravanija • Richard Long • Tseng Kwong Chi Roni Horn • Ken Lum • Ellsworth Kelly • Yayoi Kusama • Martin Kippenberger • Sherrie Levine

TRAVEL & LEISURE

A GROUP EXHIBITION

MAY – JUNE 1998

PAULA COOPER GALLERY

534 W 21 NY 10011 TEL 212 255 1105

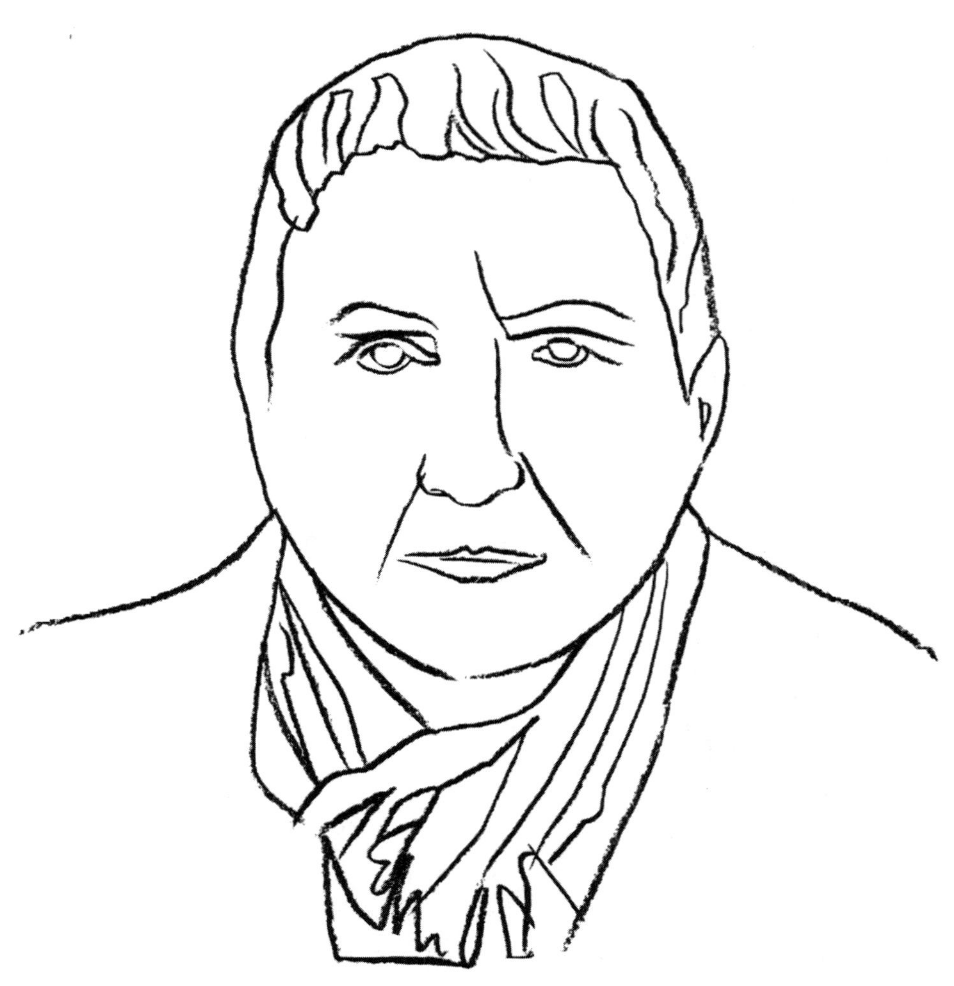

Andy Warhol *Portrait Drawings*

Fully Illustrated Catalogue Available

Brooke Alexander

59 Wooster St. New York, N Y 10012 Tel. 212.925.4338 Fax 212.941.9565 brookealex@earthlink.net

Gertrude Stein, 1980, graphite on HMP paper, 31 1/2 x 23 3/4 inches (80 x 60 cm)

OPENING
MAY 21, 1998

LUHRING AUGUSTINE
531 West 24th Street

ANDREA ROSEN
525 West 24th Street

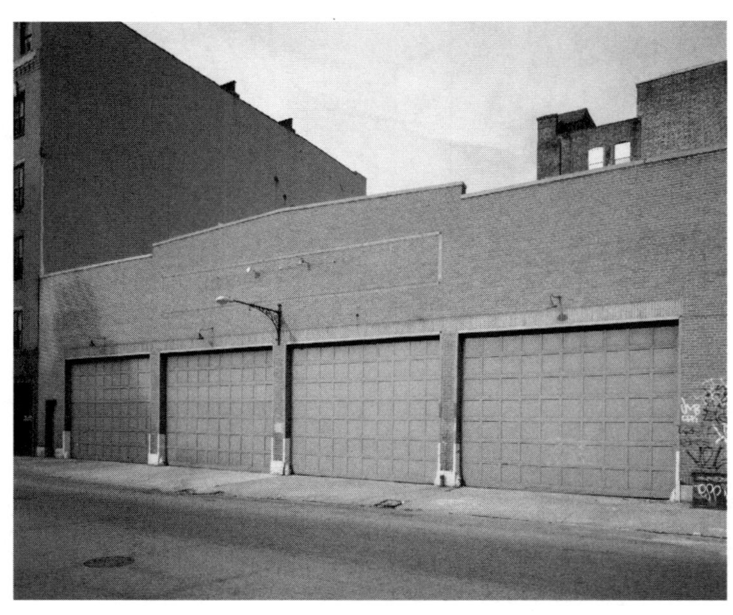

NYC 10011

THOMAS AMMANN FINE ART AG ZURICH

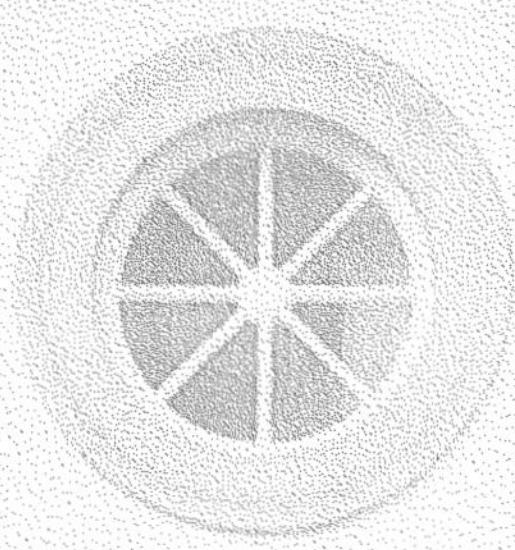

PHILIP TAAFFE

NEW WORKS

June 8 – September 30, 1998

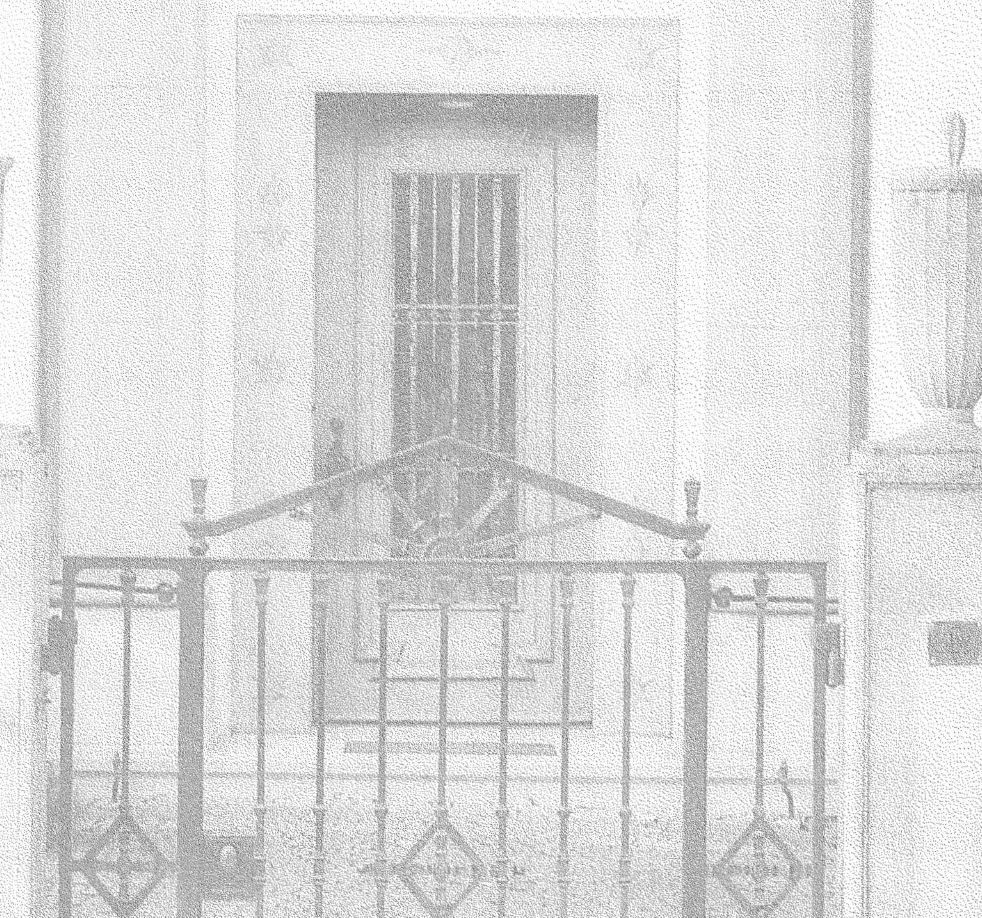

RESTELBERGSTRASSE 97 CH-8044 ZÜRICH TEL. (411) 360 51 60 FAX (411) 360 51 61

georg baselitz
max bill
john chamberlain
nicola de maria
dan flavin
christian herdeg
jahanguir
donald judd
roy lichtenstein
catherine lee
brice marden
mimmo paladino
darryl pottorf
robert rauschenberg
sean scully
richard serra
joel shapiro
frank stella
jean tinguely

galerie jamileh weber

waldmannstrasse 6
ch-8001 zürich
telefon 01 252 10 66
telefax 01 252 11 32